GOOD NEWS BIBLE

THE COMPLETE DEADLINE strips of

SHAKY KANE

**Breakdown Press**

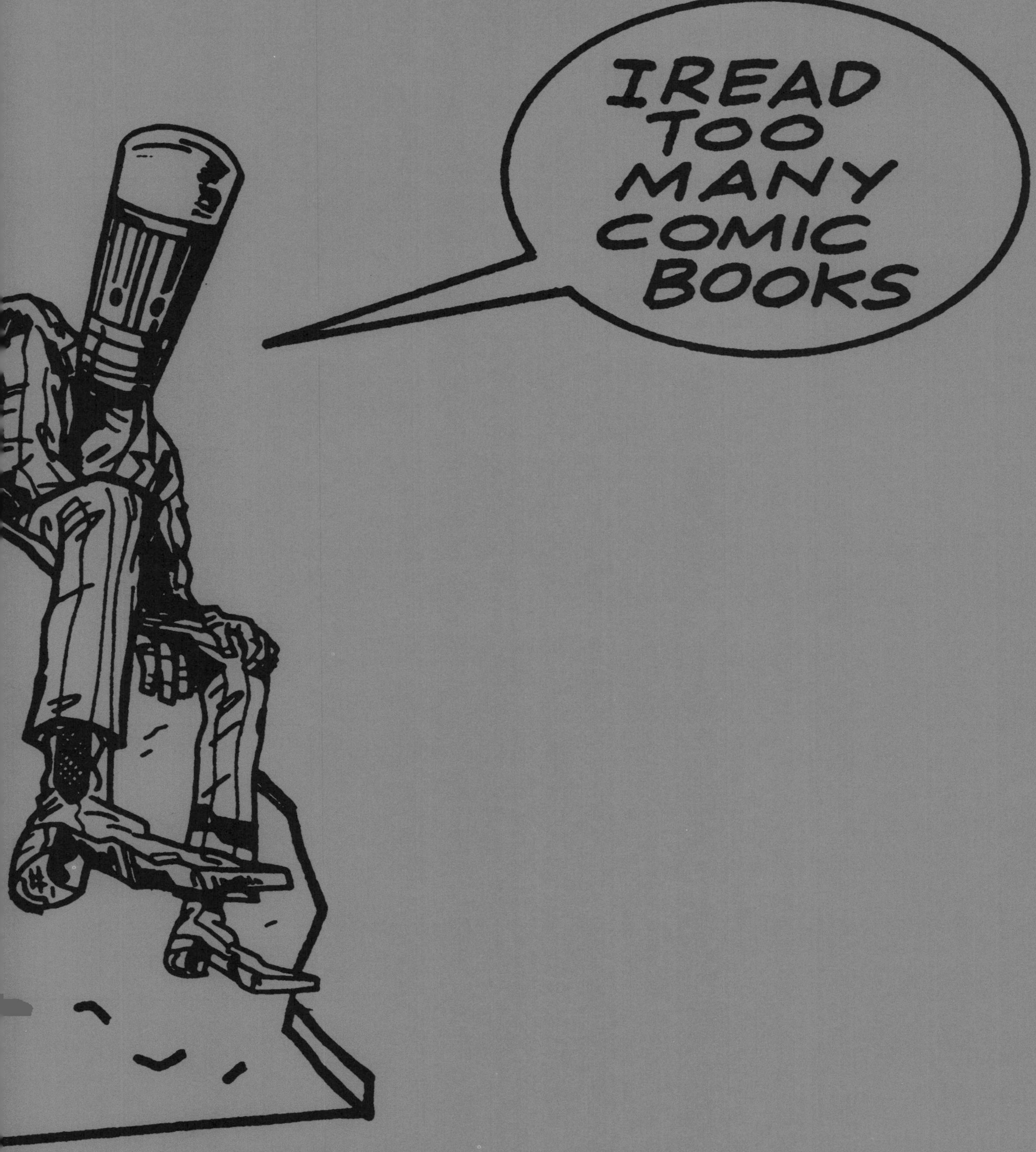
I READ TOO MANY COMIC BOOKS

He Wore a Mask of Craters

Shaky

The Complete Deadline Strips of

Beyond Belief

Your Pal Shaky

# He Wore a Mask of Craters

Foreword by

## David Quantick

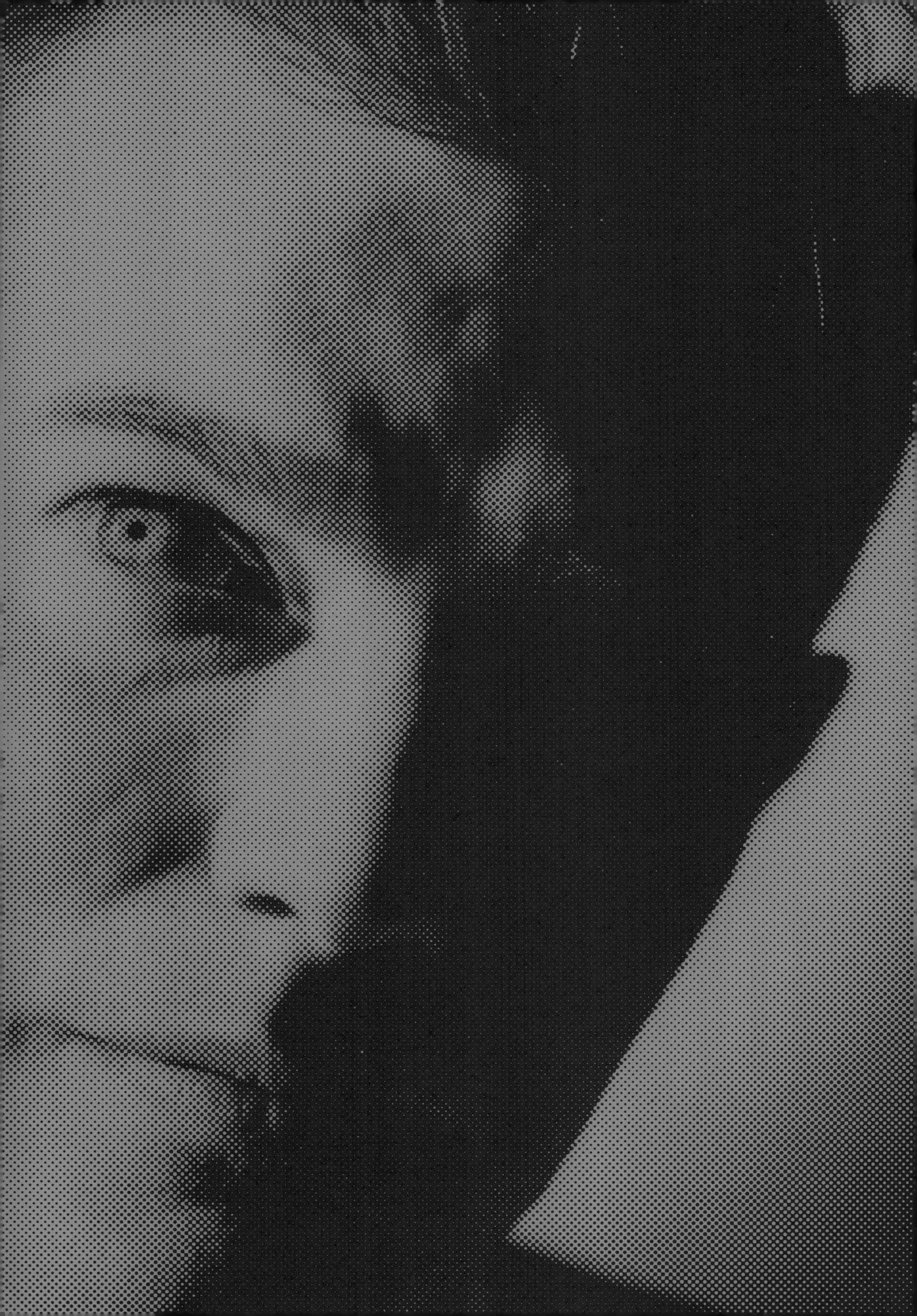

He wore
a mask
of craters

He wore a thousand gallon hat

He walked in and everything in the world started shooting at him. Guns, lasers, phasers, cannons, rifles, pistols, crossbows, bows, capguns, slingshots, waterpistols. He threw them all off like they were a shower of teddy bears.

He came up to me. By now we were the only people in the bar. Everyone else had fled or was dead.

# "Hi,"

# he said,

# "I'm Shaky

# Kane"

"Shaky Kane?" I said. "You're not Shaky Kane." And I turned back to my carving. I was carving a thousand pinheads onto the face of an angel. It was hard work and I didn't care to be interrupted by some stranger claiming to be Shaky Kane.

"If I'm not Shaky Kane," he said, "I wouldn't be able to do this."

And he shot out his hand so fast that the thumb was a blur and the fingers never had a chance, and a fireball filled the air, a fireball with a ray of light shooting out like a column of pure nuclear blindness. And out of that fireball walked a woman.

She had blonde hair, a beehive of spun crazy gold. She wore a Sigue Sigue Sputnik t-shirt ripped at the ribs. Her breasts contained galaxies. Her nipples were suns. She winked at me and all my problems apologised for bothering me and went away.

The man who called himself Shaky whispered something in the woman's ear and she left, her hips swaying like a big band.

I signalled for another drink. I was pretty much drinking anything at that point, so when the barman eventually crawled out from under the counter and said there was no more whisky, I drank him.

"Anyone could do that," I said as I drained the barman.

The stranger shrugged.

"If I wasn't Shaky Kane," he said, "I couldn't do this."

He shot out his other hand so fast that his fingers didn't even see it coming and his thumb let out a silent thumb scream and a ball of bubbling lava exploded out, full of light and colour and lightning and for some reason subway tokens. And out of that lava, with a scream of melting rubber and the howl of a thousand dead bikers crucified on iron cactuses, came the biggest truck I had ever seen. It rode on wheels bigger than the rings of Saturn with chrome hubs shinier than the cheeks of a new born robot. It had the suspension of a rocket gantry and a radiator grille the size of Detroit. The paintwork was redder than the Devil's backside and the upholstery was made from every leather jacket that Elvis ever wore. The driver's face looked like James Dean's, or at least half of it did. The other half was made of glass, but it was full of cogs and gears and for some reason subway tokens.

The half-faced James Dean nodded at the man who called himself Shaky and, with another scream, the truck spun on a dime and roared out into the dog-spattered afternoon.

I made myself a bacon sandwich. I love bacon even more than I love sandwiches. And I love sandwiches.

"Trucks," I said. "Trucks and tricks."

I took a big bite out of the bacon sandwich. Ketchup went everywhere.

The stranger just stood there, flexing his hands. There was smoke and sparks coming off his fingers. He looked like a man who was trying to control something, possibly his temper.

"If I wasn't Shaky Kane…" he began.

"Yeah, I understand," I said. "If you weren't Shaky Kane da diddly dada dum dum do. I get it. But I don't think you do."

And I got to my feet. I was wearing my unbearable boots that day, the ones that make me look seventy thousand feet tall. They had spurs attached to them the size of – well, spurs, what else would they be? They were made of the finest Spanish leather and decorated with the faces of the Four Horsemen of the Apocalypse and the Four Freshmen and four guys I met in a bar one night and I liked their faces.

I drew myself up to my full height. I was wearing my intolerable waistcoat, made from the skins of everything extinct ever. It got bigger every morning.

I took off my inconceivable sunglasses. They were darker than the bottom of a well in a disused silver mine in the furthest away black hole in the galaxy. I had won them off Roy Orbison's ghost in a poker game, because they were so dark it couldn't see the cards.

I looked at the stranger. I could see the purple irises of my own eyes reflected in the veiny dishes of his. I looked great.

"You claim to be Shaky Kane," I said.

"Yes," he said, nervously.

"The artist Shaky Kane? The writer Shaky Kane? The creative *genius* Shaky Kane?"

"Yes…"

"The man who drew Bulletproof Coffin? Fornicator Terminator? The Crying Man? A-Men? Space Boss? Pinhead Nation?"

He looked me square in the eye, I'll give him that.

"Yes," he said, "I am. I am the Shaky Kane who conceived and drew and wrote all those and more."

I could stand this no more. I pulled from my pocket a battered old book. Garish images leered from the pages like gargoyles trapped in stained glass mirrors.

"You claim that you did this?"

He glanced down at the book. It was called

# Good News Bible: The Complete Deadline Strips of Shaky Kane.

"This book contains everything dear to me!" I suddenly roared, smashing the counter with my iron fist.

"Everything that ever mattered! It is the greatest book ever created! I am made of this book!"

The stranger nodded.

"I know," he said. "I know because it was me who did it. I am Shaky Kane."

I looked at him. Emotions with their own colours surged up inside me with unbelievable violence.

I was this close to killing everyone in the world.

I took the book in my fist. I held it to the stranger's face.

"In that case," I said, "Could I trouble you for your autograph, Mister Kane?" ■

David Quantick and Shaky Kane are the makers of *That's Because You're a Robot*.

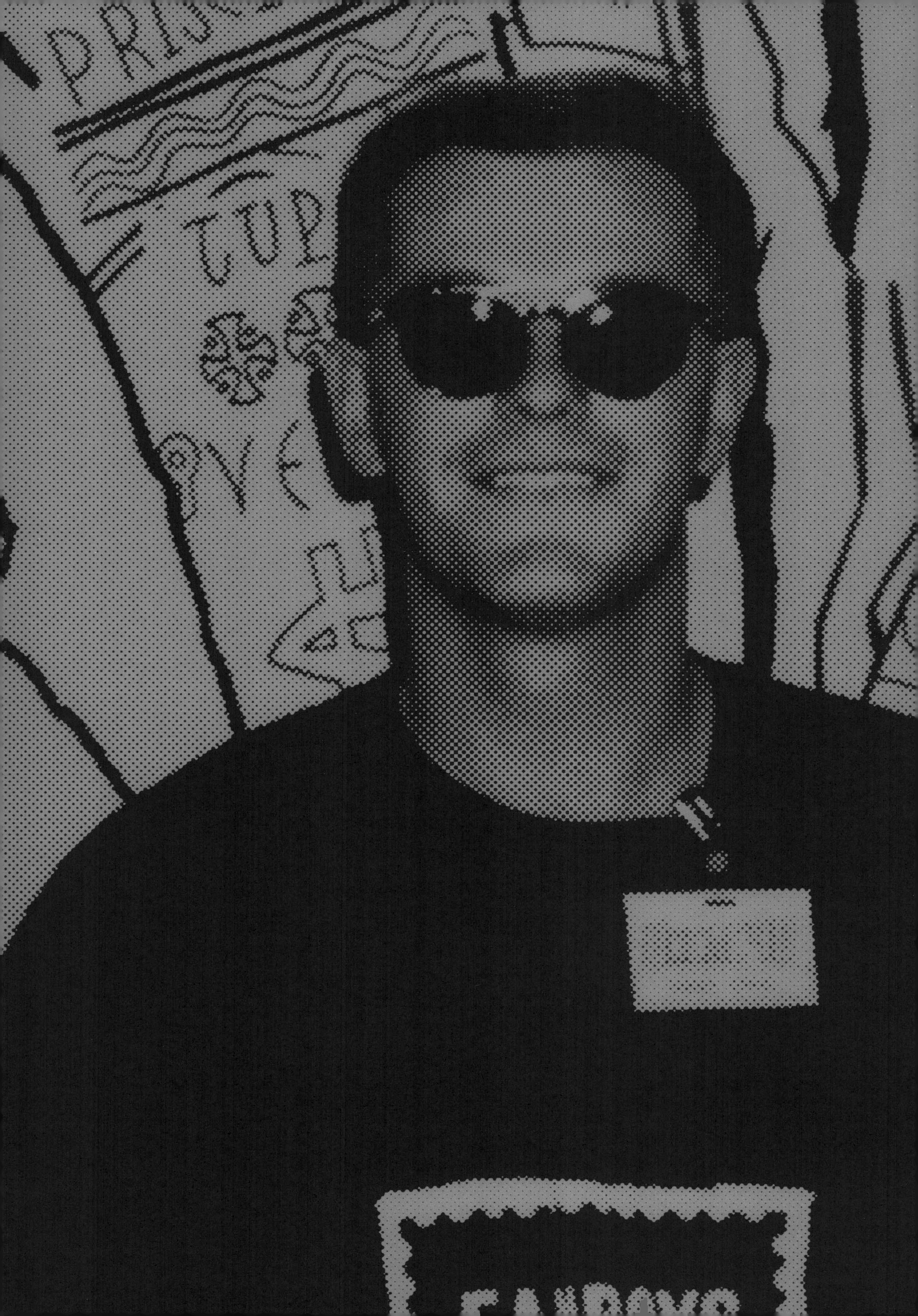

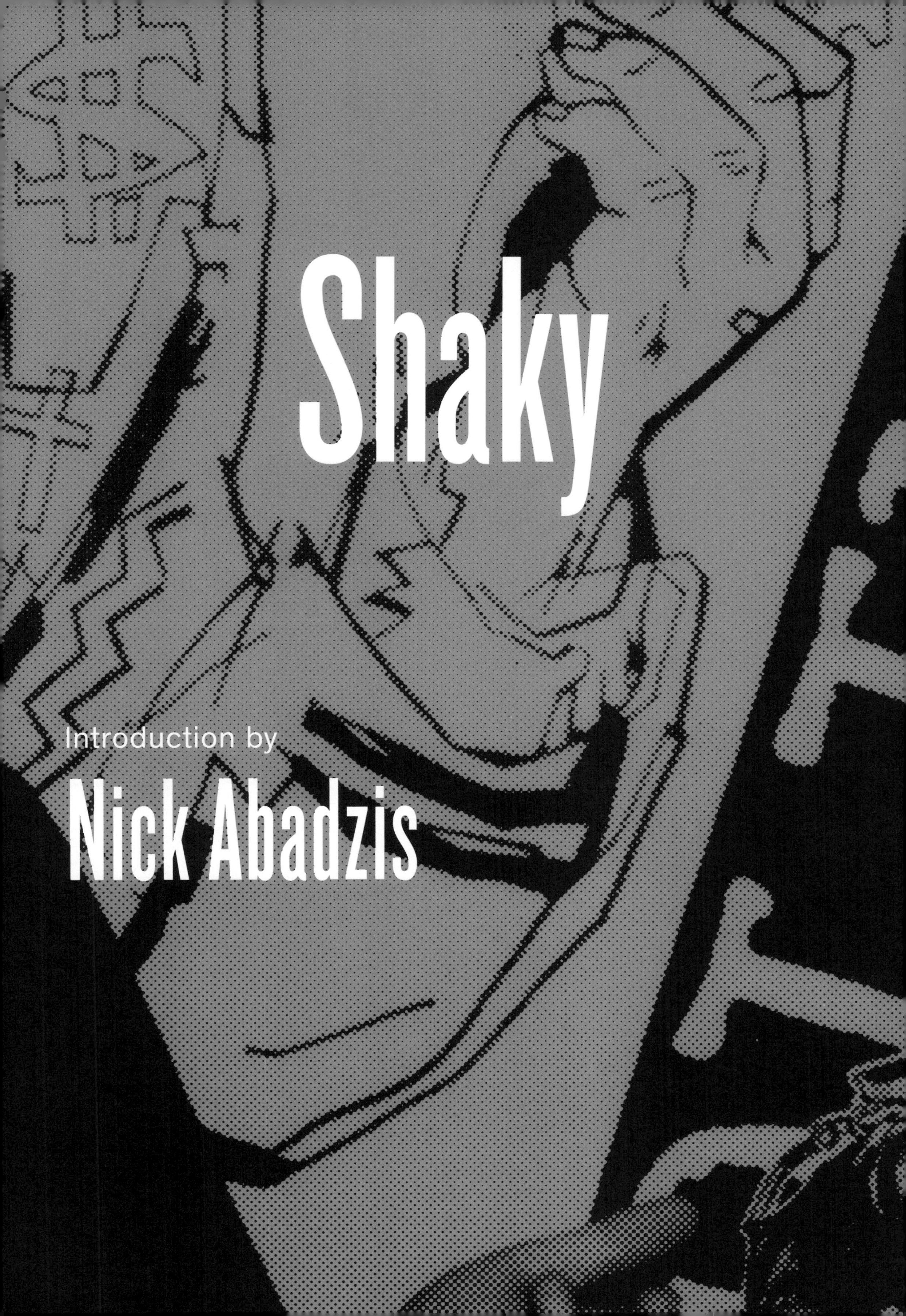

# Shaky

Introduction by

## Nick Abadzis

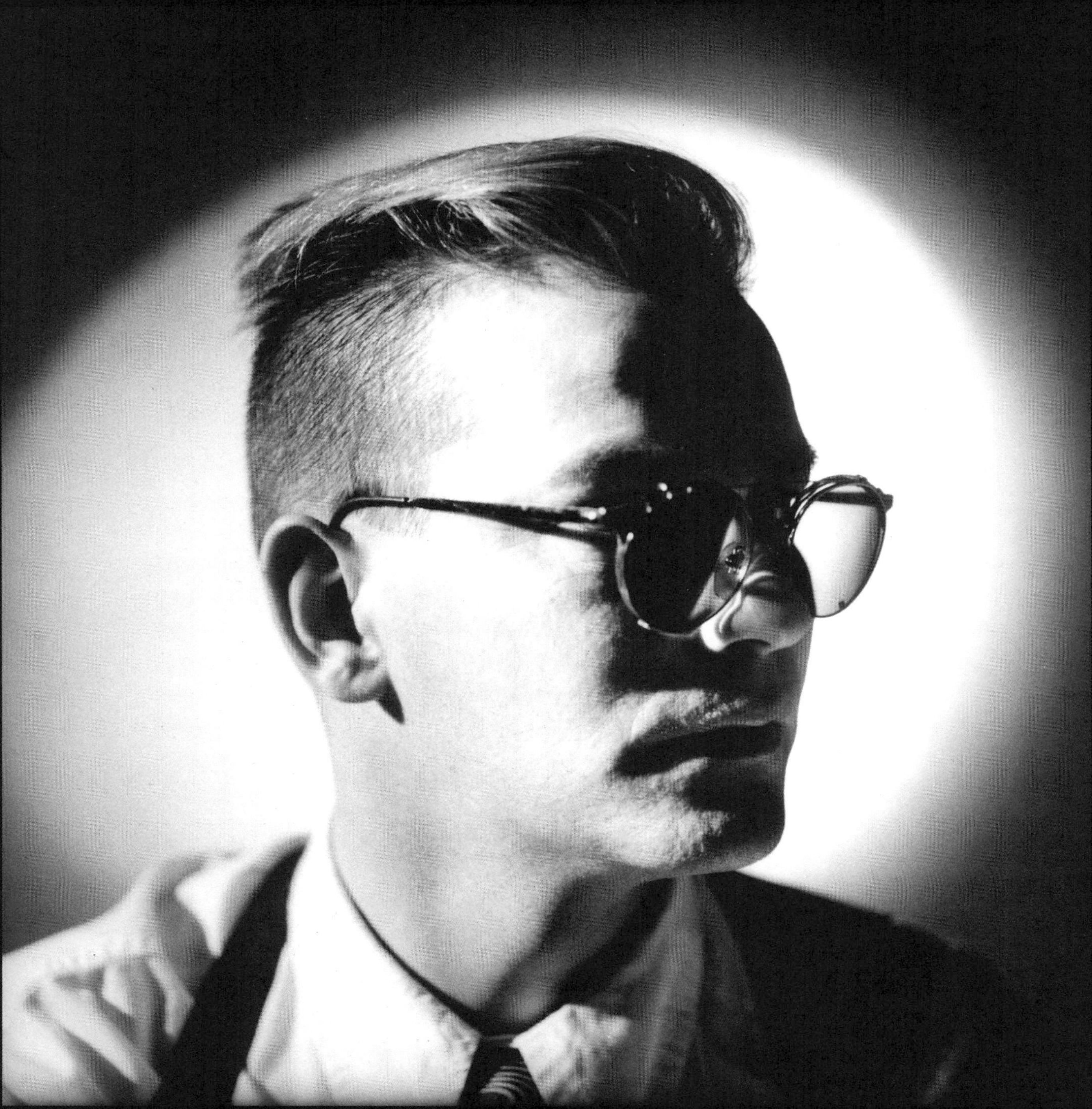

In 1988, Steve Dillon and Brett Ewins hatched an idea that would change British comics. Funded by Brett's mate Tom Astor, Deadline magazine was initially designed as a monthly anthology for comics, cartoons and features on music and pop culture. Additionally, it provided an escape route and pressure vent for its co-editors, who also worked as artists for 2000AD, the SF weekly comic that, even then, was already something of a venerable institution.

There were a few indie titles with small print runs around at the time, but nothing widely distributed, nothing regularly available on newsstands or the shelves of WH Smith to compete with the largely kid's humour or genre-based mainstream comics market. Early issues of Deadline were planned to include work by established comic artists like Steve and Brett themselves plus some of their wilder 2000AD colleagues like Peter Milligan and Brendan McCarthy, all let off the leash a little. The rest of the page count would be filled with work by younger cartoonists, each bringing their own new DIY kitchen-sink mentality that put two fingers up to the publishing status quo. Upon launch, Deadline very quickly assumed its own anarchic shape and voice, one possessed of a deep pop culture influence and awareness. Curated rather than edited per se, much of the magazine's early success was down to Steve and Brett's tastes and the contributors they selected, one of whom was Shaky Kane.

I first met Shaky when one of his drawings reached out and grabbed me by the optic nerve as I leafed through this new comics 'n' music magazine that I too contributed to.

↖ Shaky Kane, 1989. Deadline Magazine Promotional Image. Photo by Lawrence Watson.

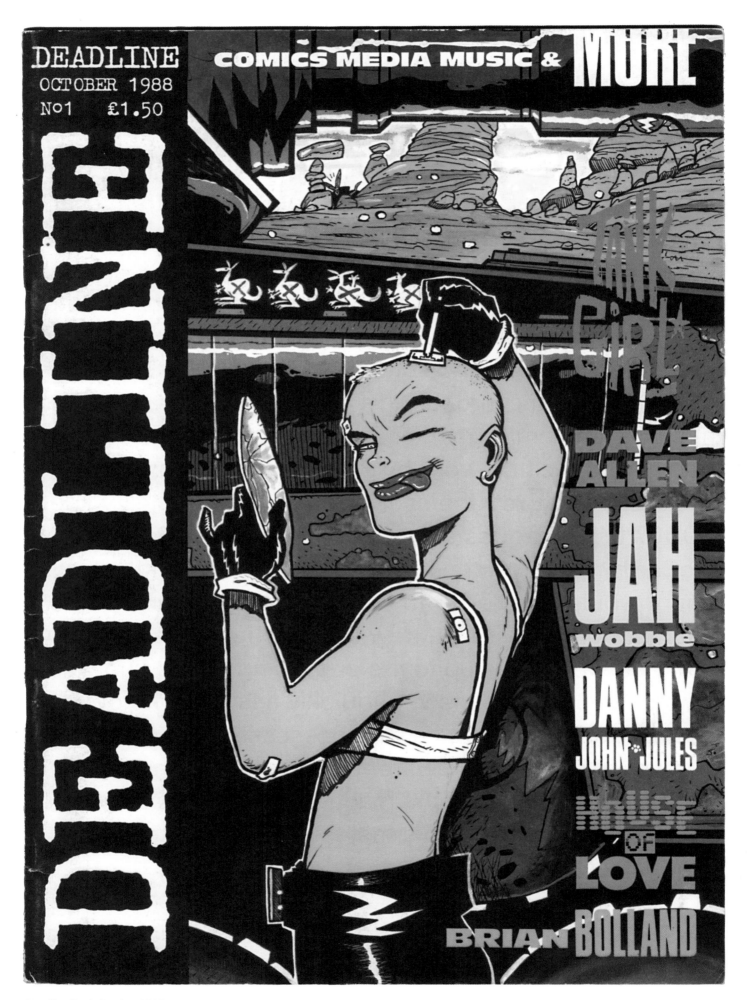

DEADLINE
OCTOBER 1988
Nº1    £1.50

COMICS MEDIA MUSIC & MORE

DEADLINE

TANK GIRL

DAVE ALLEN

JAH wobble

DANNY JOHN·JULES

HOUSE OF LOVE

BRIAN BOLLAND

Deadline No. 1, October 1988.

Our stuff appeared alongside work by Jamie Hewlett, Glyn Dillon, Philip Bond, D'Israeli, Rachael Ball and John McCrea, to name just a few of that first wave of Deadline contributors. A wise old cartoonist once said to me, "There are some people who have a way of putting themselves down on paper," and he might've been talking about any of these talents. Shaky's pages were slightly different in that there was also something else present, something autocannibalistic in the way he both channelled and repurposed a sense of the style of Jack Kirby, both mocking and loving the golden age of comics and using it as currency to comment upon the here-and-now.

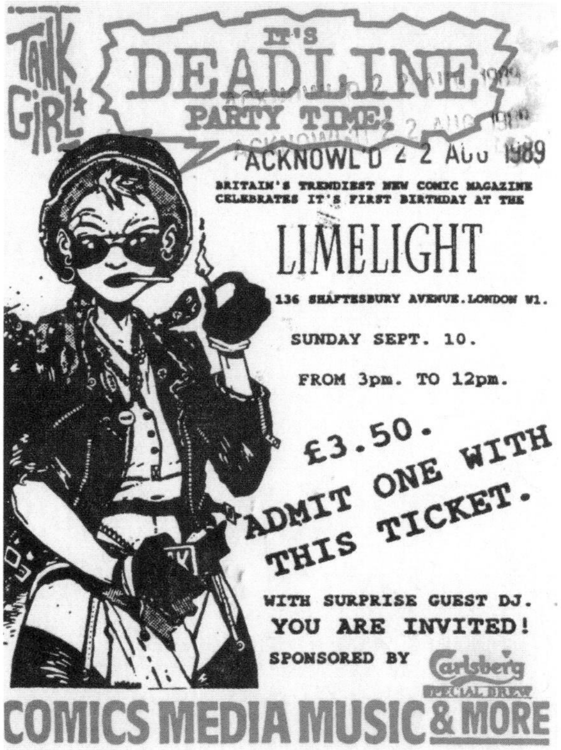
TANK GIRL*
IT'S
DEADLINE
PARTY TIME!
ACKNOWL'D 2 2 AUG 1989
BRITAIN'S TRENDIEST NEW COMIC MAGAZINE CELEBRATES IT'S FIRST BIRTHDAY AT THE
LIMELIGHT
136 SHAFTESBURY AVENUE.LONDON W1.
SUNDAY SEPT. 10.
FROM 3pm. TO 12pm.
£3.50.
ADMIT ONE WITH THIS TICKET.
WITH SURPRISE GUEST DJ.
YOU ARE INVITED!
SPONSORED BY Carlsberg SPECIAL BREW
COMICS MEDIA MUSIC & MORE

Deadline Party Ticket, 1989.

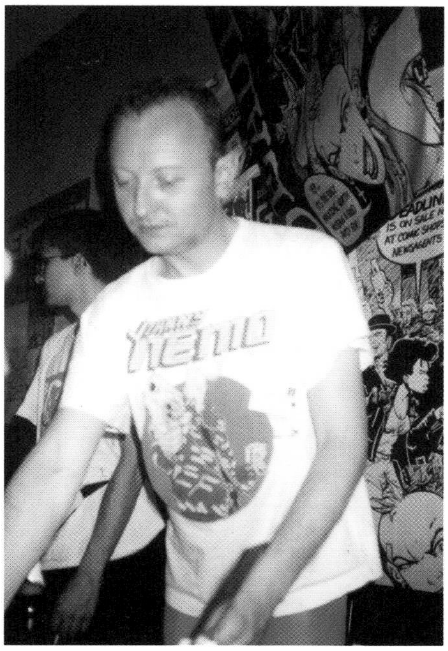

Brett Ewins, United Kingdom Comic Art Convention, 1989.

Working on Deadline in those early days felt like how I imagined it was being in a band–you came along, you jammed, you built a structure uniquely your own that added to the greater whole. A Shaky strip looked like he came at it with less of the approach of a musician and more that of a record producer, sampling things he loved, being inspired by weird shit he'd assimilated and forcing it all through the Shaky perceptual filter before mashing it all together in surreal new mixes and meanings that were somehow all his own. The end result felt gloriously subversive and was always very, very funny. Shaky's stuff exemplified the unwritten Deadline constitution—don't be like anything else out there.

Indeed, none of us working on Deadline suspected that the magazine's cultural impact would be so wide. It gave the world a lot of good things to remember as well as some truly great cartoonists whose careers continued beyond it.

I forget who eventually introduced me to Shaky in person, but I do remember being both enjoyably baffled and instantly charmed that first time. It helped that Shaky was, in person, a rakish and handsome bugger with a more than passing resemblance to David Bowie circa Scary Monsters. He spoke in riddles and playful epithets in a manner that was conversationally as insurgent as his drawings. That's the effect a Shaky Kane comic strip has — you feel as if he's coaxing out of you some new, previously unavailable level of awareness. That's Shaky's gift to the world. That's Shaky's gift to you. *A-men*. ■ January 2017

Nick Abadzis is a British, Eisner-award winning, internationally published writer and cartoonist who lives and works in the USA.

↗ Birth of Deadline, From Left Brett Ewins; Jamie Hewlett; Steve Dillon, 1988. Photo by Steve Cook / National Portrait Gallery.
→ Nick Abadzis (far right) and friends, Deadline Signing Tour, 1989.

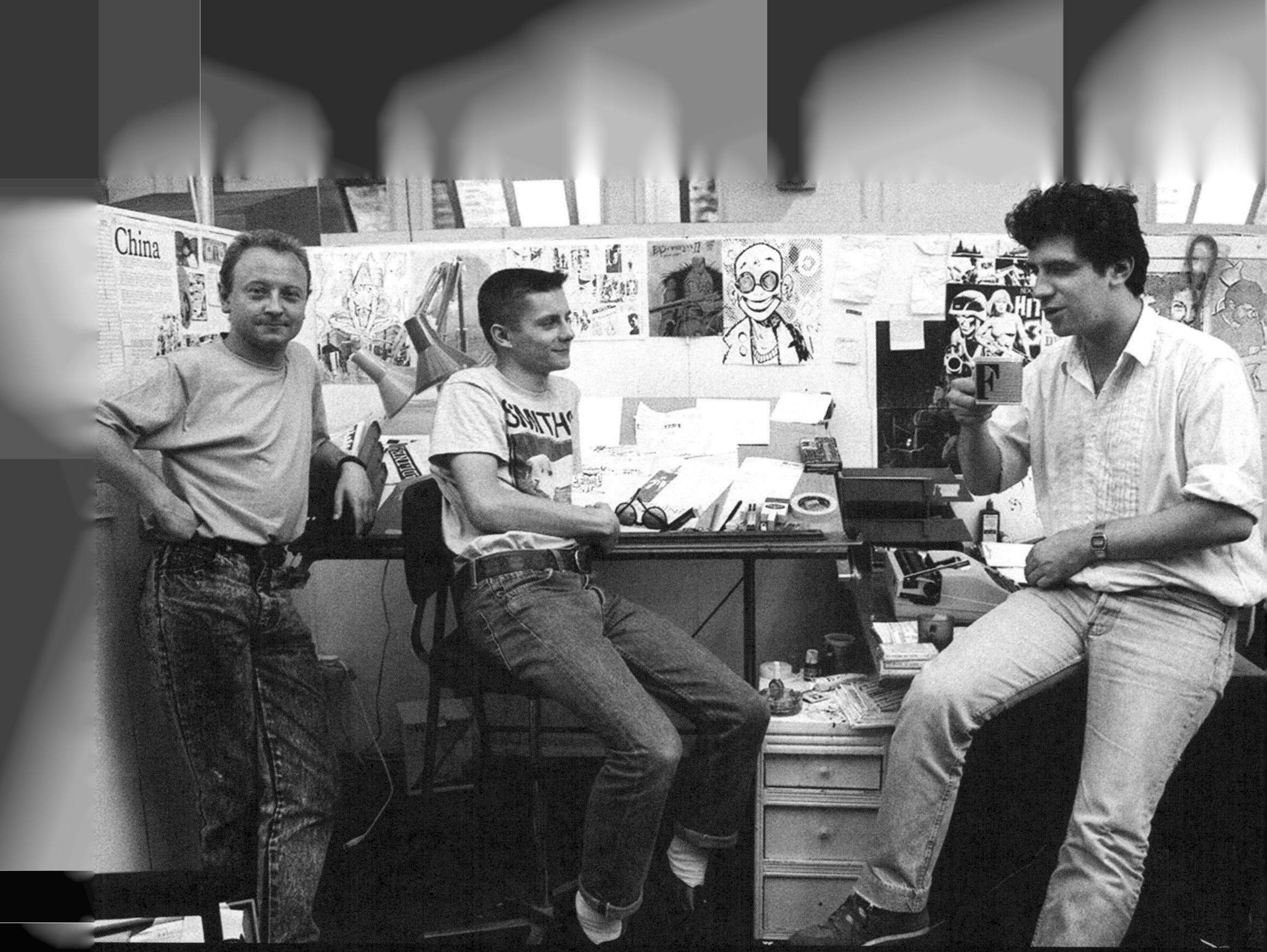
China

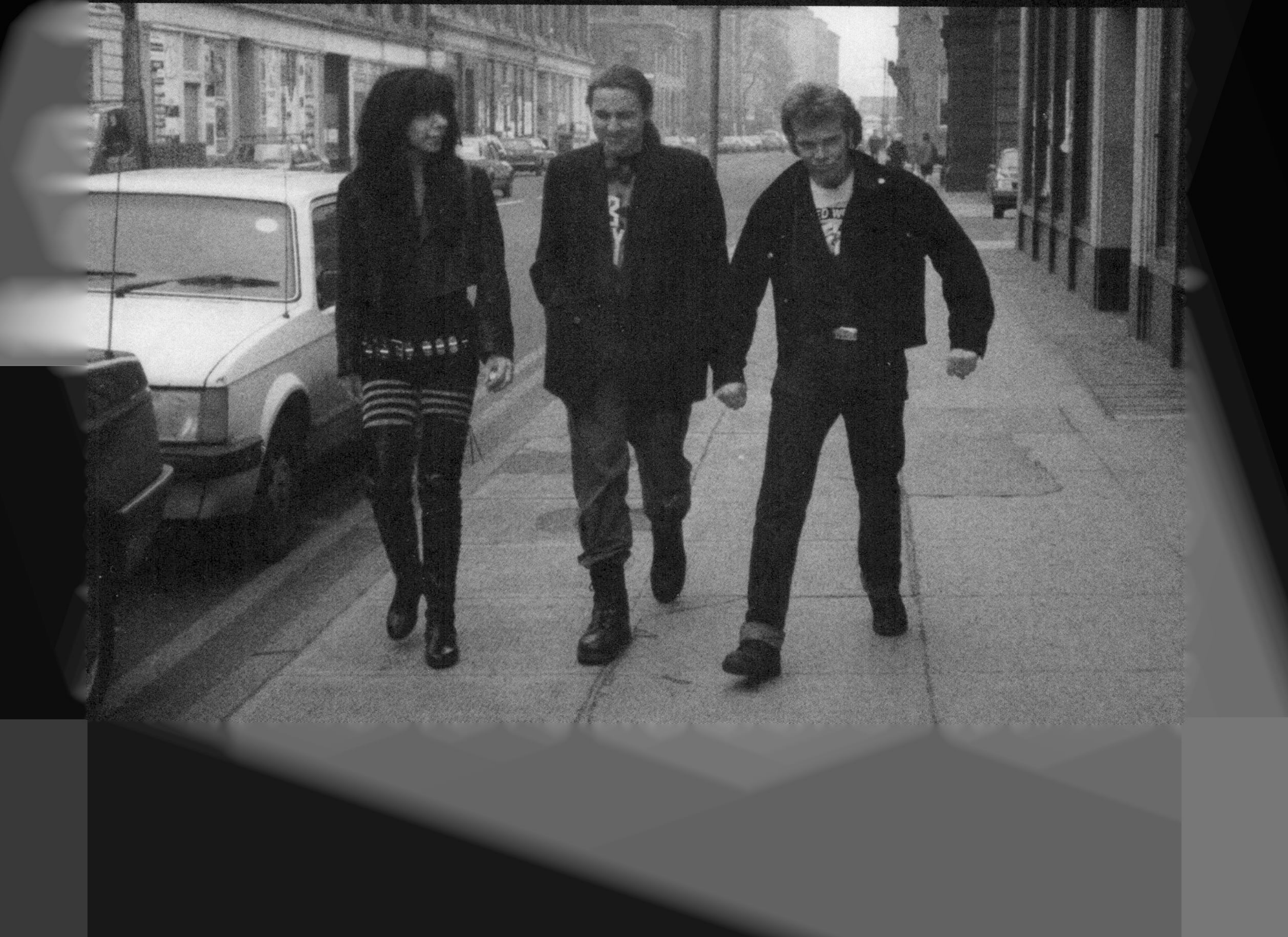

# The Complete Deadline Strips of Shaky Kane 1988 – 1995

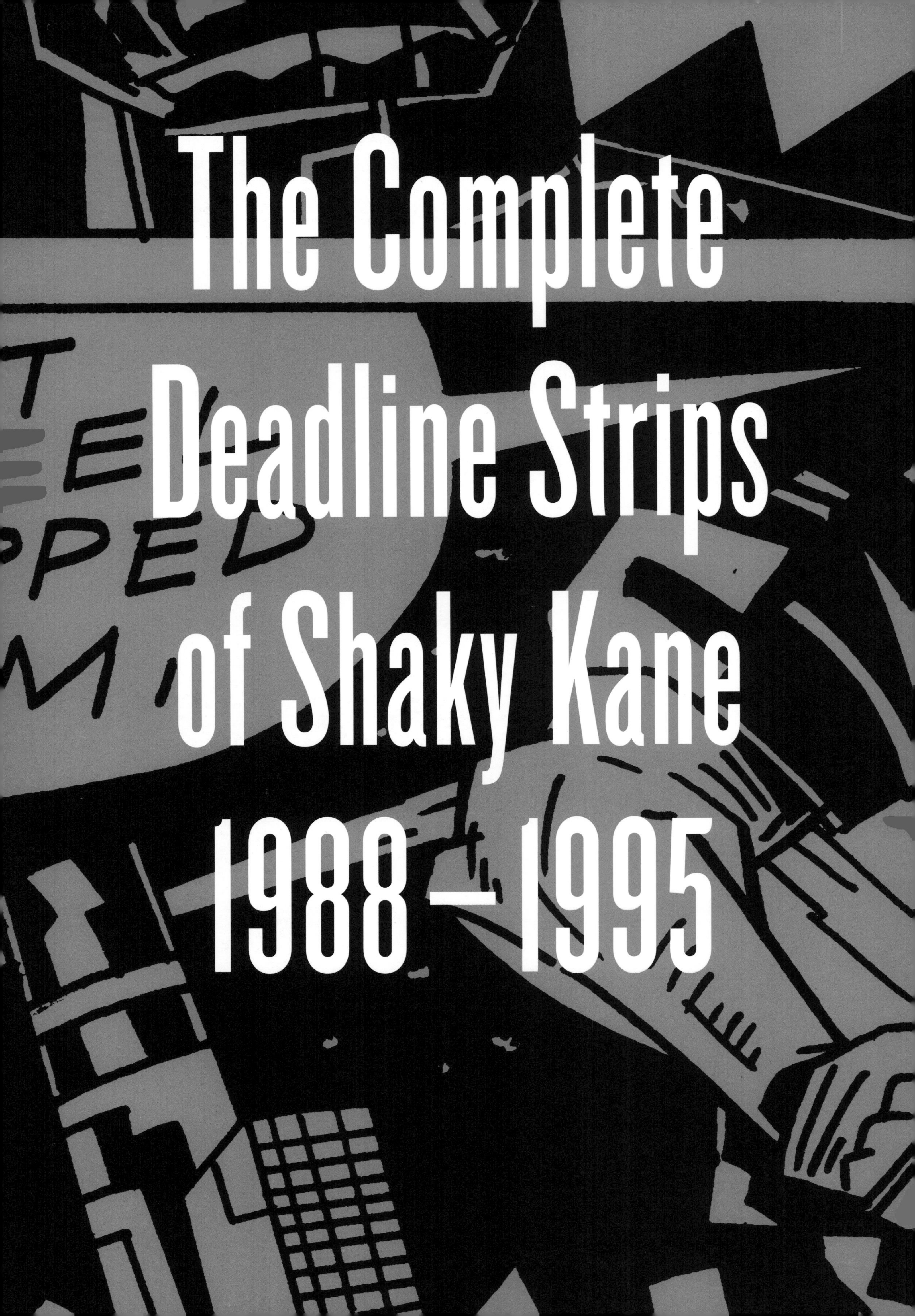

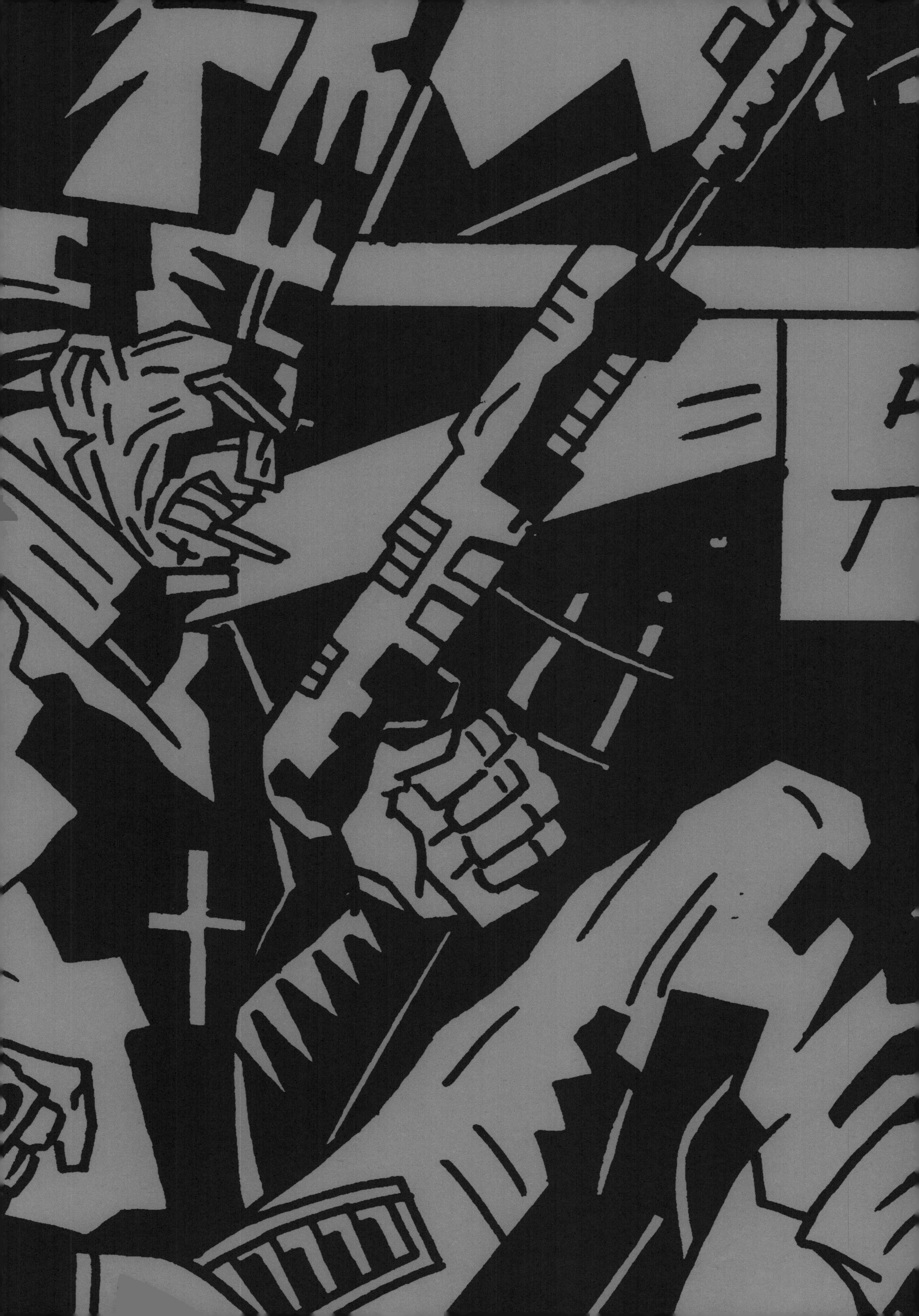

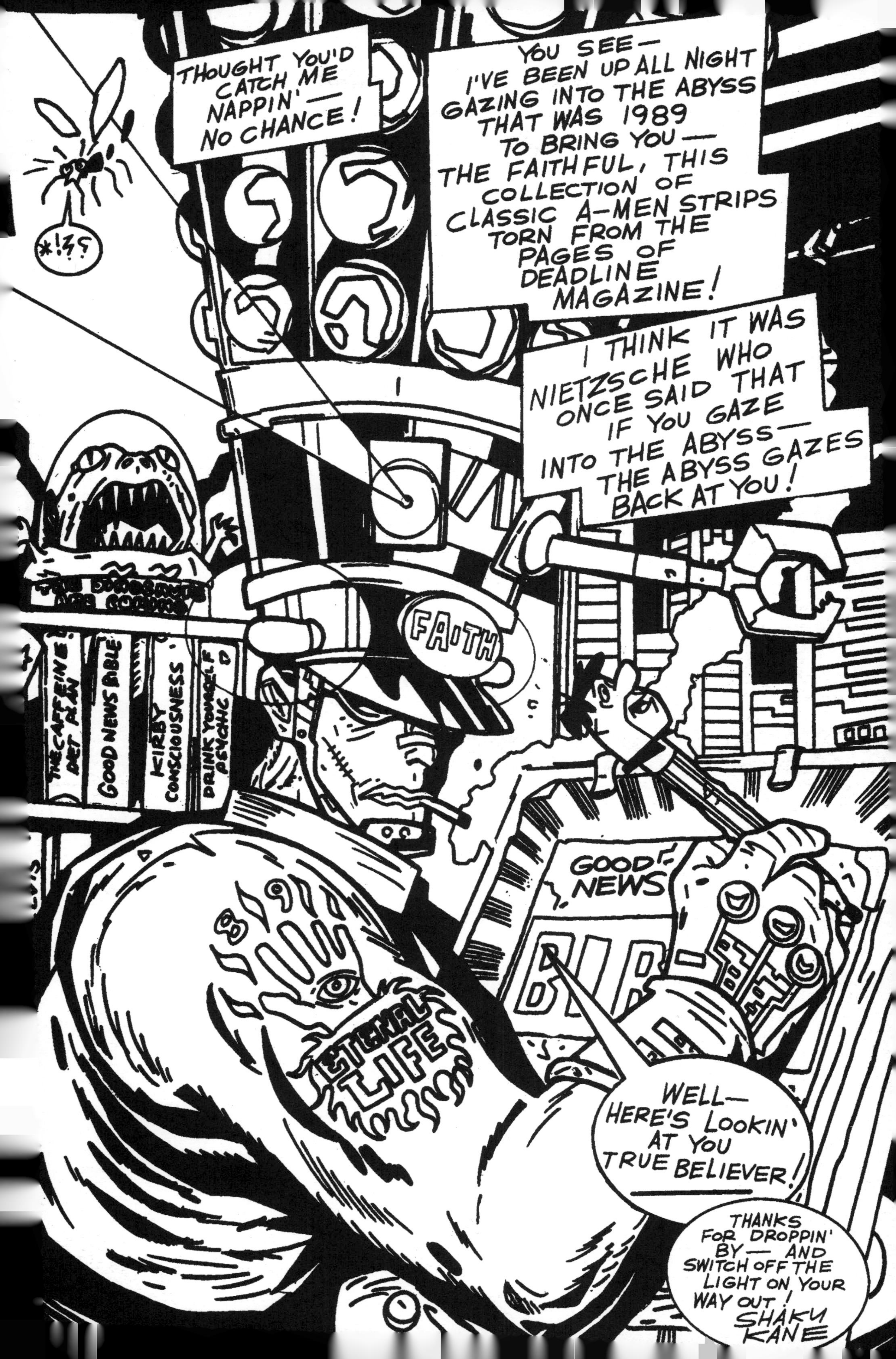

THOUGHT YOU'D CATCH ME NAPPIN' — NO CHANCE!
YOU SEE— I'VE BEEN UP ALL NIGHT GAZING INTO THE ABYSS THAT WAS 1989 TO BRING YOU— THE FAITHFUL, THIS COLLECTION OF CLASSIC A-MEN STRIPS TORN FROM THE PAGES OF DEADLINE MAGAZINE!
I THINK IT WAS NIETZSCHE WHO ONCE SAID THAT IF YOU GAZE INTO THE ABYSS— THE ABYSS GAZES BACK AT YOU!
THE CAFFEINE DIET PLAN
GOOD NEWS BIBLE
KIRBY CONSCIOUSNESS
DRINK YOURSELF PSYCHIC
FAITH
GOOD NEWS
ETERNAL LIFE
WELL— HERE'S LOOKIN' AT YOU TRUE BELIEVER!
THANKS FOR DROPPIN' BY— AND SWITCH OFF THE LIGHT ON YOUR WAY OUT!
SHAKY KANE

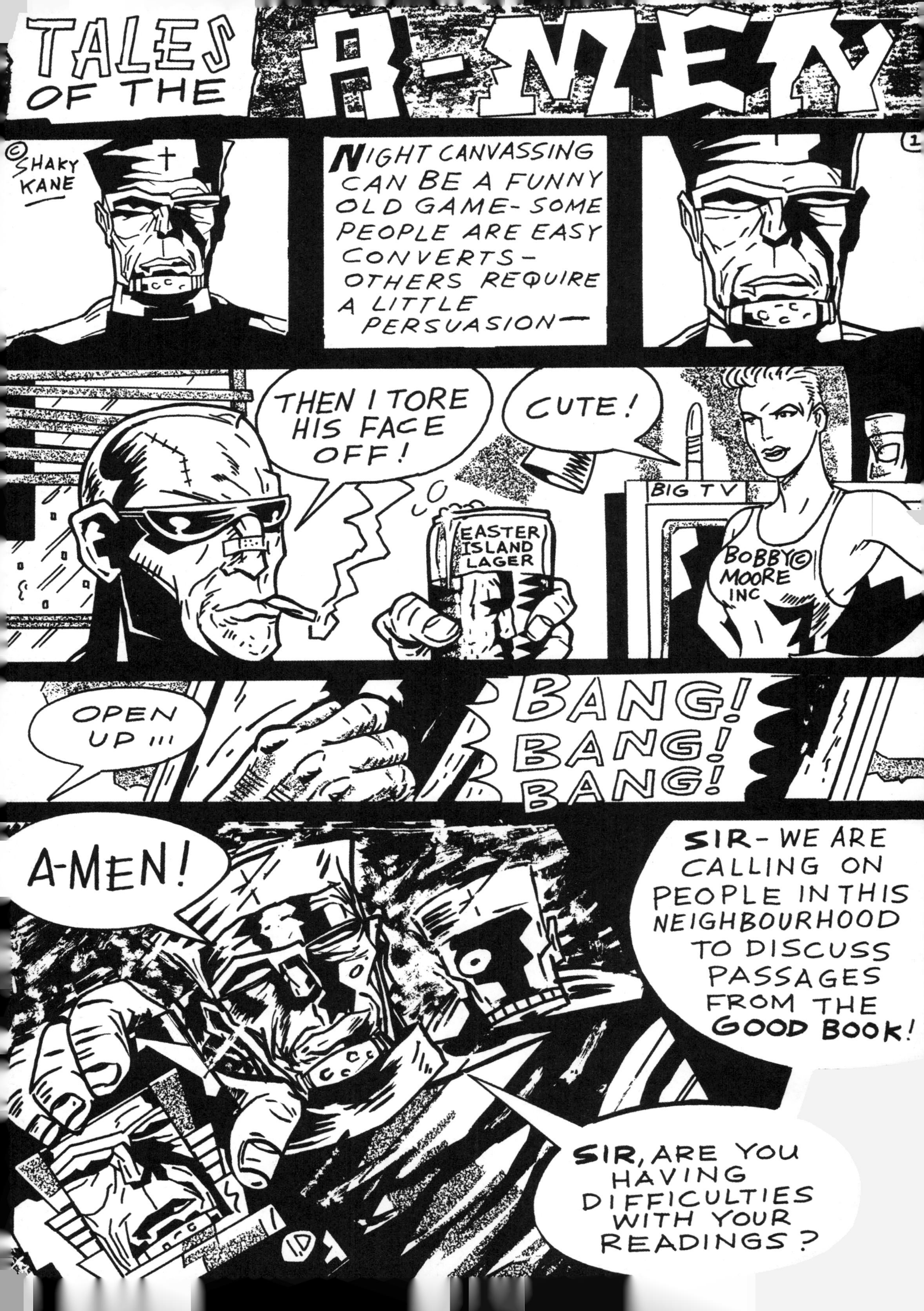

TALES OF THE A-MEN
© SHAKY KANE
1
NIGHT CANVASSING CAN BE A FUNNY OLD GAME- SOME PEOPLE ARE EASY CONVERTS- OTHERS REQUIRE A LITTLE PERSUASION—
THEN I TORE HIS FACE OFF!
CUTE!
BIG TV
EASTER ISLAND LAGER
BOBBY MOORE © INC
OPEN UP !!!
BANG! BANG! BANG!
A-MEN!
SIR- WE ARE CALLING ON PEOPLE IN THIS NEIGHBOURHOOD TO DISCUSS PASSAGES FROM THE GOOD BOOK!
SIR, ARE YOU HAVING DIFFICULTIES WITH YOUR READINGS?

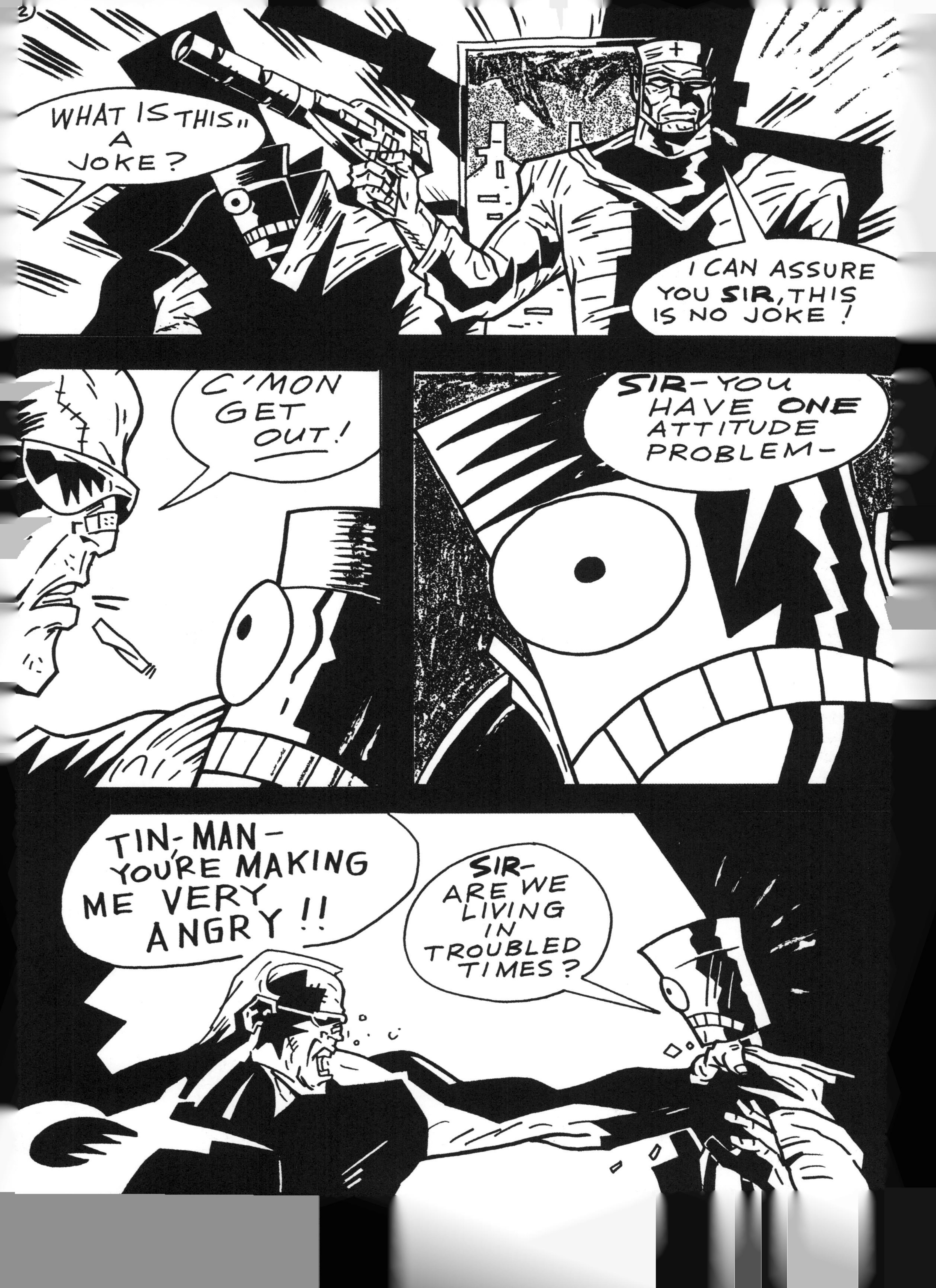
WHAT IS THIS" A JOKE?
I CAN ASSURE YOU SIR, THIS IS NO JOKE!
C'MON GET OUT!
SIR- YOU HAVE ONE ATTITUDE PROBLEM-
TIN-MAN- YOU'RE MAKING ME VERY ANGRY!!
SIR- ARE WE LIVING IN TROUBLED TIMES?

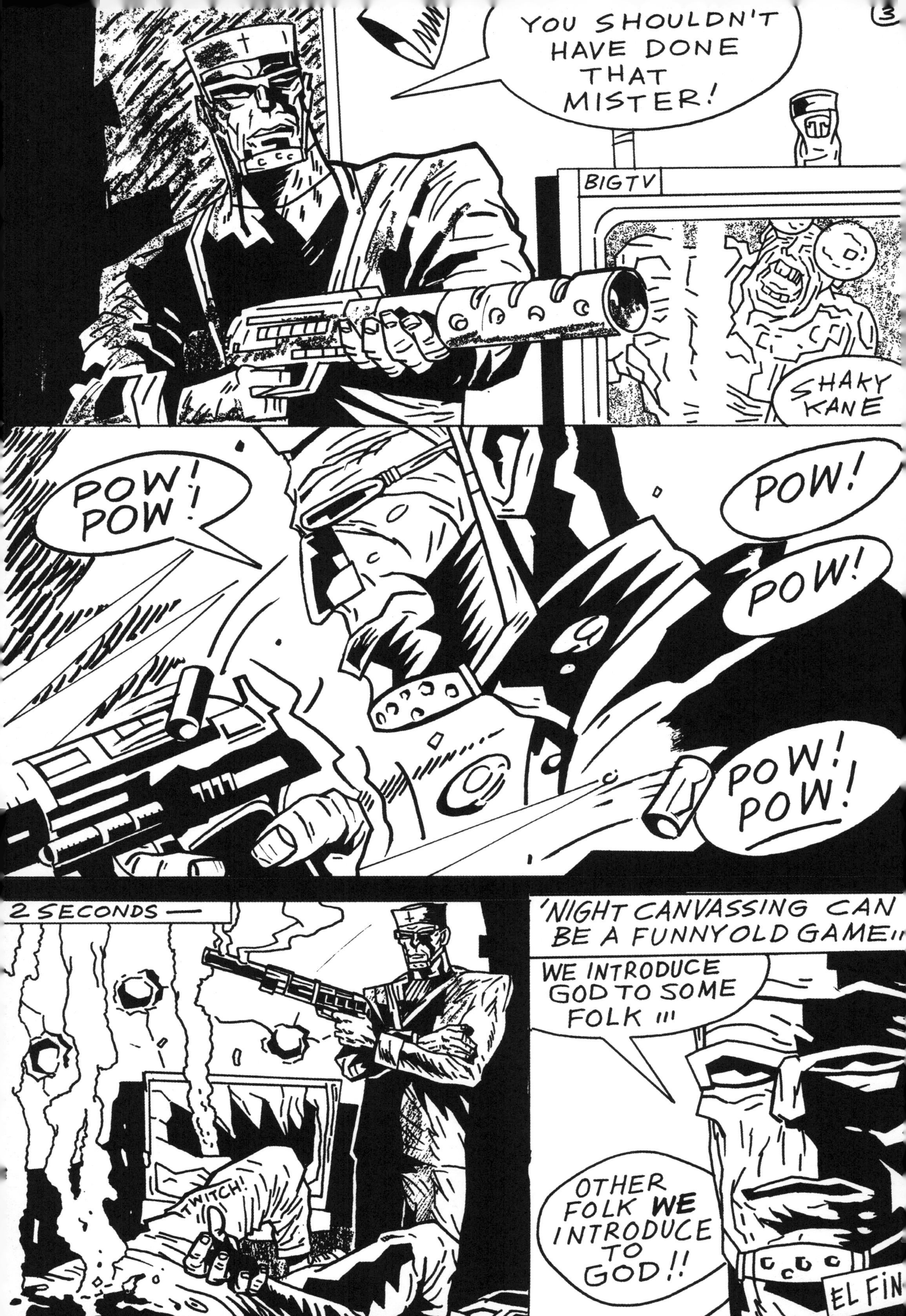

3
YOU SHOULDN'T HAVE DONE THAT MISTER!
BIGTV
SHAKY KANE
POW! POW!
POW!
POW!
POW! POW!
2 SECONDS —
TWITCH!
'NIGHT CANVASSING CAN BE A FUNNYOLD GAME...
WE INTRODUCE GOD TO SOME FOLK ...
OTHER FOLK WE INTRODUCE TO GOD!!
EL FIN

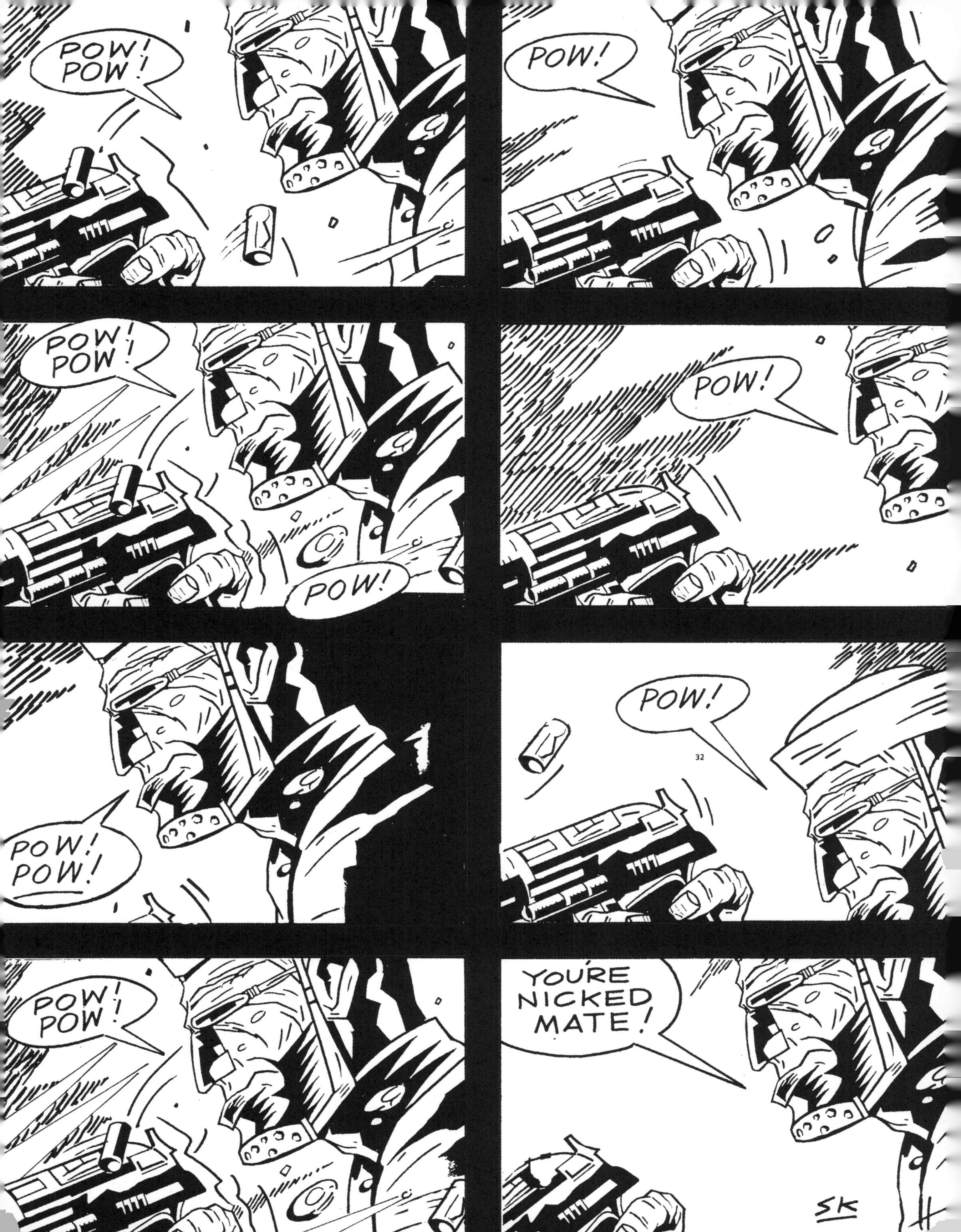
POW! POW!
POW!
POW! POW!
POW!
POW!
POW! POW!
POW!
POW! POW!
YOU'RE NICKED MATE!
SK

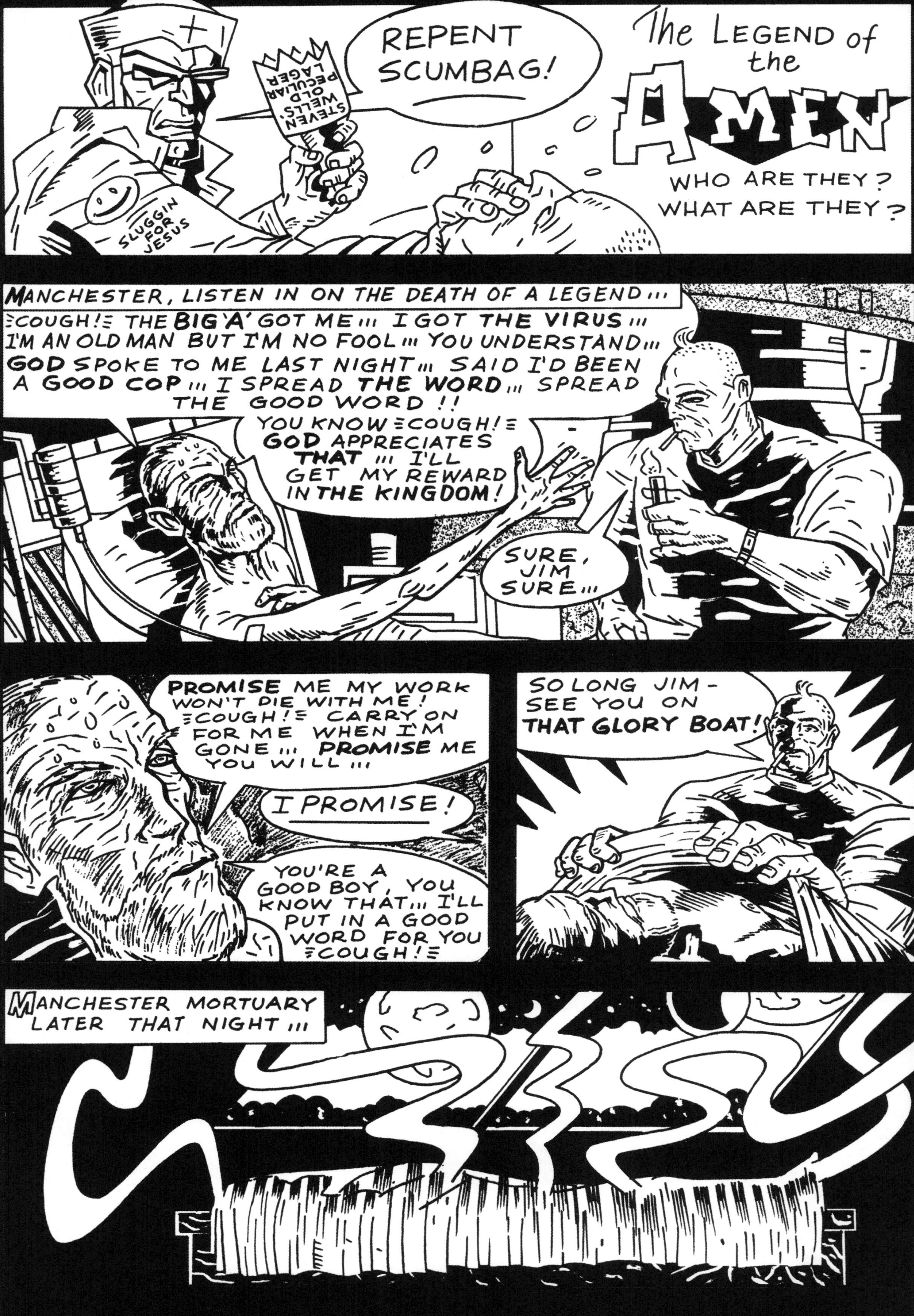
REPENT SCUMBAG!
STEVEN WELLS OLD PECULIAR LAGER
SLUGGIN FOR JESUS
The LEGEND of the AMEN
WHO ARE THEY? WHAT ARE THEY?
MANCHESTER, LISTEN IN ON THE DEATH OF A LEGEND...
≡COUGH!≡ THE BIG 'A' GOT ME... I GOT THE VIRUS... I'M AN OLD MAN BUT I'M NO FOOL... YOU UNDERSTAND... GOD SPOKE TO ME LAST NIGHT... SAID I'D BEEN A GOOD COP... I SPREAD THE WORD... SPREAD THE GOOD WORD!!
YOU KNOW ≡COUGH!≡ GOD APPRECIATES THAT... I'LL GET MY REWARD IN THE KINGDOM!
SURE, JIM SURE...
PROMISE ME MY WORK WON'T DIE WITH ME! ≡COUGH!≡ CARRY ON FOR ME WHEN I'M GONE... PROMISE ME YOU WILL...
I PROMISE!
YOU'RE A GOOD BOY, YOU KNOW THAT... I'LL PUT IN A GOOD WORD FOR YOU ≡COUGH!≡
SO LONG JIM - SEE YOU ON THAT GLORY BOAT!
MANCHESTER MORTUARY LATER THAT NIGHT...

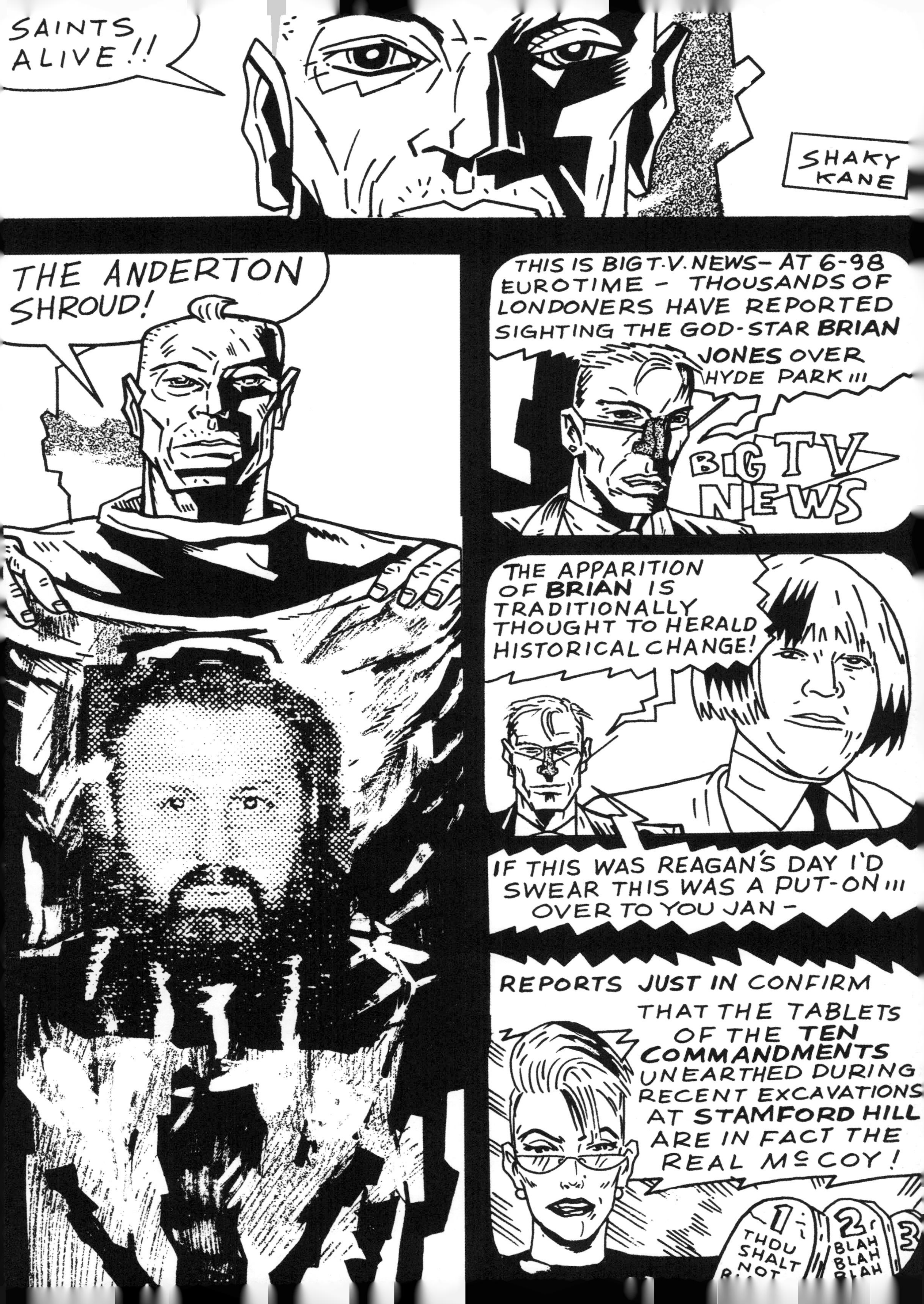
SAINTS ALIVE!!
SHAKY KANE
THE ANDERTON SHROUD!
THIS IS BIGT-V. NEWS– AT 6-98 EUROTIME – THOUSANDS OF LONDONERS HAVE REPORTED SIGHTING THE GOD-STAR BRIAN JONES OVER HYDE PARK...
BIG TV NEWS
THE APPARITION OF BRIAN IS TRADITIONALLY THOUGHT TO HERALD HISTORICAL CHANGE!
IF THIS WAS REAGAN'S DAY I'D SWEAR THIS WAS A PUT-ON... OVER TO YOU JAN –
REPORTS JUST IN CONFIRM THAT THE TABLETS OF THE TEN COMMANDMENTS UNEARTHED DURING RECENT EXCAVATIONS AT STAMFORD HILL ARE IN FACT THE REAL McCOY!
1 THOU SHALT NOT
2 BLAH BLAH
3

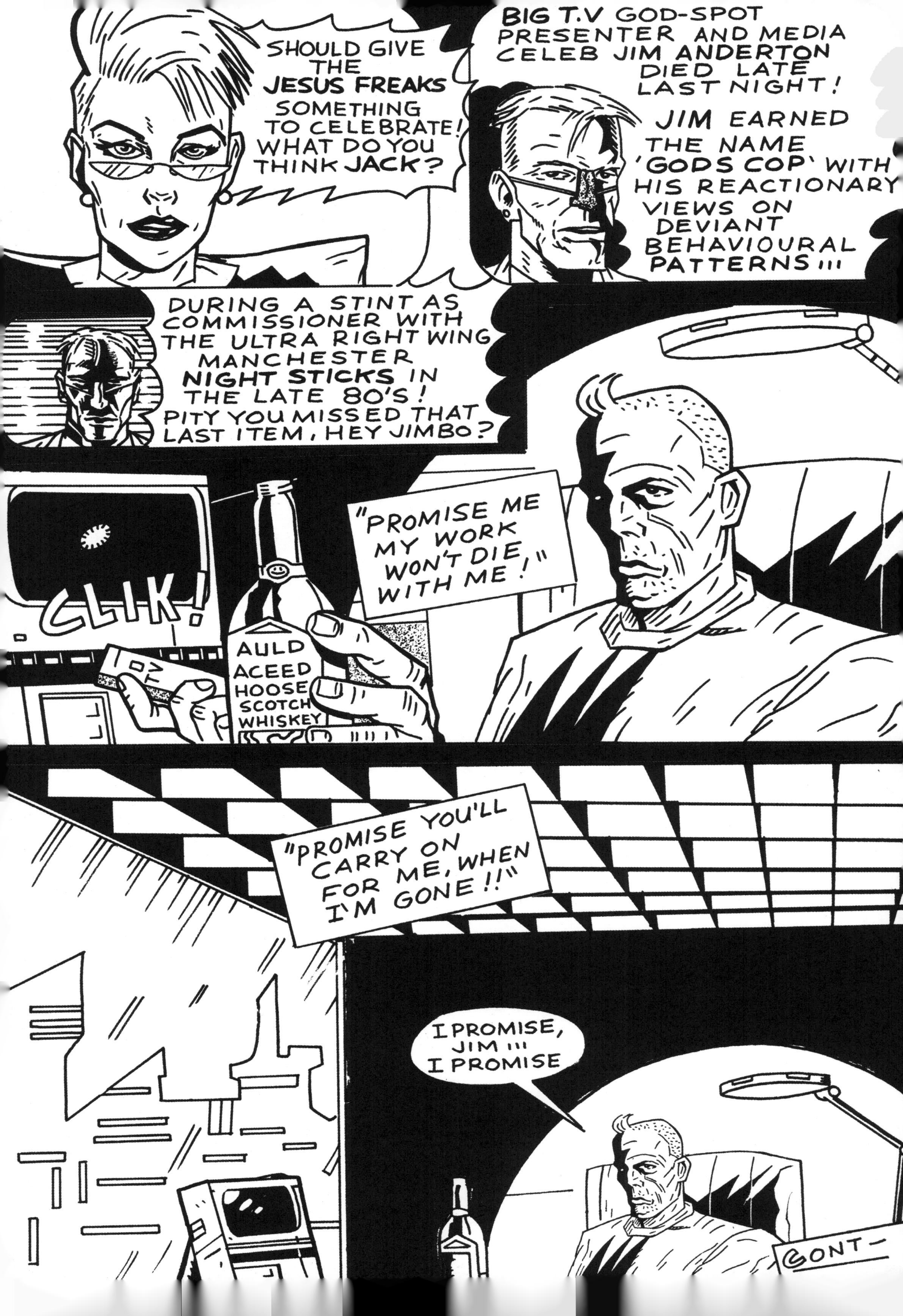
SHOULD GIVE THE JESUS FREAKS SOMETHING TO CELEBRATE! WHAT DO YOU THINK JACK?
BIG T.V GOD-SPOT PRESENTER AND MEDIA CELEB JIM ANDERTON DIED LATE LAST NIGHT!
JIM EARNED THE NAME 'GODS COP' WITH HIS REACTIONARY VIEWS ON DEVIANT BEHAVIOURAL PATTERNS ...
DURING A STINT AS COMMISSIONER WITH THE ULTRA RIGHT WING MANCHESTER NIGHT STICKS IN THE LATE 80'S!
PITY YOU MISSED THAT LAST ITEM, HEY JIMBO?
CLIK!
AULD ACEED HOOSE SCOTCH WHISKEY
"PROMISE ME MY WORK WON'T DIE WITH ME!"
"PROMISE YOU'LL CARRY ON FOR ME, WHEN I'M GONE!!"
I PROMISE, JIM ... I PROMISE
CONT-

# SHAKY KANE

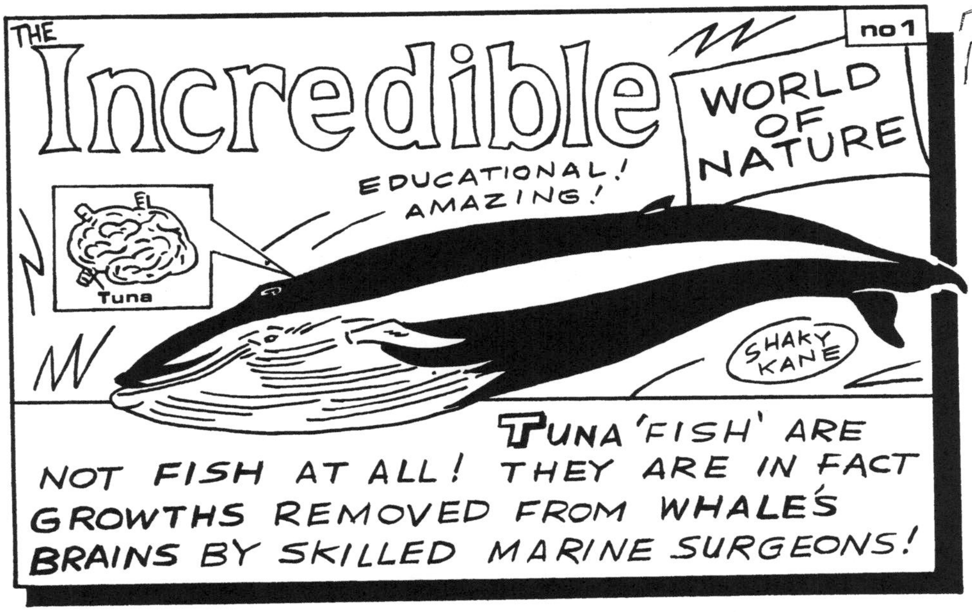

THE Incredible
no 1
WORLD OF NATURE
EDUCATIONAL! AMAZING!
Tuna
SHAKY KANE
TUNA 'FISH' ARE NOT FISH AT ALL! THEY ARE IN FACT GROWTHS REMOVED FROM WHALE'S BRAINS BY SKILLED MARINE SURGEONS!


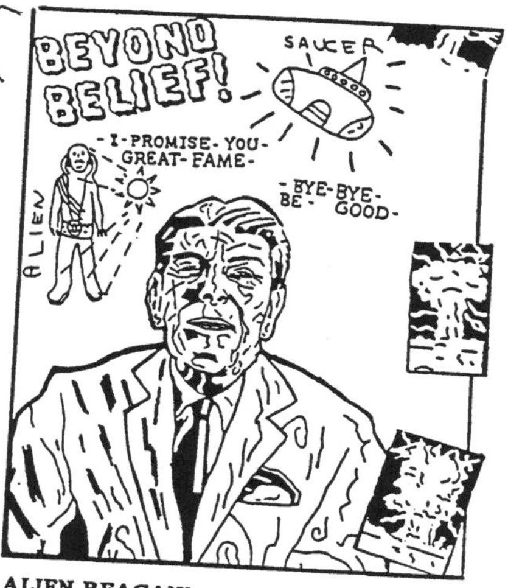

BEYOND BELIEF!
SAUCER
-I-PROMISE-YOU-GREAT-FAME-
-BYE-BYE-BE-GOOD-
ALIEN


**ALIEN REAGAN!**
BULLET DODGING B MOVIE STAR **RONALD REAGAN** CLAIMS HE WAS ONCE VISITED BY THE **OCCUPENT** OF A **FLYING SAUCER** WHO PROMISED HIM **GREAT FAME!** HE HAS SINCE APPEARED IN THE EVER POPULAR **EVE OF DESTRUCTION!**

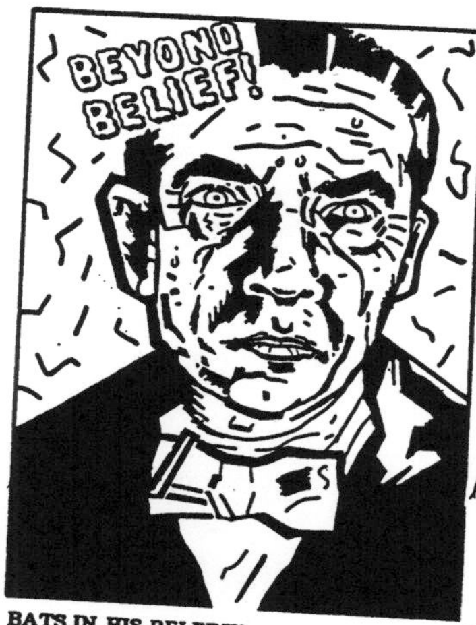

BEYOND BELIEF!


**BATS IN HIS BELFRY!**
UNDER THE INFLUENCE OF MORPHINE HOLLYWOOD WEIRDO BELA LUGOSI BELIEVED HIMSELF TO BE COUNT DRACULA!

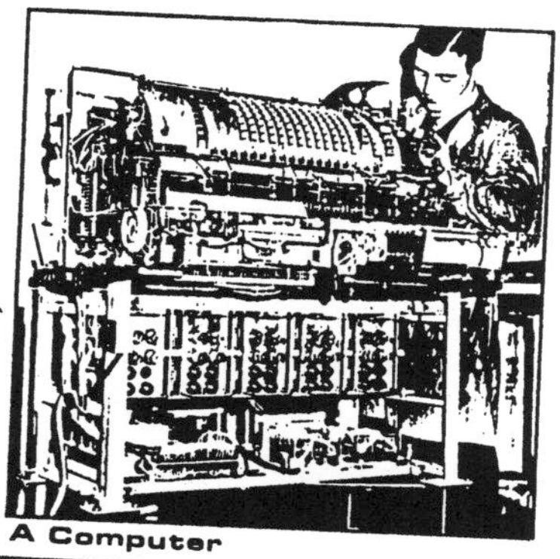

A Computer

## YOU ARE A MORMON!

— If you're not now, you'll be one pretty soon! Those Salt Lake City weirdos, the same folk that launched the Osmonds into a world too stupid to resist, have fed the names of everyone on the Planet into a super computer. Even as you read this, they're working through the list baptising us all into the Mormon faith!

So come on down! You are a Mormon!

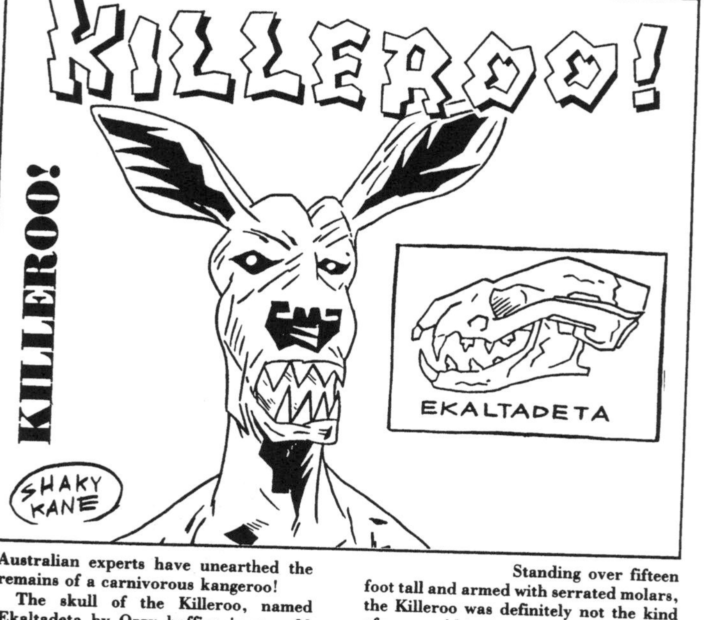

KILLEROO!
KILLEROO!
EKALTADETA
SHAKY KANE


Australian experts have unearthed the remains of a carnivorous kangeroo!

The skull of the Killeroo, named Ekaltadeta by Ozzy boffins is over 20 million years old.

Standing over fifteen foot tall and armed with serrated molars, the Killeroo was definitely not the kind of roo you'd invite to your Barby!

## RAPID BUG EYED MOVEMENT

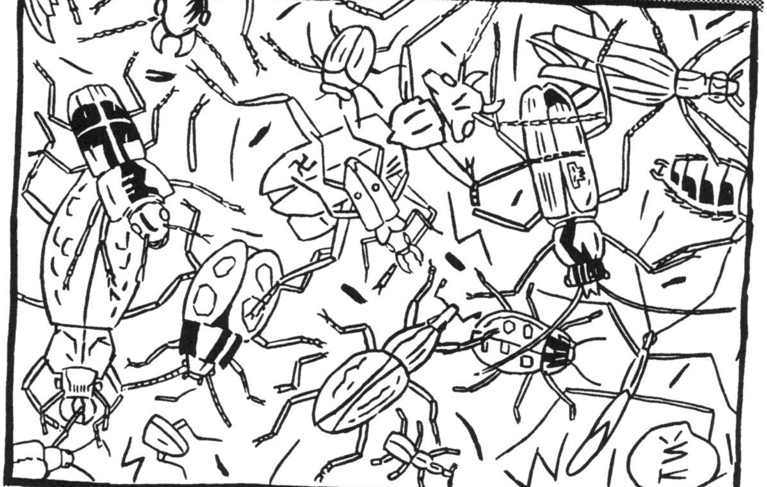

Sleep deprivation can have mind-blowing effects!
Marathon wide-awake boy, Peter Tripp, attempting 200 sleepless hours, ran screaming into the streets crawling with imaginary insects, while being chased by an 'undertaker' in a suit of worms!
Pass the pro-plus Peter!

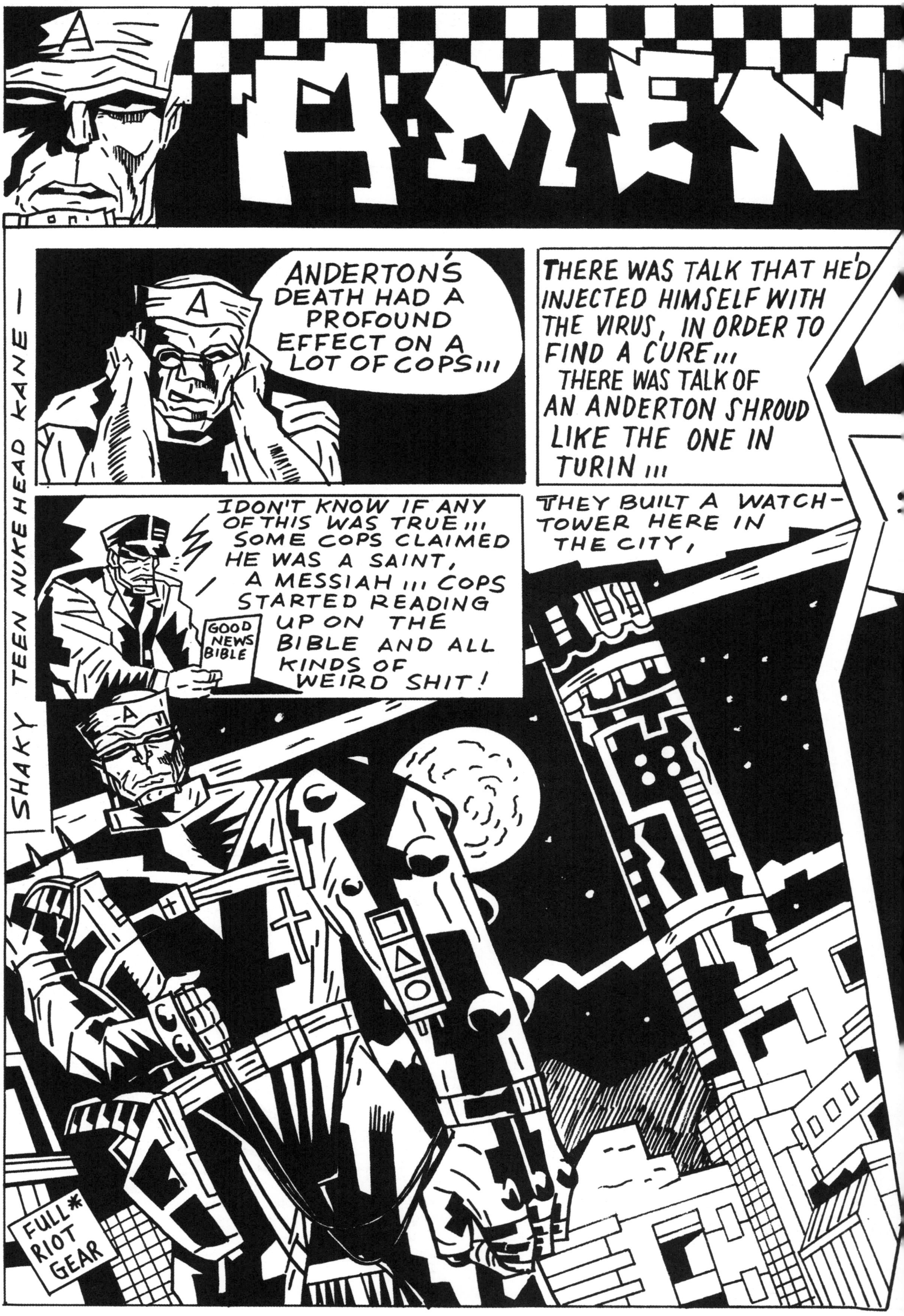
A.M.E.N
SHAKY TEEN NUKEHEAD KANE —
ANDERTON'S DEATH HAD A PROFOUND EFFECT ON A LOT OF COPS...
THERE WAS TALK THAT HE'D INJECTED HIMSELF WITH THE VIRUS, IN ORDER TO FIND A CURE... THERE WAS TALK OF AN ANDERTON SHROUD LIKE THE ONE IN TURIN...
I DON'T KNOW IF ANY OF THIS WAS TRUE... SOME COPS CLAIMED HE WAS A SAINT, A MESSIAH... COPS STARTED READING UP ON THE BIBLE AND ALL KINDS OF WEIRD SHIT!
GOOD NEWS BIBLE
THEY BUILT A WATCH-TOWER HERE IN THE CITY,
FULL* RIOT GEAR

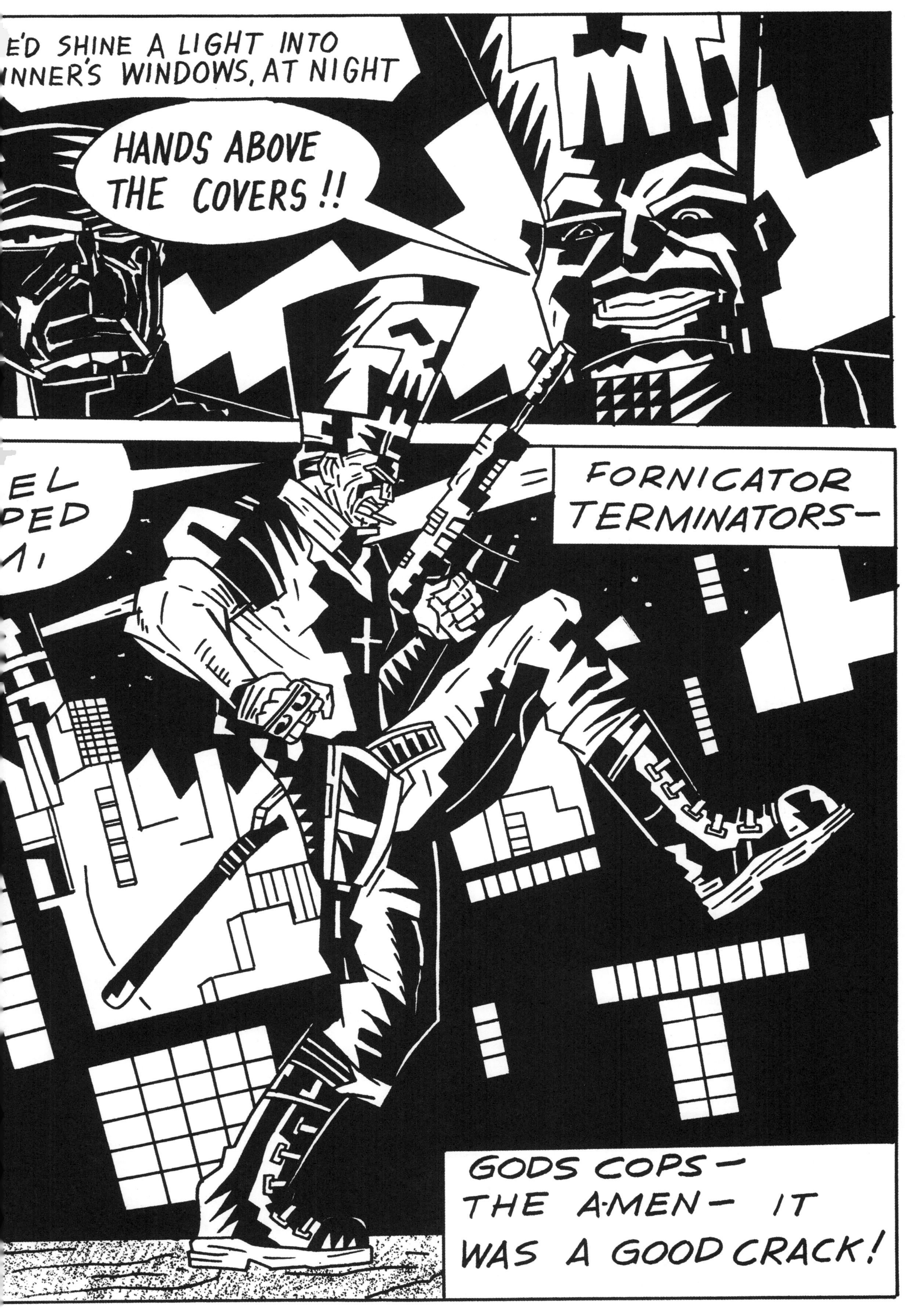
E'D SHINE A LIGHT INTO
INNER'S WINDOWS, AT NIGHT
HANDS ABOVE THE COVERS !!
FORNICATOR TERMINATORS—
GODS COPS — THE A·MEN — IT WAS A GOOD CRACK!

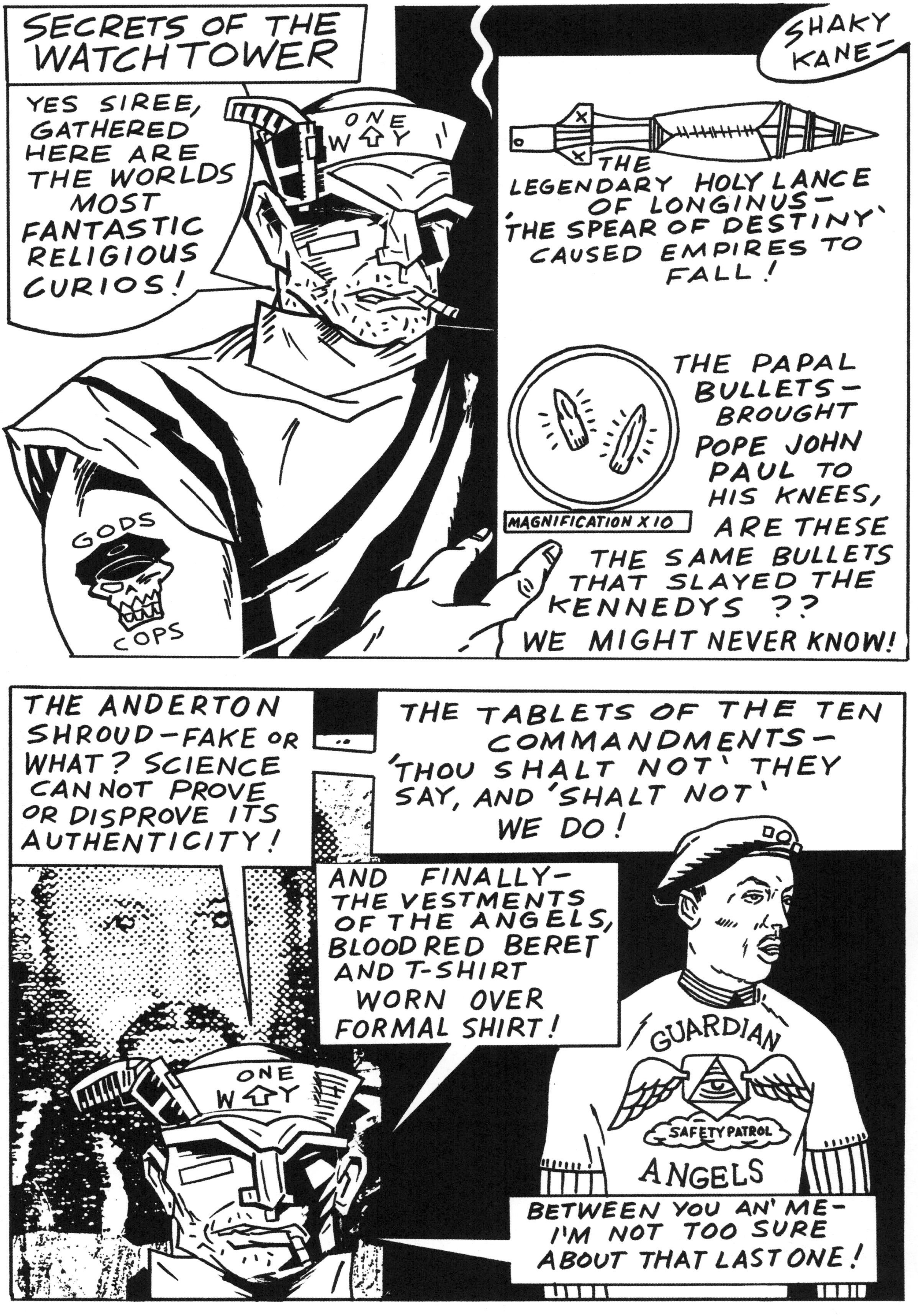

SECRETS OF THE WATCHTOWER
SHAKY KANE-
YES SIREE, GATHERED HERE ARE THE WORLDS MOST FANTASTIC RELIGIOUS CURIOS!
ONE WAY
THE LEGENDARY HOLY LANCE OF LONGINUS- 'THE SPEAR OF DESTINY' CAUSED EMPIRES TO FALL!
GODS COPS
MAGNIFICATION X 10
THE PAPAL BULLETS- BROUGHT POPE JOHN PAUL TO HIS KNEES, ARE THESE THE SAME BULLETS THAT SLAYED THE KENNEDYS ??
WE MIGHT NEVER KNOW!
THE ANDERTON SHROUD-FAKE OR WHAT? SCIENCE CAN NOT PROVE OR DISPROVE ITS AUTHENTICITY!
THE TABLETS OF THE TEN COMMANDMENTS- 'THOU SHALT NOT' THEY SAY, AND 'SHALT NOT' WE DO!
AND FINALLY- THE VESTMENTS OF THE ANGELS, BLOOD RED BERET AND T-SHIRT WORN OVER FORMAL SHIRT!
GUARDIAN
SAFETY PATROL
ANGELS
ONE WAY
BETWEEN YOU AN' ME- I'M NOT TOO SURE ABOUT THAT LAST ONE!

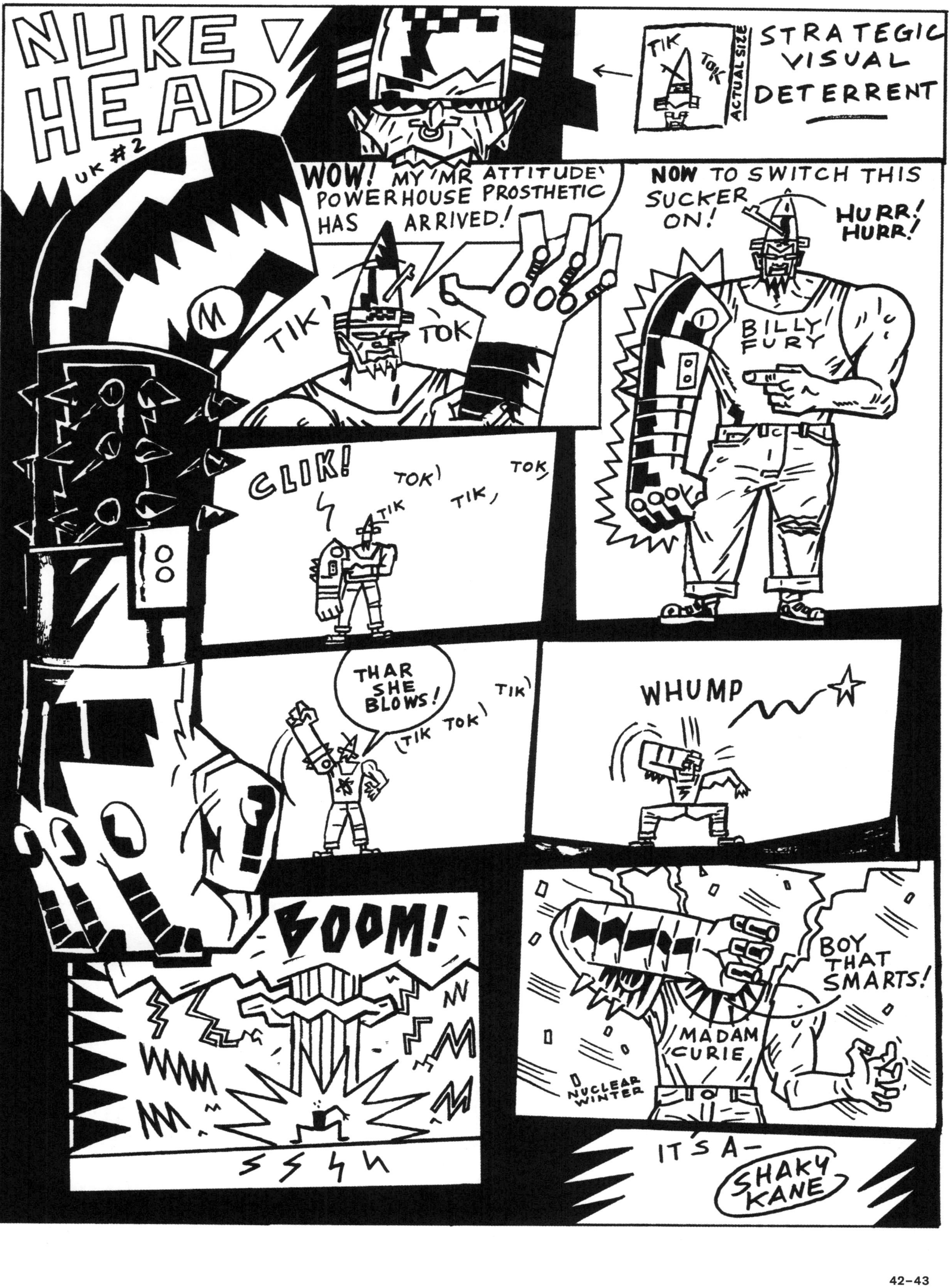
NUKE HEAD
UK #2
TIK TOK
ACTUAL SIZE
STRATEGIC VISUAL DETERRENT
WOW! MY 'MR ATTITUDE' POWERHOUSE PROSTHETIC HAS ARRIVED!
TIK TOK
NOW TO SWITCH THIS SUCKER ON!
HURR! HURR!
BILLY FURY
CLIK!
TOK TOK TIK TIK
THAR SHE BLOWS!
TIK TIK TOK
WHUMP
BOOM!
BOY THAT SMARTS!
MADAM CURIE
NUCLEAR WINTER
IT'S A—
SHAKY KANE

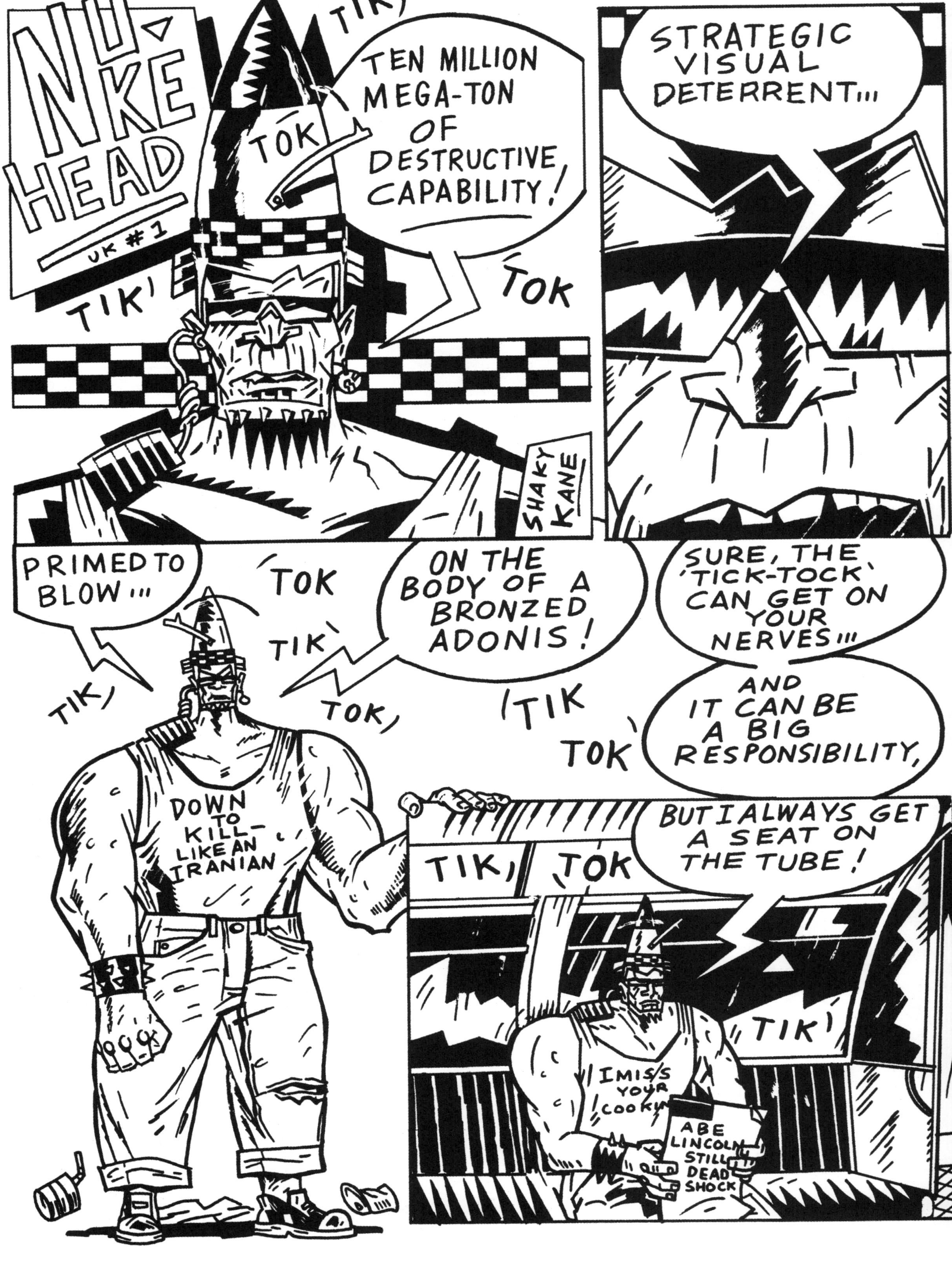
NUKE HEAD
UK #1
TIK
TOK
TEN MILLION MEGA-TON OF DESTRUCTIVE CAPABILITY!
TIK
TOK
SHAKY KANE
STRATEGIC VISUAL DETERRENT...
PRIMED TO BLOW...
TOK
TIK
TIK
TOK
ON THE BODY OF A BRONZED ADONIS!
DOWN TO KILL-LIKE AN IRANIAN
TIK
TOK
SURE, THE 'TICK-TOCK' CAN GET ON YOUR NERVES...
AND IT CAN BE A BIG RESPONSIBILITY,
BUT I ALWAYS GET A SEAT ON THE TUBE!
TIK
TOK
TIK
IMIS/S YOUR COOKIN
ABE LINCOLN STILL DEAD SHOCK

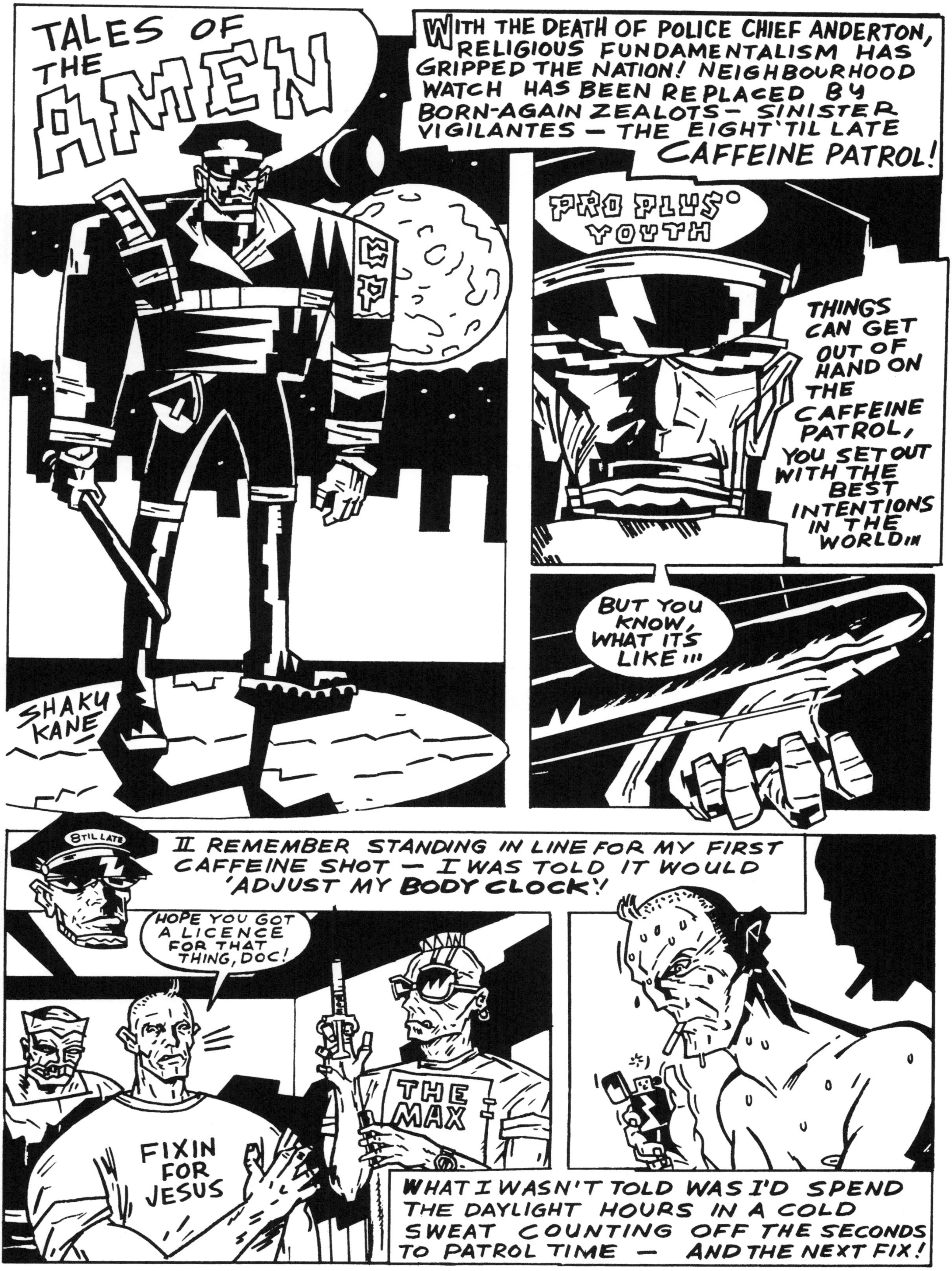

TALES OF THE AMEN
WITH THE DEATH OF POLICE CHIEF ANDERTON, RELIGIOUS FUNDAMENTALISM HAS GRIPPED THE NATION! NEIGHBOURHOOD WATCH HAS BEEN REPLACED BY BORN-AGAIN ZEALOTS– SINISTER VIGILANTES – THE EIGHT 'TIL LATE CAFFEINE PATROL!
CP
SHAKY KANE
PRO PLUS° YOUTH
THINGS CAN GET OUT OF HAND ON THE CAFFEINE PATROL, YOU SET OUT WITH THE BEST INTENTIONS IN THE WORLD...
BUT YOU KNOW, WHAT IT'S LIKE...
8 TIL LATE
I REMEMBER STANDING IN LINE FOR MY FIRST CAFFEINE SHOT – I WAS TOLD IT WOULD 'ADJUST MY BODY CLOCK'!
HOPE YOU GOT A LICENCE FOR THAT THING, DOC!
FIXIN FOR JESUS
THE MAX
WHAT I WASN'T TOLD WAS I'D SPEND THE DAYLIGHT HOURS IN A COLD SWEAT COUNTING OFF THE SECONDS TO PATROL TIME – AND THE NEXT FIX!

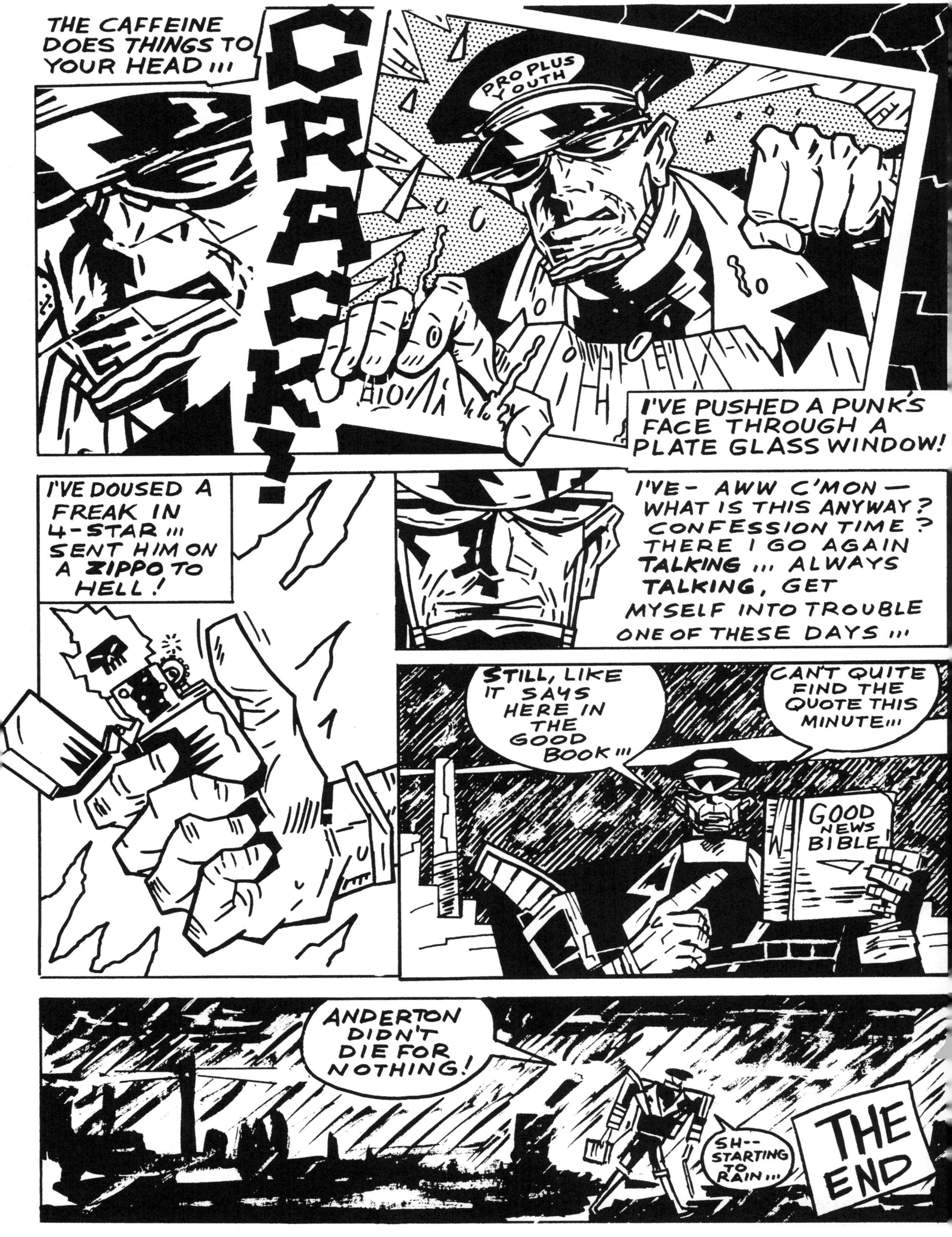

THE CAFFEINE DOES THINGS TO YOUR HEAD ...
CRACK!
PRO PLUS YOUTH
I'VE PUSHED A PUNK'S FACE THROUGH A PLATE GLASS WINDOW!
I'VE DOUSED A FREAK IN 4-STAR ... SENT HIM ON A ZIPPO TO HELL!
I'VE- AWW C'MON — WHAT IS THIS ANYWAY? CONFESSION TIME? THERE I GO AGAIN TALKING ... ALWAYS TALKING, GET MYSELF INTO TROUBLE ONE OF THESE DAYS ...
STILL, LIKE IT SAYS HERE IN THE GOOD BOOK ...
CAN'T QUITE FIND THE QUOTE THIS MINUTE ...
GOOD NEWS BIBLE
ANDERTON DIDN'T DIE FOR NOTHING!
SH-- STARTING TO RAIN ...
THE END

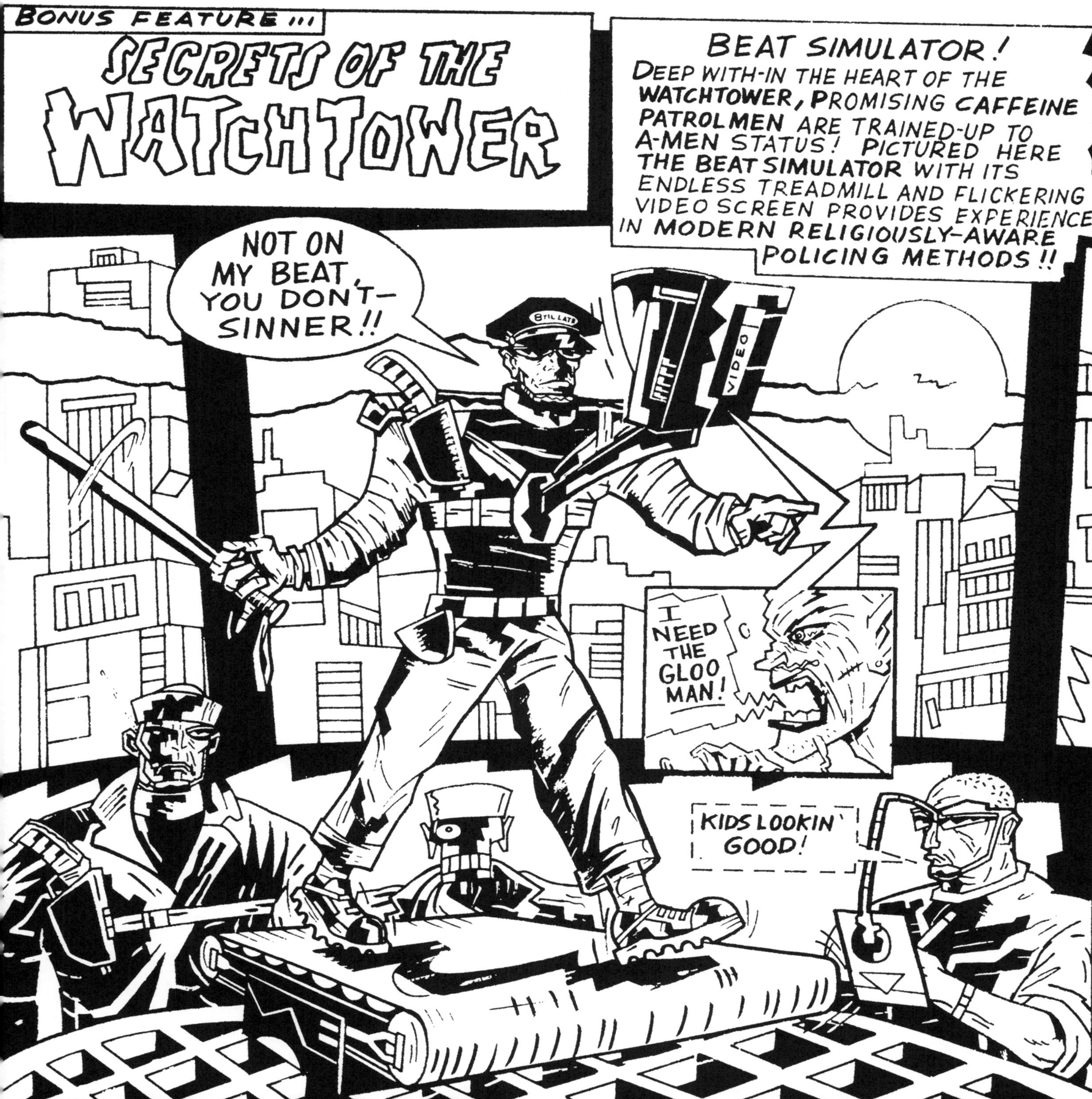
BONUS FEATURE!!!
SECRETS OF THE WATCHTOWER
BEAT SIMULATOR! DEEP WITH-IN THE HEART OF THE WATCHTOWER, PROMISING CAFFEINE PATROLMEN ARE TRAINED-UP TO A-MEN STATUS! PICTURED HERE THE BEAT SIMULATOR WITH ITS ENDLESS TREADMILL AND FLICKERING VIDEO SCREEN PROVIDES EXPERIENCE IN MODERN RELIGIOUSLY-AWARE POLICING METHODS!!
NOT ON MY BEAT, YOU DON'T-SINNER!!
VIDEO
I NEED THE GLOO MAN!
KIDS LOOKIN' GOOD!

METAL MESSIAH

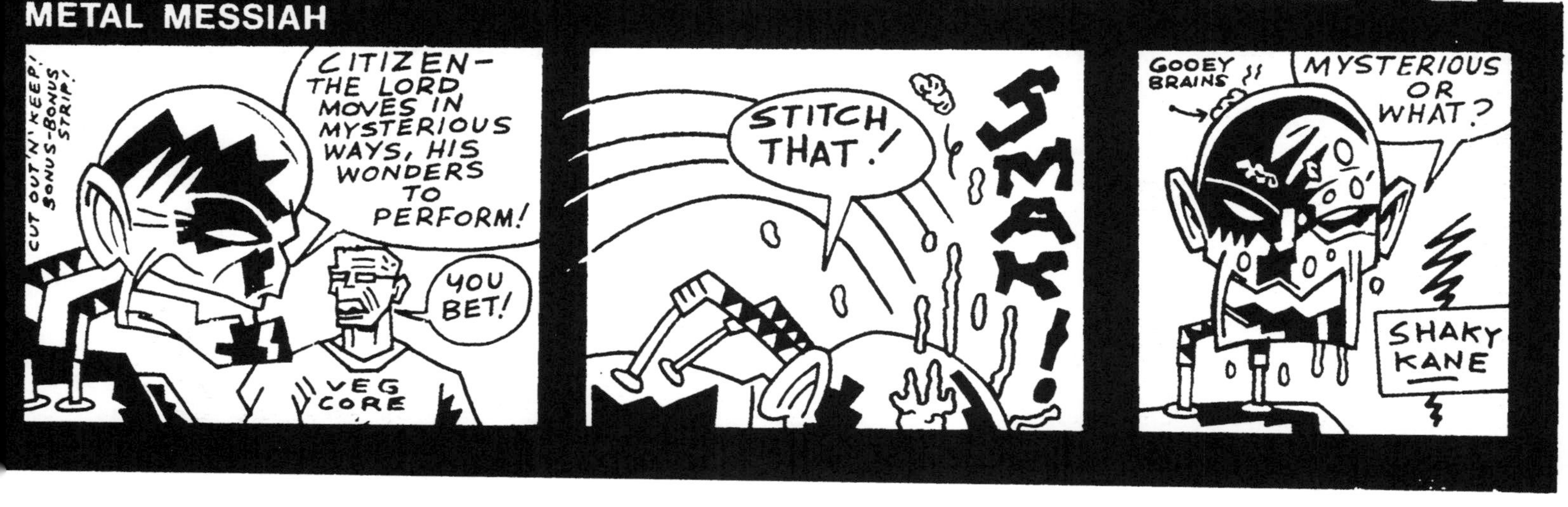
CUT OUT 'N' KEEP! BONUS-BONUS STRIP!
CITIZEN- THE LORD MOVES IN MYSTERIOUS WAYS, HIS WONDERS TO PERFORM!
YOU BET!
VEG CORE
STITCH THAT!
SMAK!
GOOEY BRAINS
MYSTERIOUS OR WHAT?
SHAKY KANE

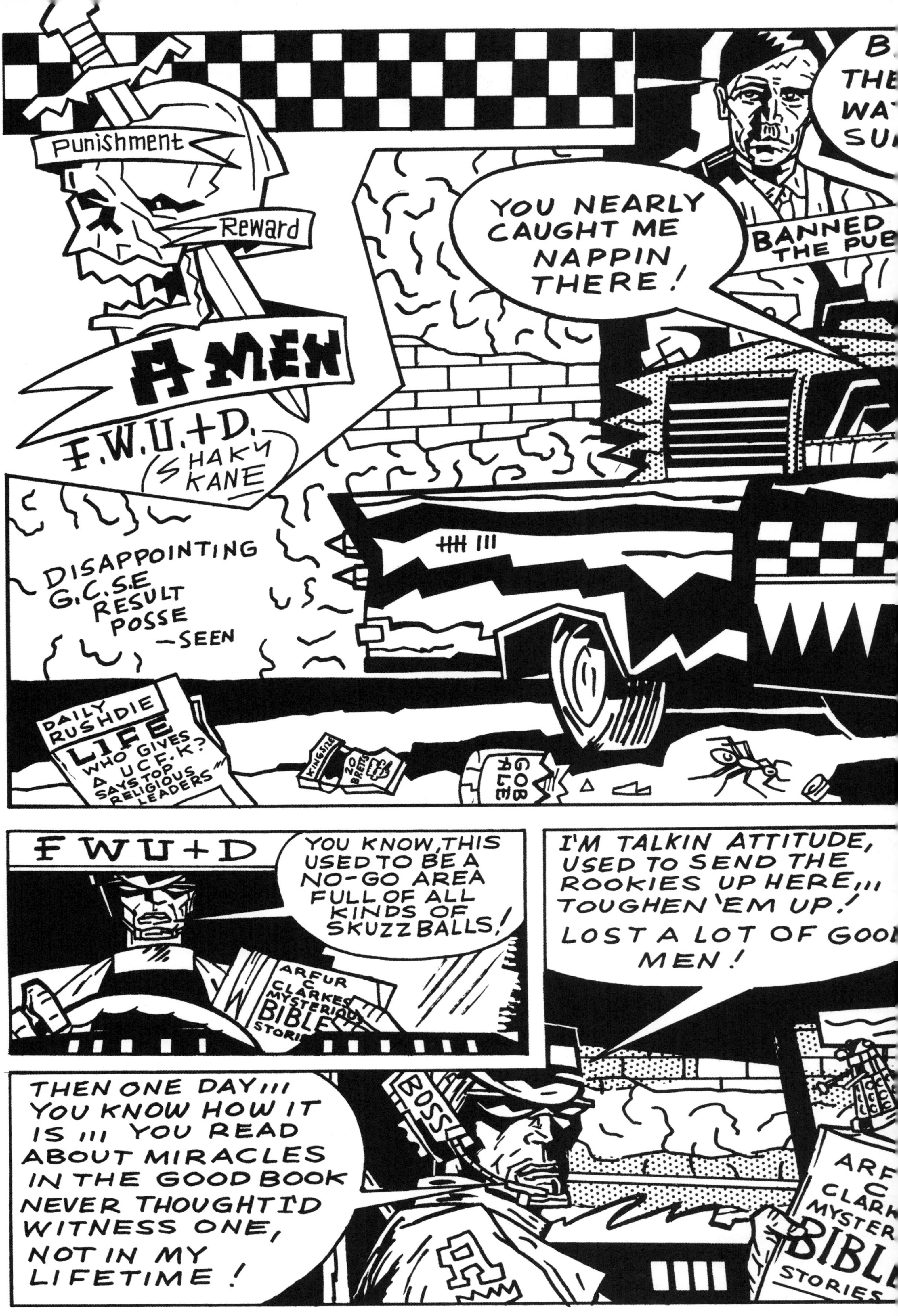
Punishment
Reward
A MEN
F.W.U.+D.
(SHAKY KANE
YOU NEARLY CAUGHT ME NAPPIN THERE!
BANNED
DISAPPOINTING G.C.S.E RESULT POSSE —SEEN
DAILY RUSHDIE
LIFE
WHO GIVES A UCF.K? SAYS TOP RELIGIOUS LEADERS
KINGSIZE 20 BRETS
GOB ALE
FWU+D
YOU KNOW, THIS USED TO BE A NO-GO AREA FULL OF ALL KINDS OF SKUZZBALLS!
ARFUR C CLARKES
BIBLE
I'M TALKIN ATTITUDE, USED TO SEND THE ROOKIES UP HERE,,, TOUGHEN 'EM UP!
LOST A LOT OF GOOD MEN!
THEN ONE DAY,,, YOU KNOW HOW IT IS ,,, YOU READ ABOUT MIRACLES IN THE GOOD BOOK NEVER THOUGHT I'D WITNESS ONE, NOT IN MY LIFETIME!
BOSS
STORIES

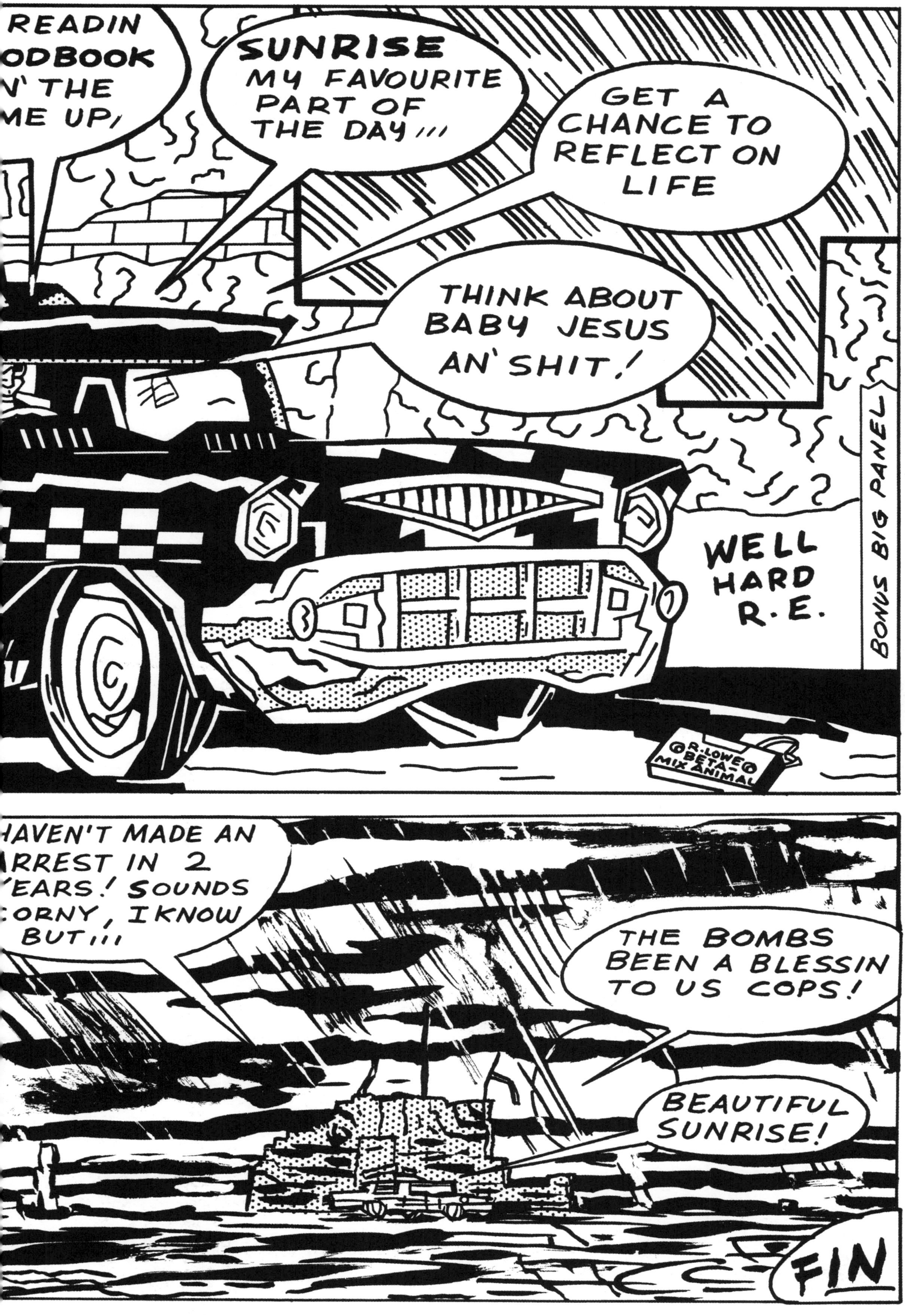

READIN ODBOOK N' THE ME UP,
SUNRISE MY FAVOURITE PART OF THE DAY,,,
GET A CHANCE TO REFLECT ON LIFE
THINK ABOUT BABY JESUS AN' SHIT!
WELL HARD R.E.
BONUS BIG PANEL
©R.LOWE© BETA-MIX ANIMAL
HAVEN'T MADE AN RREST IN 2 'EARS! SOUNDS ORNY, I KNOW BUT,,,
THE BOMBS BEEN A BLESSIN TO US COPS!
BEAUTIFUL SUNRISE!
FIN

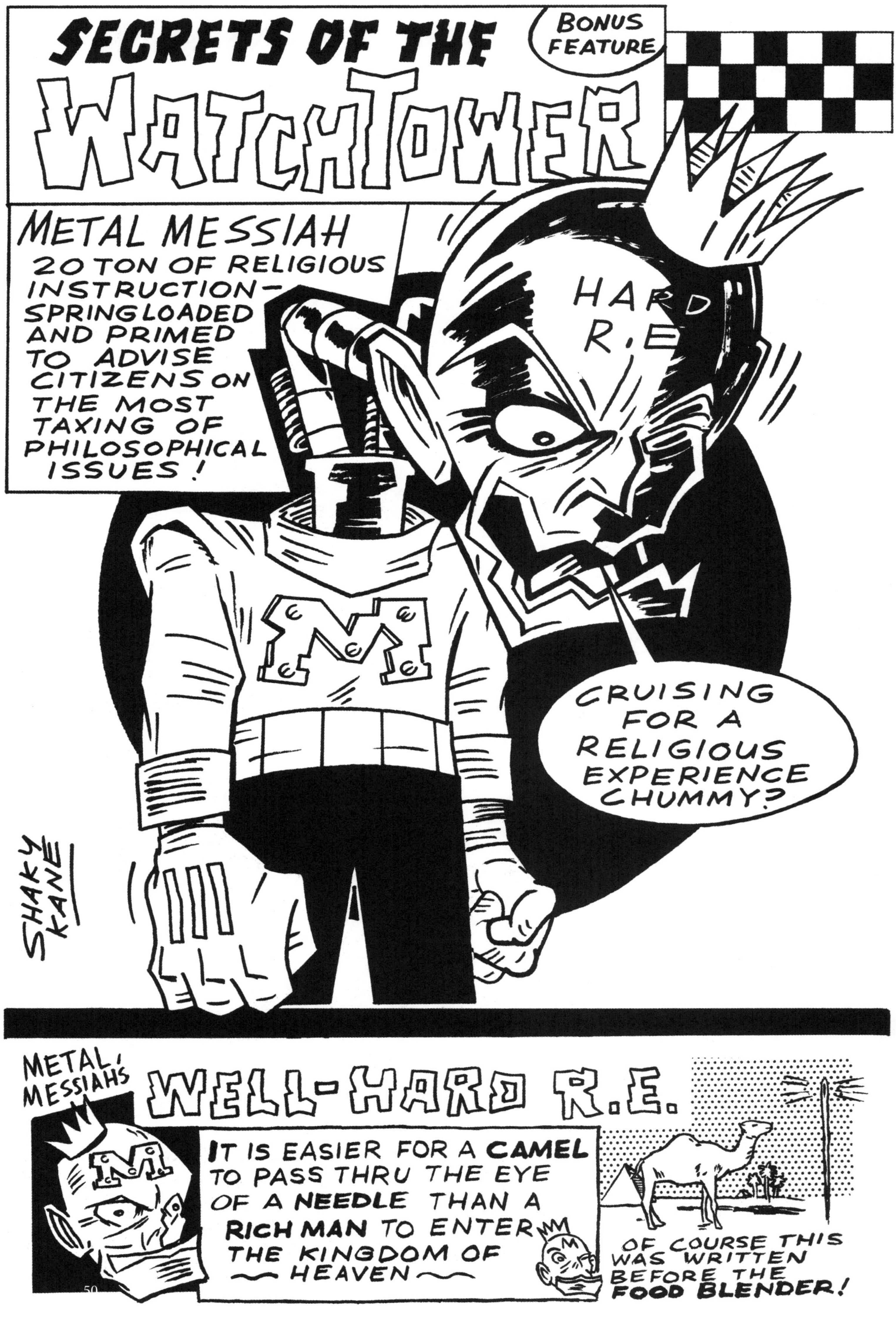
SECRETS OF THE WATCHTOWER
BONUS FEATURE
METAL MESSIAH
20 TON OF RELIGIOUS INSTRUCTION- SPRINGLOADED AND PRIMED TO ADVISE CITIZENS ON THE MOST TAXING OF PHILOSOPHICAL ISSUES!
HARD R.E
CRUISING FOR A RELIGIOUS EXPERIENCE CHUMMY?
SHAKY KANE
METAL MESSIAHS WELL-HARD R.E.
M
IT IS EASIER FOR A CAMEL TO PASS THRU THE EYE OF A NEEDLE THAN A RICH MAN TO ENTER THE KINGDOM OF HEAVEN
M
OF COURSE THIS WAS WRITTEN BEFORE THE FOOD BLENDER!

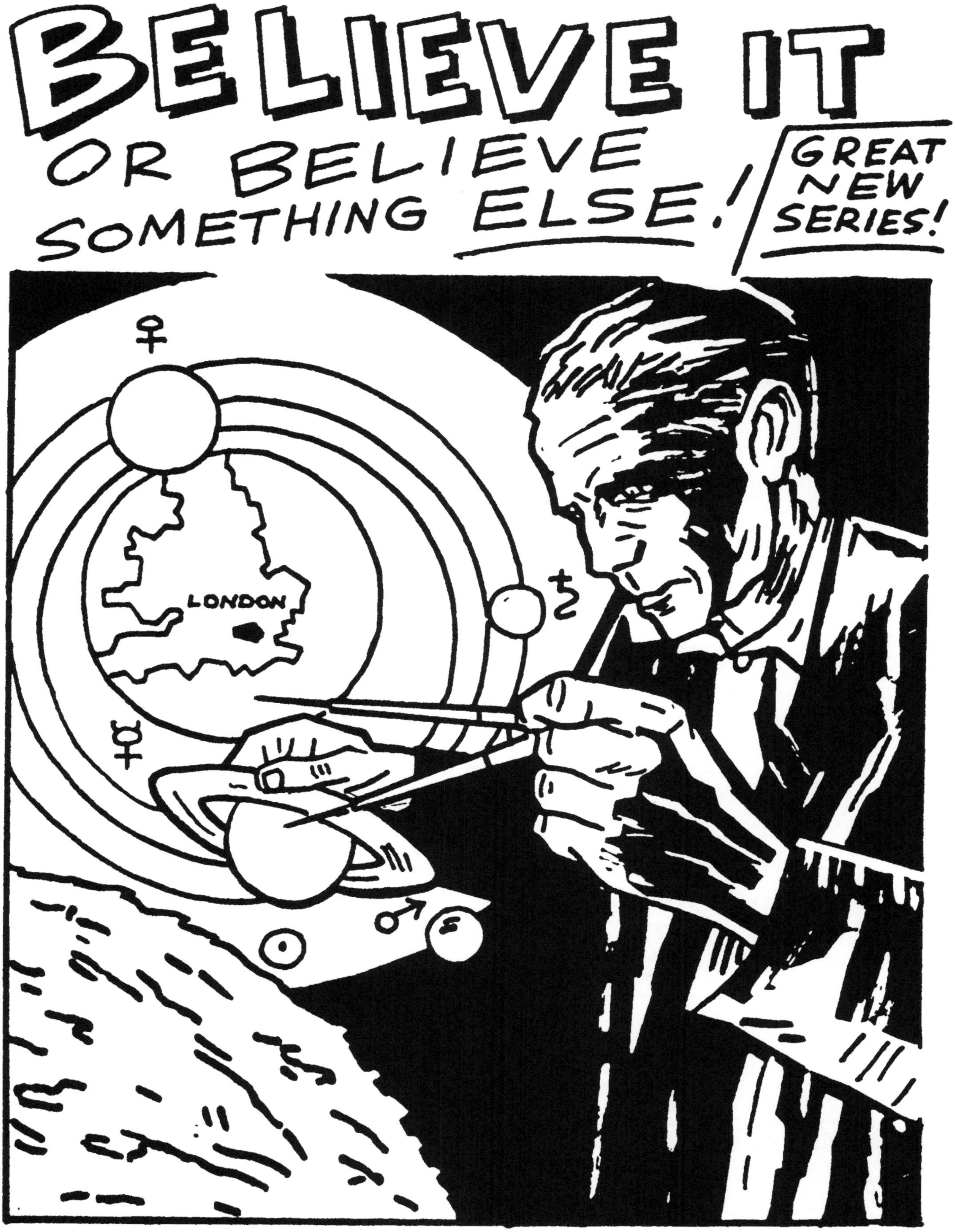
BELIEVE IT
OR BELIEVE SOMETHING ELSE!
GREAT NEW SERIES!
LONDON
LONDON NOT CENTER OF UNIVERSE! 'WE GOT IT WRONG' ADMIT BOFFINS!

Illo: Shaky Kane

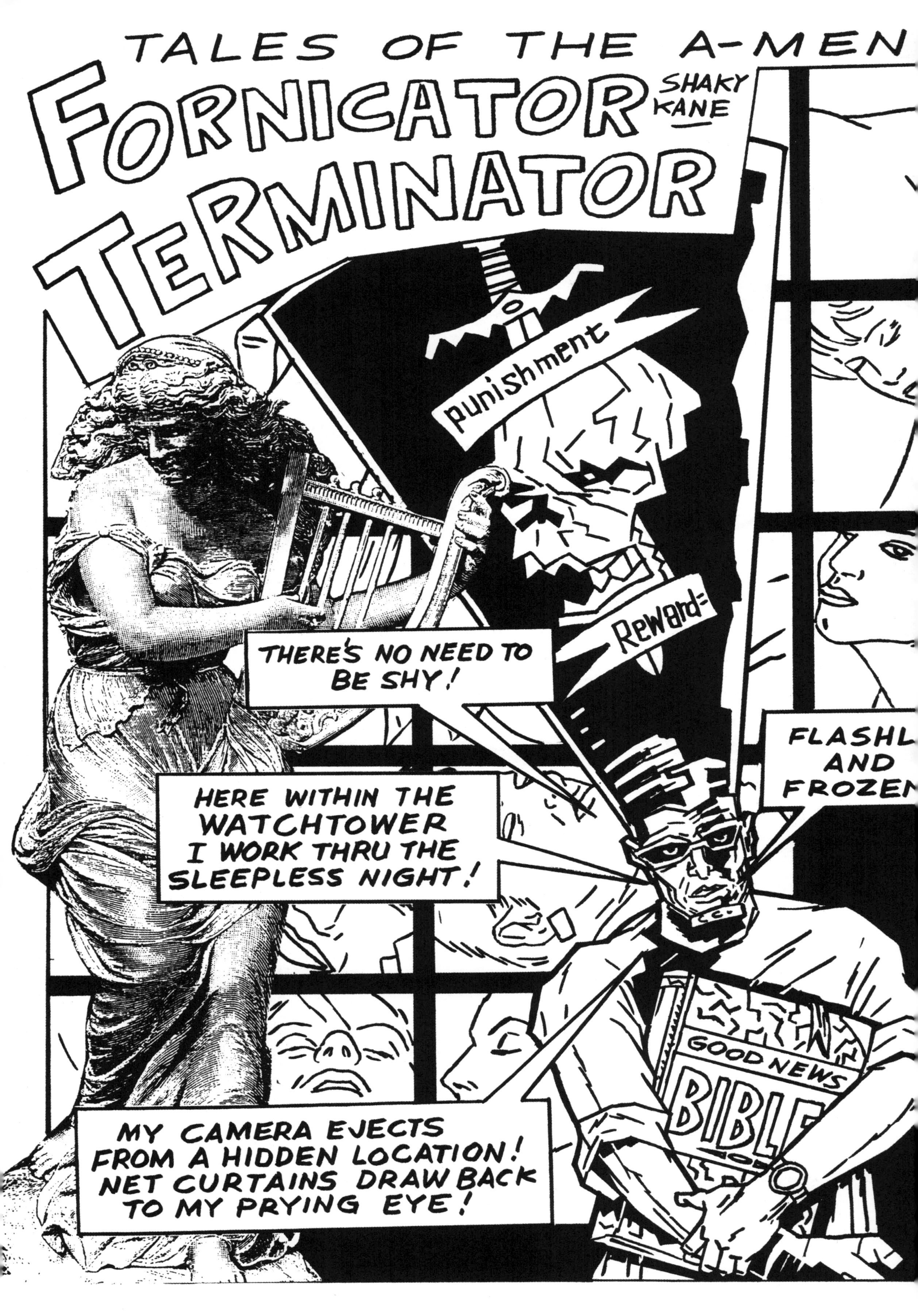
TALES OF THE A-MEN
FORNICATOR TERMINATOR
SHAKY KANE
punishment
Reward=
THERE'S NO NEED TO BE SHY!
FLASHL AND FROZEN
HERE WITHIN THE WATCHTOWER I WORK THRU THE SLEEPLESS NIGHT!
GOOD NEWS BIBLE
MY CAMERA EJECTS FROM A HIDDEN LOCATION! NET CURTAINS DRAW BACK TO MY PRYING EYE!

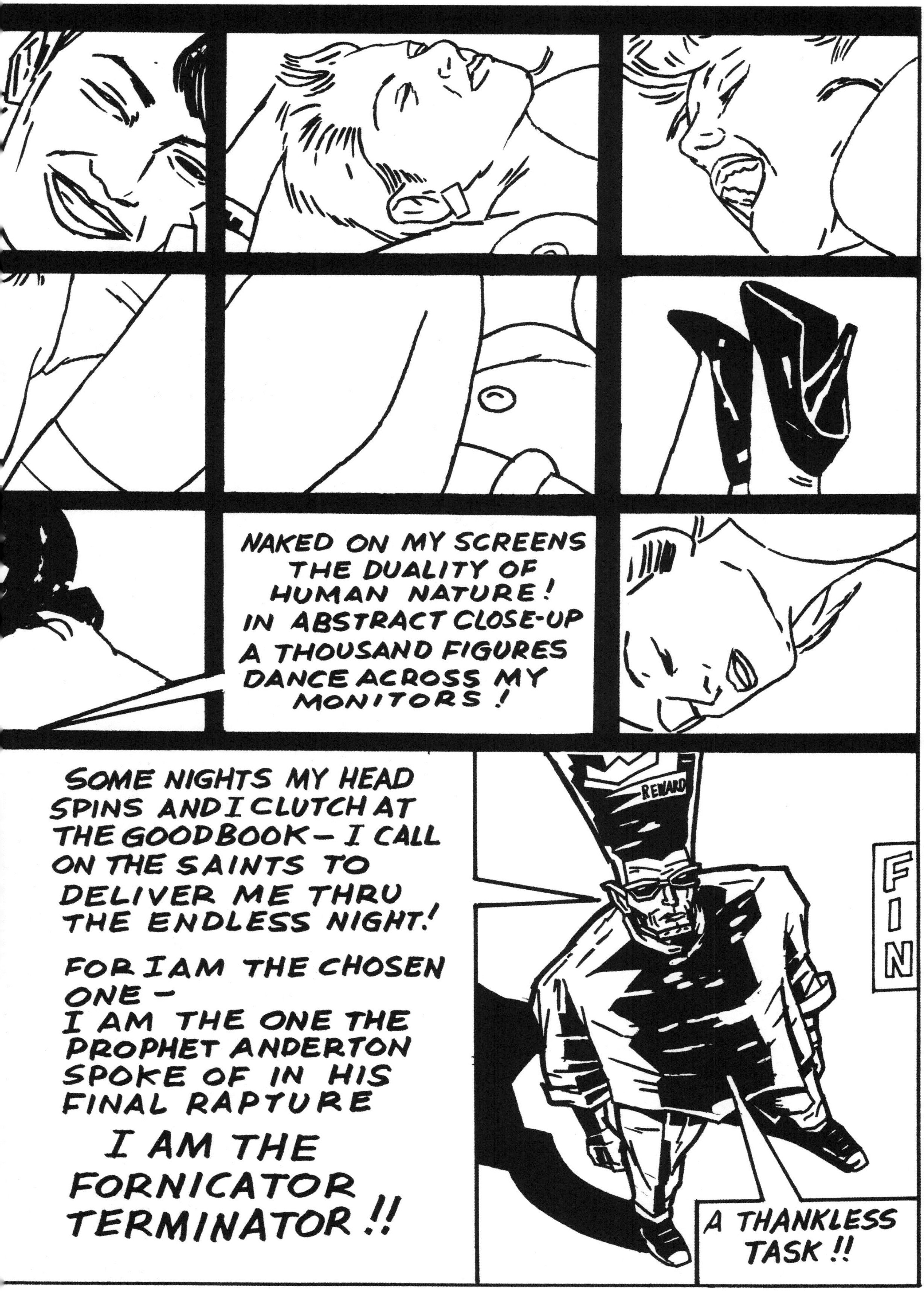
NAKED ON MY SCREENS THE DUALITY OF HUMAN NATURE! IN ABSTRACT CLOSE-UP A THOUSAND FIGURES DANCE ACROSS MY MONITORS!
SOME NIGHTS MY HEAD SPINS AND I CLUTCH AT THE GOOD BOOK – I CALL ON THE SAINTS TO DELIVER ME THRU THE ENDLESS NIGHT!
FOR I AM THE CHOSEN ONE – I AM THE ONE THE PROPHET ANDERTON SPOKE OF IN HIS FINAL RAPTURE
I AM THE FORNICATOR TERMINATOR!!
REWARD
FIN
A THANKLESS TASK!!

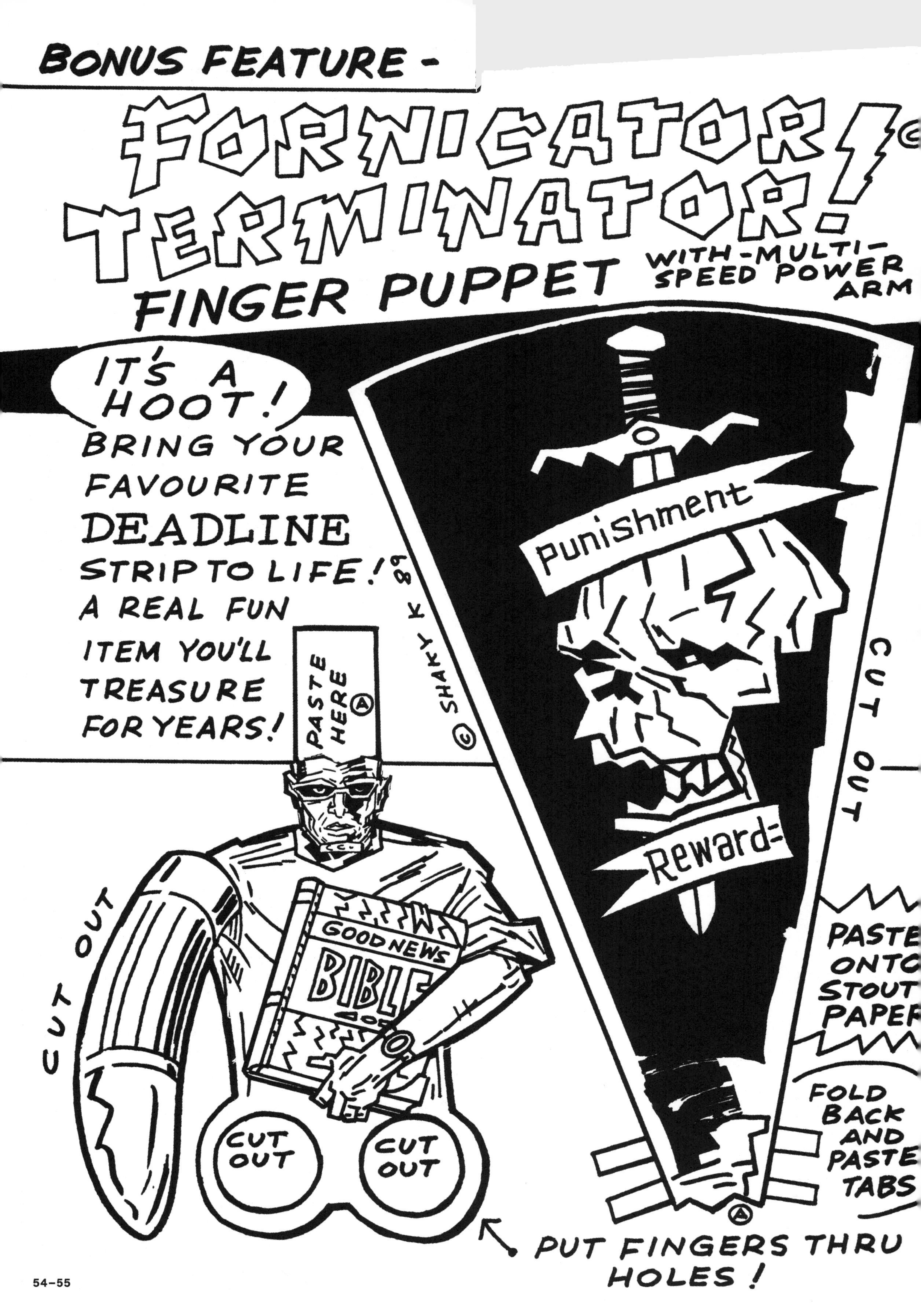
BONUS FEATURE -
FORNICATOR TERMINATOR! ©
FINGER PUPPET WITH-MULTI-SPEED POWER ARM
IT'S A HOOT!
BRING YOUR FAVOURITE DEADLINE STRIP TO LIFE! A REAL FUN ITEM YOU'LL TREASURE FOR YEARS!
PASTE HERE Ⓐ
© SHAKY K 89
Punishment
Reward=
CUT OUT
GOOD NEWS BIBLE
CUT OUT
CUT OUT
CUT OUT
PASTE ONTO STOUT PAPER
FOLD BACK AND PASTE TABS
Ⓐ
PUT FINGERS THRU HOLES!

SPECIAL BONUS PAGE!

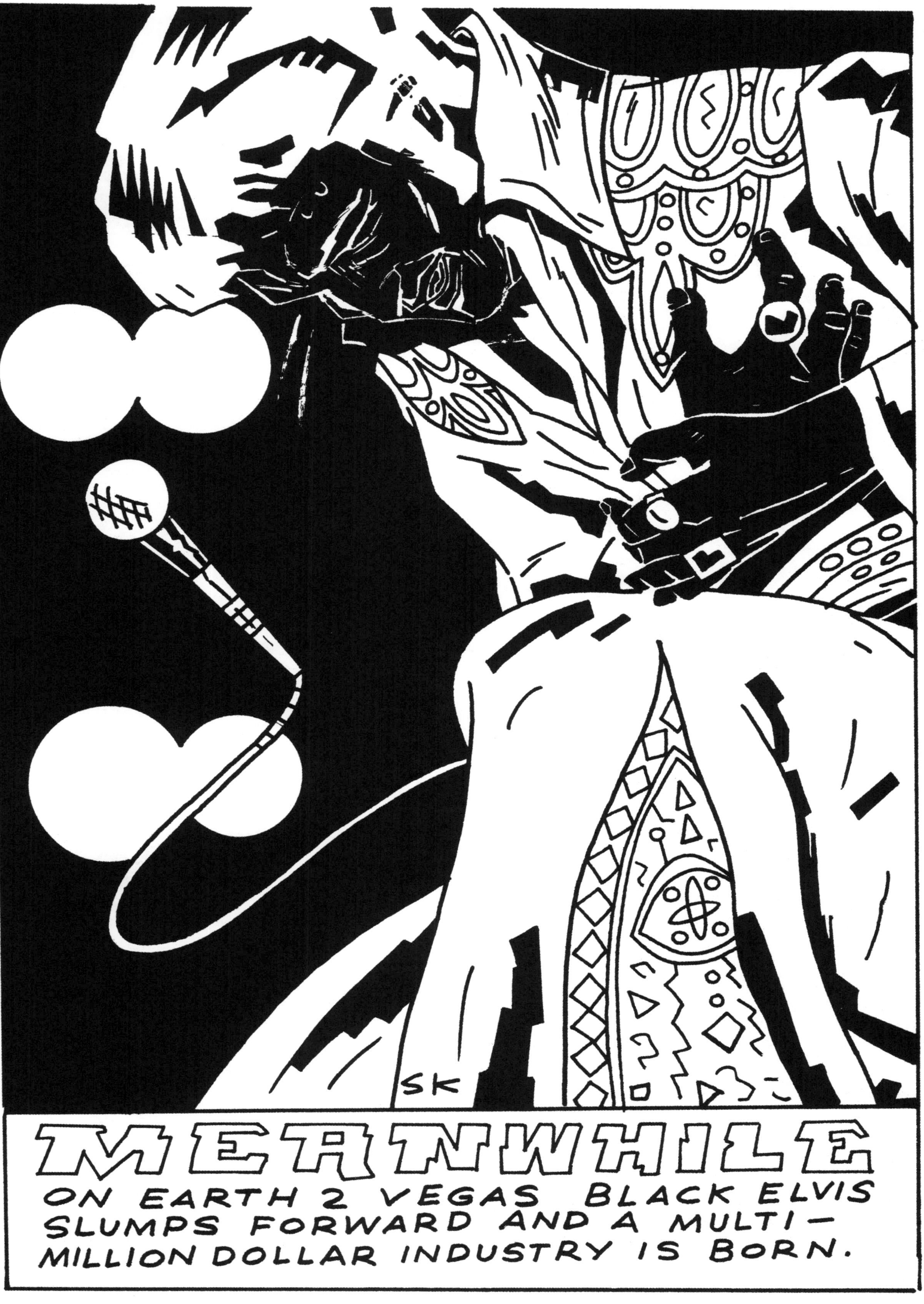
SK
MEANWHILE
ON EARTH 2 VEGAS BLACK ELVIS SLUMPS FORWARD AND A MULTI-MILLION DOLLAR INDUSTRY IS BORN.

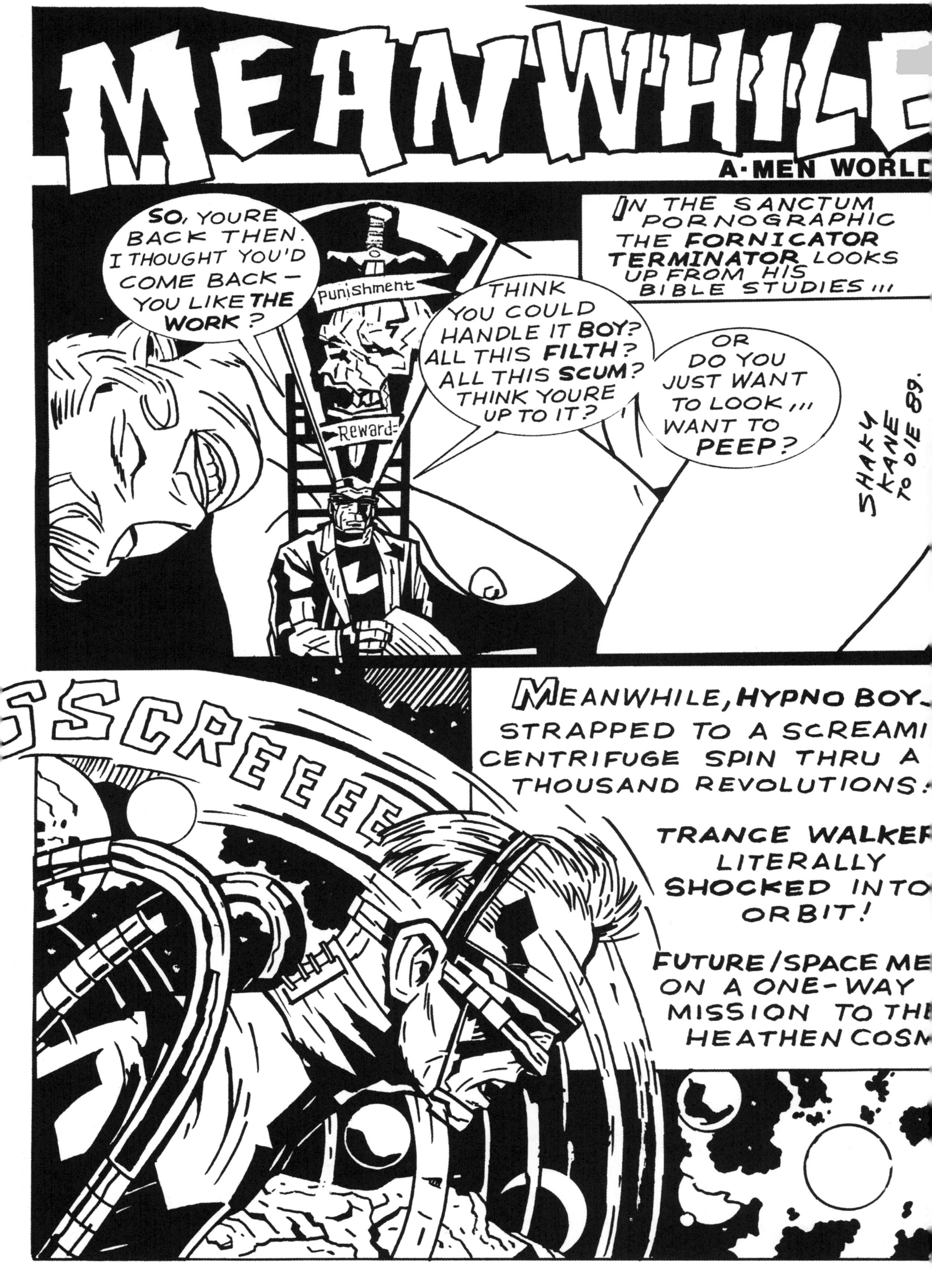
MEANWHILE
A·MEN WORLD
IN THE SANCTUM PORNOGRAPHIC THE FORNICATOR TERMINATOR LOOKS UP FROM HIS BIBLE STUDIES,,,
SO, YOURE BACK THEN. I THOUGHT YOU'D COME BACK - YOU LIKE THE WORK?
Punishment
Reward
THINK YOU COULD HANDLE IT BOY? ALL THIS FILTH? ALL THIS SCUM? THINK YOURE UP TO IT?
OR DO YOU JUST WANT TO LOOK,,, WANT TO PEEP?
SHAKY KANE TO DIE 89.
MEANWHILE, HYPNO BOY STRAPPED TO A SCREAMI CENTRIFUGE SPIN THRU A THOUSAND REVOLUTIONS:
TRANCE WALKER LITERALLY SHOCKED INTO ORBIT!
FUTURE/SPACE ME ON A ONE-WAY MISSION TO THE HEATHEN COSM
SSCREEEEE

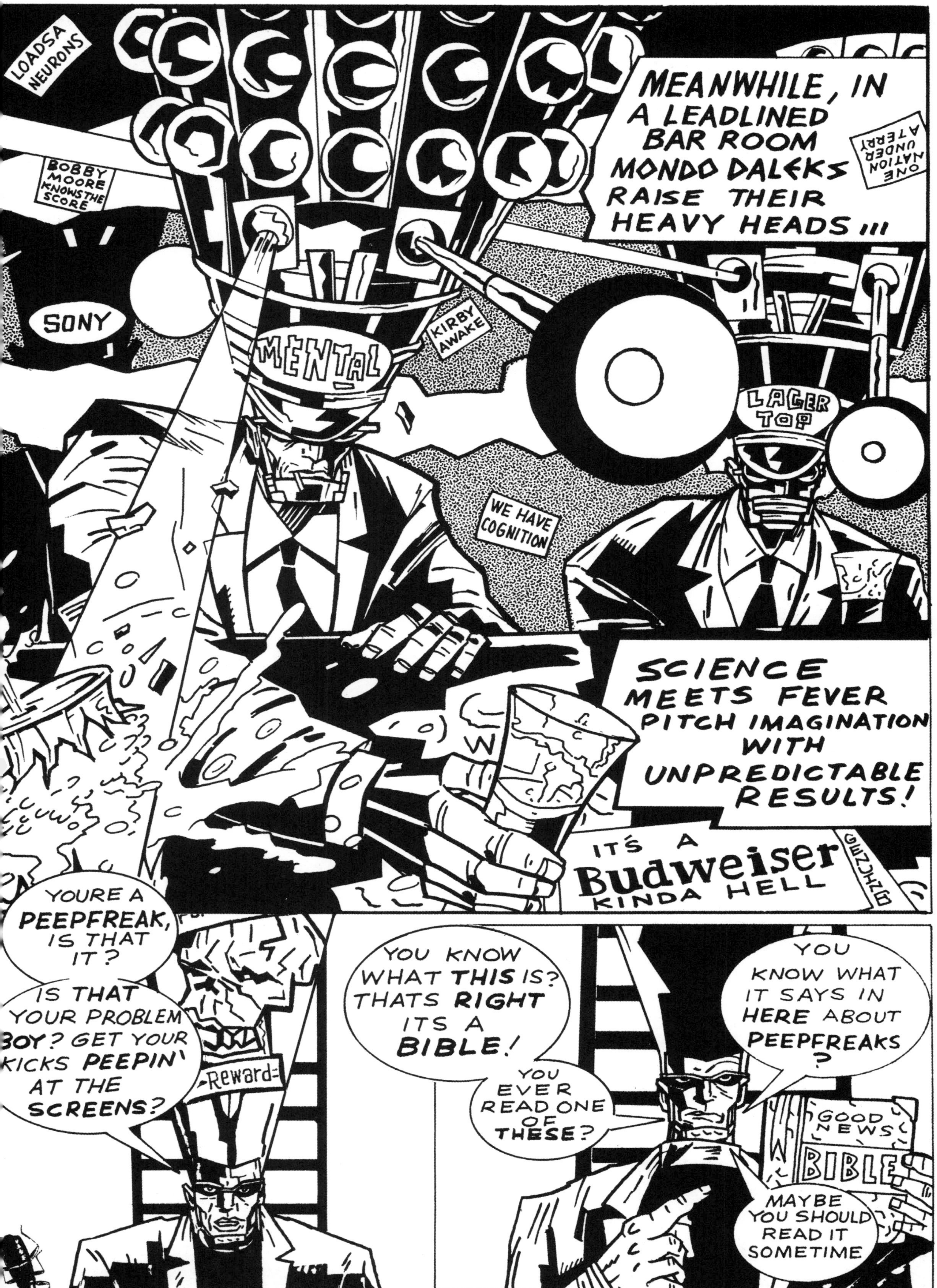
LOADSA NEURONS
MEANWHILE, IN A LEADLINED BAR ROOM MONDO DALEKS RAISE THEIR HEAVY HEADS...
ONE NATION UNDER A TERRY
BOBBY MOORE KNOWS THE SCORE
SONY
MENTAL
KIRBY AWAKE
LAGER TOP
WE HAVE COGNITION
SCIENCE MEETS FEVER PITCH IMAGINATION WITH UNPREDICTABLE RESULTS!
IT'S A Budweiser KINDA HELL
YOURE A PEEPFREAK, IS THAT IT?
IS THAT YOUR PROBLEM BOY? GET YOUR KICKS PEEPIN' AT THE SCREENS?
Reward
YOU KNOW WHAT THIS IS? THATS RIGHT ITS A BIBLE!
YOU EVER READ ONE OF THESE?
YOU KNOW WHAT IT SAYS IN HERE ABOUT PEEPFREAKS?
GOOD NEWS BIBLE
MAYBE YOU SHOULD READ IT SOMETIME

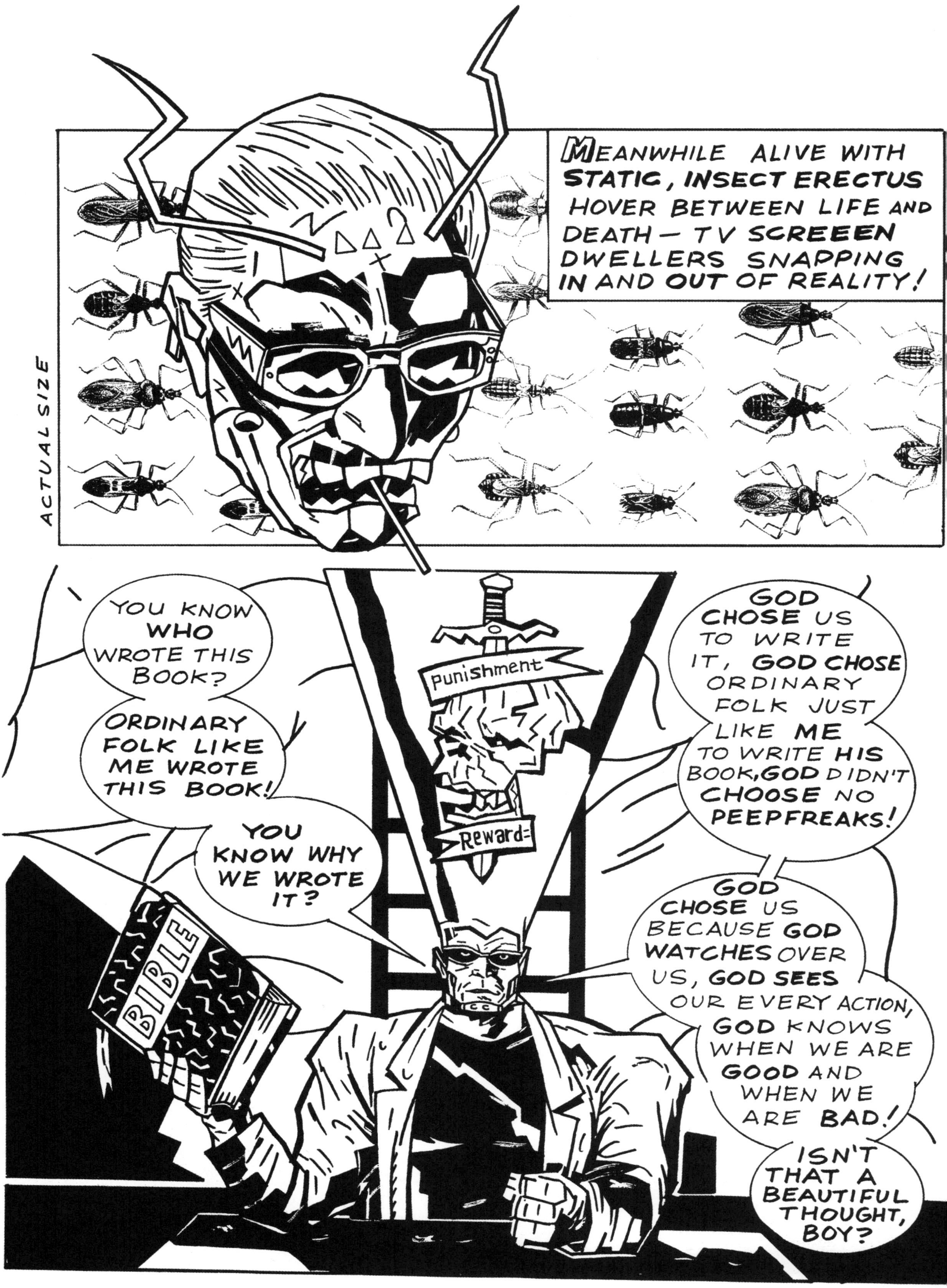

MEANWHILE ALIVE WITH STATIC, INSECT ERECTUS HOVER BETWEEN LIFE AND DEATH — TV SCREEEN DWELLERS SNAPPING IN AND OUT OF REALITY!
ACTUAL SIZE
YOU KNOW WHO WROTE THIS BOOK?
ORDINARY FOLK LIKE ME WROTE THIS BOOK!
YOU KNOW WHY WE WROTE IT?
GOD CHOSE US TO WRITE IT, GOD CHOSE ORDINARY FOLK JUST LIKE ME TO WRITE HIS BOOK, GOD DIDN'T CHOOSE NO PEEPFREAKS!
GOD CHOSE US BECAUSE GOD WATCHES OVER US, GOD SEES OUR EVERY ACTION, GOD KNOWS WHEN WE ARE GOOD AND WHEN WE ARE BAD!
ISN'T THAT A BEAUTIFUL THOUGHT, BOY?
Punishment
Reward=
BIBLE

# SPECIAL BONUS PAGE!

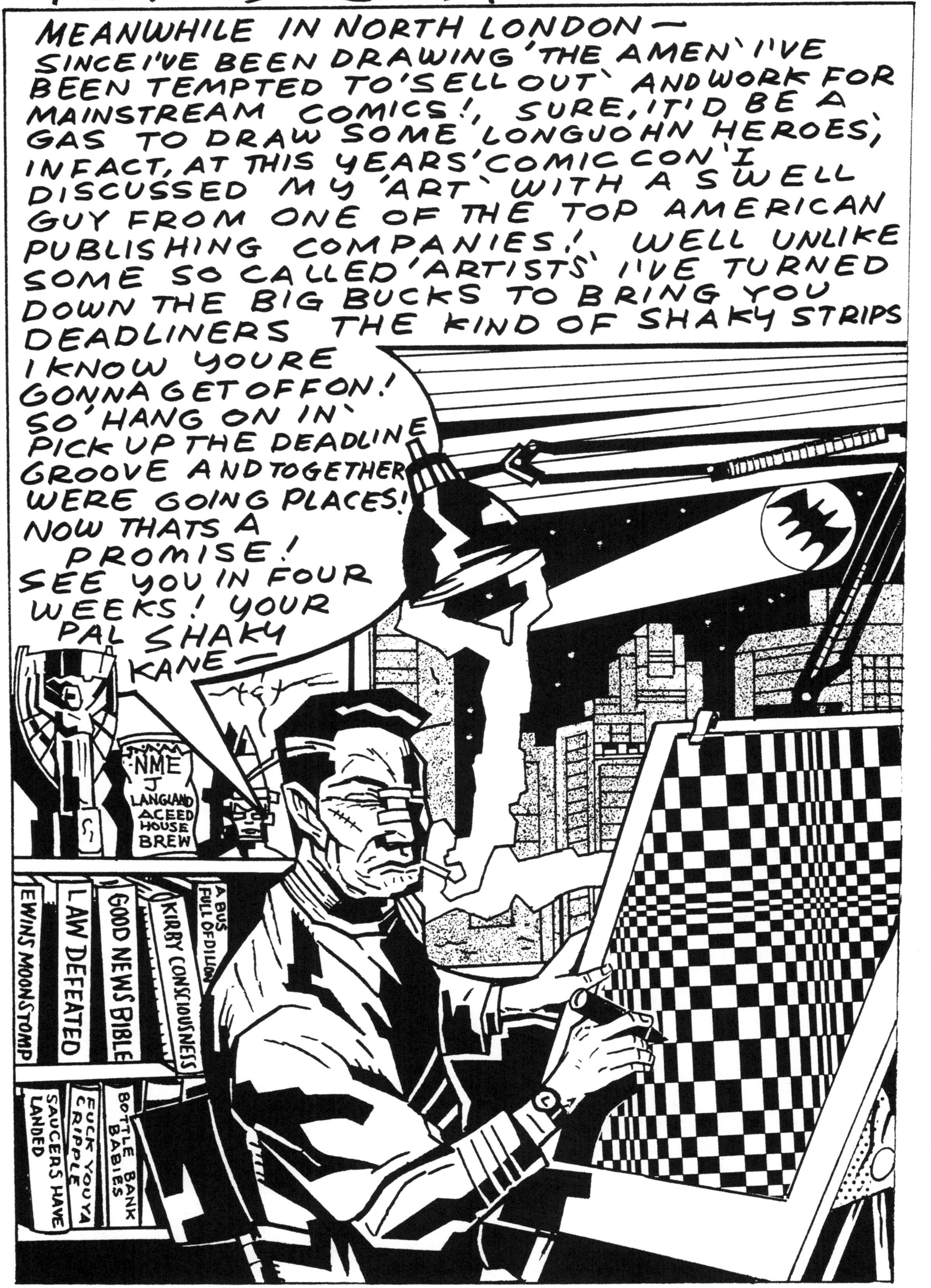
MEANWHILE IN NORTH LONDON— SINCE I'VE BEEN DRAWING 'THE AMEN' I'VE BEEN TEMPTED TO 'SELL OUT' AND WORK FOR MAINSTREAM COMICS!, SURE, IT'D BE A GAS TO DRAW SOME 'LONGJOHN HEROES', INFACT, AT THIS YEARS' COMIC CON' I DISCUSSED MY 'ART' WITH A SWELL GUY FROM ONE OF THE TOP AMERICAN PUBLISHING COMPANIES! WELL UNLIKE SOME SO CALLED 'ARTISTS' I'VE TURNED DOWN THE BIG BUCKS TO BRING YOU DEADLINERS THE KIND OF SHAKY STRIPS I KNOW YOURE GONNA GET OFF ON! SO 'HANG ON IN' PICK UP THE DEADLINE GROOVE AND TOGETHER WERE GOING PLACES! NOW THATS A PROMISE! SEE YOU IN FOUR WEEKS! YOUR PAL SHAKY KANE—
NME J LANGLAND ACEED HOUSE BREW
EWINS MOONSTOMP
LAW DEFEATED
GOOD NEWS BIBLE
KIRBY CONSCIOUSNESS
A BUS FULL OF DILLO
SAUCERS HAVE LANDED
FUCK YOU YA CRIPPLE
BOTTLE BANK BABIES

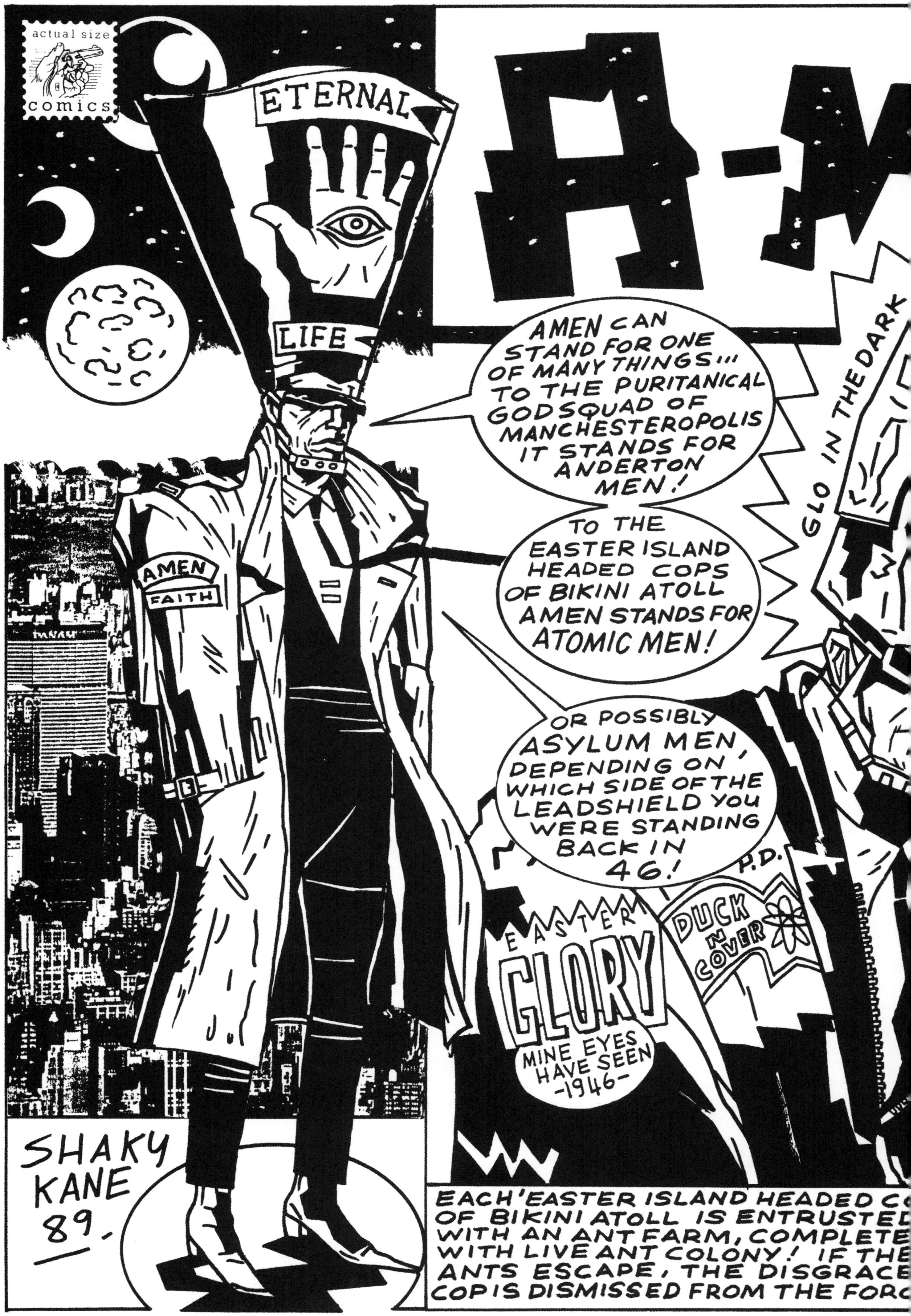
actual size comics
ETERNAL
LIFE
A-M
AMEN CAN STAND FOR ONE OF MANY THINGS... TO THE PURITANICAL GODSQUAD OF MANCHESTEROPOLIS IT STANDS FOR ANDERTON MEN!
TO THE EASTER ISLAND HEADED COPS OF BIKINI ATOLL AMEN STANDS FOR ATOMIC MEN!
OR POSSIBLY ASYLUM MEN, DEPENDING ON WHICH SIDE OF THE LEADSHIELD YOU WERE STANDING BACK IN 46!
GLO IN THE DARK
AMEN
FAITH
EASTER GLORY
MINE EYES HAVE SEEN -1946-
DUCK N COVER
P.D.
SHAKY KANE 89.
EACH 'EASTER ISLAND HEADED C
OF BIKINI ATOLL IS ENTRUSTE
WITH AN ANT FARM, COMPLETE
WITH LIVE ANT COLONY! IF THE
ANTS ESCAPE, THE DISGRACE
COP IS DISMISSED FROM THE FORC

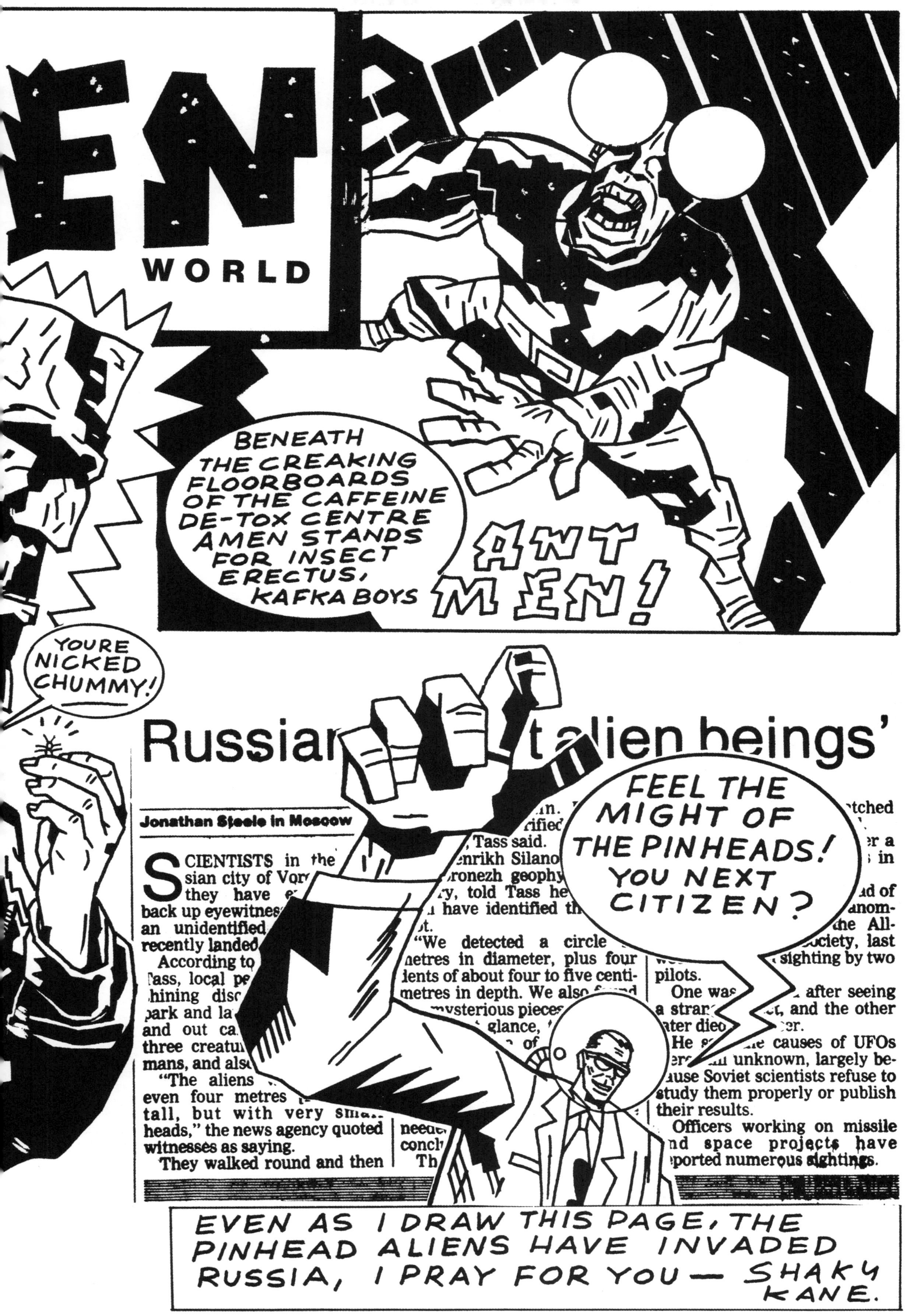
EN
WORLD
BENEATH THE CREAKING FLOORBOARDS OF THE CAFFEINE DE-TOX CENTRE AMEN STANDS FOR INSECT ERECTUS, KAFKA BOYS
ANT MEN!
YOURE NICKED CHUMMY!
Russiar t alien beings'
Jonathan Steele in Moscow
SCIENTISTS in the sian city of Vor they have back up eyewitnes an unidentified recently landed
According to Tass, local pe hining disc park and la and out ca three creatu mans, and also
"The aliens even four metres tall, but with very small heads," the news agency quoted witnesses as saying.
They walked round and then
Tass said.
enrikh Silano ronezh geophy ry, told Tass he have identified th
"We detected a circle metres in diameter, plus four lents of about four to five centimetres in depth. We also mysterious pieces glance,
neede concl Th
tched
r a in
ad of anom- the All- society, last sighting by two pilots.
One was after seeing a stran t, and the other ater died r.
He causes of UFOs unknown, largely because Soviet scientists refuse to study them properly or publish their results.
Officers working on missile nd space projects have eported numerous sightings.
FEEL THE MIGHT OF THE PINHEADS! YOU NEXT CITIZEN?
EVEN AS I DRAW THIS PAGE, THE PINHEAD ALIENS HAVE INVADED RUSSIA, I PRAY FOR YOU — SHAKY KANE.

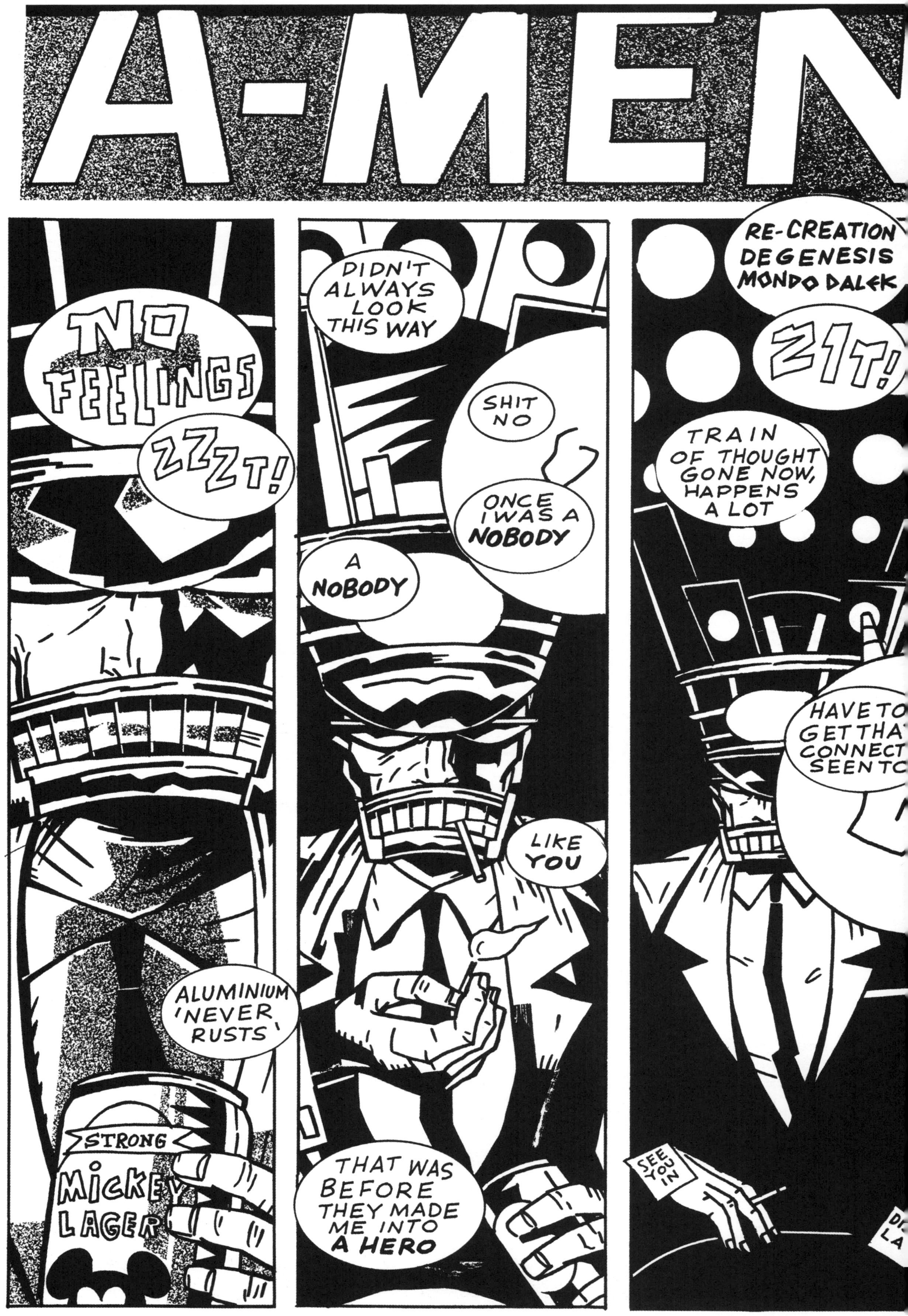
A-MEN
NO FEELINGS
ZZZT!
ALUMINIUM 'NEVER RUSTS'
STRONG
MICKEY LAGER
DIDN'T ALWAYS LOOK THIS WAY
SHIT NO
ONCE I WAS A NOBODY
A NOBODY
LIKE YOU
THAT WAS BEFORE THEY MADE ME INTO A HERO
RE-CREATION DEGENESIS MONDO DALEK
ZIT!
TRAIN OF THOUGHT GONE NOW, HAPPENS A LOT
HAVE TO GET THA CONNECT SEEN TO
SEE YOU IN

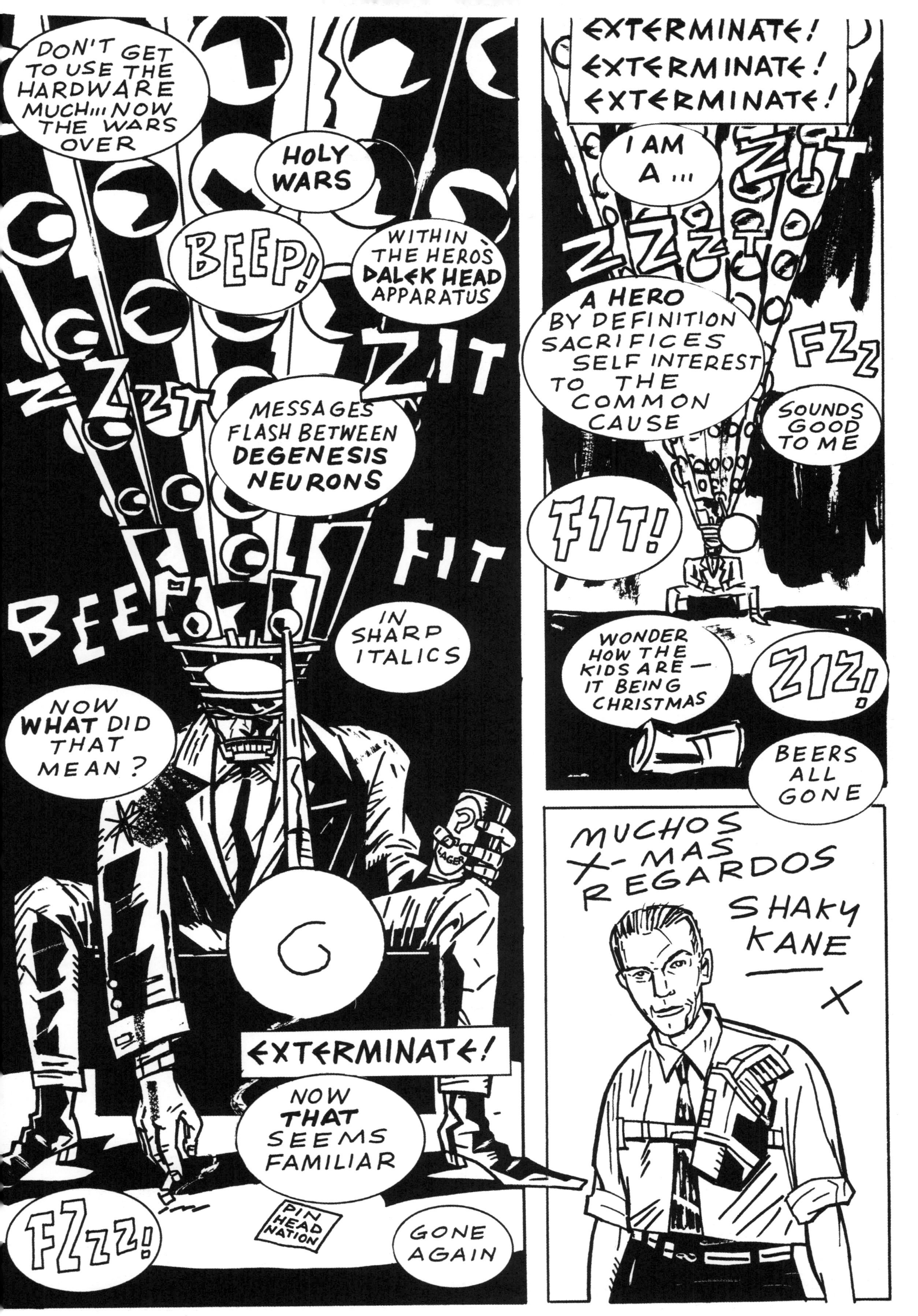
DON'T GET TO USE THE HARDWARE MUCH... NOW THE WARS OVER
HOLY WARS
BEEP!
WITHIN THE HEROS DALEK HEAD APPARATUS
ZZZT
ZIT
MESSAGES FLASH BETWEEN DEGENESIS NEURONS
FIT
BEEP
IN SHARP ITALICS
NOW WHAT DID THAT MEAN?
LAGER
EXTERMINATE!
NOW THAT SEEMS FAMILIAR
FZZZ!
PIN HEAD NATION
GONE AGAIN
EXTERMINATE! EXTERMINATE! EXTERMINATE!
I AM A...
ZIT
ZZZT
A HERO BY DEFINITION SACRIFICES SELF INTEREST TO THE COMMON CAUSE
FZZ
SOUNDS GOOD TO ME
FIT!
WONDER HOW THE KIDS ARE — IT BEING CHRISTMAS
ZIZ!
BEERS ALL GONE
MUCHOS X-MAS REGARDOS
SHAKY KANE
X

BONUS 'X-MAS BONUS' PAGE!

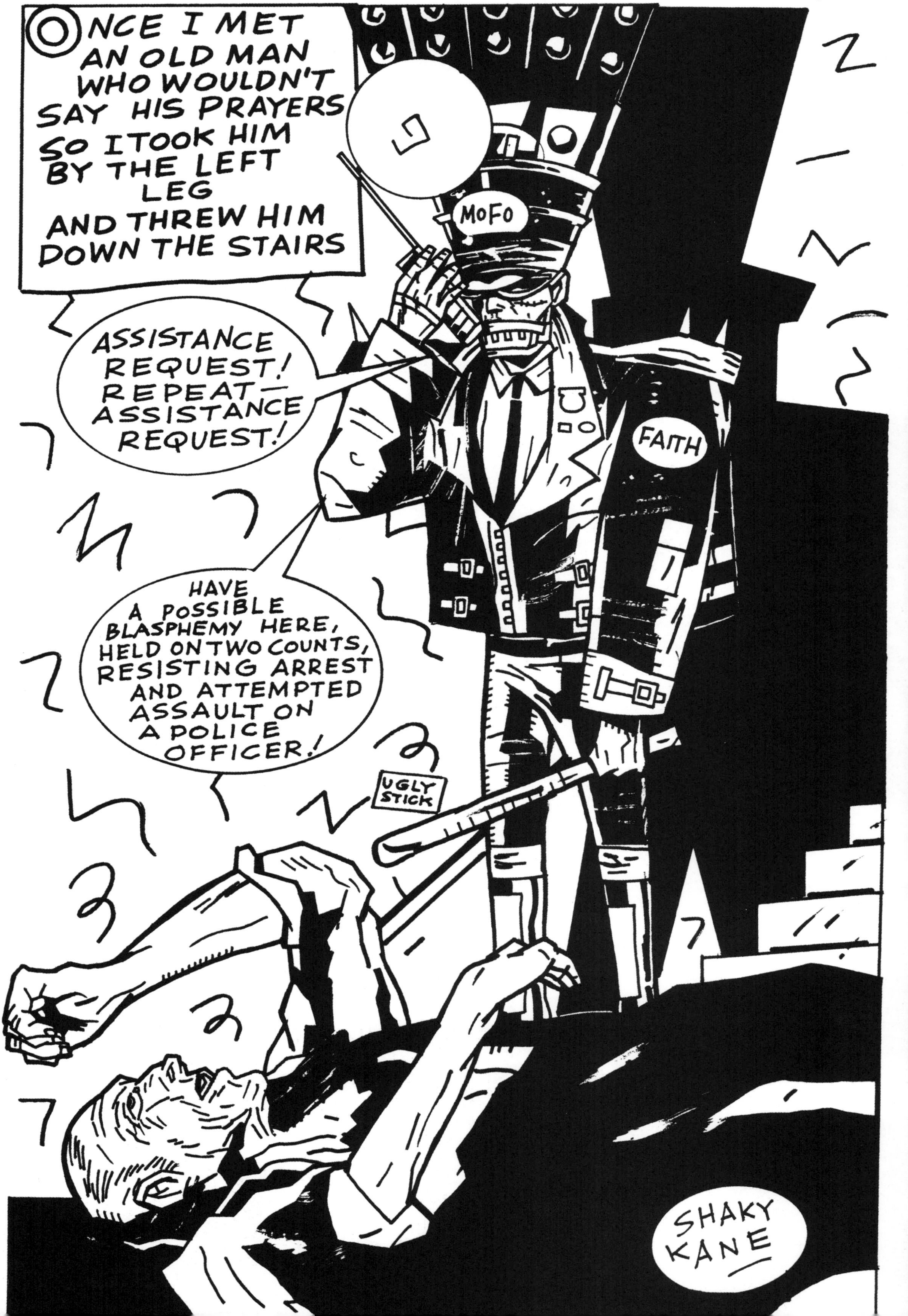
ONCE I MET AN OLD MAN WHO WOULDN'T SAY HIS PRAYERS SO I TOOK HIM BY THE LEFT LEG AND THREW HIM DOWN THE STAIRS
MOFO
ASSISTANCE REQUEST! REPEAT— ASSISTANCE REQUEST!
FAITH
HAVE A POSSIBLE BLASPHEMY HERE, HELD ON TWO COUNTS, RESISTING ARREST AND ATTEMPTED ASSAULT ON A POLICE OFFICER!
UGLY STICK
SHAKY KANE

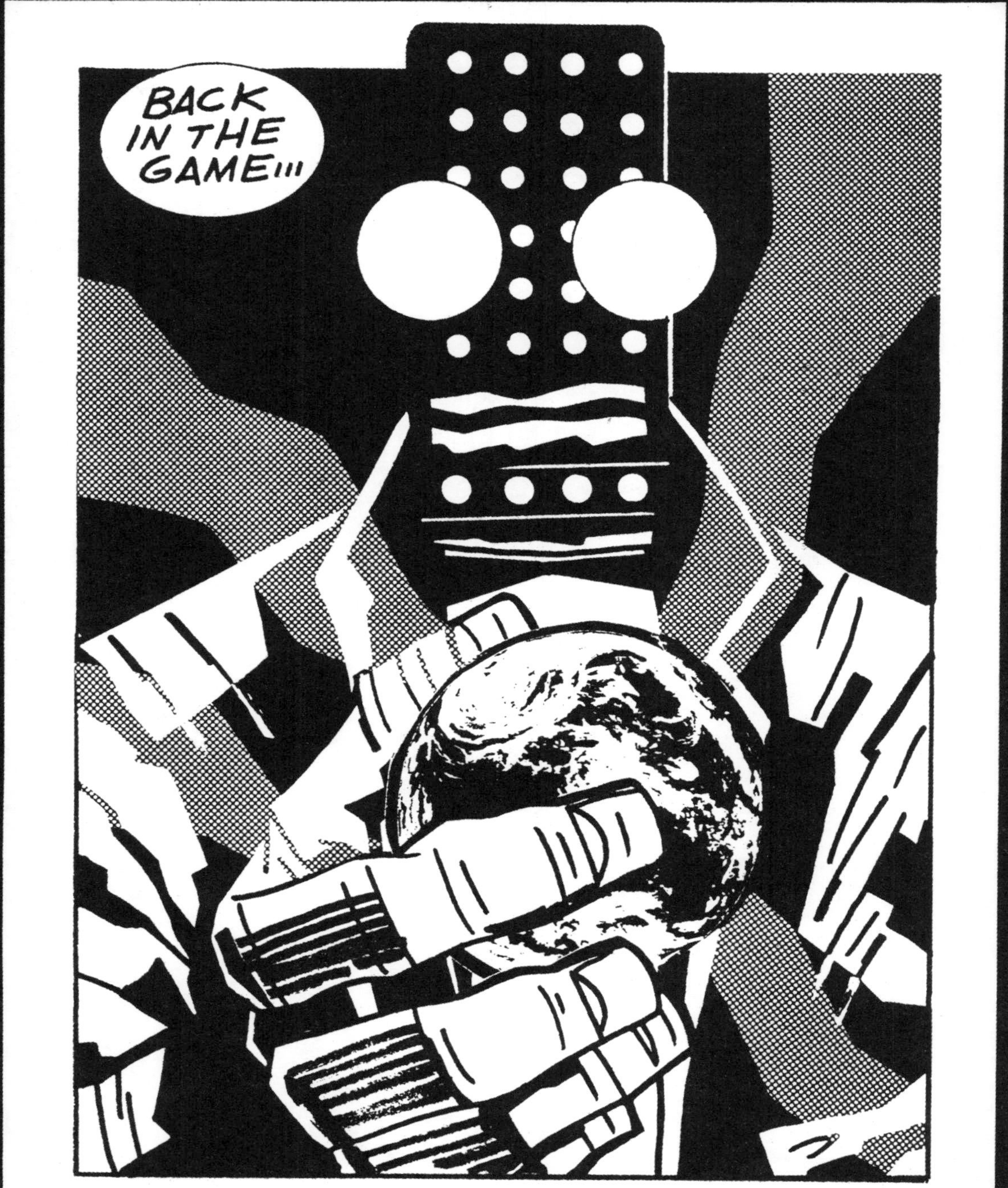
BACK IN THE GAME!!!

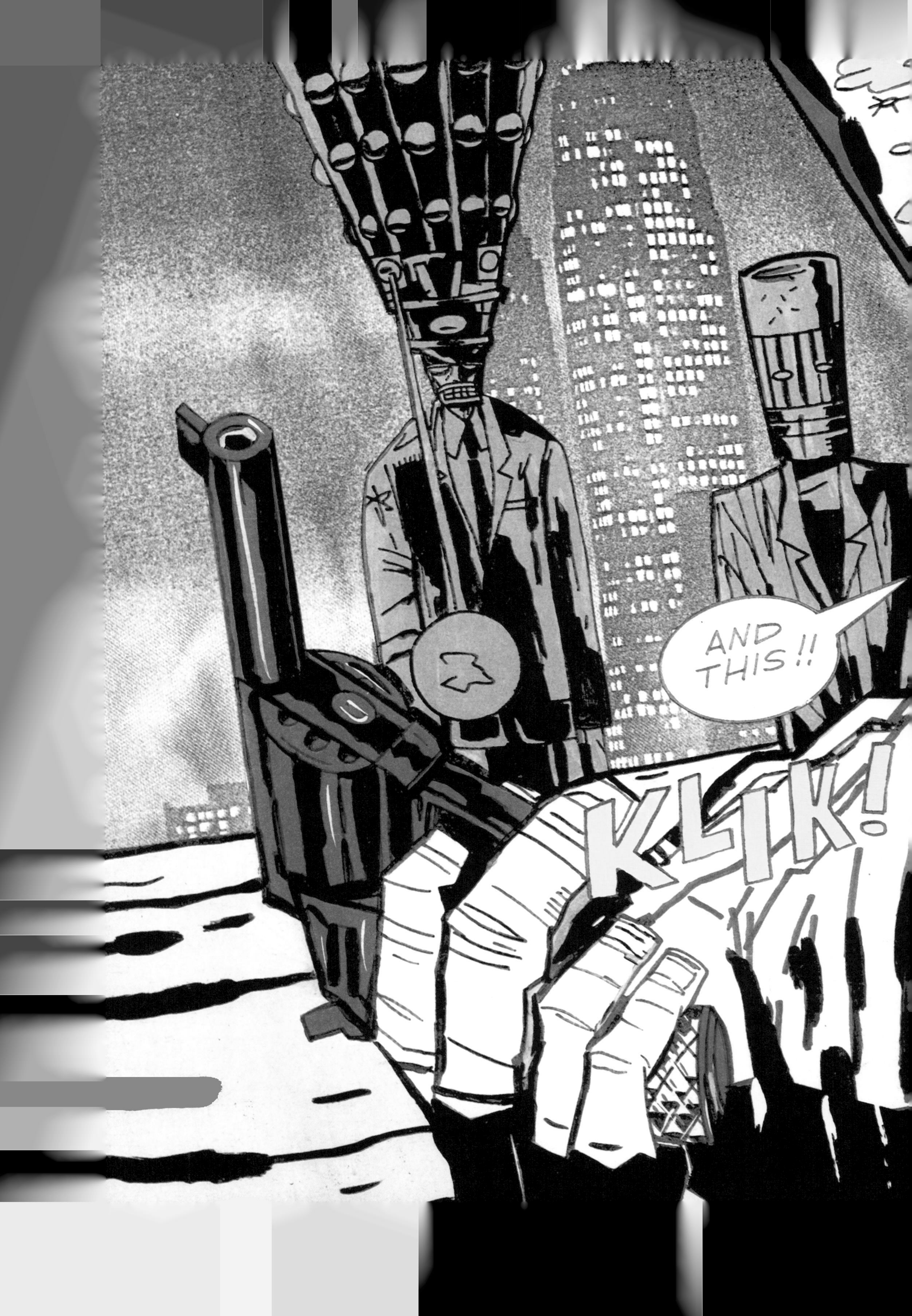
AND THIS !!
KLIK!

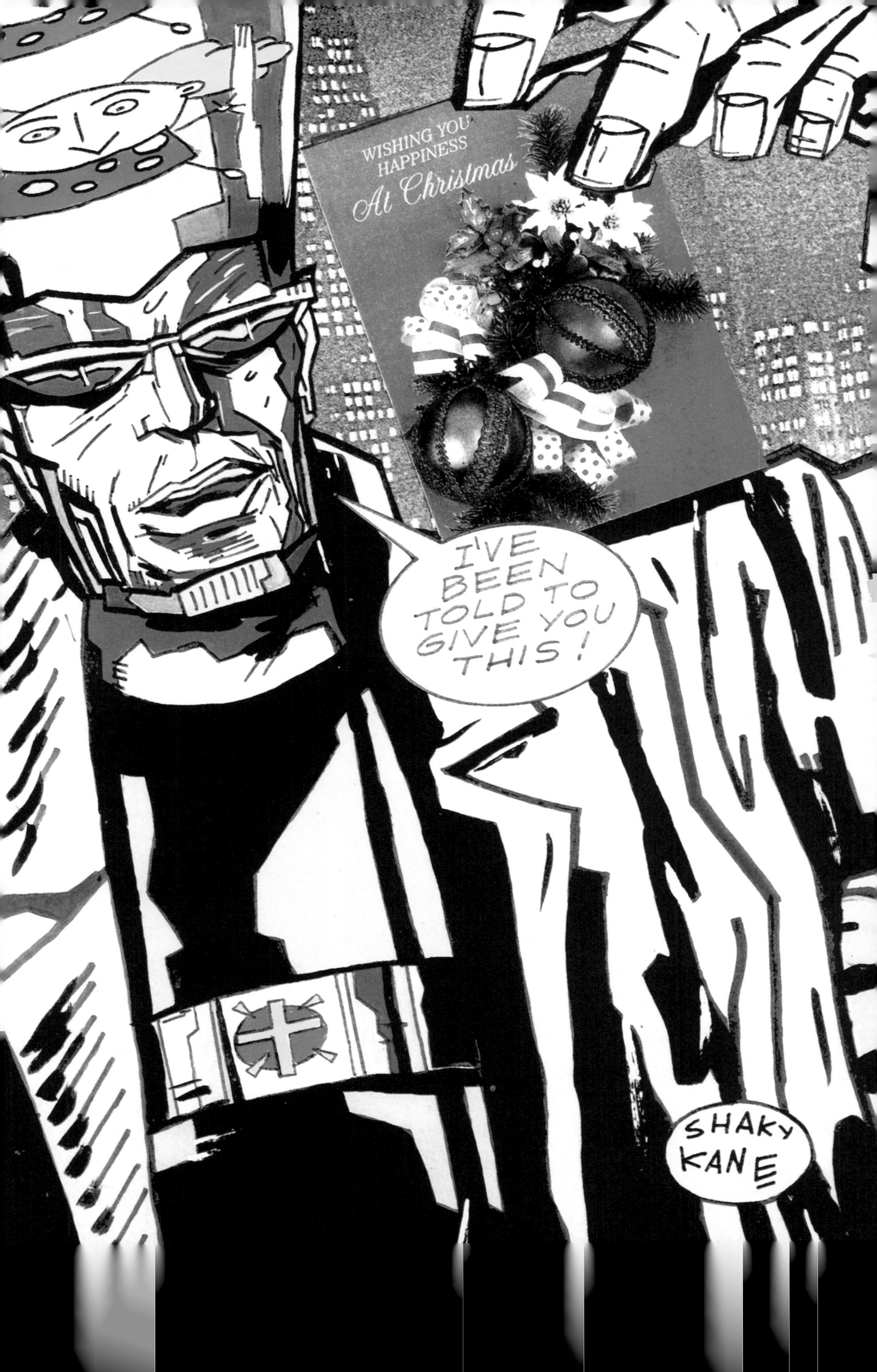

WISHING YOU HAPPINESS At Christmas
I'VE BEEN TOLD TO GIVE YOU THIS!
SHAKY KANE

ONE DAY IN DEEP SPACE ...

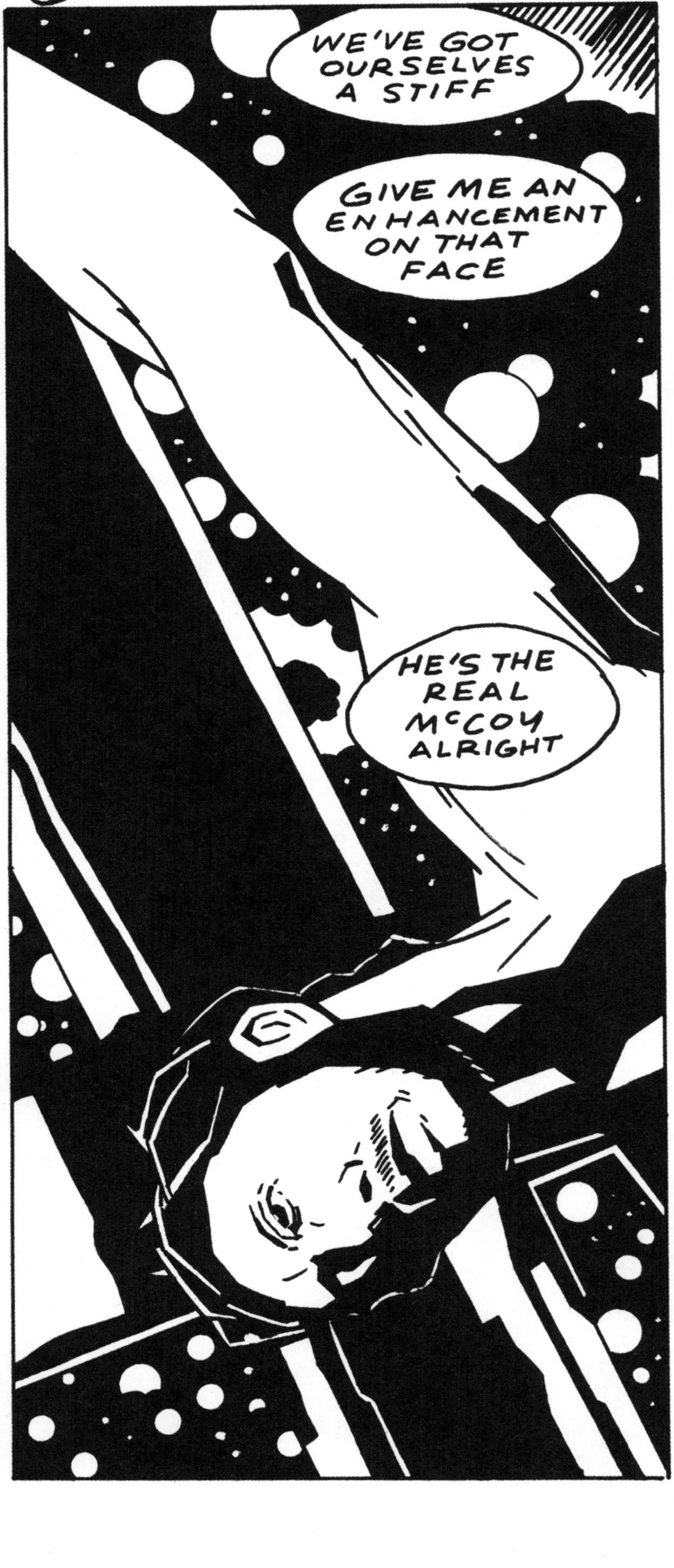
WE'VE GOT OURSELVES A STIFF
GIVE ME AN ENHANCEMENT ON THAT FACE
HE'S THE REAL McCOY ALRIGHT

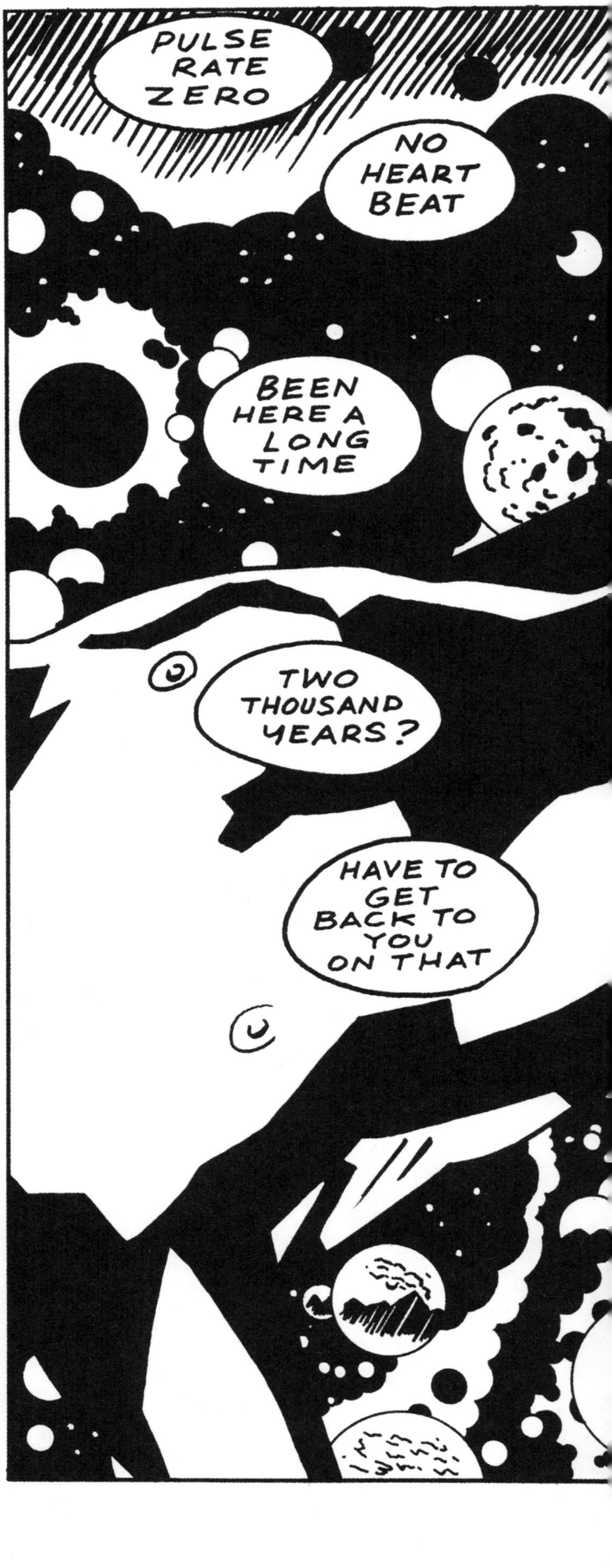
PULSE RATE ZERO
NO HEART BEAT
BEEN HERE A LONG TIME
TWO THOUSAND YEARS?
HAVE TO GET BACK TO YOU ON THAT

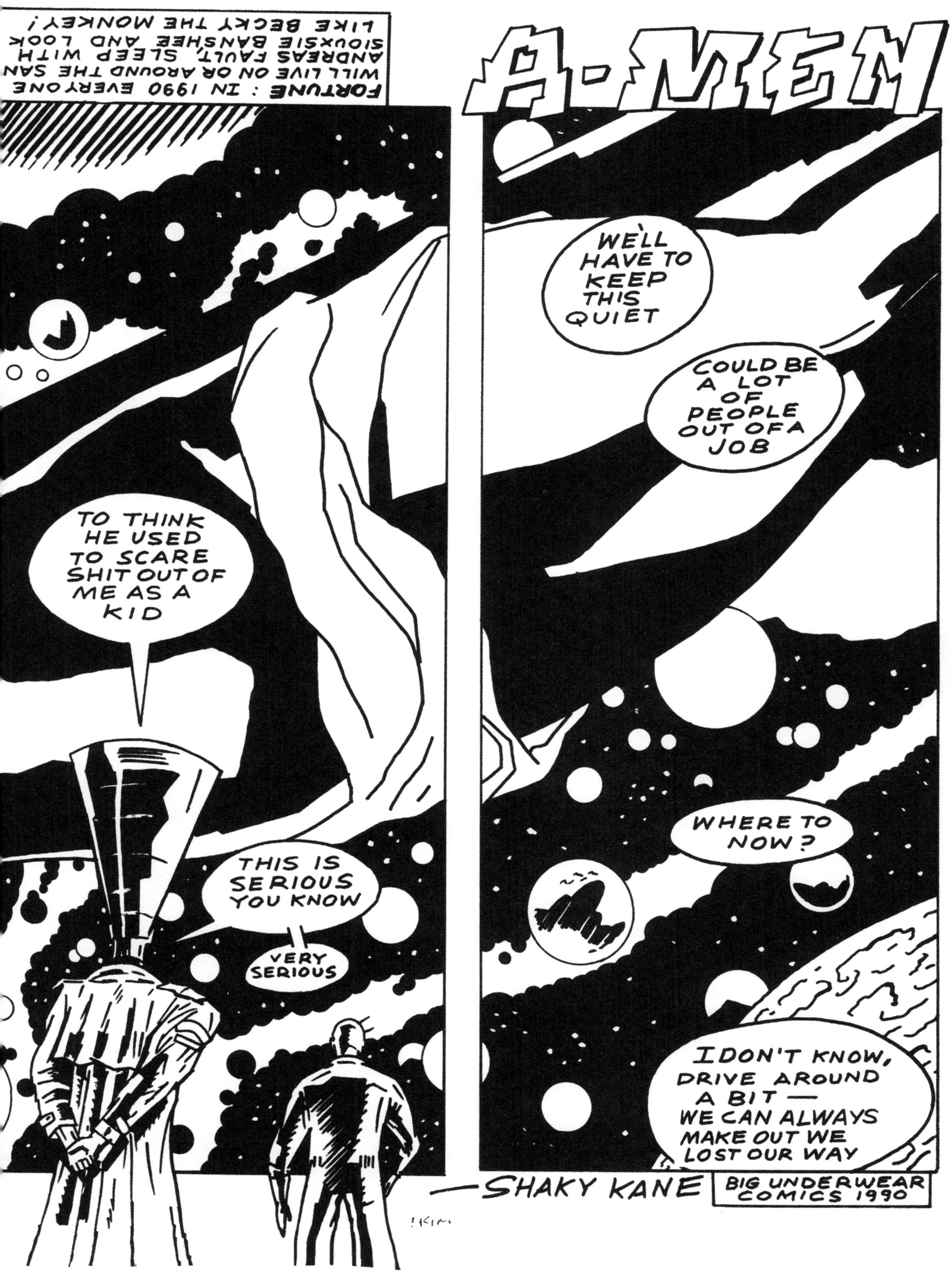

A-MEN
FORTUNE : IN 1990 EVERYONE WILL LIVE ON OR AROUND THE SAN ANDREAS FAULT, SLEEP WITH SIOUXSIE BANSHEE AND LOOK LIKE BECKY THE MONKEY!
TO THINK HE USED TO SCARE SHIT OUT OF ME AS A KID
THIS IS SERIOUS YOU KNOW
VERY SERIOUS
WE'LL HAVE TO KEEP THIS QUIET
COULD BE A LOT OF PEOPLE OUT OF A JOB
WHERE TO NOW?
I DON'T KNOW, DRIVE AROUND A BIT — WE CAN ALWAYS MAKE OUT WE LOST OUR WAY
—SHAKY KANE
BIG UNDERWEAR COMICS 1990

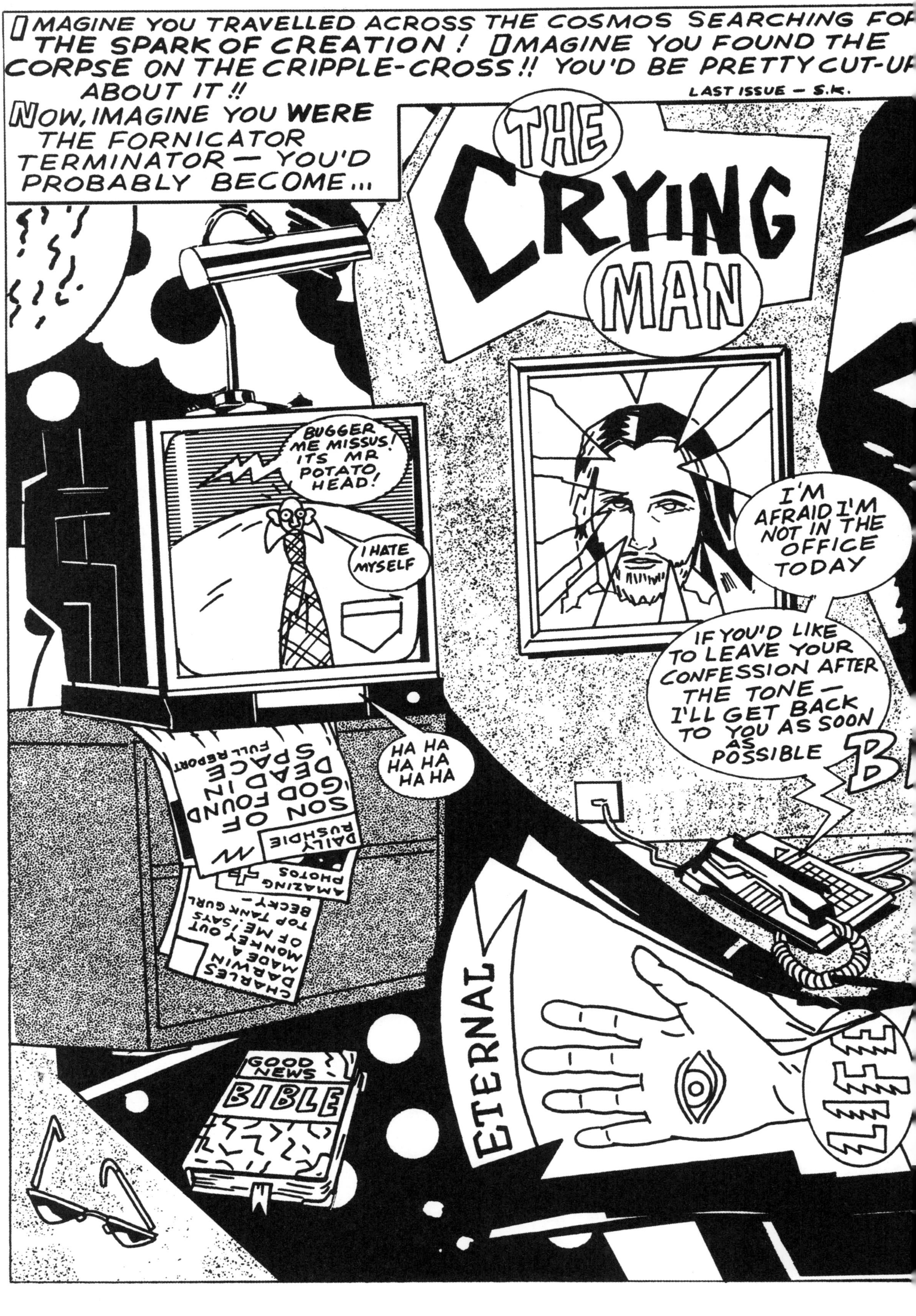
IMAGINE YOU TRAVELLED ACROSS THE COSMOS SEARCHING FOR THE SPARK OF CREATION! IMAGINE YOU FOUND THE CORPSE ON THE CRIPPLE-CROSS!! YOU'D BE PRETTY CUT-UP ABOUT IT!!
LAST ISSUE — S.K.
NOW, IMAGINE YOU WERE THE FORNICATOR TERMINATOR — YOU'D PROBABLY BECOME...
THE CRYING MAN
BUGGER ME MISSUS! ITS MR POTATO HEAD!
I HATE MYSELF
HA HA HA HA HA HA
DAILY RUSHDIE
SON OF GOD FOUND DEAD IN SPACE
FULL REPORT
AMAZING PHOTOS
CHARLES DARWIN MADE A MONKEY OUT OF ME! SAYS TOP TANK GURL BECKY
I'M AFRAID I'M NOT IN THE OFFICE TODAY
IF YOU'D LIKE TO LEAVE YOUR CONFESSION AFTER THE TONE — I'LL GET BACK TO YOU AS SOON AS POSSIBLE
B
GOOD NEWS BIBLE
ETERNAL
LIFE

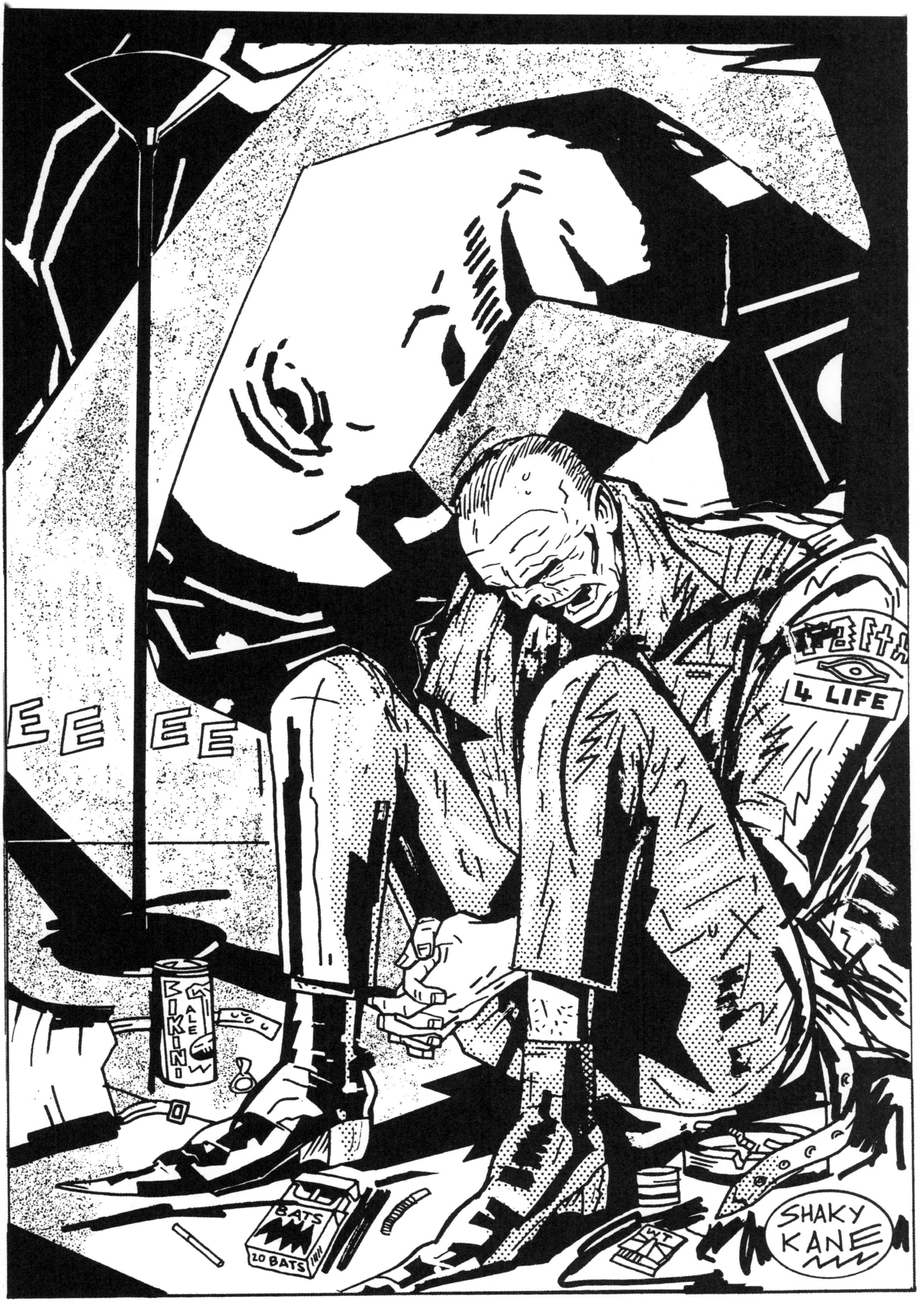
EE EE
4 LIFE
BIKINI
ALE
BATS
20 BATS
SHAKY KANE

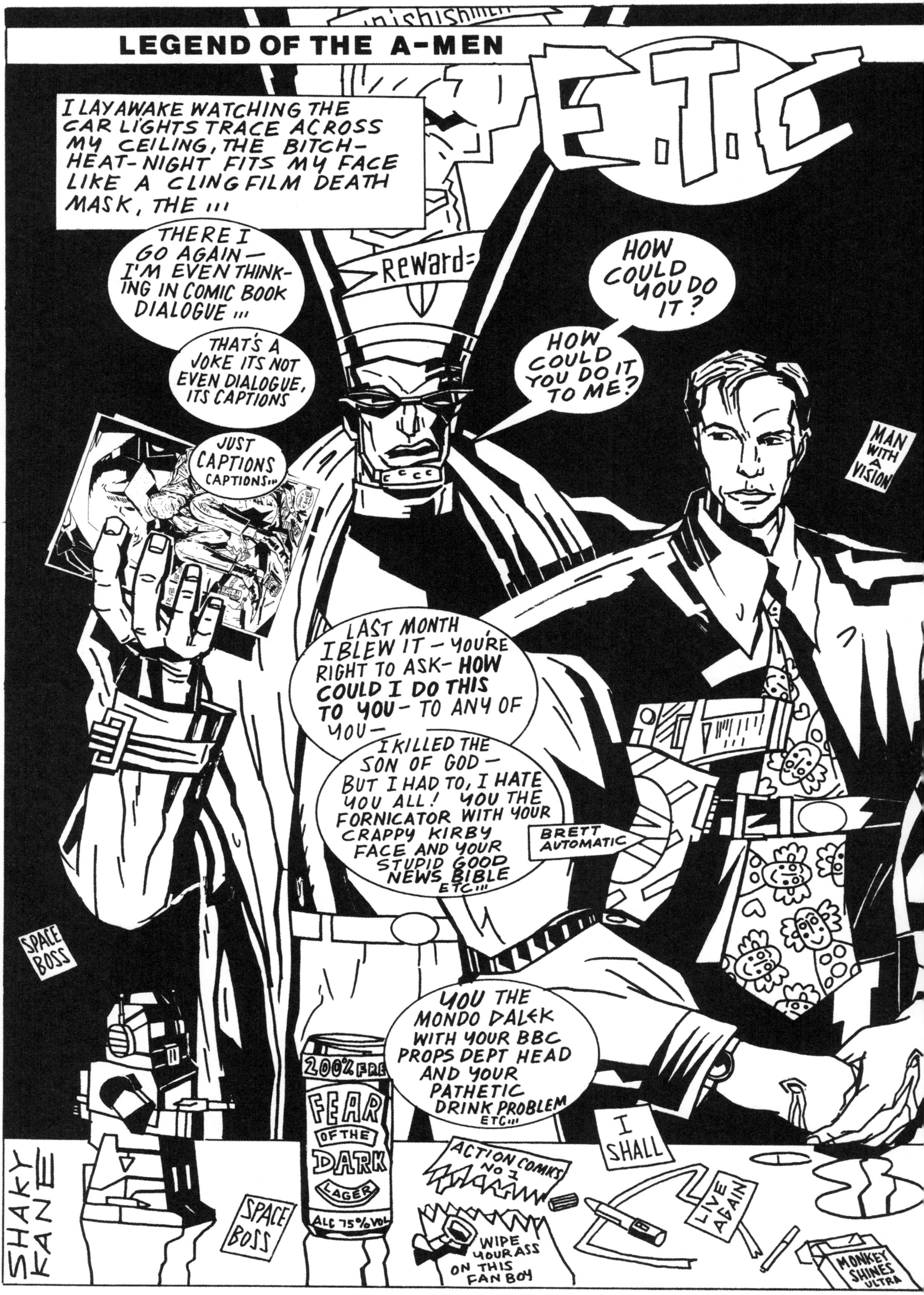
LEGEND OF THE A-MEN
E.T.C
I LAYAWAKE WATCHING THE CAR LIGHTS TRACE ACROSS MY CEILING, THE BITCH-HEAT-NIGHT FITS MY FACE LIKE A CLING FILM DEATH MASK, THE ...
THERE I GO AGAIN — I'M EVEN THINKING IN COMIC BOOK DIALOGUE ...
THAT'S A JOKE ITS NOT EVEN DIALOGUE, ITS CAPTIONS
JUST CAPTIONS CAPTIONS...
Reward=
HOW COULD YOU DO IT?
HOW COULD YOU DO IT TO ME?
MAN WITH A VISION
LAST MONTH I BLEW IT — YOU'RE RIGHT TO ASK — HOW COULD I DO THIS TO YOU — TO ANY OF YOU —
I KILLED THE SON OF GOD — BUT I HAD TO, I HATE YOU ALL! YOU THE FORNICATOR WITH YOUR CRAPPY KIRBY FACE AND YOUR STUPID GOOD NEWS BIBLE ETC...
BRETT AUTOMATIC
SPACE BOSS
YOU THE MONDO DALEK WITH YOUR BBC PROPS DEPT HEAD AND YOUR PATHETIC DRINK PROBLEM ETC...
200% FREE
FEAR OF THE DARK LAGER
ALC 75% VOL
I SHALL
ACTION COMICS No 1
LIVE AGAIN
SPACE BOSS
WIPE YOUR ASS ON THIS FAN BOY
MONKEY SHINES ULTRA
SHAKY KANE

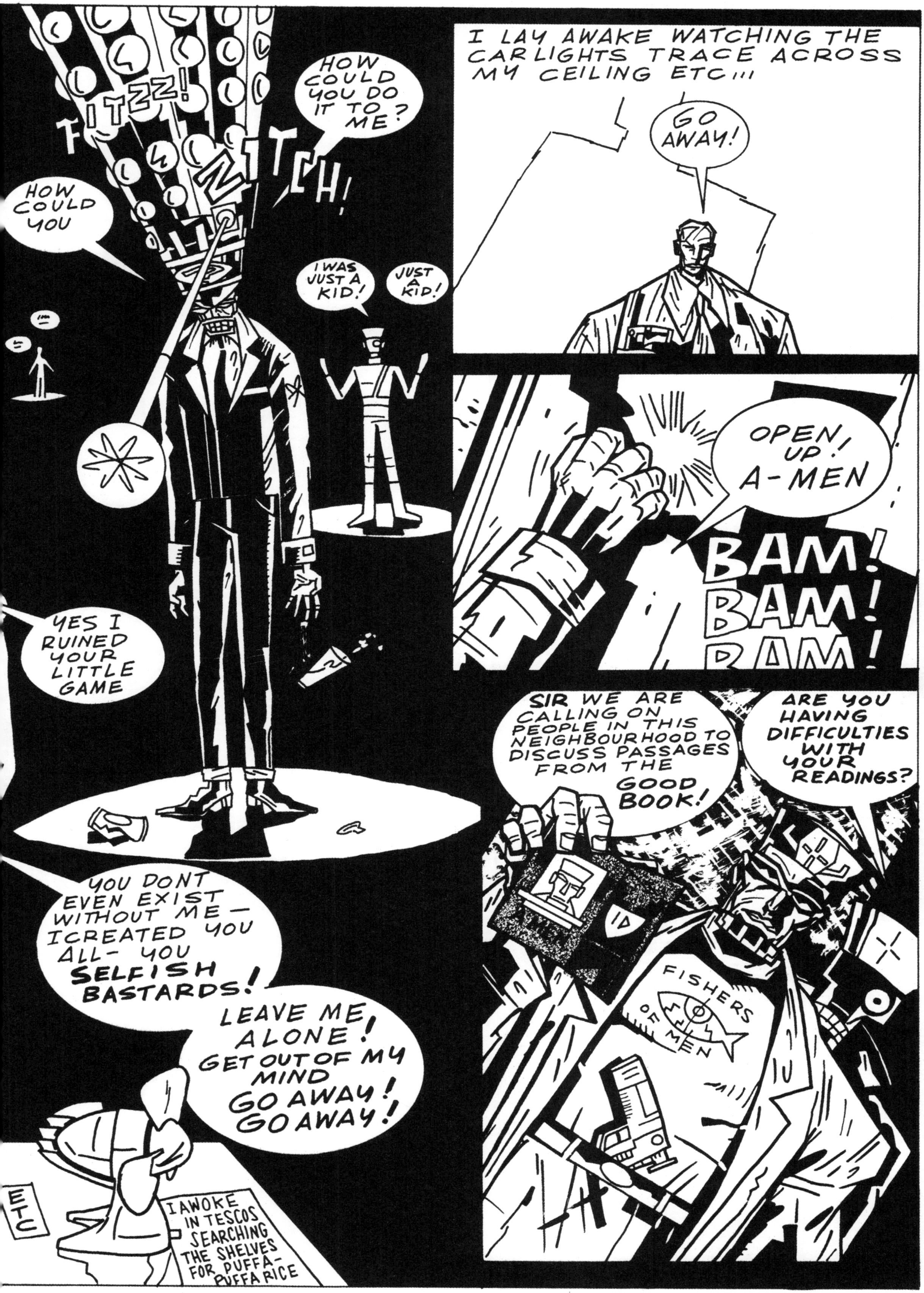
FITZZ!
HOW COULD YOU DO IT TO ME?
SNITCH!
HOW COULD YOU
I WAS JUST A KID!
JUST A KID!
YES I RUINED YOUR LITTLE GAME
YOU DONT EVEN EXIST WITHOUT ME — I CREATED YOU ALL - YOU SELFISH BASTARDS!
LEAVE ME ALONE! GET OUT OF MY MIND GO AWAY! GO AWAY!
ETC
I AWOKE IN TESCOS SEARCHING THE SHELVES FOR PUFFA-PUFFA RICE
I LAY AWAKE WATCHING THE CARLIGHTS TRACE ACROSS MY CEILING ETC...
GO AWAY!
OPEN UP! A-MEN
BAM! BAM! BAM!
SIR WE ARE CALLING ON PEOPLE IN THIS NEIGHBOURHOOD TO DISCUSS PASSAGES FROM THE GOOD BOOK!
ARE YOU HAVING DIFFICULTIES WITH YOUR READINGS?
ID
FISHERS OF MEN

# THE SHADOWMEN

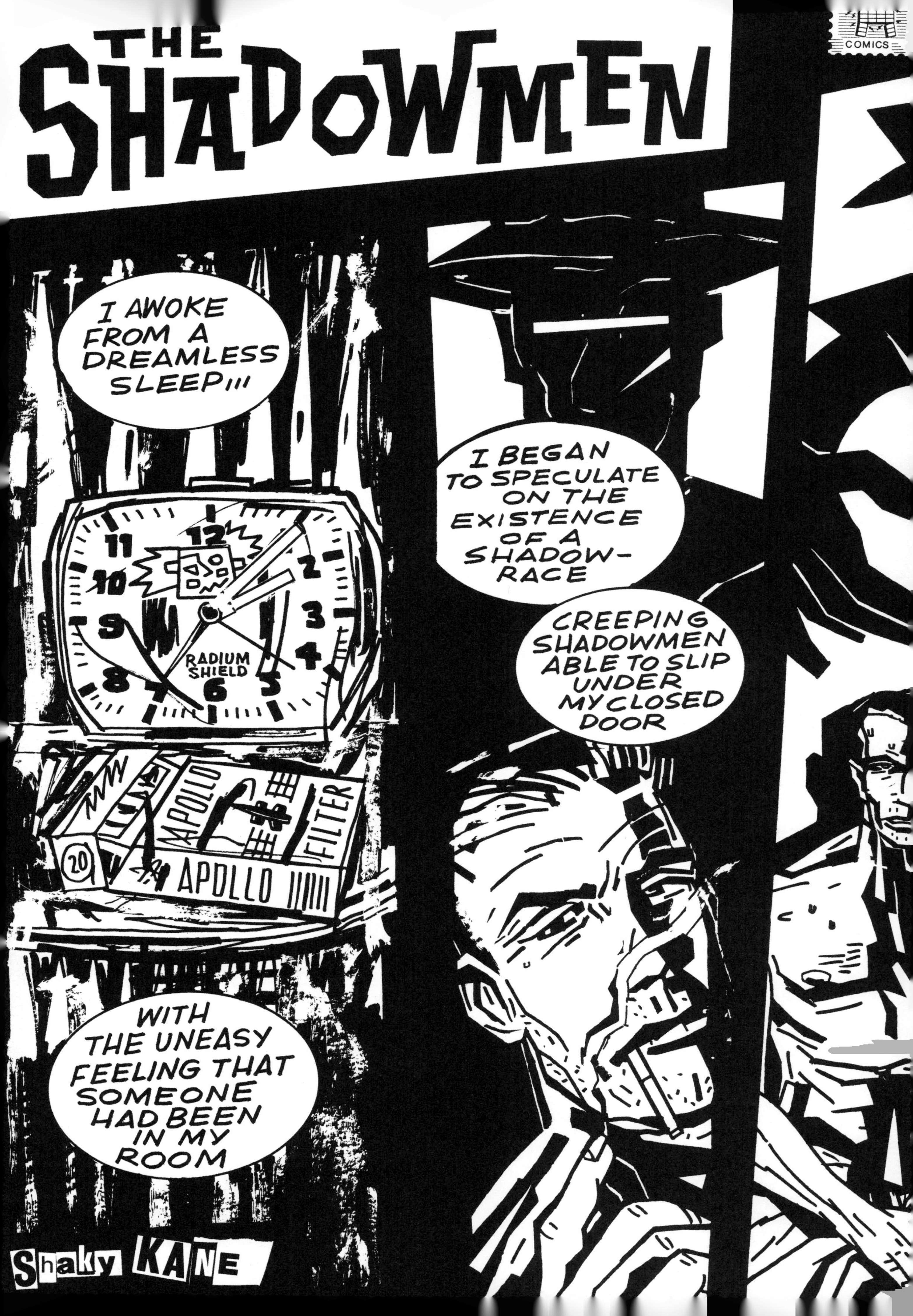
COMICS
I AWOKE FROM A DREAMLESS SLEEP...
RADIUM SHIELD
APOLLO
FILTER
20
APOLLO
WITH THE UNEASY FEELING THAT SOMEONE HAD BEEN IN MY ROOM
I BEGAN TO SPECULATE ON THE EXISTENCE OF A SHADOW-RACE
CREEPING SHADOWMEN ABLE TO SLIP UNDER MY CLOSED DOOR

Shaky KANE

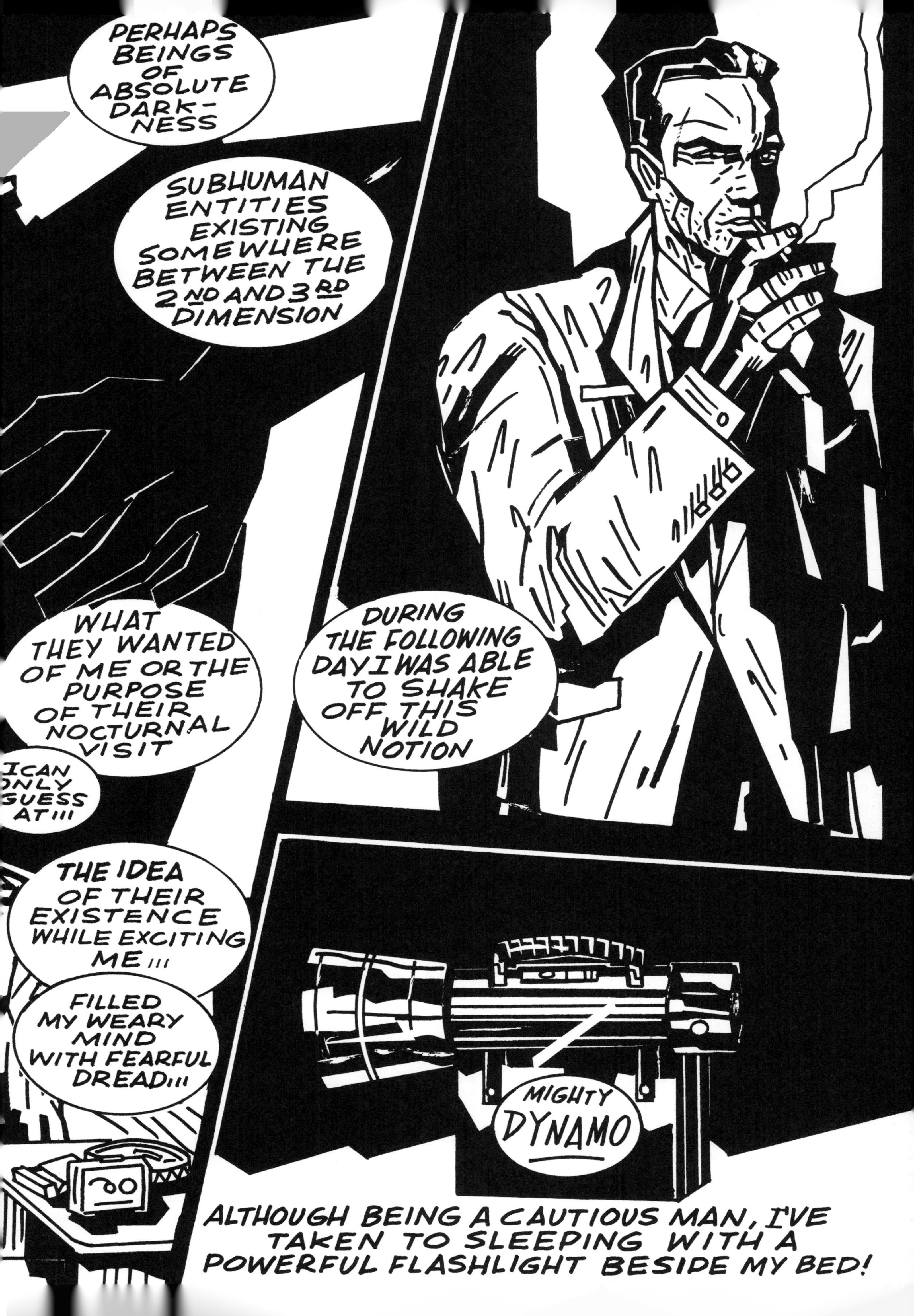
PERHAPS BEINGS OF ABSOLUTE DARK-NESS
SUBHUMAN ENTITIES EXISTING SOMEWHERE BETWEEN THE 2ND AND 3RD DIMENSION
WHAT THEY WANTED OF ME OR THE PURPOSE OF THEIR NOCTURNAL VISIT
I CAN ONLY GUESS AT...
DURING THE FOLLOWING DAY I WAS ABLE TO SHAKE OFF THIS WILD NOTION
THE IDEA OF THEIR EXISTENCE WHILE EXCITING ME...
FILLED MY WEARY MIND WITH FEARFUL DREAD...
MIGHTY DYNAMO
ALTHOUGH BEING A CAUTIOUS MAN, I'VE TAKEN TO SLEEPING WITH A POWERFUL FLASHLIGHT BESIDE MY BED!

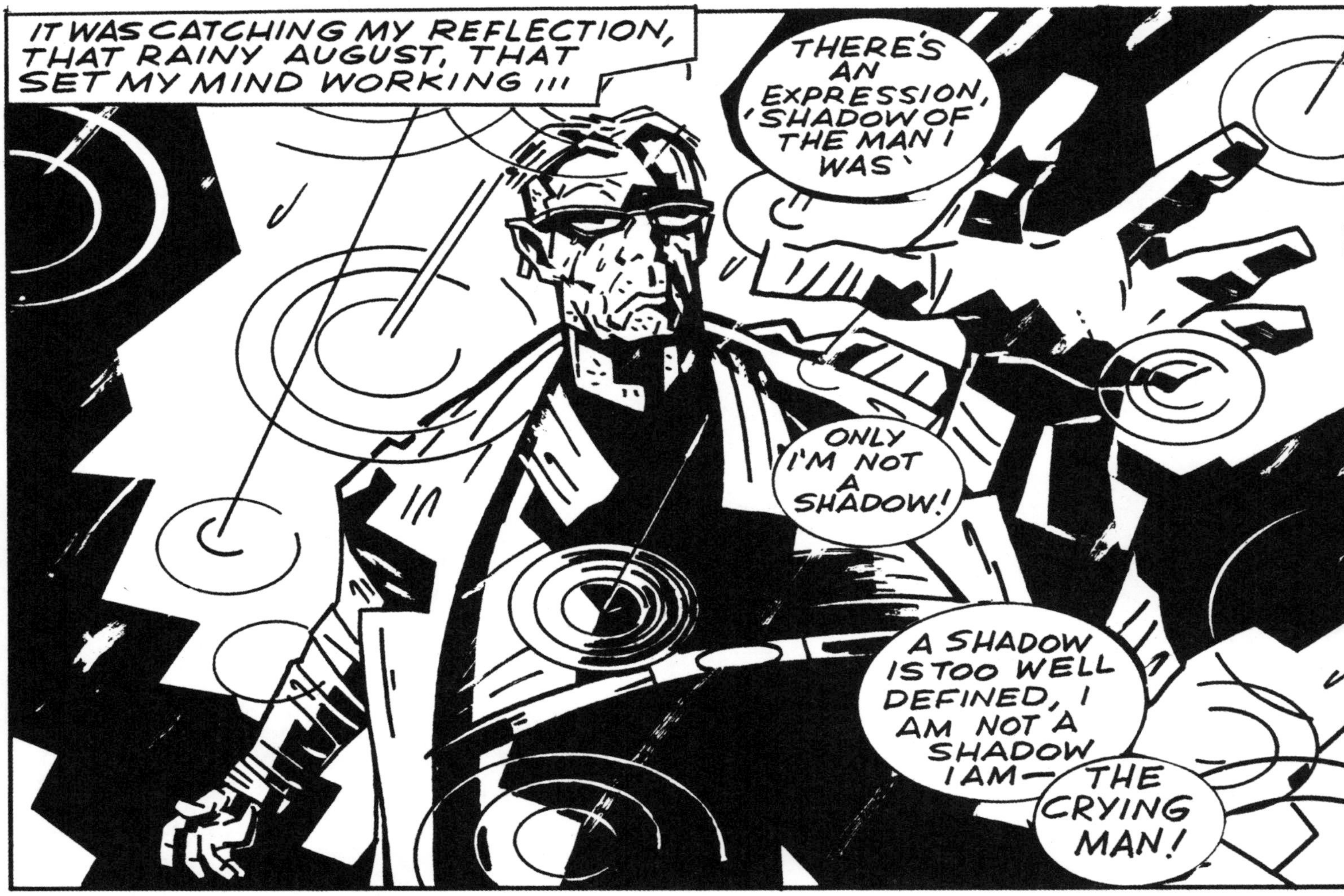
IT WAS CATCHING MY REFLECTION, THAT RAINY AUGUST, THAT SET MY MIND WORKING ...
THERE'S AN EXPRESSION, 'SHADOW OF THE MAN I WAS'
ONLY I'M NOT A SHADOW!
A SHADOW IS TOO WELL DEFINED, I AM NOT A SHADOW I AM—
THE CRYING MAN!
FOR CHESTER

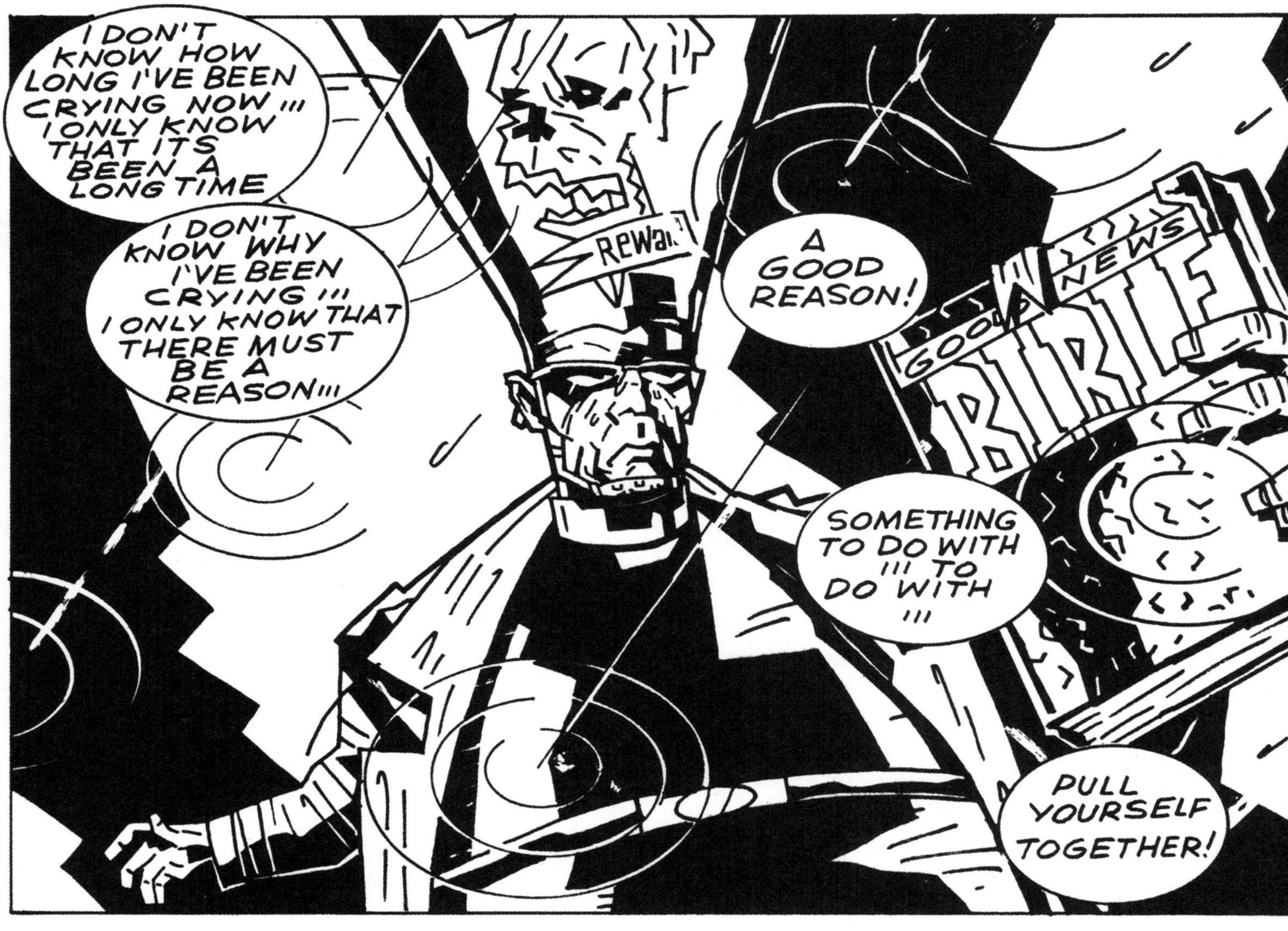
I DON'T KNOW HOW LONG I'VE BEEN CRYING NOW ... I ONLY KNOW THAT ITS BEEN A LONG TIME
I DON'T KNOW WHY I'VE BEEN CRYING ... I ONLY KNOW THAT THERE MUST BE A REASON ...
A GOOD REASON!
SOMETHING TO DO WITH ... TO DO WITH ...
PULL YOURSELF TOGETHER!
GOOD NEWS
BIBLE

EADLINE
o.12 OCT '89
1·50 MONTHLY

# DEADLINE

OBVIOUSLY THE BEST MAGAZINE IN THE OMNIVERSE*

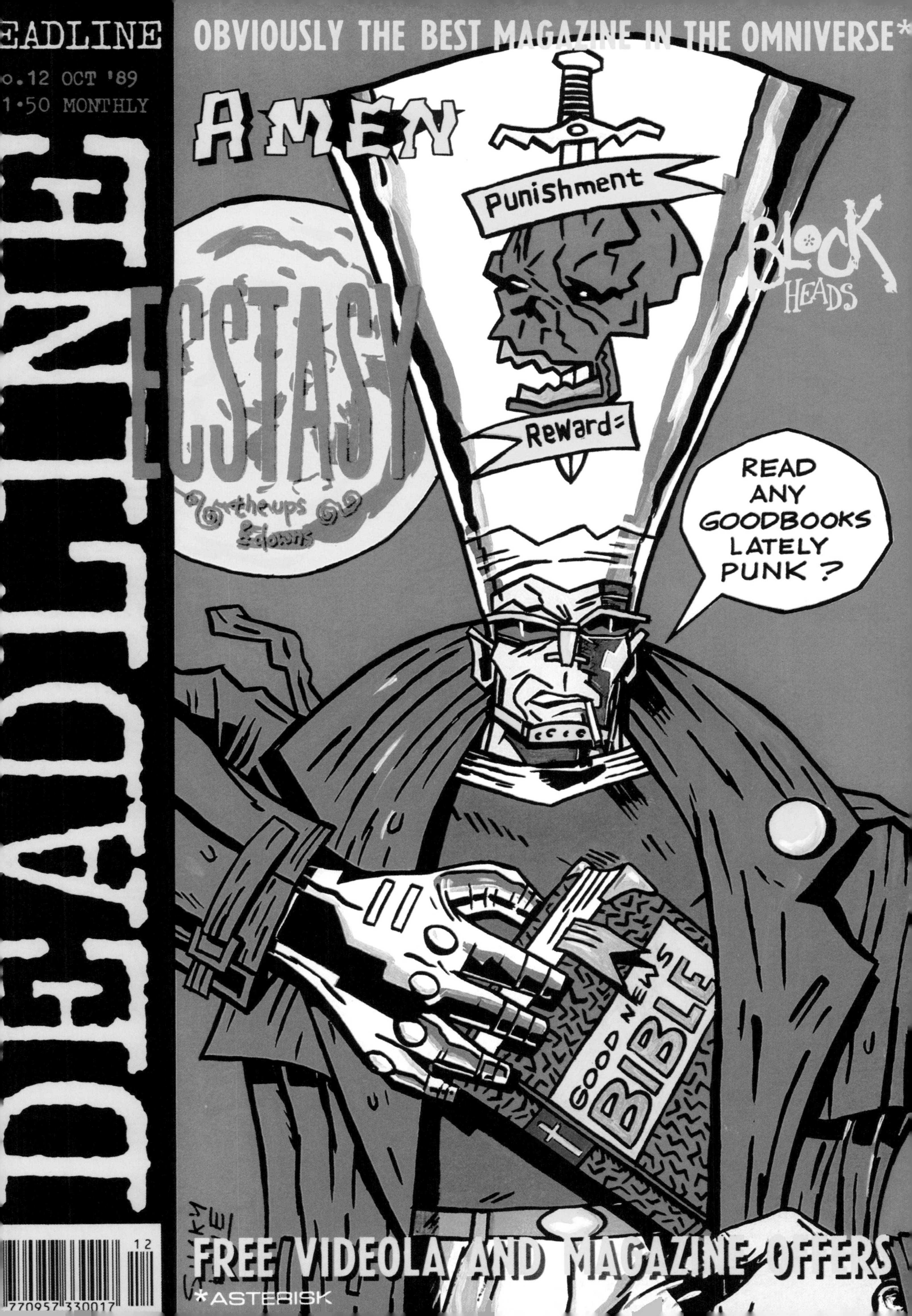

AMEN
Punishment
Reward=
ECSTASY
the ups & downs
BLOCK HEADS
READ ANY GOODBOOKS LATELY PUNK ?
GOOD NEWS BIBLE


FREE VIDEOLA AND MAGAZINE OFFERS

*ASTERISK

12
770957 330017

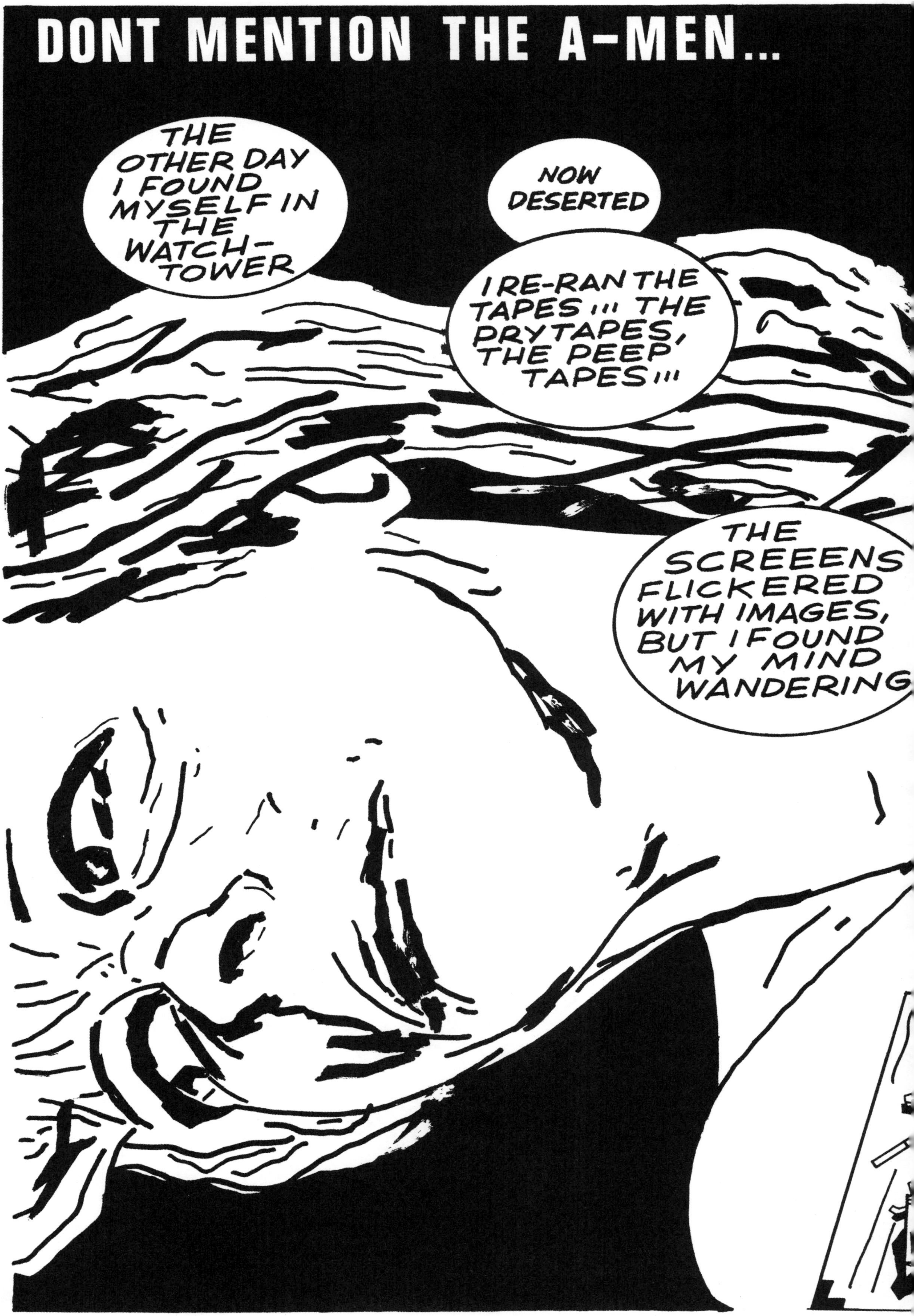
DONT MENTION THE A-MEN...
THE OTHER DAY I FOUND MYSELF IN THE WATCH-TOWER
NOW DESERTED
I RE-RAN THE TAPES ... THE PRYTAPES, THE PEEP TAPES...
THE SCREEENS FLICKERED WITH IMAGES, BUT I FOUND MY MIND WANDERING

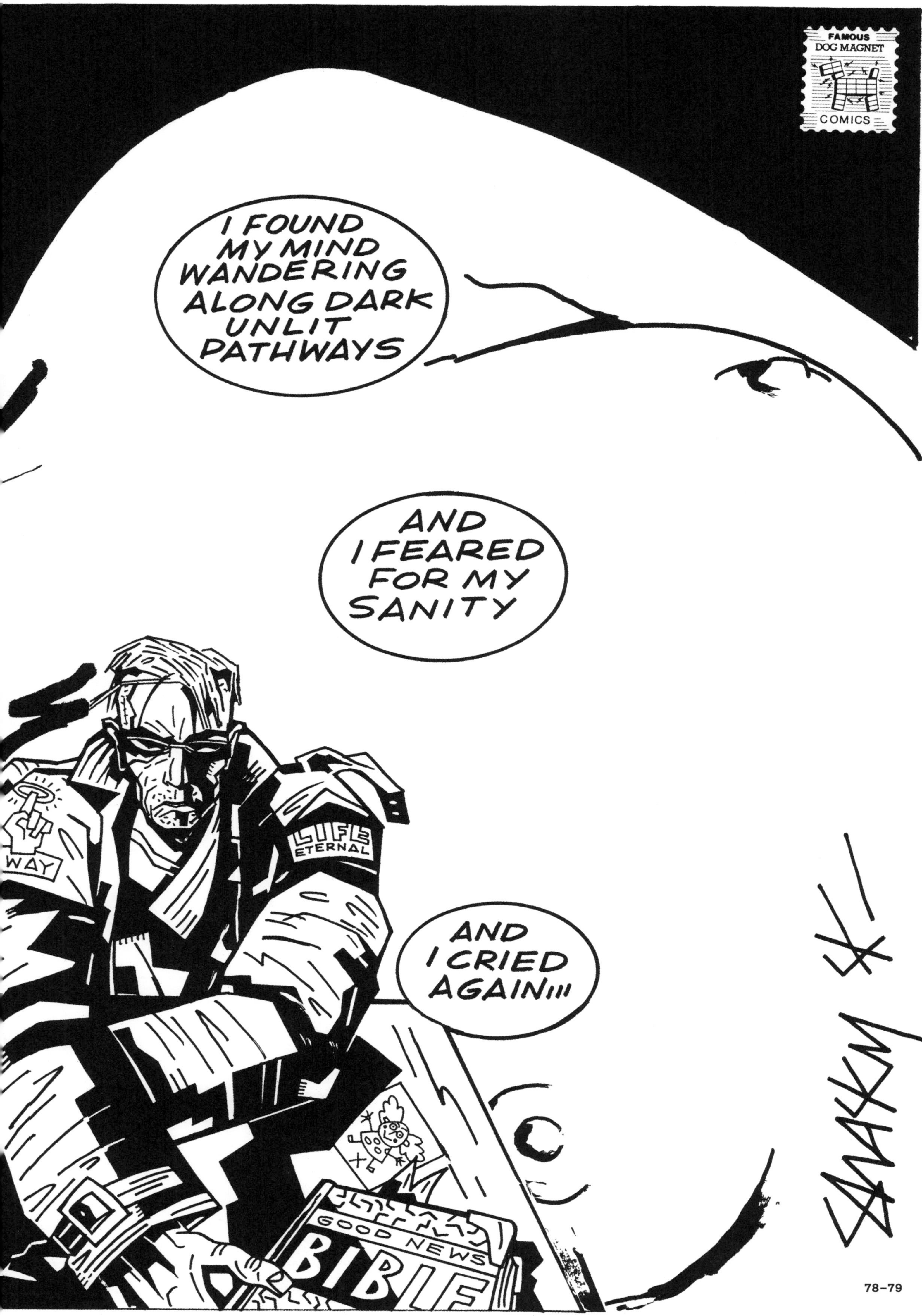
FAMOUS DOG MAGNET COMICS
I FOUND MY MIND WANDERING ALONG DARK UNLIT PATHWAYS
AND I FEARED FOR MY SANITY
AND I CRIED AGAIN...
WAY
LIFE ETERNAL
GOOD NEWS BIBLE

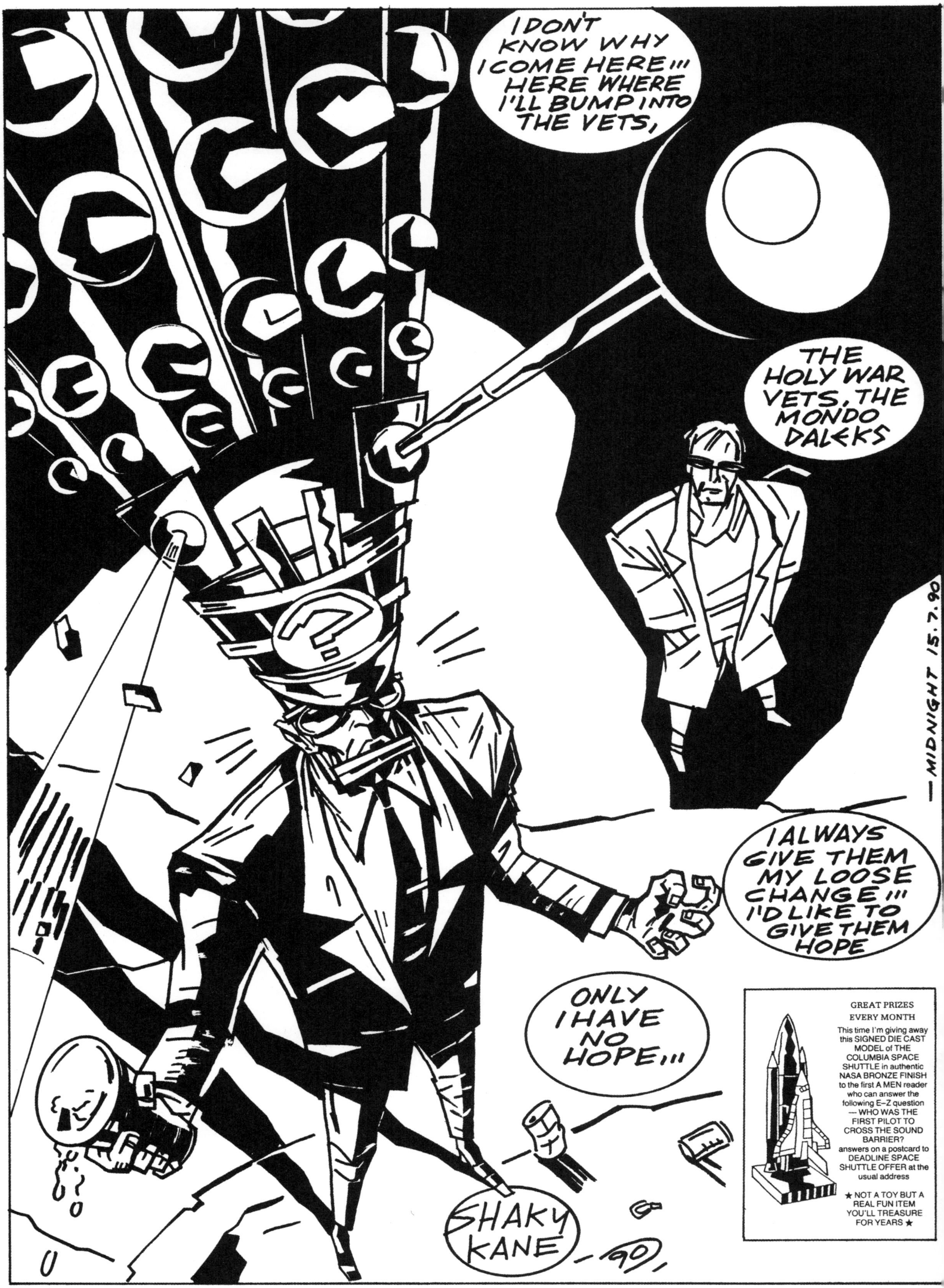
I DON'T KNOW WHY I COME HERE... HERE WHERE I'LL BUMP INTO THE VETS,
THE HOLY WAR VETS, THE MONDO DALEKS
I ALWAYS GIVE THEM MY LOOSE CHANGE... I'D LIKE TO GIVE THEM HOPE
ONLY I HAVE NO HOPE...
— MIDNIGHT 15.7.90
SHAKY KANE -90-

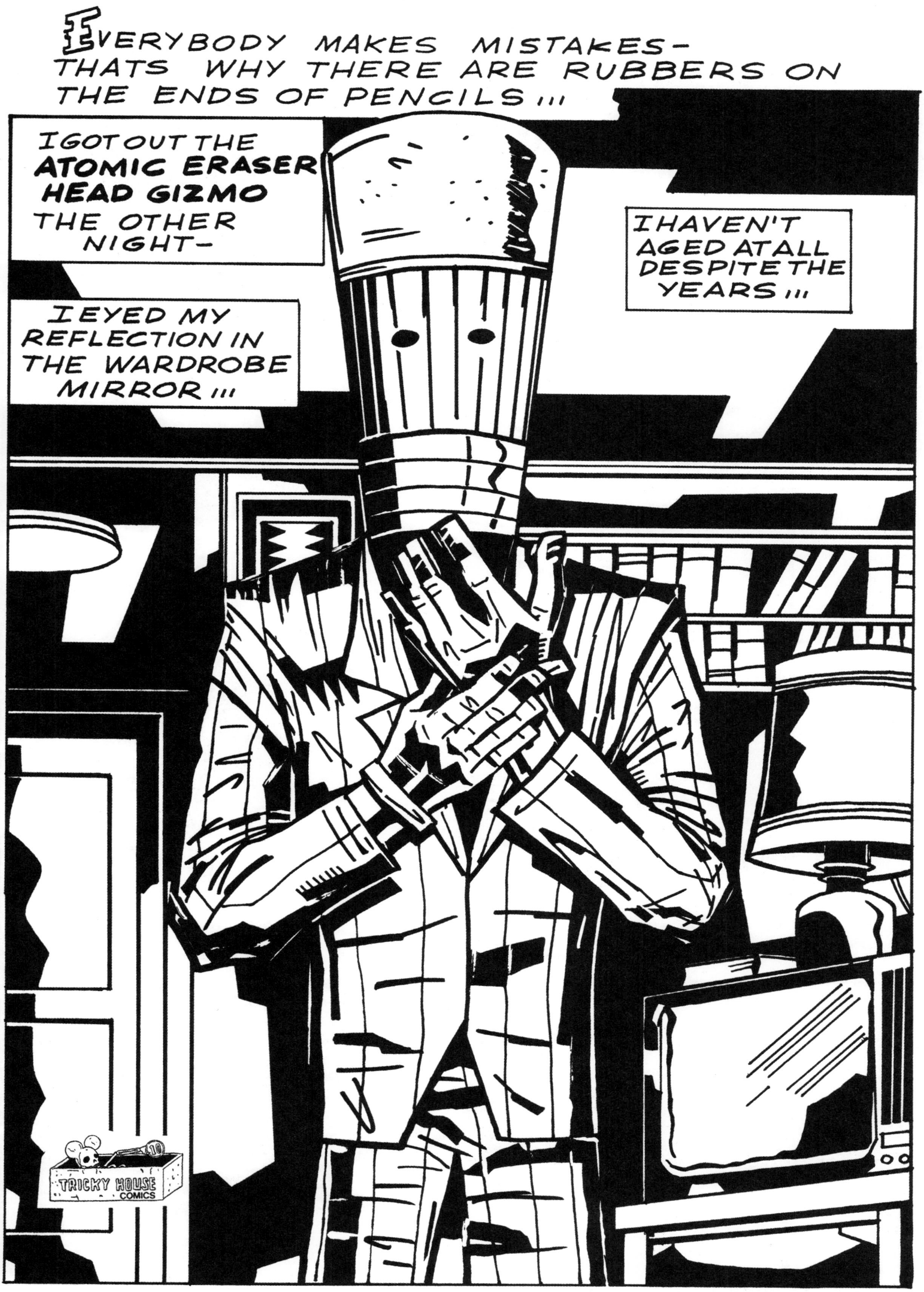
EVERYBODY MAKES MISTAKES-
THATS WHY THERE ARE RUBBERS ON
THE ENDS OF PENCILS...
I GOT OUT THE ATOMIC ERASER HEAD GIZMO THE OTHER NIGHT-
I EYED MY REFLECTION IN THE WARDROBE MIRROR...
I HAVEN'T AGED AT ALL DESPITE THE YEARS...
TRICKY HOUSE COMICS

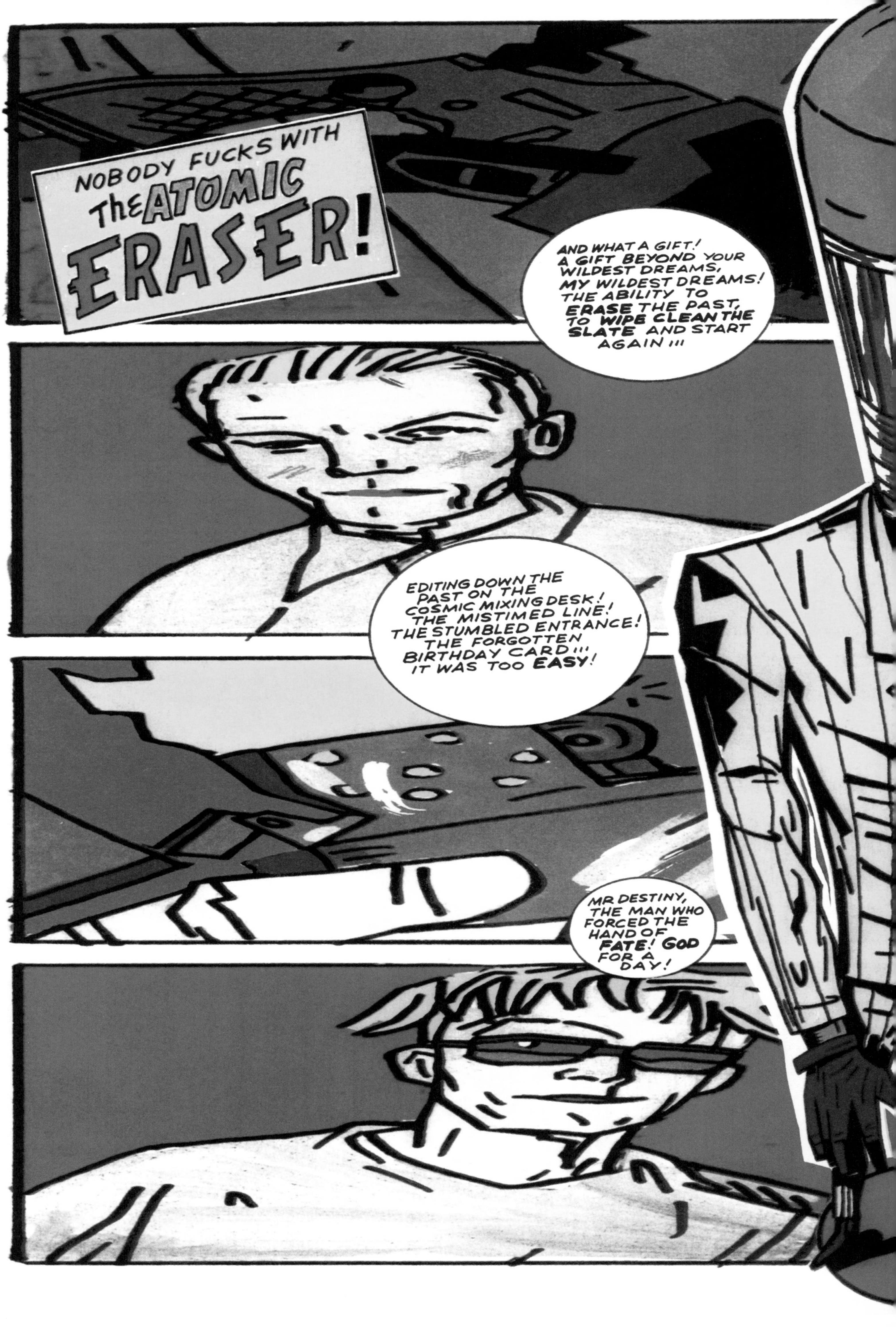
NOBODY FUCKS WITH The ATOMIC ERASER!
AND WHAT A GIFT! A GIFT BEYOND YOUR WILDEST DREAMS, MY WILDEST DREAMS! THE ABILITY TO ERASE THE PAST, TO WIPE CLEAN THE SLATE AND START AGAIN...
EDITING DOWN THE PAST ON THE COSMIC MIXING DESK! THE MISTIMED LINE! THE STUMBLED ENTRANCE! THE FORGOTTEN BIRTHDAY CARD... IT WAS TOO EASY!
MR DESTINY, THE MAN WHO FORCED THE HAND OF FATE! GOD FOR A DAY!

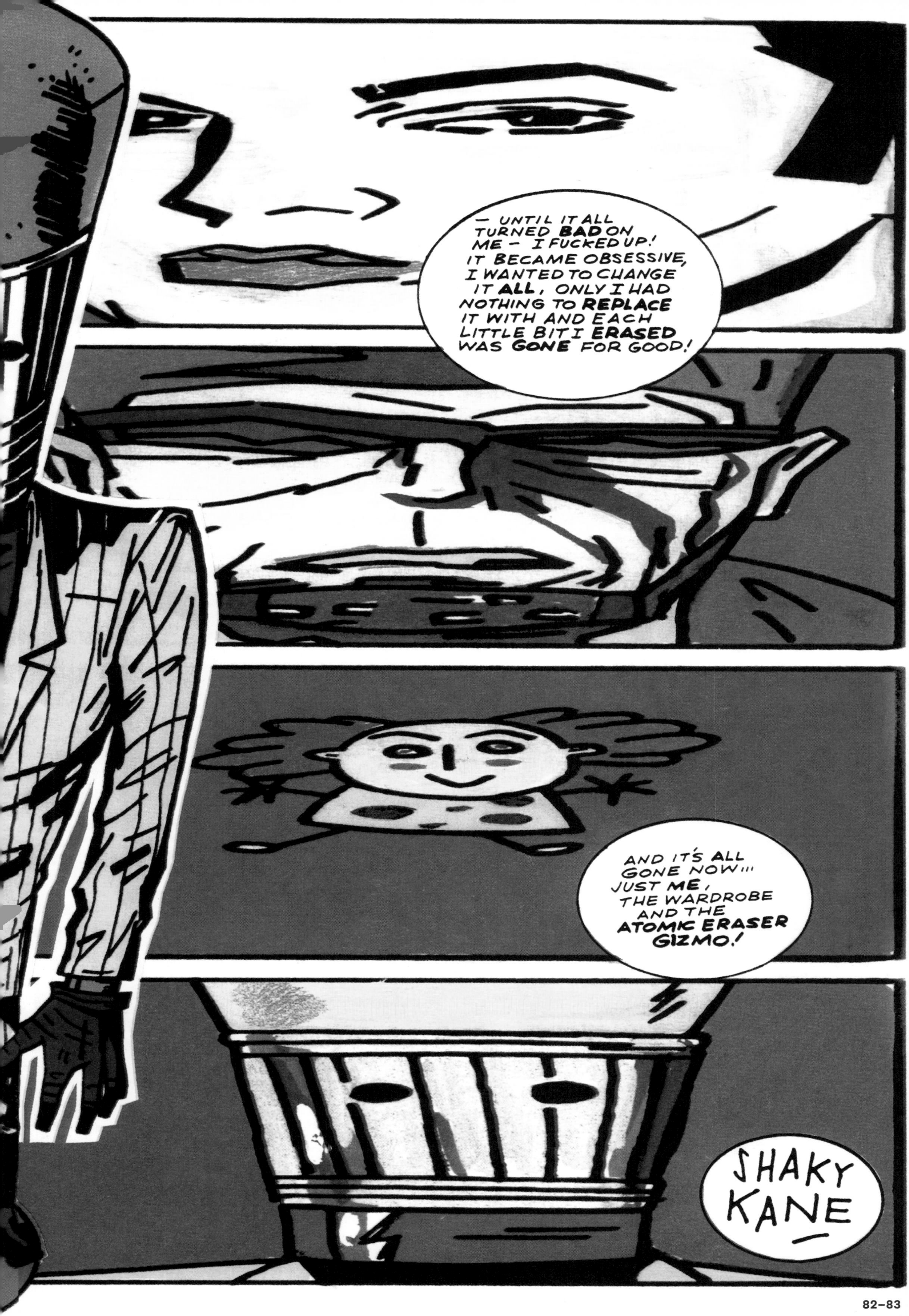
— UNTIL IT ALL TURNED BAD ON ME — I FUCKED UP! IT BECAME OBSESSIVE, I WANTED TO CHANGE IT ALL, ONLY I HAD NOTHING TO REPLACE IT WITH AND EACH LITTLE BIT I ERASED WAS GONE FOR GOOD!
AND IT'S ALL GONE NOW!!! JUST ME, THE WARDROBE AND THE ATOMIC ERASER GIZMO!
SHAKY KANE

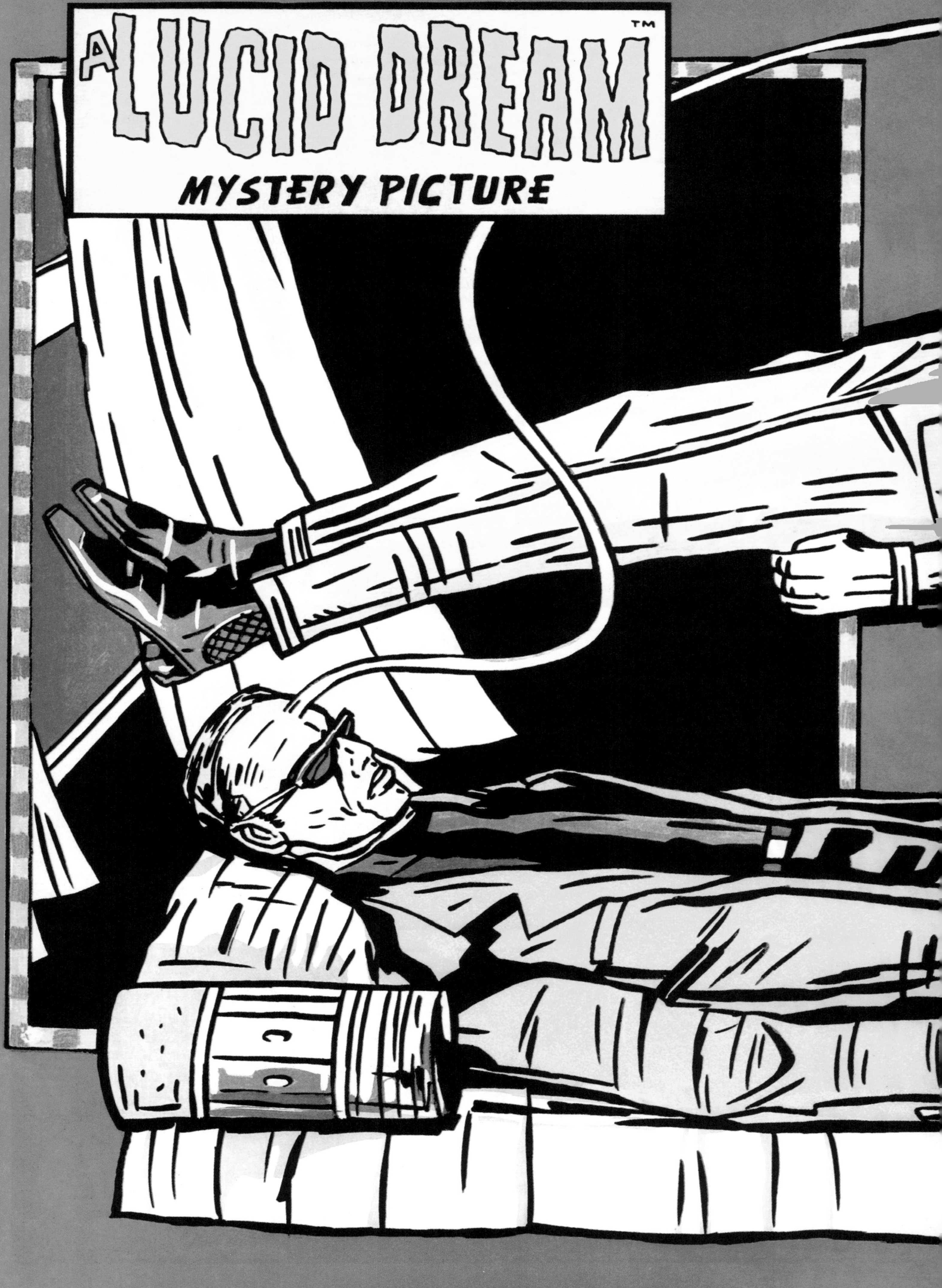
A LUCID DREAM™
MYSTERY PICTURE

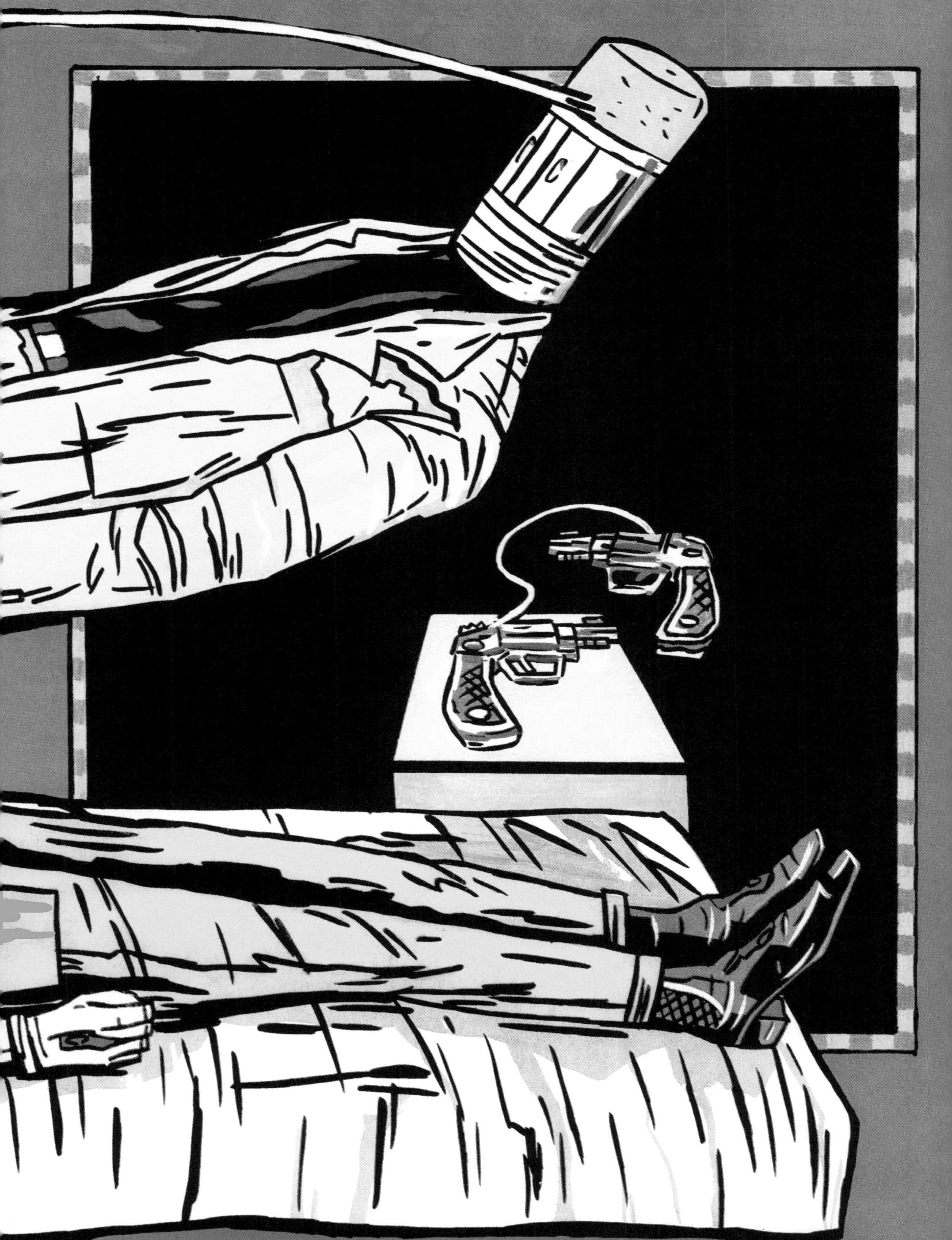

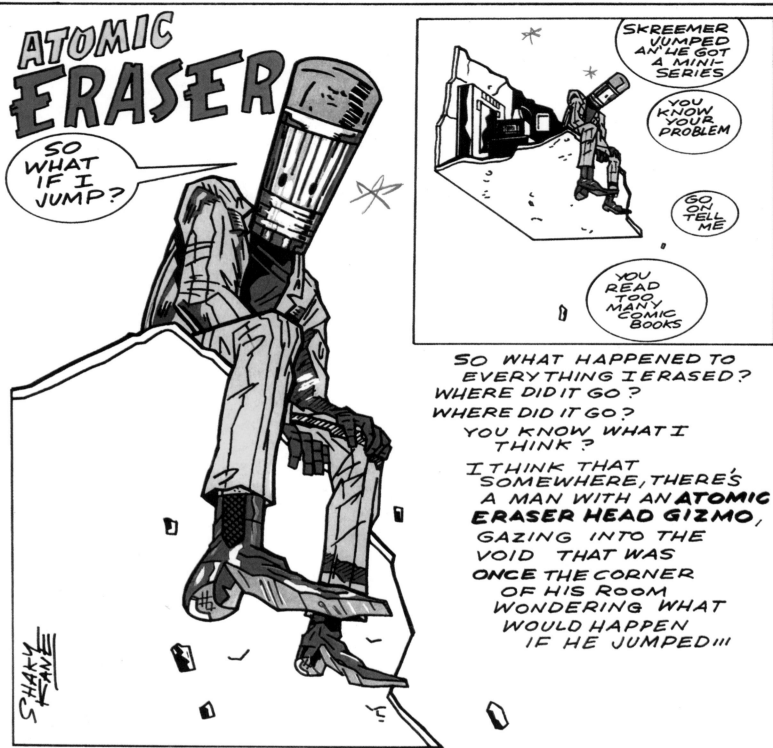

EVERYBODY MAKES MISTAKES — THATS WHY THERE ARE RUBBERS ON THE ENDS OF PENCILS!!!
ATOMIC ERASER
SO WHAT IF I JUMP?
SKREEMER JUMPED AN' HE GOT A MINI-SERIES
YOU KNOW YOUR PROBLEM
GO ON TELL ME
YOU READ TOO MANY COMIC BOOKS
SO WHAT HAPPENED TO EVERYTHING I ERASED? WHERE DID IT GO? WHERE DID IT GO? YOU KNOW WHAT I THINK? I THINK THAT SOMEWHERE, THERE'S A MAN WITH AN ATOMIC ERASER HEAD GIZMO, GAZING INTO THE VOID THAT WAS ONCE THE CORNER OF HIS ROOM WONDERING WHAT WOULD HAPPEN IF HE JUMPED!!!
SHAKY KANE
YOU KNOW WHAT MY PROBLEM IS!!!?

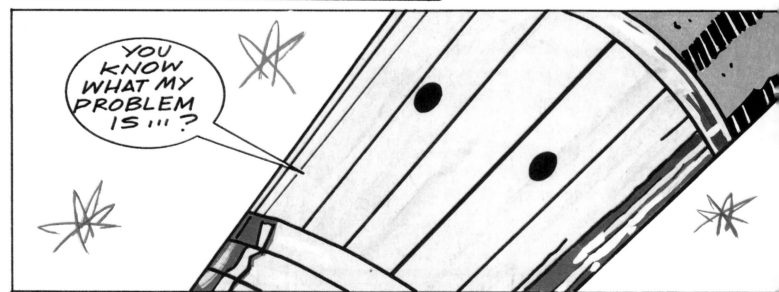

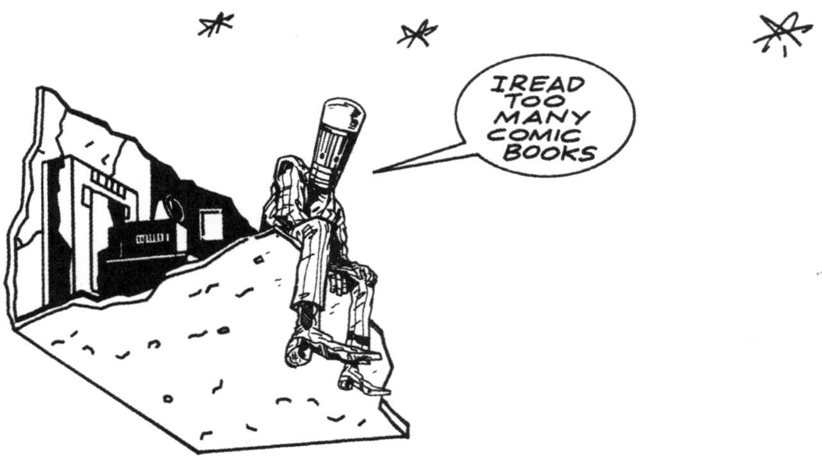
IREAD TOO MANY COMIC BOOKS

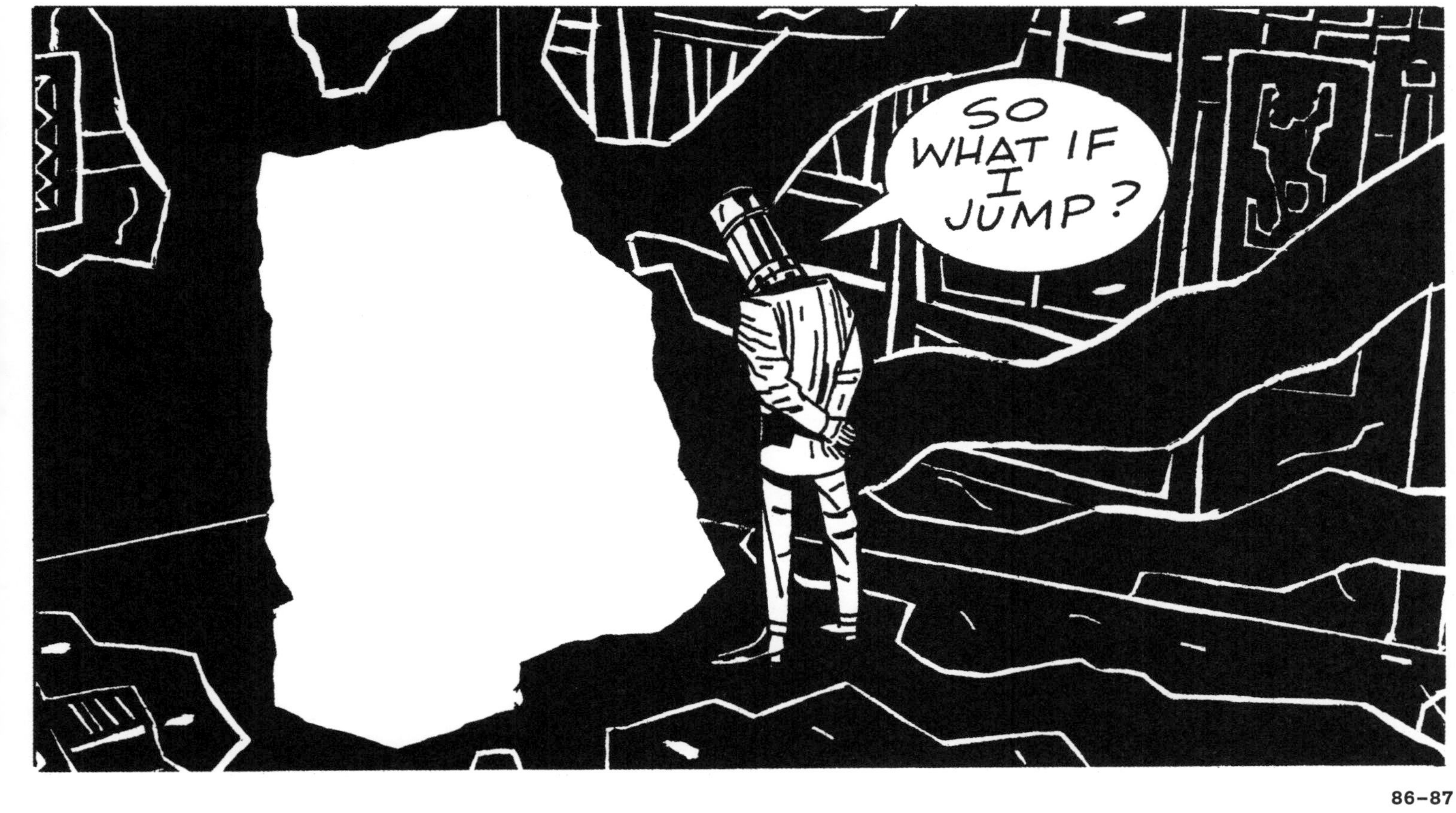
SO WHAT IF I JUMP?

MAKES YOU THINK
DOESN'T IT ?!!!

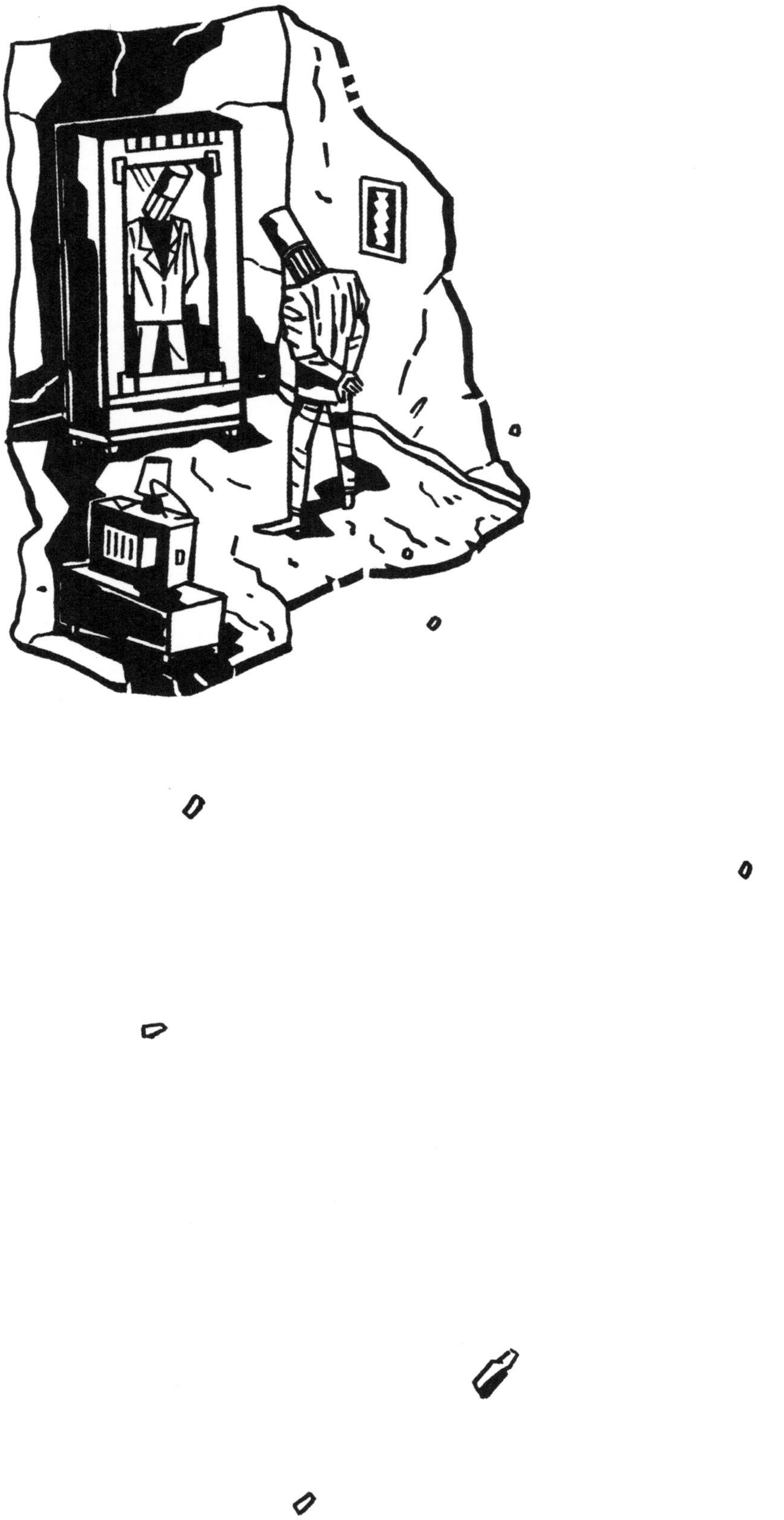

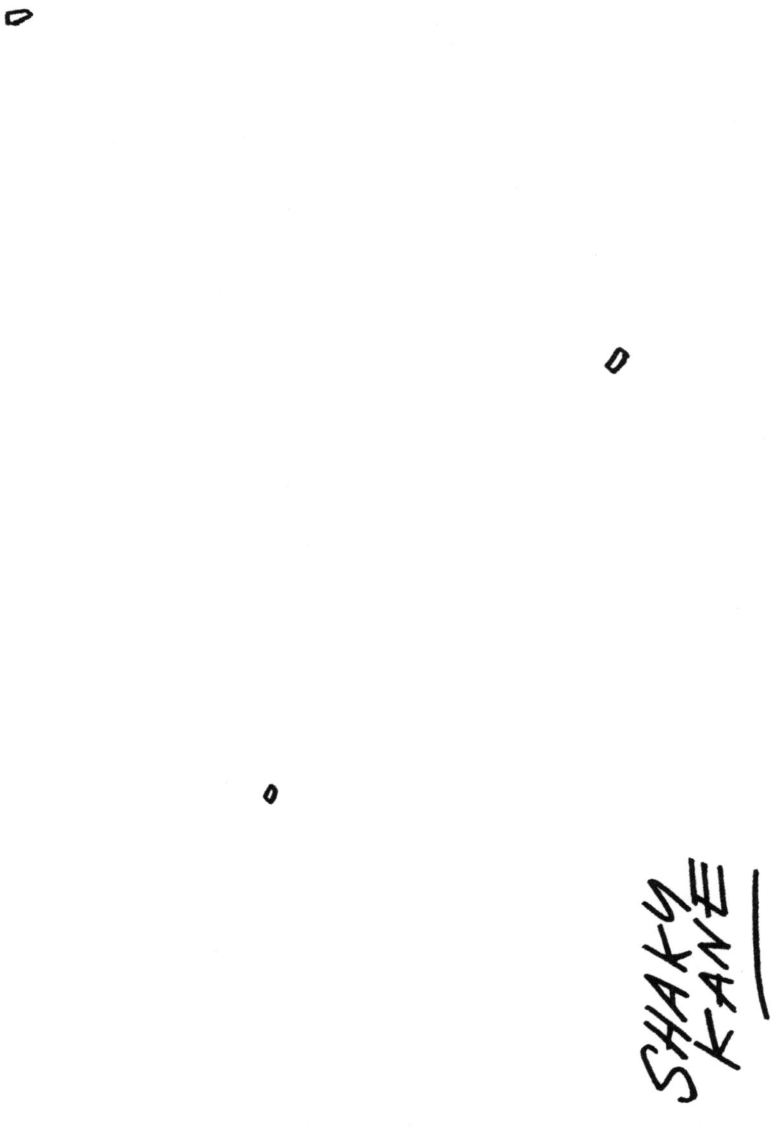
SHAKY KANE

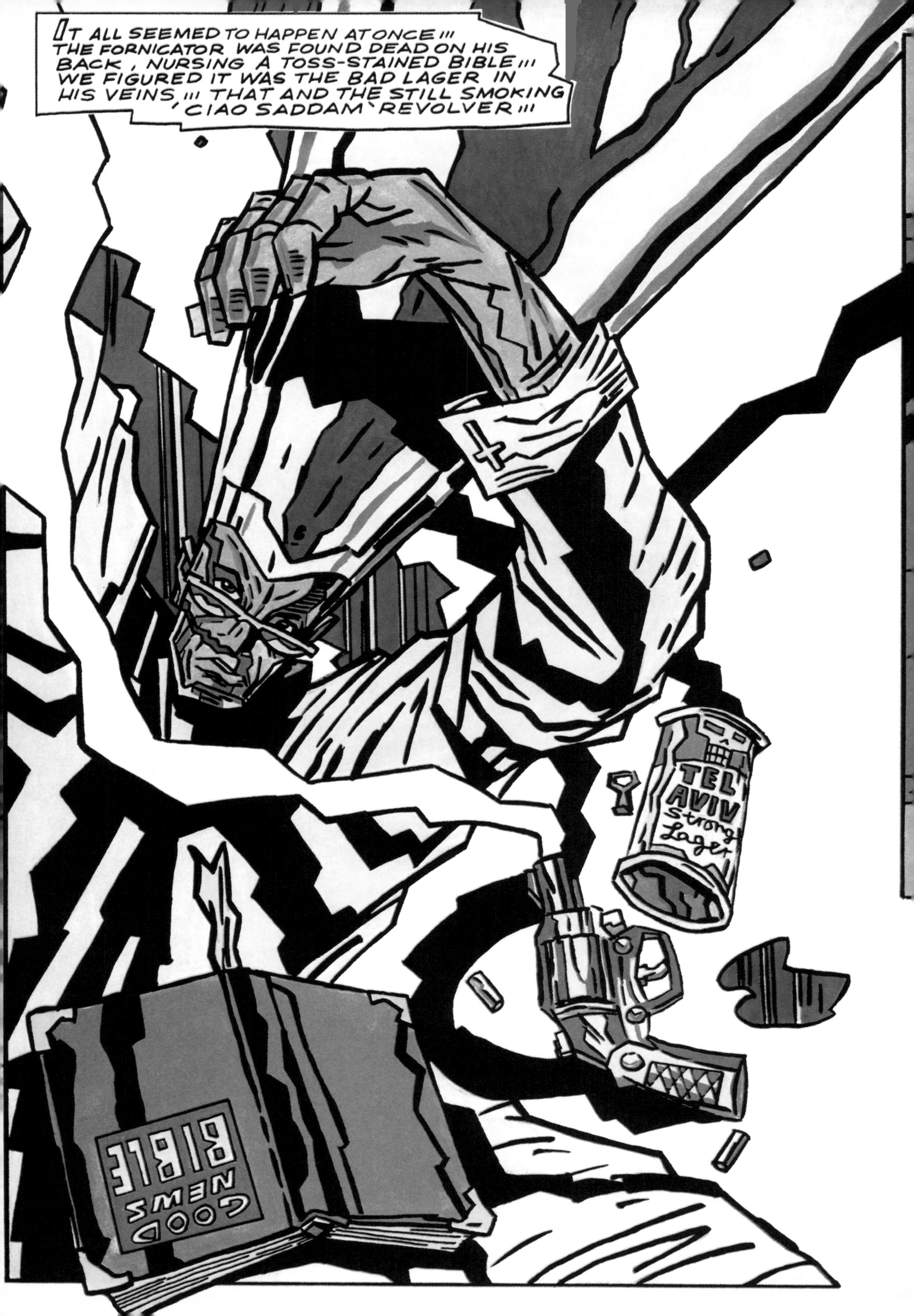
IT ALL SEEMED TO HAPPEN AT ONCE... THE FORNICATOR WAS FOUND DEAD ON HIS BACK, NURSING A TOSS-STAINED BIBLE... WE FIGURED IT WAS THE BAD LAGER IN HIS VEINS... THAT AND THE STILL SMOKING 'CIAO SADDAM' REVOLVER...
TEL AVIV Strong Lager
GOOD NEWS BIBLE

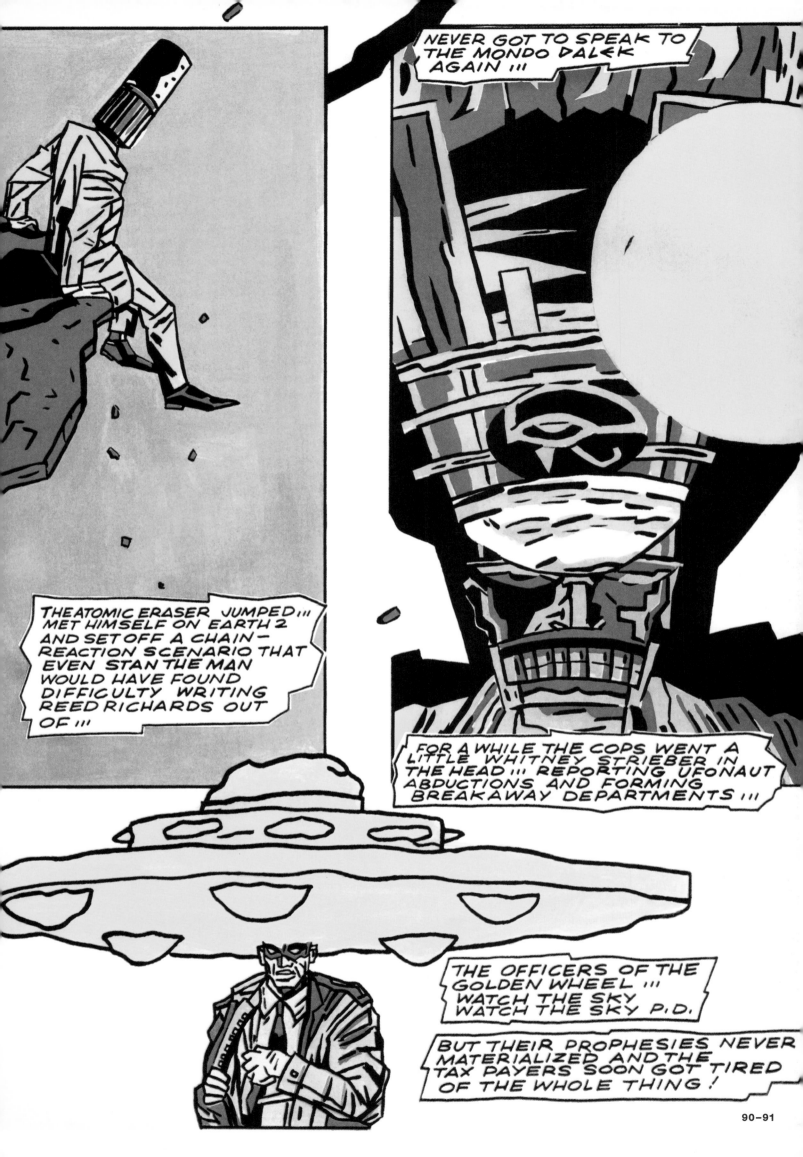

NEVER GOT TO SPEAK TO THE MONDO DALEK AGAIN !!!

THE ATOMIC ERASER JUMPED !!! MET HIMSELF ON EARTH 2 AND SET OFF A CHAIN-REACTION SCENARIO THAT EVEN STAN THE MAN WOULD HAVE FOUND DIFFICULTY WRITING REED RICHARDS OUT OF !!!

FOR A WHILE THE COPS WENT A LITTLE WHITNEY STRIEBER IN THE HEAD !!! REPORTING UFONAUT ABDUCTIONS AND FORMING BREAKAWAY DEPARTMENTS !!!

THE OFFICERS OF THE GOLDEN WHEEL !!! WATCH THE SKY WATCH THE SKY P.D.

BUT THEIR PROPHESIES NEVER MATERIALIZED AND THE TAX PAYERS SOON GOT TIRED OF THE WHOLE THING !

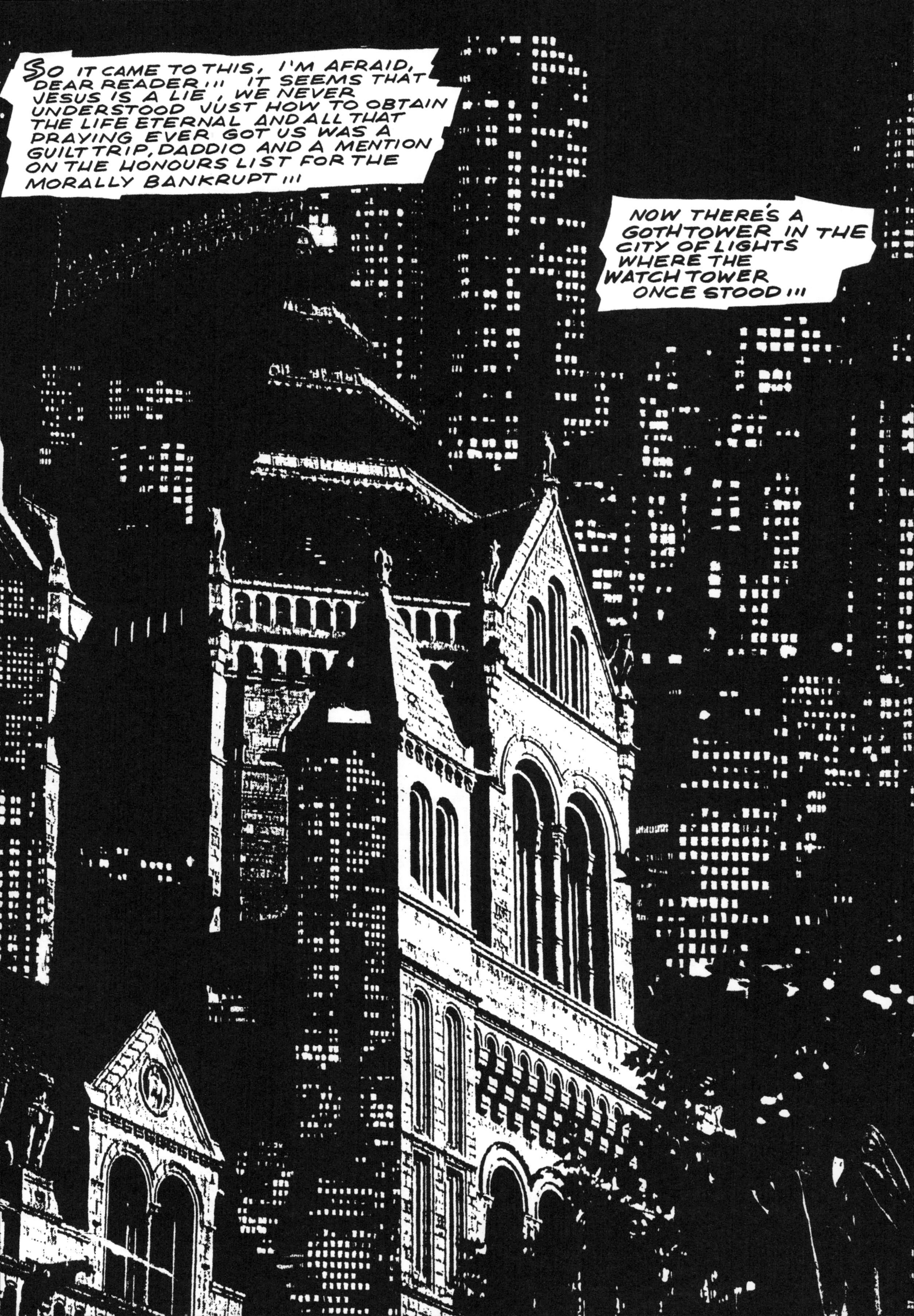
SO IT CAME TO THIS, I'M AFRAID, DEAR READER!!! IT SEEMS THAT JESUS IS A LIE, WE NEVER UNDERSTOOD JUST HOW TO OBTAIN THE LIFE ETERNAL AND ALL THAT PRAYING EVER GOT US WAS A GUILT TRIP, DADDIO AND A MENTION ON THE HONOURS LIST FOR THE MORALLY BANKRUPT!!!
NOW THERE'S A GOTHTOWER IN THE CITY OF LIGHTS WHERE THE WATCH TOWER ONCE STOOD!!!

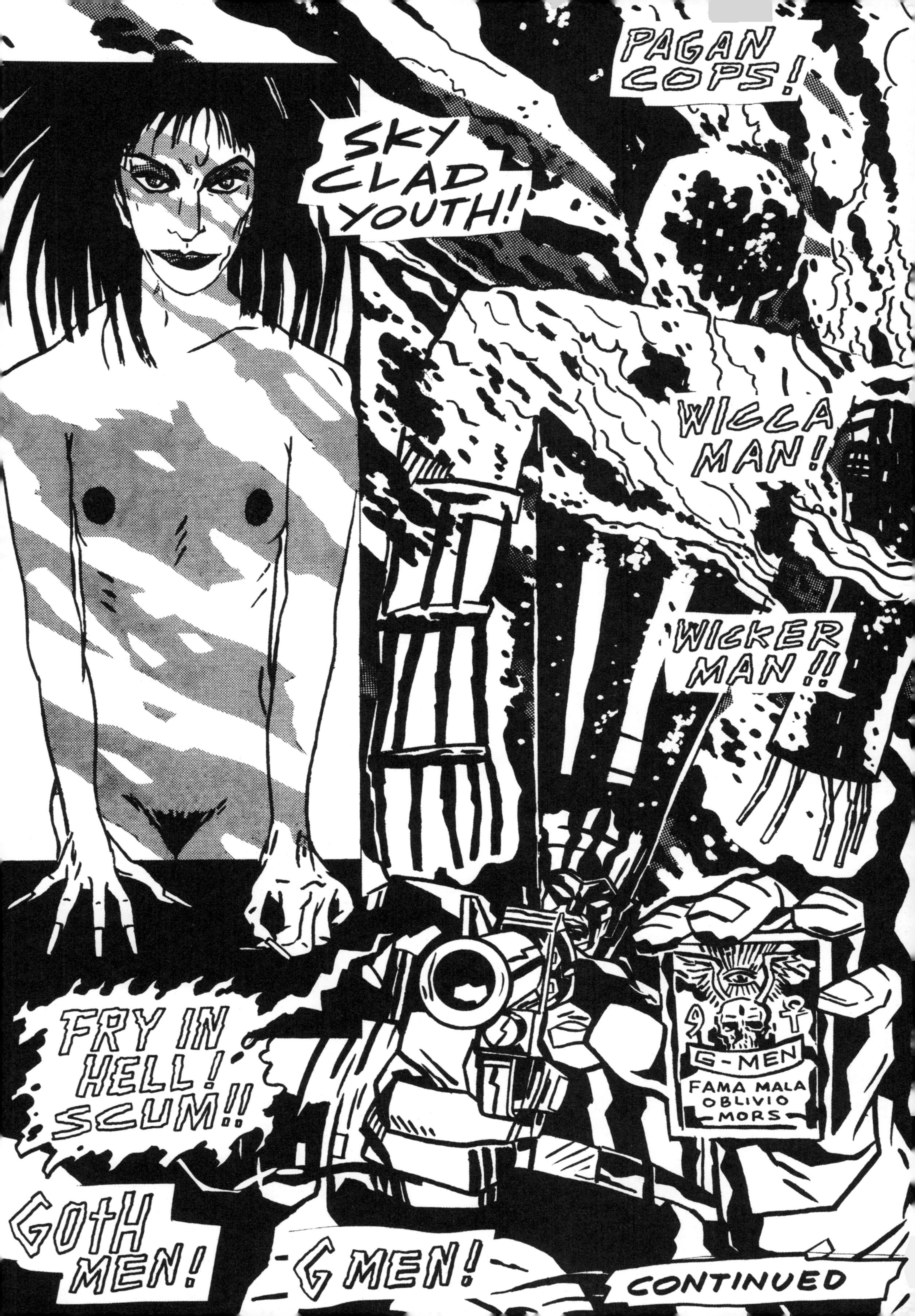
PAGAN COPS!
SKY CLAD YOUTH!
WIGGA MAN!
WICKER MAN!!
FRY IN HELL! SCUM!!
G-MEN
FAMA MALA OBLIVIO MORS
GOTH MEN!
G MEN!
CONTINUED

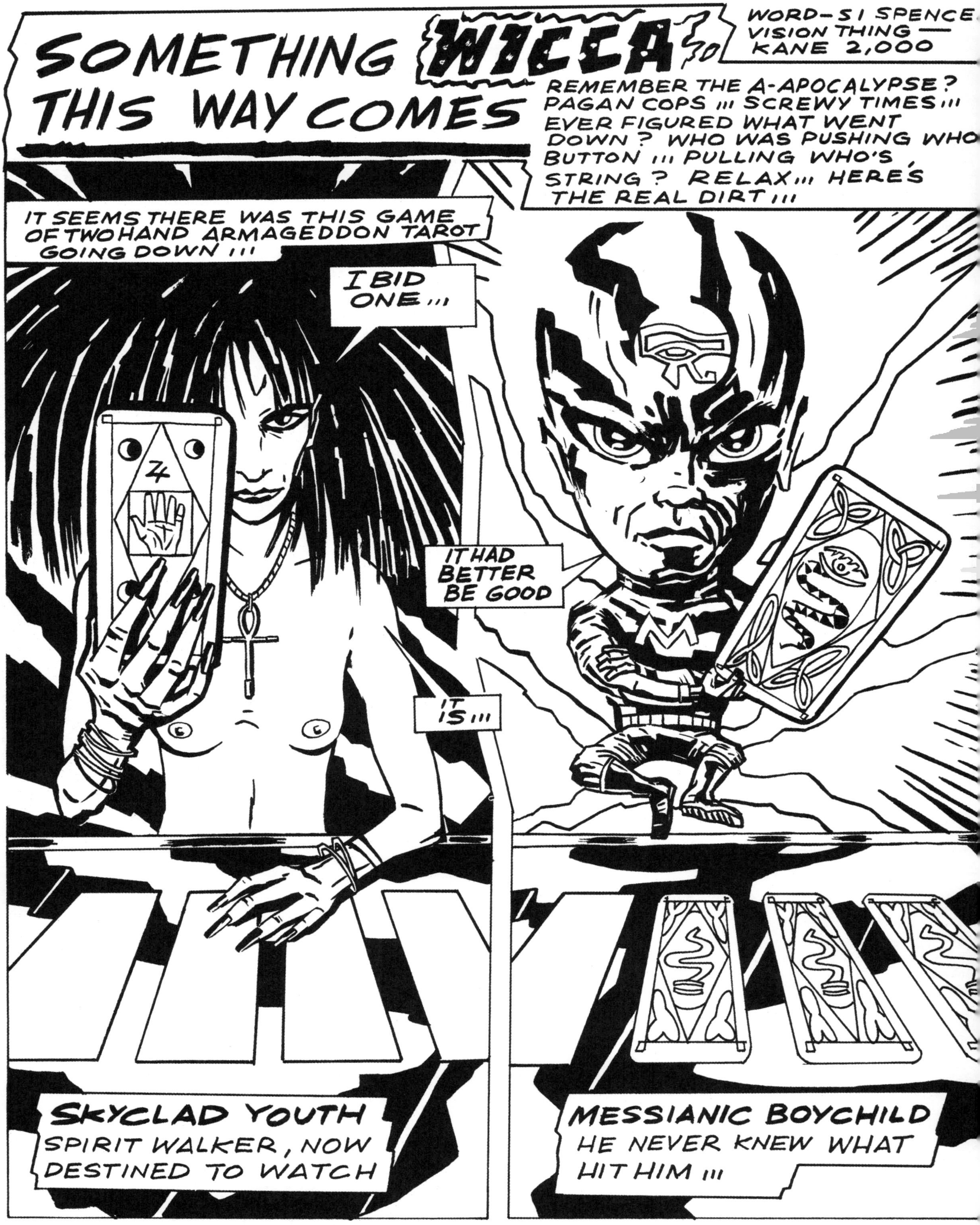
SOMETHING WICCA 'D THIS WAY COMES
WORD– SI SPENCER
VISION THING — KANE 2,000
REMEMBER THE A-APOCALYPSE? PAGAN COPS ... SCREWY TIMES ... EVER FIGURED WHAT WENT DOWN? WHO WAS PUSHING WHO'S BUTTON ... PULLING WHO'S STRING? RELAX ... HERE'S THE REAL DIRT ...
IT SEEMS THERE WAS THIS GAME OF TWO HAND ARMAGEDDON TAROT GOING DOWN ...
I BID ONE ...
IT HAD BETTER BE GOOD
IT IS ...
SKYCLAD YOUTH
SPIRIT WALKER, NOW DESTINED TO WATCH
MESSIANIC BOYCHILD
HE NEVER KNEW WHAT HIT HIM ...

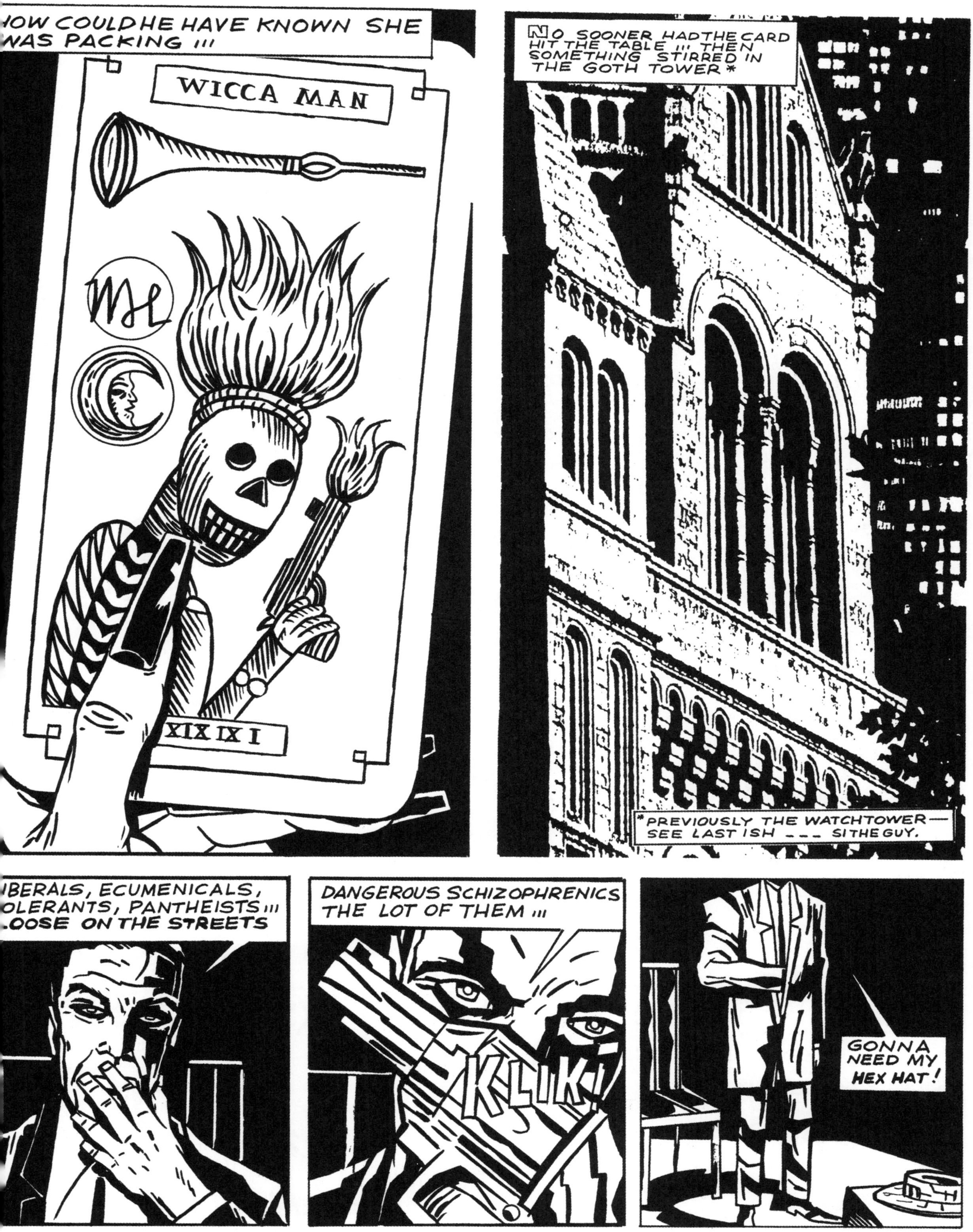

HOW COULD HE HAVE KNOWN SHE
WAS PACKING ...
WICCA MAN
XIX IX I
NO SOONER HAD THE CARD HIT THE TABLE ... THEN SOMETHING STIRRED IN THE GOTH TOWER*
*PREVIOUSLY THE WATCHTOWER— SEE LAST ISH --- SI THE GUY.
IBERALS, ECUMENICALS, OLERANTS, PANTHEISTS ... LOOSE ON THE STREETS
DANGEROUS SCHIZOPHRENICS THE LOT OF THEM ...
KLIK!
GONNA NEED MY HEX HAT!

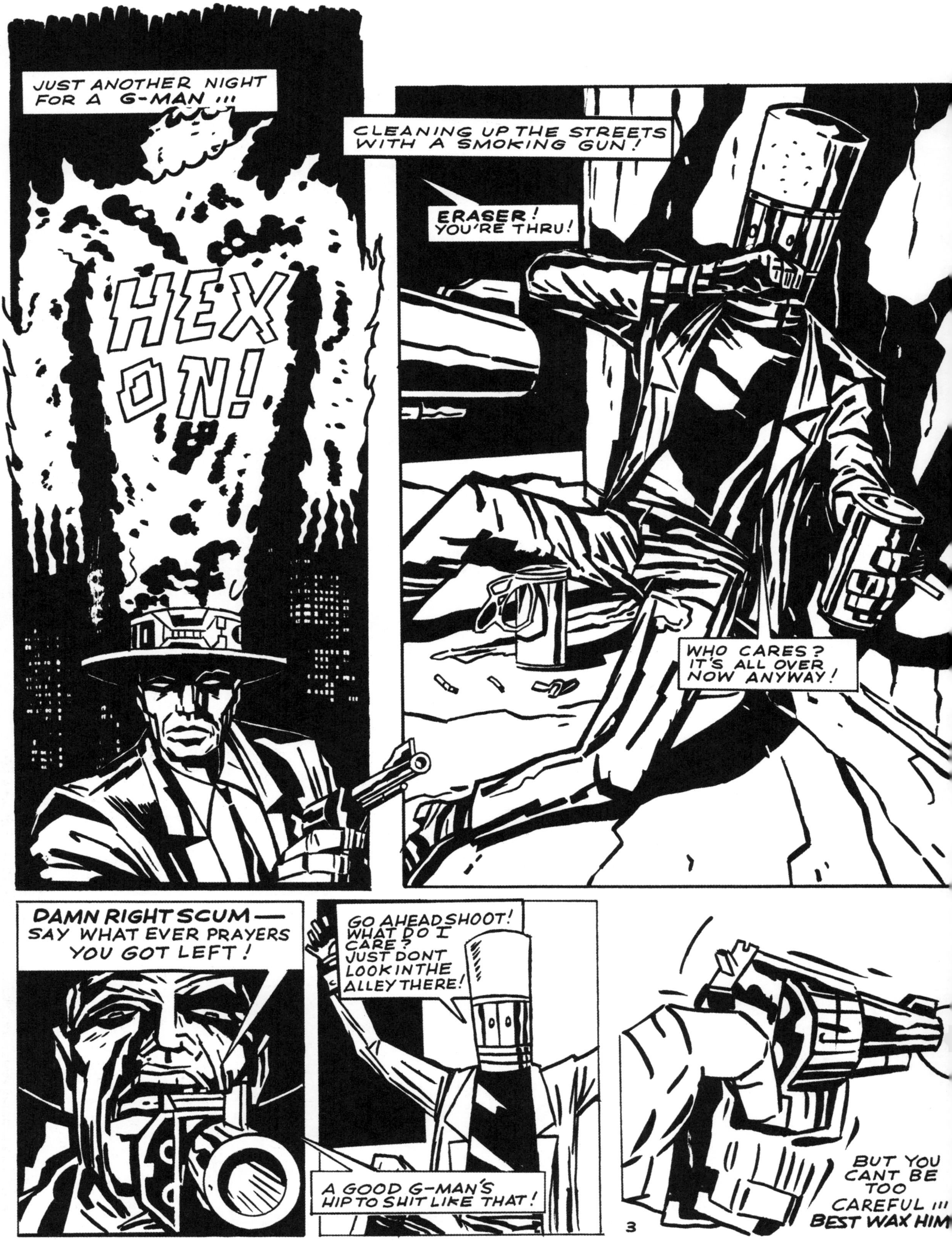

JUST ANOTHER NIGHT FOR A G-MAN ...
HEX ON!
CLEANING UP THE STREETS WITH A SMOKING GUN!
ERASER! YOU'RE THRU!
WHO CARES? IT'S ALL OVER NOW ANYWAY!
DAMN RIGHT SCUM — SAY WHAT EVER PRAYERS YOU GOT LEFT!
GO AHEAD SHOOT! WHAT DO I CARE? JUST DONT LOOK IN THE ALLEY THERE!
A GOOD G-MAN'S HIP TO SHIT LIKE THAT!
BUT YOU CANT BE TOO CAREFUL ... BEST WAX HIM

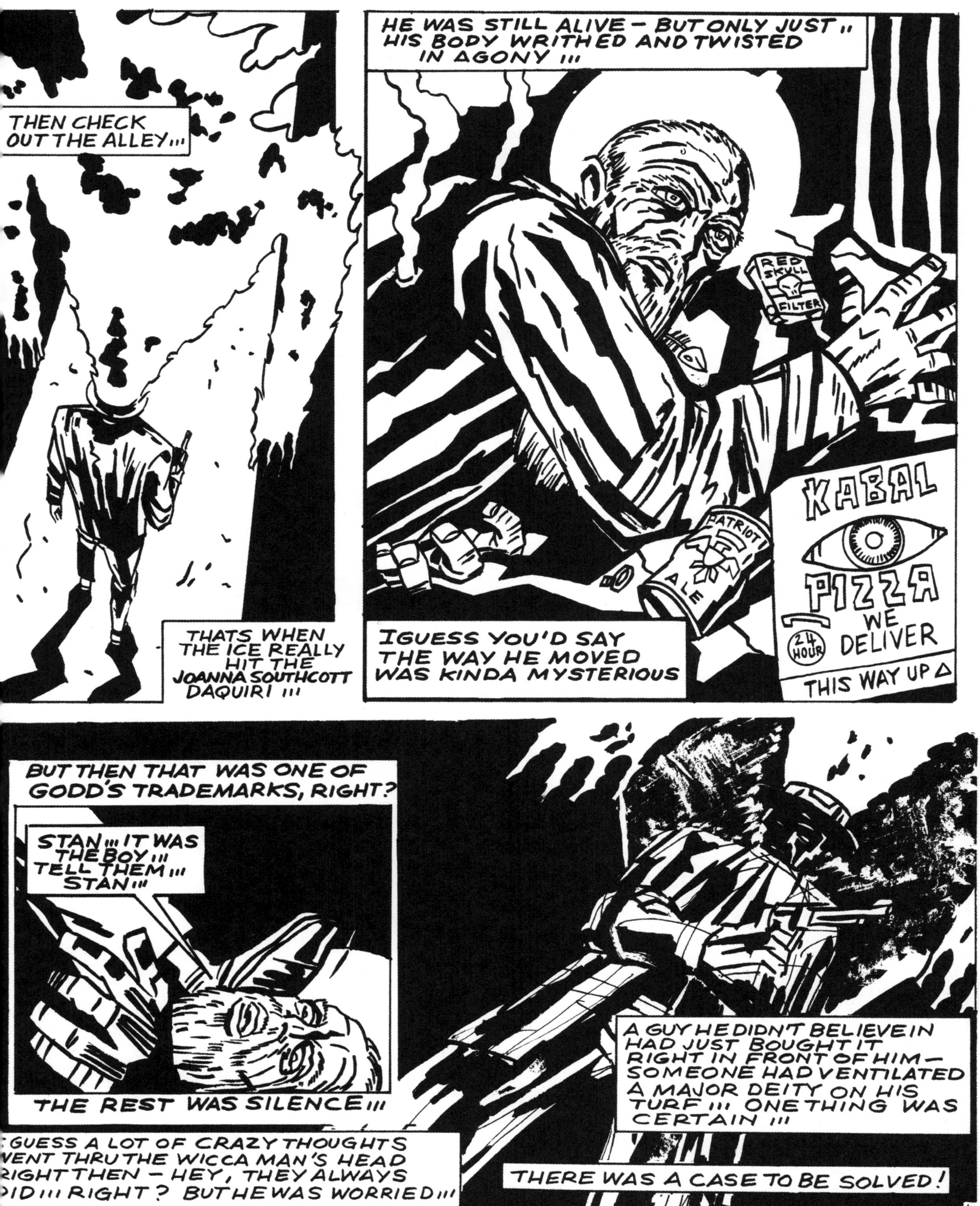
THEN CHECK OUT THE ALLEY...
THATS WHEN THE ICE REALLY HIT THE JOANNA SOUTHCOTT DAQUIRI ...
HE WAS STILL ALIVE – BUT ONLY JUST.. HIS BODY WRITHED AND TWISTED IN AGONY ...
RED SKULL FILTER
PATRIOT ALE
KABAL PIZZA
24 HOUR WE DELIVER
THIS WAY UP
I GUESS YOU'D SAY THE WAY HE MOVED WAS KINDA MYSTERIOUS
BUT THEN THAT WAS ONE OF GODD'S TRADEMARKS, RIGHT?
STAN ... IT WAS THE BOY ... TELL THEM ... STAN ...
THE REST WAS SILENCE ...
GUESS A LOT OF CRAZY THOUGHTS WENT THRU THE WICCA MAN'S HEAD RIGHT THEN – HEY, THEY ALWAYS DID ... RIGHT? BUT HE WAS WORRIED ...
A GUY HE DIDN'T BELIEVE IN HAD JUST BOUGHT IT RIGHT IN FRONT OF HIM – SOMEONE HAD VENTILATED A MAJOR DEITY ON HIS TURF ... ONE THING WAS CERTAIN ...
THERE WAS A CASE TO BE SOLVED!
4

CONTINUED ...

# G-MEN

APPROVED BY MR G

BY SHAKY AND SPENCER KANE

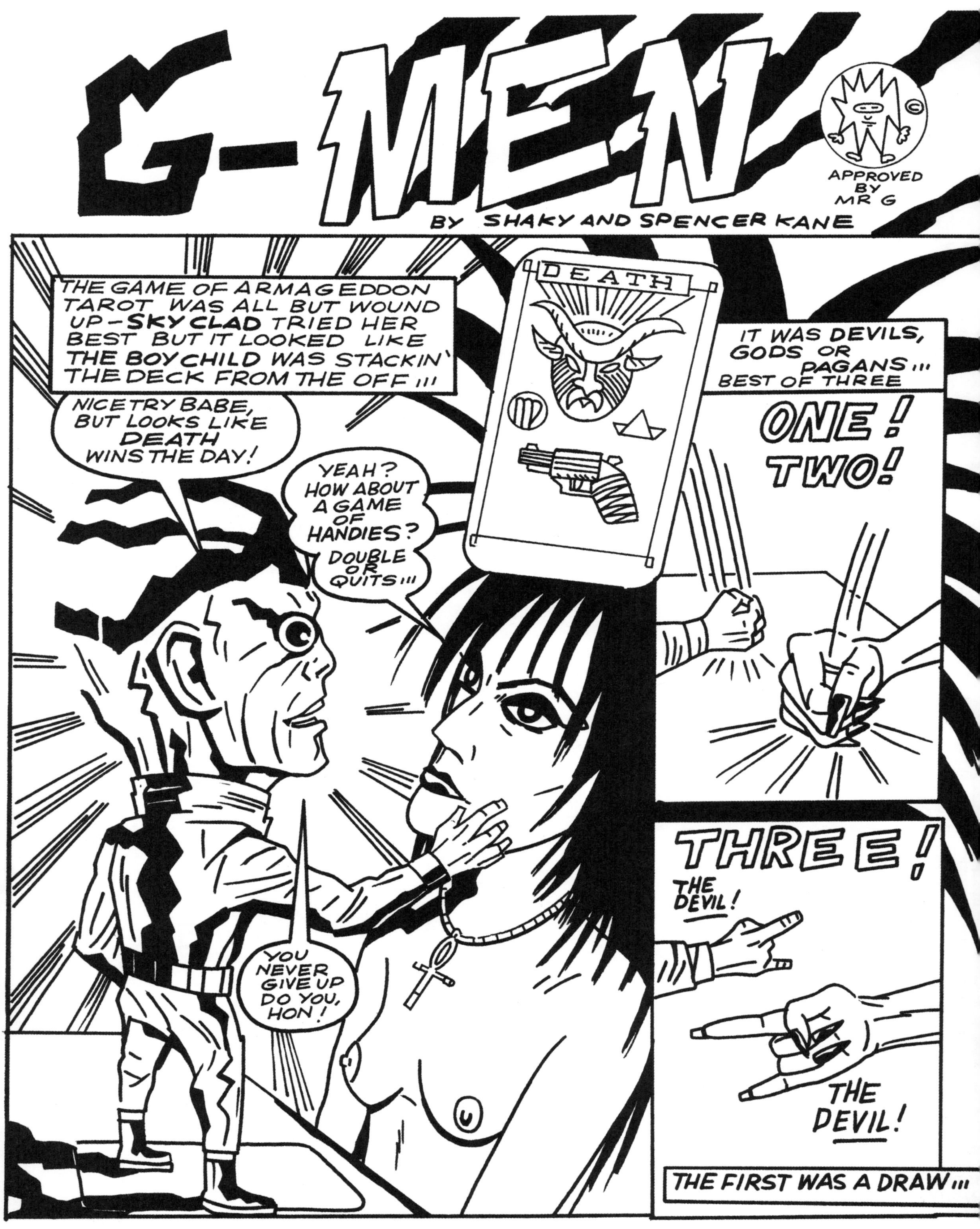

THE GAME OF ARMAGEDDON TAROT WAS ALL BUT WOUND UP - SKYCLAD TRIED HER BEST BUT IT LOOKED LIKE THE BOYCHILD WAS STACKIN' THE DECK FROM THE OFF...
NICE TRY BABE, BUT LOOKS LIKE DEATH WINS THE DAY!
DEATH
YEAH? HOW ABOUT A GAME OF HANDIES? DOUBLE OR QUITS...
YOU NEVER GIVE UP DO YOU, HON!
IT WAS DEVILS, GODS OR PAGANS... BEST OF THREE
ONE! TWO!
THREE!
THE DEVIL!
THE DEVIL!
THE FIRST WAS A DRAW...

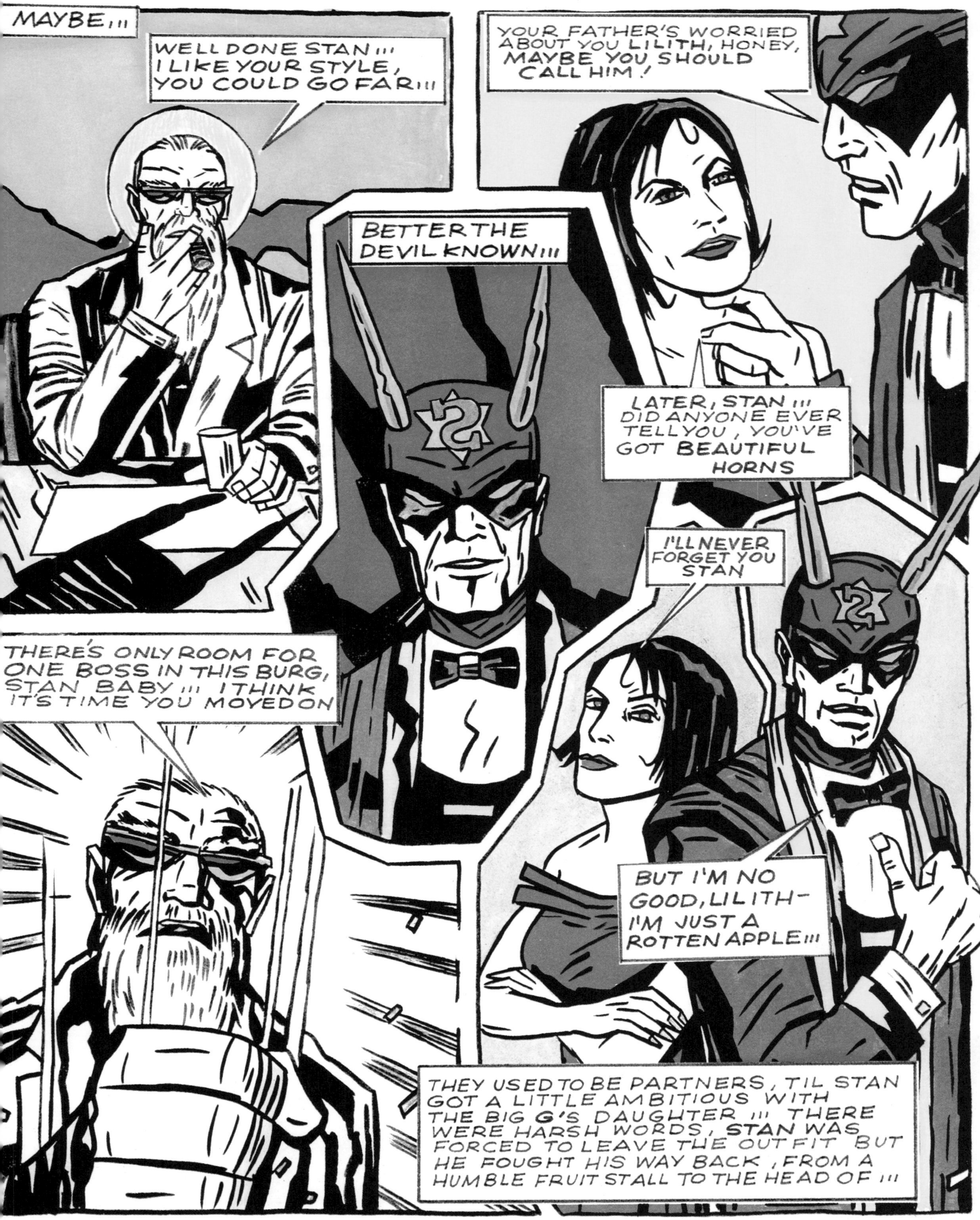
MAYBE...
WELL DONE STAN... I LIKE YOUR STYLE, YOU COULD GO FAR...
YOUR FATHER'S WORRIED ABOUT YOU LILITH, HONEY, MAYBE YOU SHOULD CALL HIM!
BETTER THE DEVIL KNOWN...
LATER, STAN... DID ANYONE EVER TELL YOU, YOU'VE GOT BEAUTIFUL HORNS
I'LL NEVER FORGET YOU STAN
THERE'S ONLY ROOM FOR ONE BOSS IN THIS BURG, STAN BABY... I THINK IT'S TIME YOU MOVED ON
BUT I'M NO GOOD, LILITH- I'M JUST A ROTTEN APPLE...
THEY USED TO BE PARTNERS, TIL STAN GOT A LITTLE AMBITIOUS WITH THE BIG G'S DAUGHTER... THERE WERE HARSH WORDS, STAN WAS FORCED TO LEAVE THE OUTFIT BUT HE FOUGHT HIS WAY BACK, FROM A HUMBLE FRUIT STALL TO THE HEAD OF...

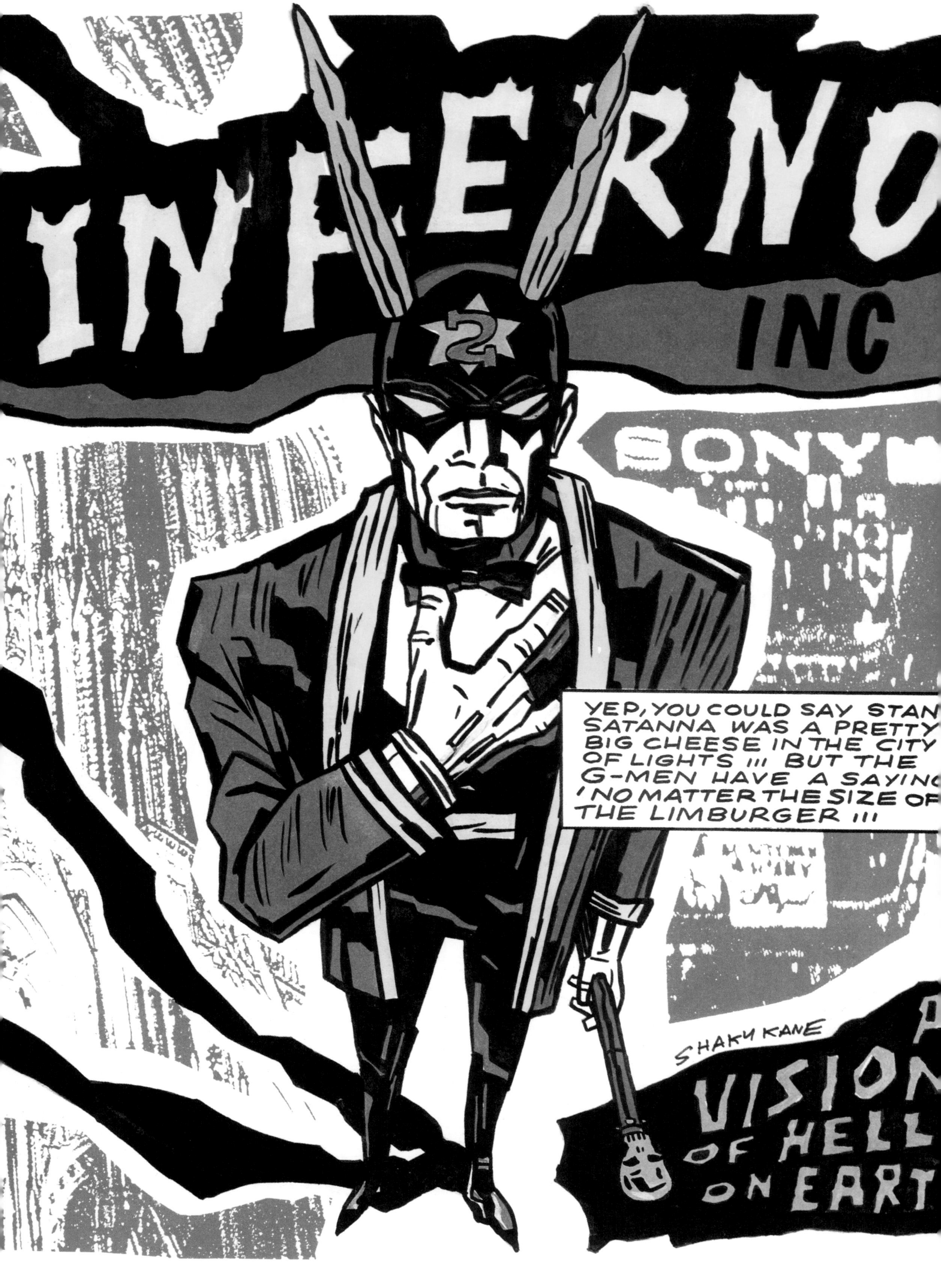
INFERNO
INC
SONY
YEP, YOU COULD SAY STAN SATANNA WAS A PRETTY BIG CHEESE IN THE CITY OF LIGHTS ... BUT THE G-MEN HAVE A SAYING 'NO MATTER THE SIZE OF THE LIMBURGER ...
SHAKY KANE
A VISION OF HELL ON EART

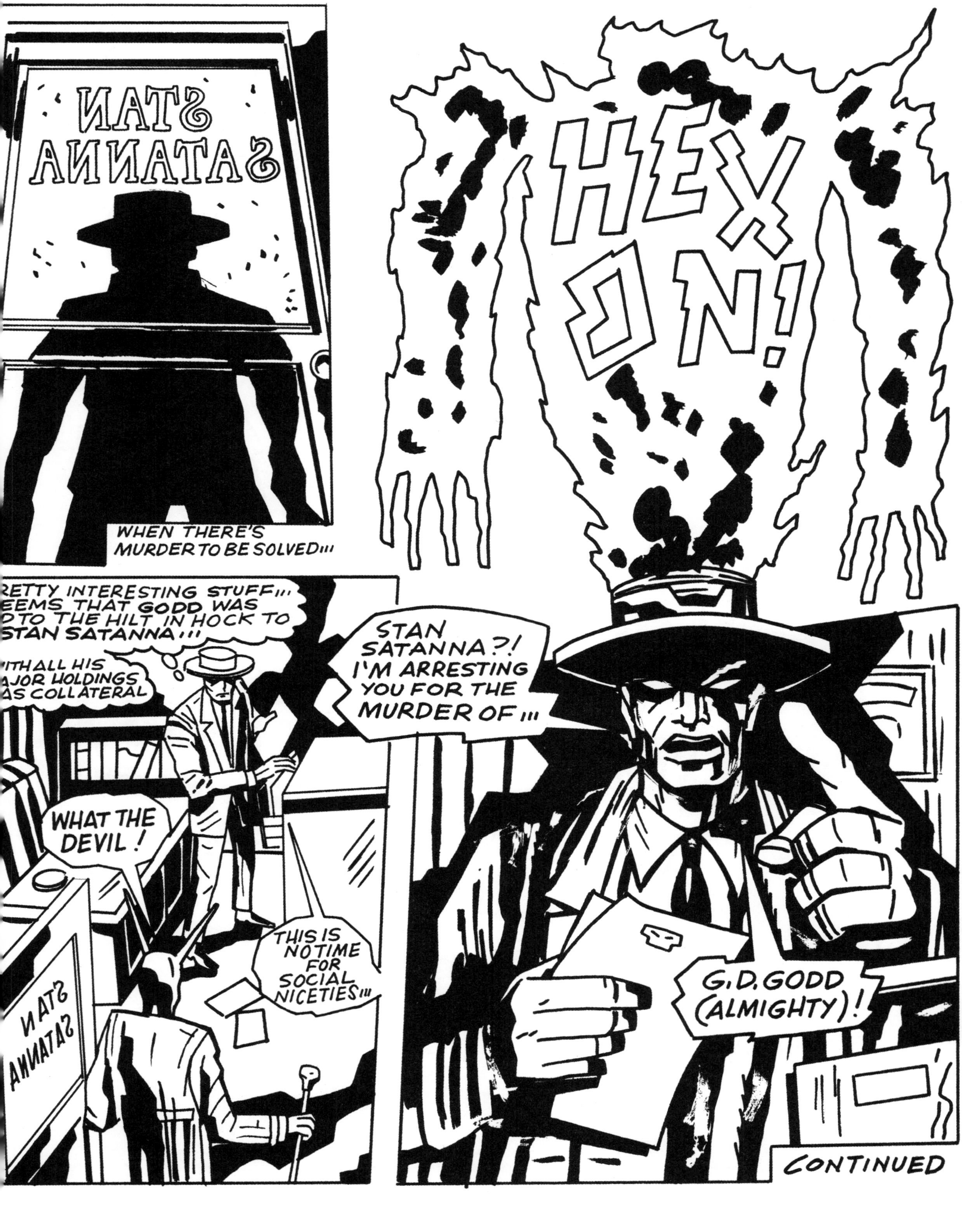
WHEN THERE'S MURDER TO BE SOLVED...
HEX ON!
RETTY INTERESTING STUFF... EEMS THAT GODD WAS D TO THE HILT IN HOCK TO STAN SATANNA...
ITH ALL HIS AJOR HOLDINGS AS COLLATERAL
WHAT THE DEVIL!
THIS IS NO TIME FOR SOCIAL NICETIES...
STAN SATANNA?! I'M ARRESTING YOU FOR THE MURDER OF...
G.D. GODD (ALMIGHTY)!
CONTINUED

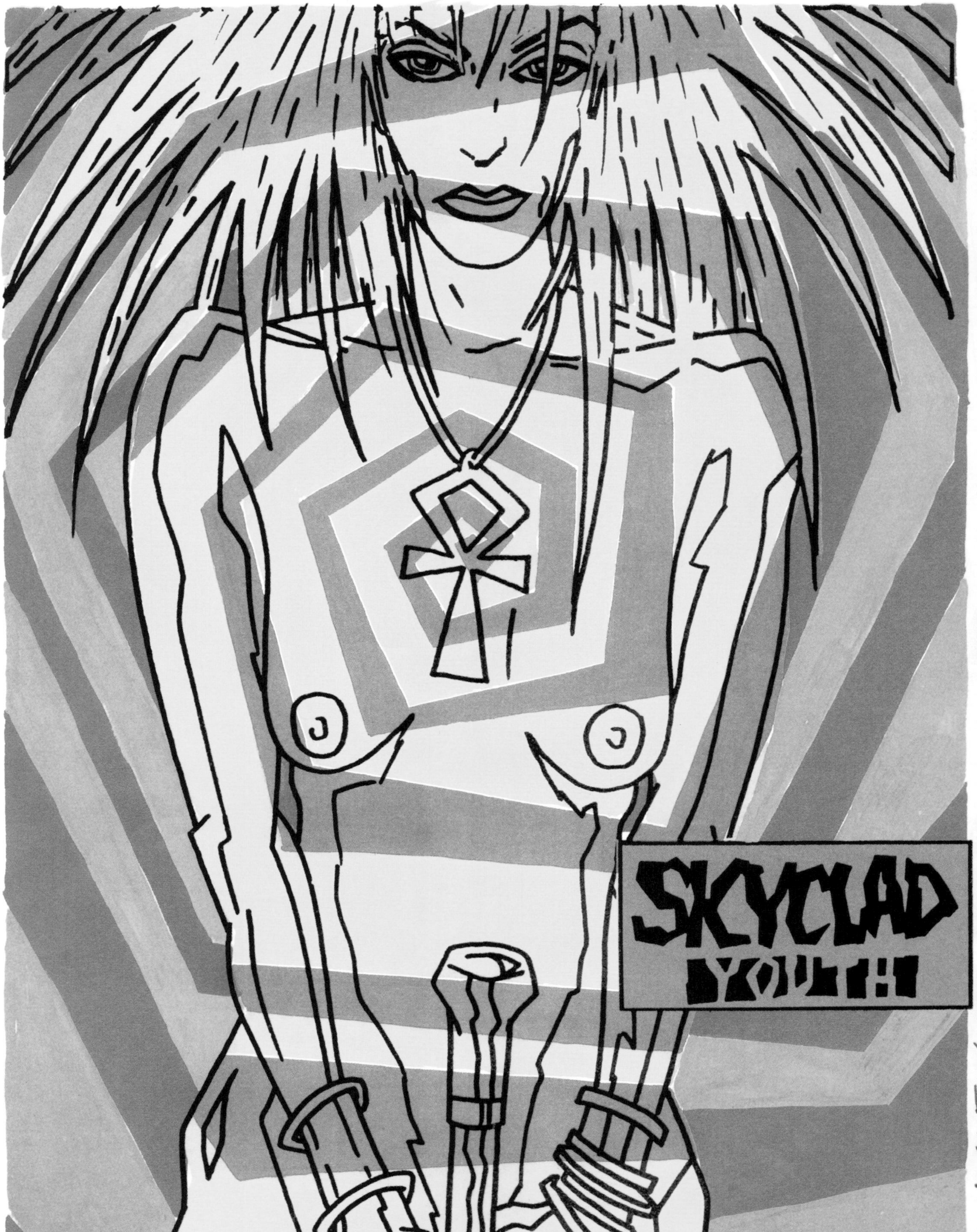
SKYCLAD
YOUTH

# A LUCID DREAM

*MYSTERY PIN-UP*

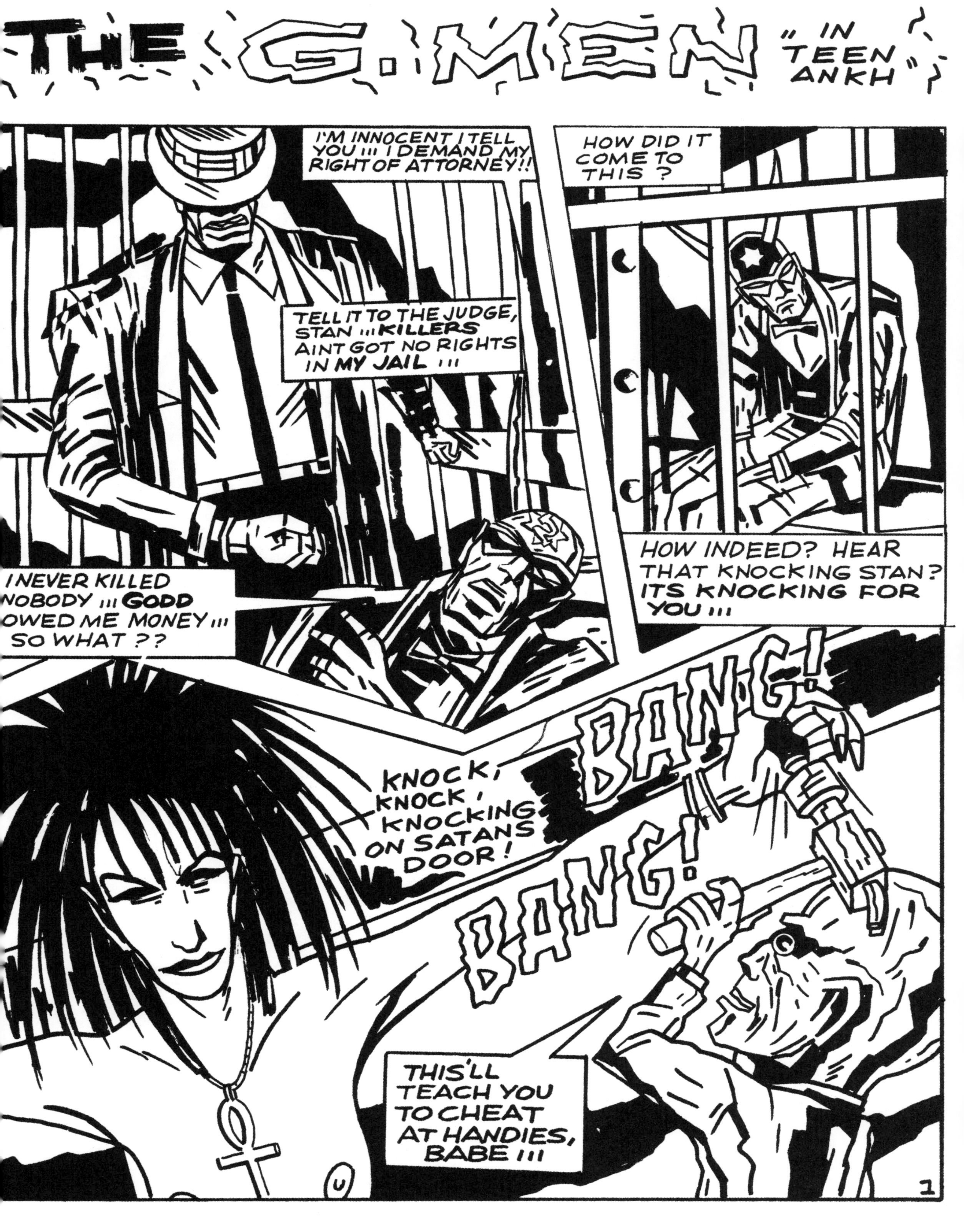
THE G. MEN "IN TEEN ANKH"
I'M INNOCENT I TELL YOU ... I DEMAND MY RIGHT OF ATTORNEY!!
TELL IT TO THE JUDGE, STAN ... KILLERS AINT GOT NO RIGHTS IN MY JAIL ...
I NEVER KILLED NOBODY ... GODD OWED ME MONEY ... SO WHAT??
HOW DID IT COME TO THIS ?
HOW INDEED? HEAR THAT KNOCKING STAN? ITS KNOCKING FOR YOU ...
KNOCK, KNOCK, KNOCKING ON SATANS DOOR!
BANG!
BANG!
THIS'LL TEACH YOU TO CHEAT AT HANDIES, BABE ...
1

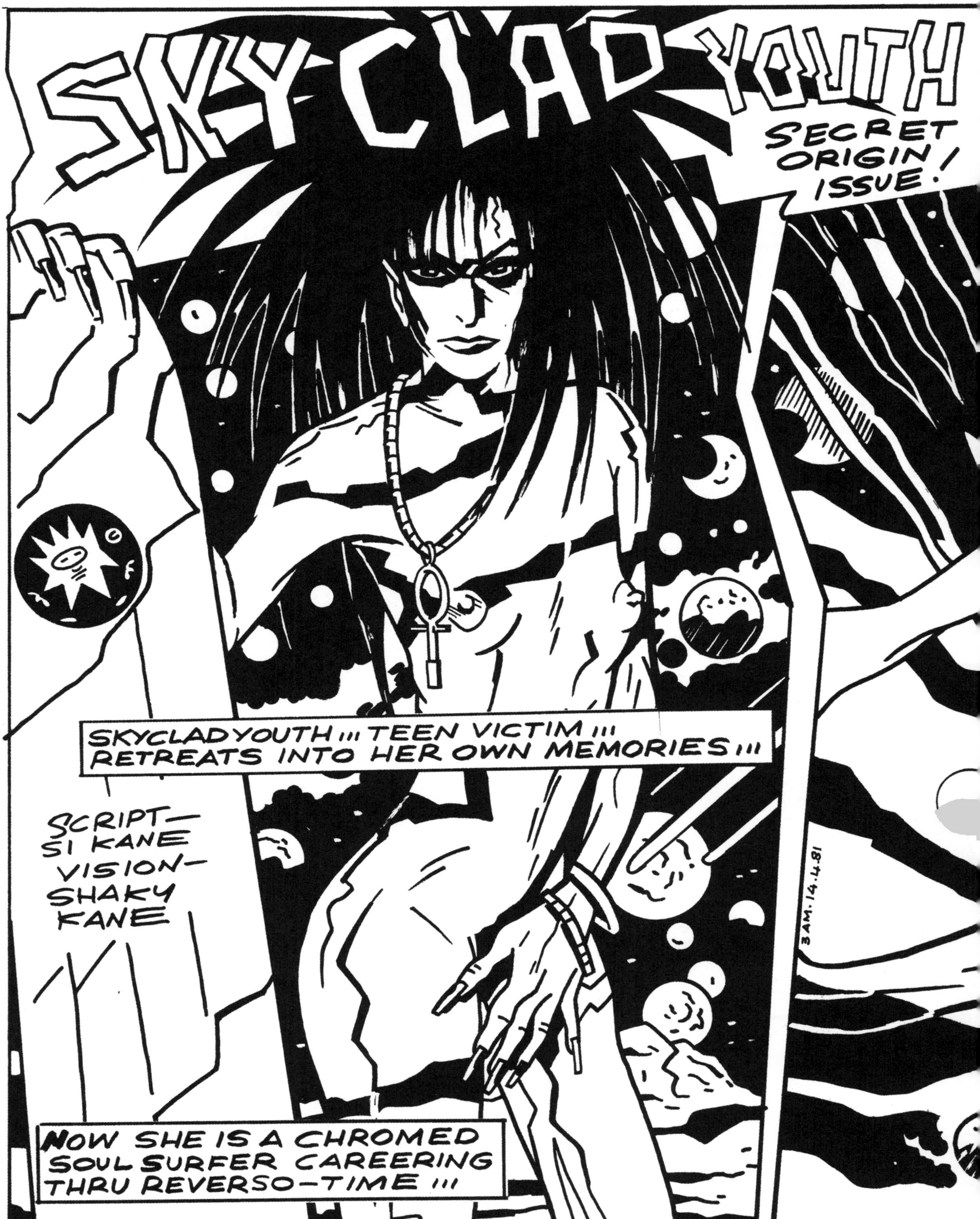
SKY CLAD YOUTH
SECRET ORIGIN ! ISSUE !
SKYCLADYOUTH ::: TEEN VICTIM ::: RETREATS INTO HER OWN MEMORIES :::
SCRIPT— SI KANE VISION— SHAKY KANE
3 AM. 14.4.81
NOW SHE IS A CHROMED SOUL SURFER CAREERING THRU REVERSO-TIME :::

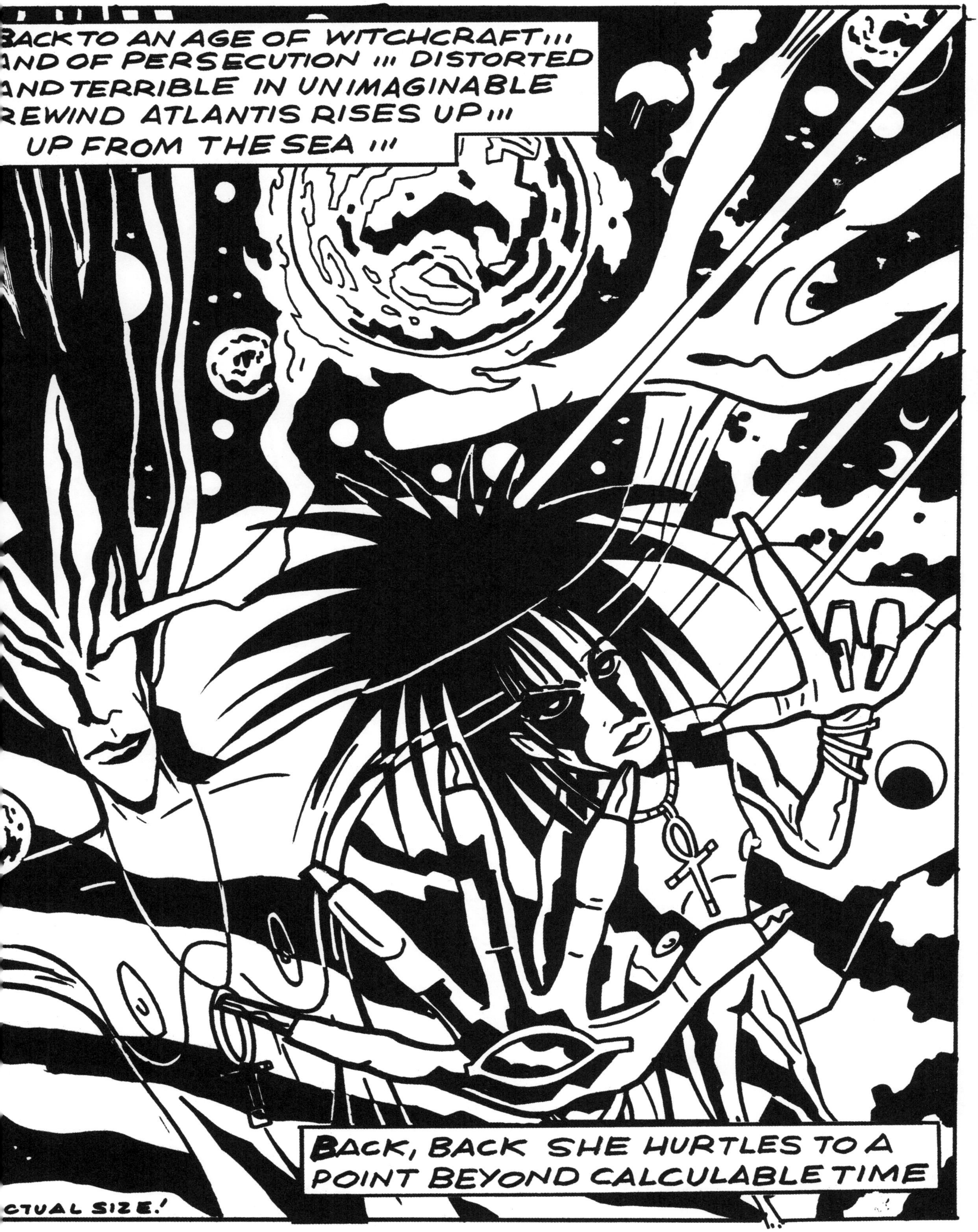
BACK TO AN AGE OF WITCHCRAFT ... AND OF PERSECUTION ... DISTORTED AND TERRIBLE IN UNIMAGINABLE REWIND ATLANTIS RISES UP ... UP FROM THE SEA ...
BACK, BACK SHE HURTLES TO A POINT BEYOND CALCULABLE TIME
CTUAL SIZE!

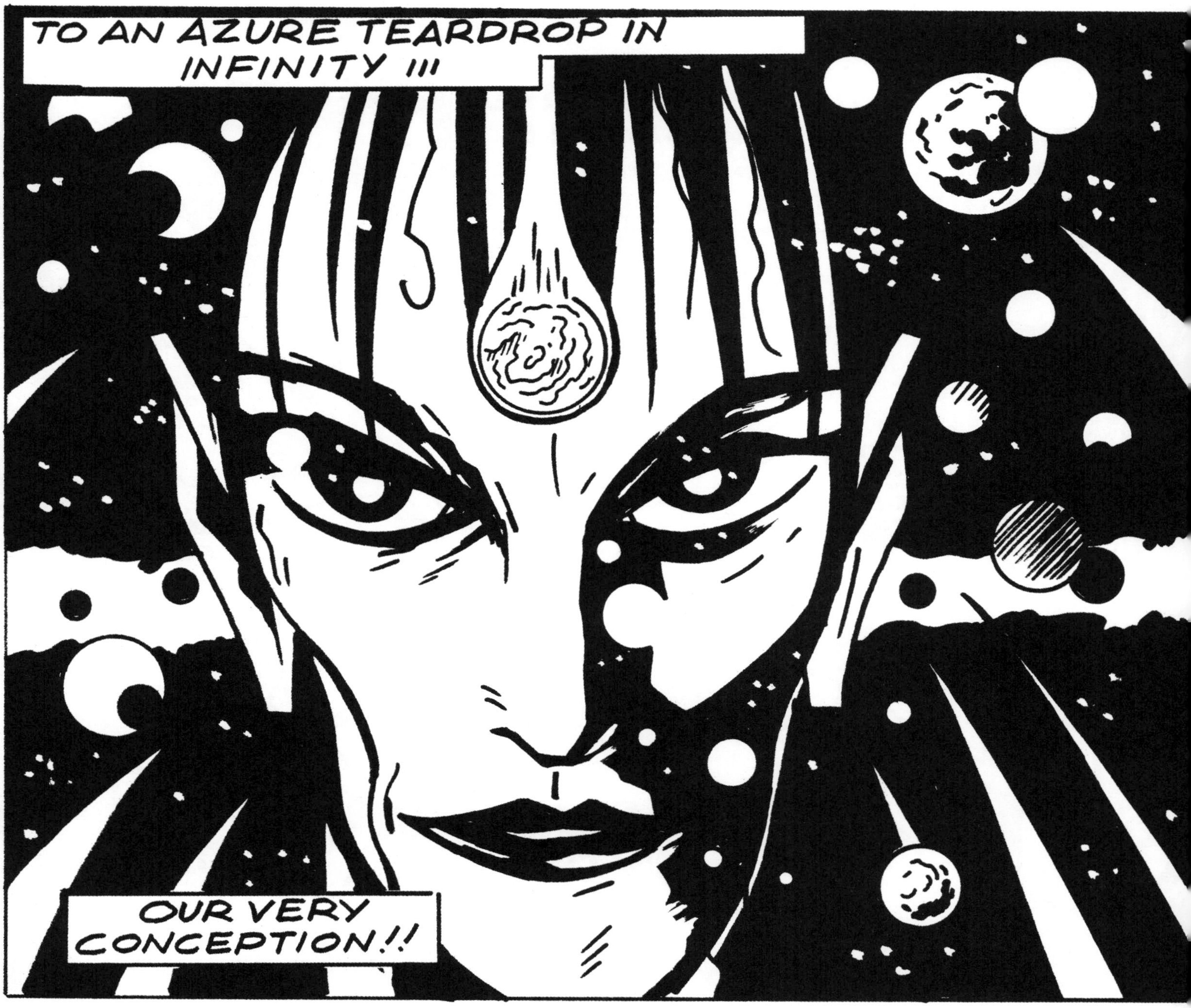
TO AN AZURE TEARDROP IN INFINITY !!!
OUR VERY CONCEPTION!!

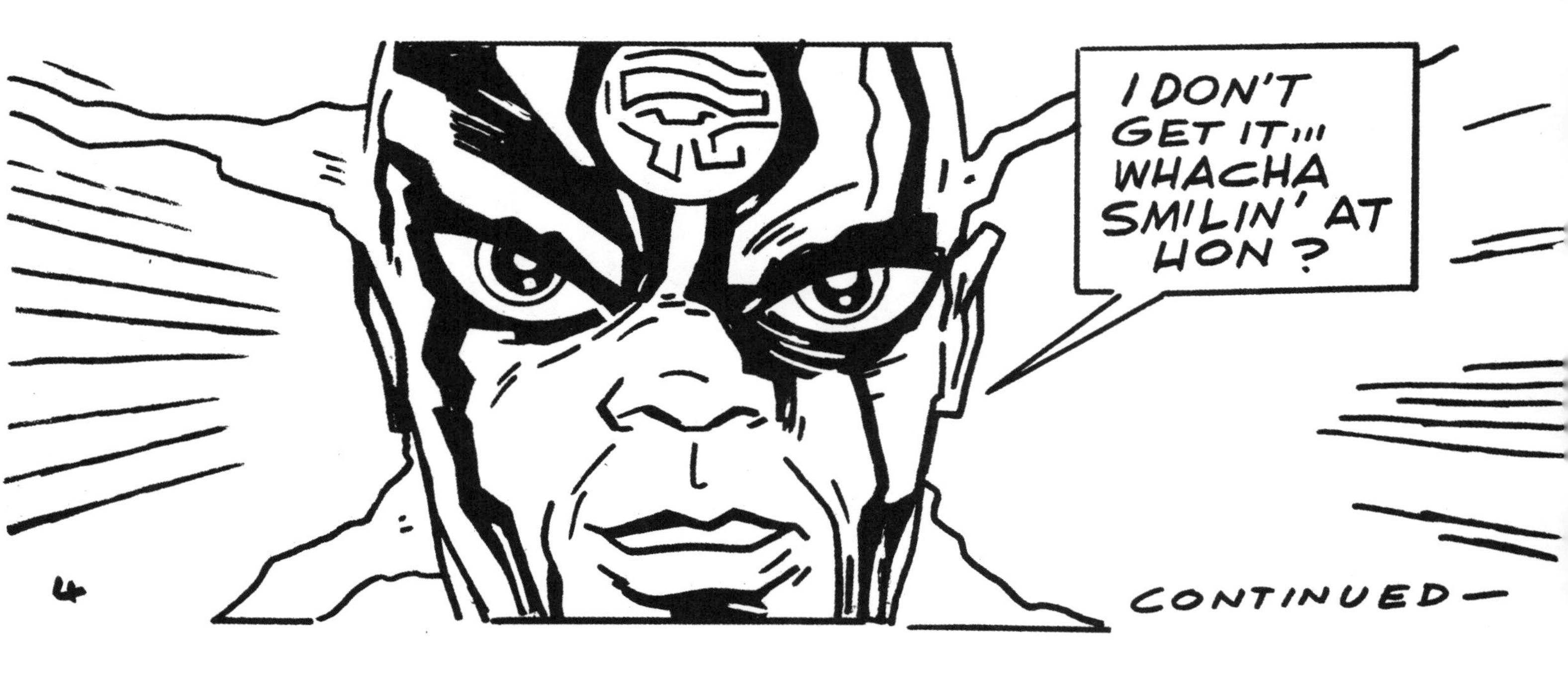
I DON'T GET IT!!! WHACHA SMILIN' AT HON?



CONTINUED—

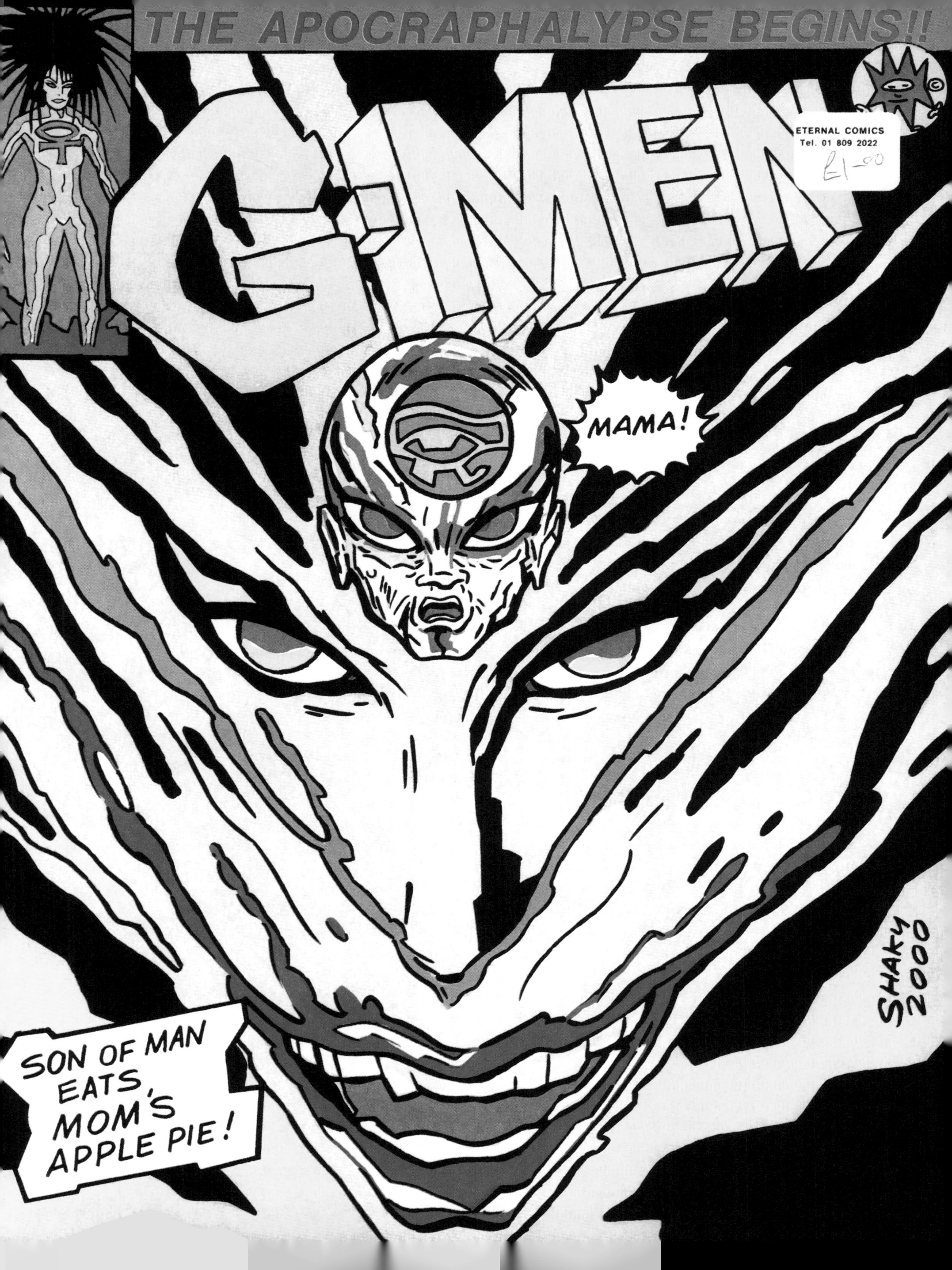
THE APOCRAPHALYPSE BEGINS!!
G-MEN
ETERNAL COMICS
Tel. 01 809 2022
£1-00
MAMA!
SON OF MAN EATS MOM'S APPLE PIE!
SHAKY 2000

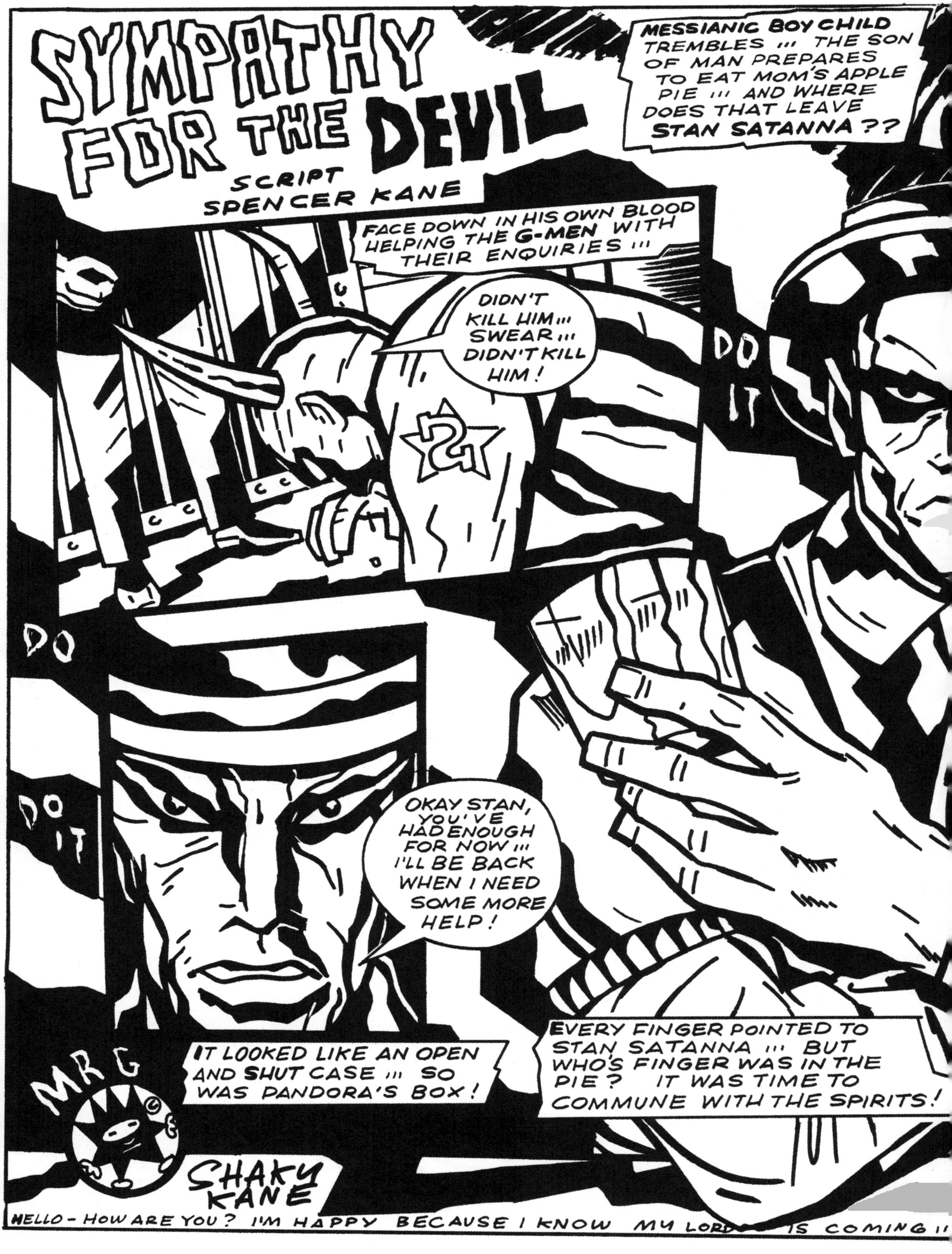

SYMPATHY FOR THE DEVIL
SCRIPT SPENCER KANE
MESSIANIC BOY CHILD TREMBLES ... THE SON OF MAN PREPARES TO EAT MOM'S APPLE PIE ... AND WHERE DOES THAT LEAVE STAN SATANNA ??
FACE DOWN IN HIS OWN BLOOD HELPING THE G-MEN WITH THEIR ENQUIRIES ...
DIDN'T KILL HIM ... SWEAR ... DIDN'T KILL HIM!
DO IT
DO
DO IT
OKAY STAN, YOU'VE HAD ENOUGH FOR NOW ... I'LL BE BACK WHEN I NEED SOME MORE HELP!
IT LOOKED LIKE AN OPEN AND SHUT CASE ... SO WAS PANDORA'S BOX!
EVERY FINGER POINTED TO STAN SATANNA ... BUT WHO'S FINGER WAS IN THE PIE? IT WAS TIME TO COMMUNE WITH THE SPIRITS!
MRG
SHAKY KANE
HELLO - HOW ARE YOU? I'M HAPPY BECAUSE I KNOW MY LORD IS COMING !!

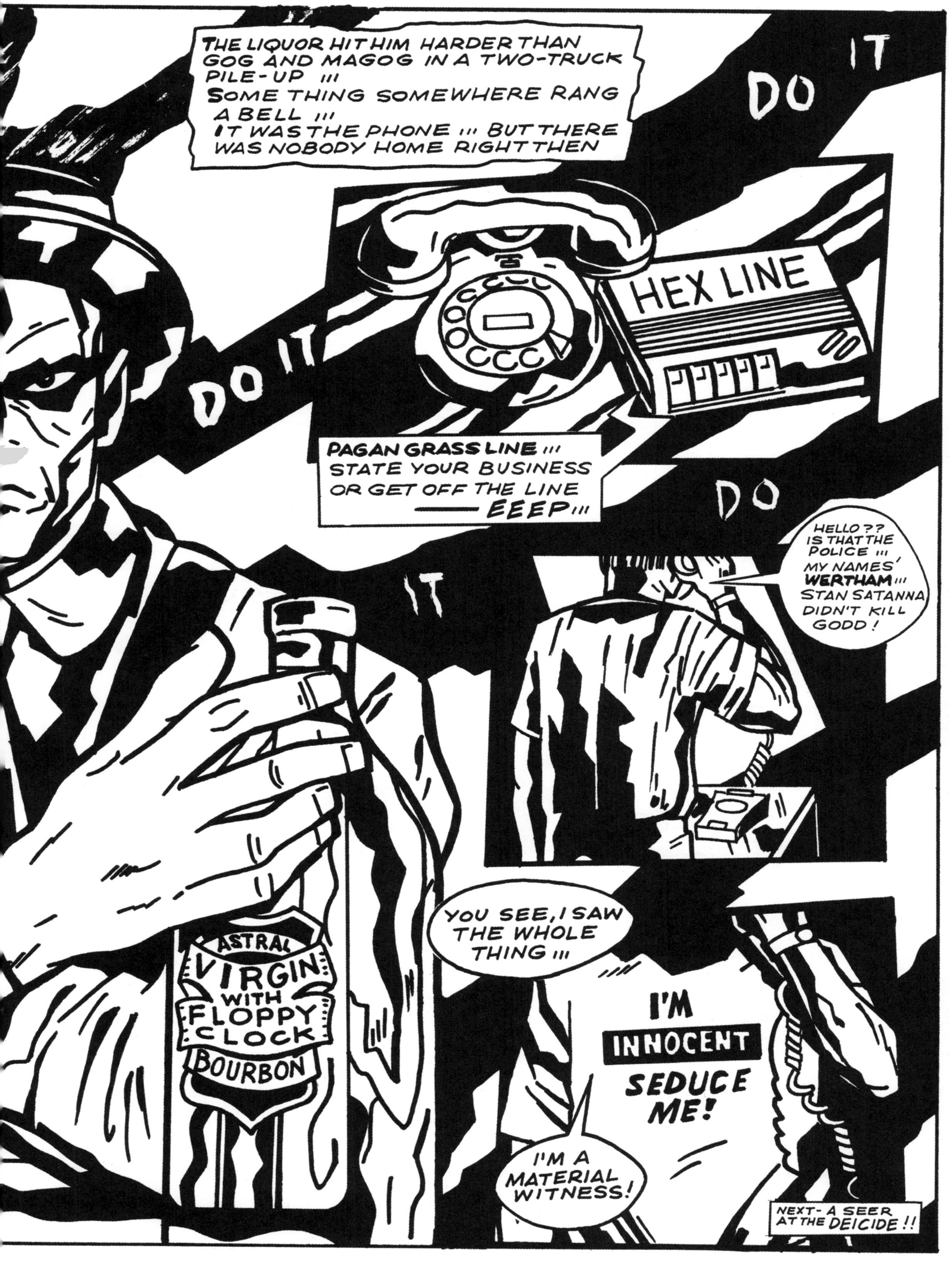
THE LIQUOR HIT HIM HARDER THAN GOG AND MAGOG IN A TWO-TRUCK PILE-UP ... SOME THING SOMEWHERE RANG A BELL ... IT WAS THE PHONE ... BUT THERE WAS NOBODY HOME RIGHT THEN
DO IT
HEX LINE
DO IT
PAGAN GRASS LINE ... STATE YOUR BUSINESS OR GET OFF THE LINE —— EEEP ...
DO
IT
HELLO ?? IS THAT THE POLICE ... MY NAMES' WERTHAM ... STAN SATANNA DIDN'T KILL GODD !
ASTRAL VIRGIN WITH FLOPPY CLOCK BOURBON
YOU SEE, I SAW THE WHOLE THING ...
I'M INNOCENT SEDUCE ME!
I'M A MATERIAL WITNESS!
NEXT- A SEER AT THE DEICIDE !!

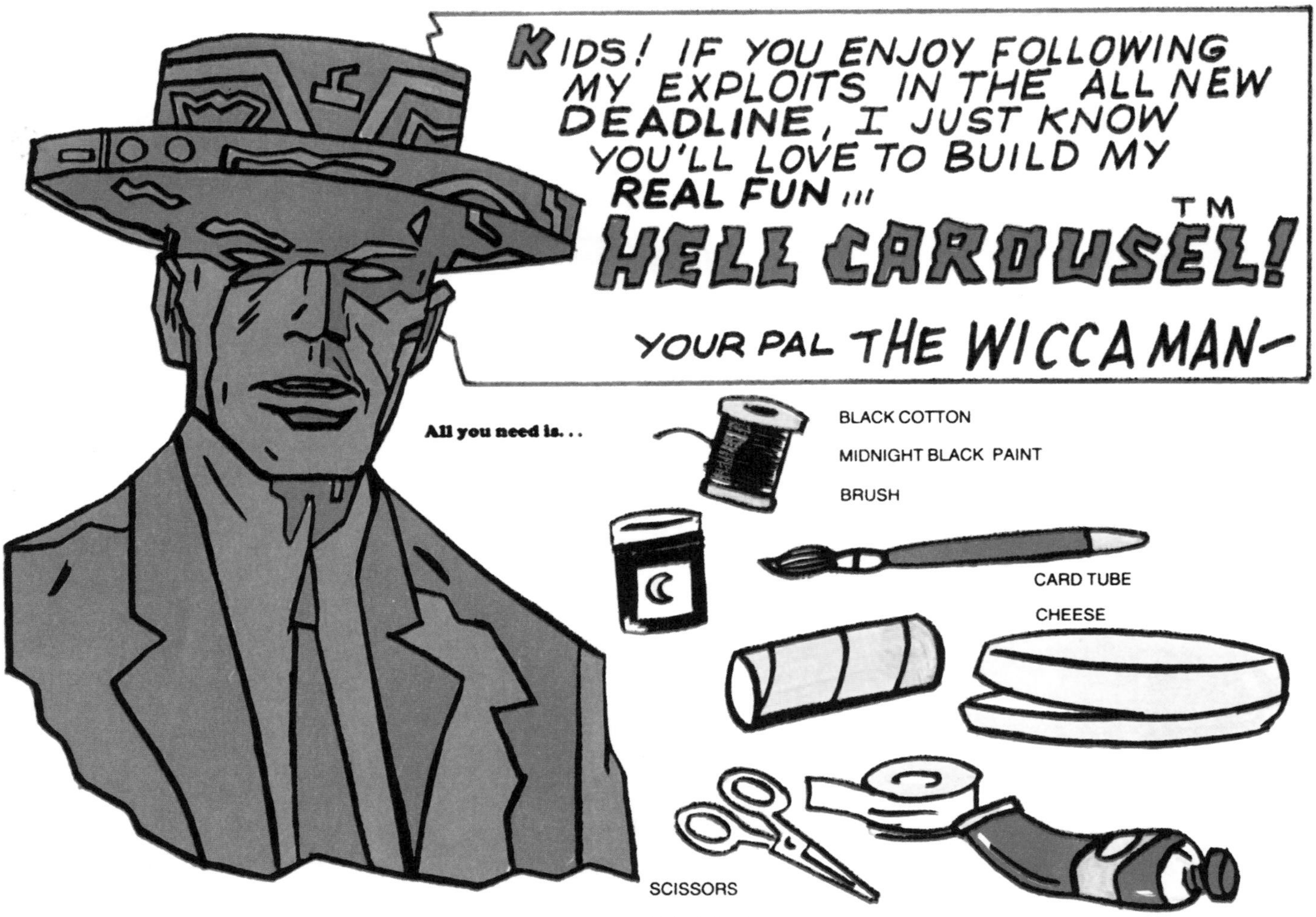
KIDS! IF YOU ENJOY FOLLOWING MY EXPLOITS IN THE ALL NEW DEADLINE, I JUST KNOW YOU'LL LOVE TO BUILD MY REAL FUN ...
HELL CAROUSEL! TM
YOUR PAL THE WICCA MAN-

**All you need is...**

BLACK COTTON

MIDNIGHT BLACK PAINT

BRUSH

CARD TUBE

CHEESE

SCISSORS

CLEAR TAPE

STRONG GLUE

**All you have to do is...**

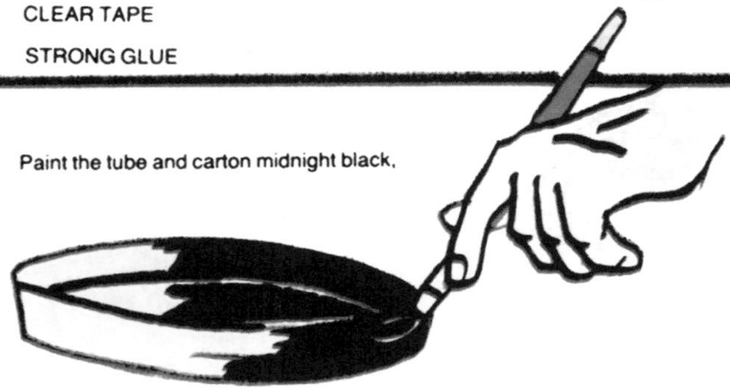

Paint the tube and carton midnight black,

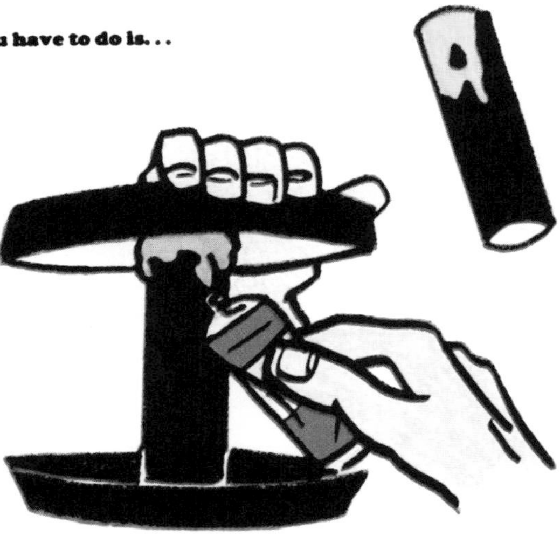

Fix the top between the top and bottom of the carton with the strong glue. . Don't inhale the vapour.

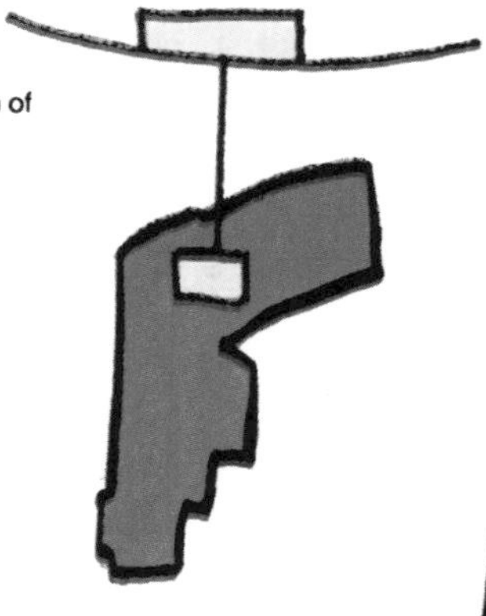

Attach the figures (Printed overleaf) using the black cotton and clear tape to the inside rim.

Finally decorate the top of your Hell Carousel with the large "LOVE SATAN BABY" OR "HEX ON" logos.

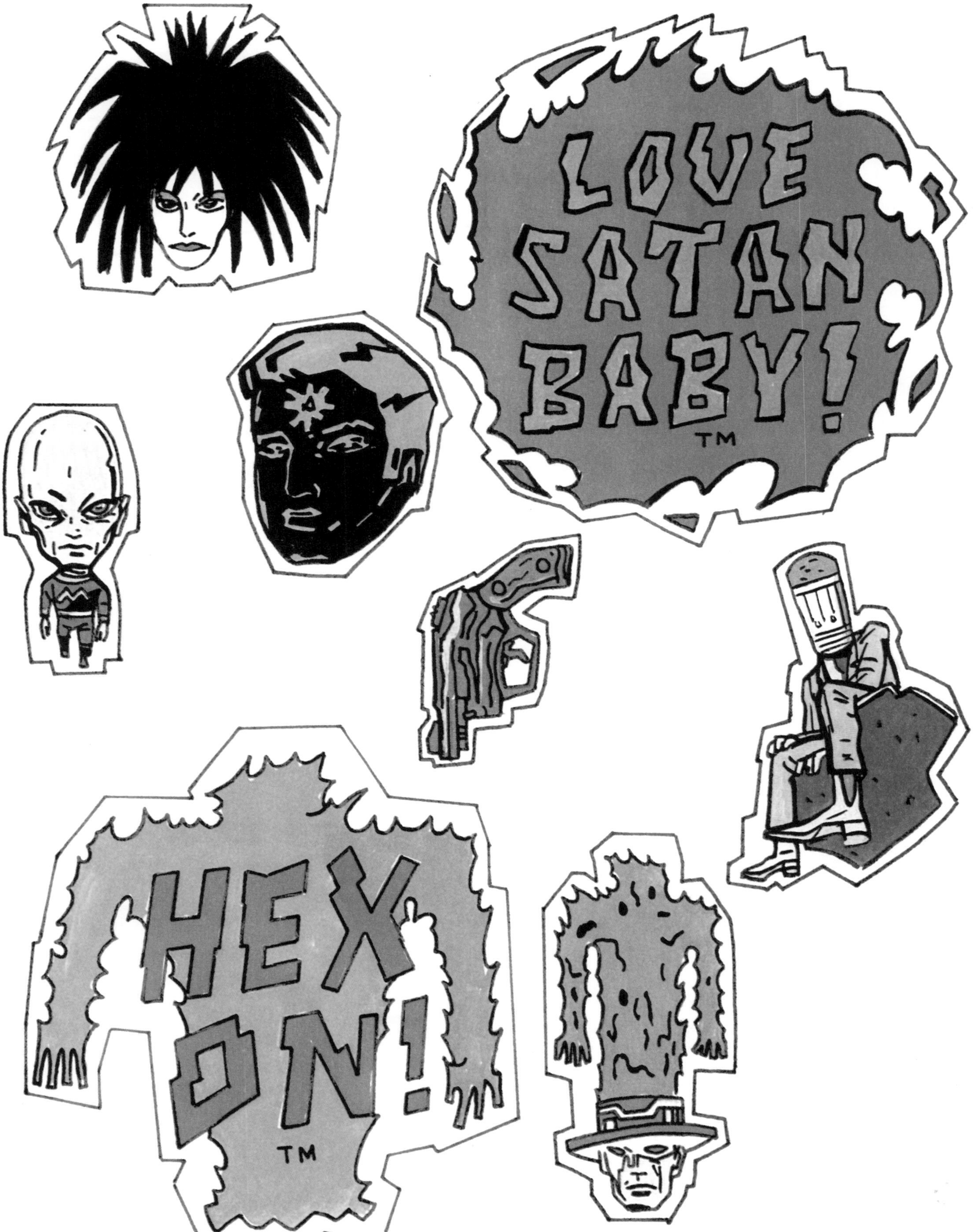
LOVE SATAN BABY!
TM
HEX ON!
TM

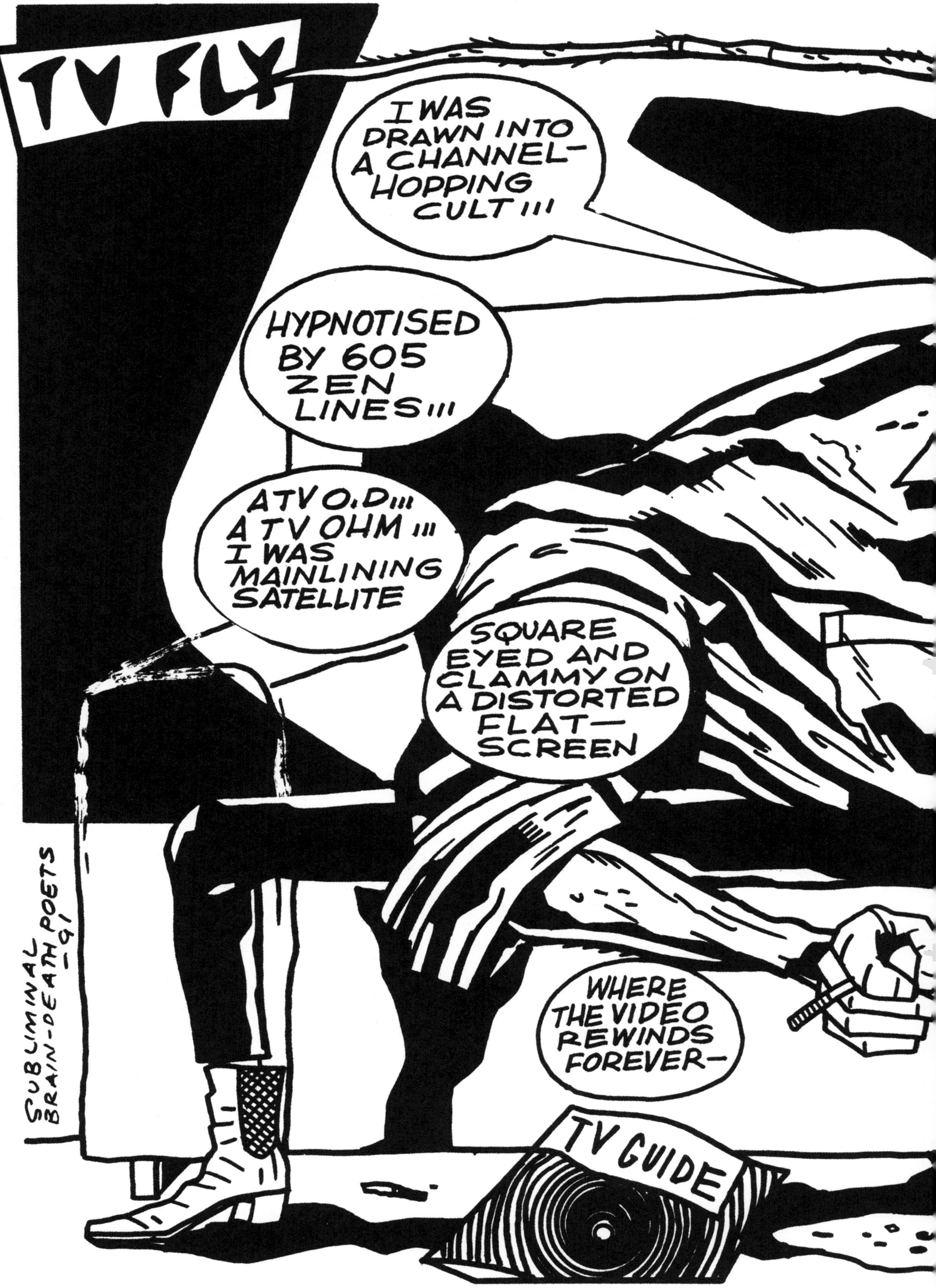
TV FLY
I WAS DRAWN INTO A CHANNEL-HOPPING CULT!!!
HYPNOTISED BY 605 ZEN LINES!!!
A TV O.D!!! A TV OHM!!! I WAS MAINLINING SATELLITE
SQUARE EYED AND CLAMMY ON A DISTORTED FLAT—SCREEN
WHERE THE VIDEO REWINDS FOREVER—
TV GUIDE
SUBLIMINAL BRAIN-DEATH POETS —91

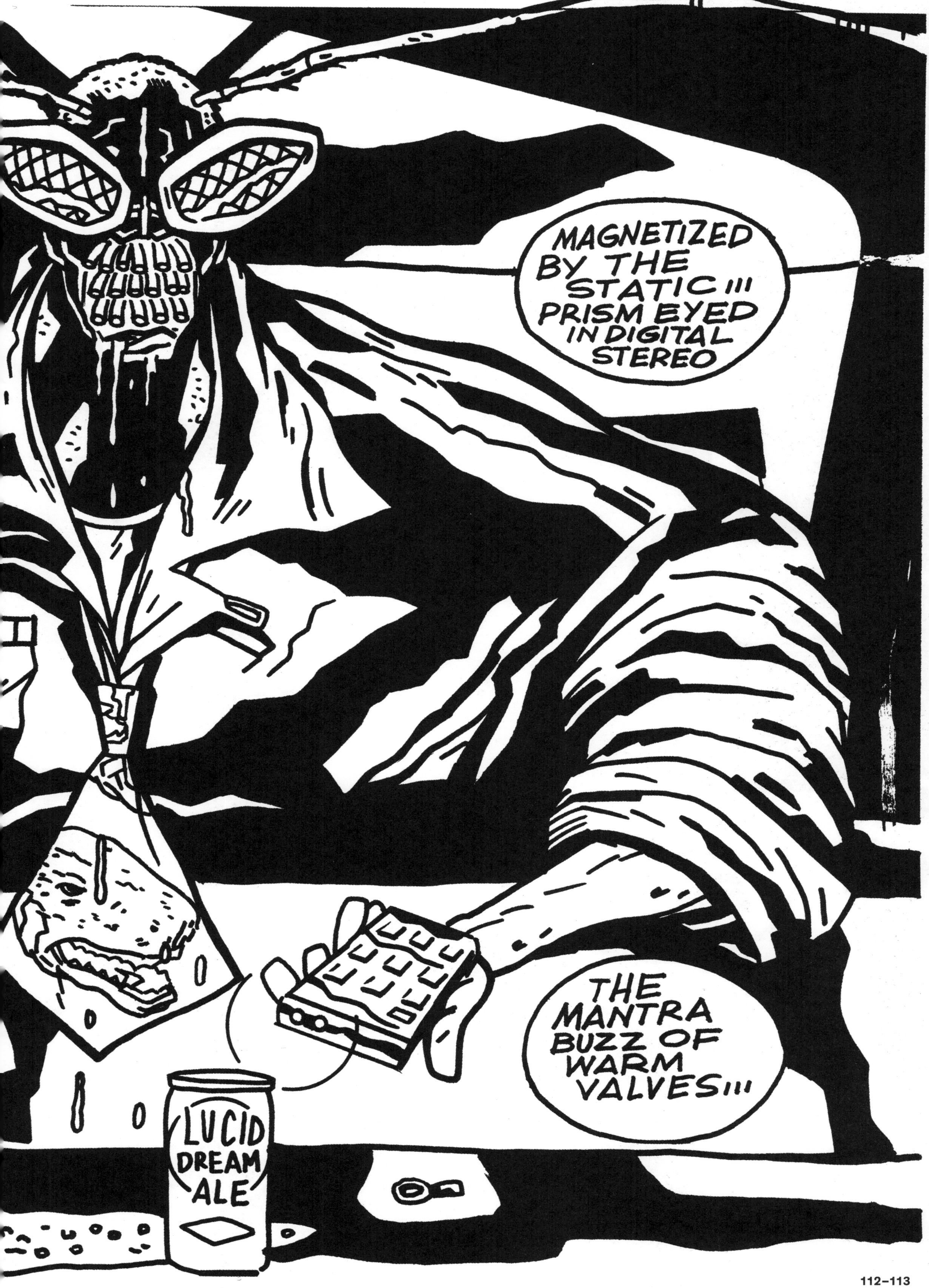
MAGNETIZED BY THE STATIC... PRISM EYED IN DIGITAL STEREO
THE MANTRA BUZZ OF WARM VALVES...
LUCID DREAM ALE

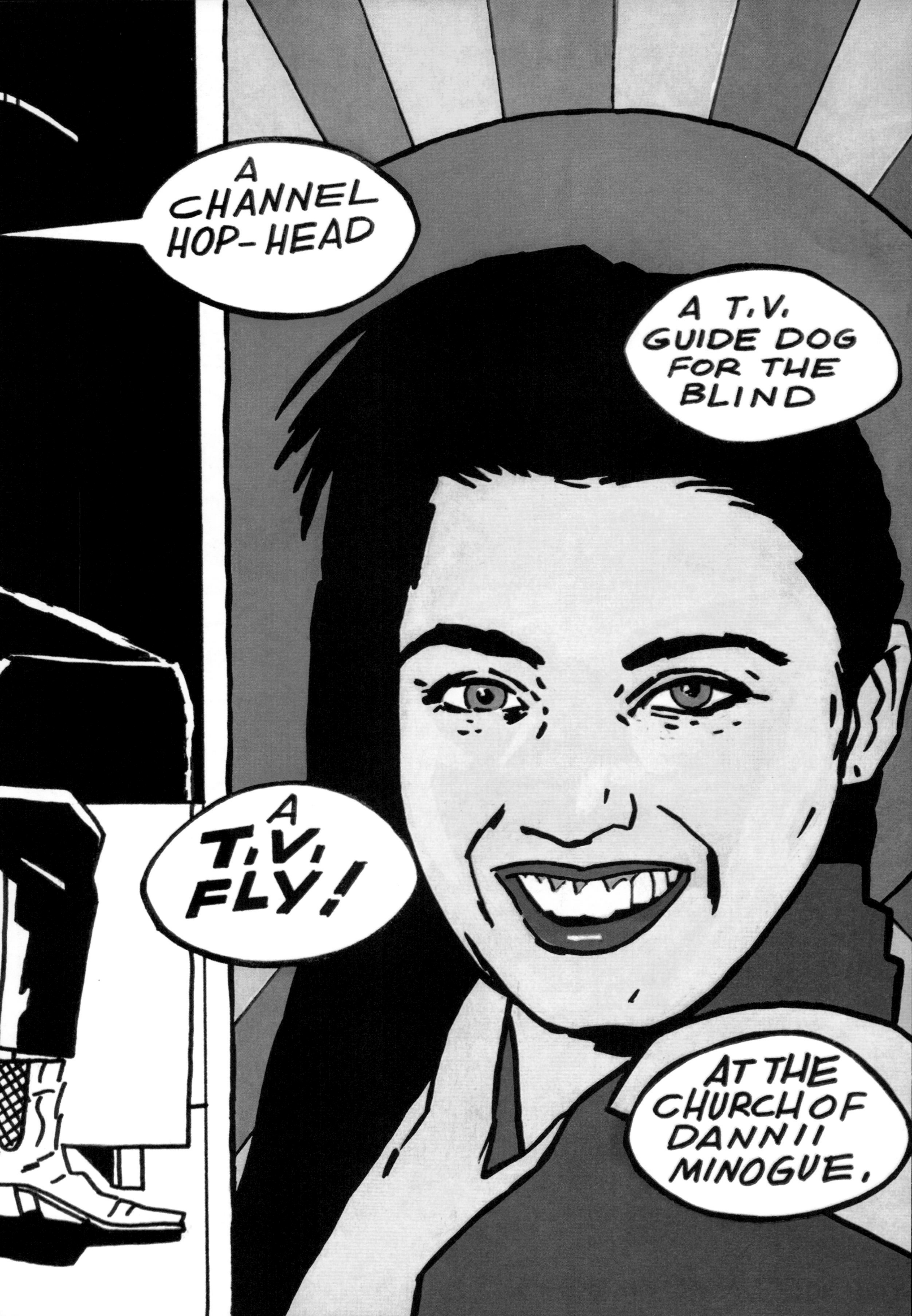
A CHANNEL HOP-HEAD
A T.V. GUIDE DOG FOR THE BLIND
A T.V. FLY!
AT THE CHURCH OF DANNII MINOGUE.

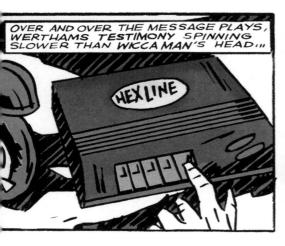

OVER AND OVER THE MESSAGE PLAYS, WERTHAMS TESTIMONY SPINNING SLOWER THAN WICCA MAN'S HEAD...

WICCAMAN GETS THE MESSAGE ALRIGHT... BUT HE DOESN'T LIKE THE TONE...

THE APOCRAPHALYPSE... HE'S NAILED HER BANG TO RIGHTS... IT'S THE SON, THE CHILD IS FATHER TO THE MAN... STAN SATANNA DIDN'T DO IT EEEP!

SOMEONE HAD TRIED TO FINGER STAN SATANNA

SOMEONE HIGH-UP SOMEONE IN THE FAMILY

HEX ON!

HE HAD A NEW SUSPECT, OFF HIS TURF...

HE WAS GOING TO BE PREPARED

A SEER AT THE DEICIDE CAN I GET A WITNESS?

SHAKY 2000.

THE LAST SURVIVING TEMPLE OF THE CREED OF THE WEEPING NAZARENE

SI SPENCER THE SAGE OF THE DEADLINE AGE!

SHAKY KANE THE RAGE OF THE DEADLINE AGE!

BAMBOS FROM HIS CAGE IN THE DEADLINE AGE!

HE DIDN'T LIKE IT... THERE WAS A STIGMA ATTACHED

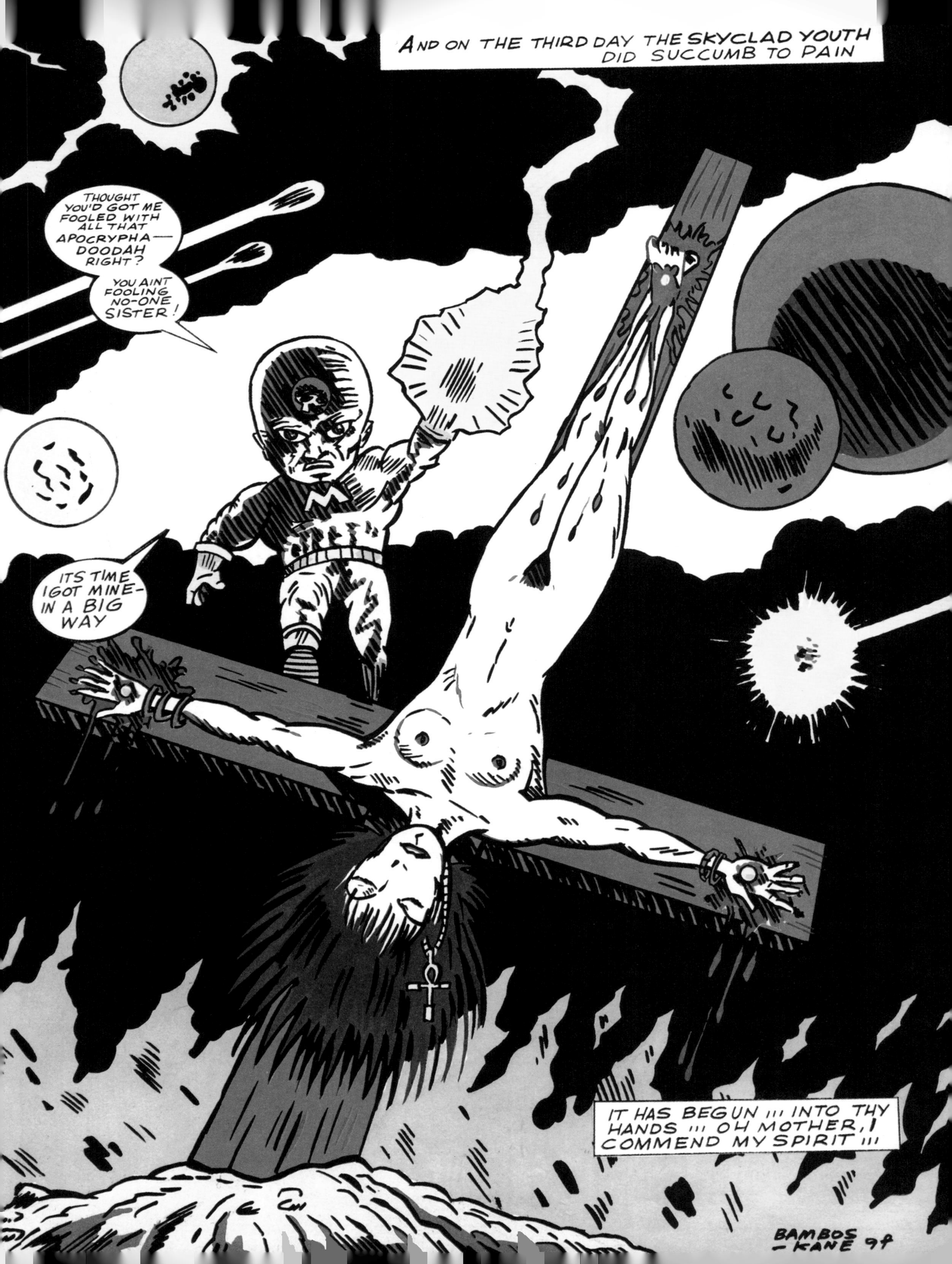
AND ON THE THIRD DAY THE SKYCLAD YOUTH DID SUCCUMB TO PAIN
THOUGHT YOU'D GOT ME FOOLED WITH ALL THAT APOCRYPHA-DOODAH RIGHT?
YOU AINT FOOLING NO-ONE SISTER!
ITS TIME I GOT MINE- IN A BIG WAY
IT HAS BEGUN ... INTO THY HANDS ... OH MOTHER, I COMMEND MY SPIRIT ...
BAMBOS -KANE 94

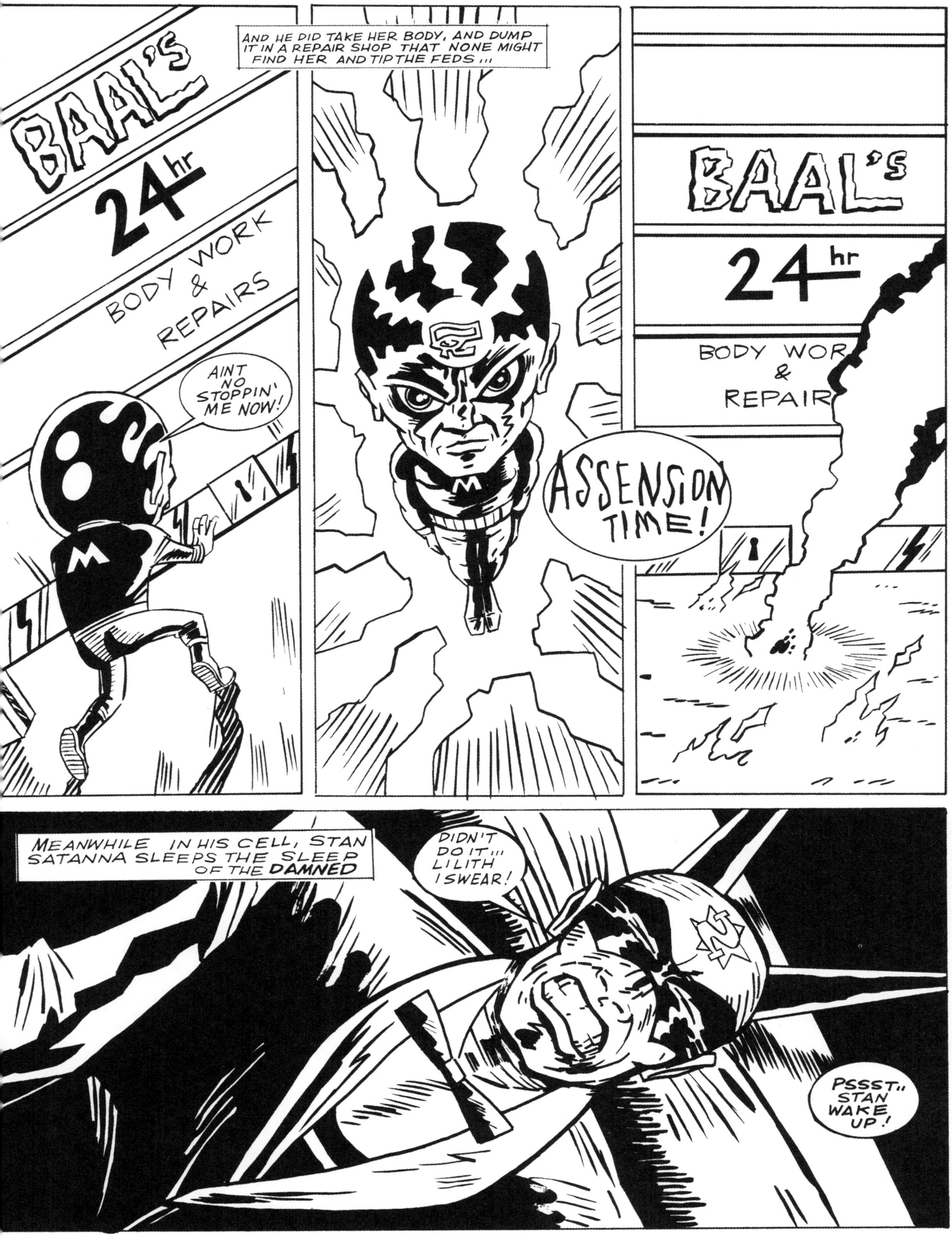
BAAL'S
24 hr
BODY WORK & REPAIRS
AINT NO STOPPIN' ME NOW!
AND HE DID TAKE HER BODY, AND DUMP IT IN A REPAIR SHOP THAT NONE MIGHT FIND HER AND TIP THE FEDS ...
ASSENSION TIME!
BAAL'S
24 hr
BODY WOR & REPAIR
MEANWHILE IN HIS CELL, STAN SATANNA SLEEPS THE SLEEP OF THE DAMNED
DIDN'T DO IT... LILITH I SWEAR!
PSSST.. STAN WAKE UP!

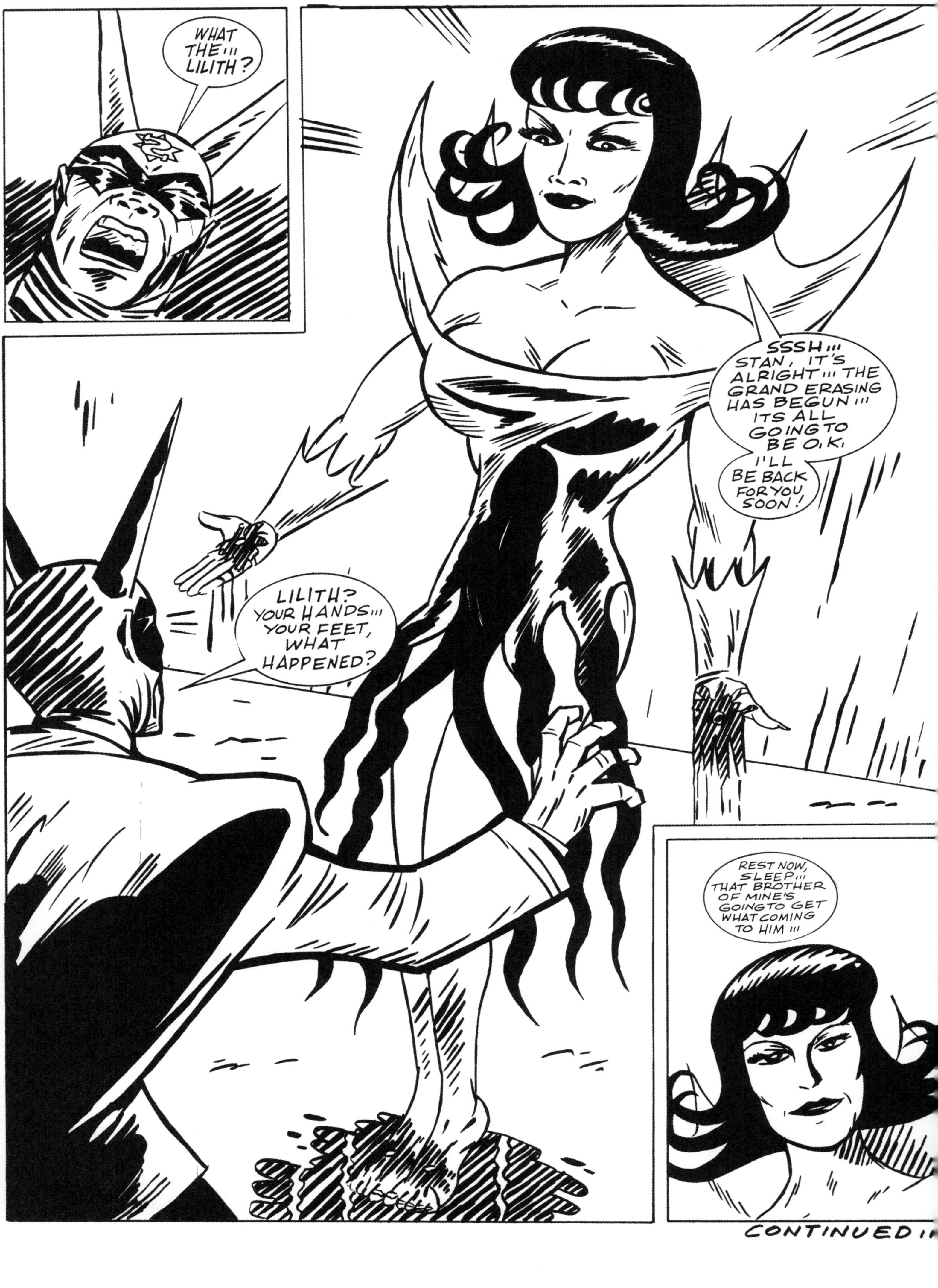
WHAT THE... LILITH?
SSSH... STAN, IT'S ALRIGHT... THE GRAND ERASING HAS BEGUN... ITS ALL GOING TO BE O.K.
I'LL BE BACK FOR YOU SOON!
LILITH? YOUR HANDS... YOUR FEET, WHAT HAPPENED?
REST NOW, SLEEP... THAT BROTHER OF MINE'S GOING TO GET WHAT COMING TO HIM...
CONTINUED...

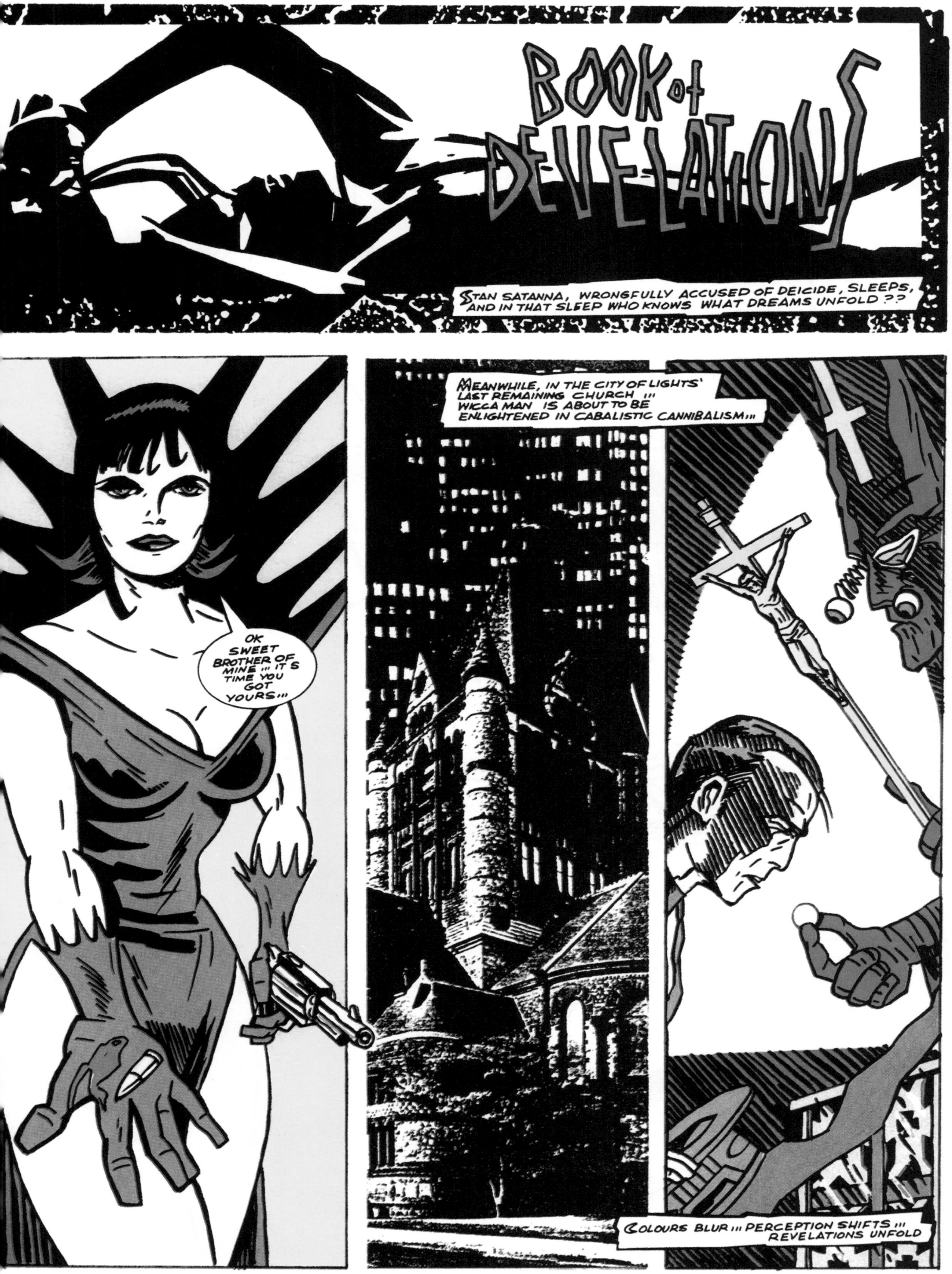
BOOK of REVELATIONS
STAN SATANNA, WRONGFULLY ACCUSED OF DEICIDE, SLEEPS, AND IN THAT SLEEP WHO KNOWS WHAT DREAMS UNFOLD ??
OK SWEET BROTHER OF MINE ... IT'S TIME YOU GOT YOURS...
MEANWHILE, IN THE CITY OF LIGHTS' LAST REMAINING CHURCH ... WICCA MAN IS ABOUT TO BE ENLIGHTENED IN CABALISTIC CANNIBALISM...
COLOURS BLUR ... PERCEPTION SHIFTS ... REVELATIONS UNFOLD

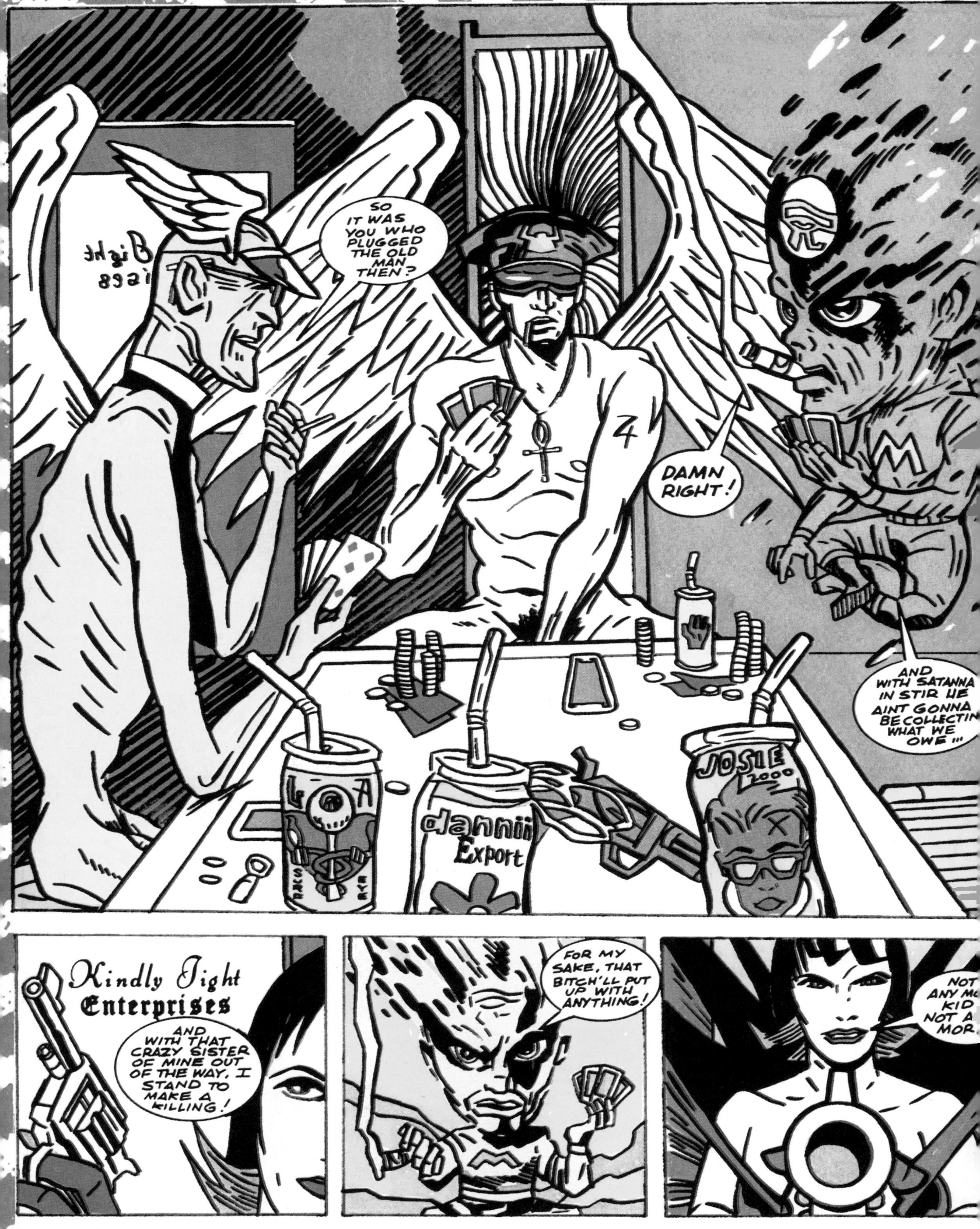
SO IT WAS YOU WHO PLUGGED THE OLD MAN THEN?
DAMN RIGHT!
AND WITH SATANNA IN STIR HE AINT GONNA BECOLLECTIN WHAT WE OWE...
JOSIE 2000
dannii Export
Kindly Light Enterprises
AND WITH THAT CRAZY SISTER OF MINE OUT OF THE WAY, I STAND TO MAKE A KILLING!
FOR MY SAKE, THAT BITCH'LL PUT UP WITH ANYTHING!
NOT ANY MO KID NOT A MOR

DURING THE MIDDLE AGES, AN ESTIMATED FOUR MILLION WOMEN WERE PUT DEATH FOR A VARIETY OF CRIMES SUCH AS LEARNING TO READ, PRACTIS MEDICINE, HAVING SEXUAL INTERCOURSE AND PREACHING THE DOCTRINES THEIR PERSECUTORS...

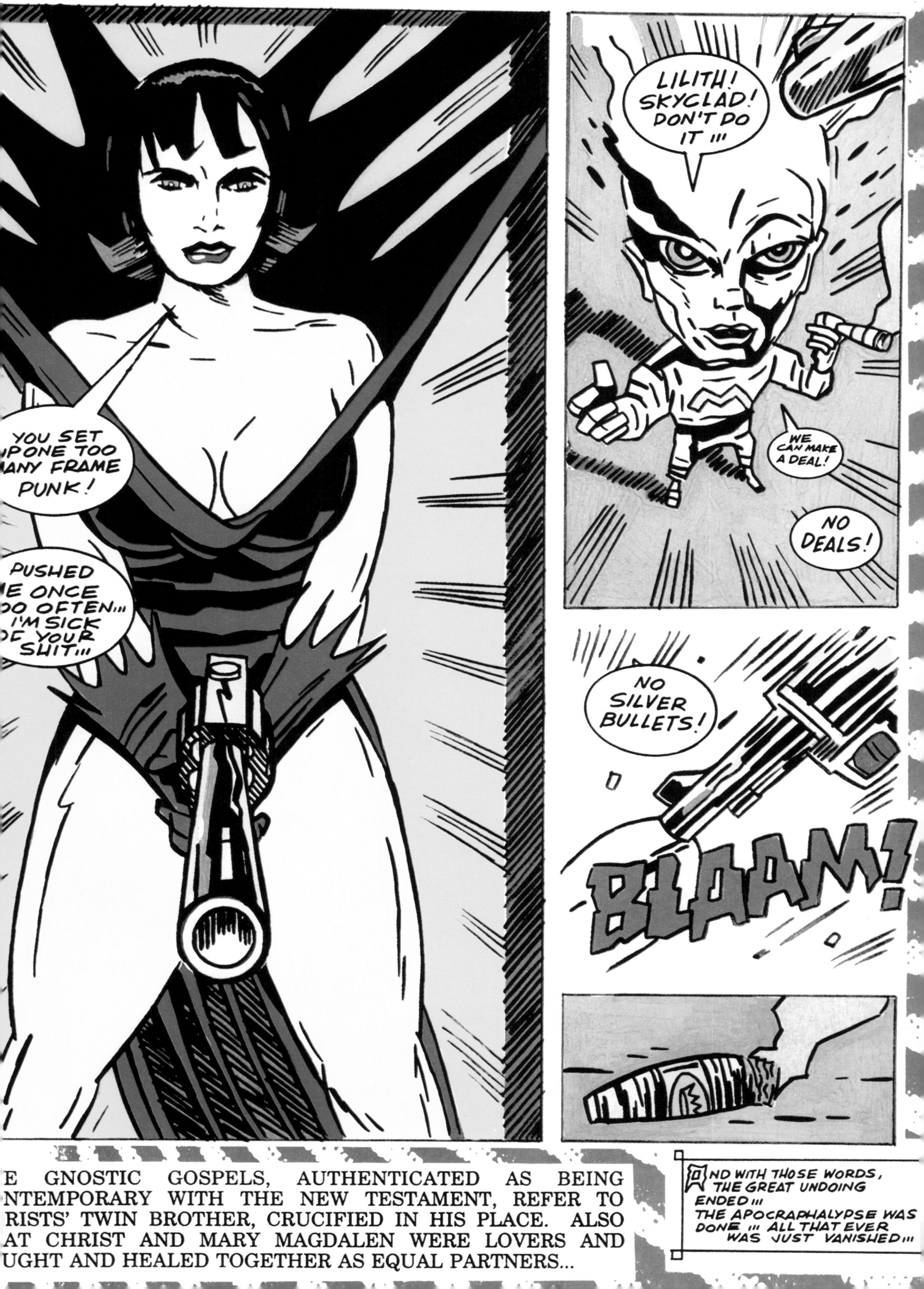

YOU SET PONE TOO ANY FRAME PUNK!
PUSHED E ONCE OO OFTEN... I'M SICK OF YOUR SHIT...
LILITH! SKYCLAD! DON'T DO IT...
WE CAN MAKE A DEAL!
NO DEALS!
NO SILVER BULLETS!
BLAAM!


E GNOSTIC GOSPELS, AUTHENTICATED AS BEING NTEMPORARY WITH THE NEW TESTAMENT, REFER TO RISTS' TWIN BROTHER, CRUCIFIED IN HIS PLACE. ALSO AT CHRIST AND MARY MAGDALEN WERE LOVERS AND UGHT AND HEALED TOGETHER AS EQUAL PARTNERS...

AND WITH THOSE WORDS, THE GREAT UNDOING ENDED... THE APOCRAPHALYPSE WAS DONE... ALL THAT EVER WAS JUST VANISHED...

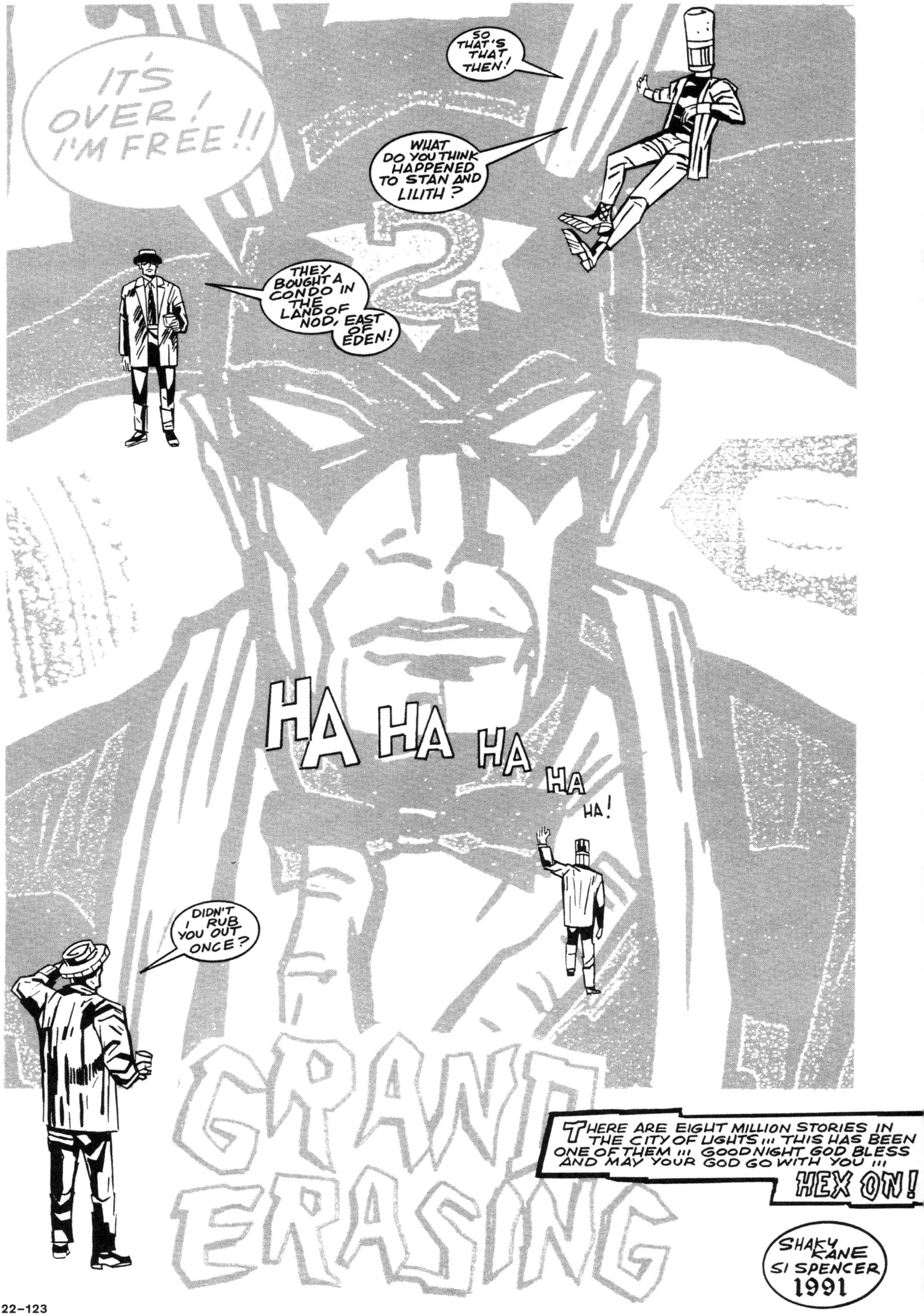
IT'S OVER! I'M FREE!!
SO THAT'S THAT, THEN!
WHAT DO YOU THINK HAPPENED TO STAN AND LILITH?
THEY BOUGHT A CONDO IN THE LAND OF NOD, EAST OF EDEN!
HA HA HA HA HA!
DIDN'T I RUB YOU OUT ONCE?
GRANT ERASING
THERE ARE EIGHT MILLION STORIES IN THE CITY OF LIGHTS ... THIS HAS BEEN ONE OF THEM ... GOODNIGHT GOD BLESS AND MAY YOUR GOD GO WITH YOU ...
HEX ON!
SHAKY KANE
SI SPENCER
1991

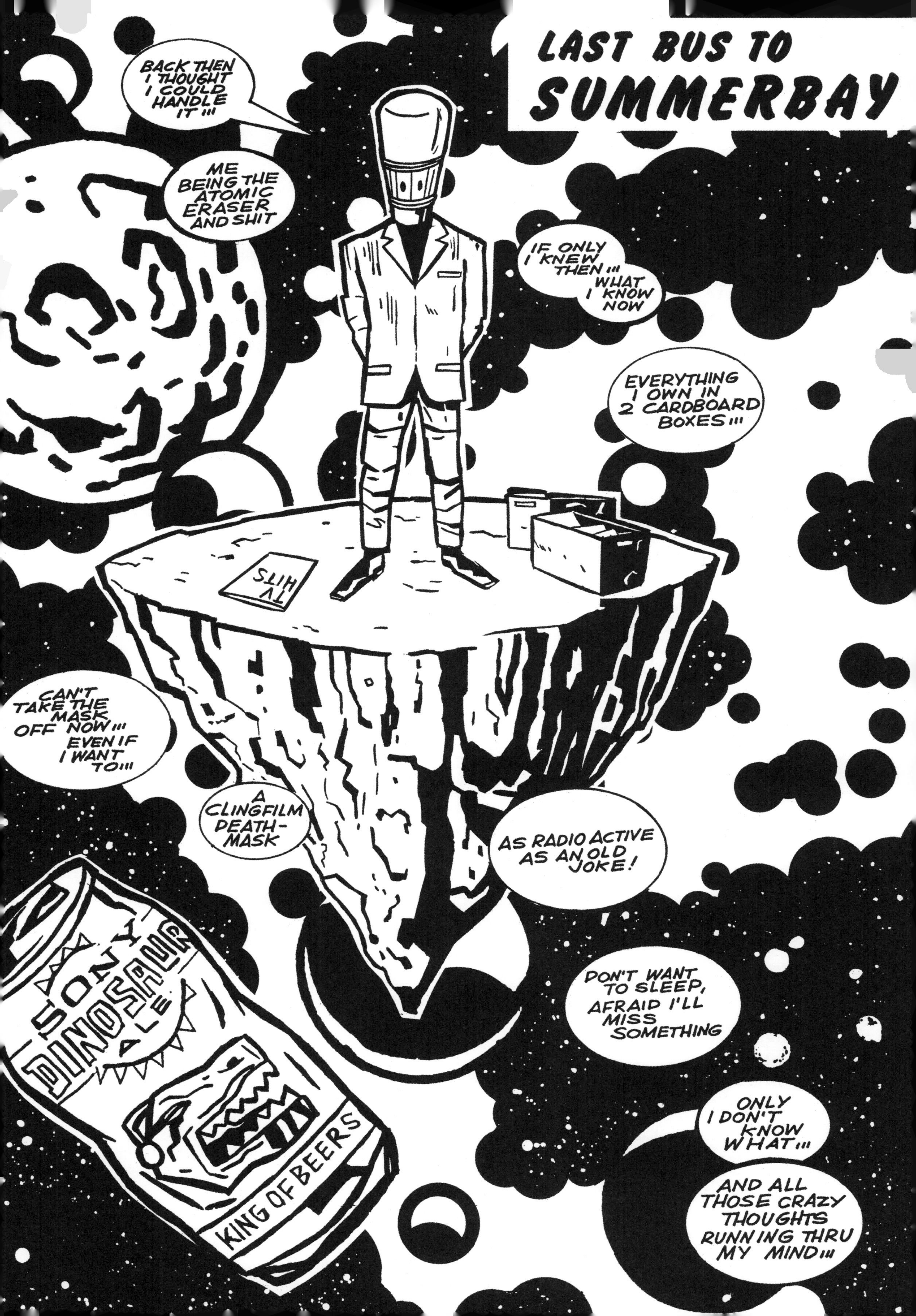
LAST BUS TO SUMMERBAY
BACK THEN I THOUGHT I COULD HANDLE IT...
ME BEING THE ATOMIC ERASER AND SHIT
IF ONLY I KNEW THEN... WHAT I KNOW NOW
EVERYTHING I OWN IN 2 CARDBOARD BOXES...
TV HITS
CAN'T TAKE THE MASK OFF NOW... EVEN IF I WANT TO...
A CLINGFILM DEATH-MASK
AS RADIO ACTIVE AS AN OLD JOKE!
SONY DINOSAUR ALE
KING OF BEERS
DON'T WANT TO SLEEP, AFRAID I'LL MISS SOMETHING
ONLY I DON'T KNOW WHAT...
AND ALL THOSE CRAZY THOUGHTS RUNNING THRU MY MIND...

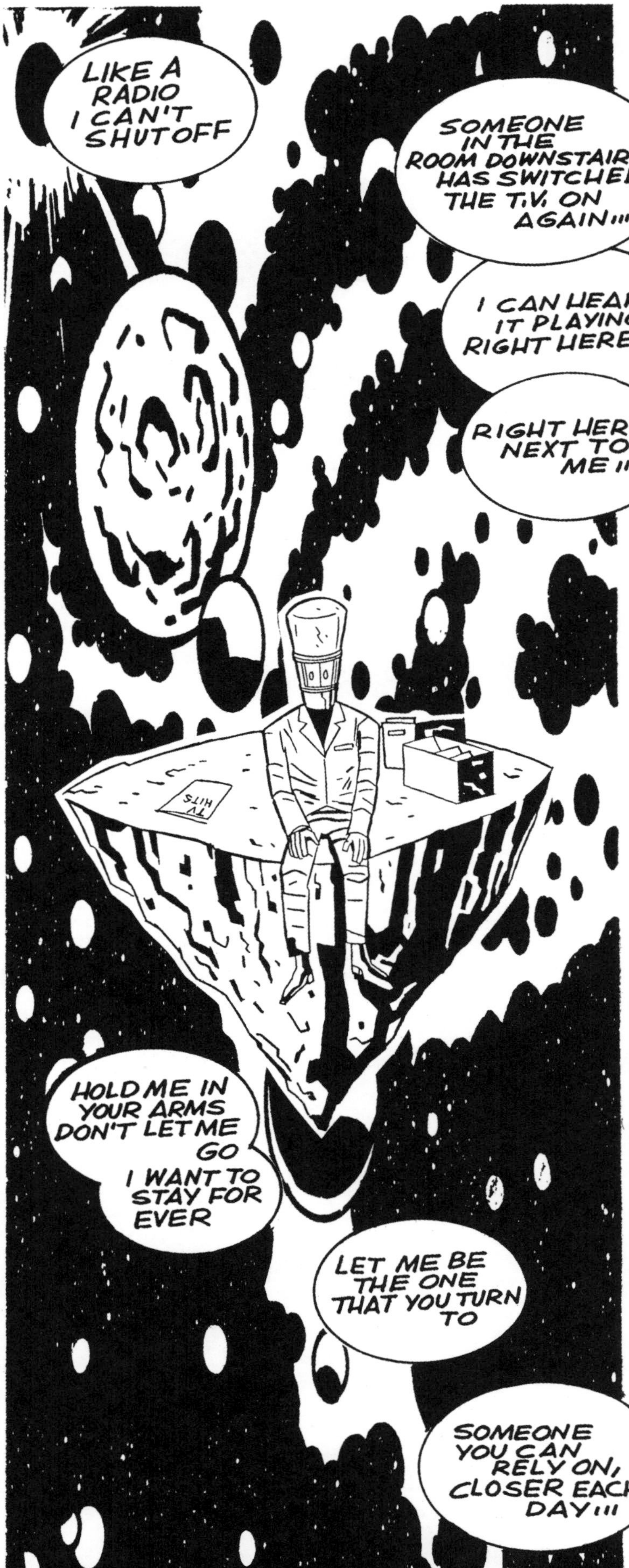
LIKE A RADIO I CAN'T SHUTOFF
SOMEONE IN THE ROOM DOWNSTAIRS HAS SWITCHED THE T.V. ON AGAIN...
I CAN HEAR IT PLAYING RIGHT HERE...
RIGHT HERE NEXT TO ME...
HOLD ME IN YOUR ARMS DON'T LET ME GO
I WANT TO STAY FOR EVER
LET ME BE THE ONE THAT YOU TURN TO
SOMEONE YOU CAN RELY ON, CLOSER EACH DAY...

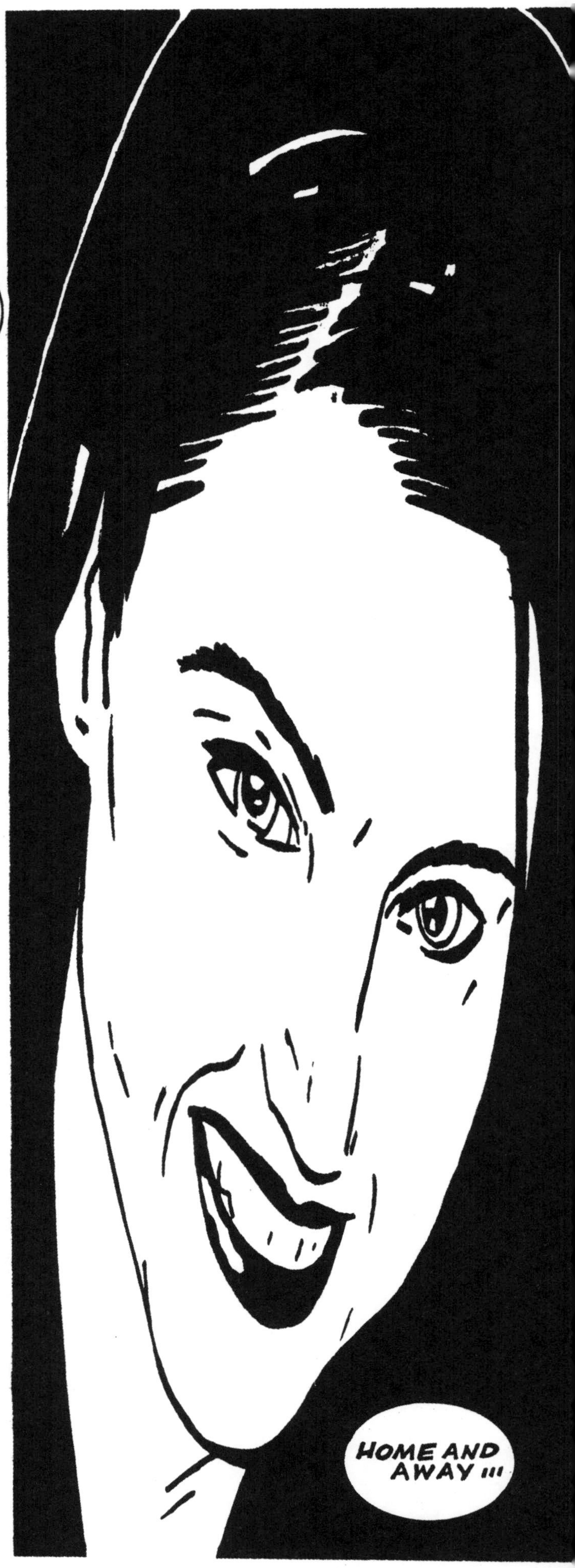
HOME AND AWAY...

FOR DANNII, ALAN, MATTY MATT AND THE FUNKY BUNCH WHO FIXED MY ZIP ON THE SUSSEX COAST X.

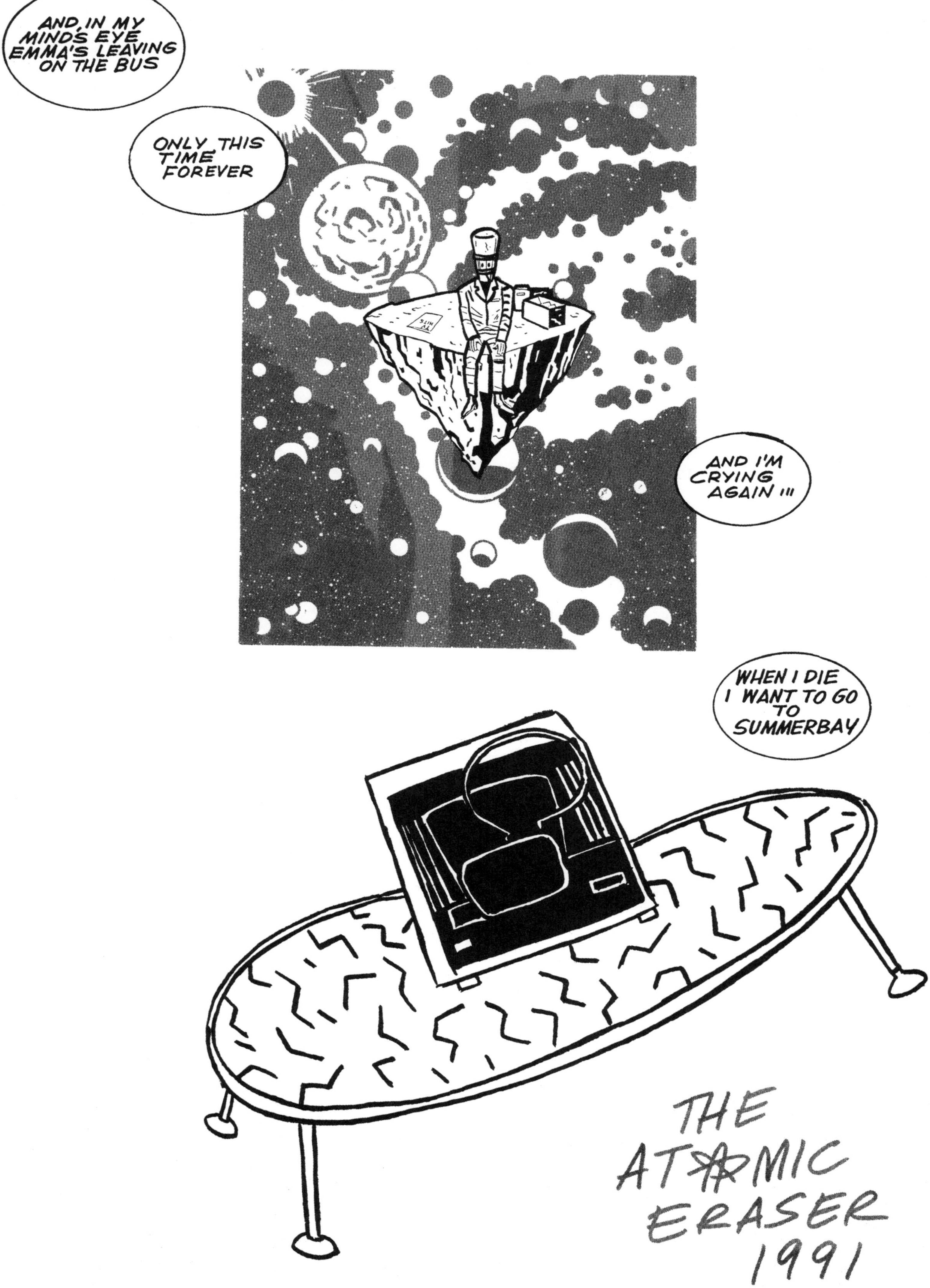
AND, IN MY MIND'S EYE EMMA'S LEAVING ON THE BUS
ONLY THIS TIME FOREVER
AND I'M CRYING AGAIN !!!
WHEN I DIE I WANT TO GO TO SUMMERBAY
THE ATOMIC ERASER 1991

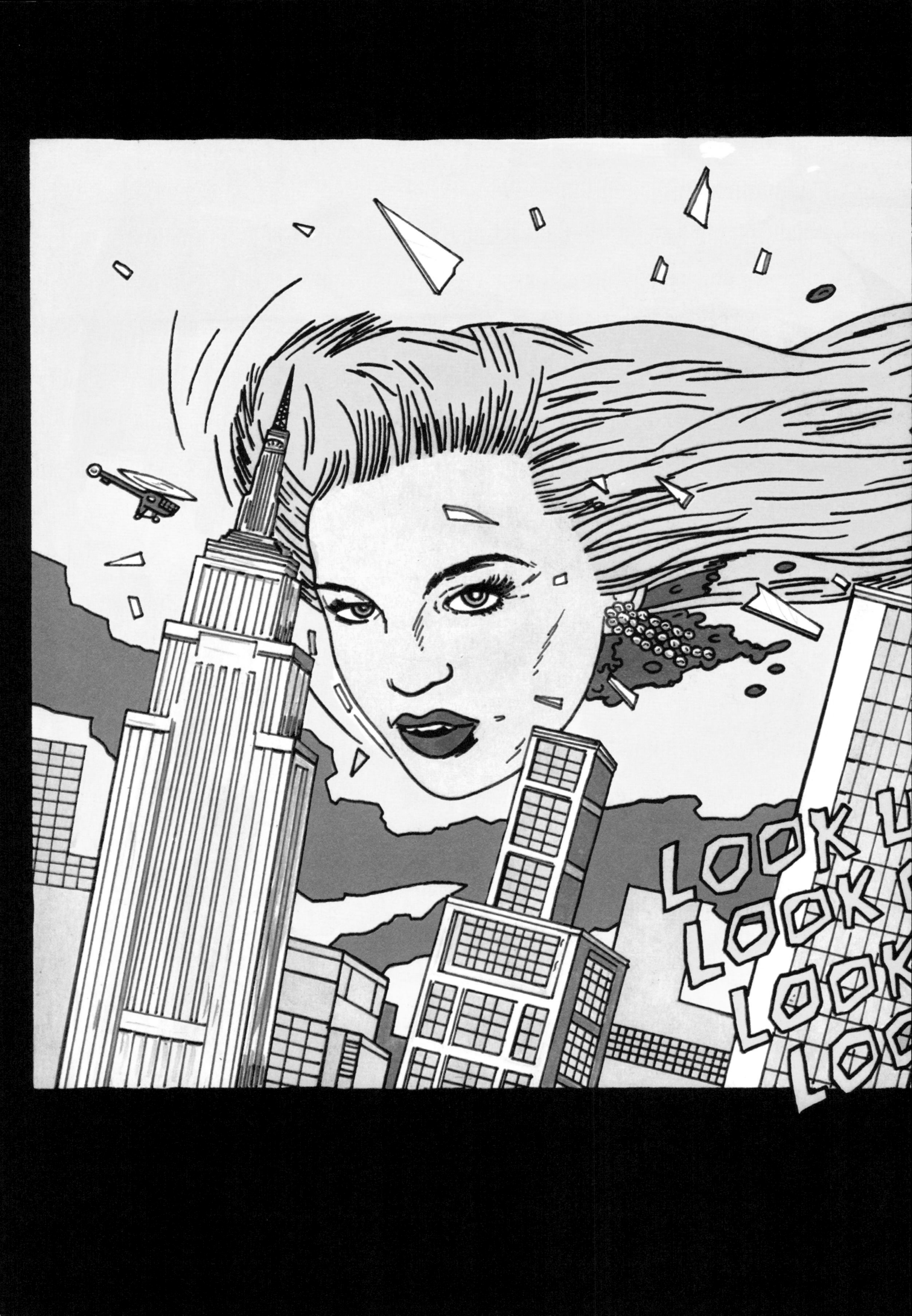
LOOK
LOOK

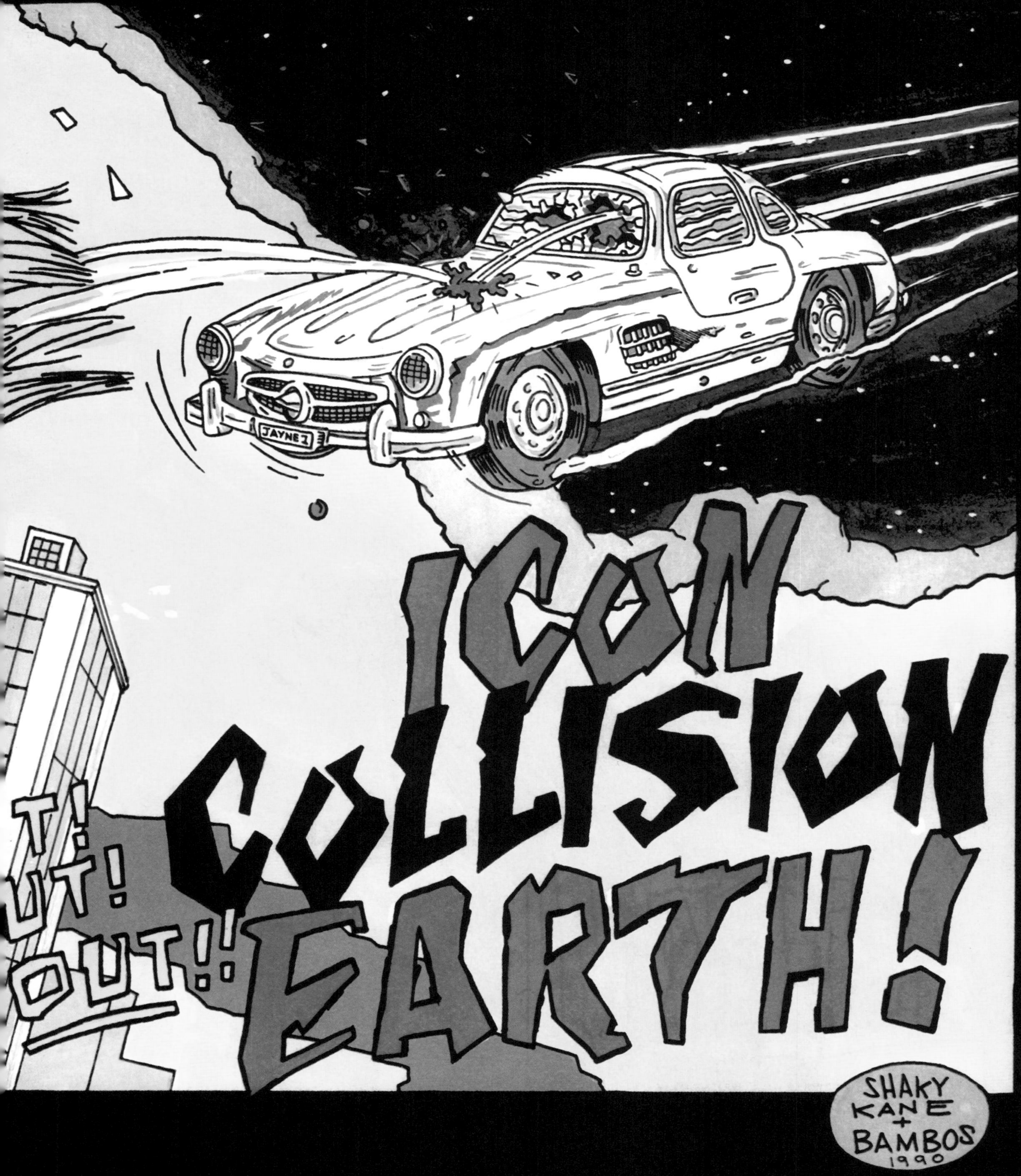
JAYNE 1
ICON COLLISION EARTH!
T!
UT!
OUT!!
SHAKY KANE + BAMBOS 1990

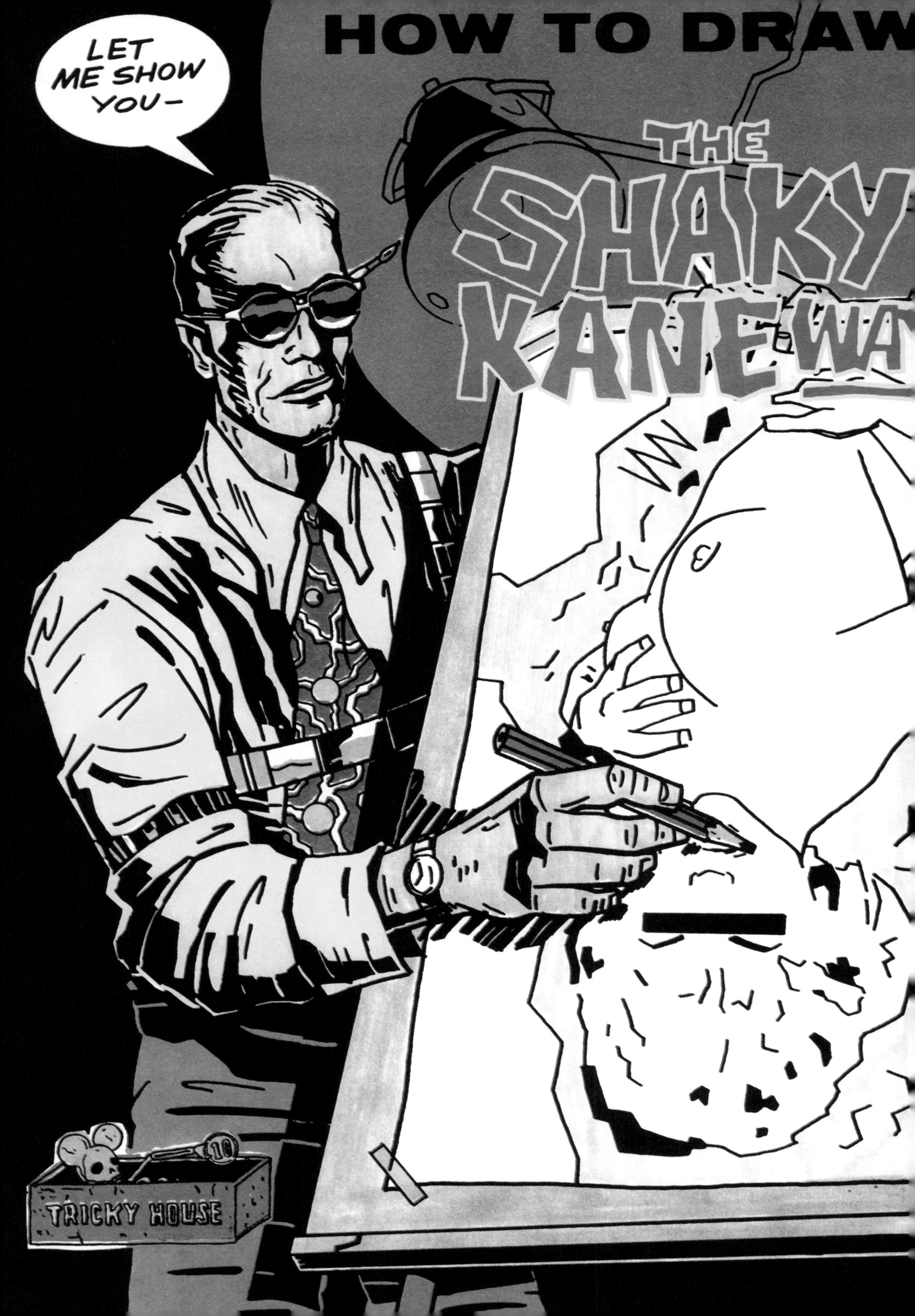
HOW TO DRAW
LET ME SHOW YOU-
THE SHAKY KANE WA
TRICKY HOUSE
10

# STEP 1: FINDING THE INSPIRATION

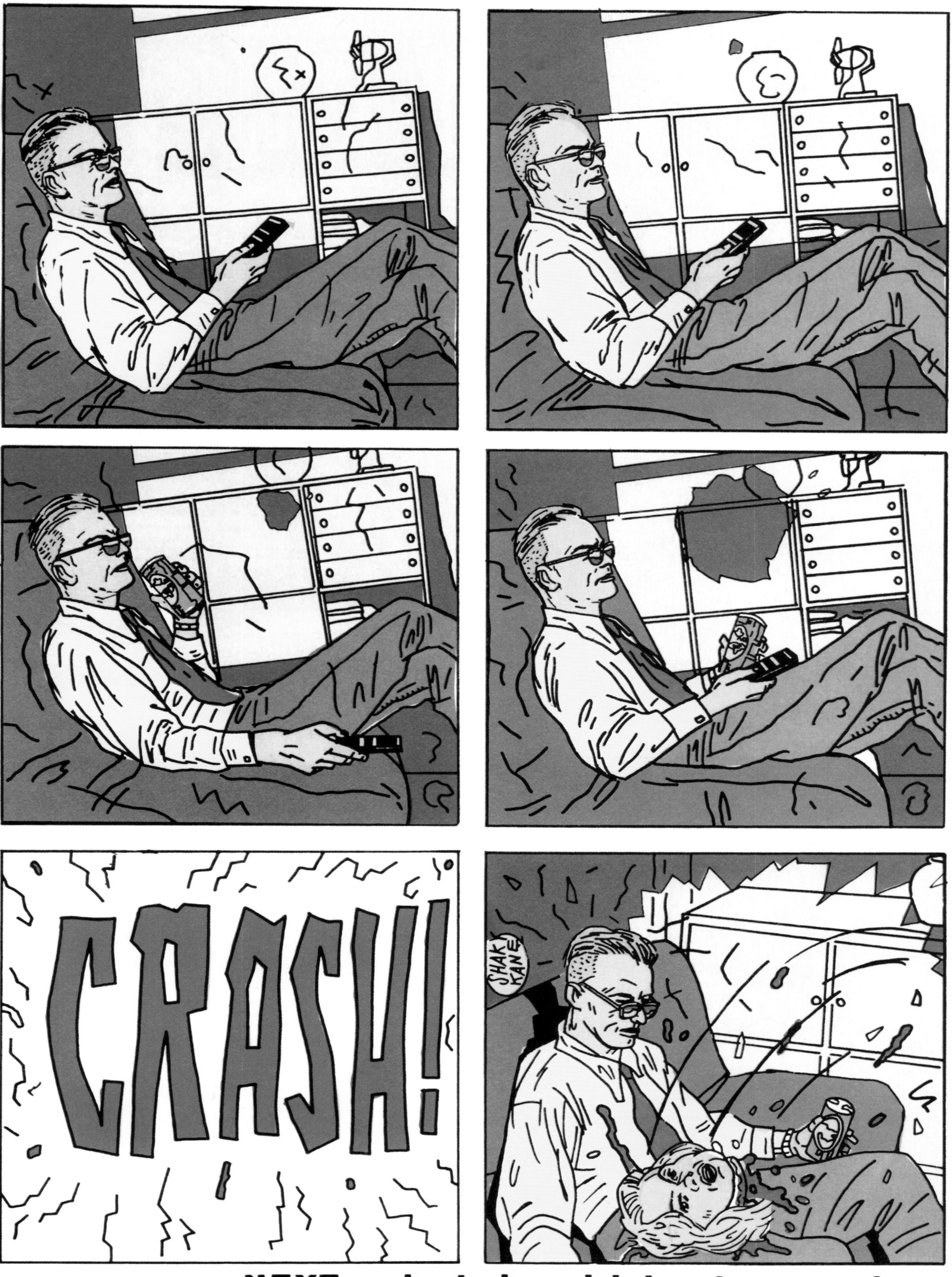
CRASH!
SHAK KANE

**NEXT: who to buy drinks at conventions**

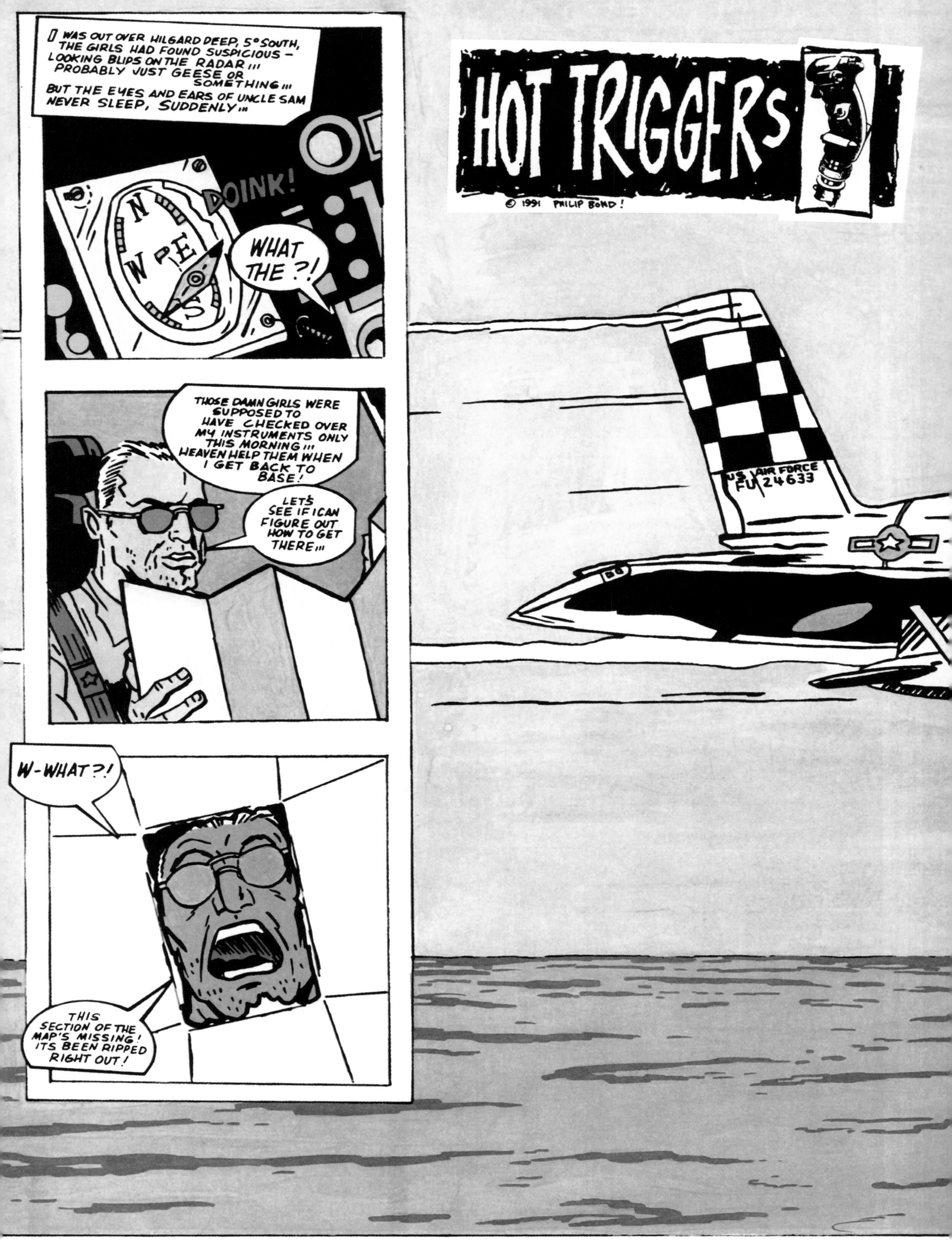
HOT TRIGGERS
© 1991 PHILIP BOND!
I WAS OUT OVER HILGARD DEEP, 5° SOUTH, THE GIRLS HAD FOUND SUSPICIOUS-LOOKING BLIPS ON THE RADAR ... PROBABLY JUST GEESE OR SOMETHING ... BUT THE EYES AND EARS OF UNCLE SAM NEVER SLEEP, SUDDENLY ...
DOINK!
WHAT THE ?!
THOSE DAMN GIRLS WERE SUPPOSED TO HAVE CHECKED OVER MY INSTRUMENTS ONLY THIS MORNING ... HEAVEN HELP THEM WHEN I GET BACK TO BASE!
LET'S SEE IF I CAN FIGURE OUT HOW TO GET THERE ...
W-WHAT?!
THIS SECTION OF THE MAP'S MISSING! ITS BEEN RIPPED RIGHT OUT!
US AIR FORCE
FU 24633

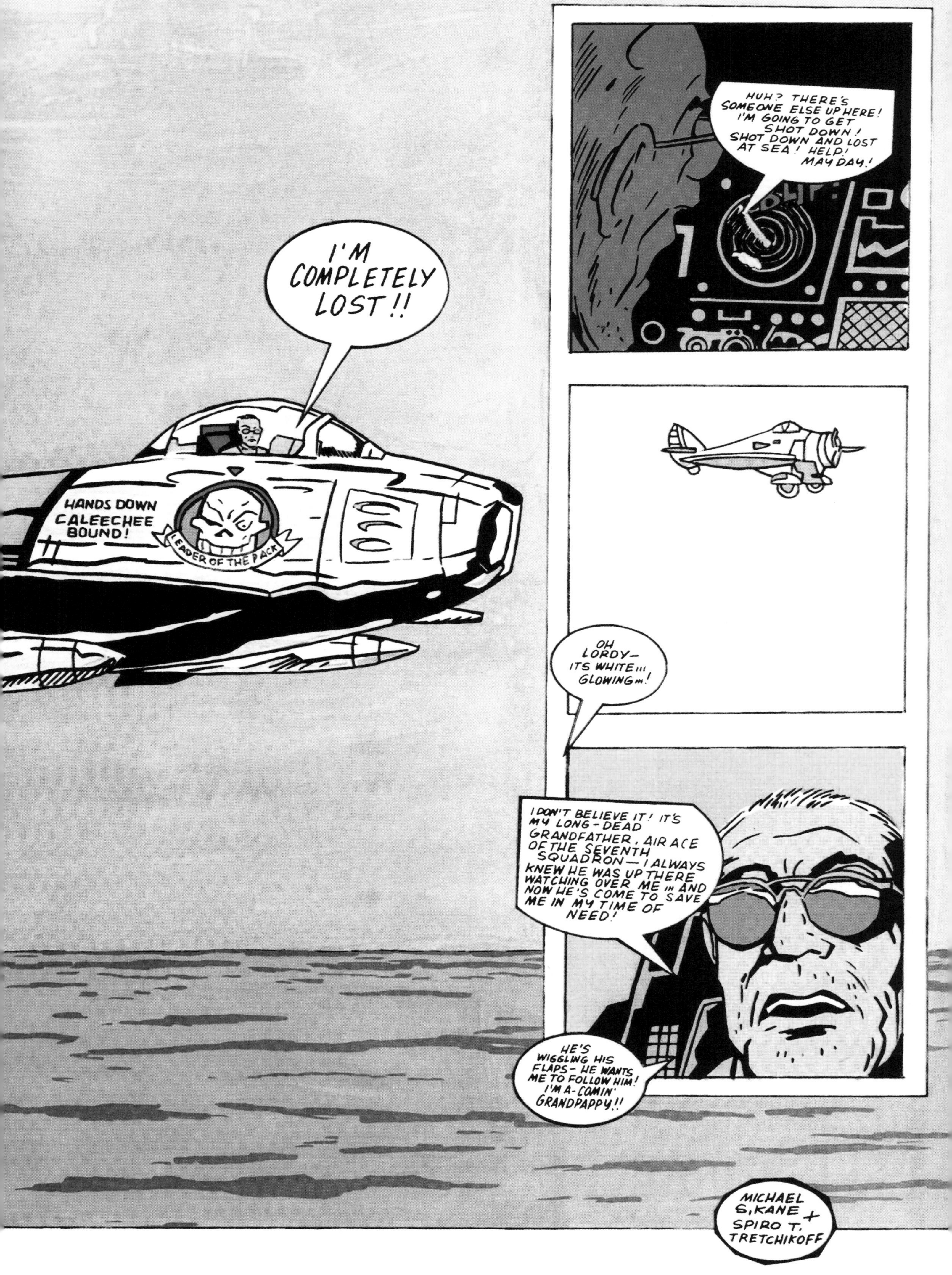
I'M COMPLETELY LOST!!
HANDS DOWN CALEECHEE BOUND!
LEADER OF THE PACK
HUH? THERE'S SOMEONE ELSE UP HERE! I'M GOING TO GET SHOT DOWN! SHOT DOWN AND LOST AT SEA! HELP! MAY DAY!
OH LORDY– ITS WHITE... GLOWING...!
I DON'T BELIEVE IT! IT'S MY LONG-DEAD GRANDFATHER, AIR ACE OF THE SEVENTH SQUADRON— I ALWAYS KNEW HE WAS UP THERE WATCHING OVER ME... AND NOW HE'S COME TO SAVE ME IN MY TIME OF NEED!
HE'S WIGGLING HIS FLAPS– HE WANTS ME TO FOLLOW HIM! I'M A-COMIN' GRANDPAPPY!!
MICHAEL S. KANE + SPIRO T. TRETCHIKOFF

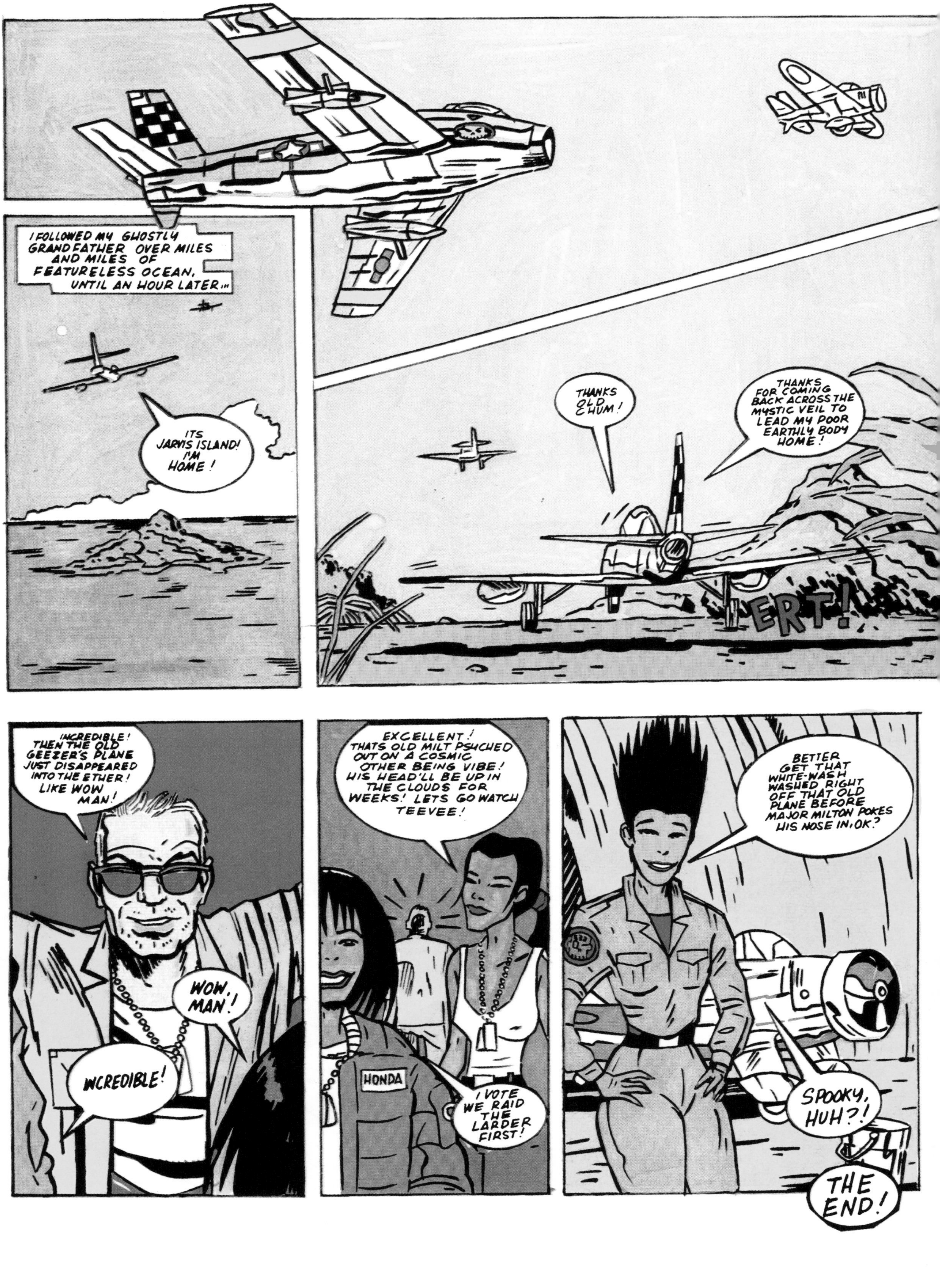
I FOLLOWED MY GHOSTLY GRANDFATHER OVER MILES AND MILES OF FEATURELESS OCEAN, UNTIL AN HOUR LATER...
ITS JARVIS ISLAND! I'M HOME!
THANKS OLD CHUM!
THANKS FOR COMING BACK ACROSS THE MYSTIC VEIL TO LEAD MY POOR EARTHLY BODY HOME!
ERT!
INCREDIBLE! THEN THE OLD GEEZER'S PLANE JUST DISAPPEARED INTO THE ETHER! LIKE WOW MAN!
WOW, MAN!
INCREDIBLE!
EXCELLENT! THATS OLD MILT PSYCHED OUT ON A COSMIC OTHER BEING VIBE! HIS HEAD'LL BE UP IN THE CLOUDS FOR WEEKS! LETS GO WATCH TEEVEE!
HONDA
I VOTE WE RAID THE LARDER FIRST!
BETTER GET THAT WHITE-WASH WASHED RIGHT OFF THAT OLD PLANE BEFORE MAJOR MILTON POKES HIS NOSE IN, OK?
SPOOKY, HUH?!
THE END!

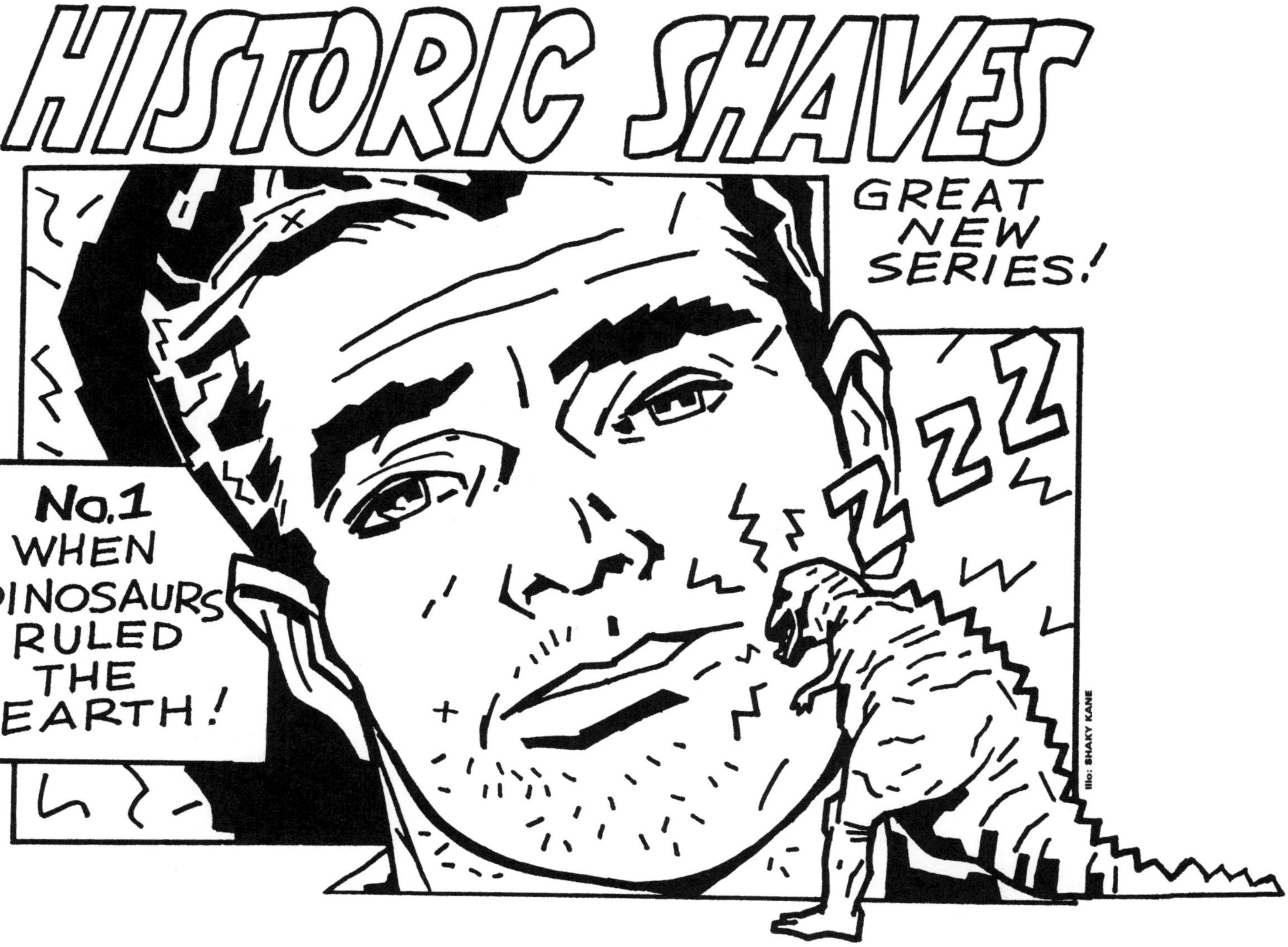
HISTORIC SHAVES
GREAT NEW SERIES!
No.1 WHEN DINOSAURS RULED THE EARTH!
ZZZ
Illo: SHAKY KANE

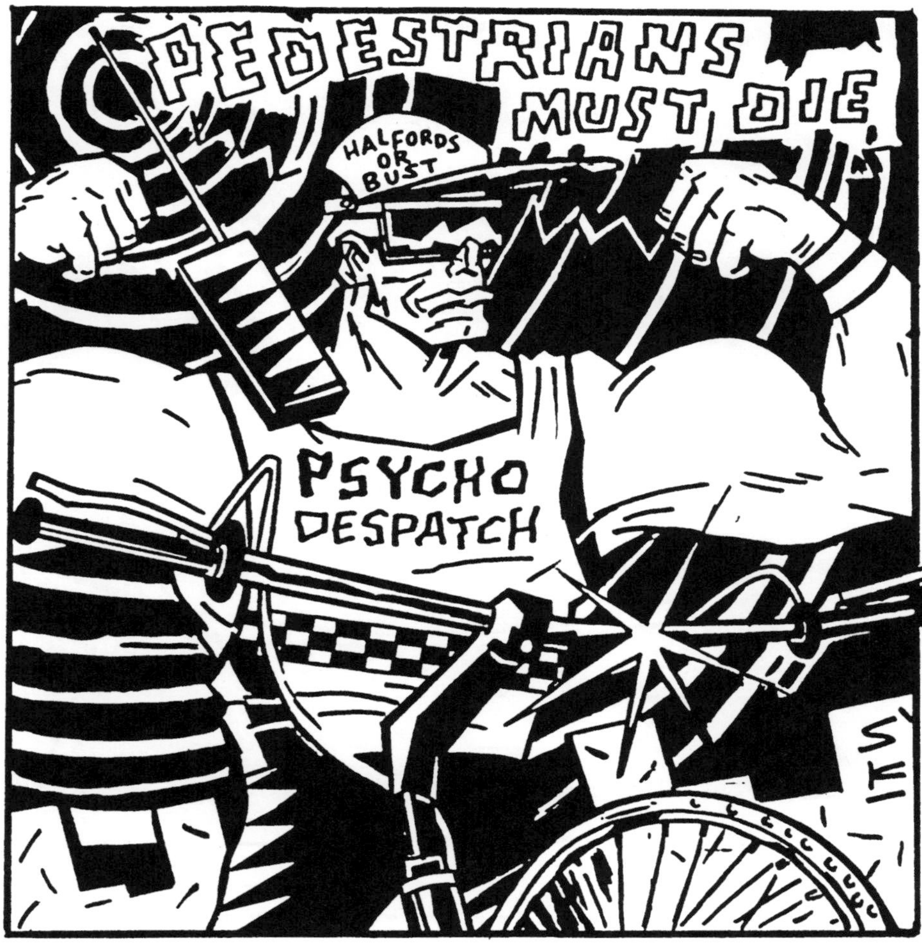
PEDESTRIANS MUST DIE
HALFORDS OR BUST
PSYCHO DESPATCH

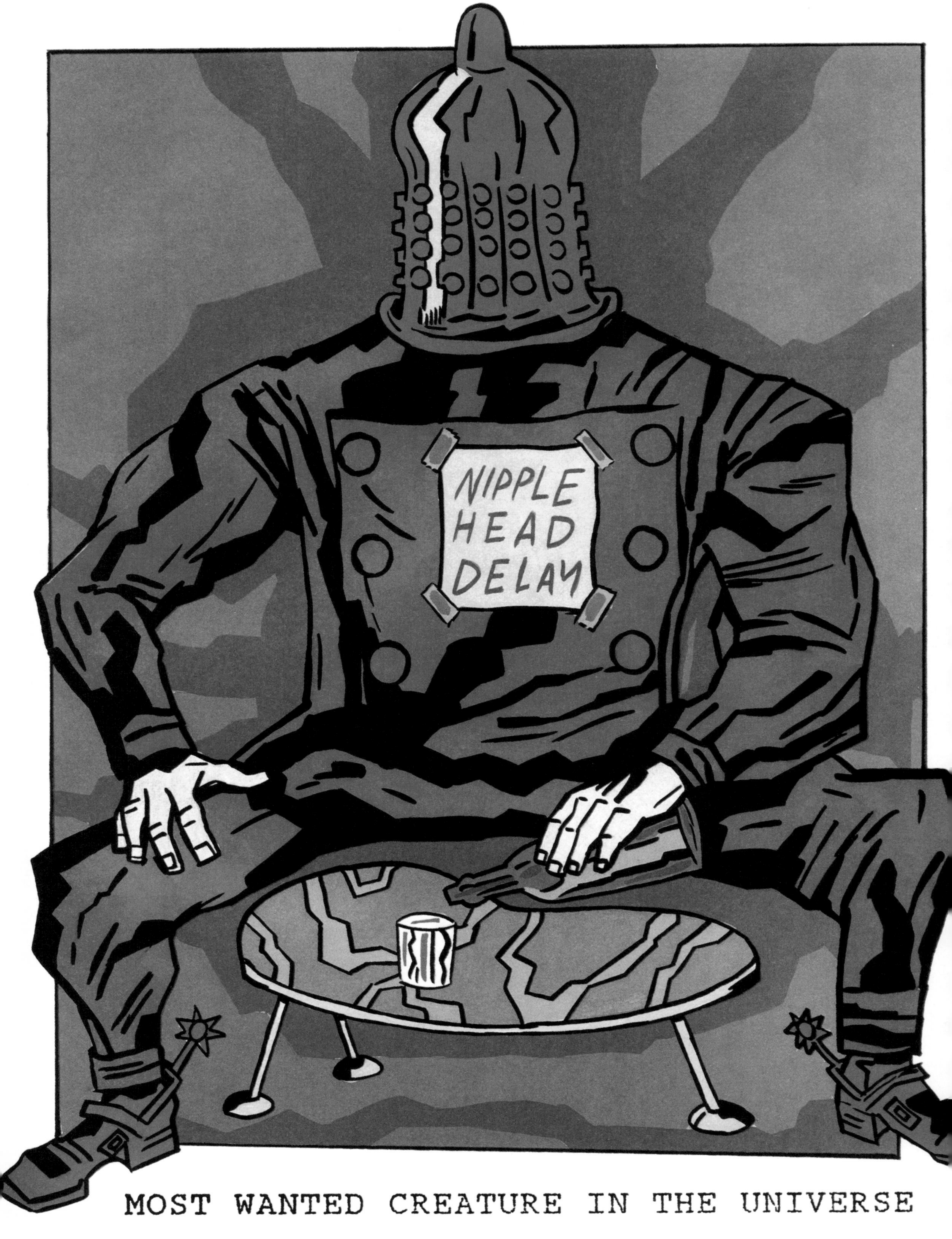
NIPPLE
HEAD
DELAY

MOST WANTED CREATURE IN THE UNIVERSE

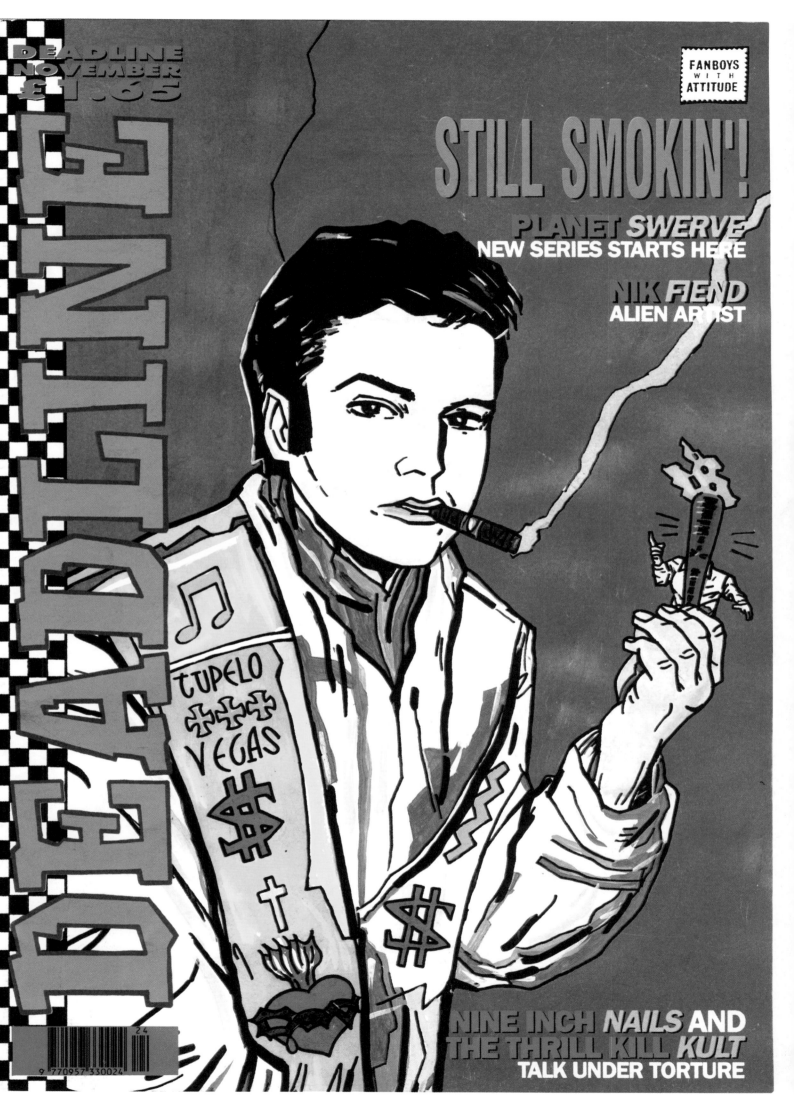

DEADLINE
NOVEMBER
£1.65

FANBOYS
WITH
ATTITUDE

STILL SMOKIN'!

PLANET *SWERVE*
NEW SERIES STARTS HERE

NIK *FIEND*
ALIEN ARTIST

TUPELO ✝✝✝ VEGAS $

NINE INCH *NAILS* AND
THE THRILL KILL *KULT*
TALK UNDER TORTURE

9 770957 330024
24

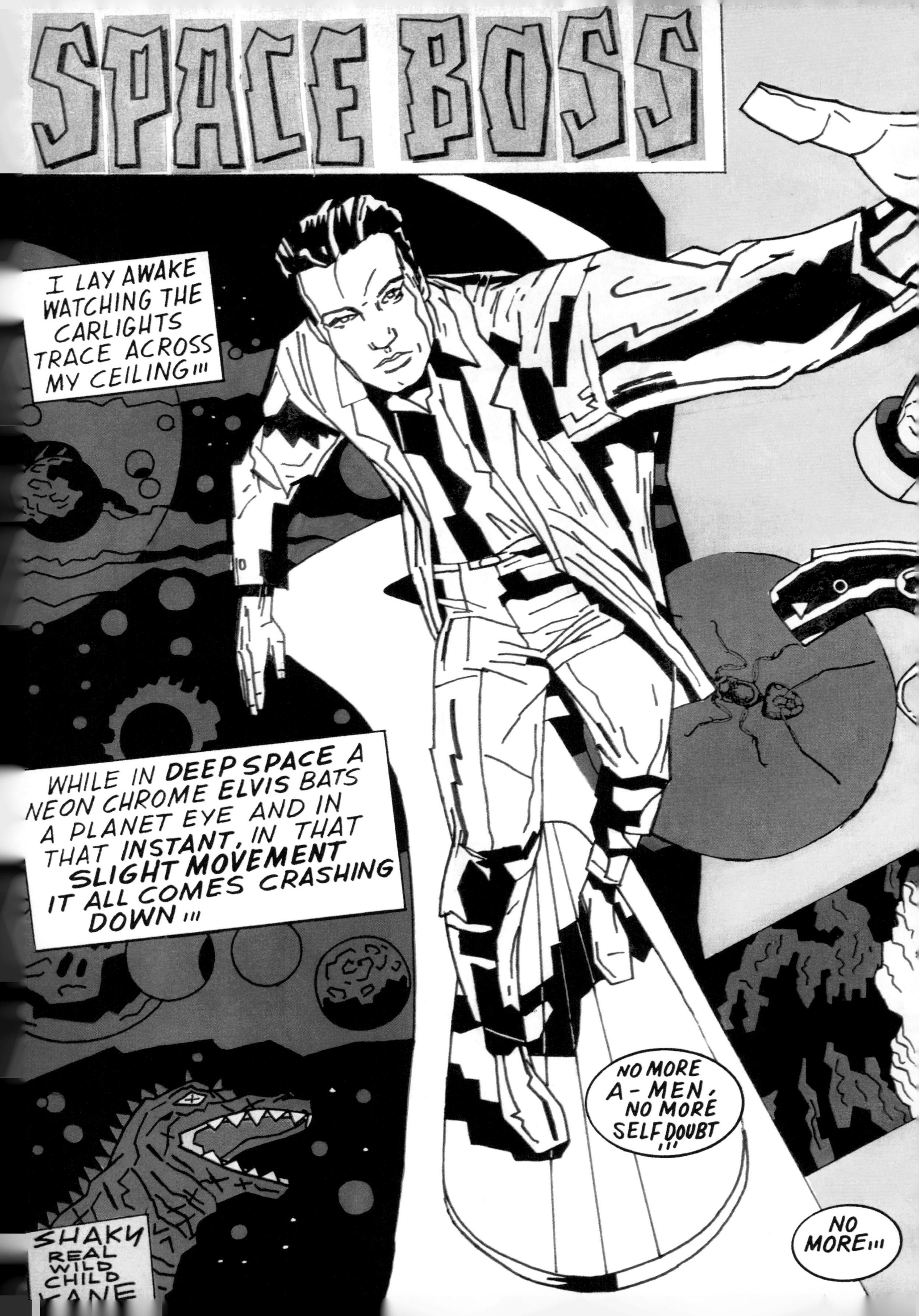
SPACE BOSS
I LAY AWAKE WATCHING THE CARLIGHTS TRACE ACROSS MY CEILING...
WHILE IN DEEP SPACE A NEON CHROME ELVIS BATS A PLANET EYE AND IN THAT INSTANT, IN THAT SLIGHT MOVEMENT IT ALL COMES CRASHING DOWN...
NO MORE A-MEN, NO MORE SELF DOUBT...
NO MORE...
SHAKY REAL WILD CHILD LANE

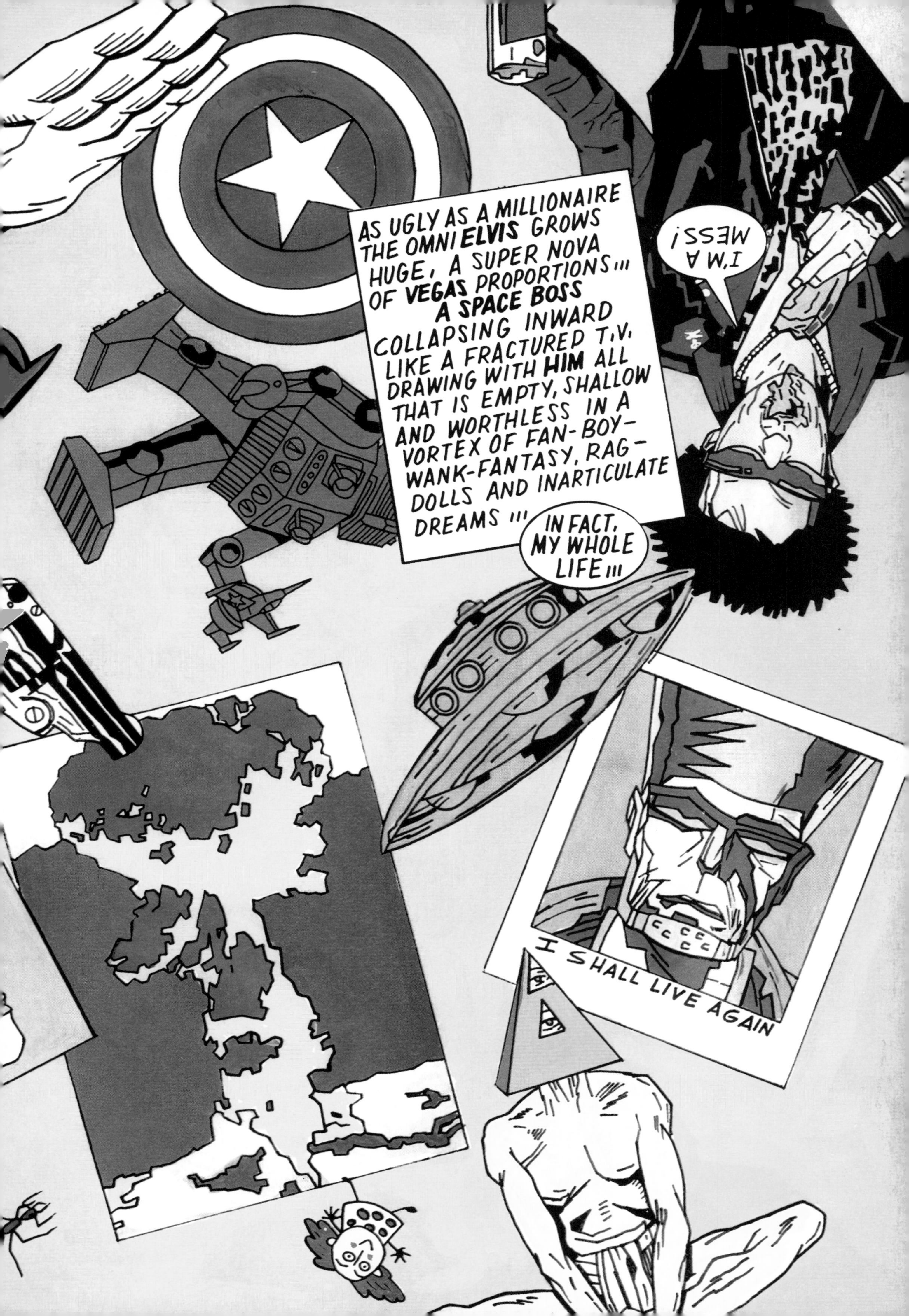
AS UGLY AS A MILLIONAIRE THE OMNI ELVIS GROWS HUGE, A SUPER NOVA OF VEGAS PROPORTIONS... A SPACE BOSS COLLAPSING INWARD LIKE A FRACTURED T.V. DRAWING WITH HIM ALL THAT IS EMPTY, SHALLOW AND WORTHLESS IN A VORTEX OF FAN-BOY-WANK-FANTASY, RAG-DOLLS AND INARTICULATE DREAMS...
I'M A MESS!
IN FACT, MY WHOLE LIFE...
I SHALL LIVE AGAIN

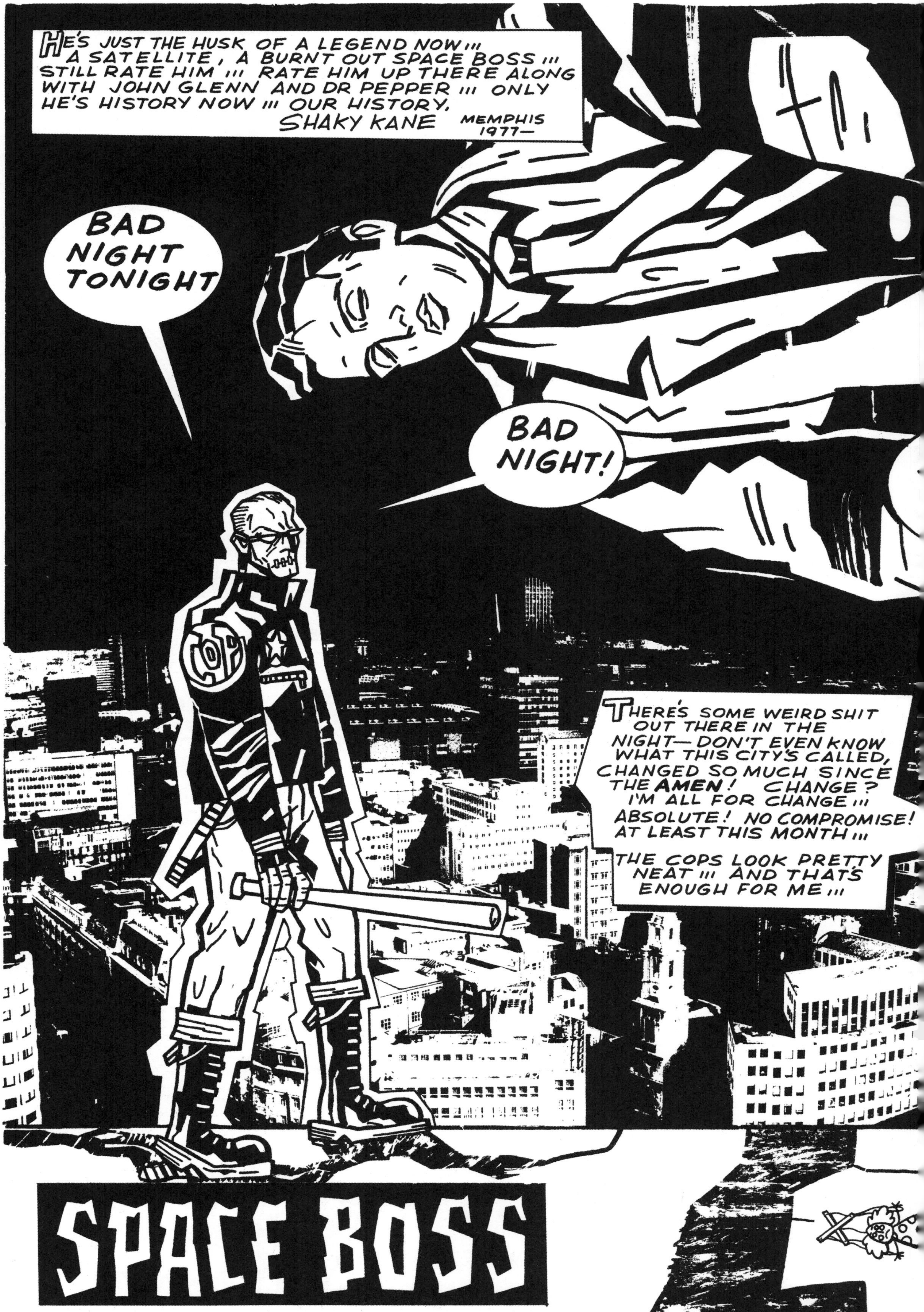
HE'S JUST THE HUSK OF A LEGEND NOW... A SATELLITE, A BURNT OUT SPACE BOSS... STILL RATE HIM... RATE HIM UP THERE ALONG WITH JOHN GLENN AND DR PEPPER... ONLY HE'S HISTORY NOW... OUR HISTORY.
SHAKY KANE MEMPHIS 1977—
BAD NIGHT TONIGHT
BAD NIGHT!
THERE'S SOME WEIRD SHIT OUT THERE IN THE NIGHT— DON'T EVEN KNOW WHAT THIS CITY'S CALLED, CHANGED SO MUCH SINCE THE AMEN! CHANGE? I'M ALL FOR CHANGE... ABSOLUTE! NO COMPROMISE! AT LEAST THIS MONTH...
THE COPS LOOK PRETTY NEAT... AND THAT'S ENOUGH FOR ME...
SPACE BOSS

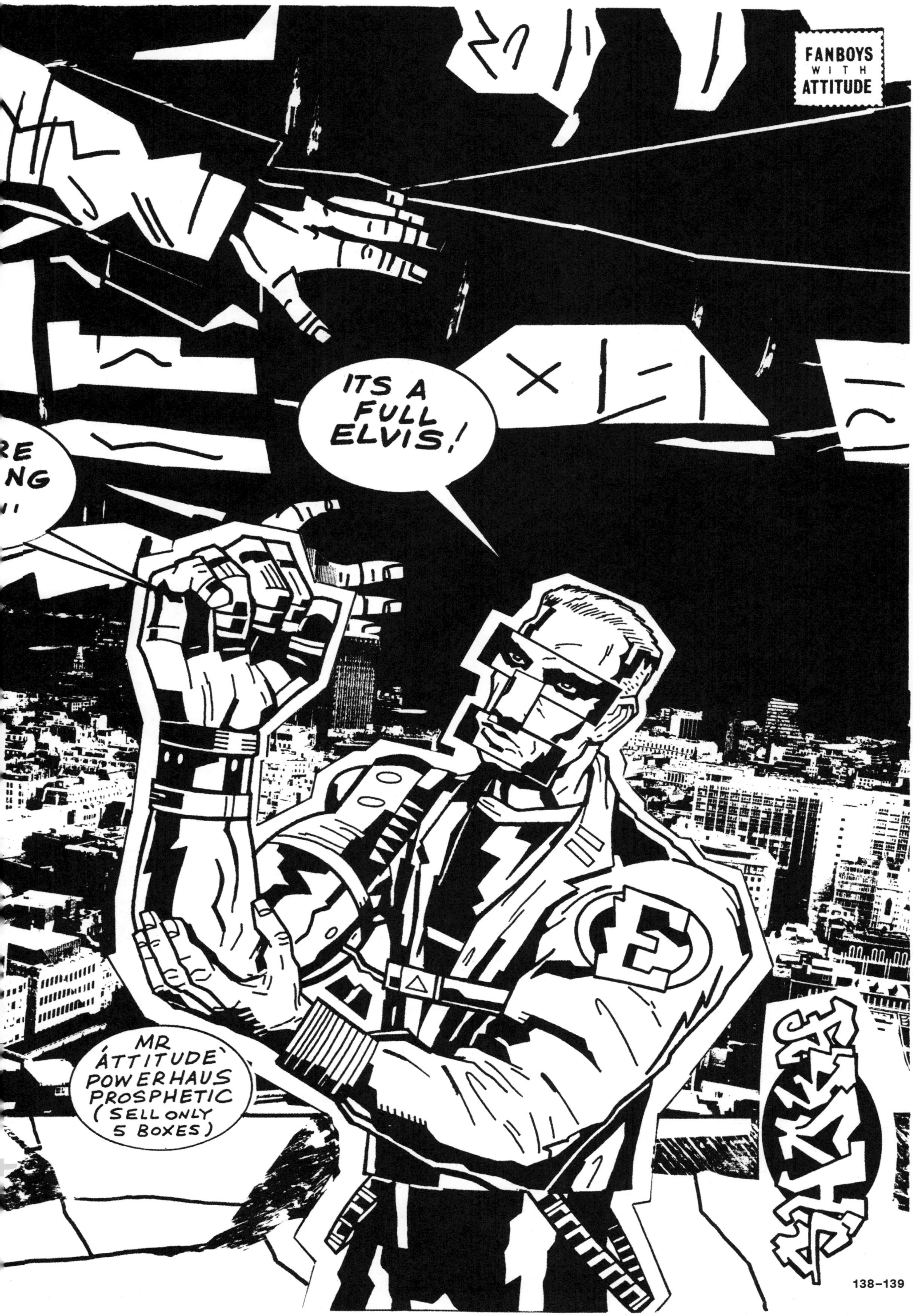
ITS A FULL ELVIS!
MR ÁTTITUDE` POWERHAUS PROSPHETIC (SELL ONLY 5 BOXES)

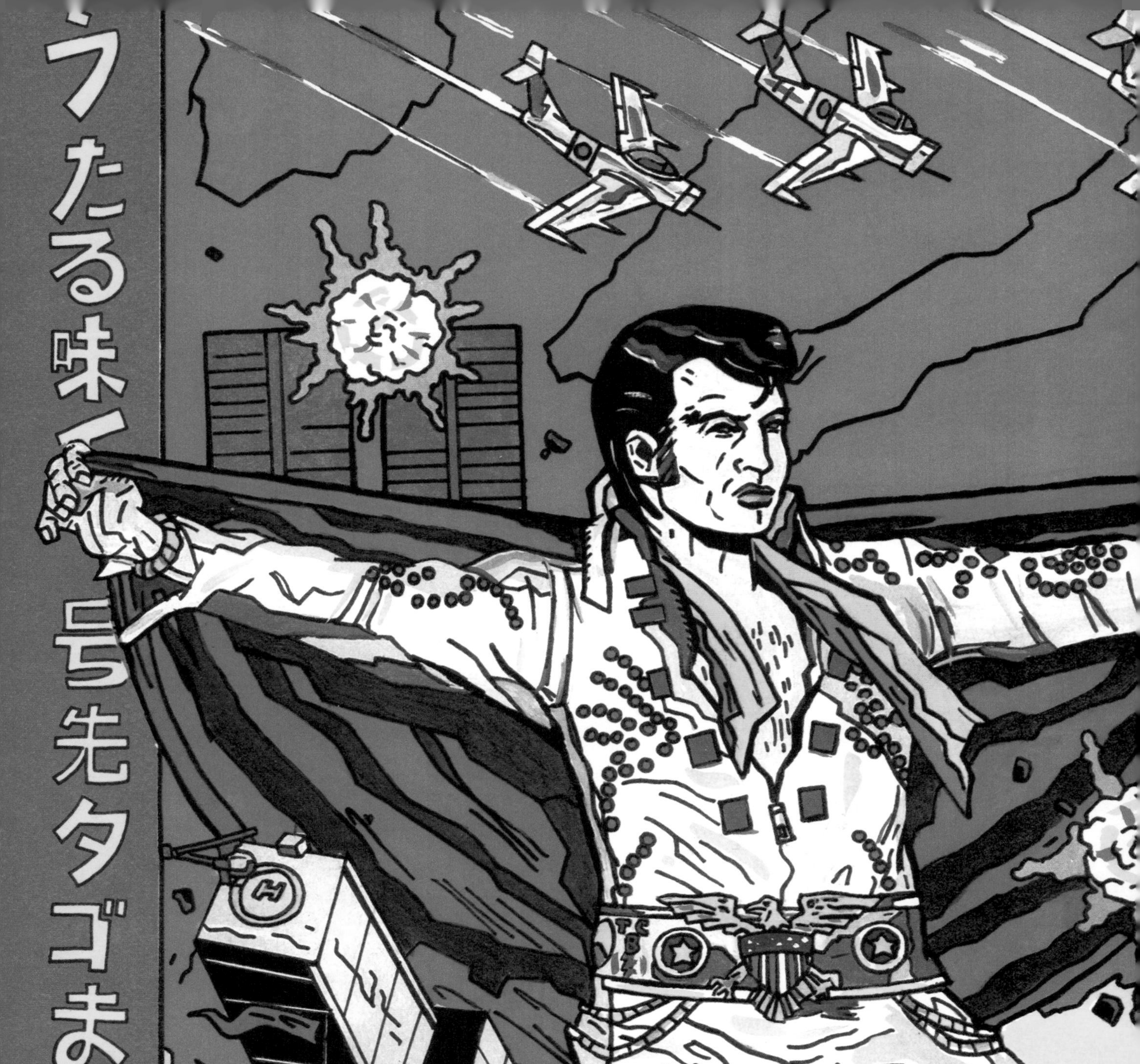

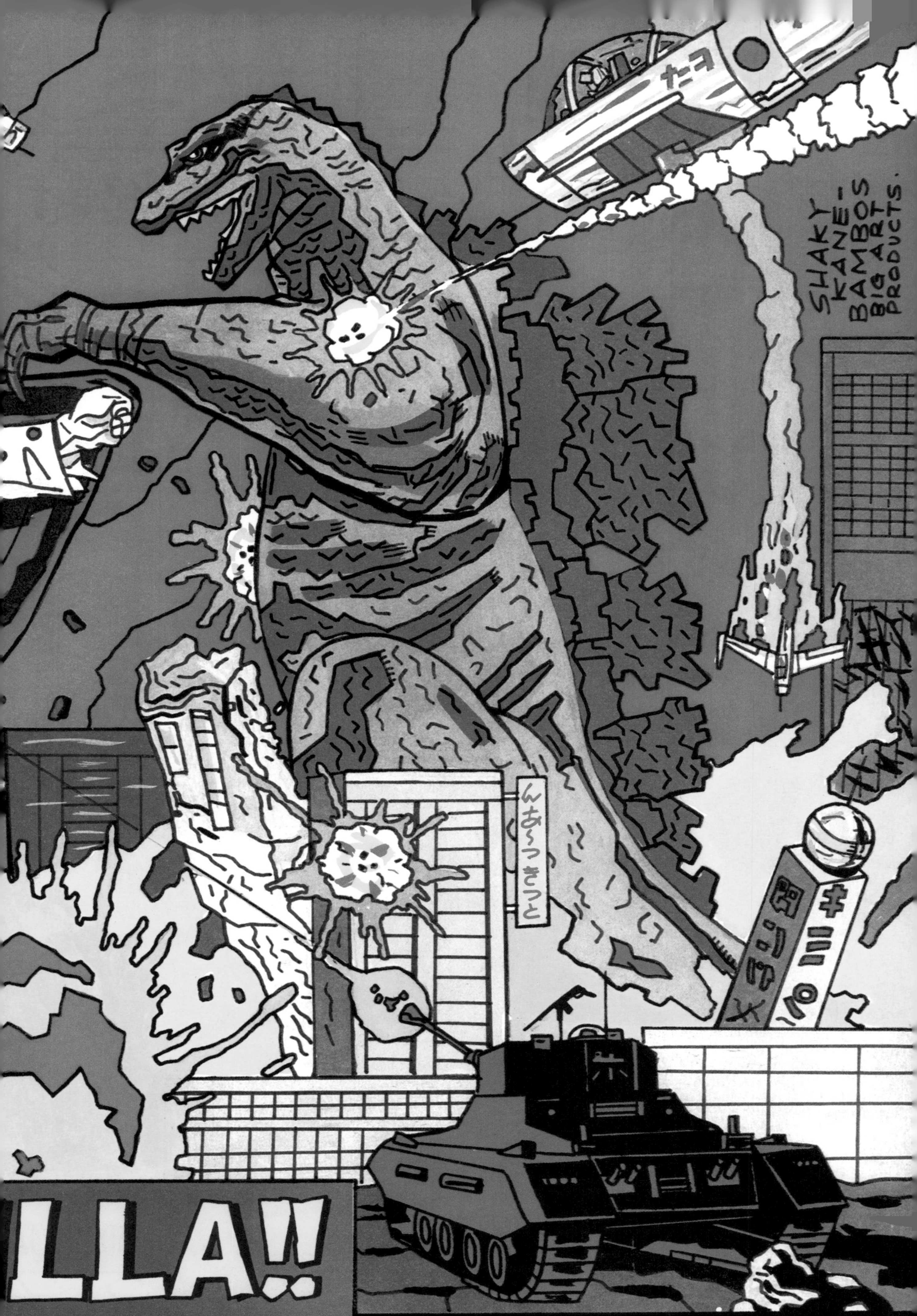
SHAKY KANE-BAMBOS BIG ART PRODUCTS.
LLA!!

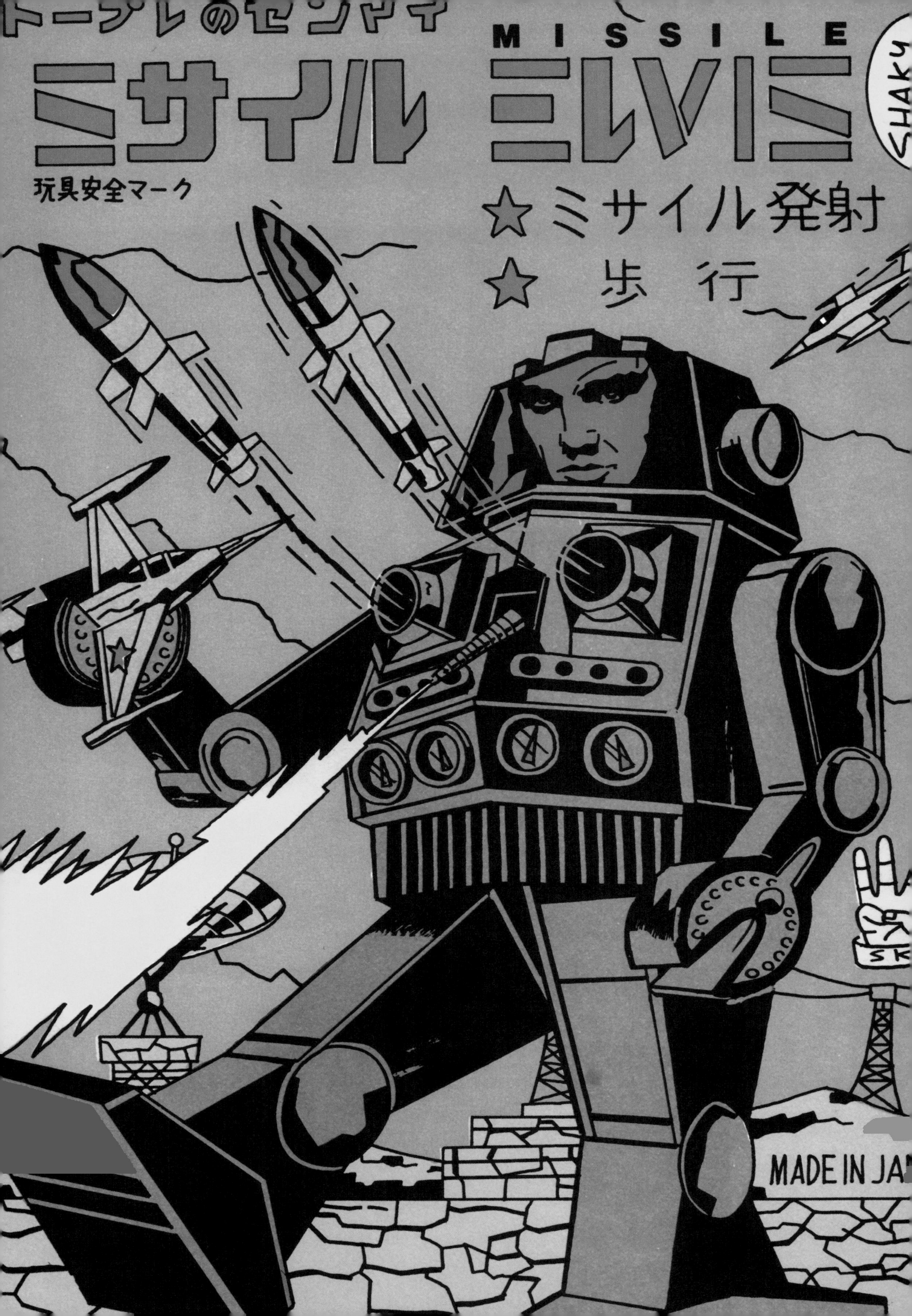
MISSILE
ミサイル
玩具安全マーク
★ミサイル発射
★歩行
SHAKY
MADE IN JA

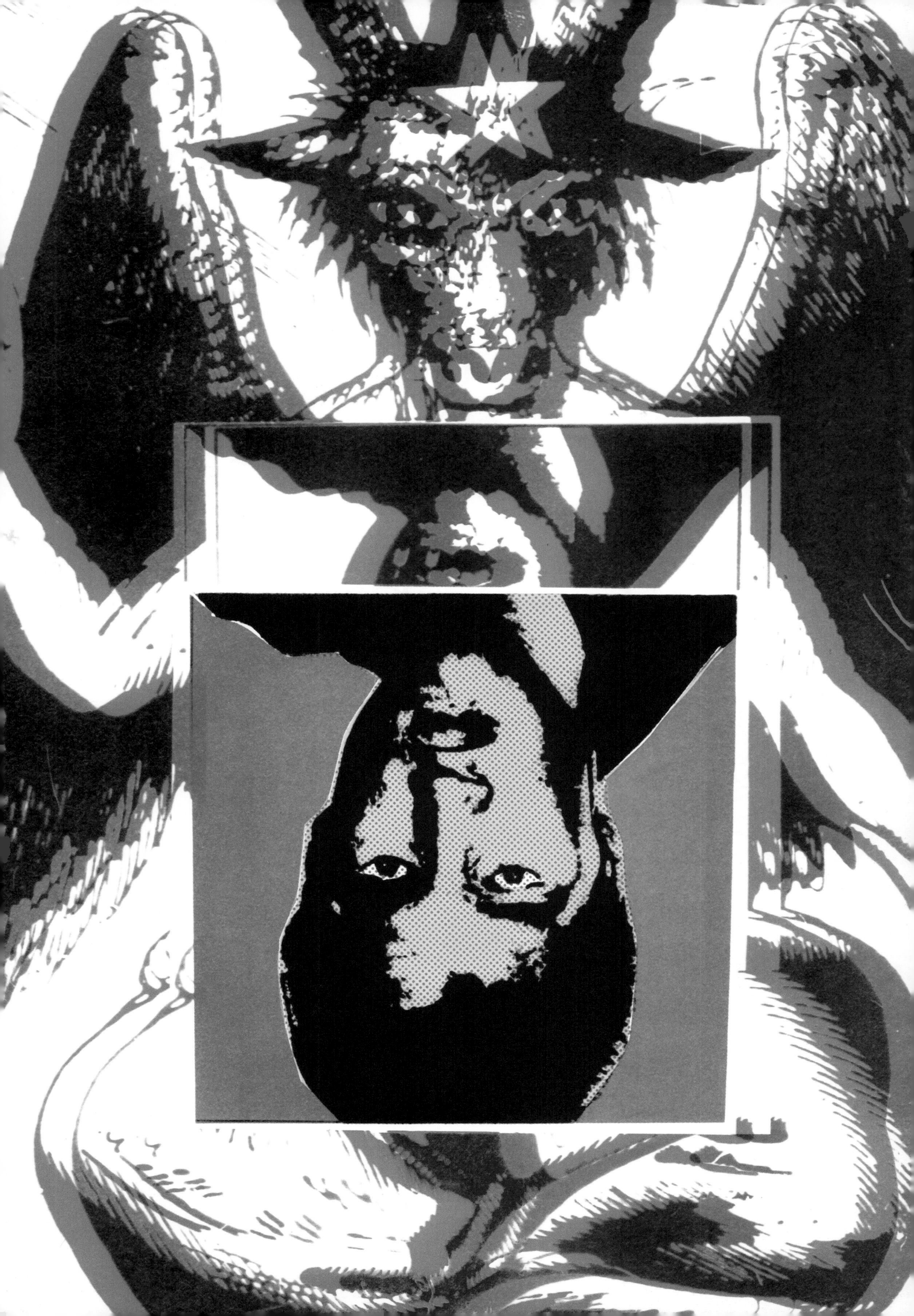

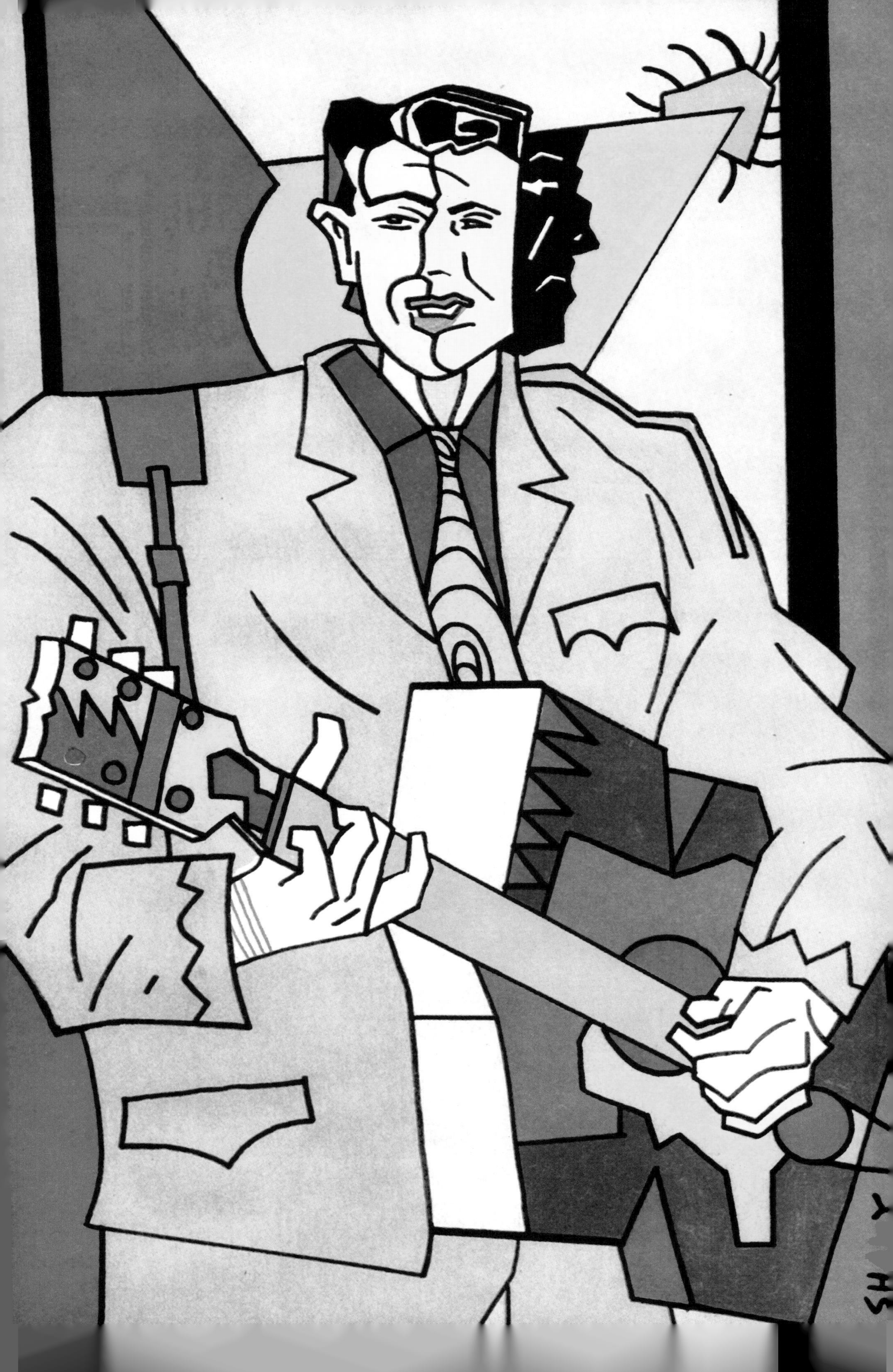

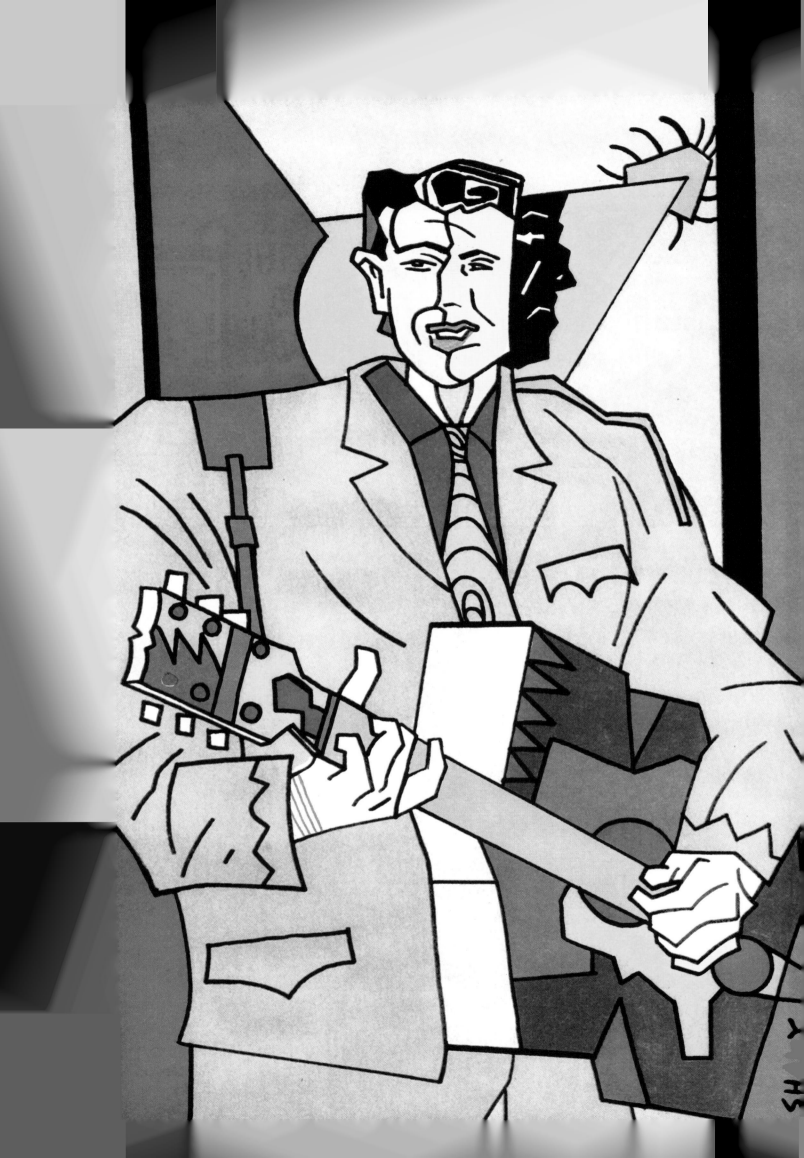

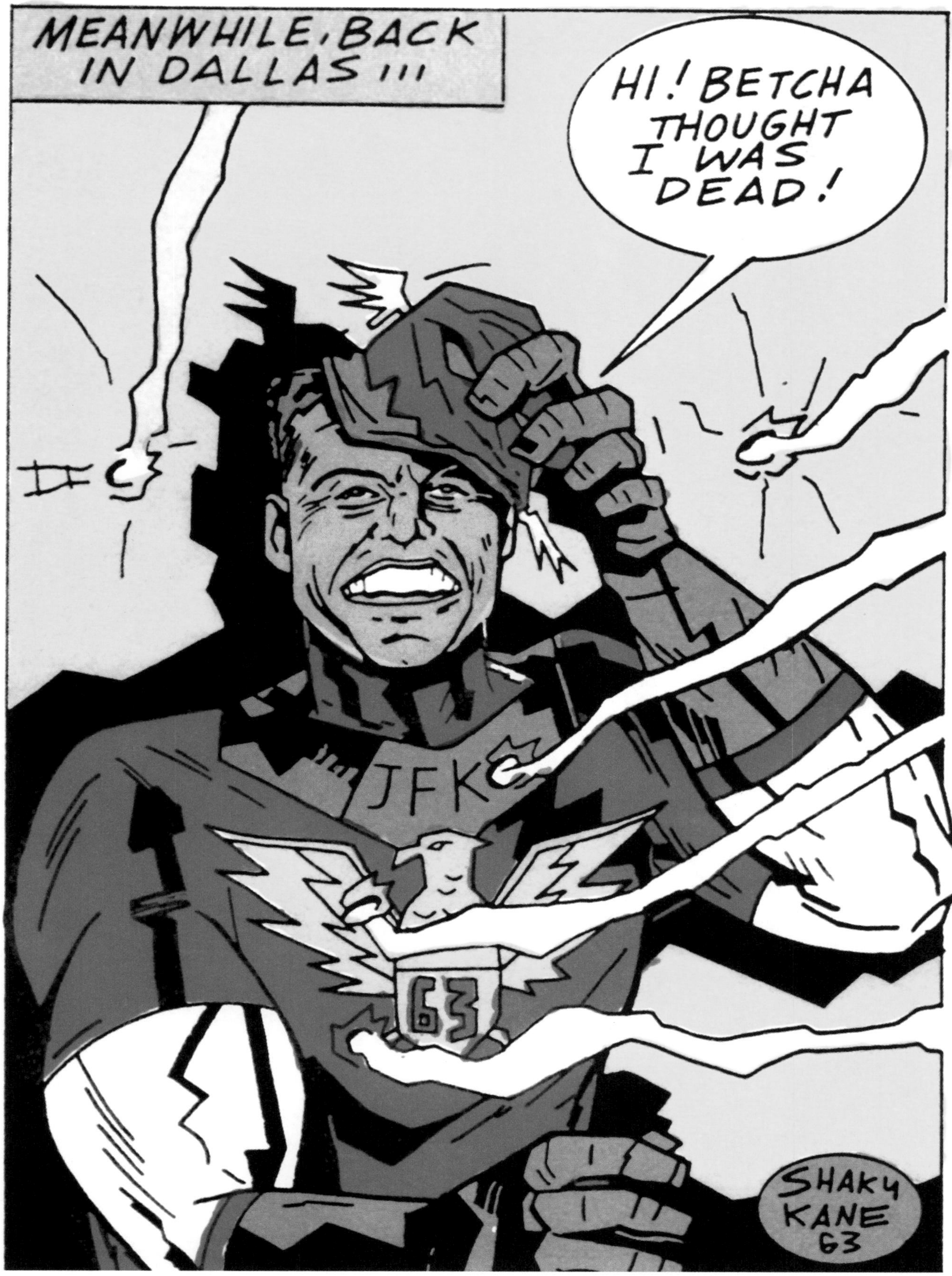
MEANWHILE, BACK IN DALLAS ...
HI! BETCHA THOUGHT I WAS DEAD!
JFK
63
SHAKY KANE 63

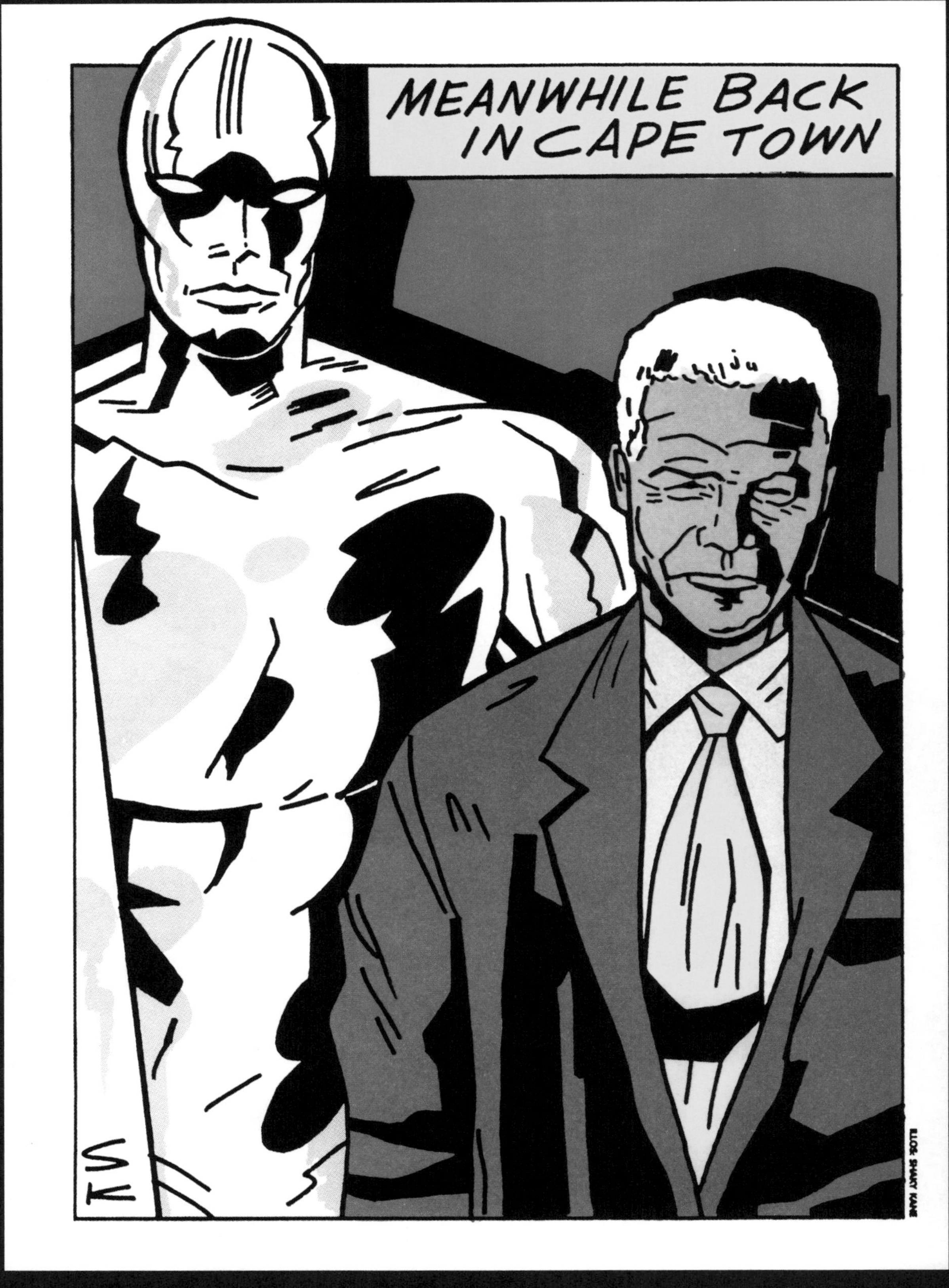
MEANWHILE BACK
IN CAPE TOWN

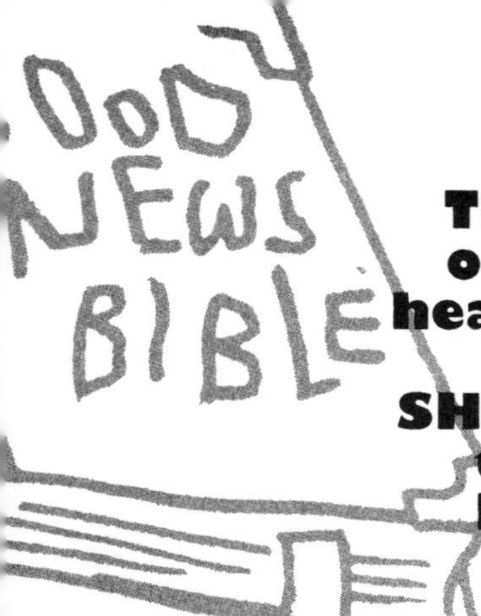
NEWS
BIBLE

**The first of a regular series in which our artists share a few words on the heady world of pop. And who did we ask first, who else but the legendary SHAKY KANE. This recorded interview tells all we need to know about the history of Rock. Read it and weep.**

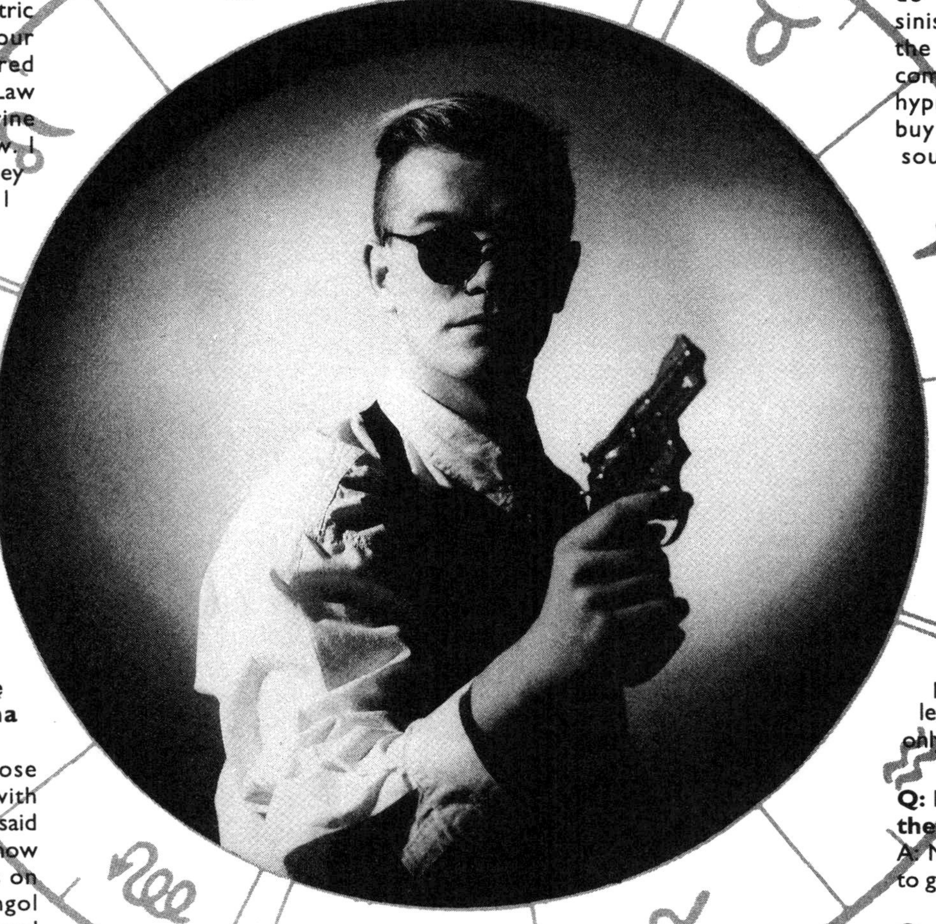

# SHAKY
## PLAYS POP

**"I'm the Godfather of all Western religion, I'm the Crucifix Kid, I'm the night porter with terminal acne, I'm the tattooed snakeshot Madonna and I know what I'm talking about..."**

**'ere YOU ever in a band?**
as in a band in my head for over years playing electric sky guitar underbolt pyrotechnic electric Fifteen foot of pure glamour an effected lisp and mirrored :t lenses. We were called Law ted or maybe the Submarine s - I can't remember now. I see the other guys now. They n and out of television - I you'd call them static - like s of shadowmen. My t never phones me back.

**it true that you're Godfather of the revival?**
es, just like I'm the ther of all Western n. I'm the Crucifix Kid, ne night porter with nal acne, I'm the ed snakeshot madonna know what I'm talking , cos I read a lot of ines.

**Do you know the rence between Nirvana Guns and Roses?**
course I do. I saw Axl Rose ing on "Beat My Spleen" with Van Warcry back in 1957. I said guy's got something" and now at him. Thirty three years on ne's headlining the Mongol ut, two miles out of Lesbograd Nirvana humping the gear. He's ivor, like me.

**Who's going to be big in '92?**
an't tell you, I don't want to ruin . Anyway it doesn't do you any to see these things. I tried it and it's scary shit you're ng with. I can only say this - Russel Grant's got a lot of ning to do.

**Do you see an increase in nic backmasking in '92?**
u don't fool me with this one r. Look what happened to Mr. otlk. Mess with this one and you set off a chain reaction that will Black Elvis Day look like an ion handgun.

**Whatever happened to Goth?**
went the same way as all other for living. It moved out to the and got the shit kicked out of it e great British inebriate, our nal institution.

**Q: What do you think of World Music?**
A: Never heard of it. Is it anything to do with Peter Gabriel. It sounds sinister to me like flying saucers in the hollow Arctic or something, coming out drifting into the air and hypnotising people so they go and buy crappy CD's. Don't like the sound of it - World Music, eh?

**Q: Where does Dannii fit into all this?**
A: She's an inspirational figure and she is the promise of sex that has the ability to change lives. She's cosmetic reality, the backing track to the advert that sells us our sanity again and again. I don't know how you could ask me this question, Dannii is a fact.

**Q: When did you last stage-dive?**
A: I never have but I once touched Sparks' Russel Mael's plastic sandal and on a molecular level I became the 1970's, but sadly only briefly.

**Q: Is there too much suffering in the world?**
A: No, there's just the right amount to go around.

**Q: Who are your musical influences?**
A: Everyone - I never shut down for the night. I'm the dreamer who's reached the end of dreams, the man from Maybe. Like Adam Ant said back in 1957, "Lock up your brain I'm here again. I'm never bored, I'll steal your chords as long as it seems like a good idea at the time."

**Q: Where were you the day Elvis died?**
A: I was on the bus writing next week's Deadline script on the inside sleeve of a Park Drive packet. I remember it clearly now..A girl my age went off her head and hit some tiny children. A cop knelt and kissed the feet of a priest and Freddie Mercury crossed himself and turned tearfully to gaze at his reflection in the now darkened window. I think he wrote something in the condensation - a date or something. I never found out. I'd reached my stop and made my way off the bus and into the now deserted street. ■

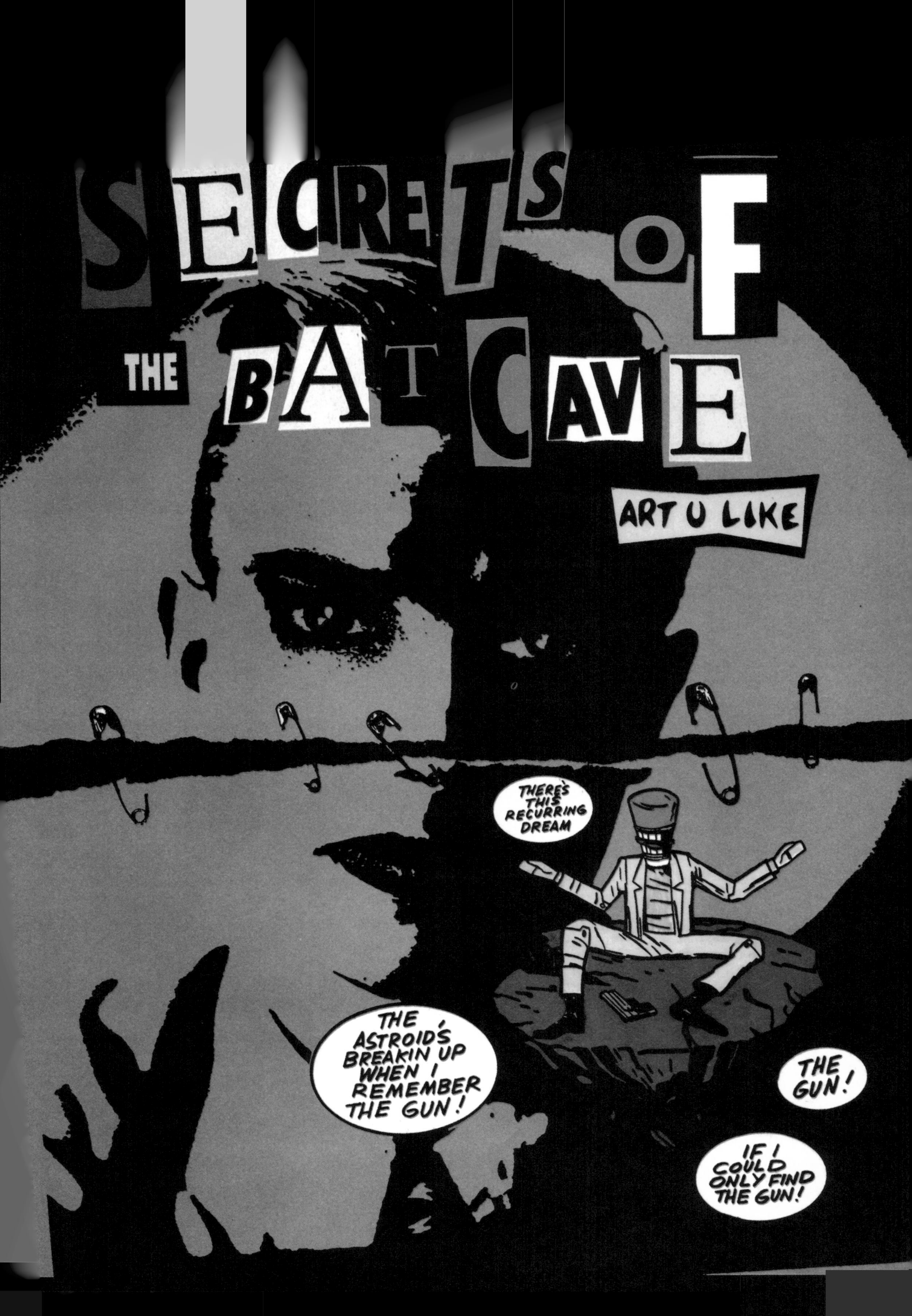
SECRETS OF THE BAT CAVE
ART U LIKE
THERE'S THIS RECURRING DREAM
THE ASTROID'S BREAKIN UP WHEN I REMEMBER THE GUN!
THE GUN!
IF I COULD ONLY FIND THE GUN!

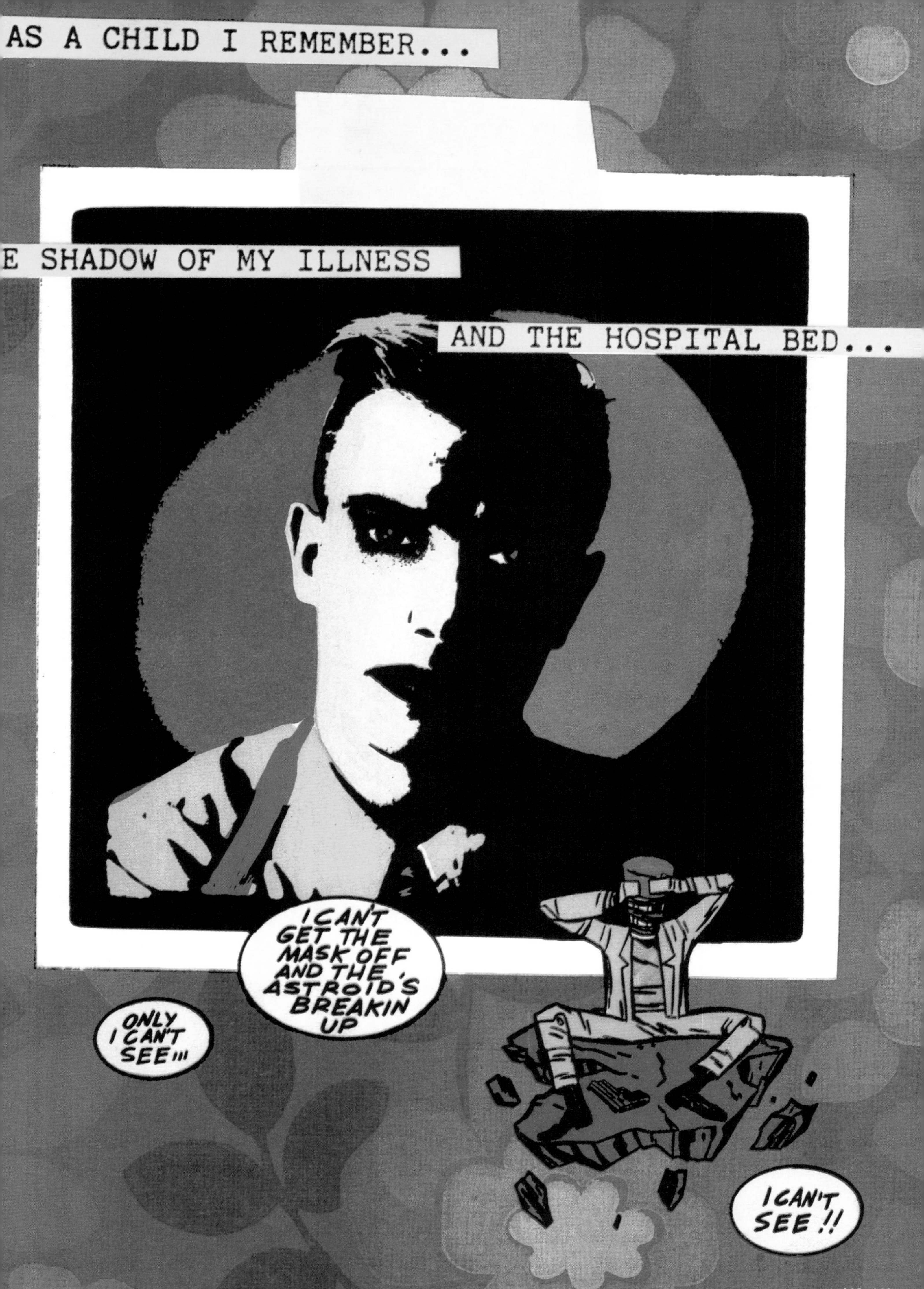
AS A CHILD I REMEMBER...
E SHADOW OF MY ILLNESS
AND THE HOSPITAL BED...
I CAN'T GET THE MASK OFF AND THE ASTROID'S BREAKIN UP
ONLY I CAN'T SEE!!!
I CAN'T SEE!!

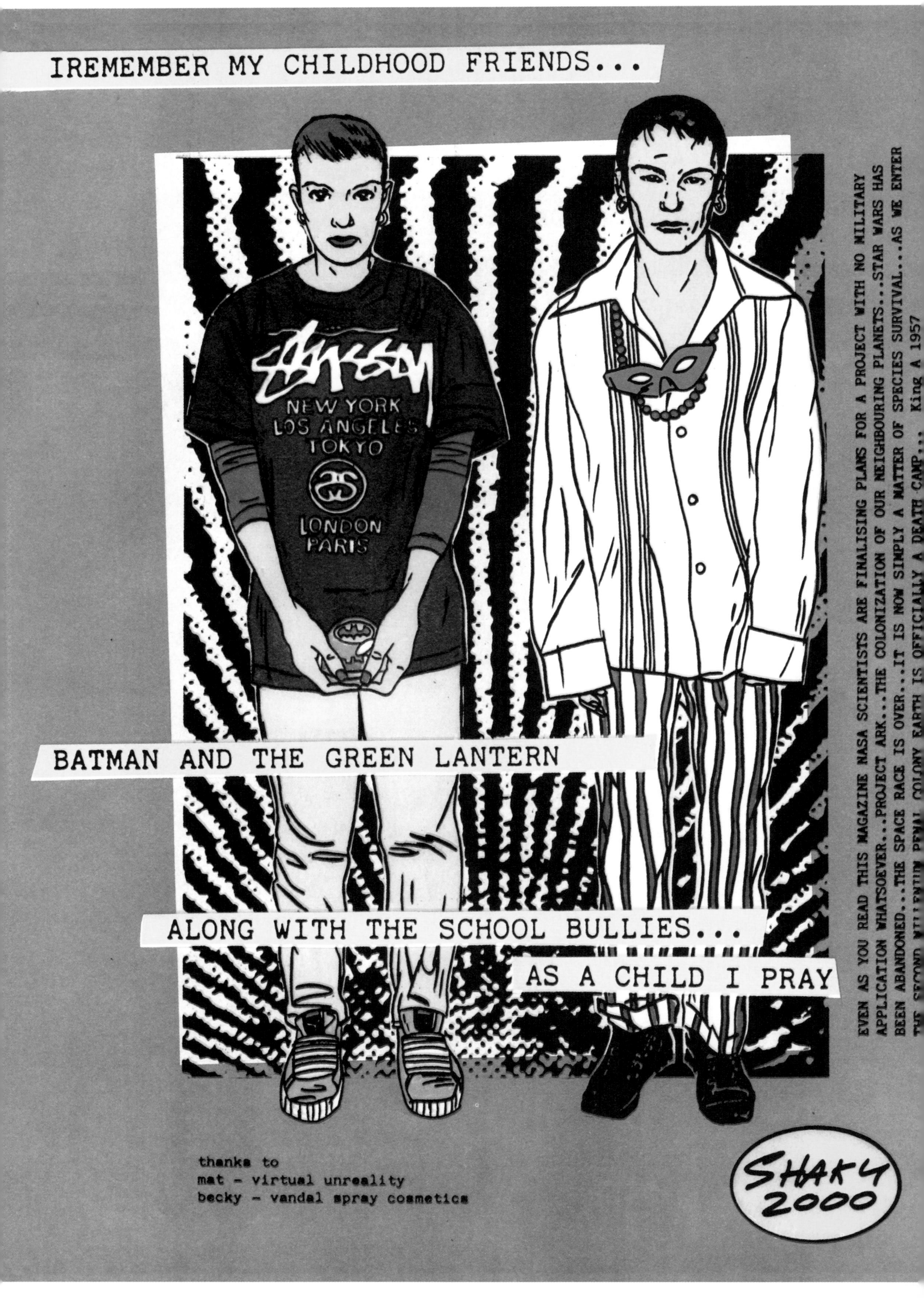
IREMEMBER MY CHILDHOOD FRIENDS...
BATMAN AND THE GREEN LANTERN
ALONG WITH THE SCHOOL BULLIES...
AS A CHILD I PRAY

EVEN AS YOU READ THIS MAGAZINE NASA SCIENTISTS ARE FINALISING PLANS FOR A PROJECT WITH NO MILITARY APPLICATION WHATSOEVER...PROJECT ARK...THE COLONIZATION OF OUR NEIGHBOURING PLANETS...STAR WARS HAS BEEN ABANDONED...THE SPACE RACE IS OVER...IT IS NOW SIMPLY A MATTER OF SPECIES SURVIVAL...AS WE ENTER THE SECOND MILLENNIUM PENAL COLONY EARTH IS OFFICIALLY A DEATH CAMP... King A 1957

thanks to
mat - virtual unreality
becky - vandal spray cosmetics

SHAKY 2000

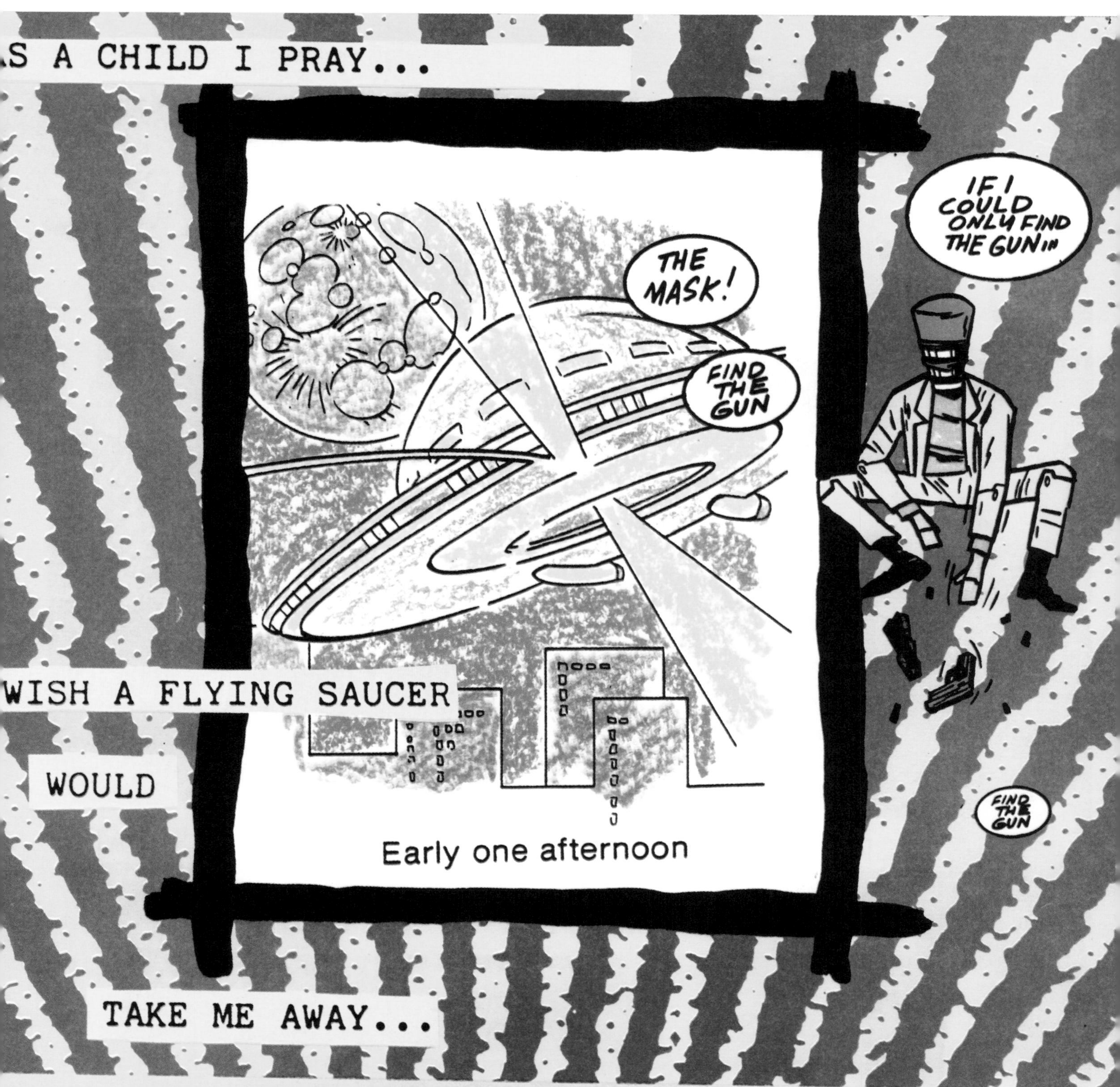
S A CHILD I PRAY...
THE MASK!
FIND THE GUN
IF I COULD ONLY FIND THE GUN...
WISH A FLYING SAUCER
WOULD
FIND THE GUN
Early one afternoon
TAKE ME AWAY...

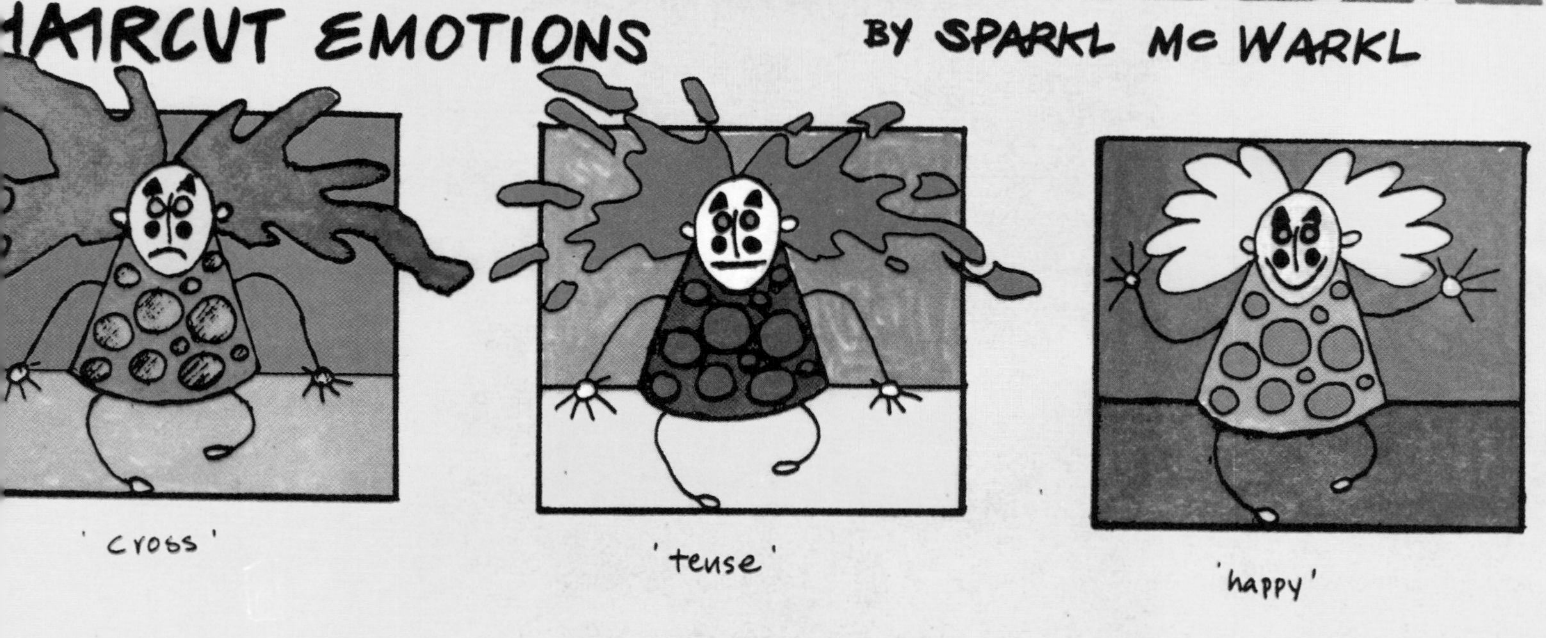
HAIRCUT EMOTIONS
BY SPARKL MC WARKL
'cross'
'tense'
'happy'

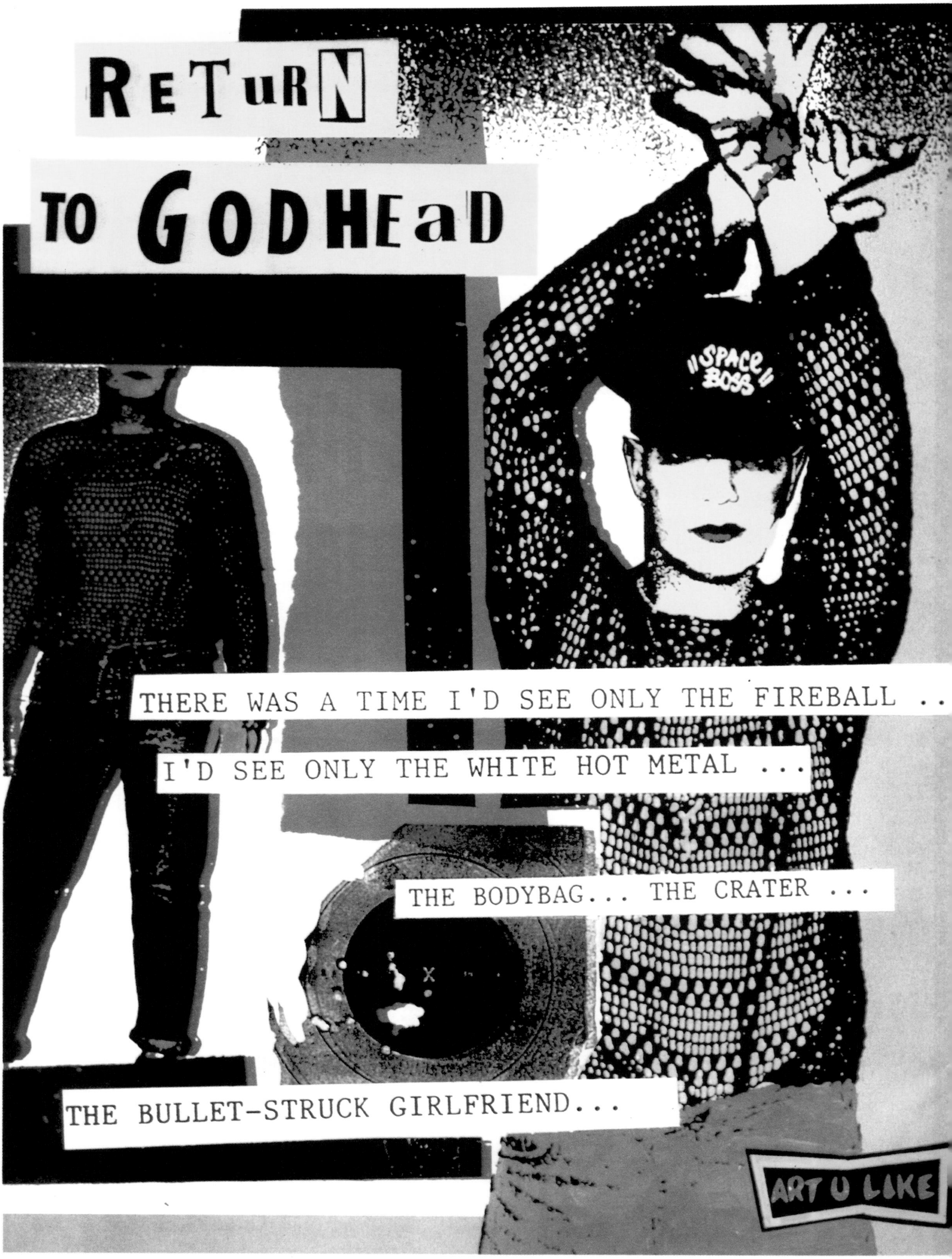
RETURN
TO GODHEAD
"SPACE" BOSS
THERE WAS A TIME I'D SEE ONLY THE FIREBALL ..
I'D SEE ONLY THE WHITE HOT METAL ...
THE BODYBAG... THE CRATER ...
THE BULLET-STRUCK GIRLFRIEND...
ART U LIKE

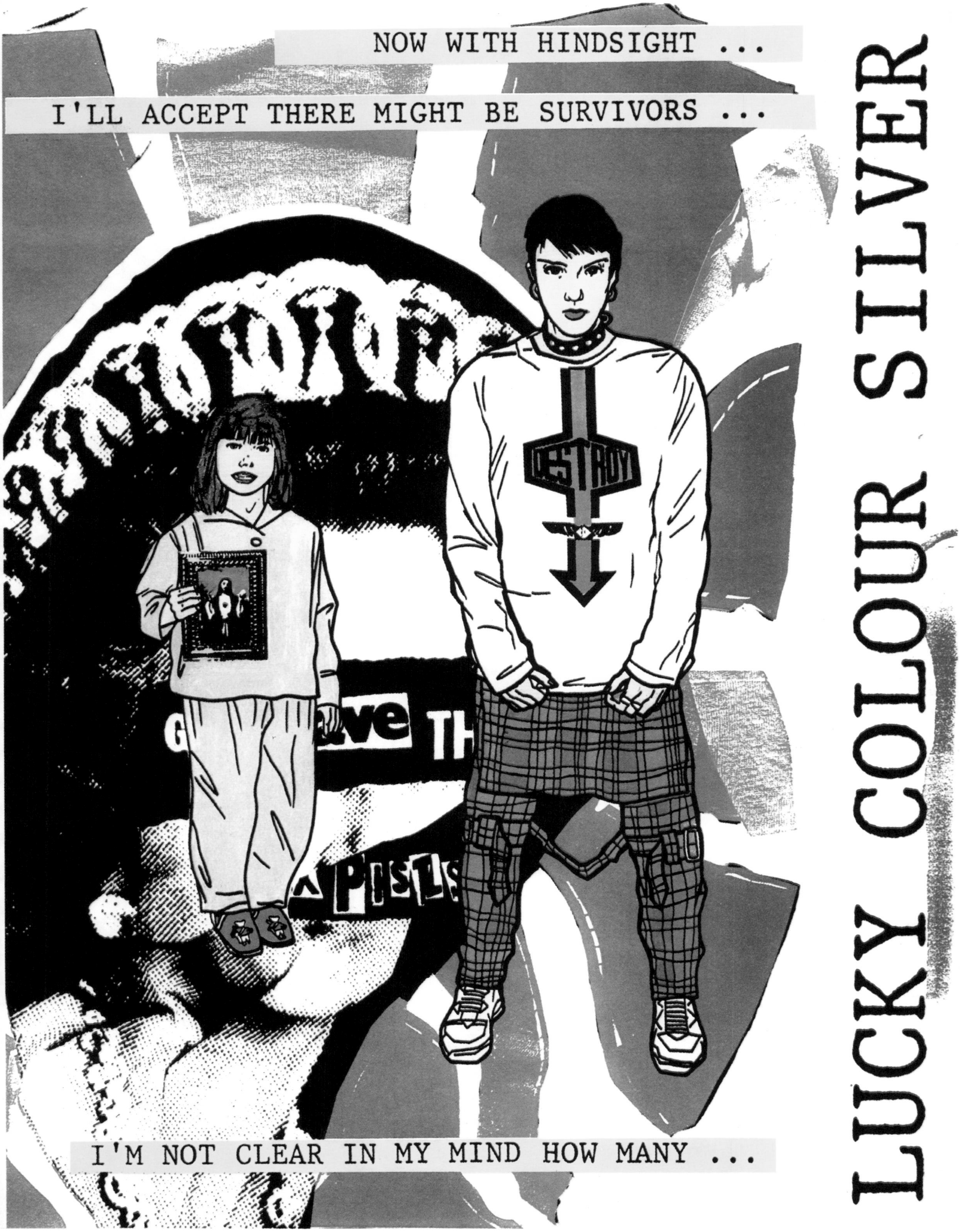
NOW WITH HINDSIGHT ...
I'LL ACCEPT THERE MIGHT BE SURVIVORS ...
DESTROY
ave TH
PISTLS
I'M NOT CLEAR IN MY MIND HOW MANY ...
LUCKY COLOUR SILVER

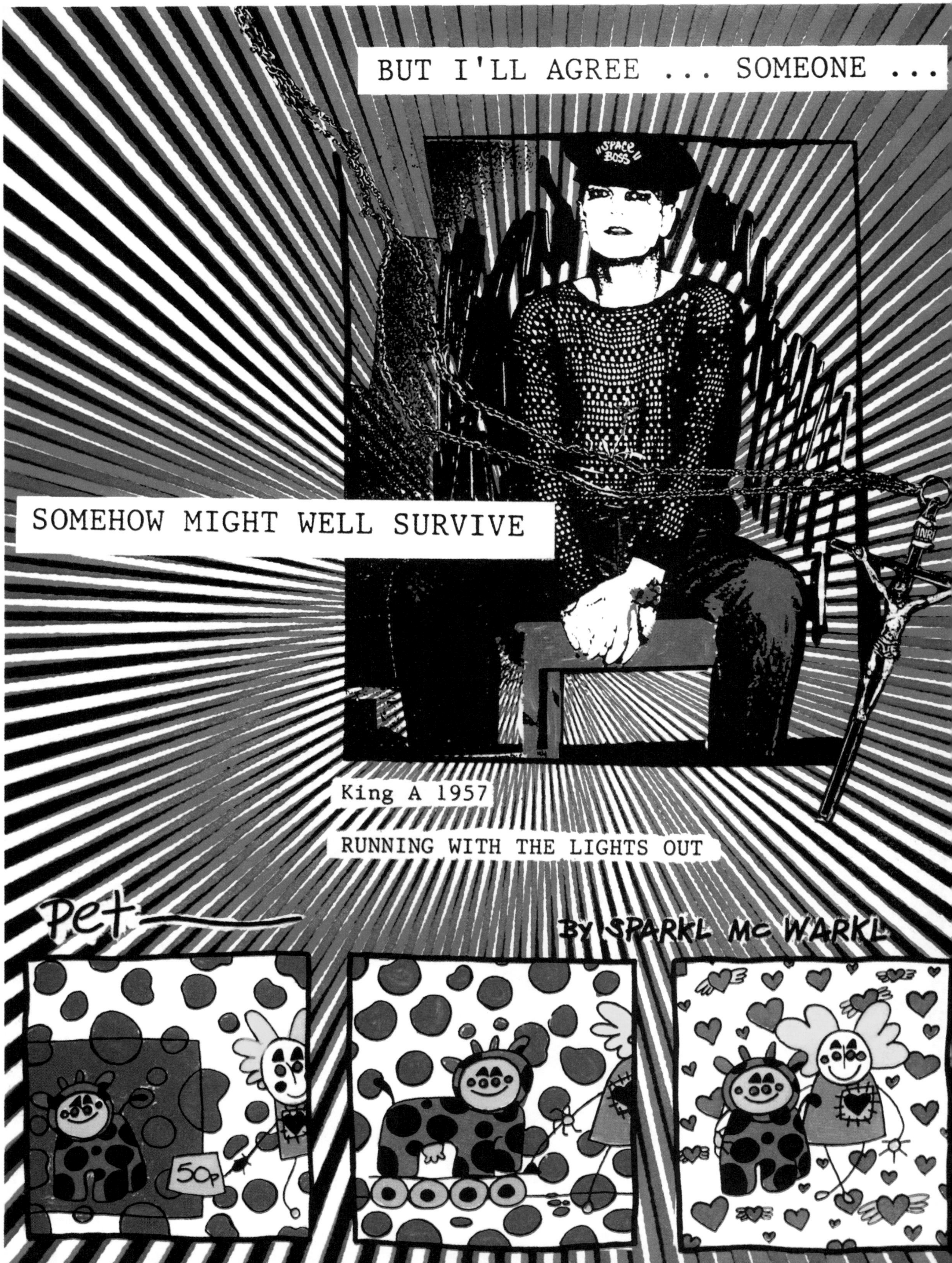
BUT I'LL AGREE ... SOMEONE ...
SOMEHOW MIGHT WELL SURVIVE
King A 1957
RUNNING WITH THE LIGHTS OUT
SPACE BOSS
INRI
Pet
BY SPARKL Mc WARKL
50p

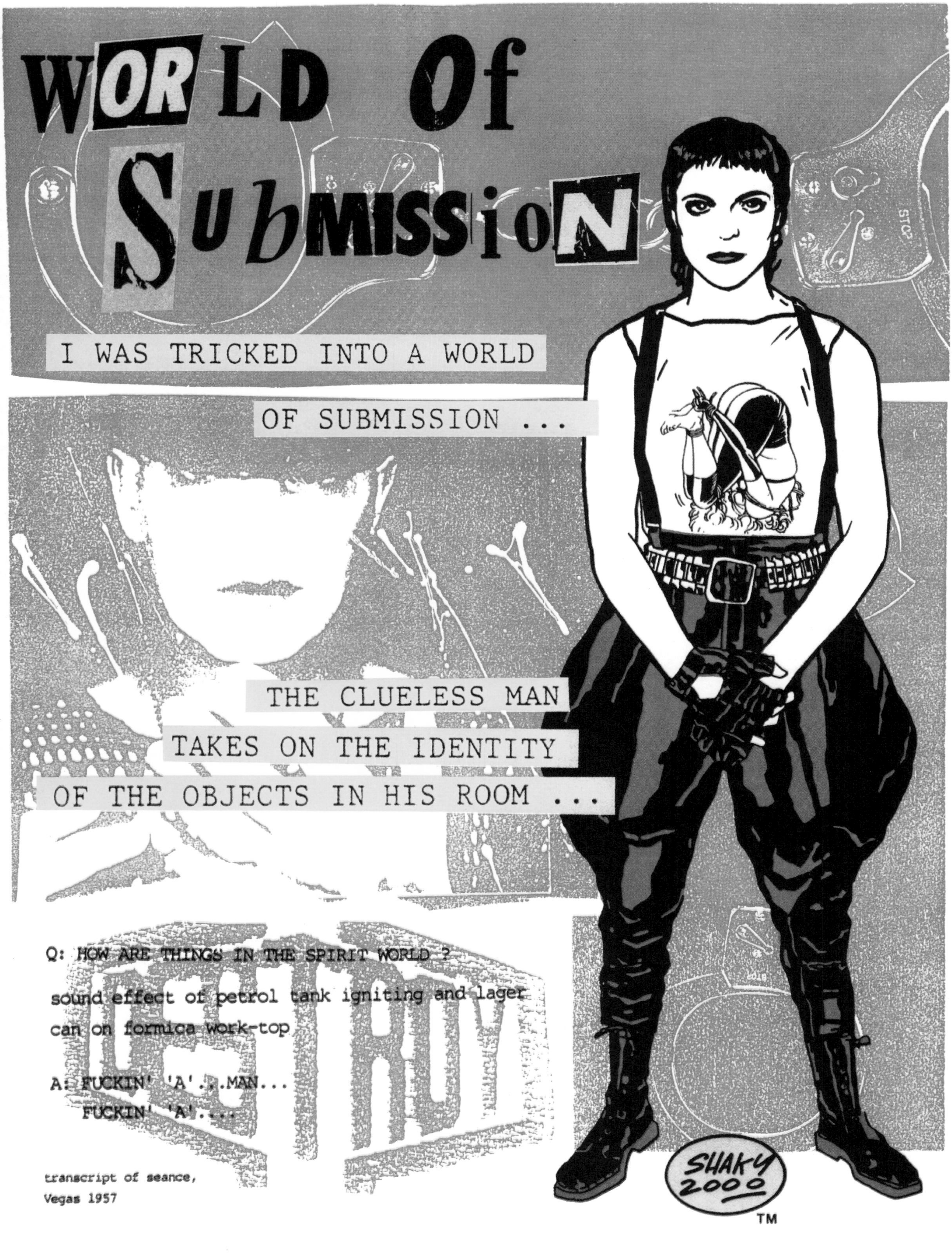
WORLD OF SUBMISSION
I WAS TRICKED INTO A WORLD
OF SUBMISSION ...
THE CLUELESS MAN
TAKES ON THE IDENTITY
OF THE OBJECTS IN HIS ROOM ...
Q: HOW ARE THINGS IN THE SPIRIT WORLD ?
sound effect of petrol tank igniting and lager
can on formica work-top
A: FUCKIN' 'A'...MAN...
FUCKIN' 'A'...
transcript of seance,
Vegas 1957
SHAKY 2000
TM

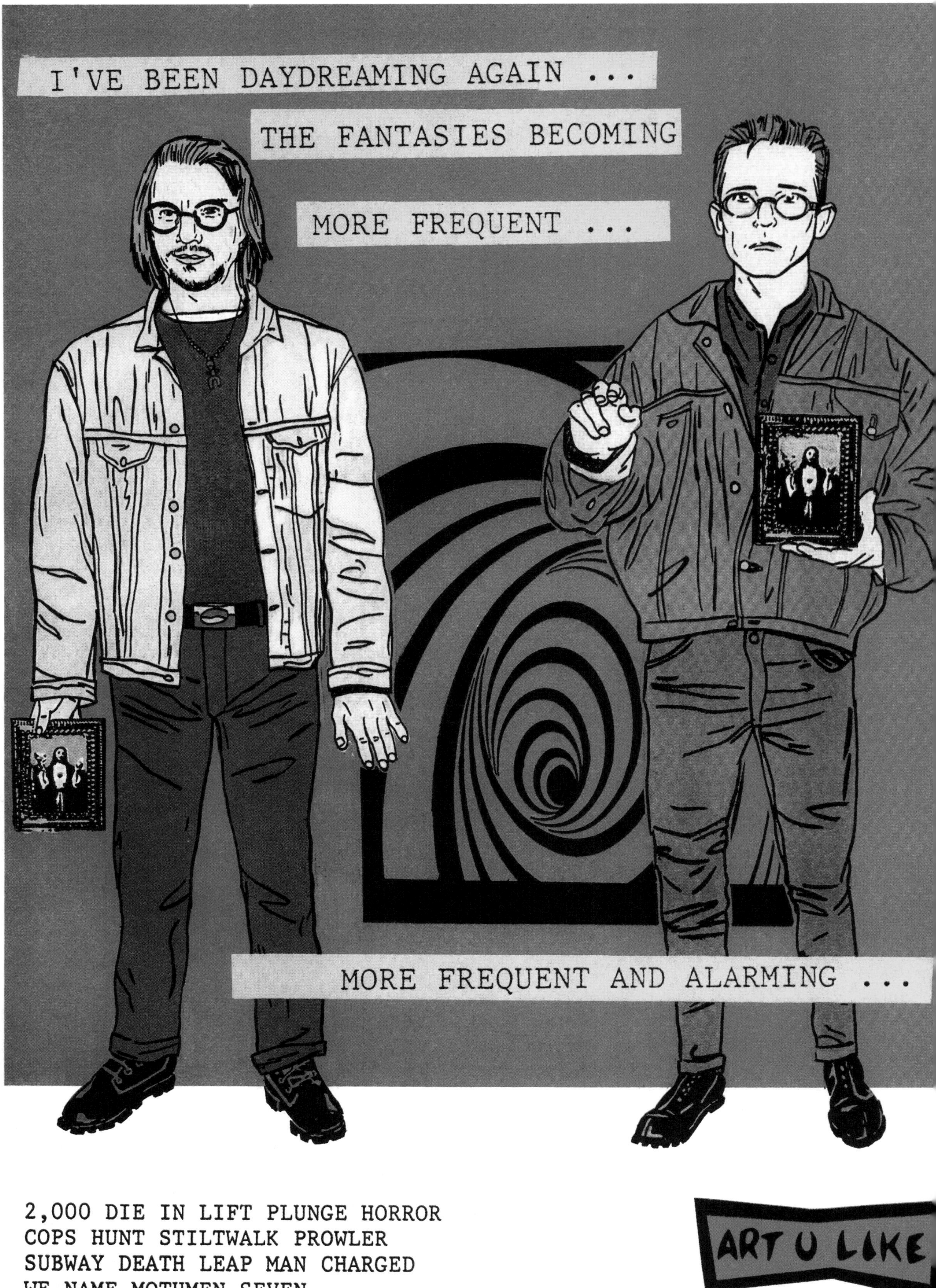
I'VE BEEN DAYDREAMING AGAIN ...
THE FANTASIES BECOMING
MORE FREQUENT ...
MORE FREQUENT AND ALARMING ...

2,000 DIE IN LIFT PLUNGE HORROR
COPS HUNT STILTWALK PROWLER
SUBWAY DEATH LEAP MAN CHARGED
WE NAME MOTHMEN SEVEN

ART U LIKE

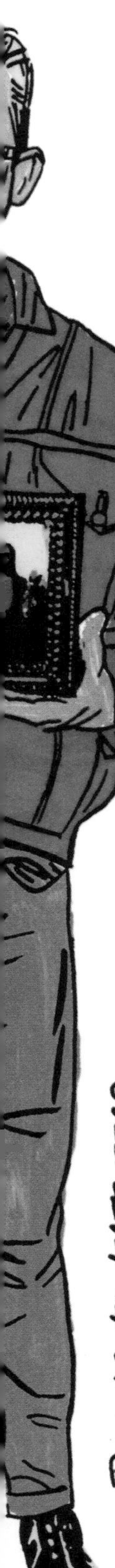

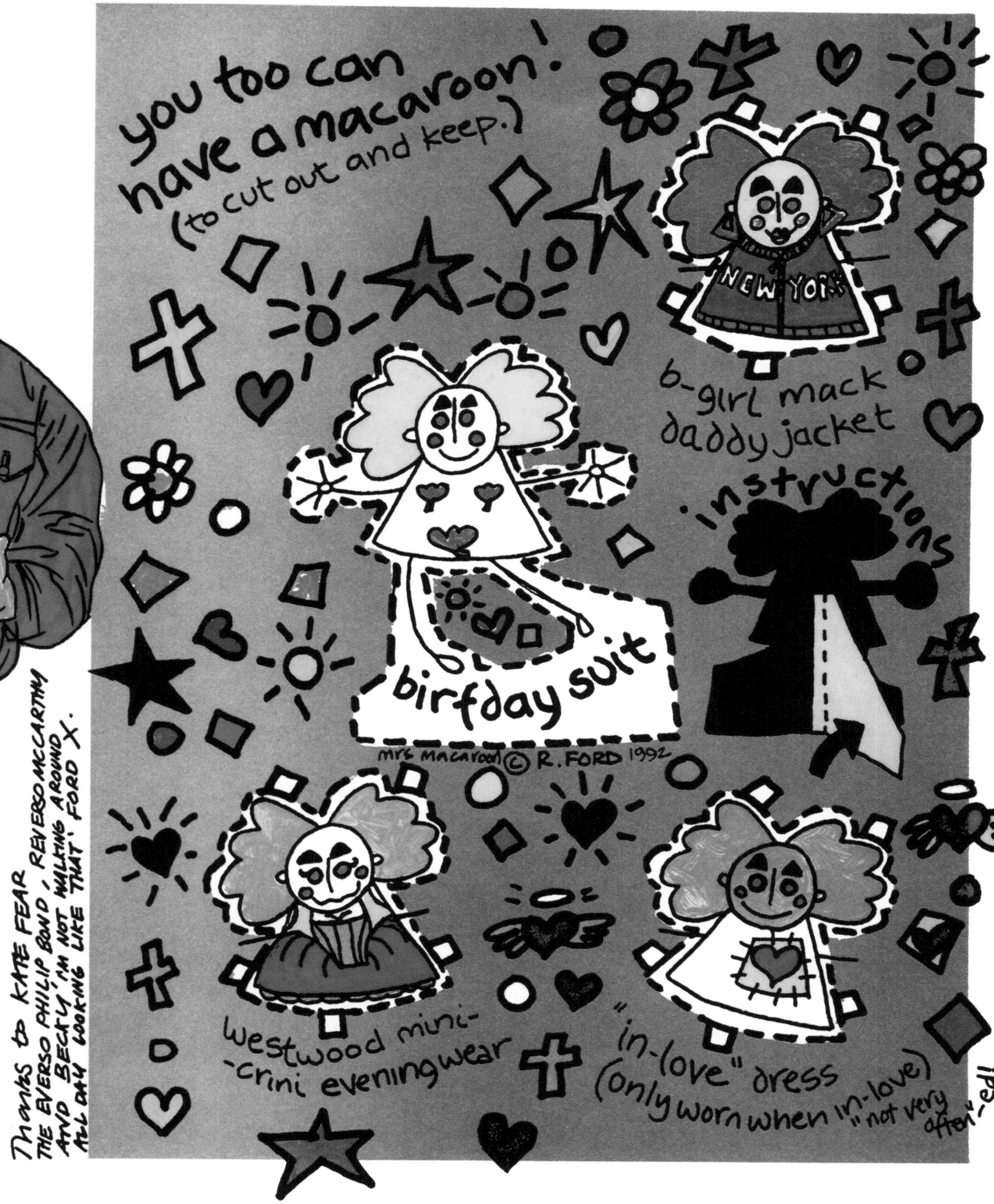

you too can have a macaroon!
(to cut out and keep.)
NEW YORK
b-girl mack daddy jacket
instructions
birfday suit
mrs macaroon © R. FORD 1992
westwood mini--crini eveningwear
"in-love" dress (only worn when in-love) "not very often" - ed!
Thanks to KATE FEAR THE EVERSO PHILIP BOND, REVERSO MCCARTHY AND BECKY, 'I'M NOT WALKING AROUND ALL DAY LOOKING LIKE THAT' FORD X.


"SUITS ME" inscription on tomb stone VEGAS 1957

LIKE

I WAS TRICKED INTO A WORLD OF SUBMISSION ...

A WORLD OF GLAMOUR ...

A WORLD OF GLAMOUR AND DESPAIR ...

# CEASE TO EXIST

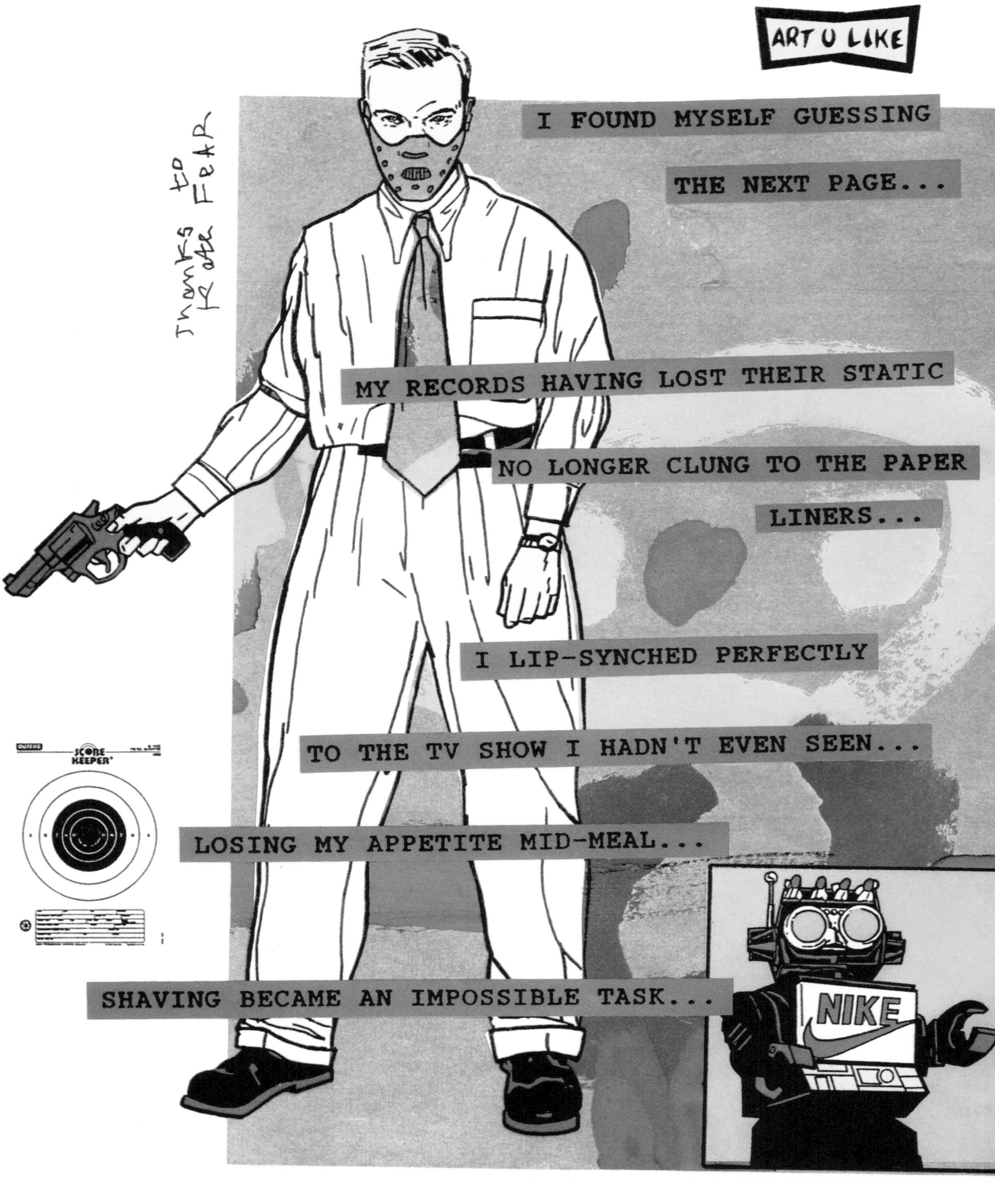
ART U LIKE
Thanks to Kate Fear
I FOUND MYSELF GUESSING
THE NEXT PAGE...
MY RECORDS HAVING LOST THEIR STATIC
NO LONGER CLUNG TO THE PAPER
LINERS...
I LIP-SYNCHED PERFECTLY
TO THE TV SHOW I HADN'T EVEN SEEN...
LOSING MY APPETITE MID-MEAL...
SHAVING BECAME AN IMPOSSIBLE TASK...
SCORE KEEPER
NIKE

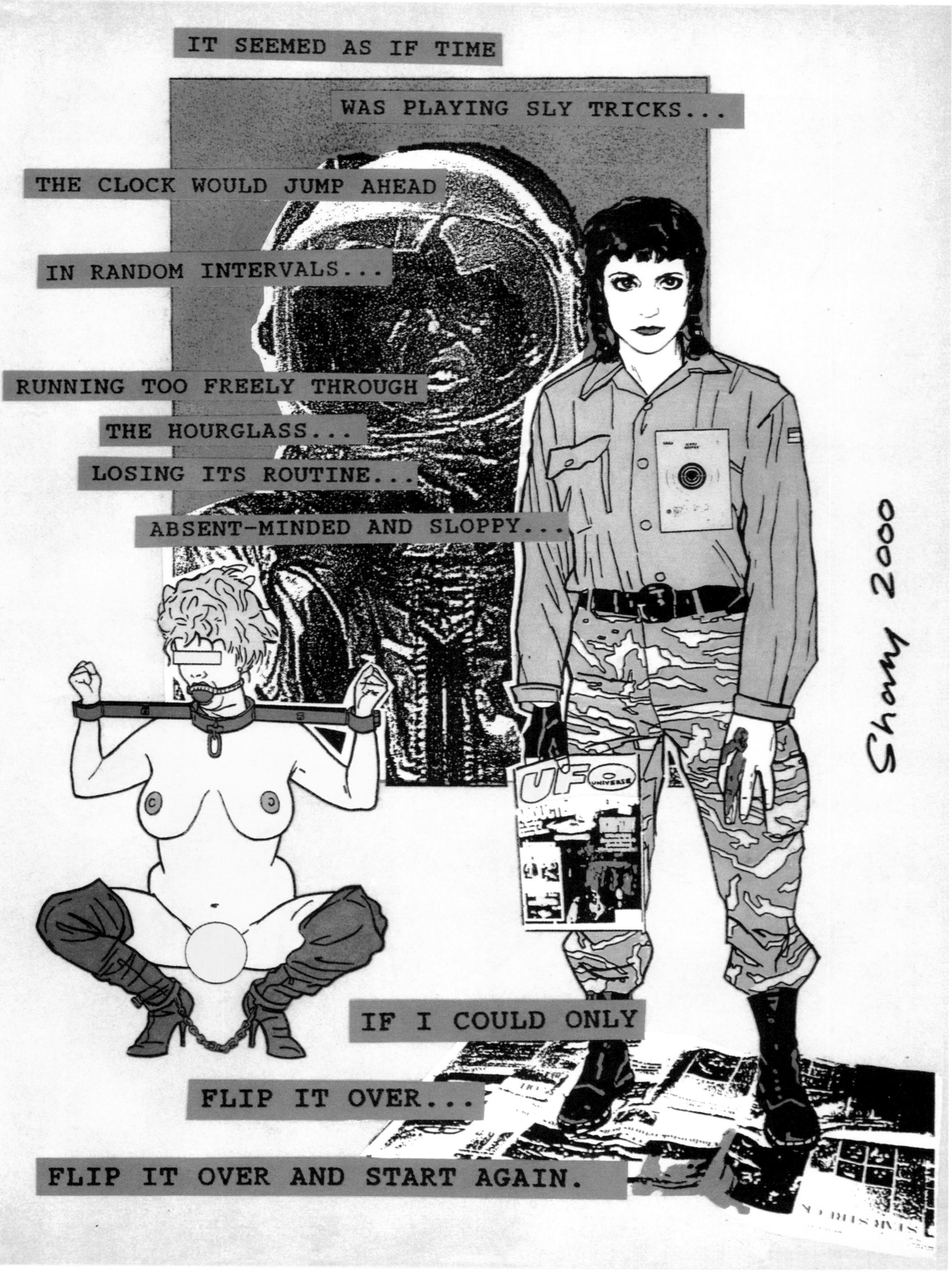
IT SEEMED AS IF TIME
WAS PLAYING SLY TRICKS...
THE CLOCK WOULD JUMP AHEAD
IN RANDOM INTERVALS...
RUNNING TOO FREELY THROUGH
THE HOURGLASS...
LOSING ITS ROUTINE...
ABSENT-MINDED AND SLOPPY...
IF I COULD ONLY
FLIP IT OVER...
FLIP IT OVER AND START AGAIN.
UFO

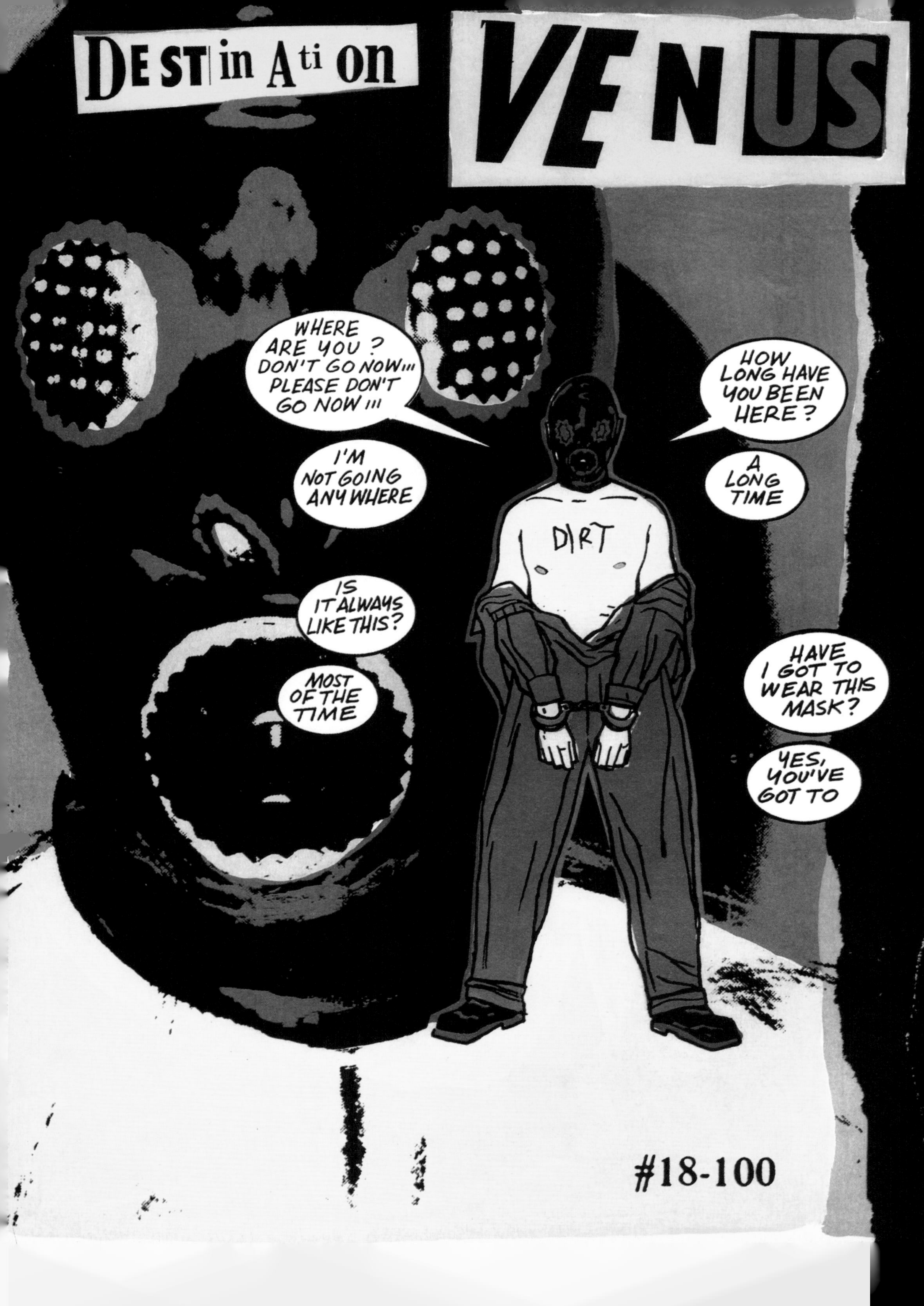
DEST in Ati on
VENUS
WHERE ARE YOU ? DON'T GO NOW!!! PLEASE DON'T GO NOW !!!
HOW LONG HAVE YOU BEEN HERE ?
I'M NOT GOING ANYWHERE
A LONG TIME
DIRT
IS IT ALWAYS LIKE THIS?
MOST OF THE TIME
HAVE I GOT TO WEAR THIS MASK?
YES, YOU'VE GOT TO
#18-100

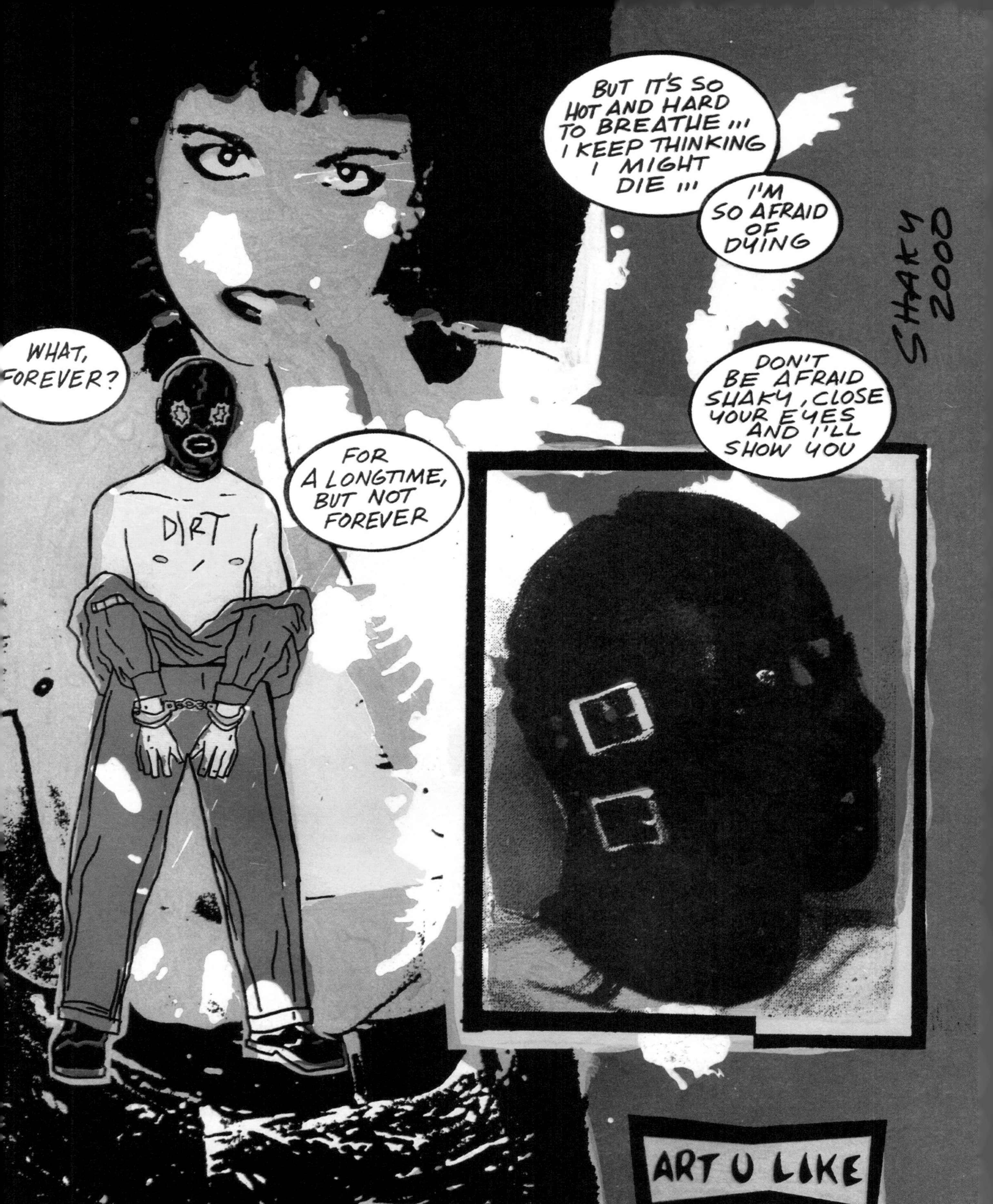
BUT IT'S SO HOT AND HARD TO BREATHE ... I KEEP THINKING I MIGHT DIE ...
I'M SO AFRAID OF DYING
WHAT, FOREVER?
FOR A LONGTIME, BUT NOT FOREVER
DON'T BE AFRAID SHAKY, CLOSE YOUR EYES AND I'LL SHOW YOU
DIRT
SHAKY 2000
ART U LIKE

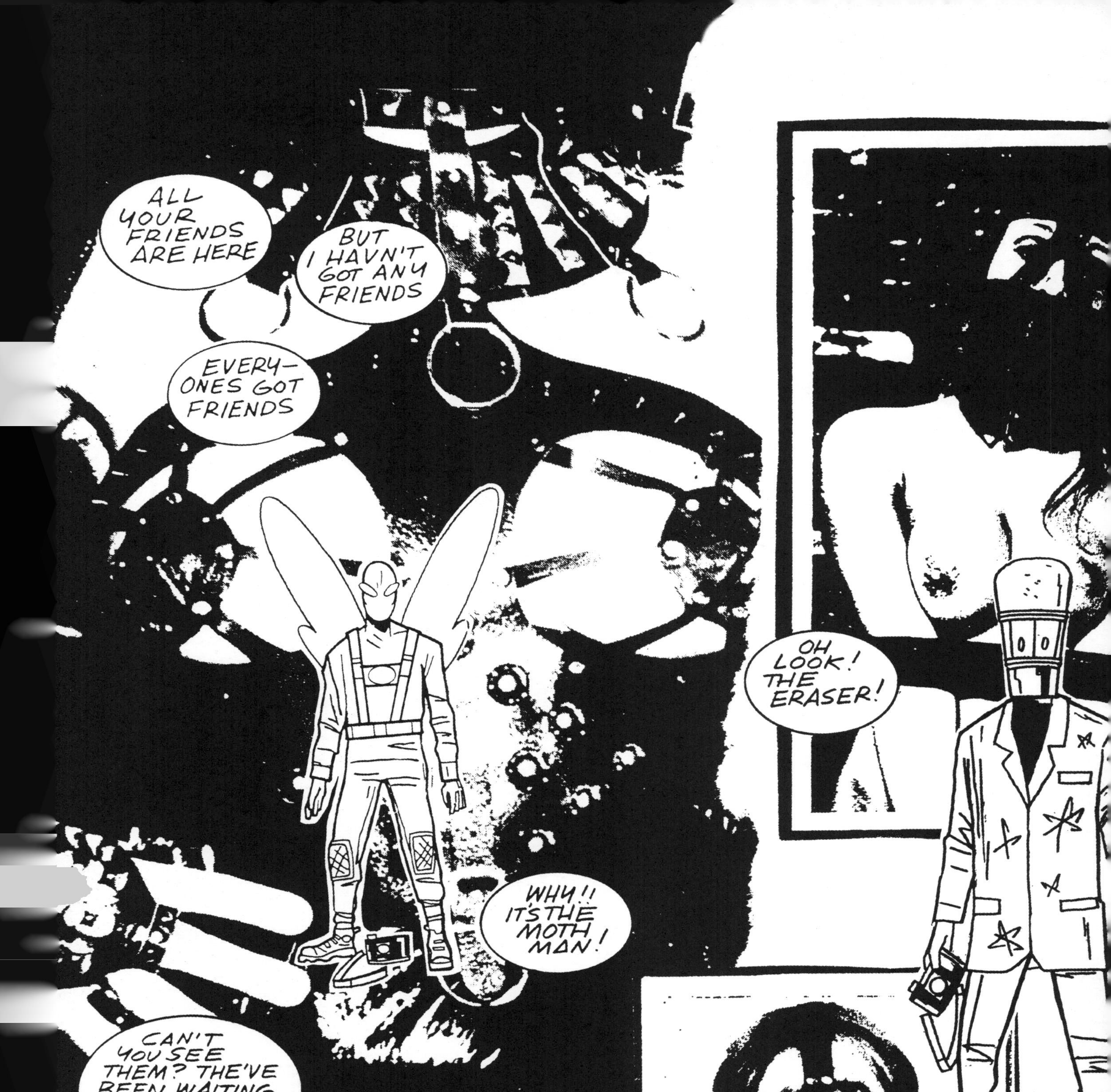


Thanks to—
VISUAL DISCIPLIN : KATE
HOT DATE : BECKY F

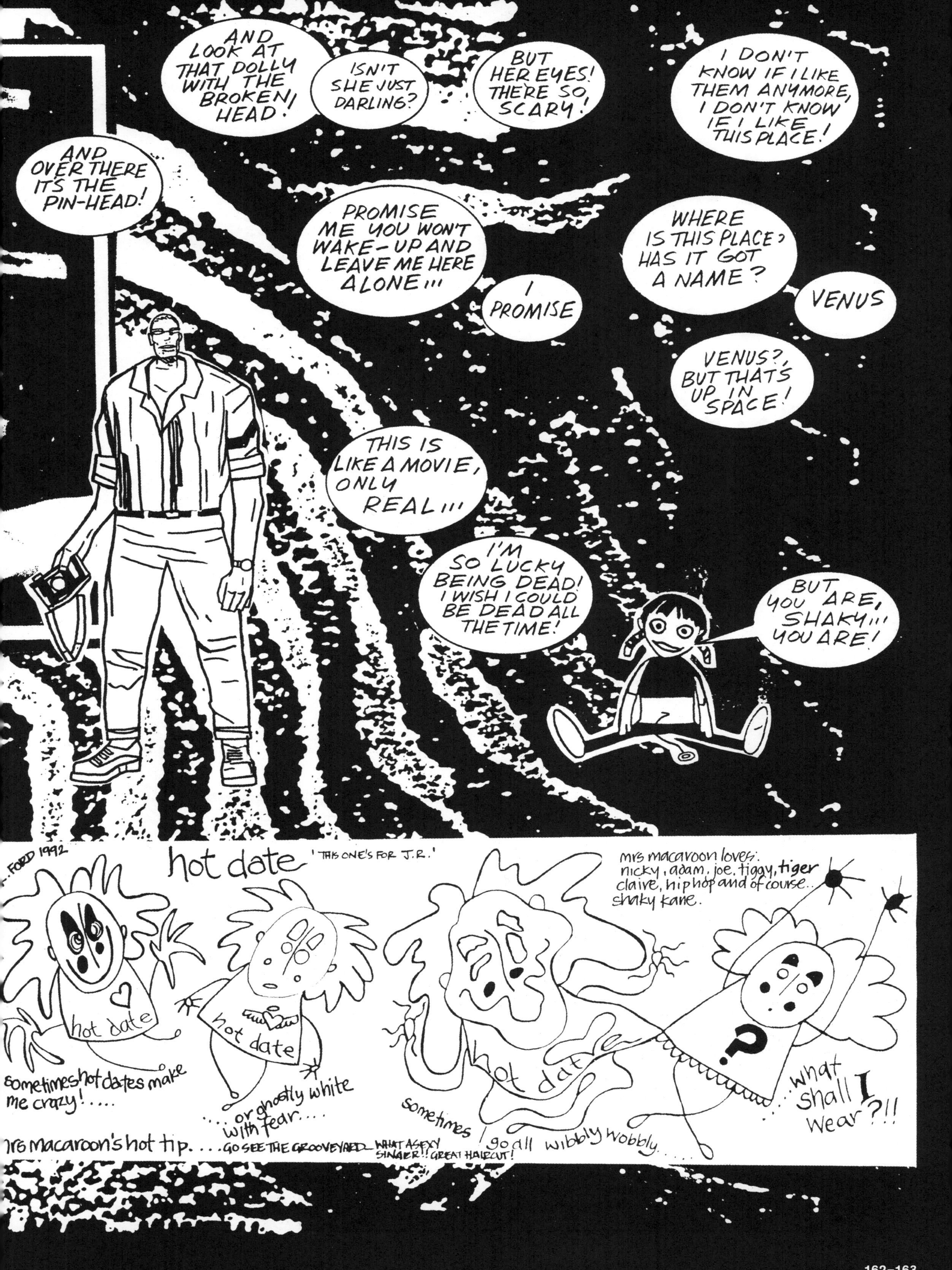

AND LOOK AT THAT DOLLY WITH THE BROKEN HEAD!
ISN'T SHE JUST DARLING?
BUT HER EYES! THERE SO, SCARY!
I DON'T KNOW IF I LIKE THEM ANYMORE, I DON'T KNOW IF I LIKE THIS PLACE!
AND OVER THERE IT'S THE PIN-HEAD!
PROMISE ME YOU WON'T WAKE-UP AND LEAVE ME HERE ALONE...
I PROMISE
WHERE IS THIS PLACE? HAS IT GOT A NAME?
VENUS
VENUS?, BUT THAT'S UP IN SPACE!
THIS IS LIKE A MOVIE, ONLY REAL...
I'M SO LUCKY BEING DEAD! I WISH I COULD BE DEAD ALL THE TIME!
BUT YOU ARE, SHAKY... YOU ARE!
FORD 1992
hot date
'THIS ONE'S FOR J.R.'
mrs macaroon loves: nicky, adam, joe, tiggy, tiger claire, hip hop and of course.. shaky kane.
hot date
hot date
hot date
sometimes hot dates make me crazy!....
....or ghostly white with fear....
sometimes I go all wibbly wobbly.....
...what shall I wear?!!
mrs macaroon's hot tip....GO SEE THE GROOVEYARD WHAT A SEXY SINGER!! GREAT HAIRCUT!

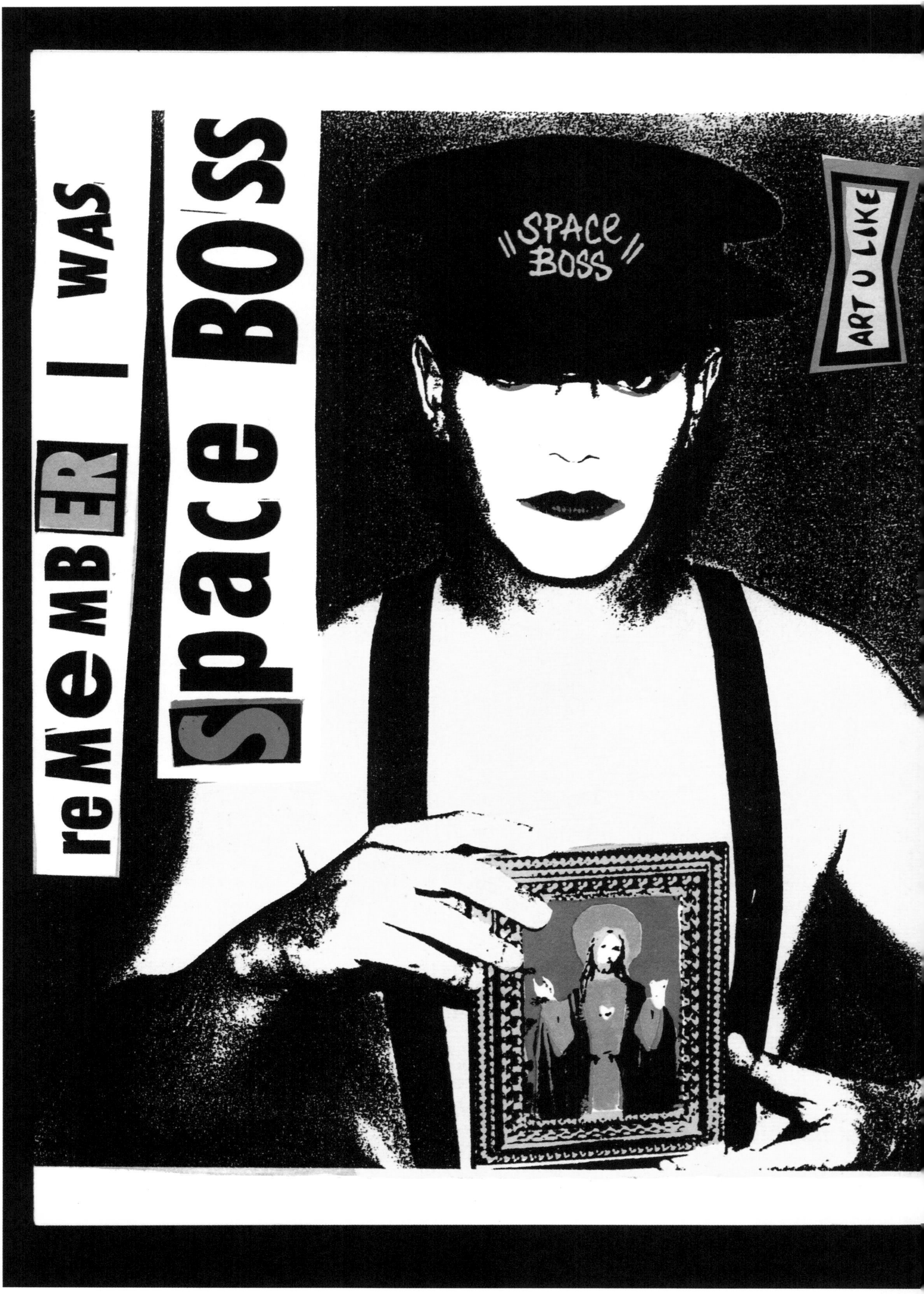
reMEMBER I WAS
Space BOSS
SPACE BOSS
ART U LIKE

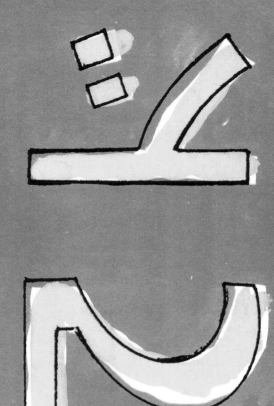

SHAKY
2000

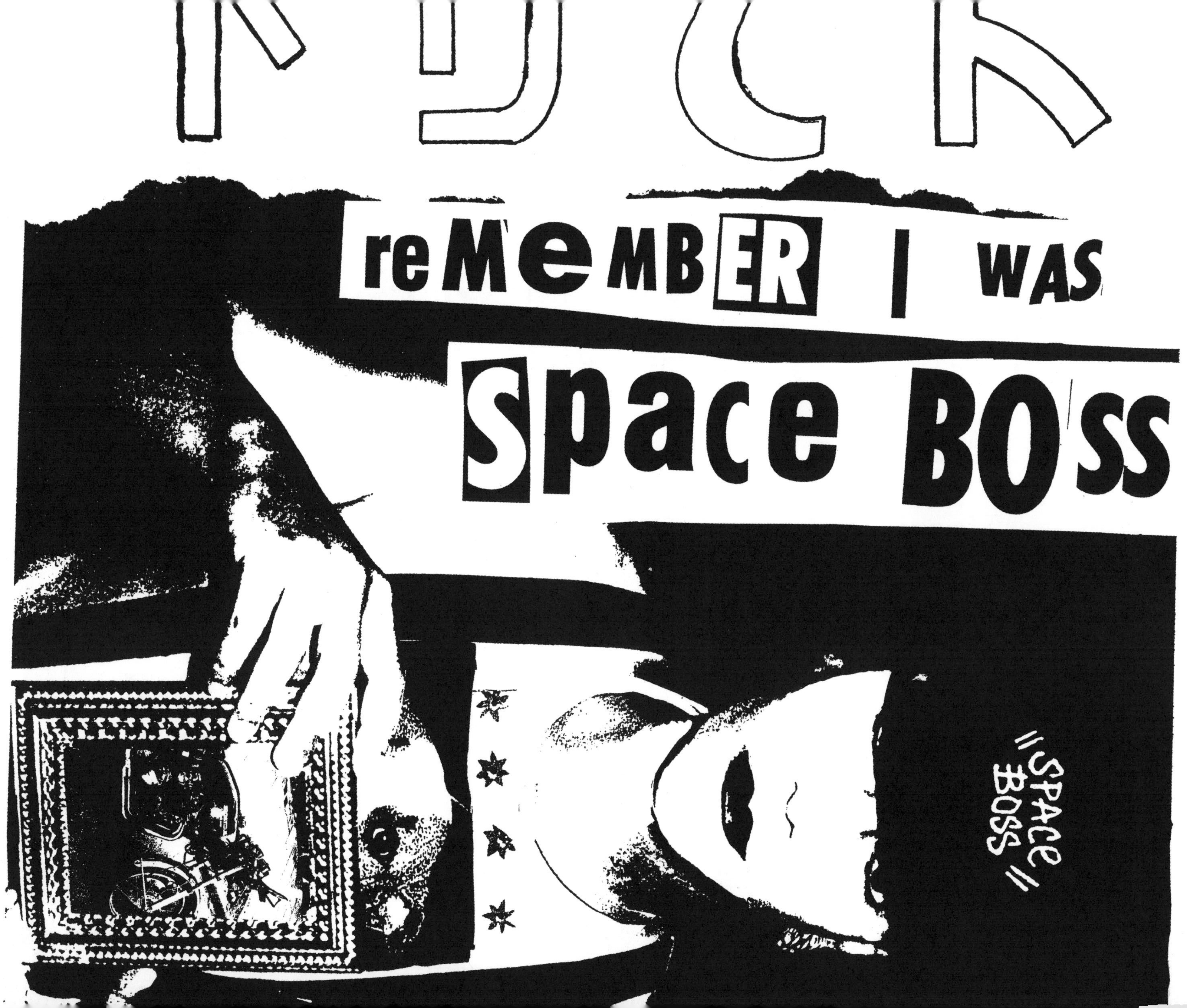
reMEMBER I WAS
SPACE BOSS
SPACE BOSS

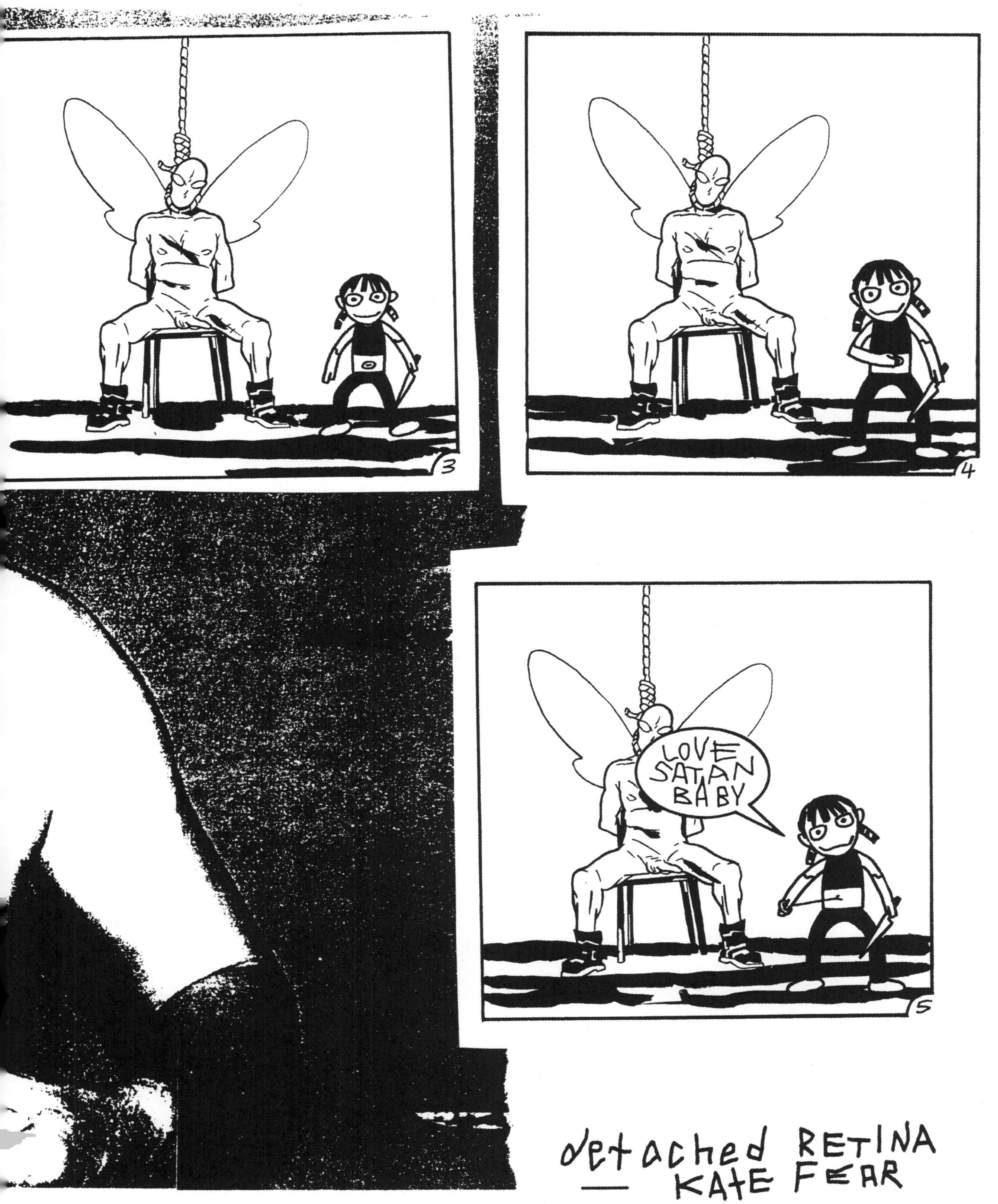
3
4
LOVE SATAN BABY
5

detached RETINA
— KATE FEAR

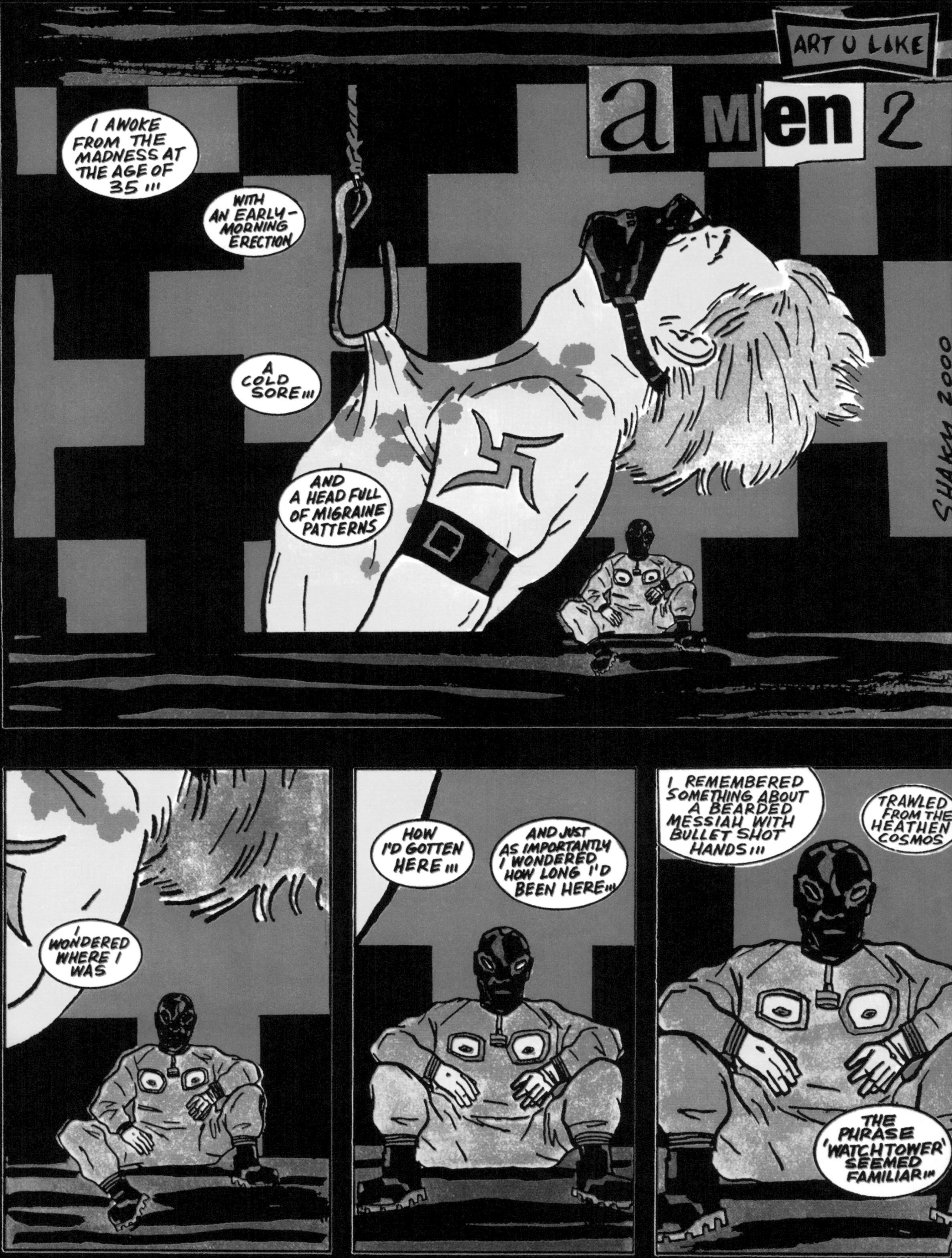

ART U LIKE
a Men 2
I AWOKE FROM THE MADNESS AT THE AGE OF 35...
WITH AN EARLY-MORNING ERECTION
A COLD SORE...
AND A HEAD FULL OF MIGRAINE PATTERNS
I WONDERED WHERE I WAS
HOW I'D GOTTEN HERE...
AND JUST AS IMPORTANTLY I WONDERED HOW LONG I'D BEEN HERE...
I REMEMBERED SOMETHING ABOUT A BEARDED MESSIAH WITH BULLET SHOT HANDS...
TRAWLED FROM THE HEATHEN COSMOS
THE PHRASE 'WATCHTOWER' SEEMED FAMILIAR...

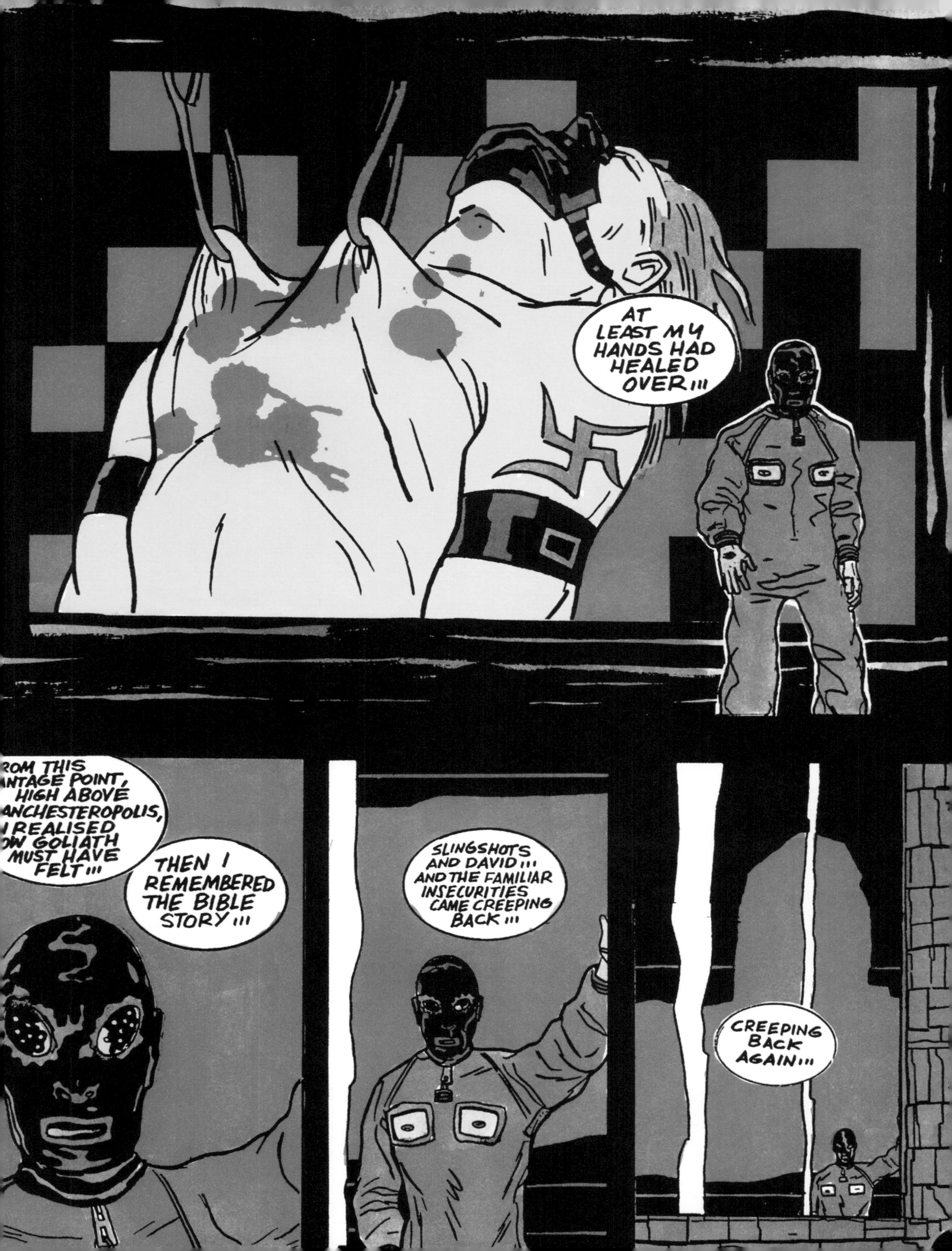
AT LEAST MY HANDS HAD HEALED OVER...
ROM THIS ANTAGE POINT, HIGH ABOVE ANCHESTEROPOLIS, I REALISED OW GOLIATH MUST HAVE FELT...
THEN I REMEMBERED THE BIBLE STORY...
SLINGSHOTS AND DAVID... AND THE FAMILIAR INSECURITIES CAME CREEPING BACK...
CREEPING BACK AGAIN...

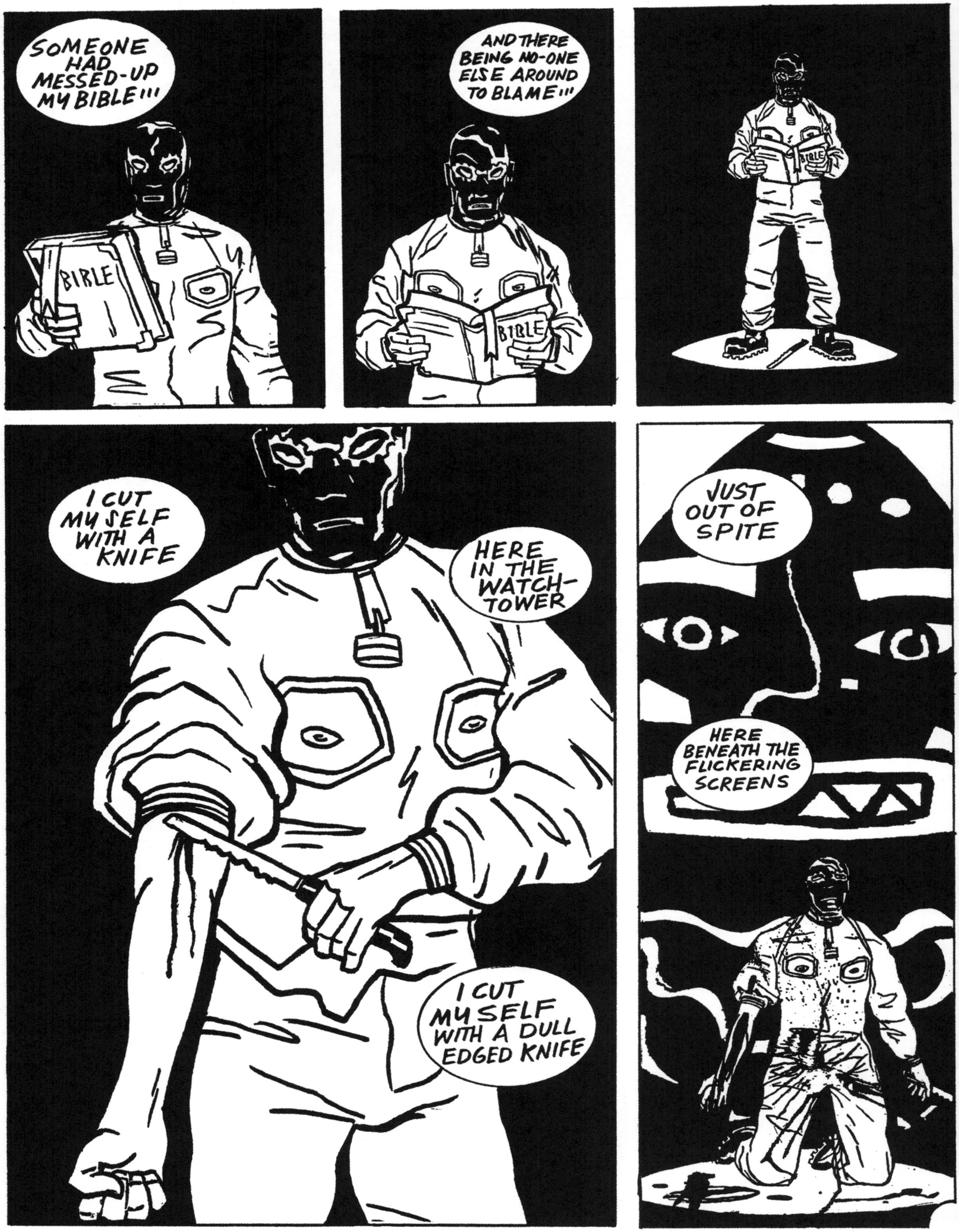
SOMEONE HAD MESSED-UP MY BIBLE!!!
BIBLE
AND THERE BEING NO-ONE ELSE AROUND TO BLAME!!!
BIBLE
BIBLE
I CUT MYSELF WITH A KNIFE
HERE IN THE WATCH-TOWER
I CUT MYSELF WITH A DULL EDGED KNIFE
JUST OUT OF SPITE
HERE BENEATH THE FLICKERING SCREENS

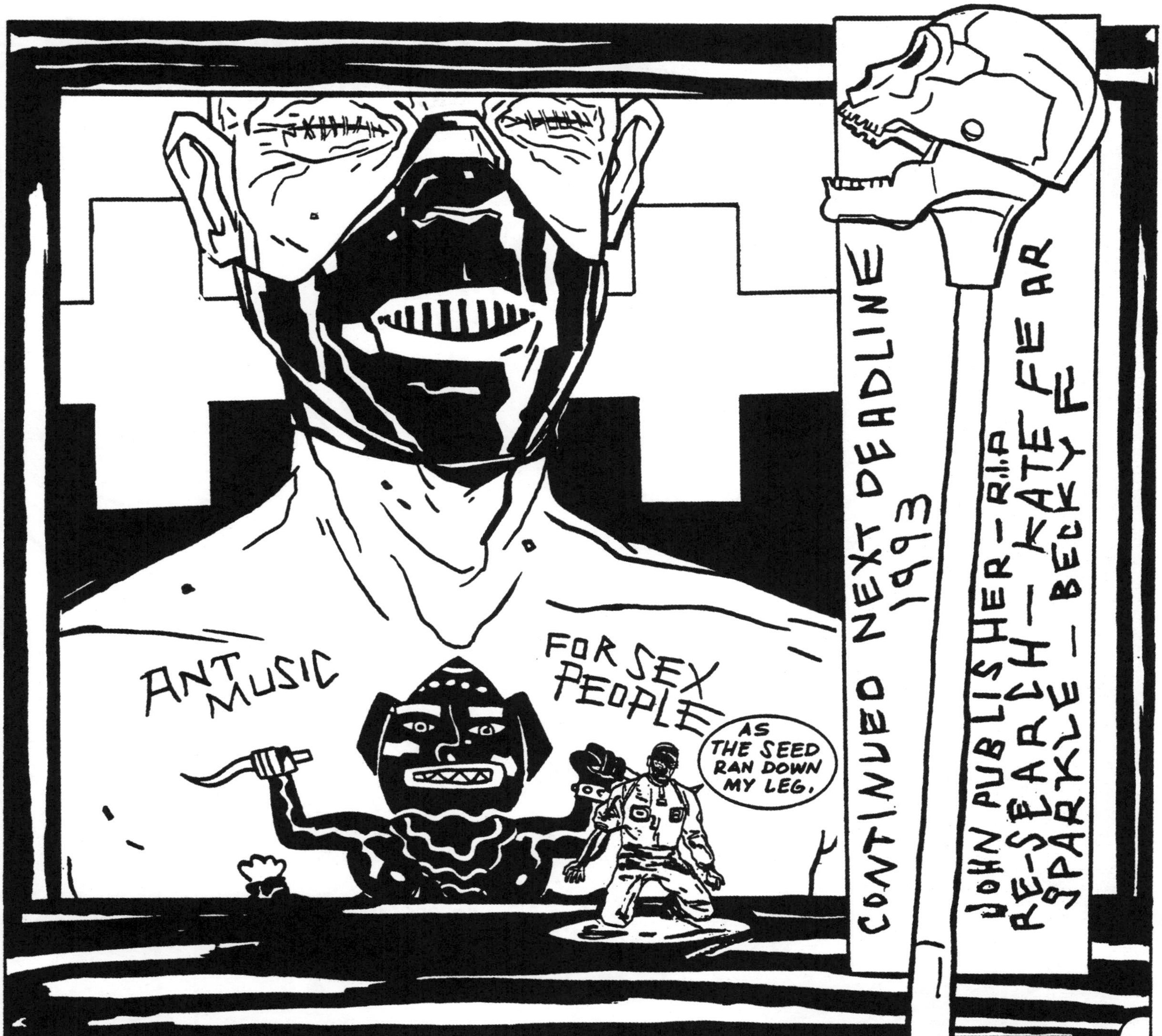
ANT MUSIC
FOR SEX PEOPLE
AS THE SEED RAN DOWN MY LEG.
CONTINUED NEXT DEADLINE 1993
JOHN PUBLISHER - R.I.P
RE-SEARCH - KATE FEAR
SPARKLE - BECKY F

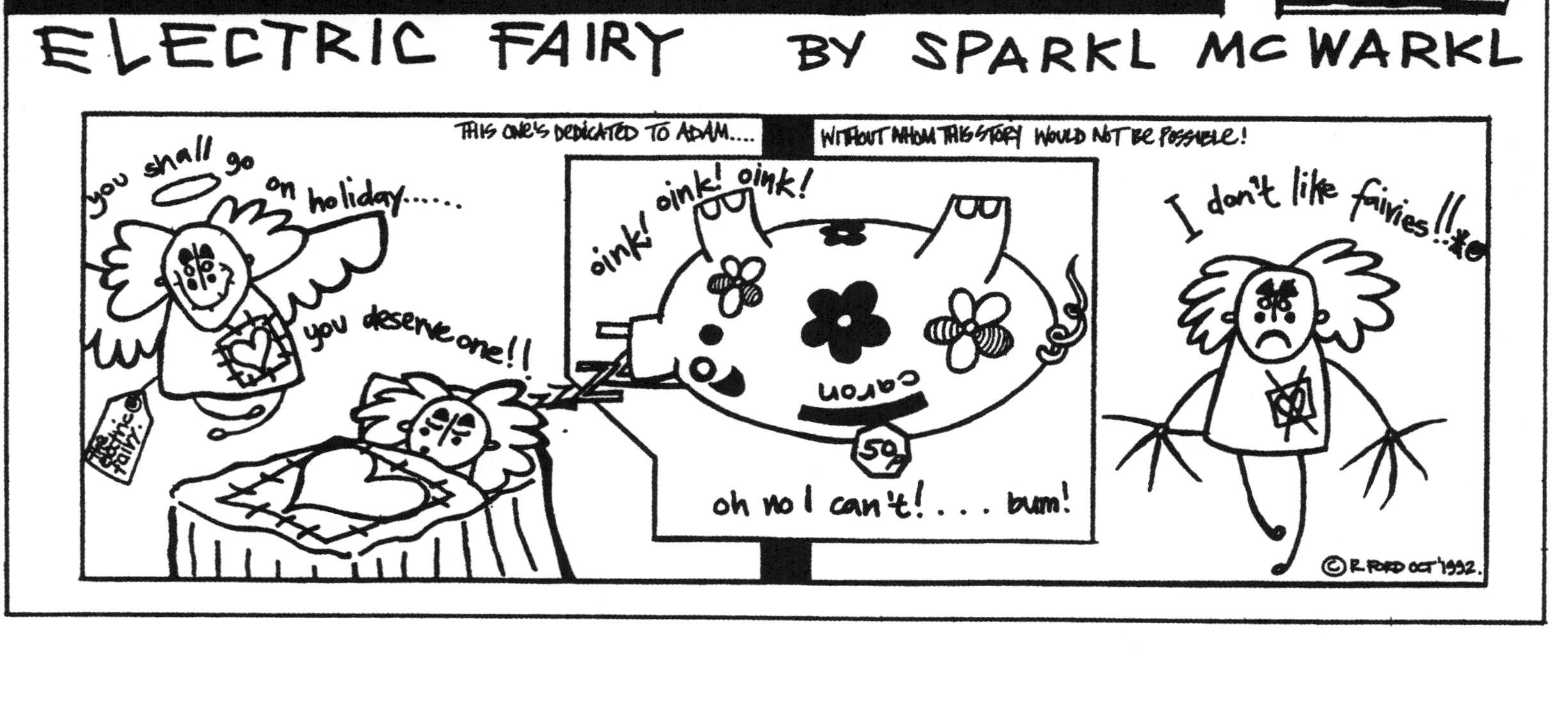
ELECTRIC FAIRY BY SPARKL MCWARKL
THIS ONE'S DEDICATED TO ADAM....
WITHOUT WHOM THIS STORY WOULD NOT BE POSSIBLE!
you shall go on holiday......
you deserve one!!
oink! oink! oink!
caron
50p
oh no I can't! . . . bum!
I don't like fairies!!
© R. FORD OCT '1992.

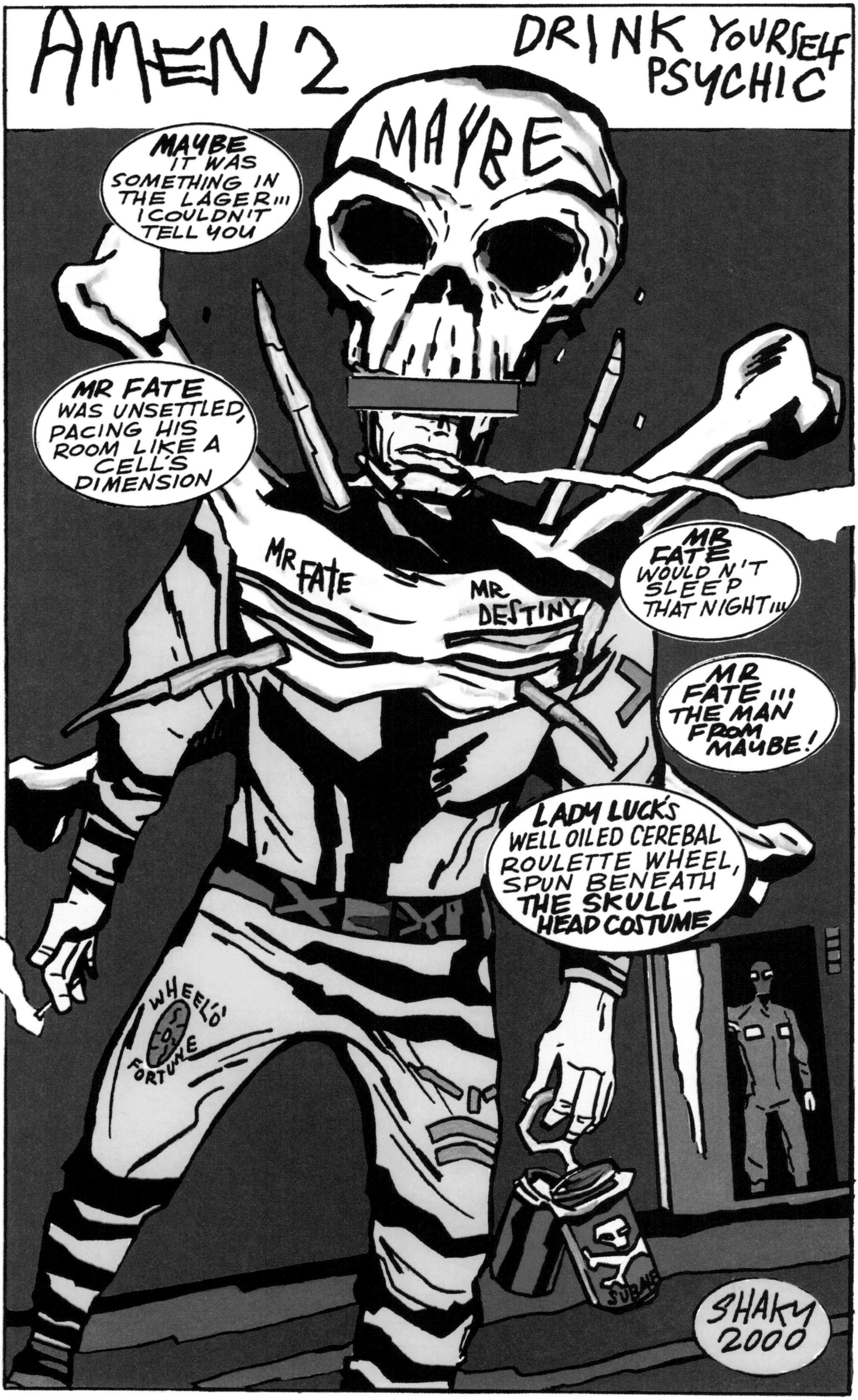
AMEN 2
DRINK YOURSELF PSYCHIC
MAYBE
MAYBE IT WAS SOMETHING IN THE LAGER... I COULDN'T TELL YOU
MR FATE WAS UNSETTLED, PACING HIS ROOM LIKE A CELL'S DIMENSION
MR FATE
MR DESTINY
MR FATE WOULDN'T SLEEP THAT NIGHT...
MR FATE... THE MAN FROM MAYBE!
LADY LUCK'S WELL OILED CEREBAL ROULETTE WHEEL, SPUN BENEATH THE SKULL-HEAD COSTUME
WHEEL 'O' FORTUNE
SHAKY 2000

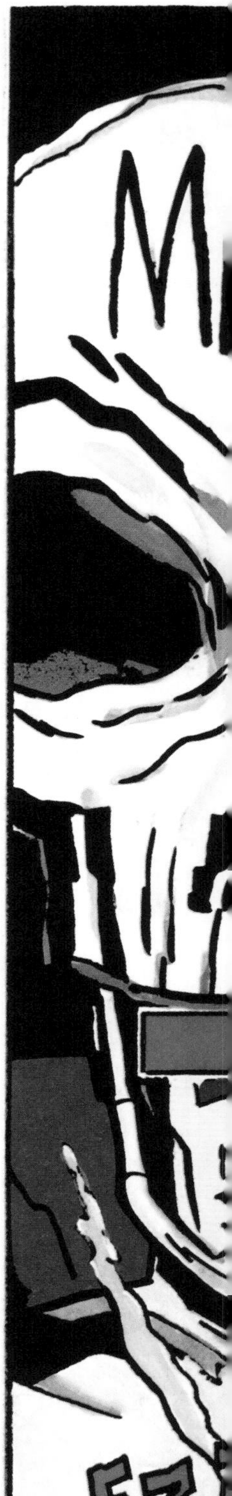

"you

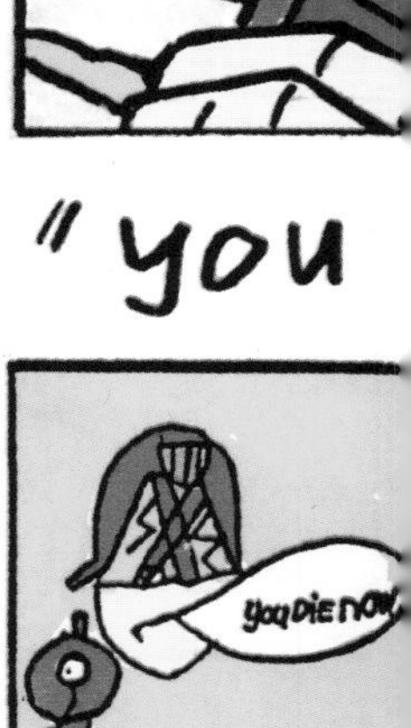
you die now

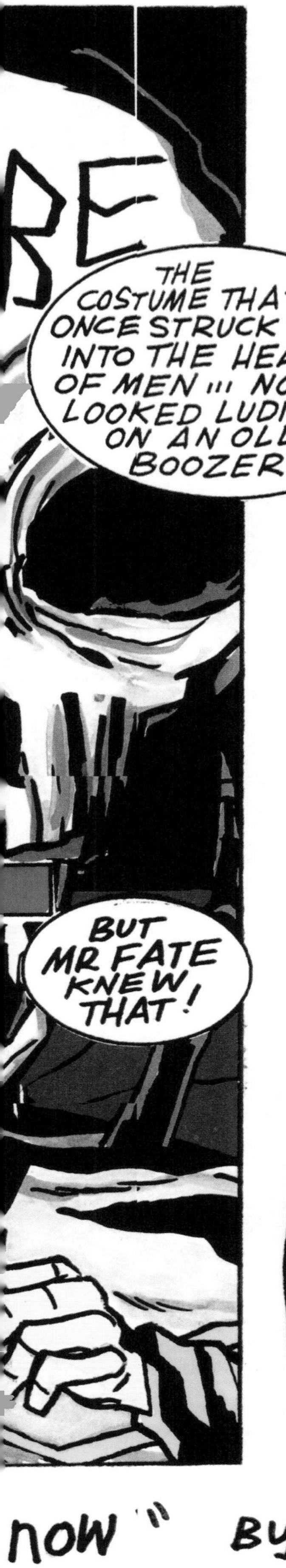
THE COSTUME THAT ONCE STRUCK FEAR INTO THE HEARTS OF MEN ... NOW LOOKED LUDICROUS ON AN OLD BOOZER
BUT MR FATE KNEW THAT!

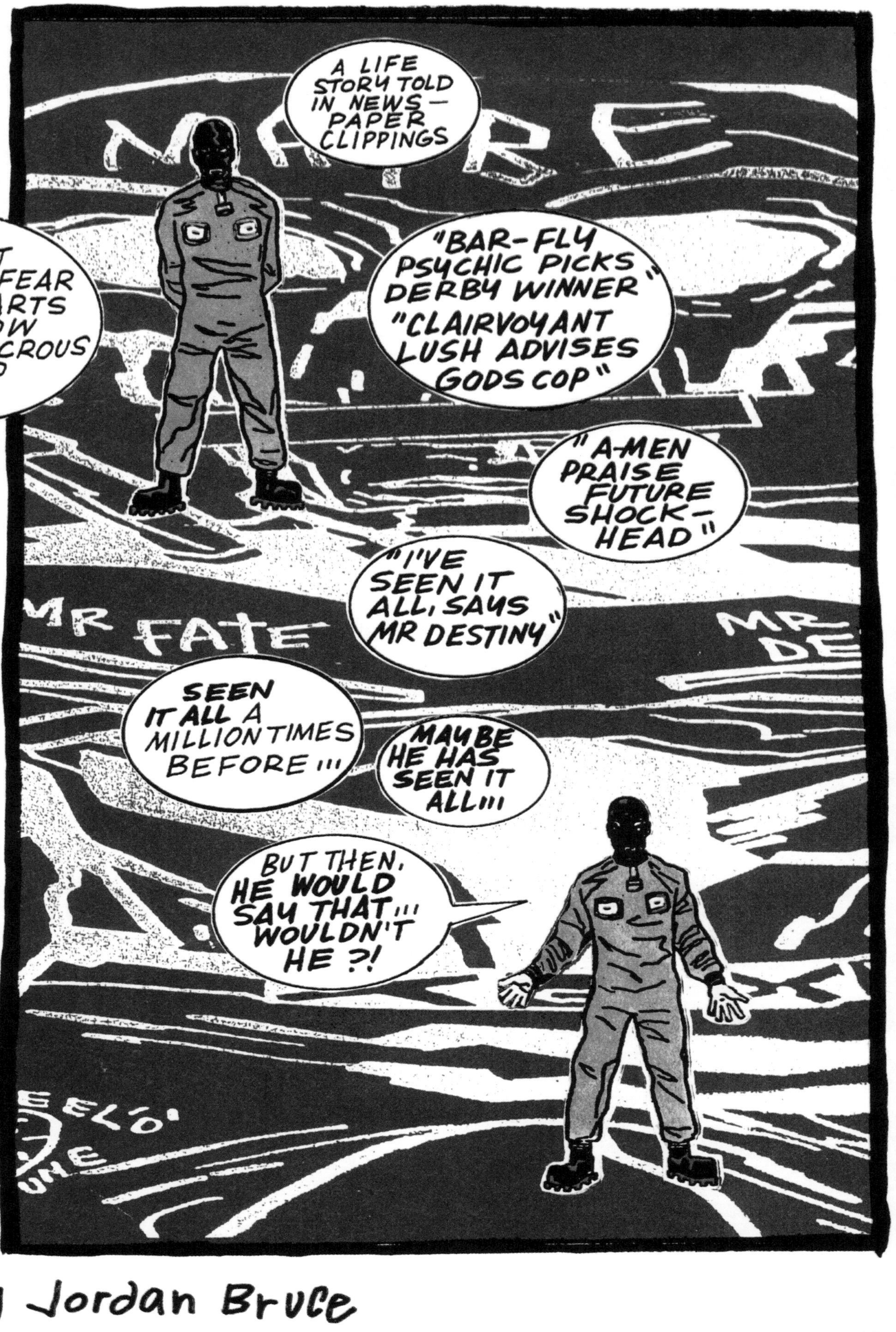
A LIFE STORY TOLD IN NEWS-PAPER CLIPPINGS
"BAR-FLY PSYCHIC PICKS DERBY WINNER"
"CLAIRVOYANT LUSH ADVISES GODS COP"
"A-MEN PRAISE FUTURE SHOCK-HEAD"
"I'VE SEEN IT ALL, SAYS MR DESTINY"
MR FATE
SEEN IT ALL A MILLION TIMES BEFORE ...
MAYBE HE HAS SEEN IT ALL ...
BUT THEN, HE WOULD SAY THAT ... WOULDN'T HE ?!

now" By Jordan Bruce

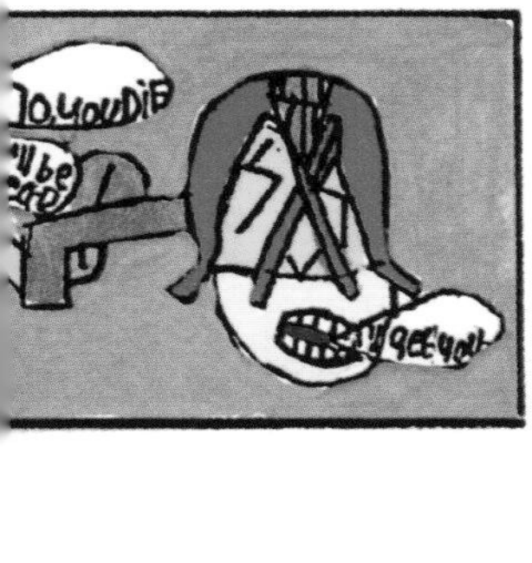

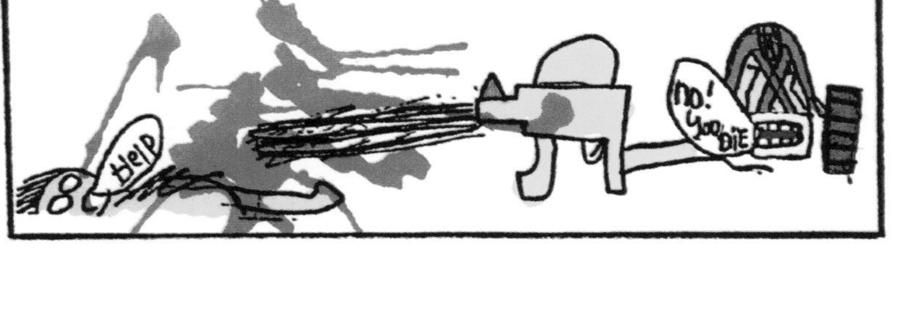
Help
no! you DIE

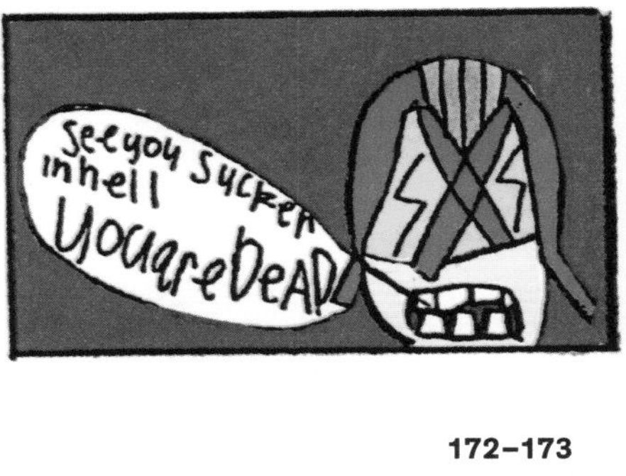
See you Sucker in hell
You are DEAD

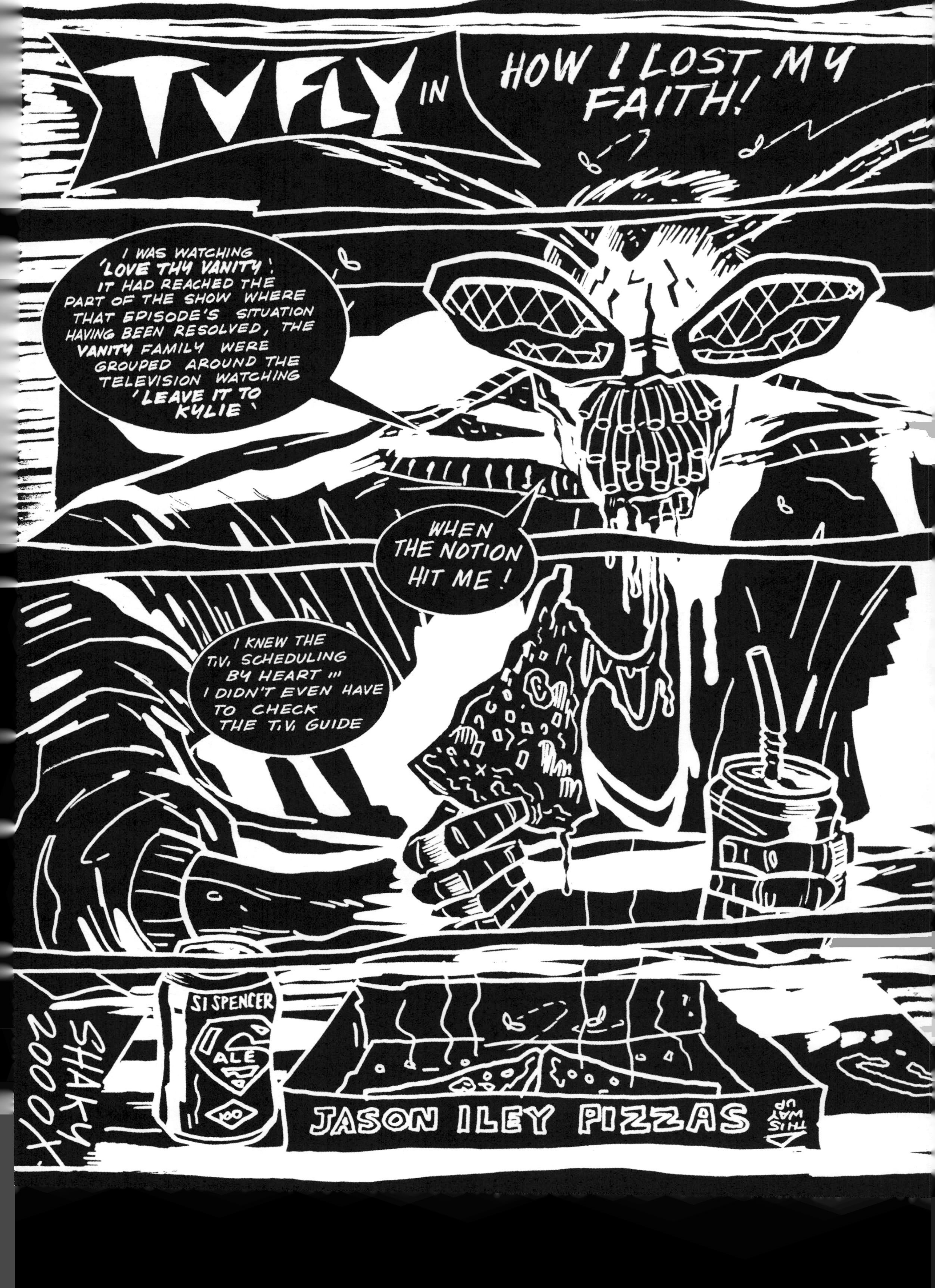
TVFLY IN
HOW I LOST MY FAITH!
I WAS WATCHING 'LOVE THY VANITY'. IT HAD REACHED THE PART OF THE SHOW WHERE THAT EPISODE'S SITUATION HAVING BEEN RESOLVED, THE VANITY FAMILY WERE GROUPED AROUND THE TELEVISION WATCHING 'LEAVE IT TO KYLIE'
WHEN THE NOTION HIT ME!
I KNEW THE T.V. SCHEDULING BY HEART !!! I DIDN'T EVEN HAVE TO CHECK THE T.V. GUIDE
SI SPENCER
ALE
100
JASON ILEY PIZZAS
THIS WAY UP
SHAKY 2000.

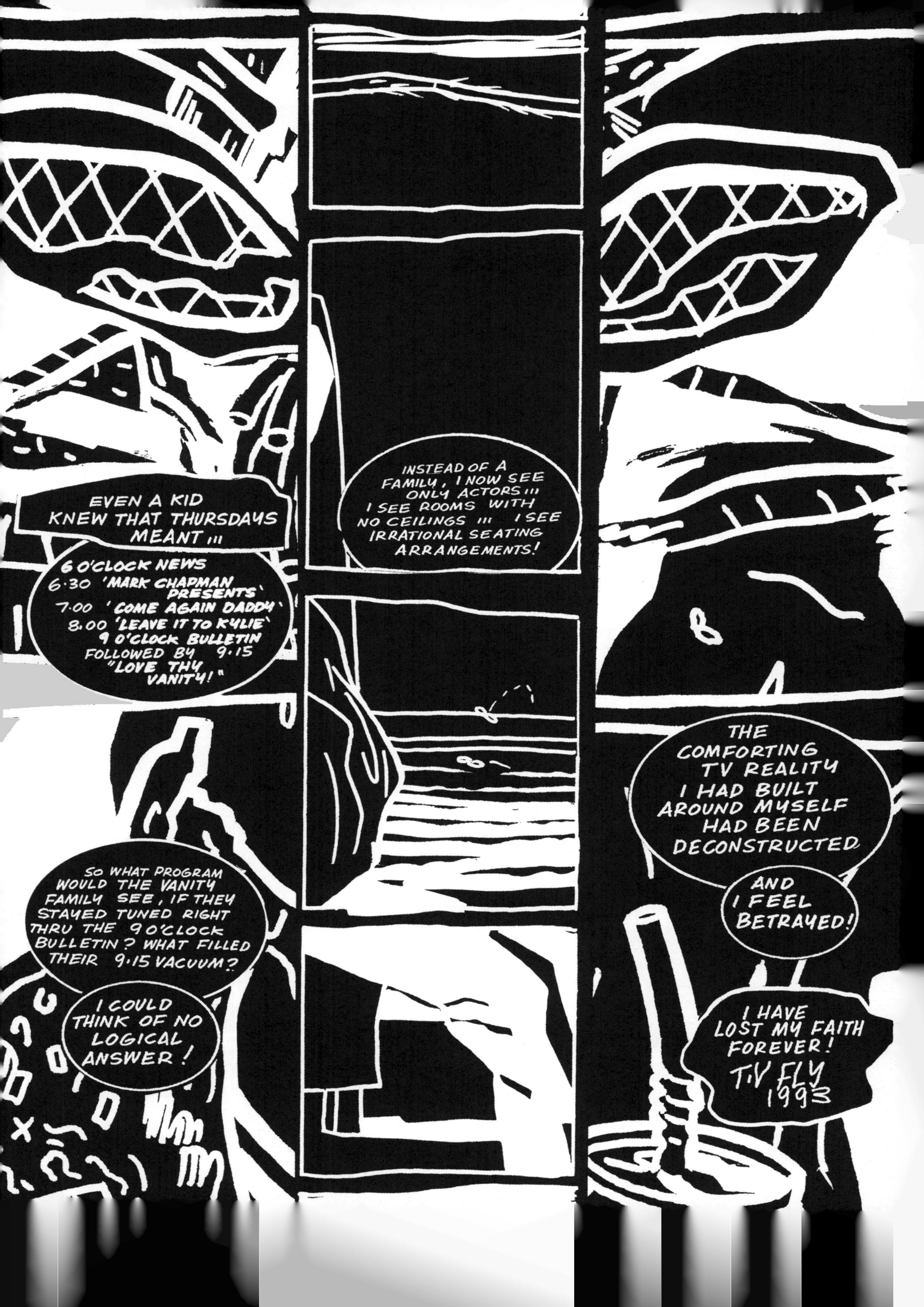
EVEN A KID KNEW THAT THURSDAYS MEANT ...
6 O'CLOCK NEWS 6.30 'MARK CHAPMAN PRESENTS' 7.00 'COME AGAIN DADDY' 8.00 'LEAVE IT TO KYLIE' 9 O'CLOCK BULLETIN FOLLOWED BY 9.15 "LOVE THY VANITY!"
SO WHAT PROGRAM WOULD THE VANITY FAMILY SEE, IF THEY STAYED TUNED RIGHT THRU THE 9 O'CLOCK BULLETIN? WHAT FILLED THEIR 9.15 VACUUM?
I COULD THINK OF NO LOGICAL ANSWER!
INSTEAD OF A FAMILY, I NOW SEE ONLY ACTORS ... I SEE ROOMS WITH NO CEILINGS ... I SEE IRRATIONAL SEATING ARRANGEMENTS!
THE COMFORTING TV REALITY I HAD BUILT AROUND MYSELF HAD BEEN DECONSTRUCTED
AND I FEEL BETRAYED!
I HAVE LOST MY FAITH FOREVER!
T.V FLY 1993

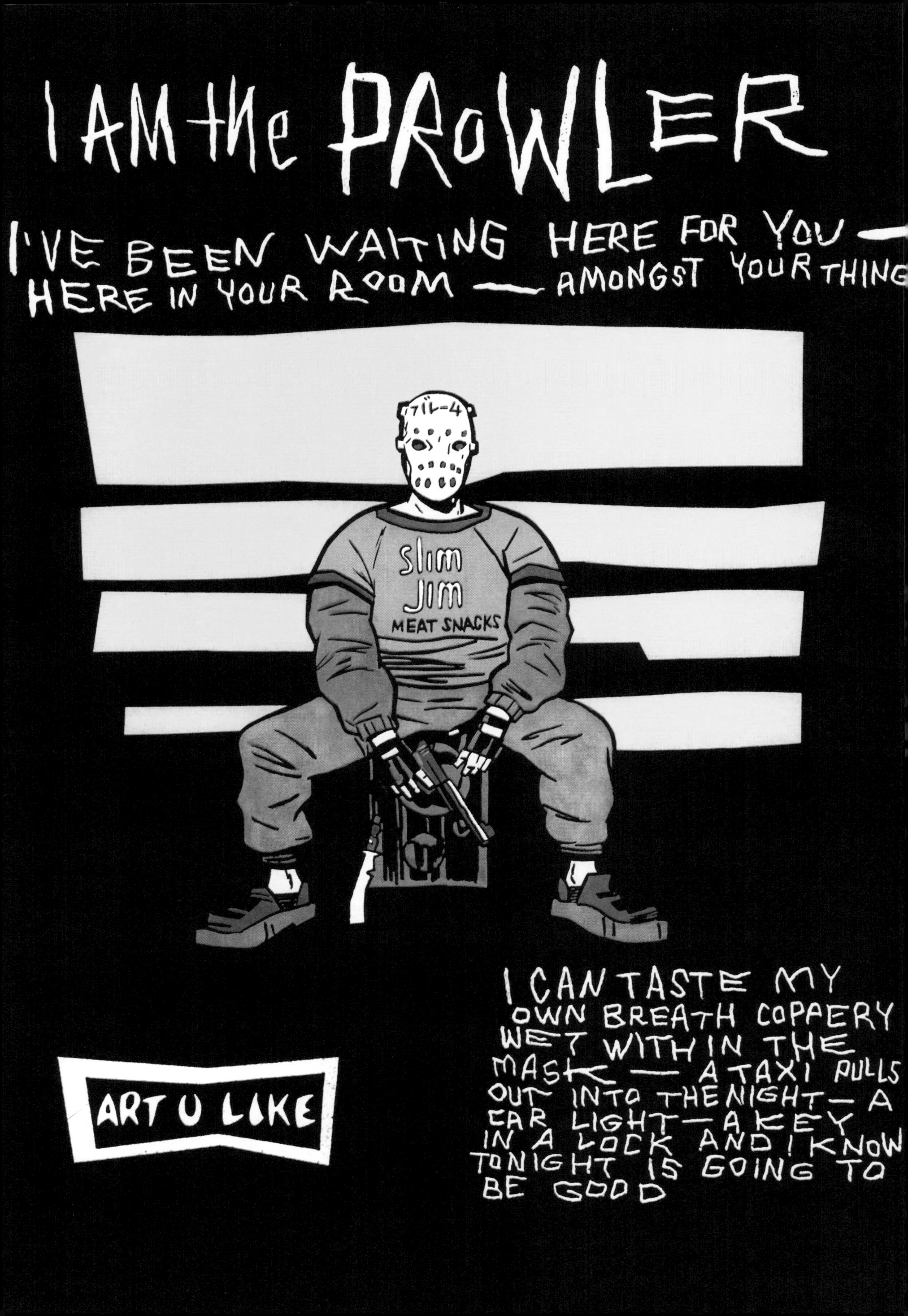
I AM the PROWLER
I'VE BEEN WAITING HERE FOR YOU — HERE IN YOUR ROOM — AMONGST YOUR THING
slim Jim MEAT SNACKS
I CAN TASTE MY OWN BREATH COPPERY WET WITH IN THE MASK — A TAXI PULLS OUT INTO THE NIGHT — A CAR LIGHT — A KEY IN A LOCK AND I KNOW TONIGHT IS GOING TO BE GOOD
ART U LIKE

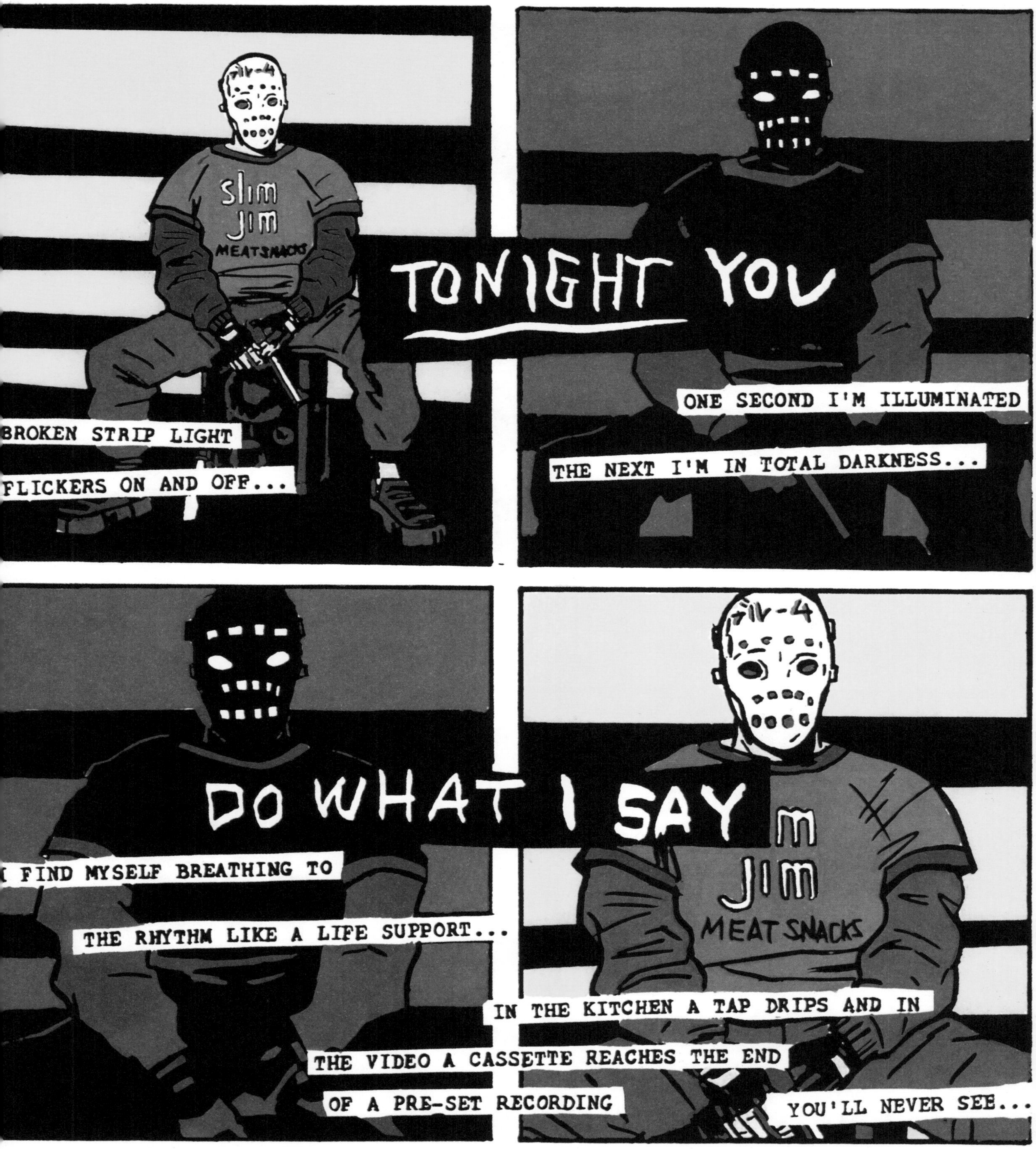
slim jim MEATSNACKS
TONIGHT YOU
BROKEN STRIP LIGHT
FLICKERS ON AND OFF...
ONE SECOND I'M ILLUMINATED
THE NEXT I'M IN TOTAL DARKNESS...
DO WHAT I SAY
I FIND MYSELF BREATHING TO
THE RHYTHM LIKE A LIFE SUPPORT...
IN THE KITCHEN A TAP DRIPS AND IN
THE VIDEO A CASSETTE REACHES THE END
OF A PRE-SET RECORDING
YOU'LL NEVER SEE...

"3 minutes"
By
Jordan
Bruce

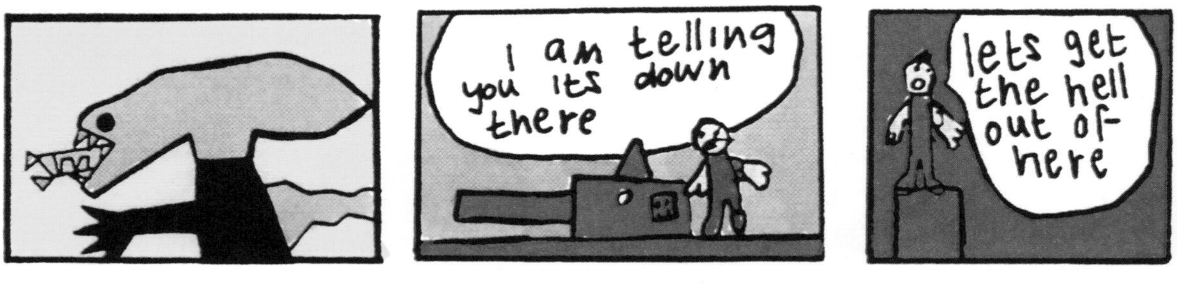
I am telling you its down there
lets get the hell out of here

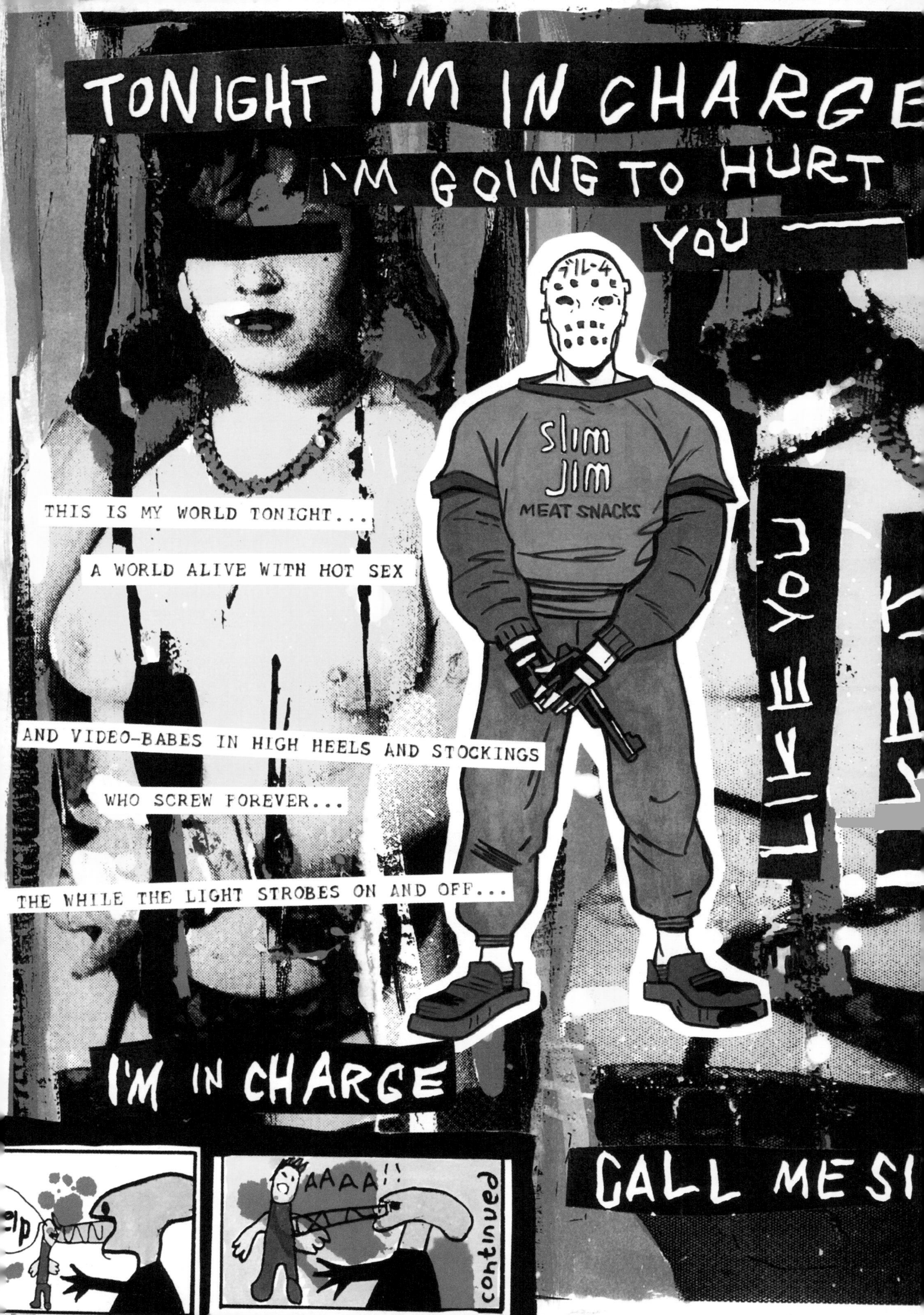

TONIGHT I'M IN CHARGE
I'M GOING TO HURT
YOU —
THIS IS MY WORLD TONIGHT...
A WORLD ALIVE WITH HOT SEX
AND VIDEO-BABES IN HIGH HEELS AND STOCKINGS
WHO SCREW FOREVER...
THE WHILE THE LIGHT STROBES ON AND OFF...
slim
jim
MEAT SNACKS
LIKE YOU
I'M IN CHARGE
AAAA!!
continued
CALL ME SI

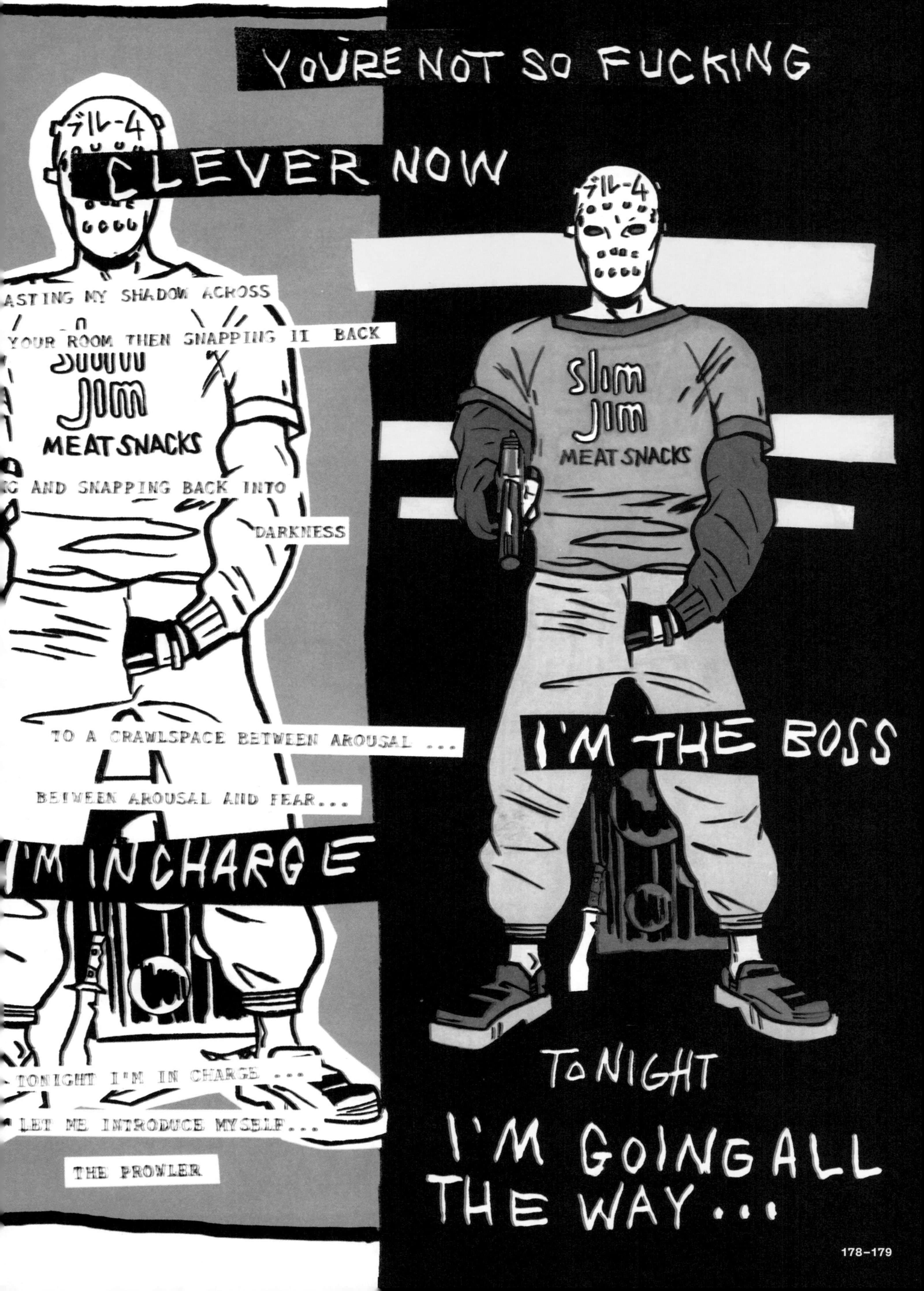
YOU'RE NOT SO FUCKING
CLEVER NOW
ASTING MY SHADOW ACROSS
YOUR ROOM THEN SNAPPING IT BACK
G AND SNAPPING BACK INTO
DARKNESS
slim
jim
MEAT SNACKS
TO A CRAWLSPACE BETWEEN AROUSAL ...
BETWEEN AROUSAL AND FEAR...
I'M INCHARGE
TONIGHT I'M IN CHARGE ...
LET ME INTRODUCE MYSELF...
THE PROWLER
I'M THE BOSS
TONIGHT
I'M GOING ALL
THE WAY...

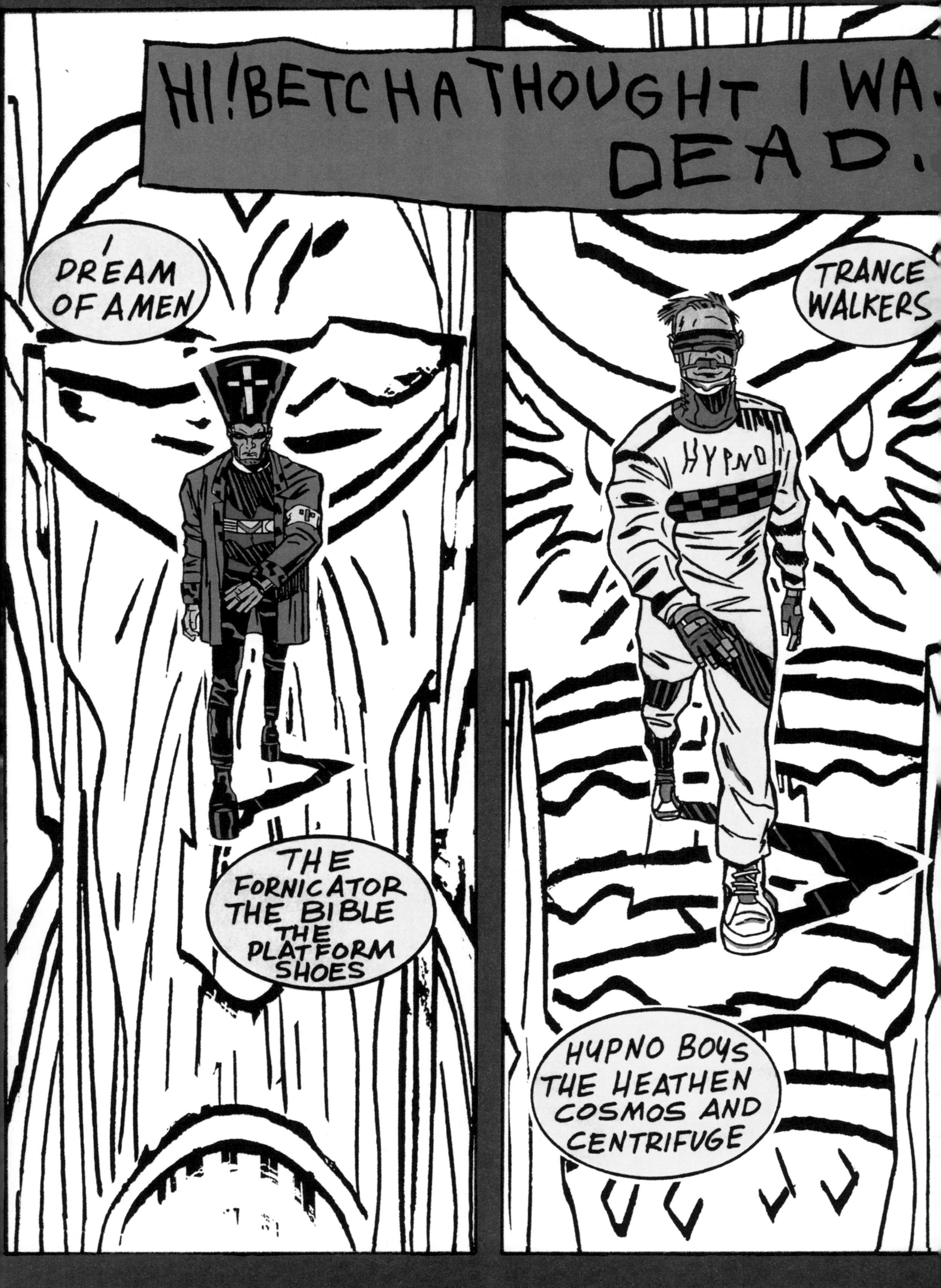
HI! BETCHA THOUGHT I WAS DEAD..
I DREAM OF AMEN
THE FORNICATOR THE BIBLE THE PLATFORM SHOES
TRANCE WALKERS
HYPNO
HYPNO BOYS THE HEATHEN COSMOS AND CENTRIFUGE

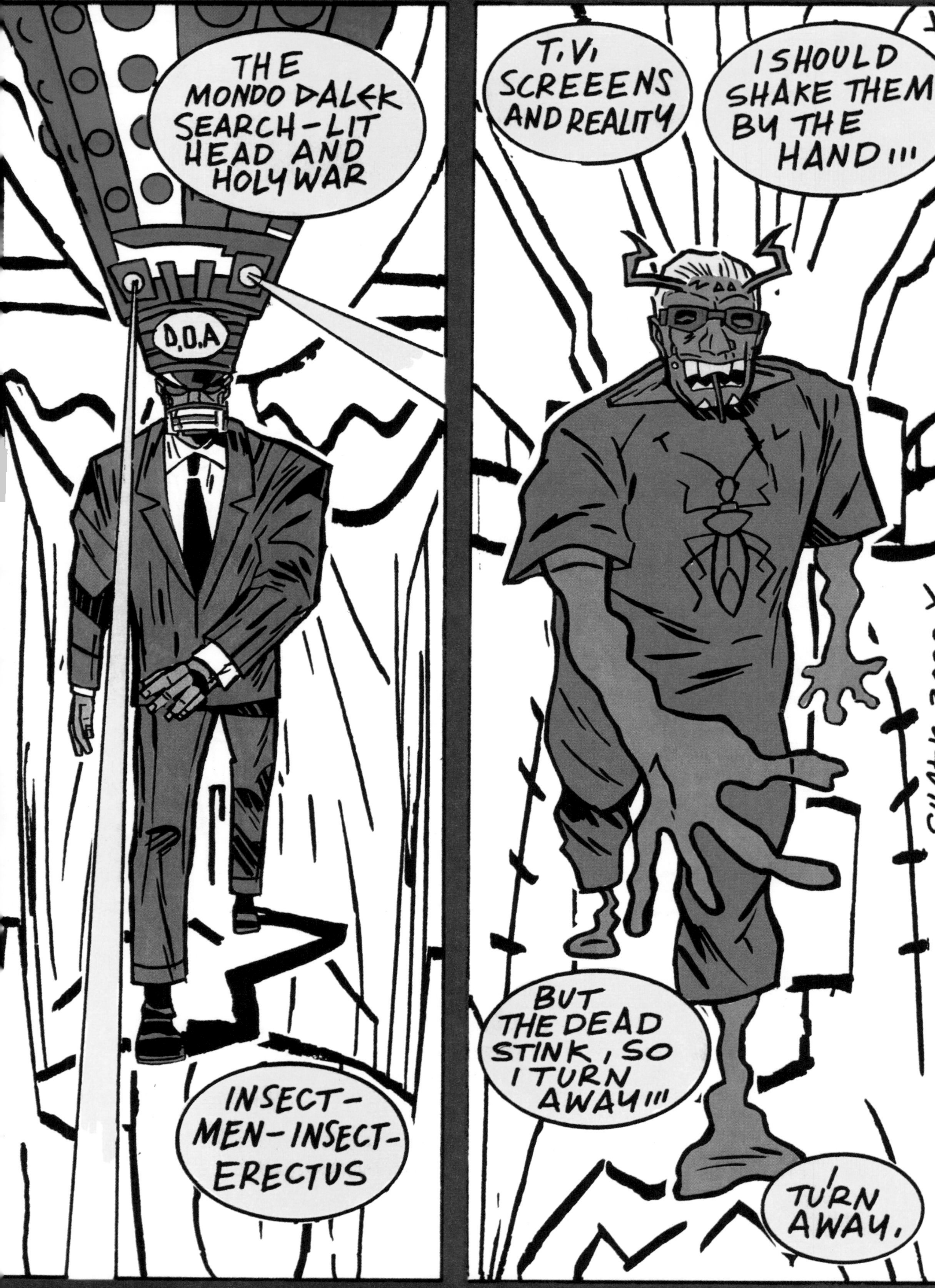
THE MONDO DALEK SEARCH-LIT HEAD AND HOLY WAR
D.O.A
INSECT-MEN-INSECT-ERECTUS
T.V. SCREEENS AND REALITY
I SHOULD SHAKE THEM BY THE HAND...
BUT THE DEAD STINK, SO I TURN AWAY...
I TURN AWAY.
SHAKY 2000 X.

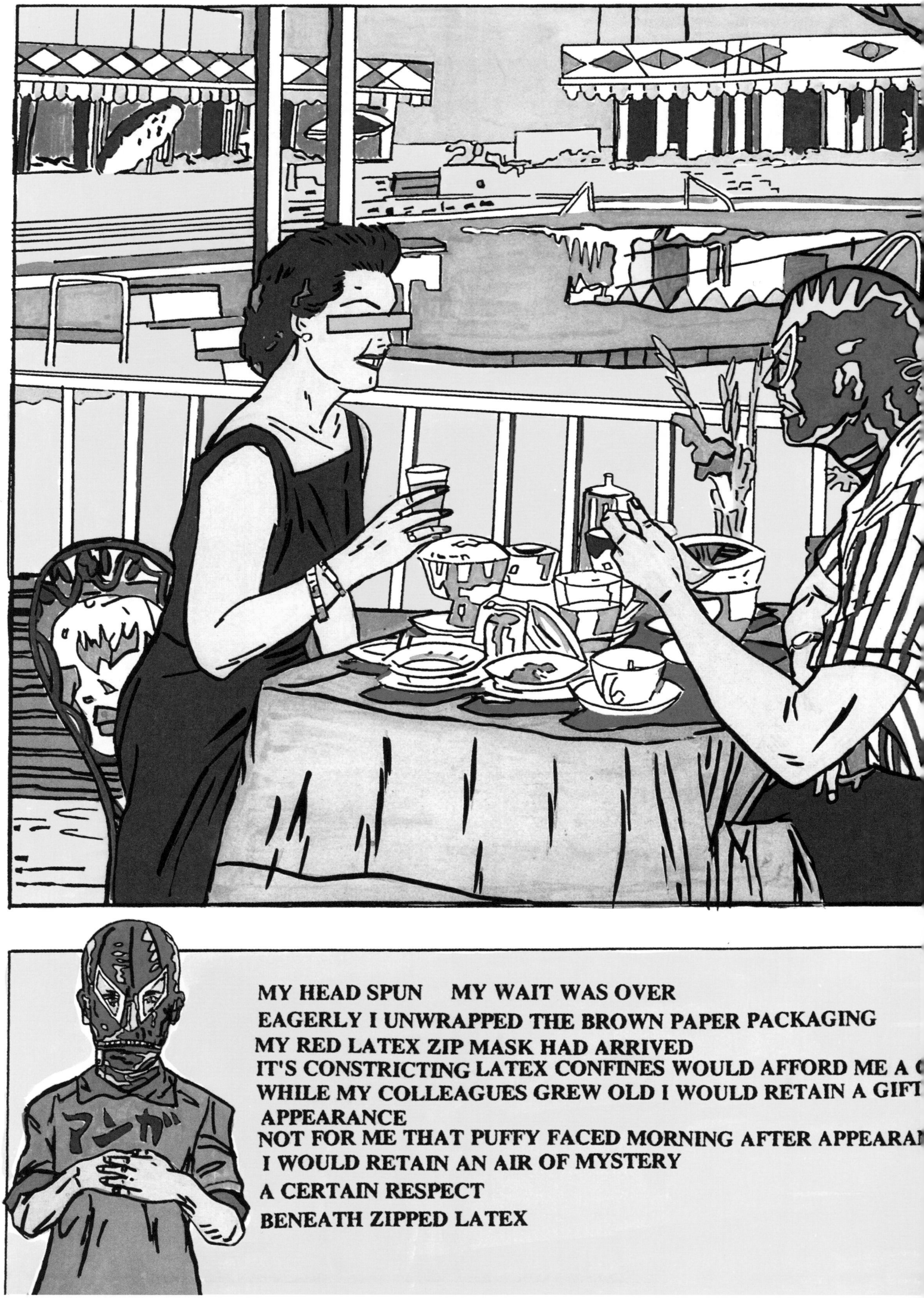
MY HEAD SPUN MY WAIT WAS OVER
EAGERLY I UNWRAPPED THE BROWN PAPER PACKAGING
MY RED LATEX ZIP MASK HAD ARRIVED
IT'S CONSTRICTING LATEX CONFINES WOULD AFFORD ME A C
WHILE MY COLLEAGUES GREW OLD I WOULD RETAIN A GIFT
APPEARANCE
NOT FOR ME THAT PUFFY FACED MORNING AFTER APPEARAN
I WOULD RETAIN AN AIR OF MYSTERY
A CERTAIN RESPECT
BENEATH ZIPPED LATEX
アンガ

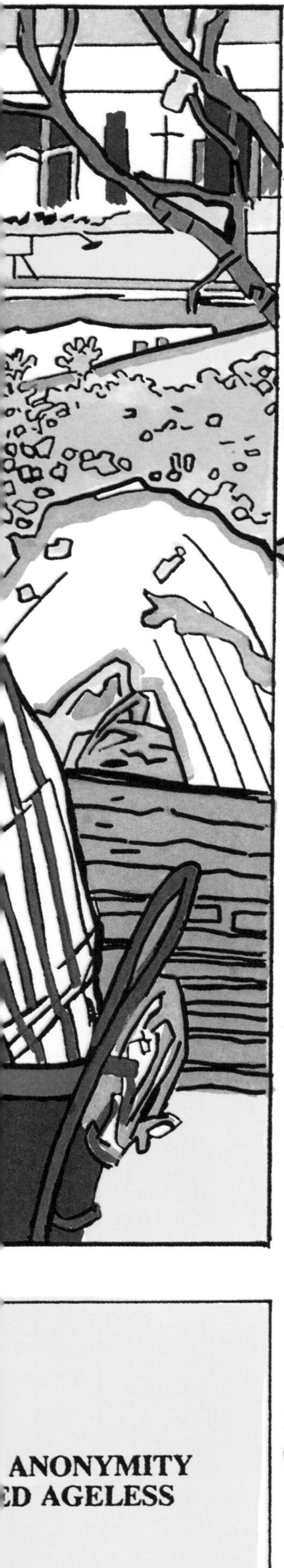
ANONYMITY
ED AGELESS

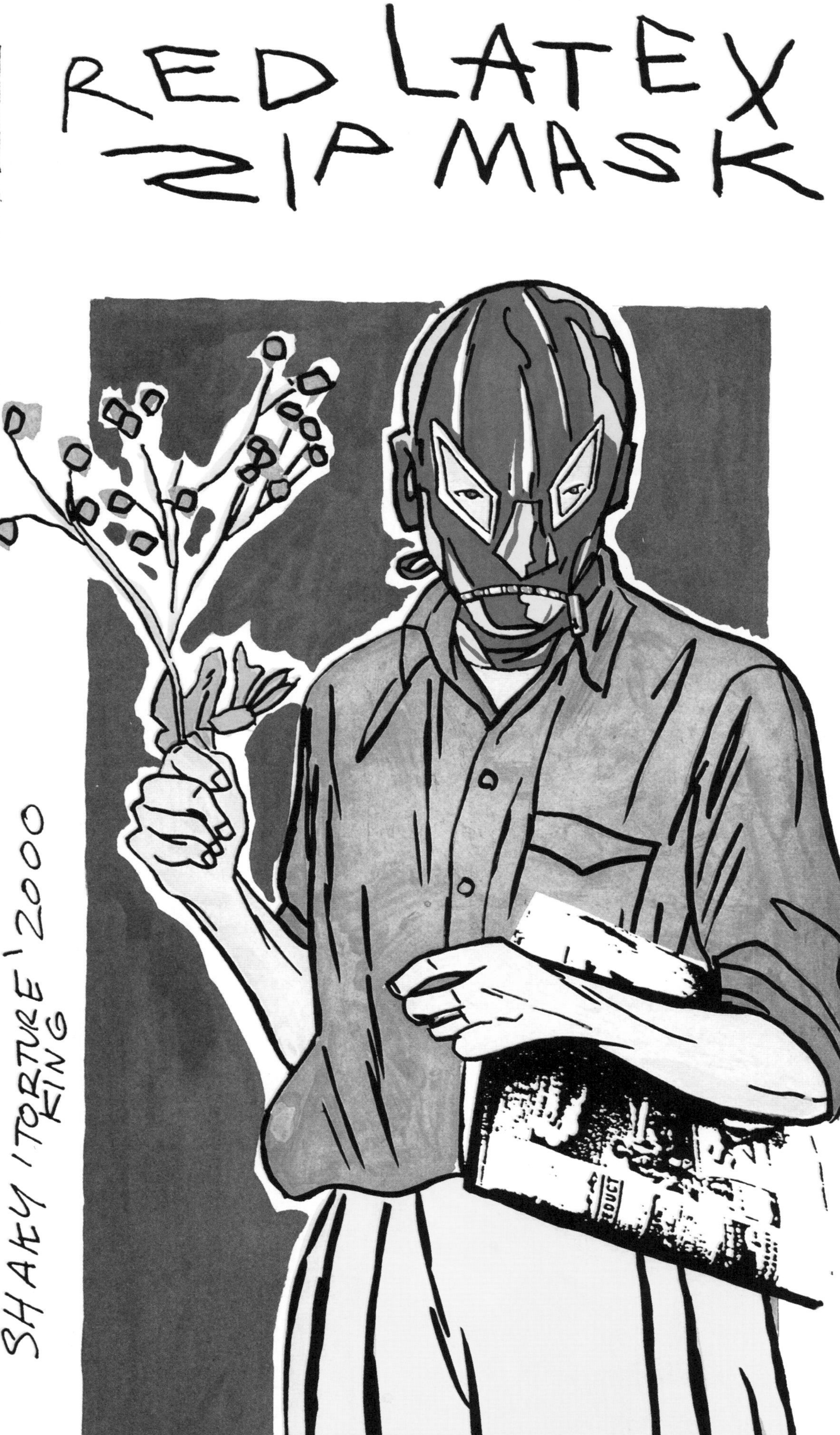
RED LATEX
ZIP MASK
SHAKY 'TORTURE' KING 2000

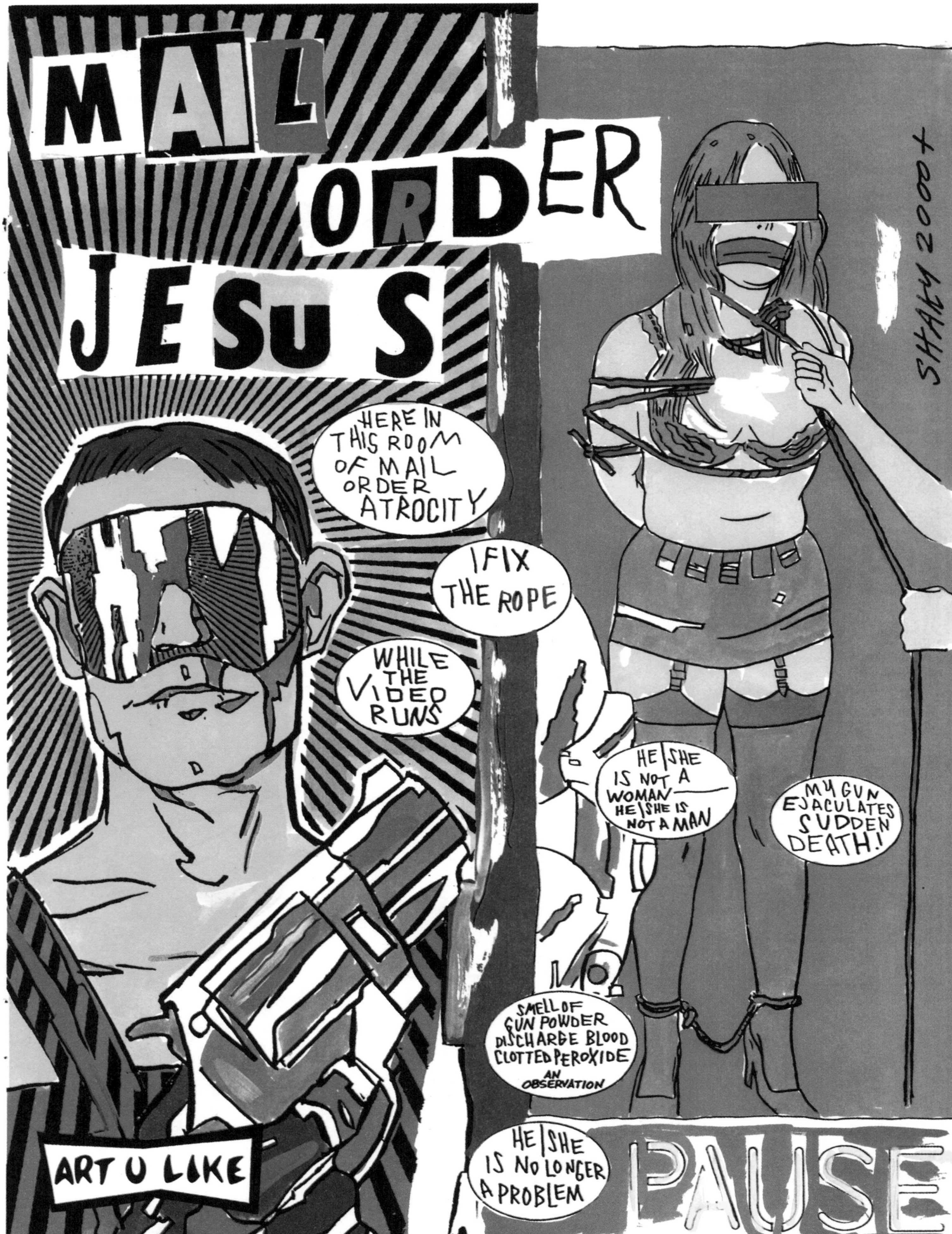
MAIL ORDER JESUS
HERE IN THIS ROOM OF MAIL ORDER ATROCITY
I FIX THE ROPE
WHILE THE VIDEO RUNS
SHAKY 2000+
HE|SHE IS NOT A WOMAN HE|SHE IS NOT A MAN
MY GUN EJACULATES SUDDEN DEATH!
SMELL OF GUN POWDER DISCHARGE BLOOD CLOTTED PEROXIDE
AN OBSERVATION
ART U LIKE
HE|SHE IS NO LONGER A PROBLEM
PAUSE

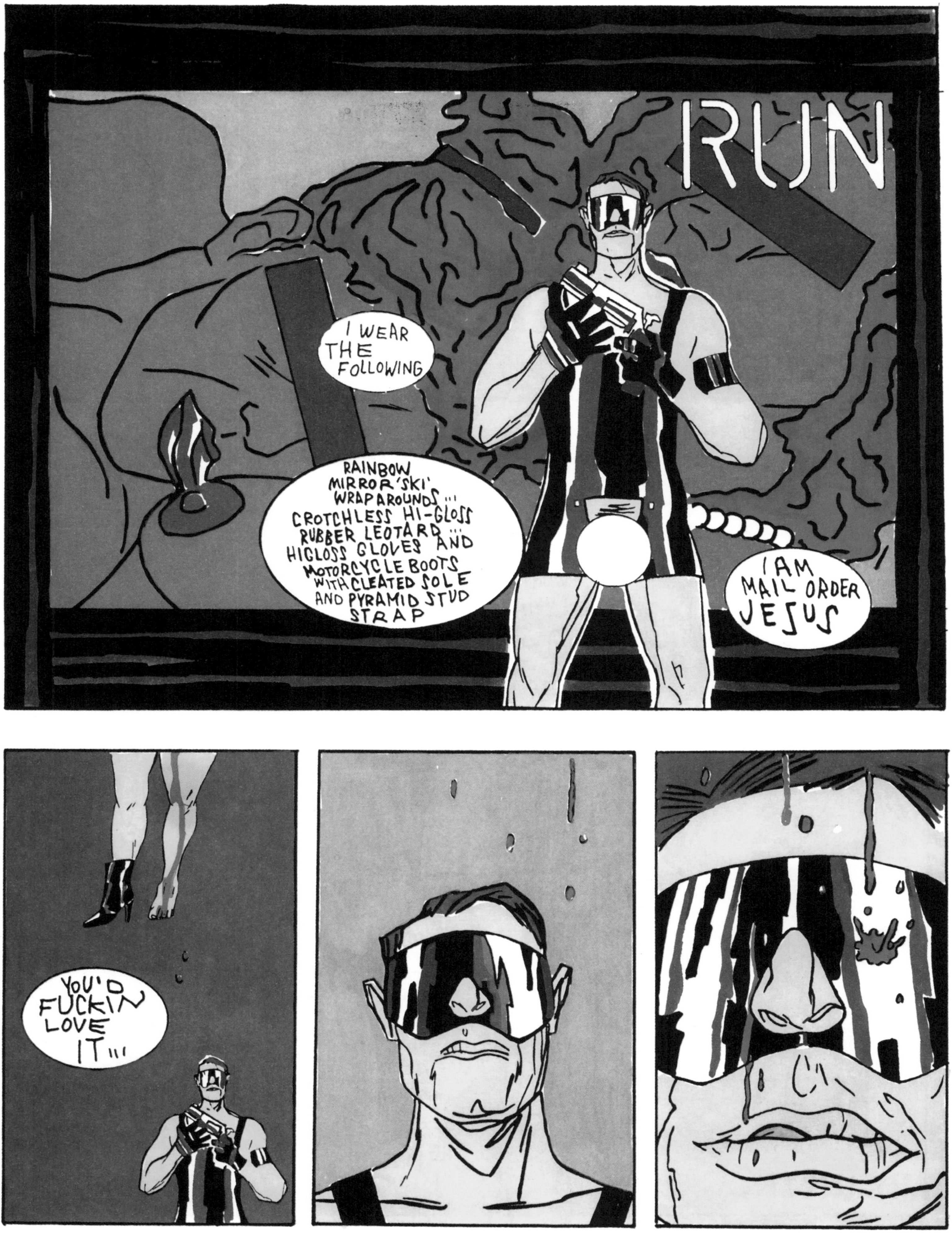
RUN
I WEAR THE FOLLOWING
RAINBOW MIRROR 'SKI' WRAPAROUNDS... CROTCHLESS HI-GLOSS RUBBER LEOTARD... HIGLOSS GLOVES AND MOTORCYCLE BOOTS WITH CLEATED SOLE AND PYRAMID STUD STRAP
I AM MAIL ORDER JESUS
YOU'D FUCKIN LOVE IT...

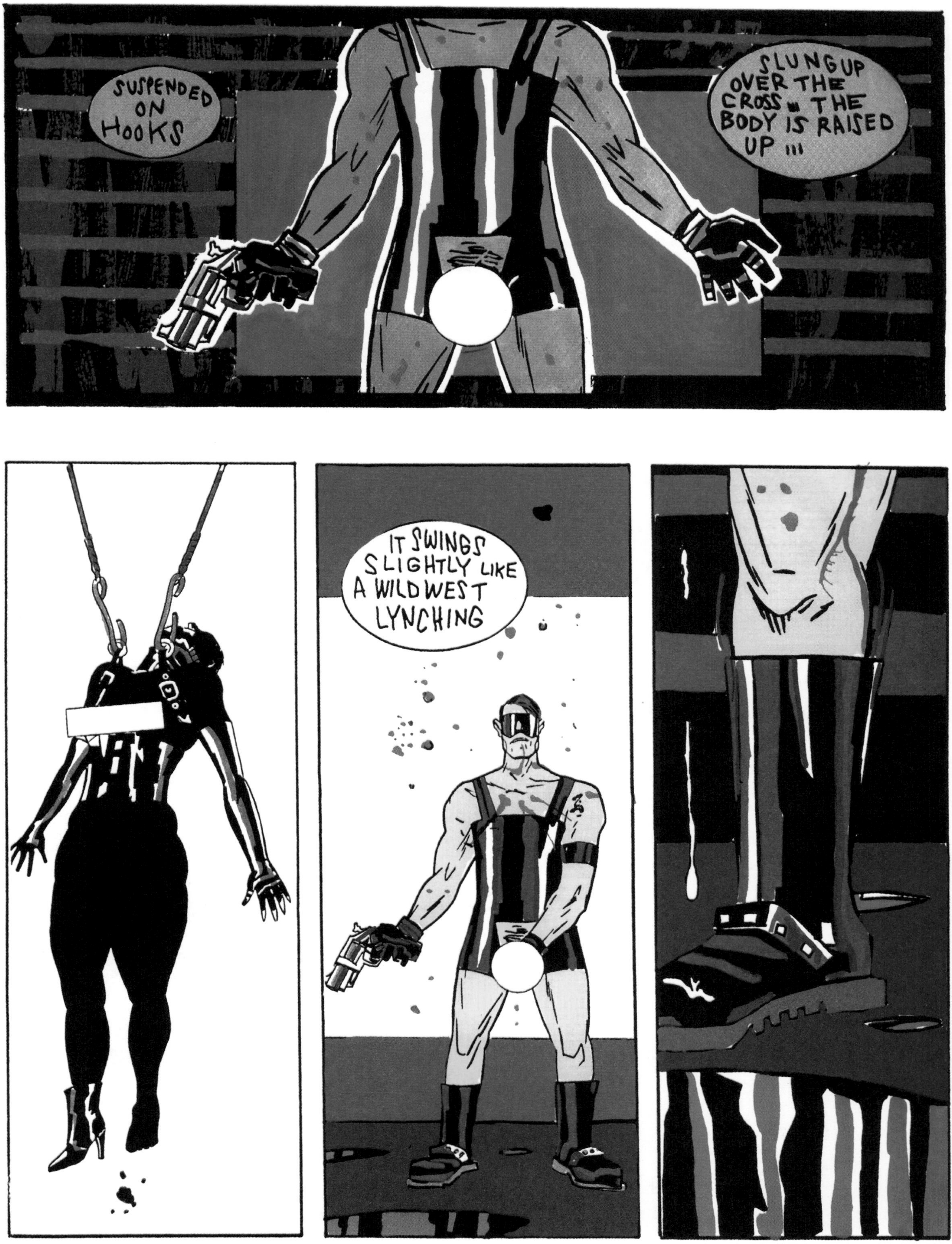
SUSPENDED ON HOOKS
SLUNG UP OVER THE CROSS ... THE BODY IS RAISED UP ...
IT SWINGS SLIGHTLY LIKE A WILD WEST LYNCHING

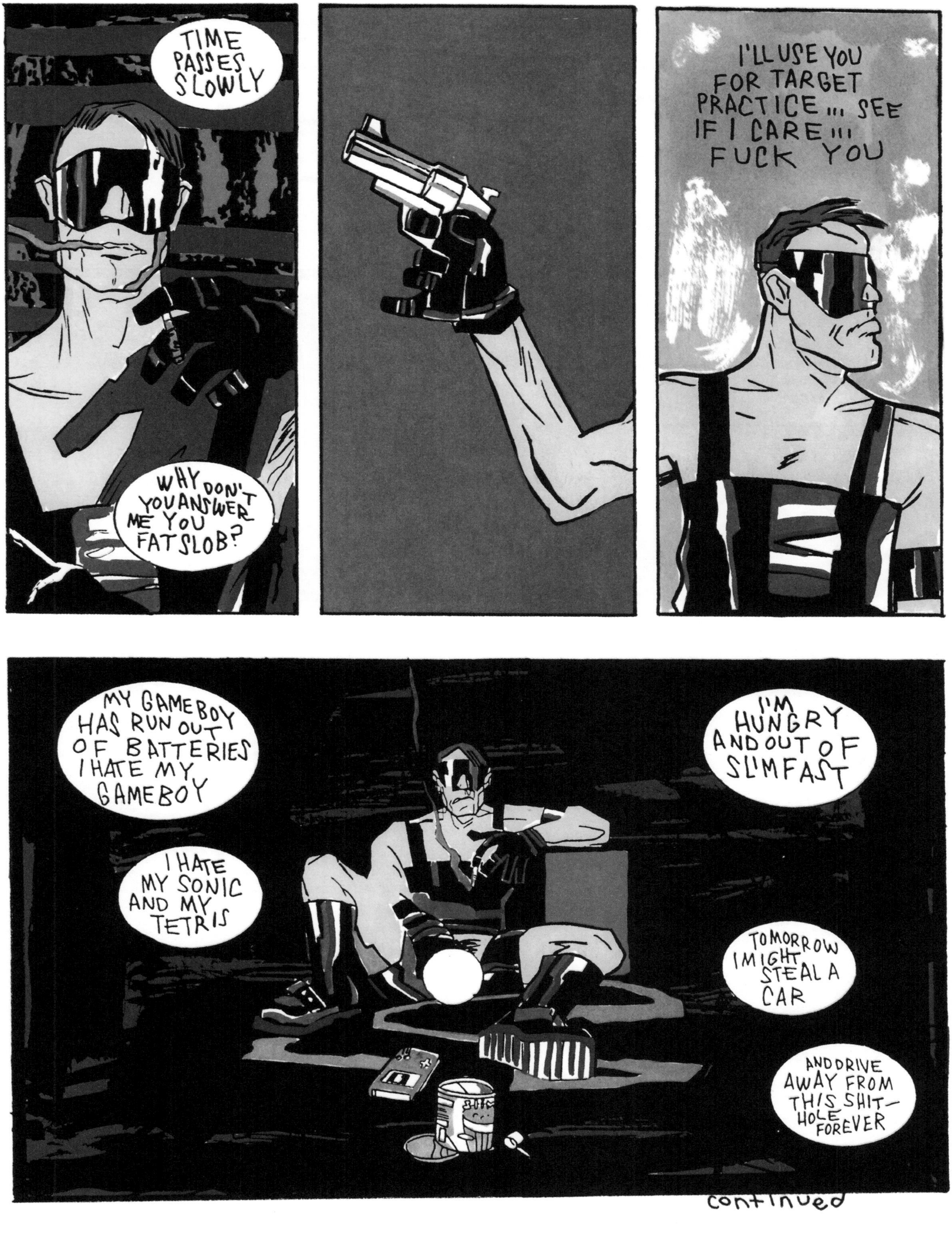
TIME PASSES SLOWLY
WHY DON'T YOU ANSWER ME YOU FAT SLOB?
I'LL USE YOU FOR TARGET PRACTICE ... SEE IF I CARE ... FUCK YOU
MY GAMEBOY HAS RUN OUT OF BATTERIES I HATE MY GAMEBOY
I HATE MY SONIC AND MY TETRIS
I'M HUNGRY AND OUT OF SLIMFAST
TOMORROW I MIGHT STEAL A CAR
AND DRIVE AWAY FROM THIS SHIT-HOLE FOREVER

continued

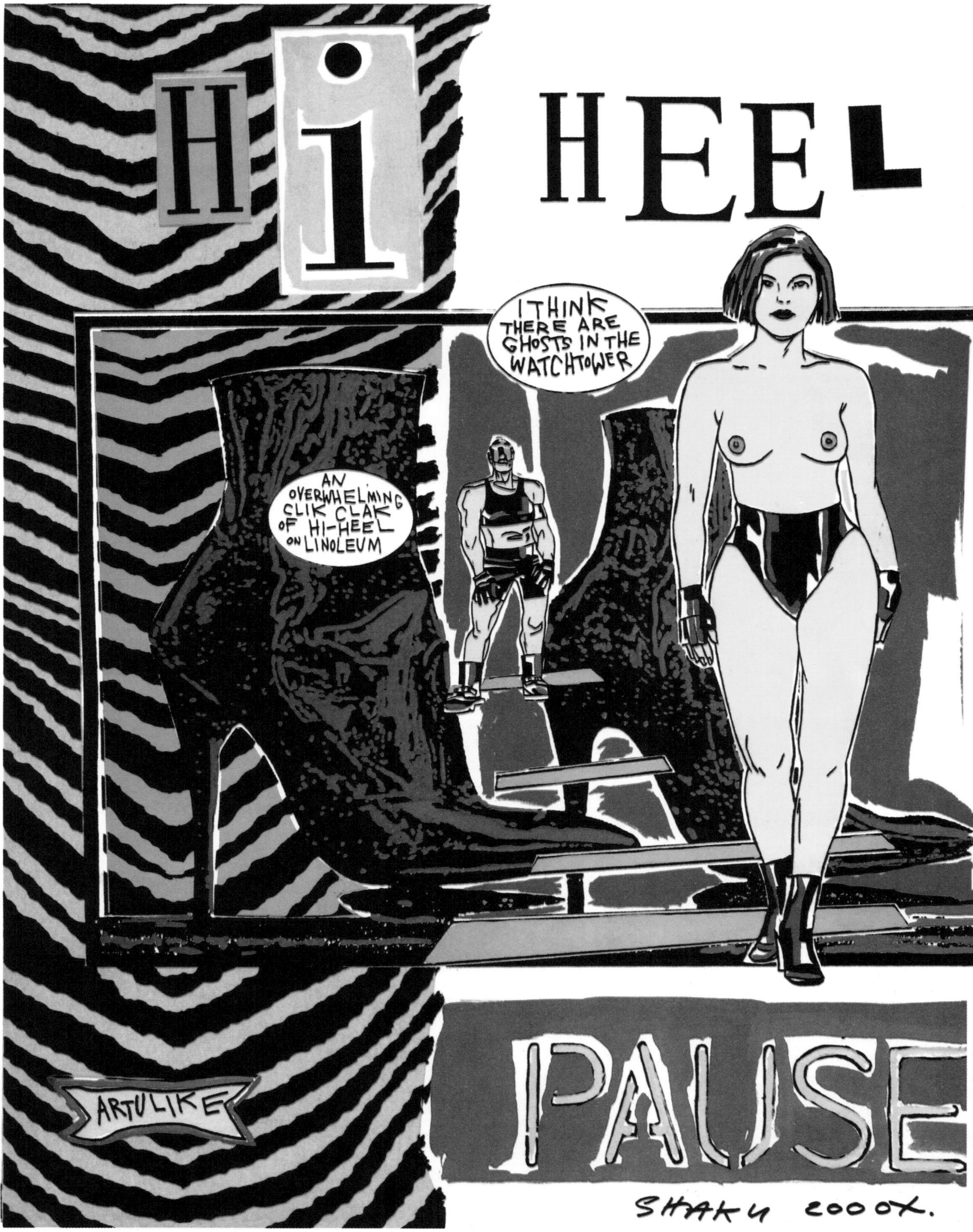

Hi HEEL
I THINK THERE ARE GHOSTS IN THE WATCHTOWER
AN OVERWHELMING CLIK CLAK OF HI-HEEL ON LINOLEUM
ARTULIKE
PAUSE
SHAKU 2000X.

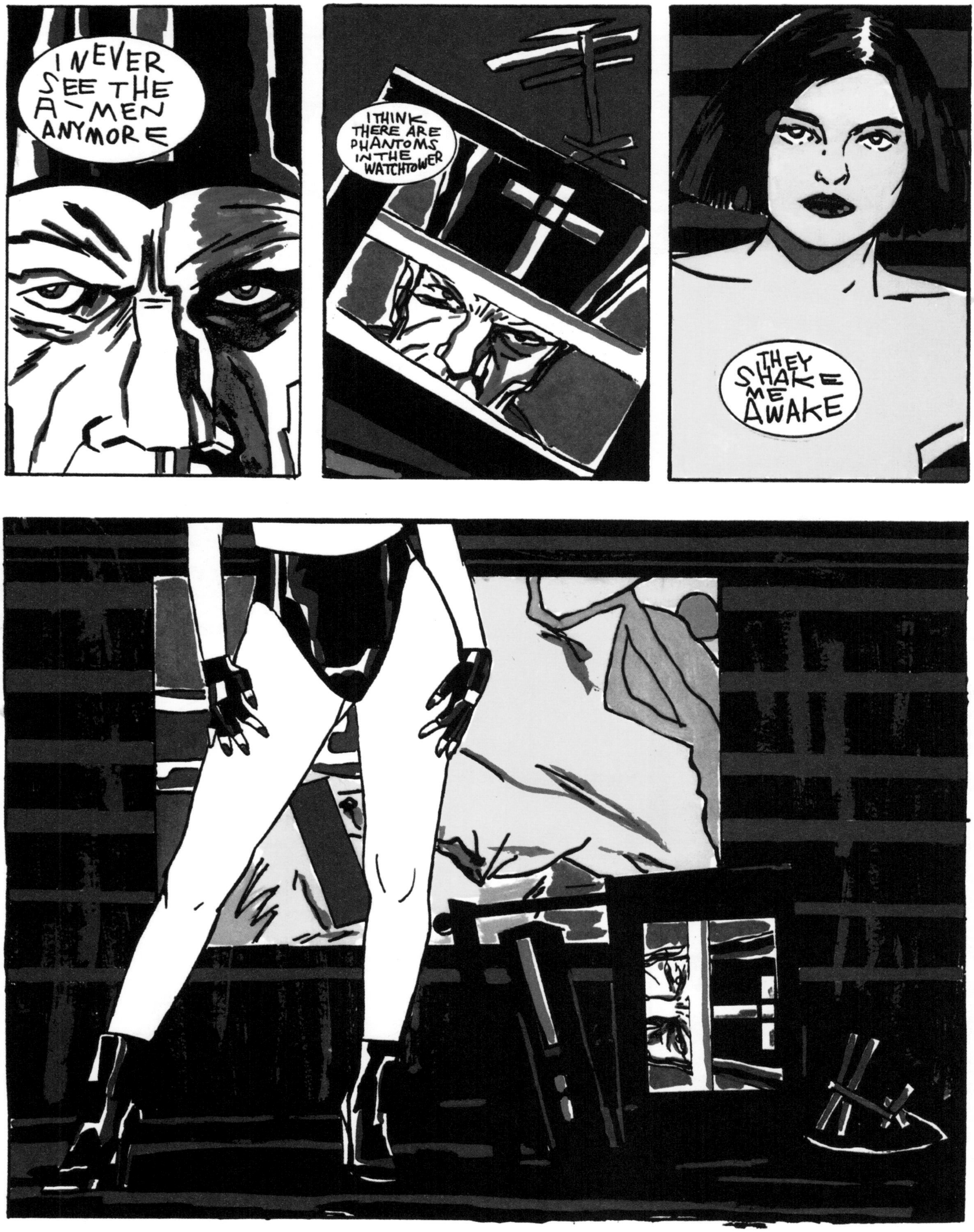
I NEVER SEE THE A-MEN ANYMORE
I THINK THERE ARE PHANTOMS IN THE WATCHTOWER
THEY SHAKE ME AWAKE

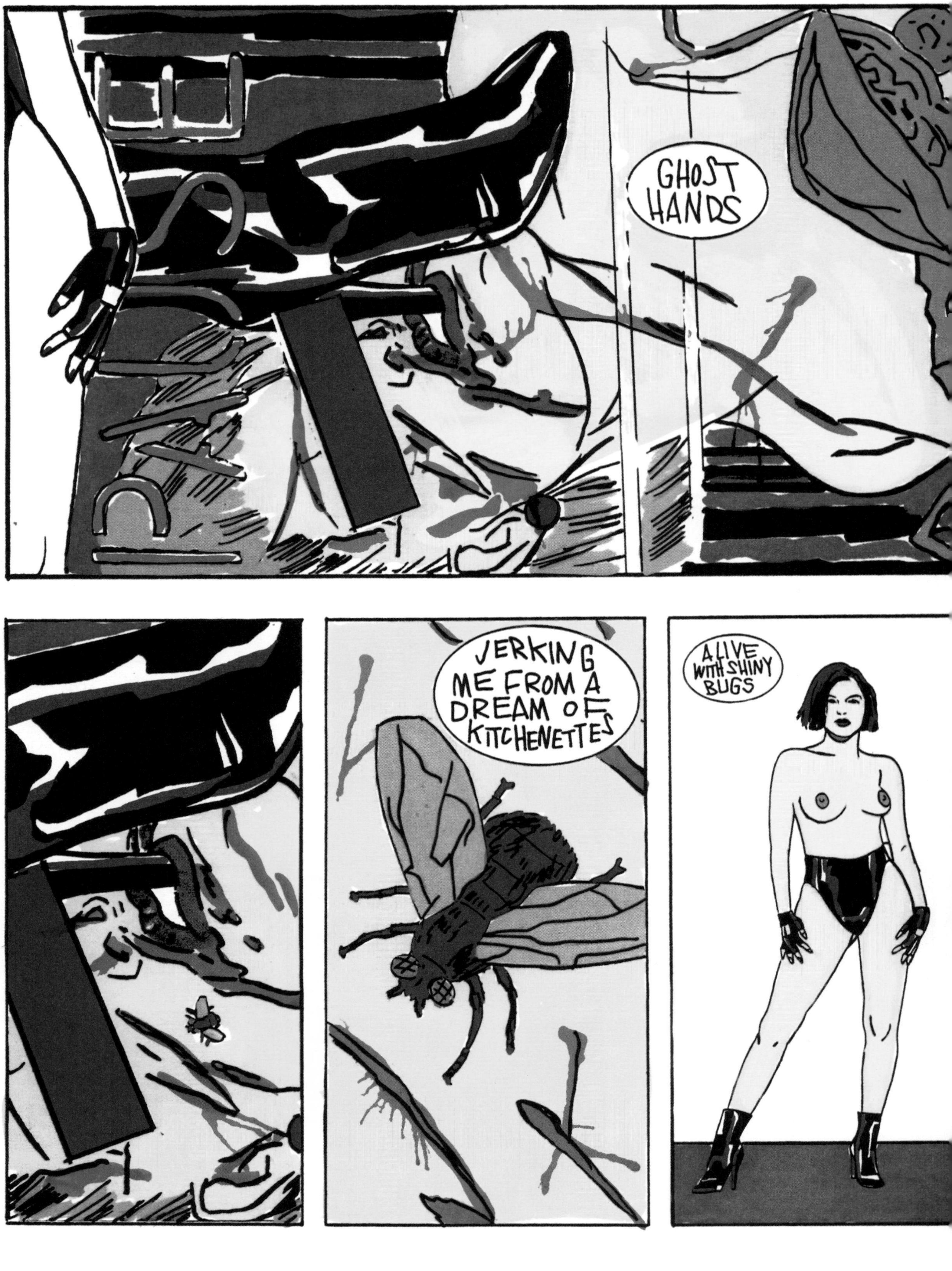
GHOST HANDS
JERKING ME FROM A DREAM OF KITCHENETTES
ALIVE WITH SHINY BUGS

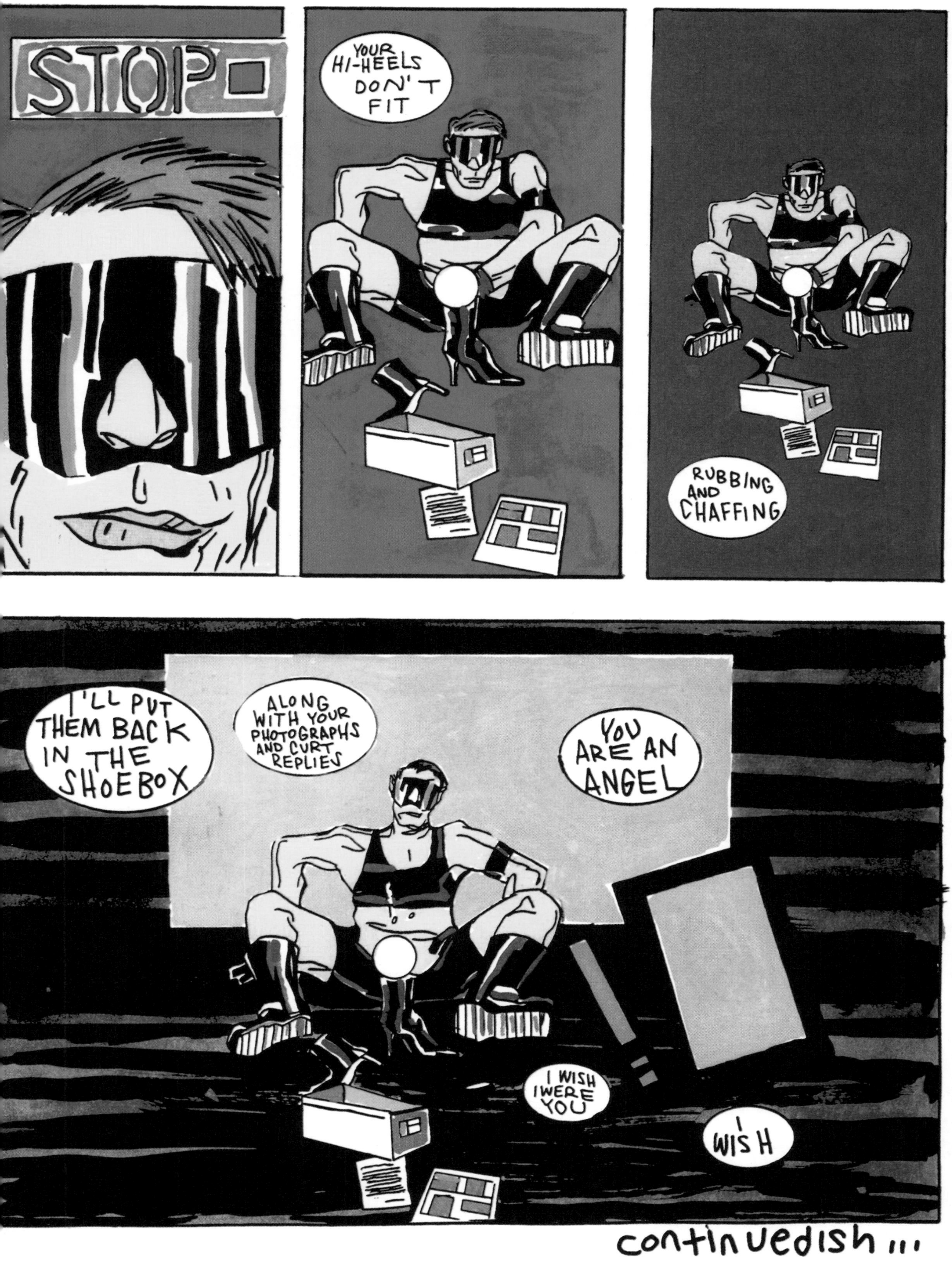
STOP
YOUR HI-HEELS DON'T FIT
RUBBING AND CHAFFING
I'LL PUT THEM BACK IN THE SHOEBOX
ALONG WITH YOUR PHOTOGRAPHS AND CURT REPLIES
YOU ARE AN ANGEL
I WISH I WERE YOU
I WISH
continuedish...

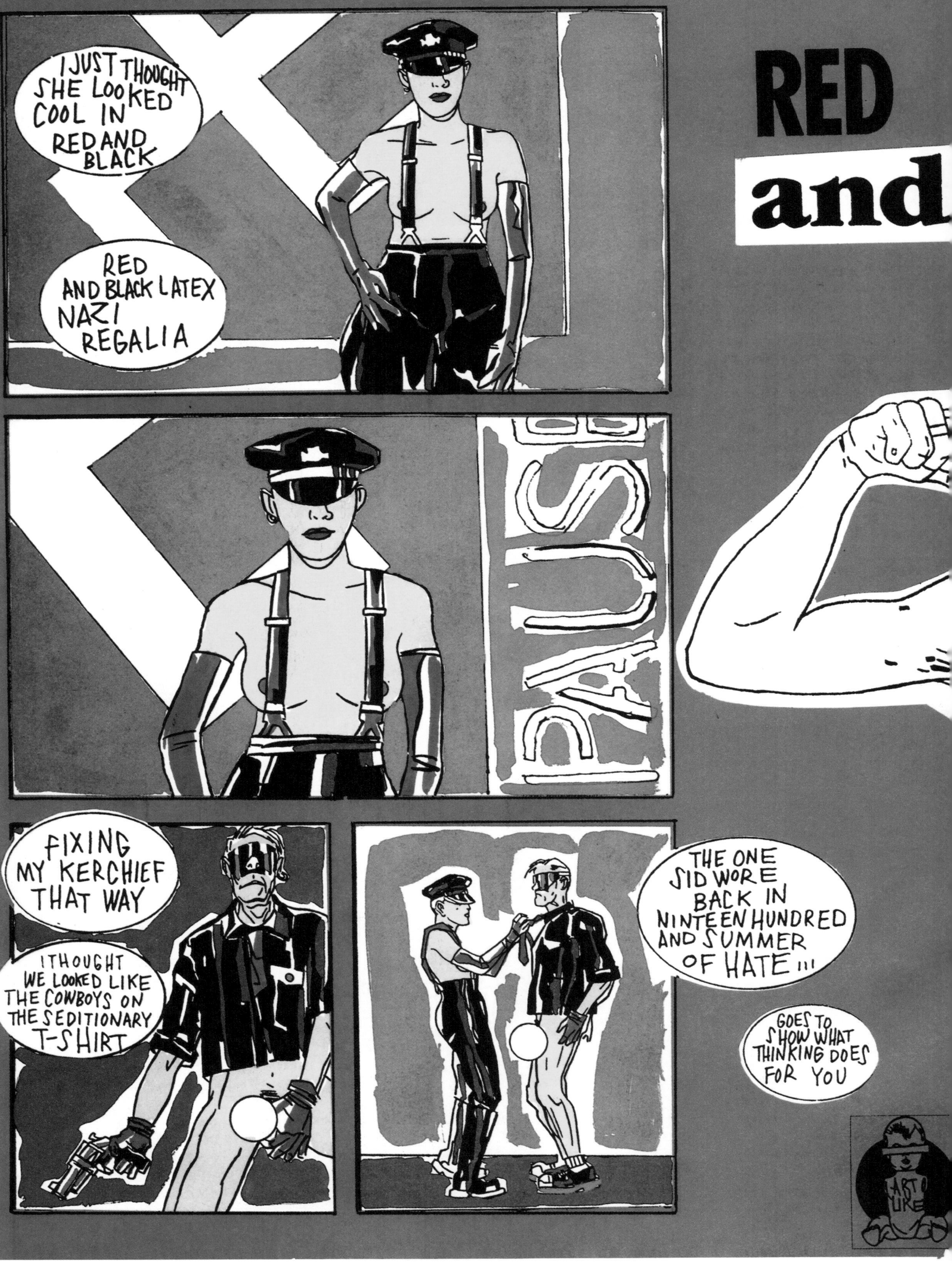

RED
and
I JUST THOUGHT SHE LOOKED COOL IN RED AND BLACK
RED AND BLACK LATEX NAZI REGALIA
PAUSE
FIXING MY KERCHIEF THAT WAY
I THOUGHT WE LOOKED LIKE THE COWBOYS ON THE SEDITIONARY T-SHIRT
THE ONE SID WORE BACK IN NINTEEN HUNDRED AND SUMMER OF HATE !!!
GOES TO SHOW WHAT THINKING DOES FOR YOU

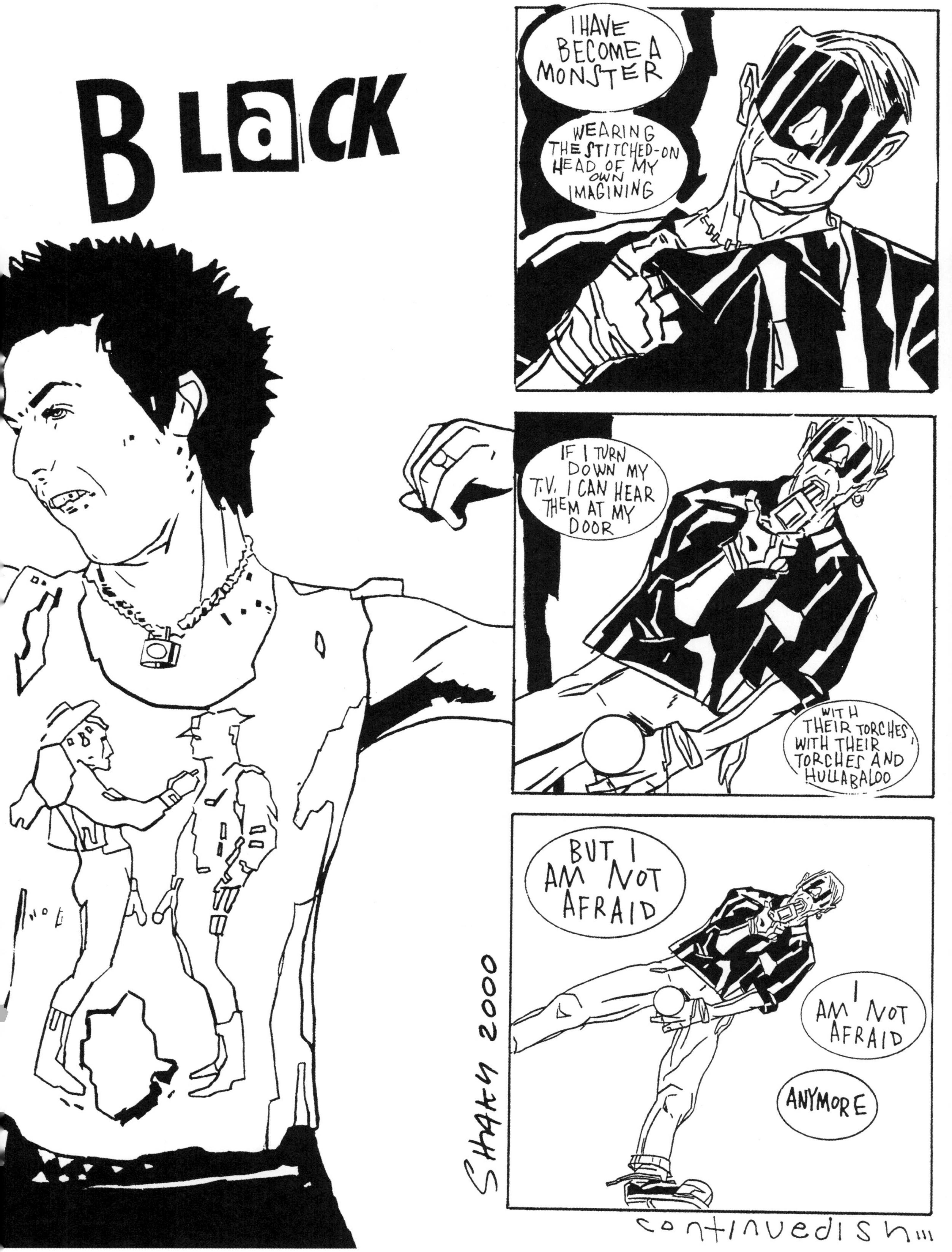
BLACK
I HAVE BECOME A MONSTER
WEARING THE STITCHED-ON HEAD OF MY OWN IMAGINING
IF I TURN DOWN MY T.V. I CAN HEAR THEM AT MY DOOR
WITH THEIR TORCHES, WITH THEIR TORCHES AND HULLABALOO
BUT I AM NOT AFRAID
I AM NOT AFRAID
ANYMORE
SHAKY 2000
continuedish...

GOD knew BLACK ELVIS
was tired,
So he took him to Rest.

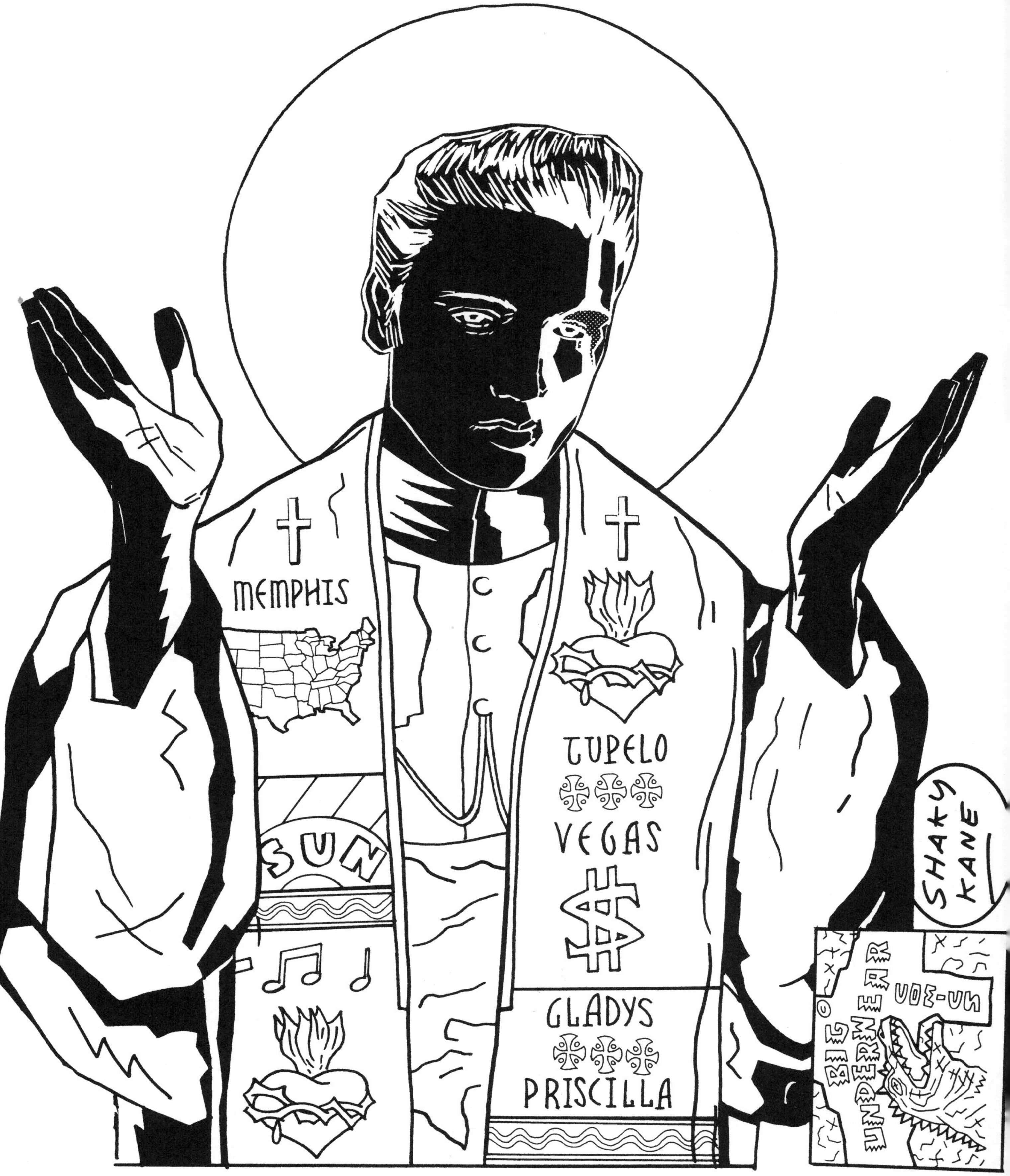

MEMPHIS
TUPELO
VEGAS
GLADYS
PRISCILLA
SUN
SHAKY KANE
BIG UNDERWEAR
UDE-UN

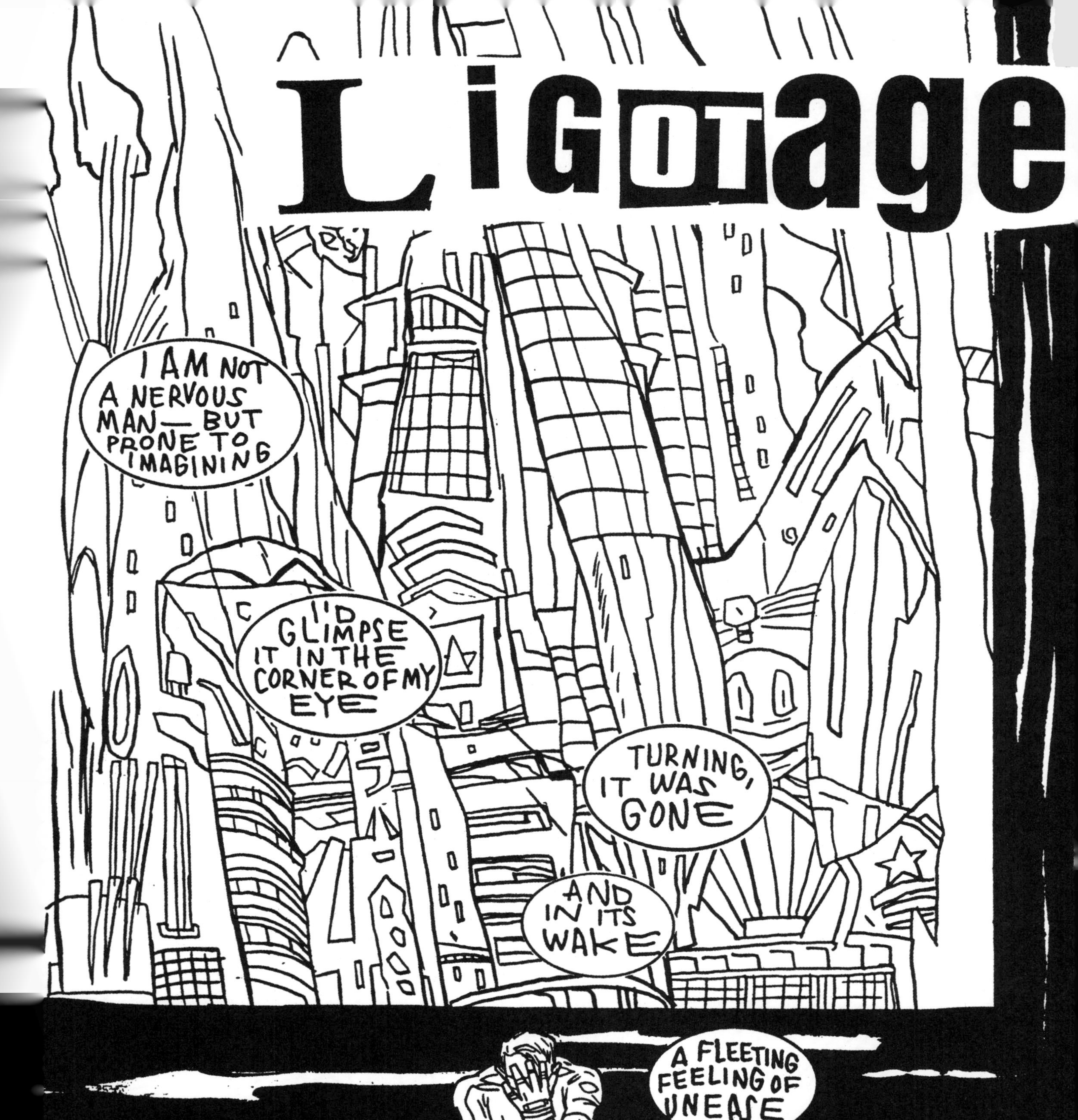
LiGOTage
I AM NOT A NERVOUS MAN— BUT PRONE TO IMAGINING
I'D GLIMPSE IT IN THE CORNER OF MY EYE
TURNING, IT WAS GONE
AND IN ITS WAKE
A FLEETING FEELING OF UNEASE

NNING FOR PHANTOMS

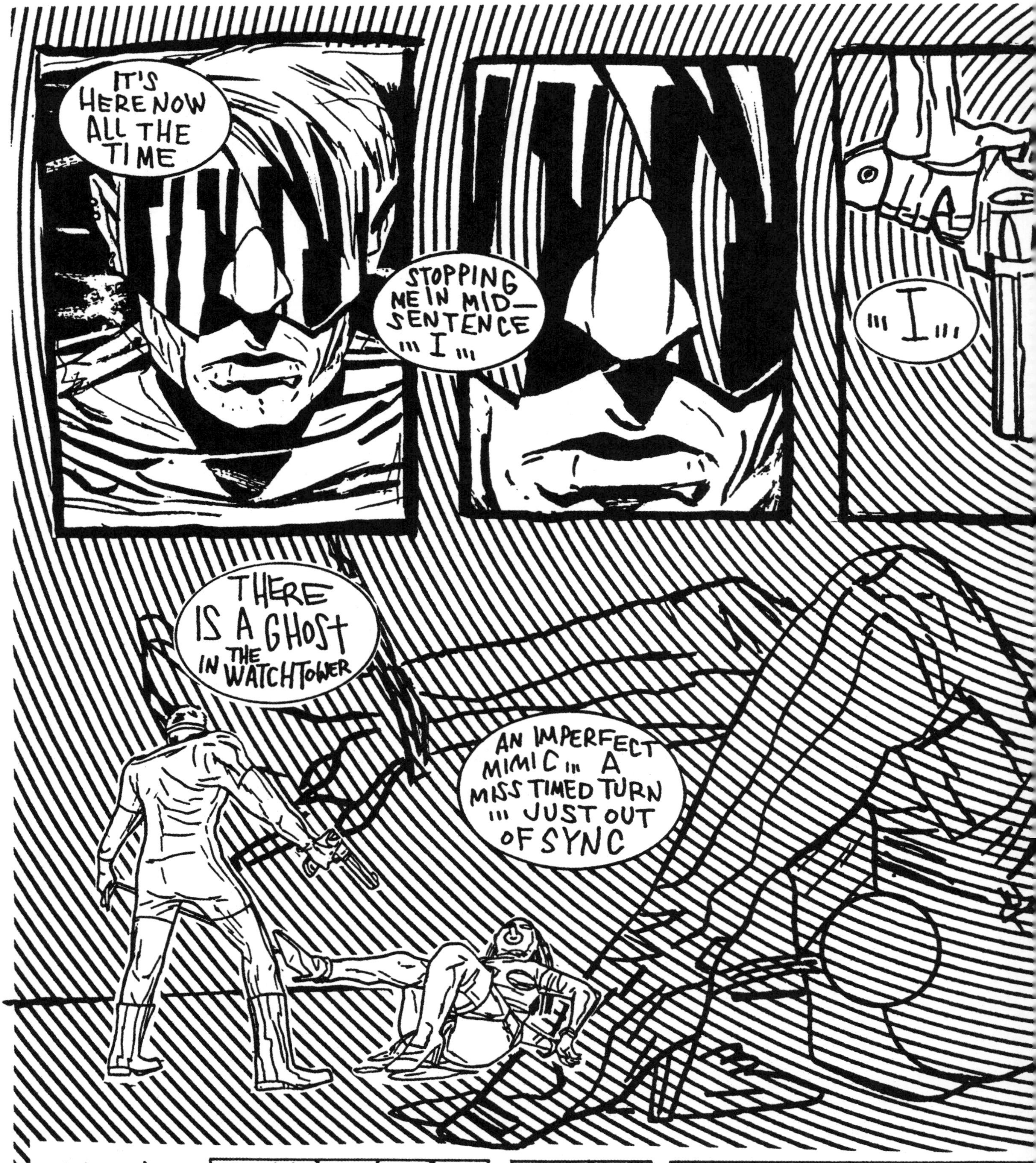
IT'S HERE NOW ALL THE TIME
STOPPING ME IN MID_SENTENCE ... I ...
... I ...
THERE IS A GHOST IN THE WATCHTOWER
AN IMPERFECT MIMIC ... A MISS TIMED TURN ... JUST OUT OF SYNC

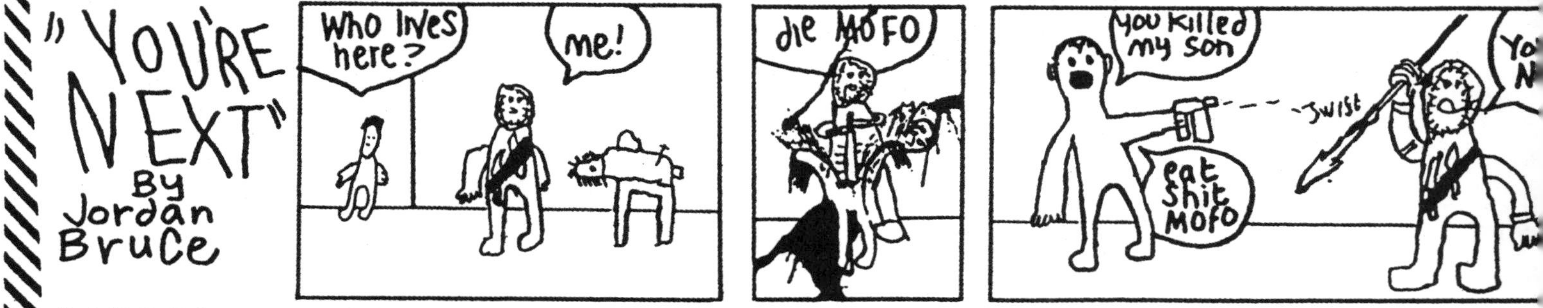
"YOU'RE NEXT"
By Jordan Bruce
Who lives here?
me!
die MOFO
You killed my son
eat shit MOFO

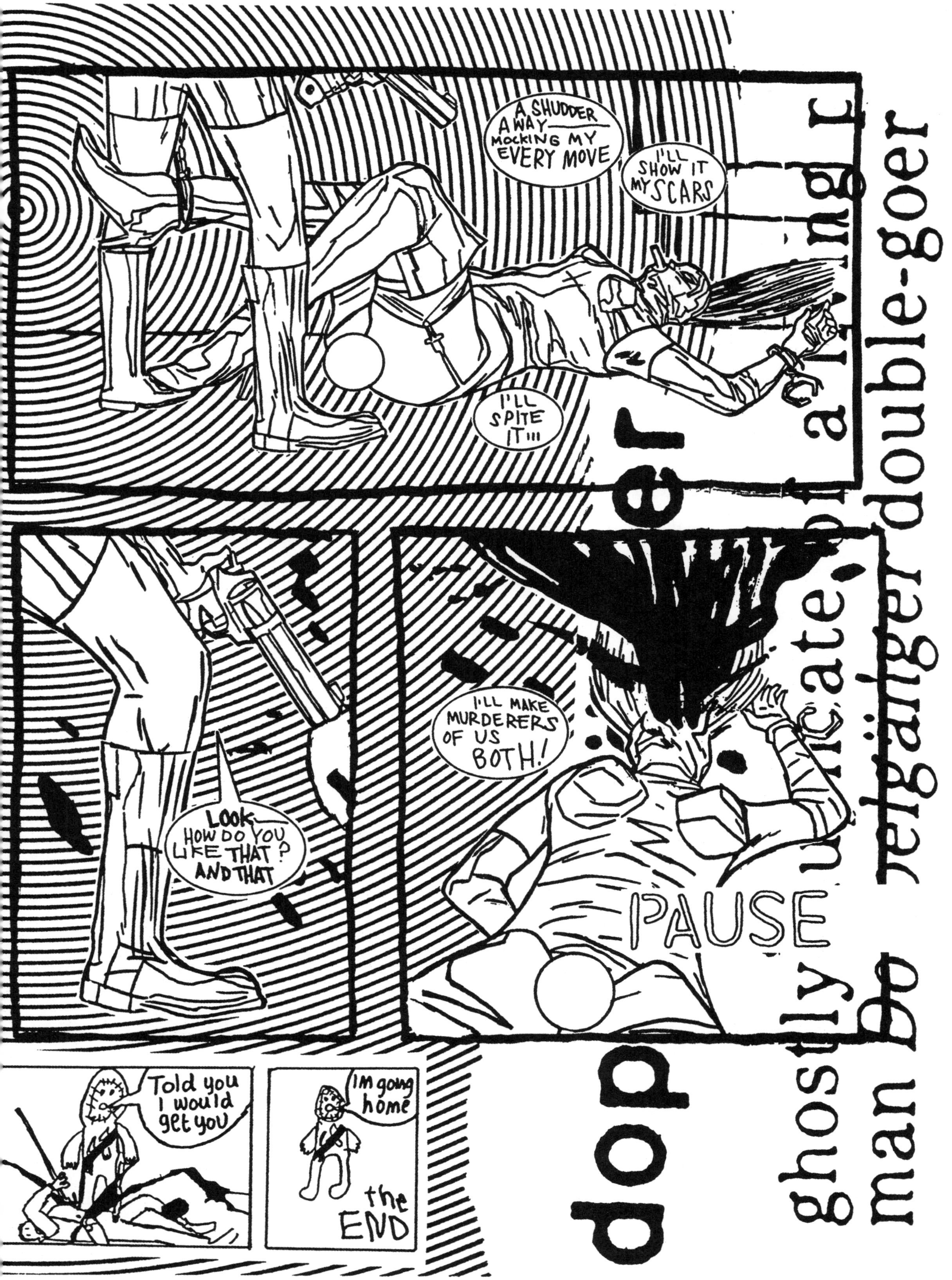
A SHUDDER AWAY—— MOCKING MY EVERY MOVE
I'LL SHOW IT MY SCARS
I'LL SPITE IT!!!
I'LL MAKE MURDERERS OF US BOTH!
LOOK HOW DO YOU LIKE THAT? AND THAT
PAUSE
Told you I would get you
Im going home
the END
dop
ghostly
man
double-goer
a

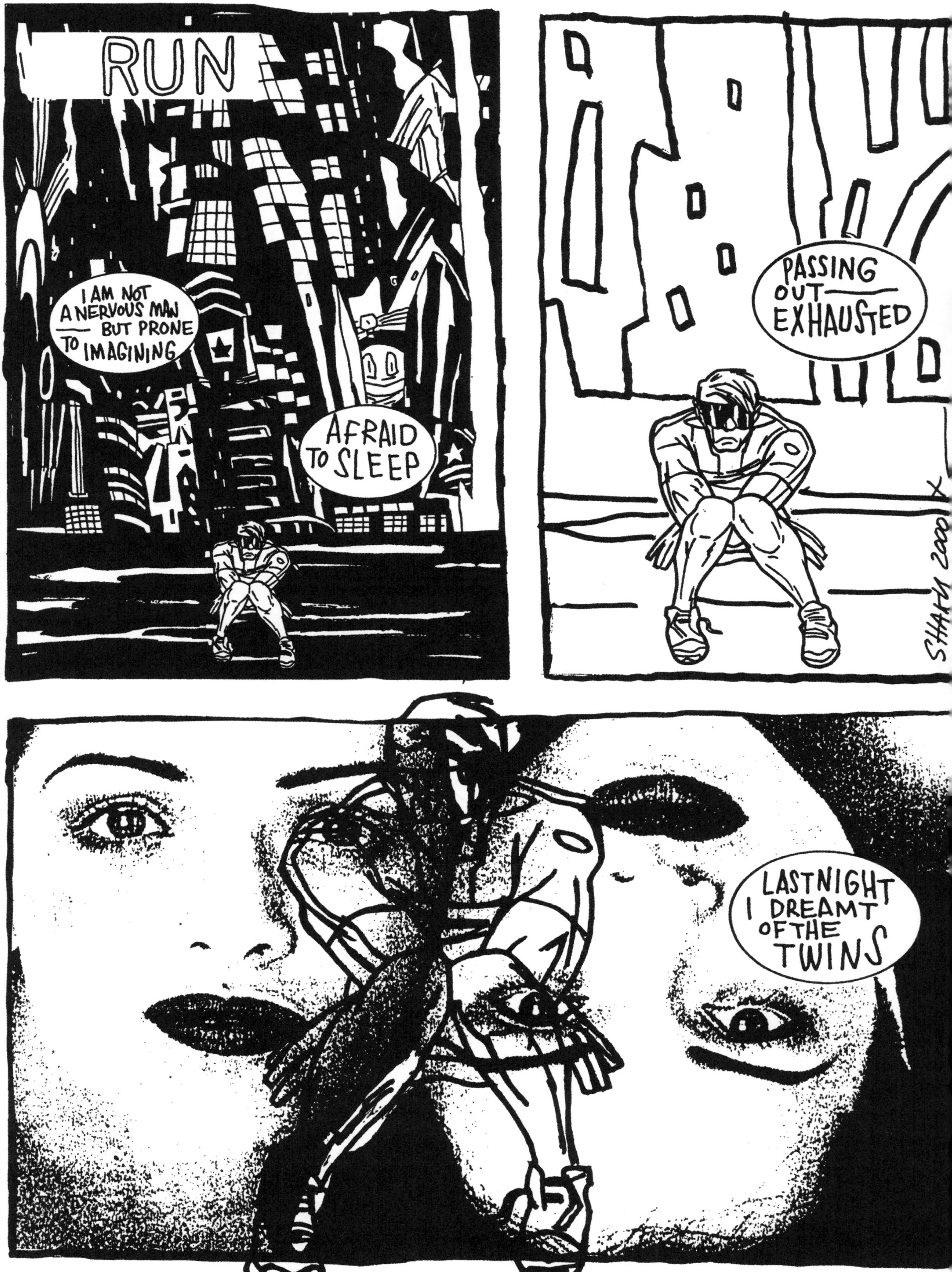
RUN
I AM NOT A NERVOUS MAN — BUT PRONE TO IMAGINING
AFRAID TO SLEEP
PASSING OUT — EXHAUSTED
SHAKY 2000
LASTNIGHT I DREAMT OF THE TWINS

# THIS IS WHAT WE LOOK LIKE WHEN WE DIE

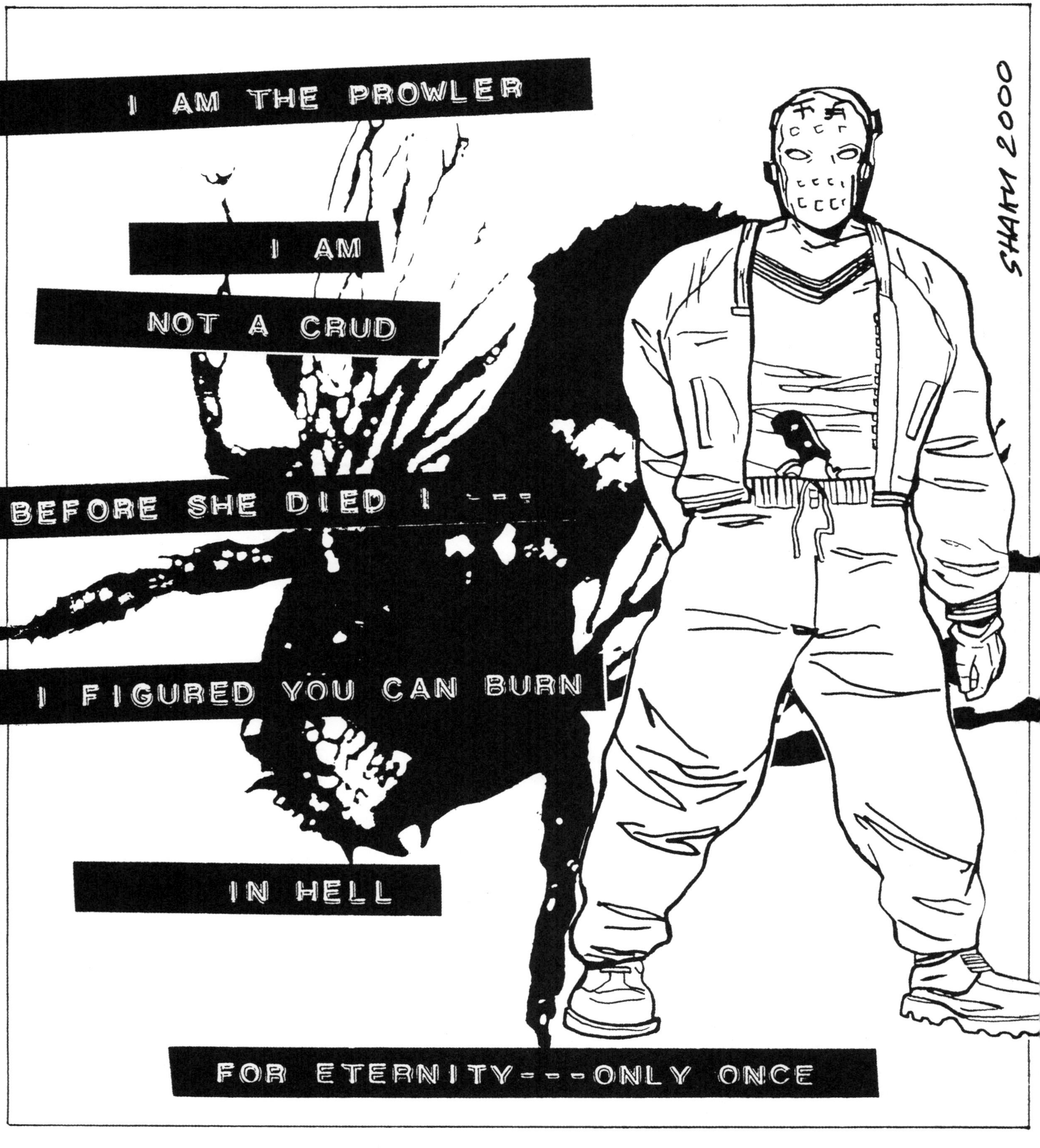
I AM THE PROWLER
I AM
NOT A CRUD
BEFORE SHE DIED I ---
I FIGURED YOU CAN BURN
IN HELL
FOR ETERNITY---ONLY ONCE
SHAM 2000

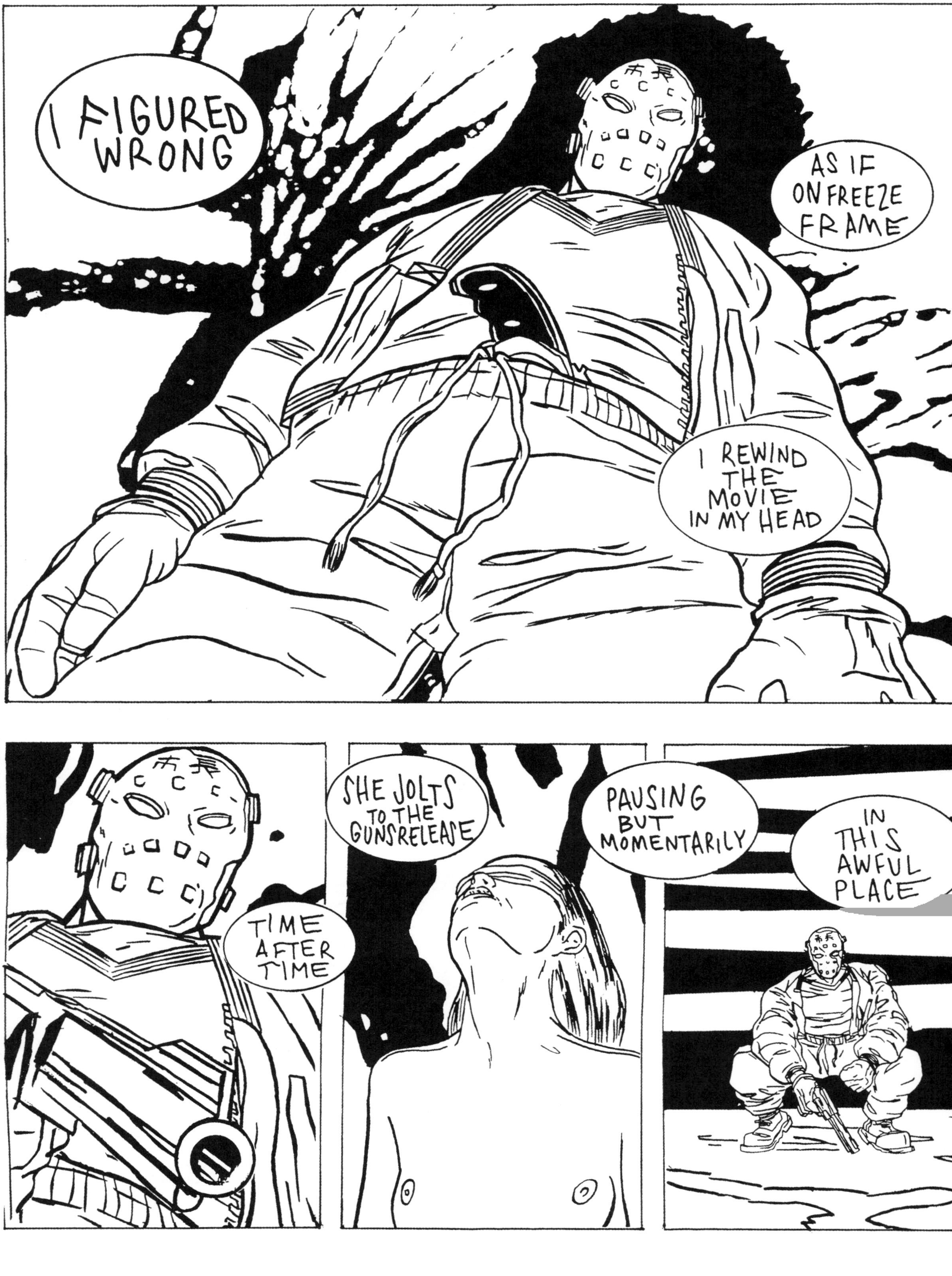
I FIGURED WRONG
AS IF ON FREEZE FRAME
I REWIND THE MOVIE IN MY HEAD
TIME AFTER TIME
SHE JOLTS TO THE GUNS RELEASE
PAUSING BUT MOMENTARILY
IN THIS AWFUL PLACE

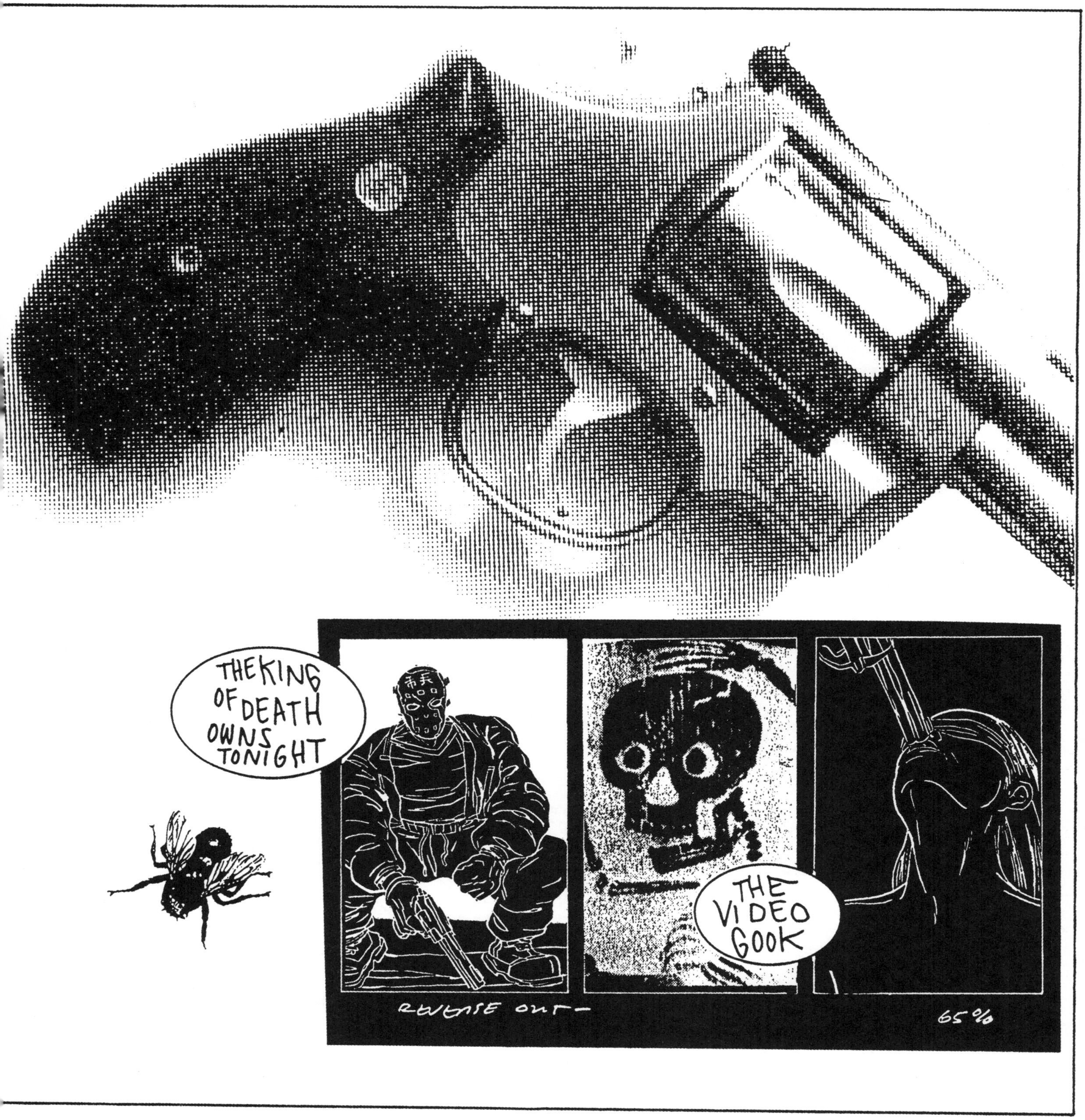
THE KING OF DEATH OWNS TONIGHT
THE VIDEO GOOK
65%

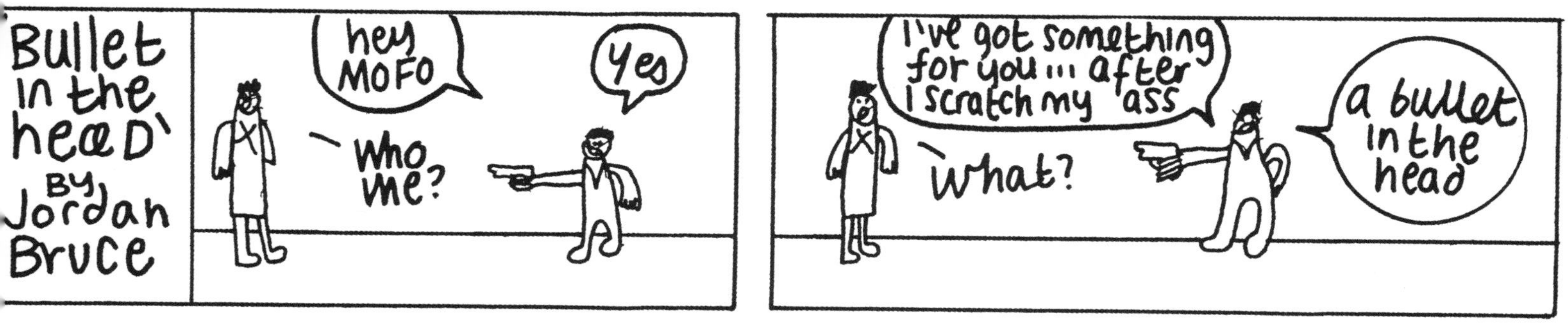
Bullet in the heaD'
By Jordan Bruce
hey MOFO
Yes
Who me?
I've got something for you ... after I scratch my ass
What?
a bullet in the head

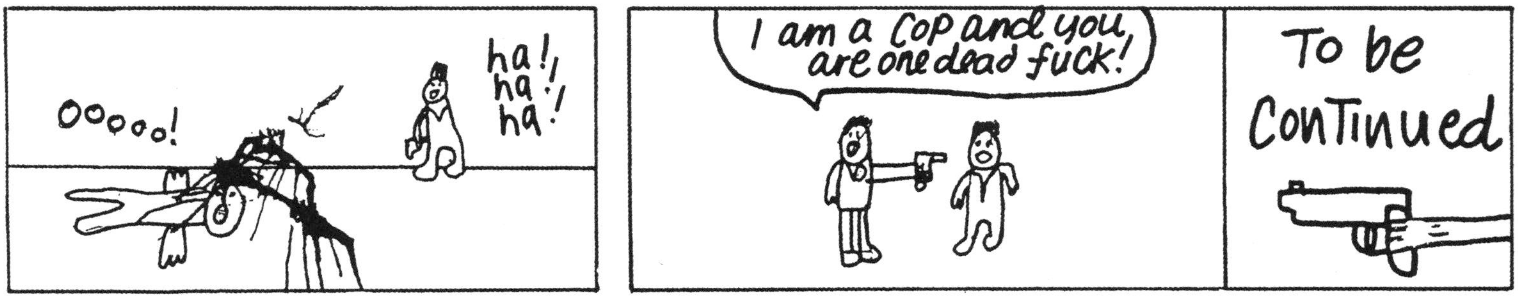
Ooooo!
ha! ha! ha!
I am a cop and you are one dead fuck!
To be Continued
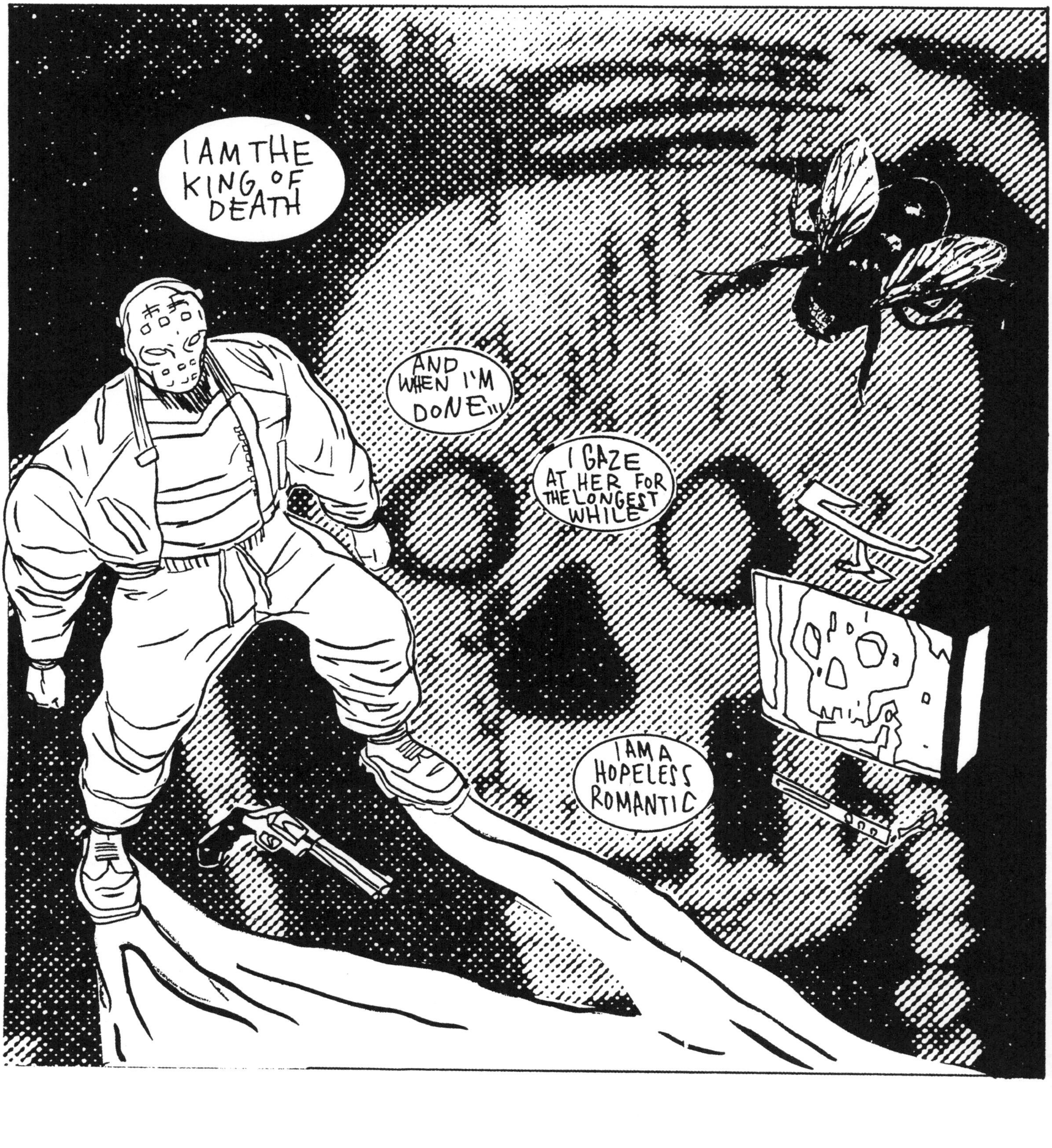
I AM THE KING OF DEATH
AND WHEN I'M DONE...
I GAZE AT HER FOR THE LONGEST WHILE
I AM A HOPELESS ROMANTIC

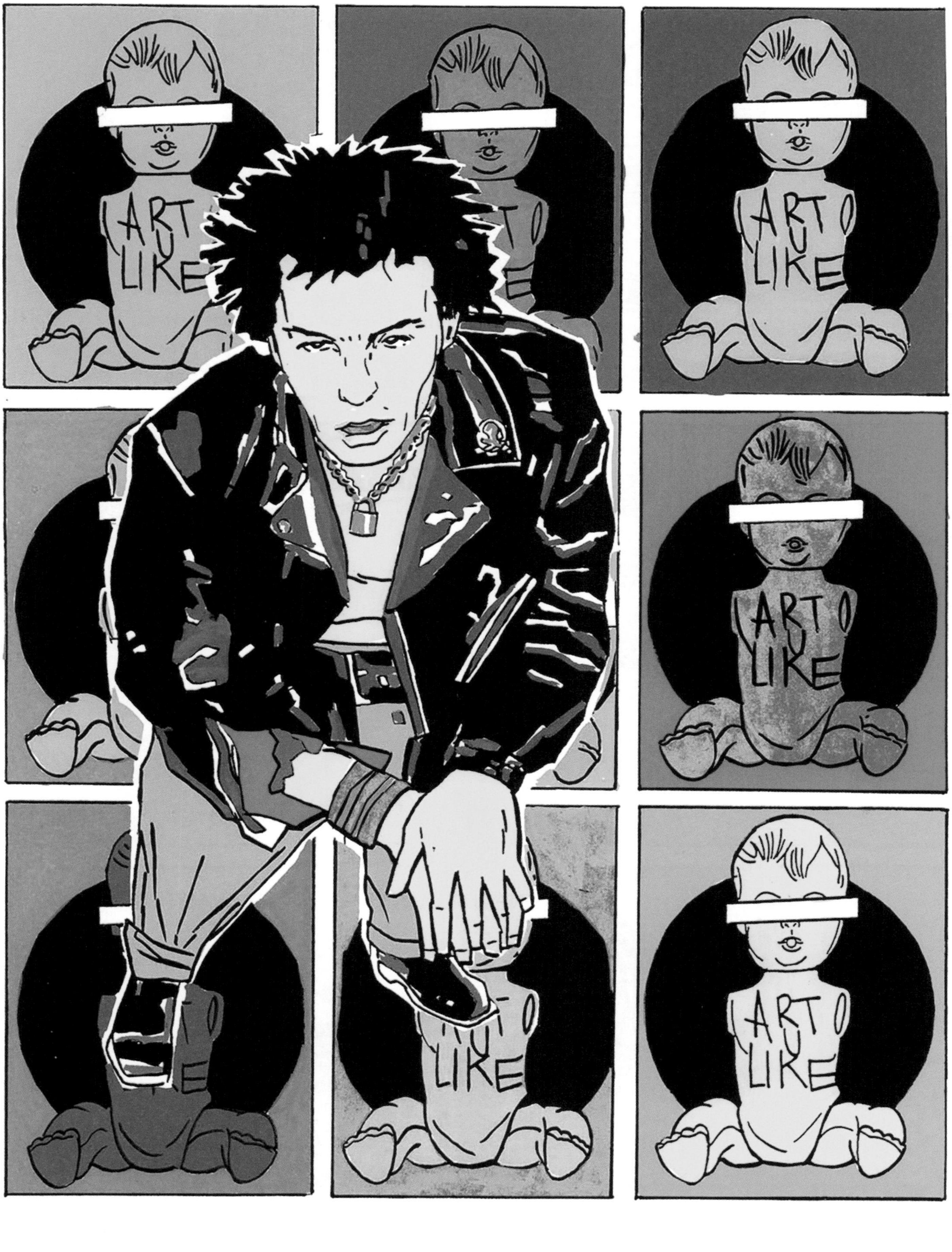
ART
U
LIKE

TED WAS AN INCURABLE ROMANTIC

JENNY AND CAROL HIT IT OFF IMMEDIATELY

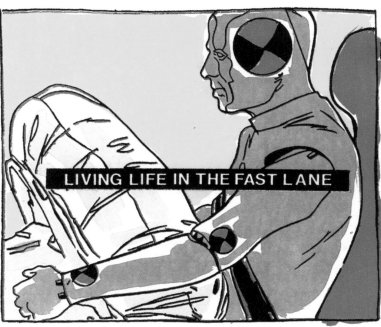

LIVING LIFE IN THE FAST LANE

SALLY HAD THE STRANGEST DREAM

KATE WOULD ALWAYS LAND ON HER FEET

JACK KNEW EXACTLY WHAT HE WANTED OUT OF LIFE

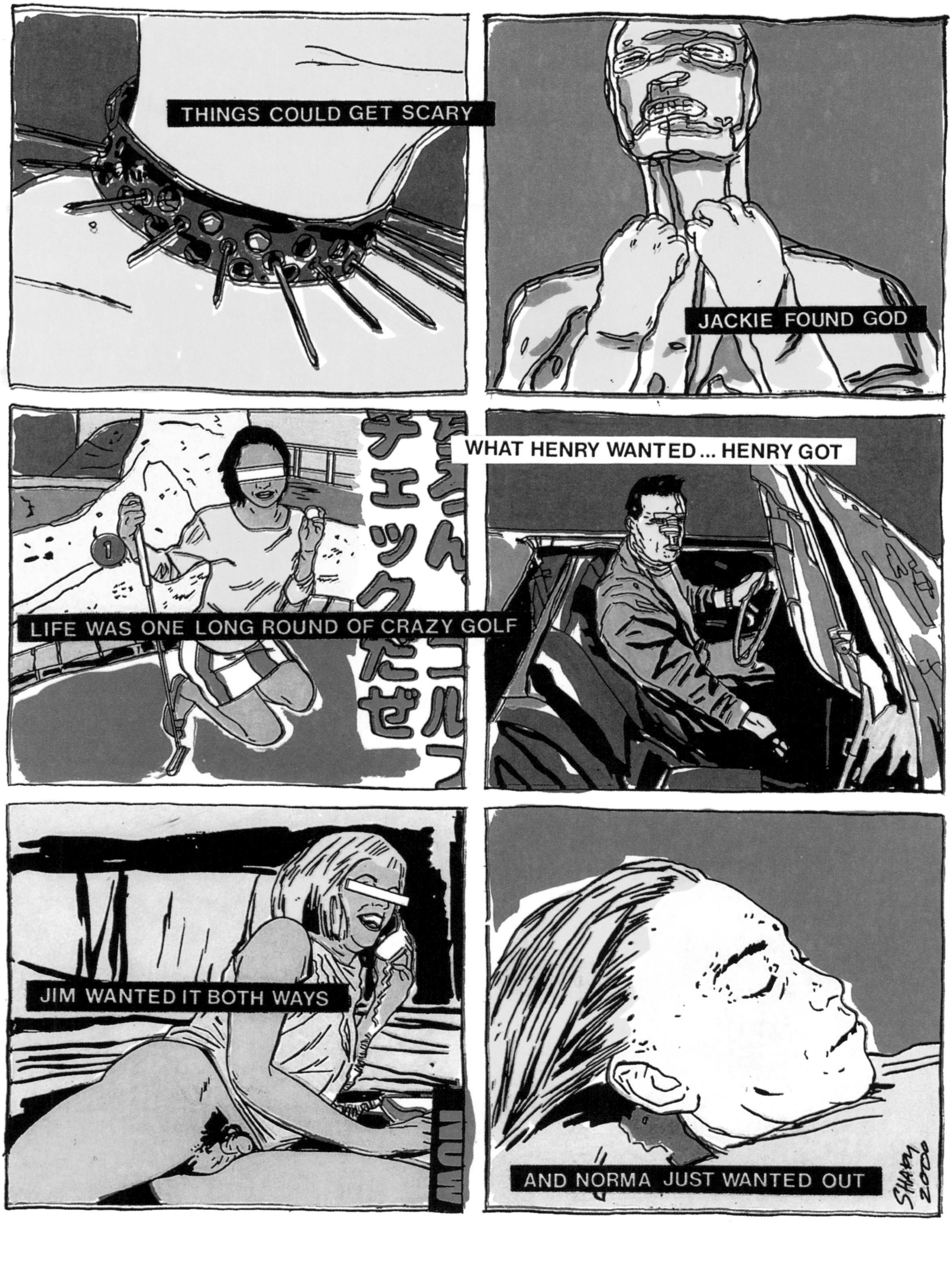
THINGS COULD GET SCARY
JACKIE FOUND GOD
LIFE WAS ONE LONG ROUND OF CRAZY GOLF
WHAT HENRY WANTED... HENRY GOT
JIM WANTED IT BOTH WAYS
AND NORMA JUST WANTED OUT
SHAW 2000

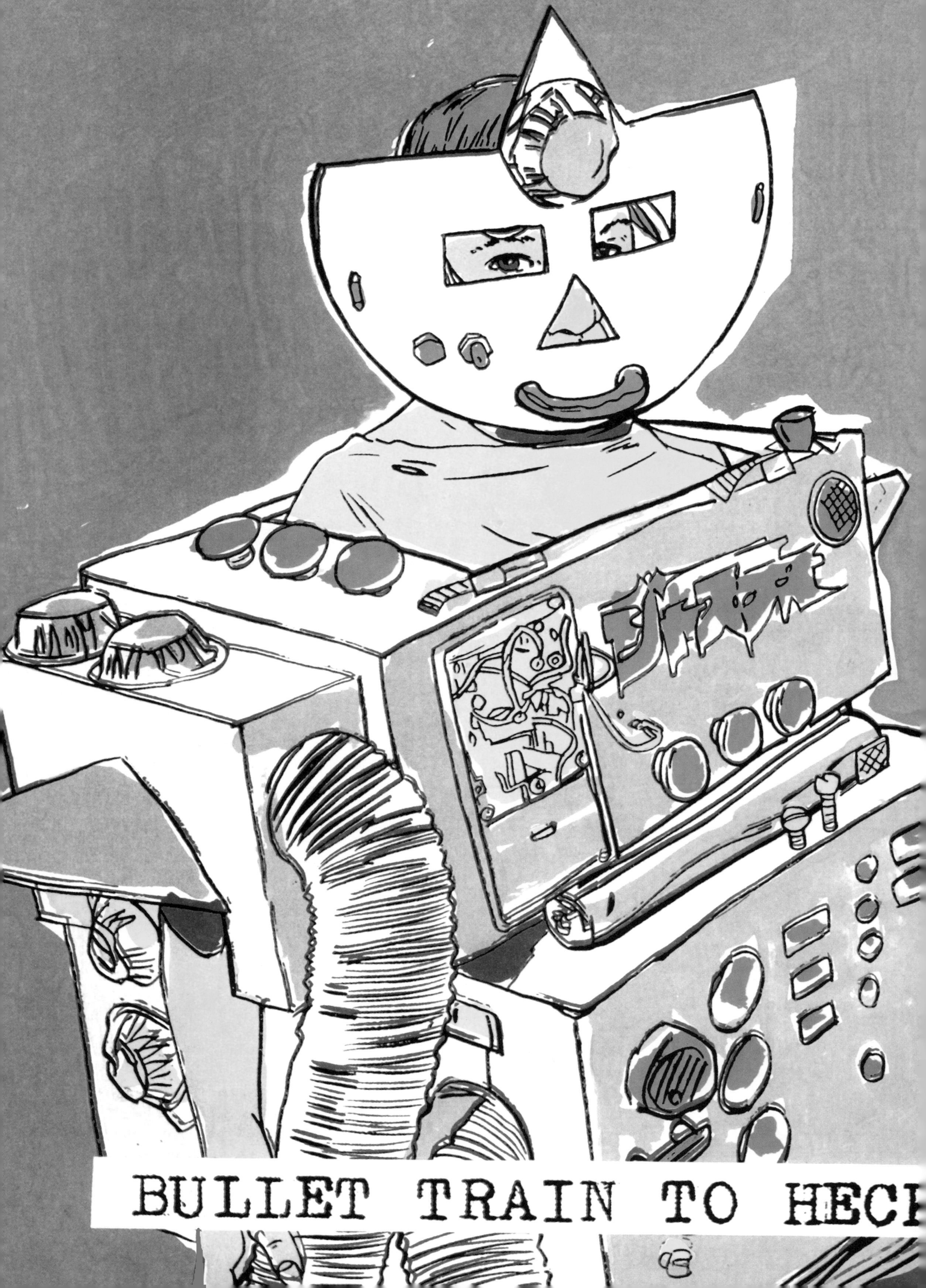
BULLET TRAIN TO HEC

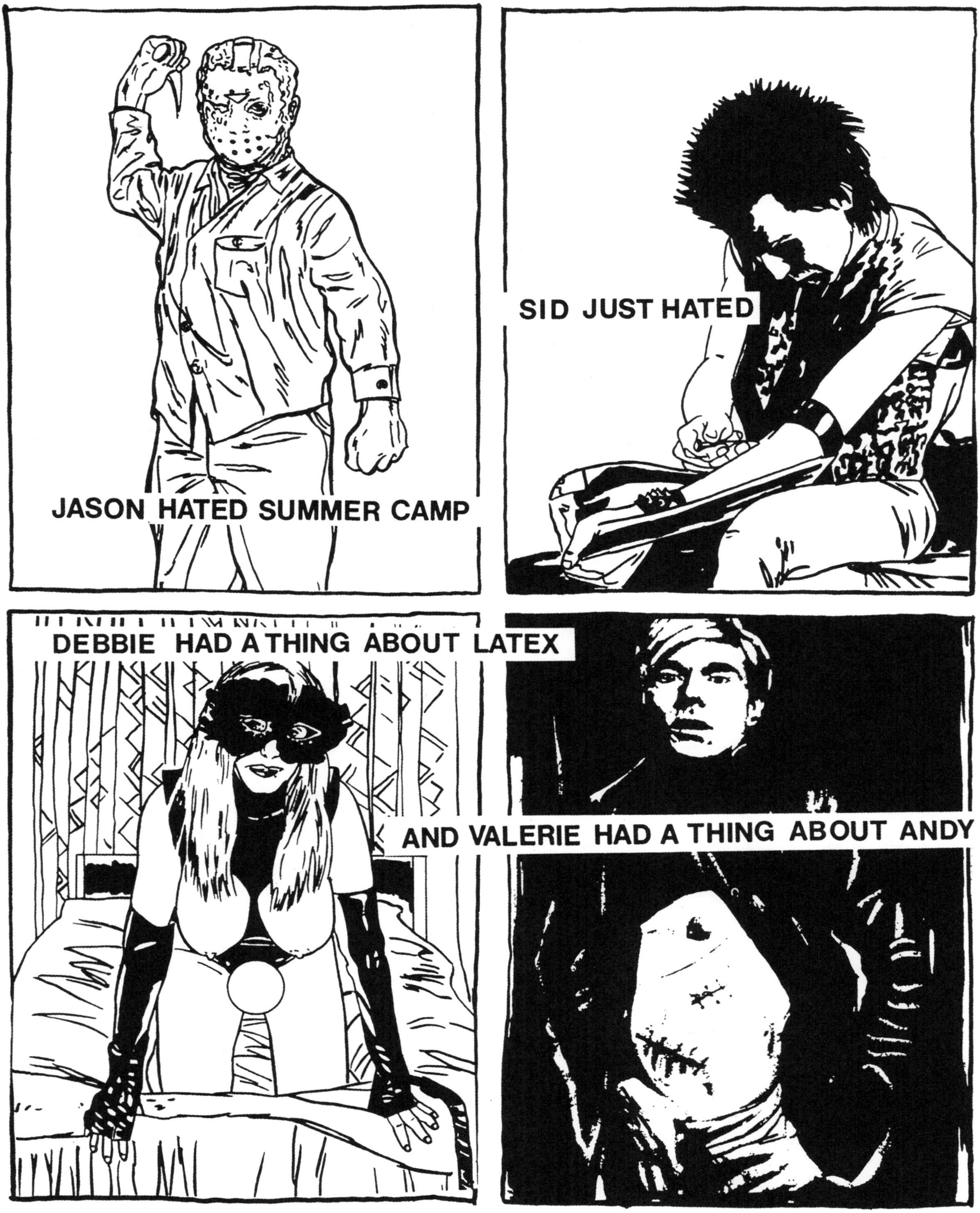
JASON HATED SUMMER CAMP
SID JUST HATED
DEBBIE HAD A THING ABOUT LATEX
AND VALERIE HAD A THING ABOUT ANDY

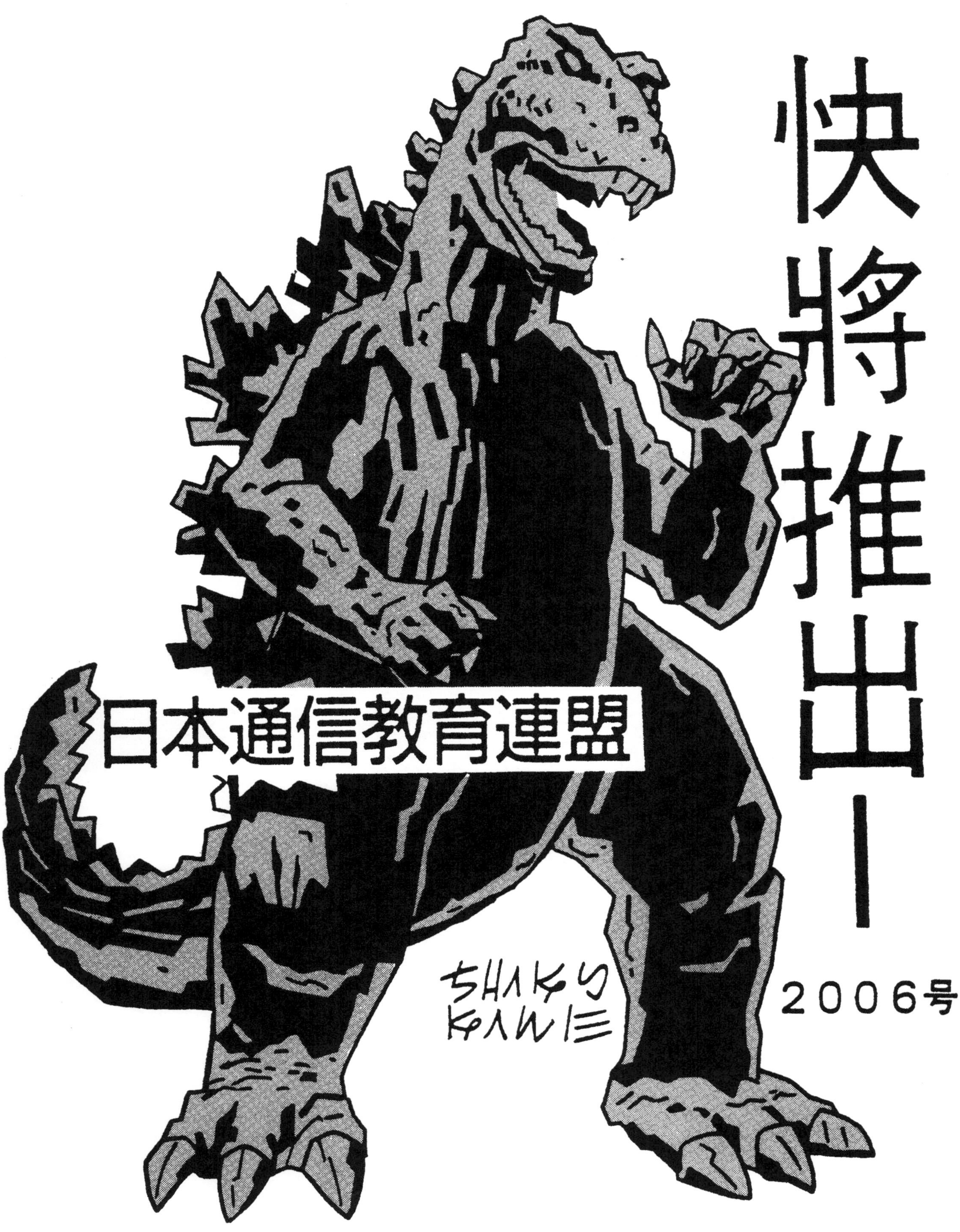
快將推出ー
2006号
日本通信教育連盟
SHAKY KANE

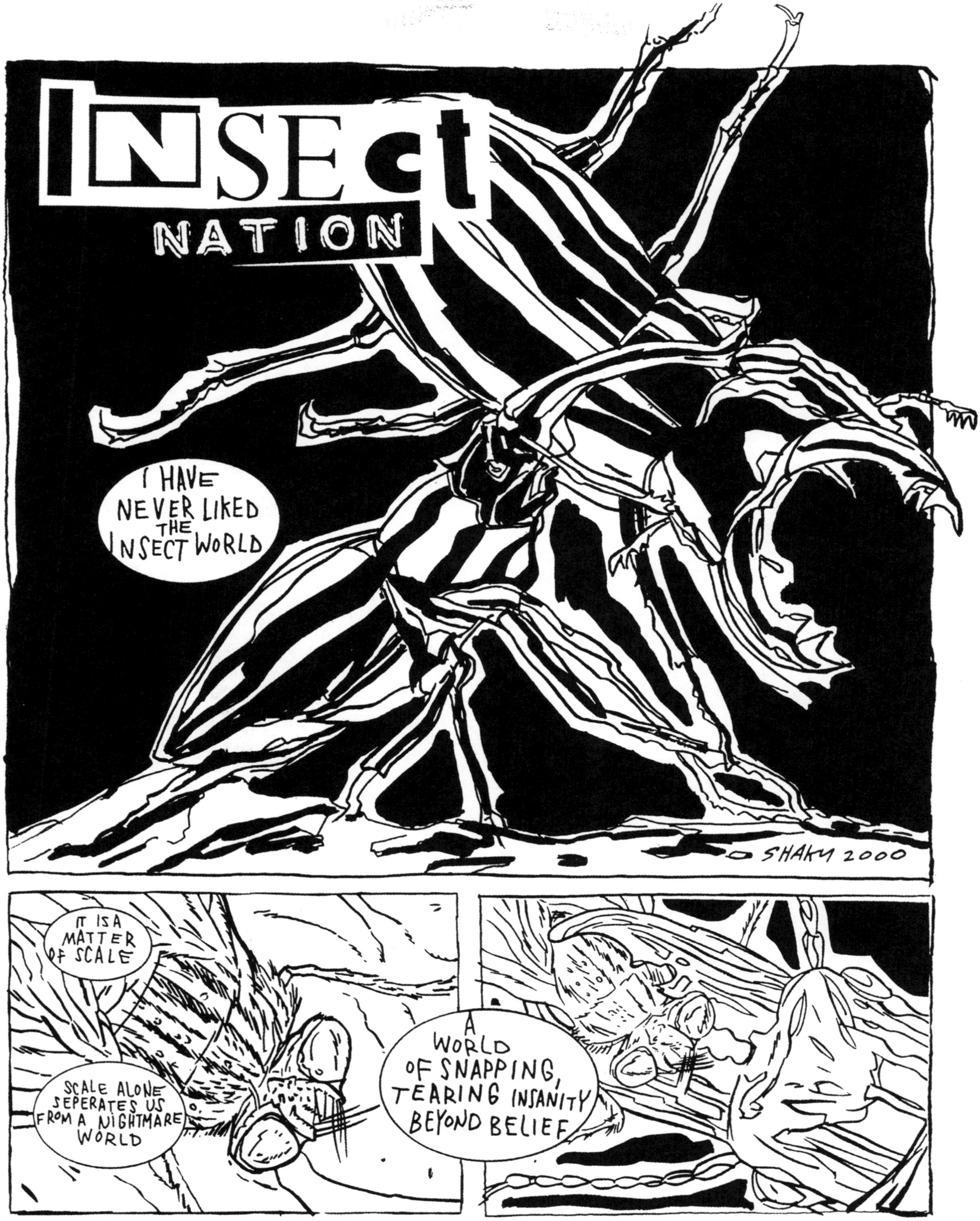
INSECT NATION
I HAVE NEVER LIKED THE INSECT WORLD
© SHAKY 2000
IT IS A MATTER OF SCALE
SCALE ALONE SEPERATES US FROM A NIGHTMARE WORLD
A WORLD OF SNAPPING, TEARING INSANITY BEYOND BELIEF

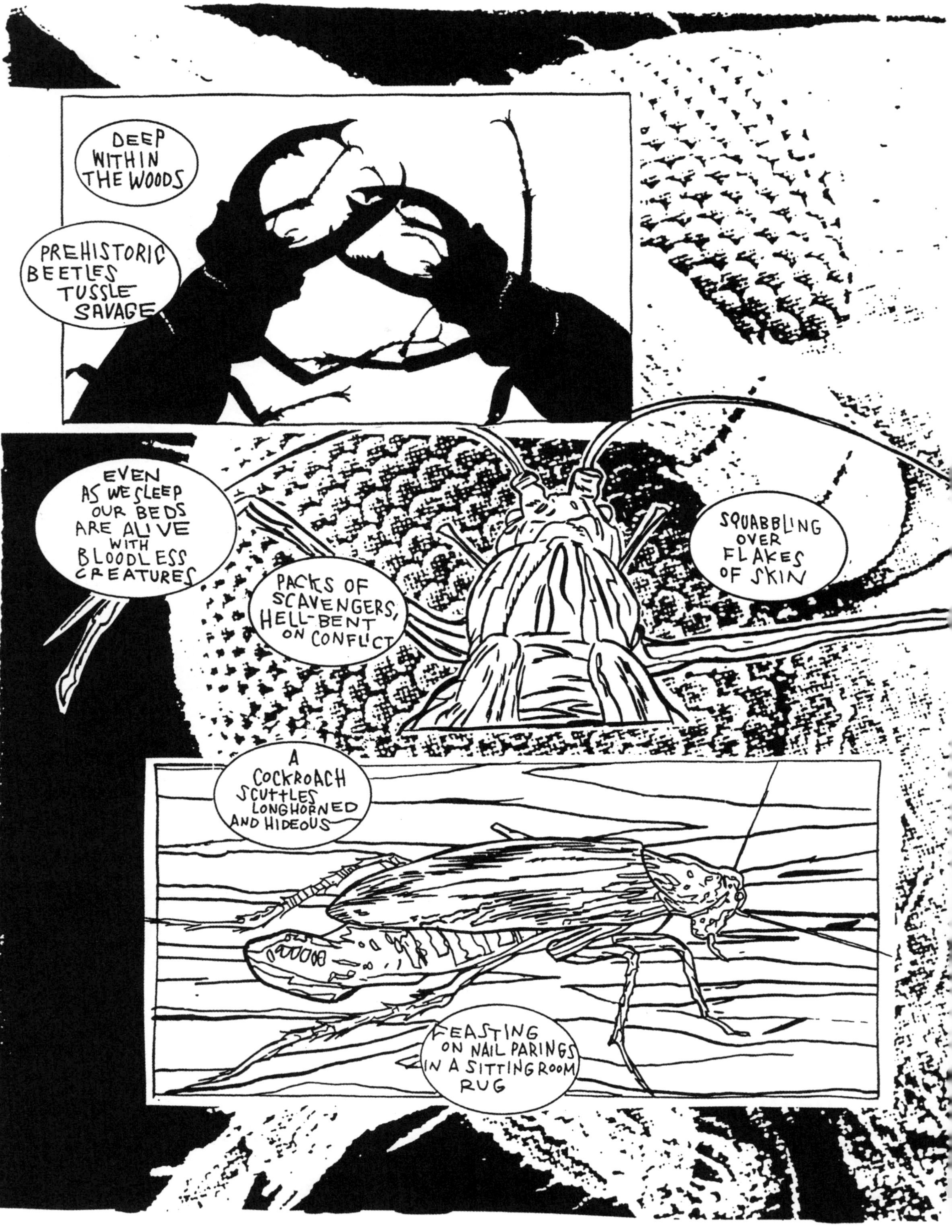
DEEP WITHIN THE WOODS
PREHISTORIC BEETLES TUSSLE SAVAGE
EVEN AS WE SLEEP OUR BEDS ARE ALIVE WITH BLOODLESS CREATURES
PACKS OF SCAVENGERS, HELL-BENT ON CONFLICT
SQUABBLING OVER FLAKES OF SKIN
A COCKROACH SCUTTLES LONGHORNED AND HIDEOUS
FEASTING ON NAIL PARINGS IN A SITTING ROOM RUG

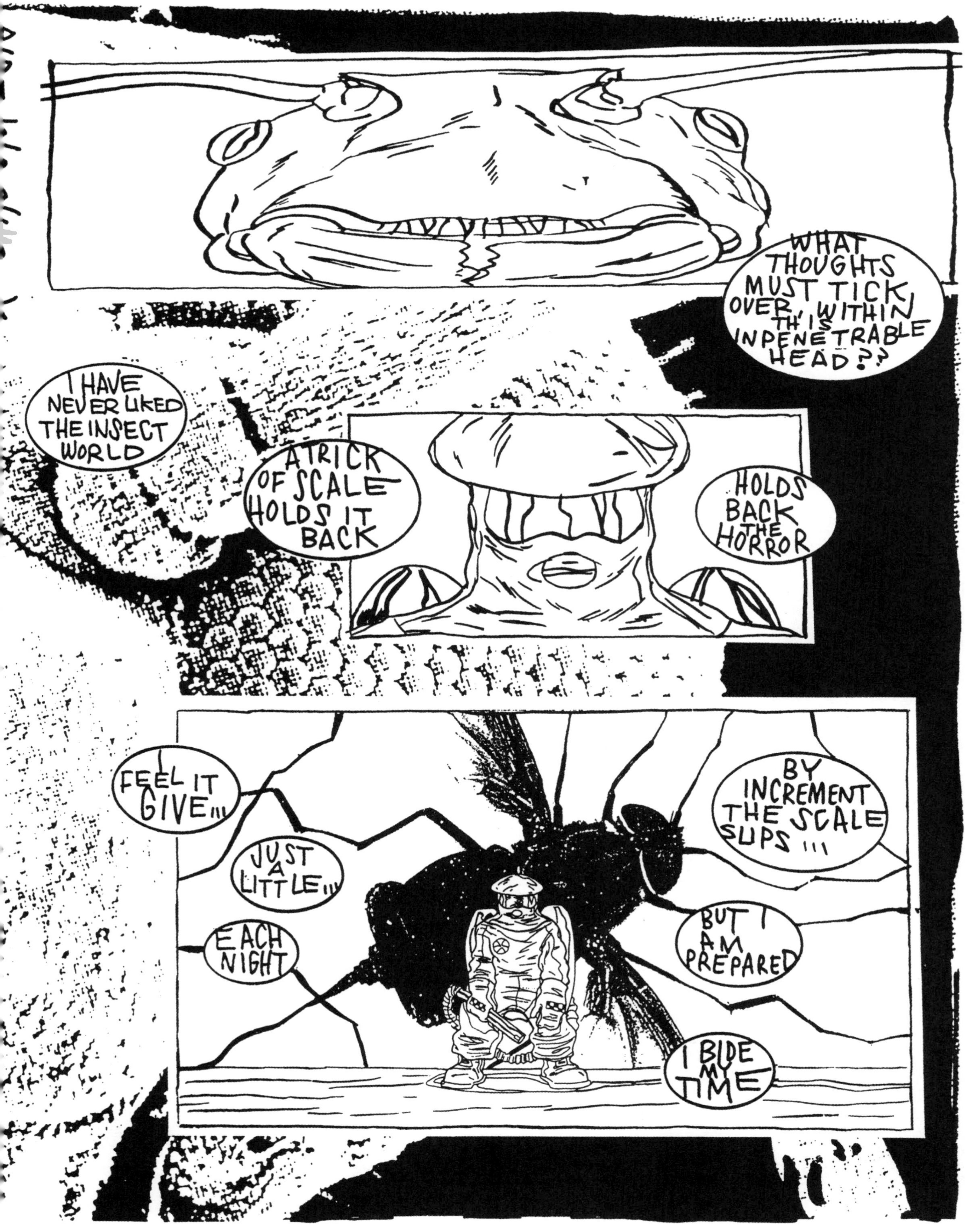
WHAT THOUGHTS MUST TICK OVER, WITHIN TH'IS INPENETRABLE HEAD??
I HAVE NEVER LIKED THE INSECT WORLD
A TRICK OF SCALE HOLDS IT BACK
HOLDS BACK THE HORROR
I FEEL IT GIVE...
JUST A LITTLE...
EACH NIGHT
BY INCREMENT THE SCALE SLIPS...
BUT I AM PREPARED
I BIDE MY TIME

# 'PINHEAD'

BY, SHAKY 'DAD' 2000

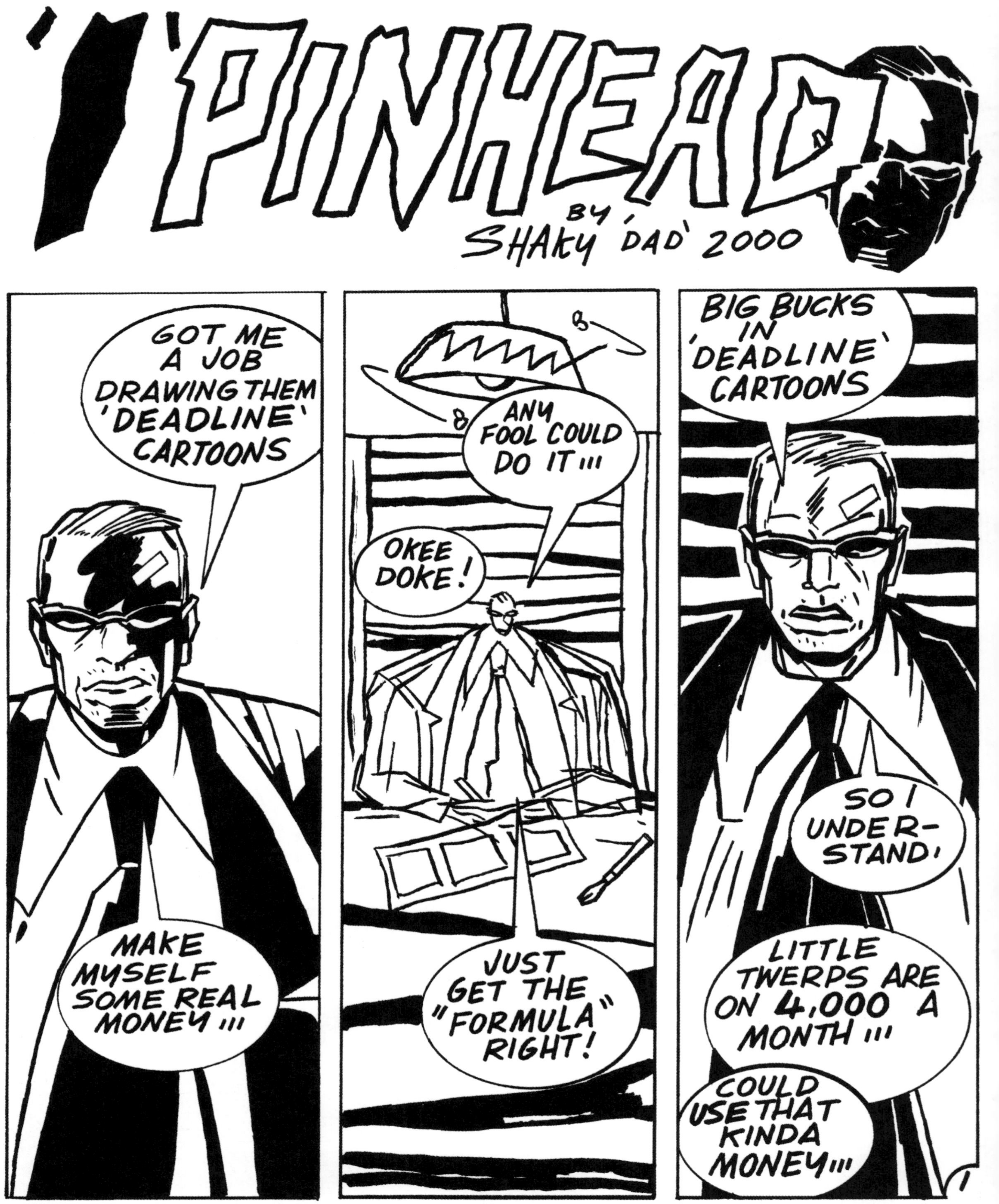
GOT ME A JOB DRAWING THEM 'DEADLINE' CARTOONS
MAKE MYSELF SOME REAL MONEY ...
ANY FOOL COULD DO IT ...
OKEE DOKE!
JUST GET THE "FORMULA" RIGHT!
BIG BUCKS IN 'DEADLINE' CARTOONS
SO I UNDER-STAND'
LITTLE TWERPS ARE ON 4,000 A MONTH ...
COULD USE THAT KINDA MONEY ...

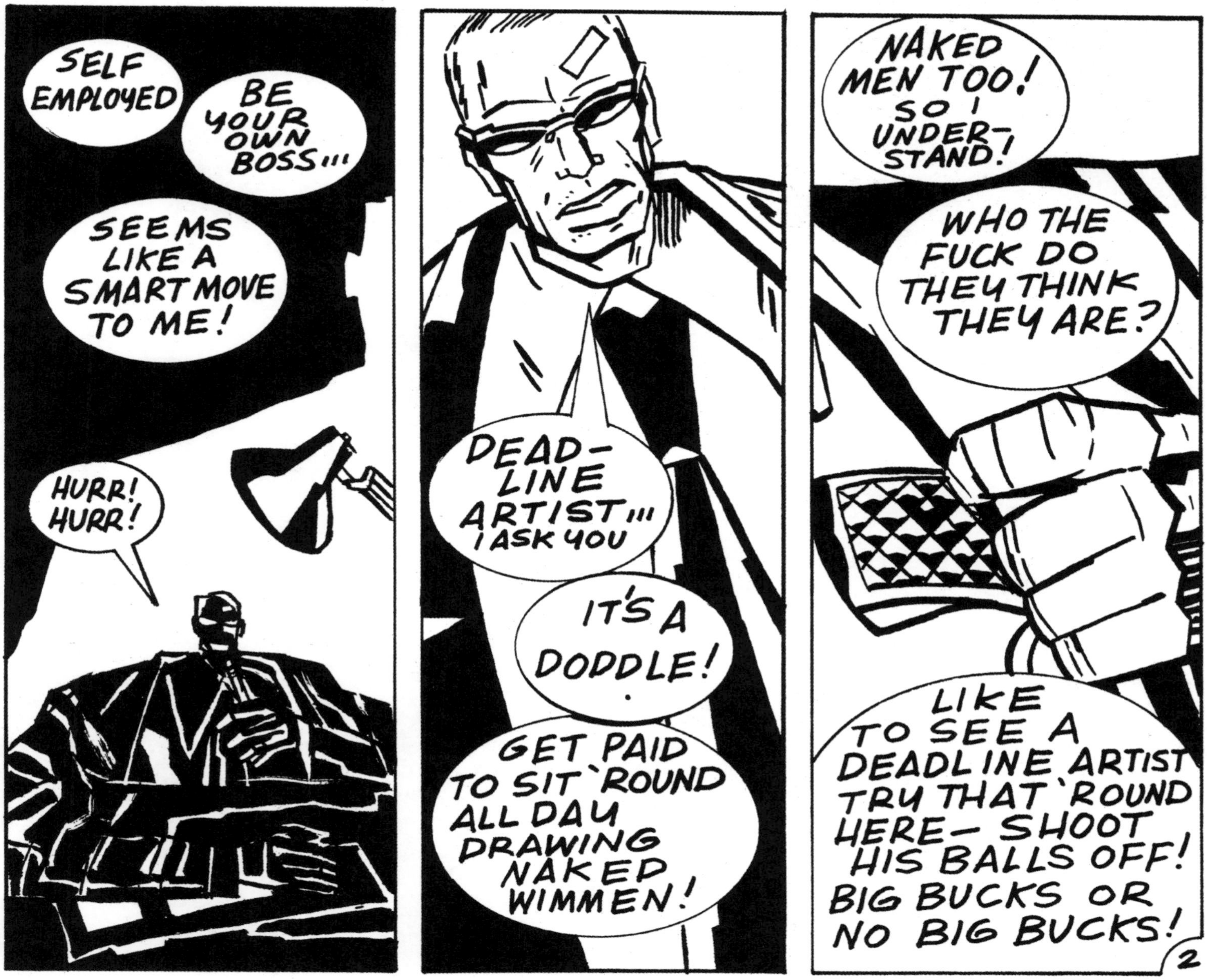
SELF EMPLOYED
BE YOUR OWN BOSS...
SEEMS LIKE A SMART MOVE TO ME!
HURR! HURR!
DEAD-LINE ARTIST... I ASK YOU
IT'S A DODDLE!
GET PAID TO SIT 'ROUND ALL DAY DRAWING NAKED WIMMEN!
NAKED MEN TOO! SO I UNDER-STAND!
WHO THE FUCK DO THEY THINK THEY ARE?
LIKE TO SEE A DEADLINE ARTIST TRY THAT 'ROUND HERE- SHOOT HIS BALLS OFF! BIG BUCKS OR NO BIG BUCKS!
2

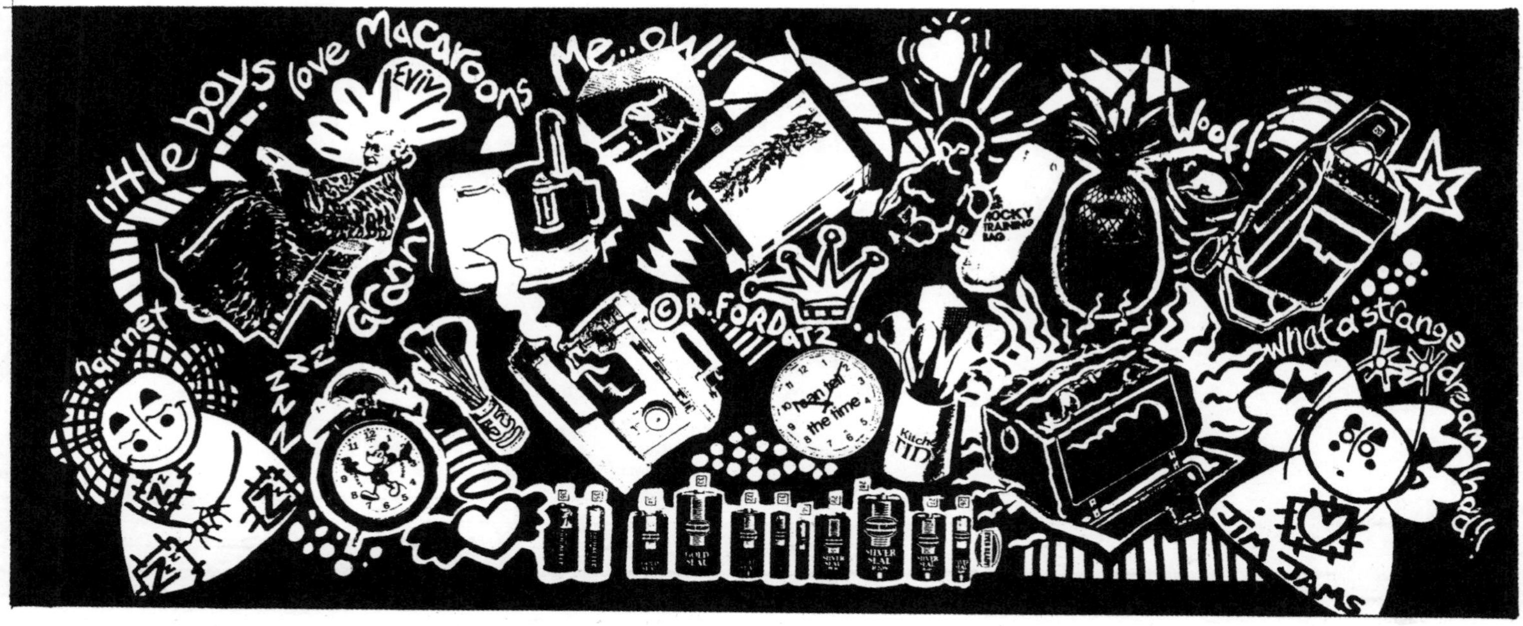
little boys love Macaroons Me..ow!!
Evil
Granny
hairnet
Z Z Z
©R.FORD '92
Woof!
ROCKY TRAINING BAG
I can tell the time
Kitchen TIDY
GOLD SEAL
SILVER SEAL
what a strange dream that!!
JIM JAMS

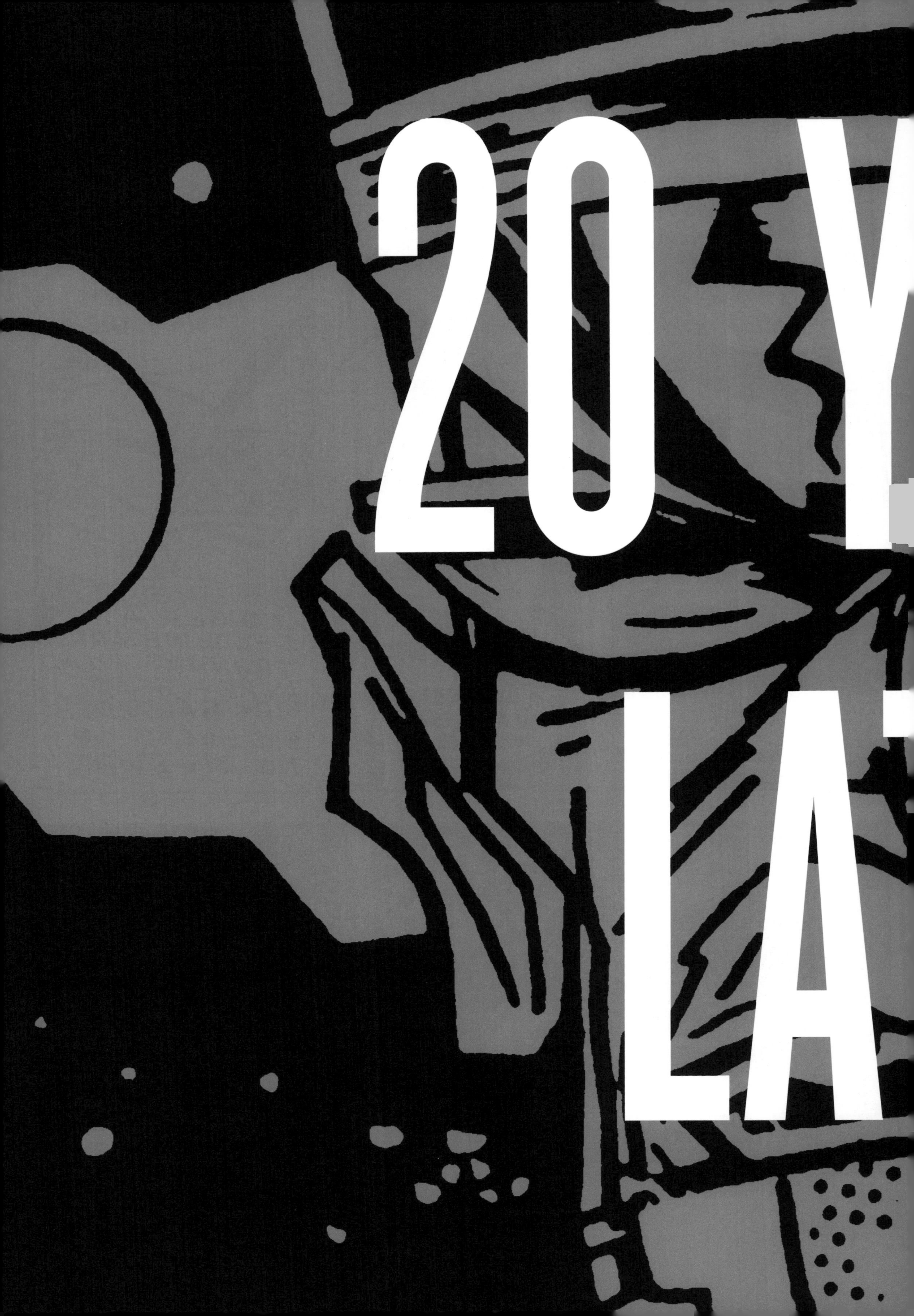
20 Y
LA

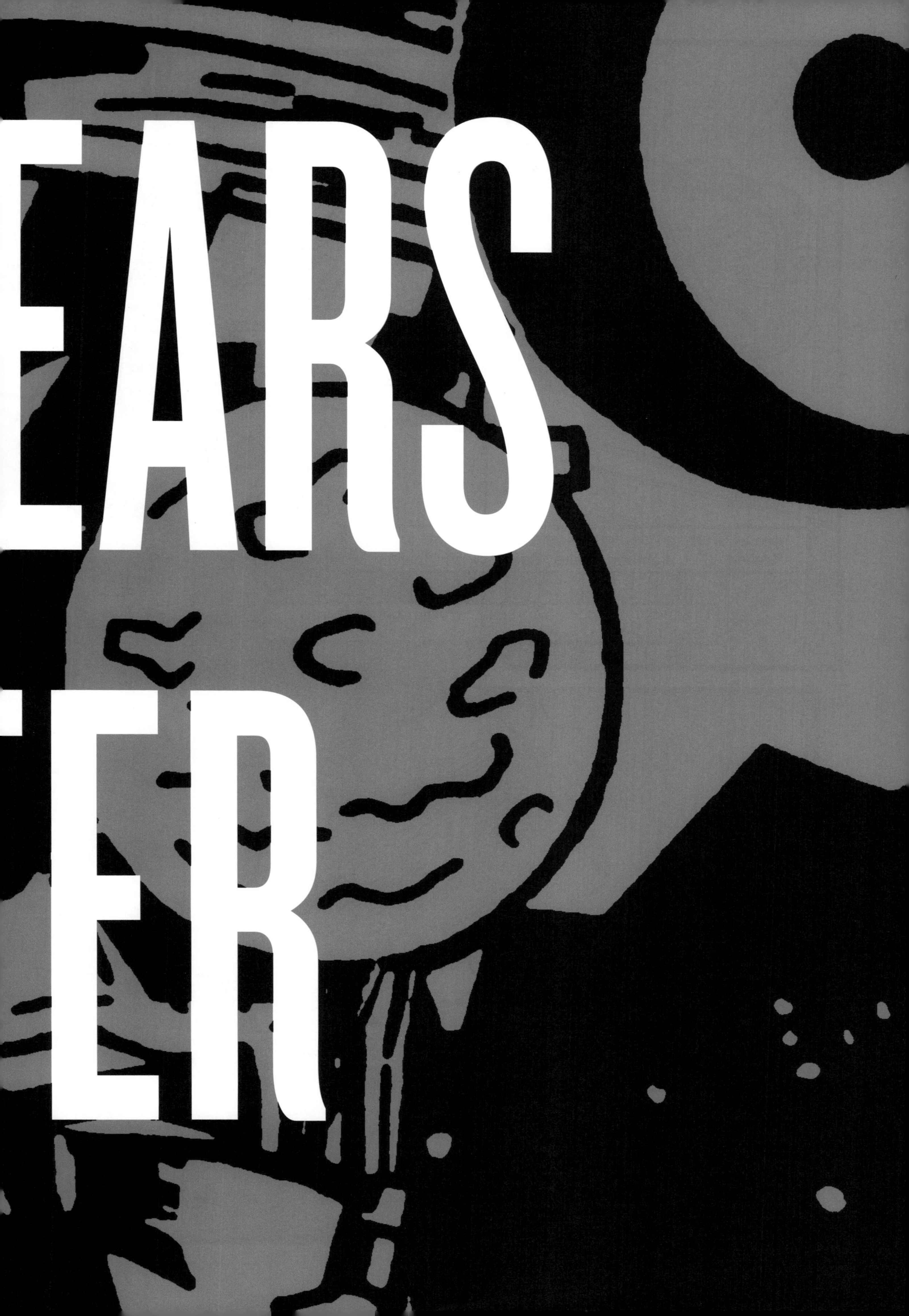
EARS
ER

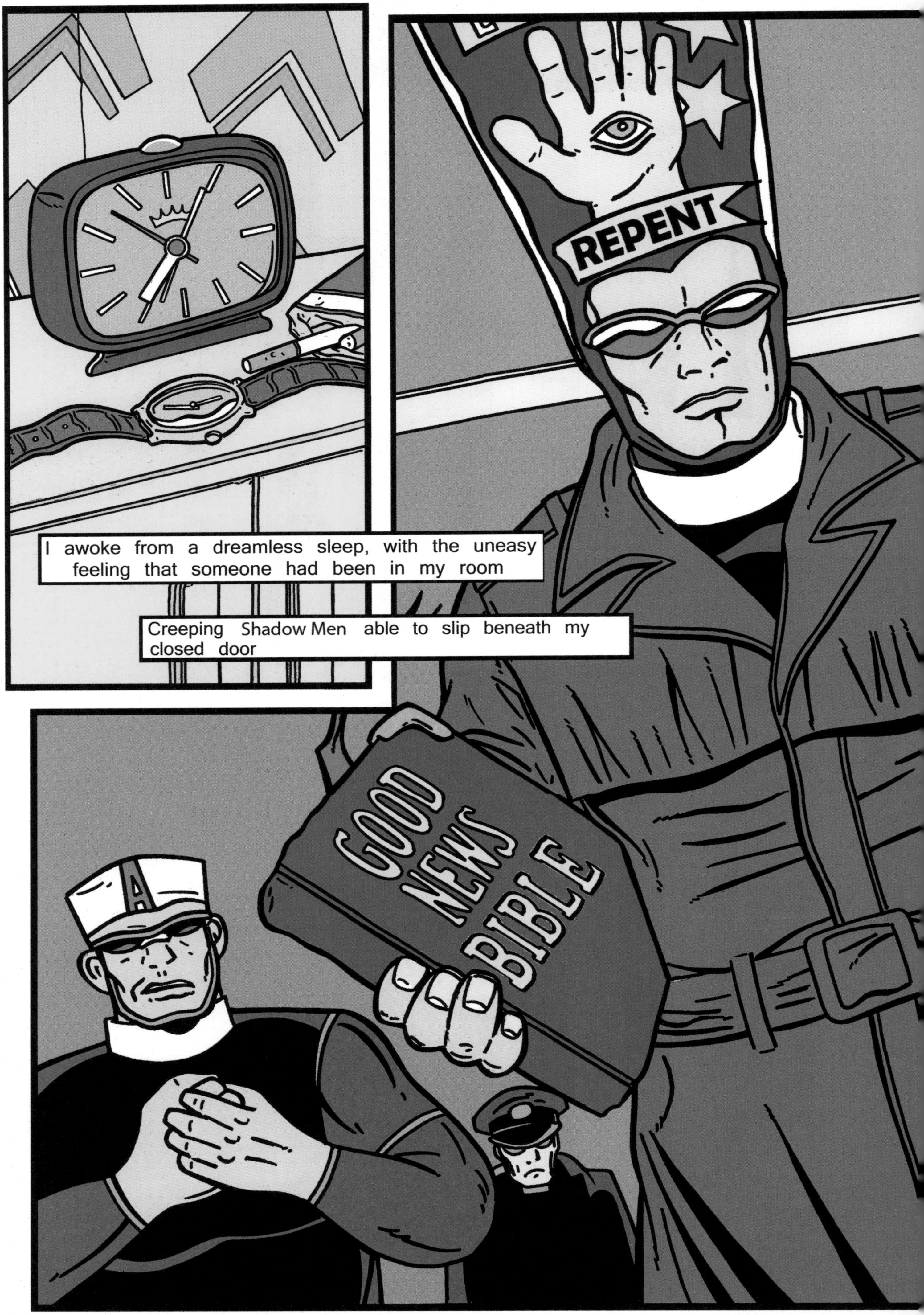
REPENT
I awoke from a dreamless sleep, with the uneasy feeling that someone had been in my room
Creeping Shadow Men able to slip beneath my closed door
GOOD NEWS BIBLE
A

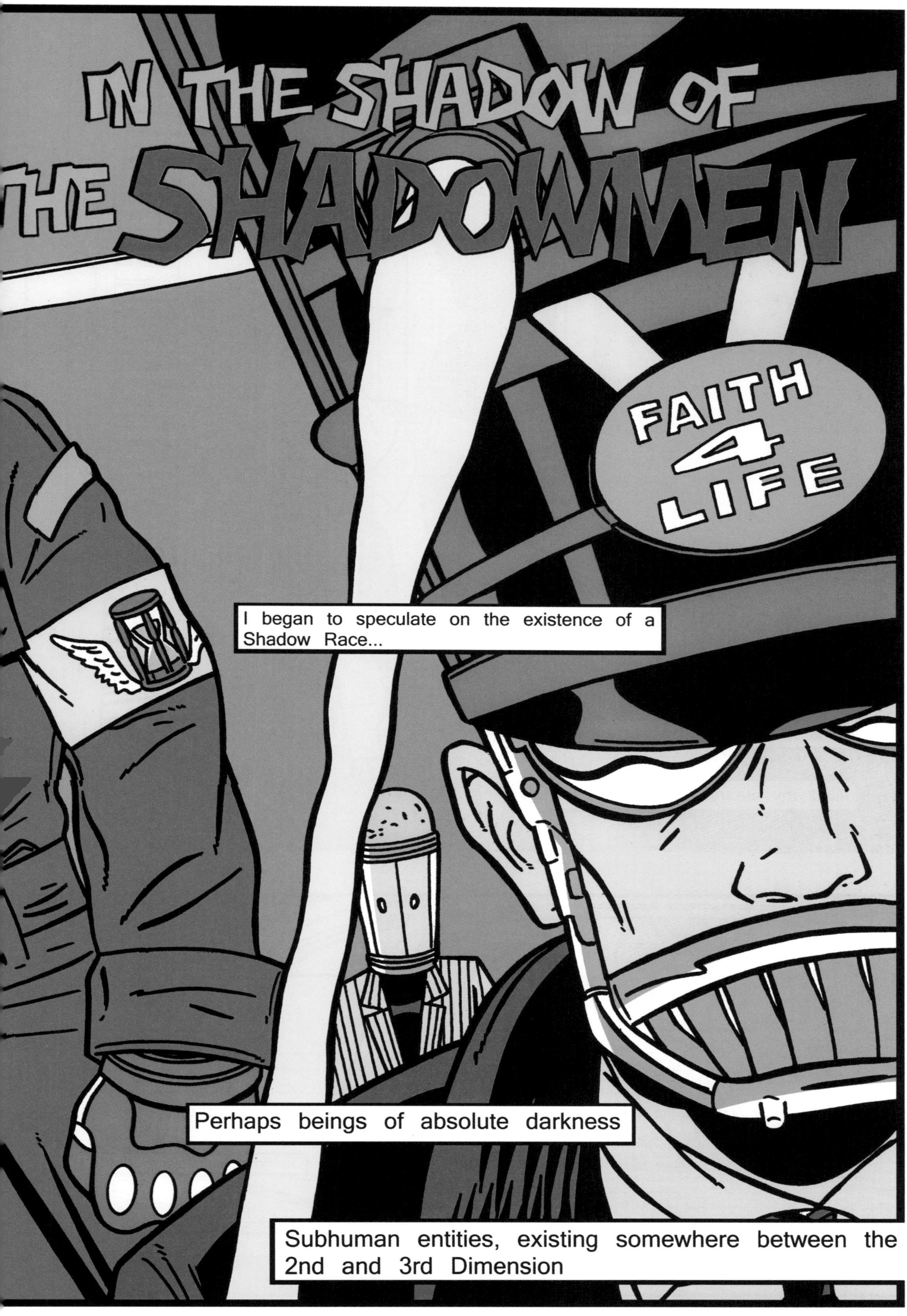
IN THE SHADOW OF
THE SHADOWMEN
FAITH 4 LIFE
I began to speculate on the existence of a Shadow Race...
Perhaps beings of absolute darkness
Subhuman entities, existing somewhere between the 2nd and 3rd Dimension

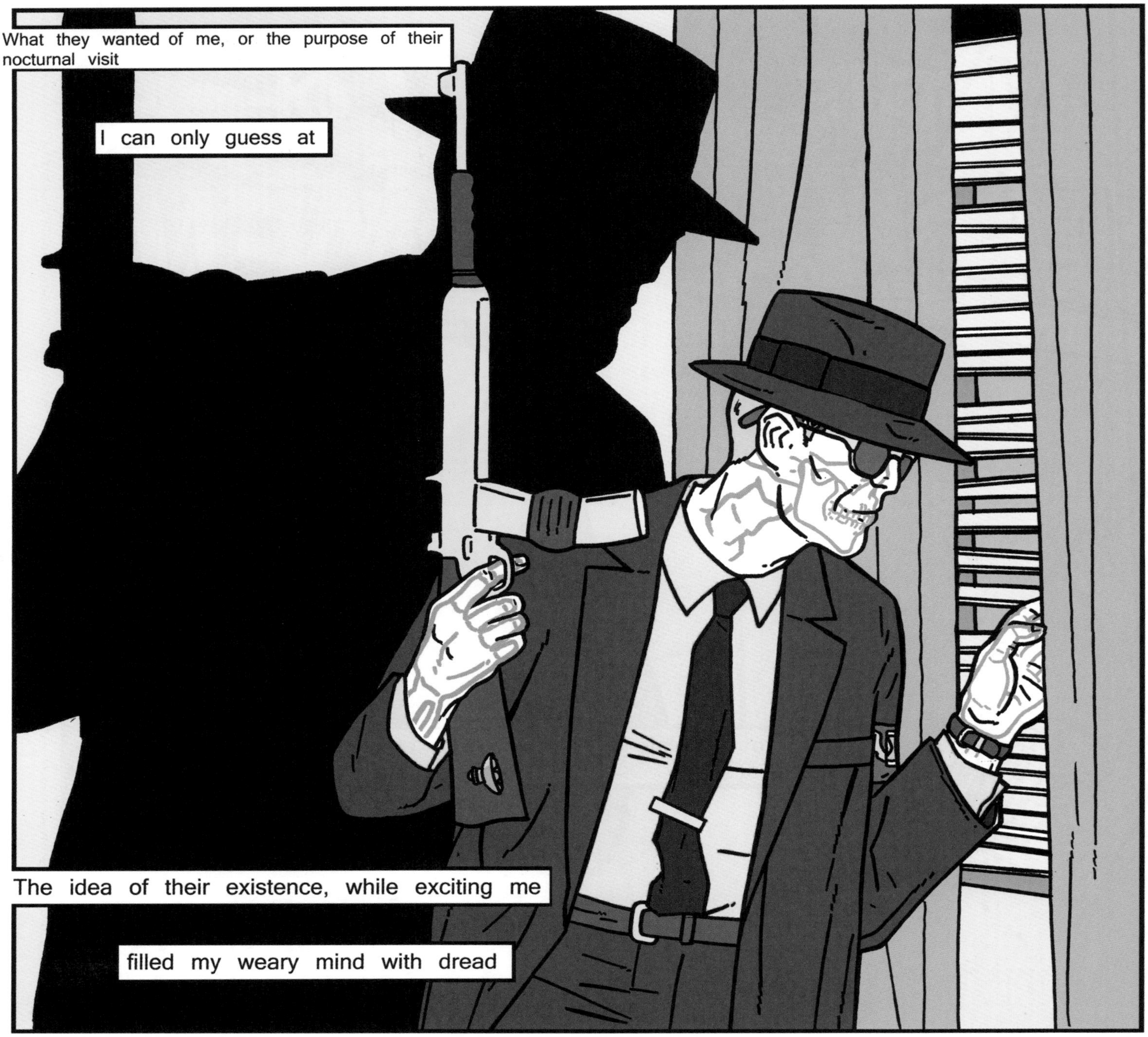
What they wanted of me, or the purpose of their nocturnal visit
I can only guess at
The idea of their existence, while exciting me
filled my weary mind with dread

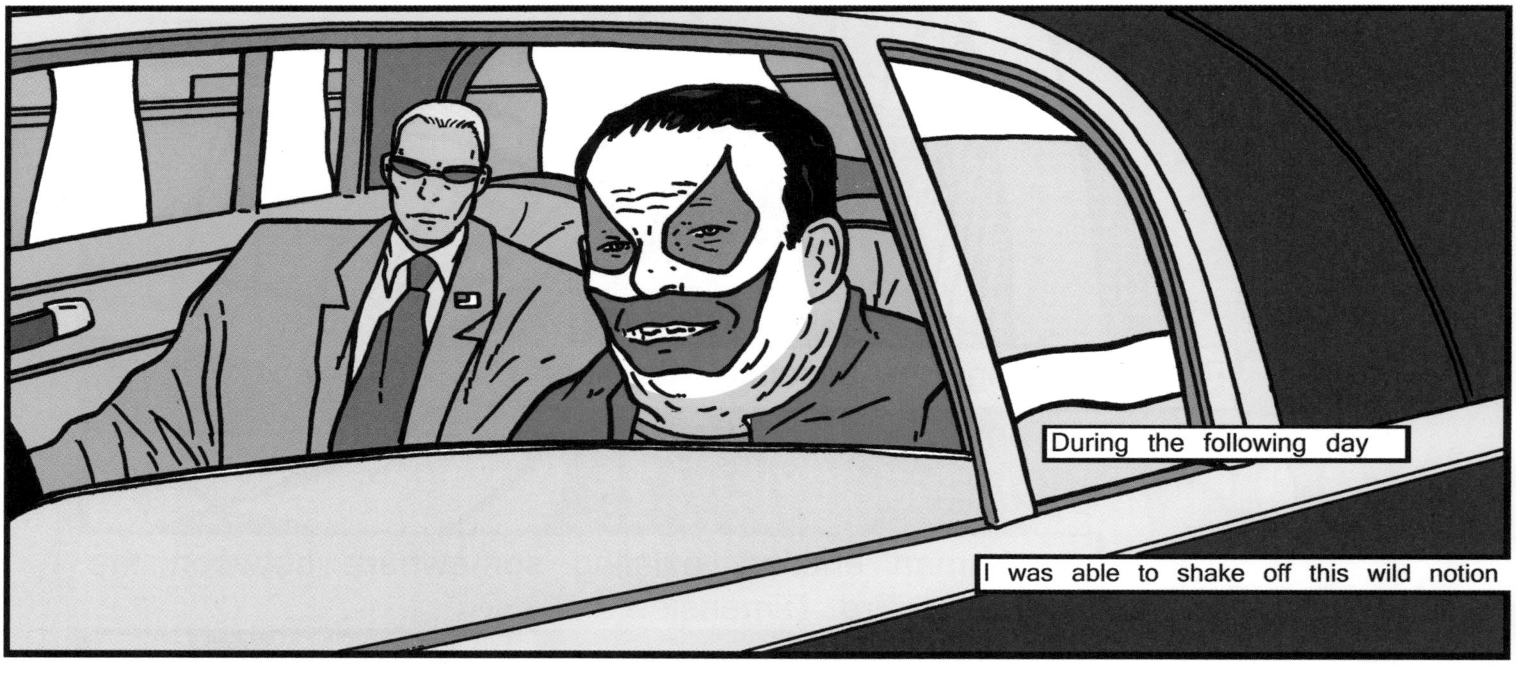
During the following day
I was able to shake off this wild notion

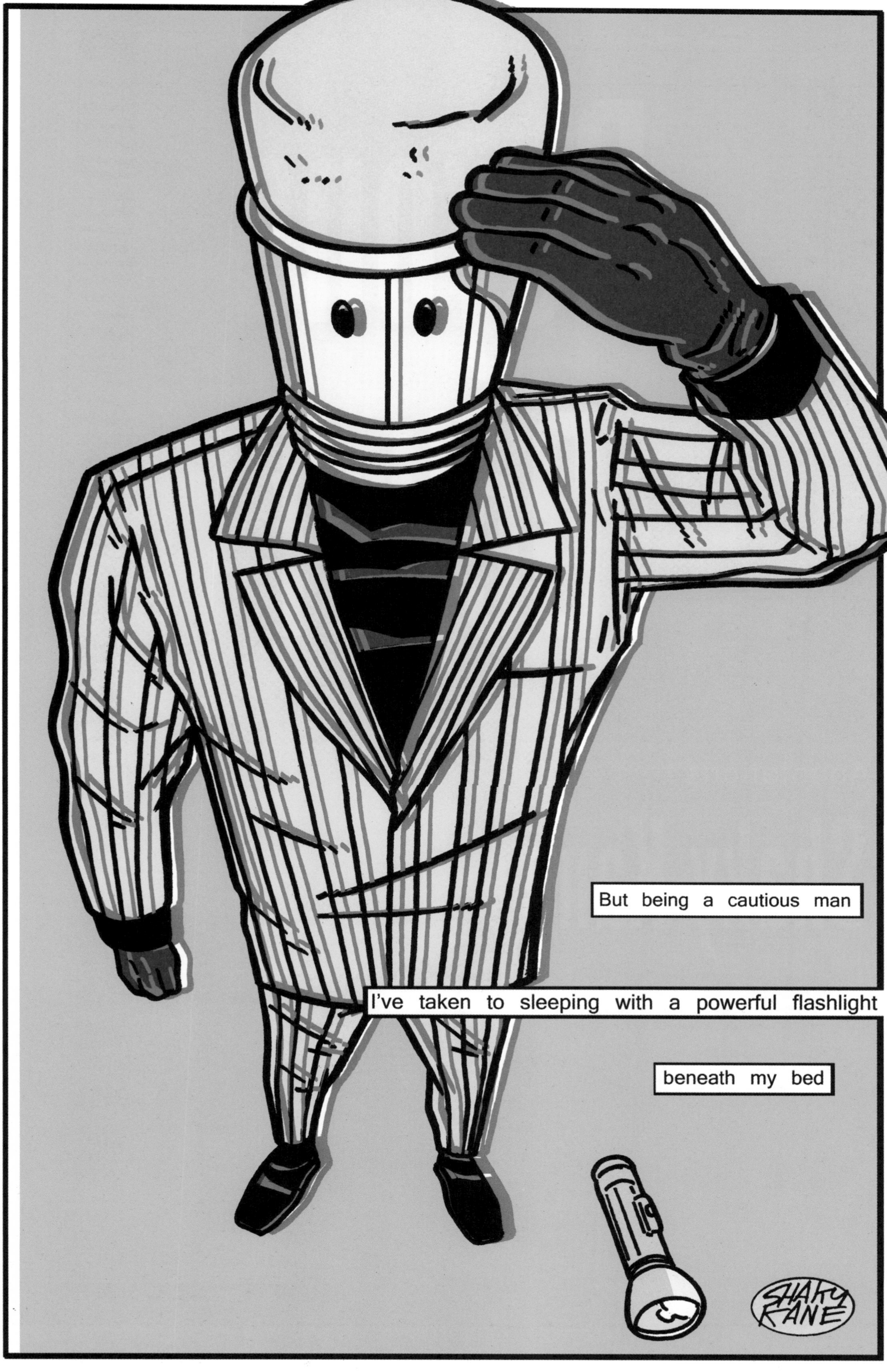
But being a cautious man
I've taken to sleeping with a powerful flashlight
beneath my bed
SHAKY KANE

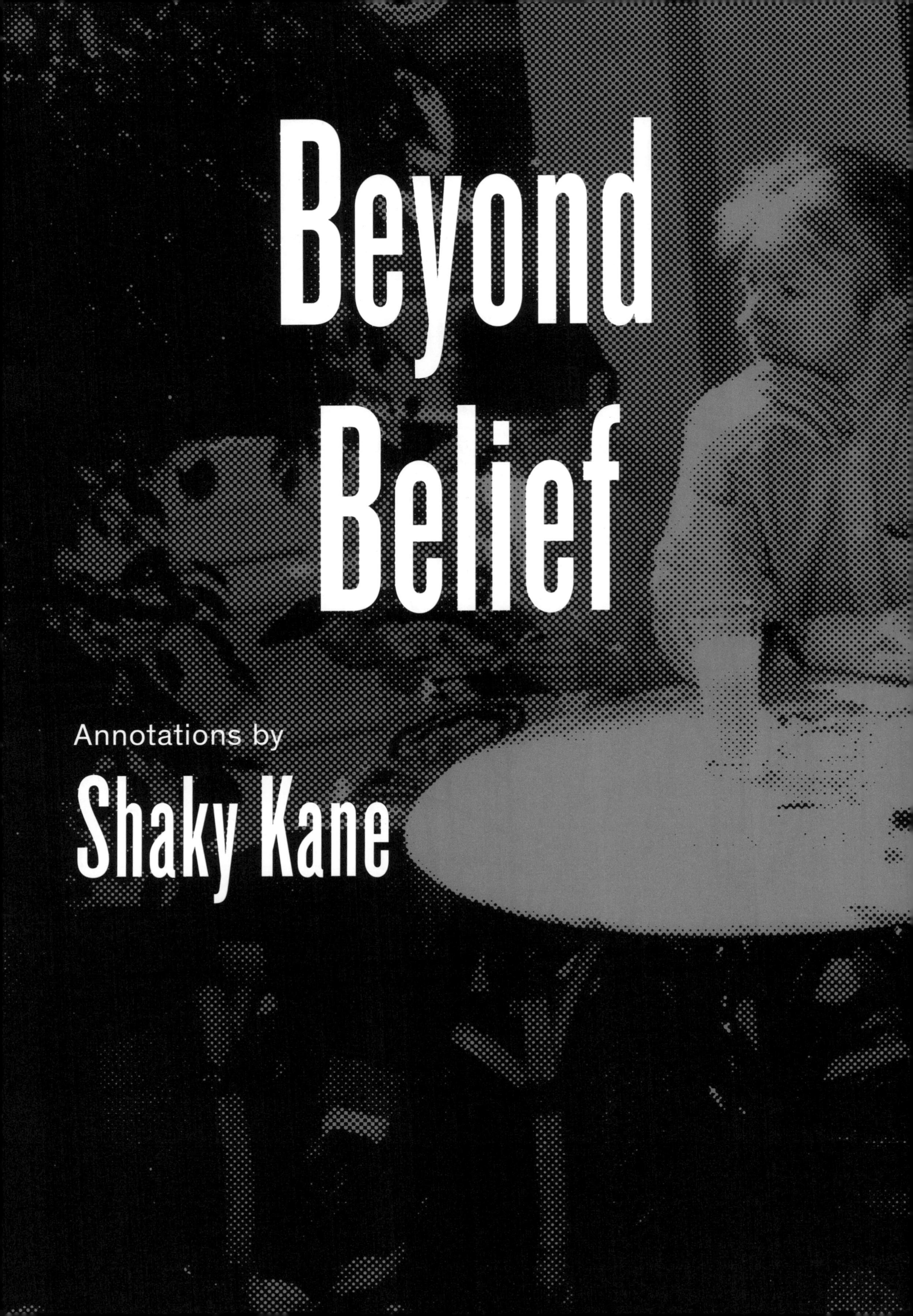

# Beyond Belief

Annotations by

## Shaky Kane

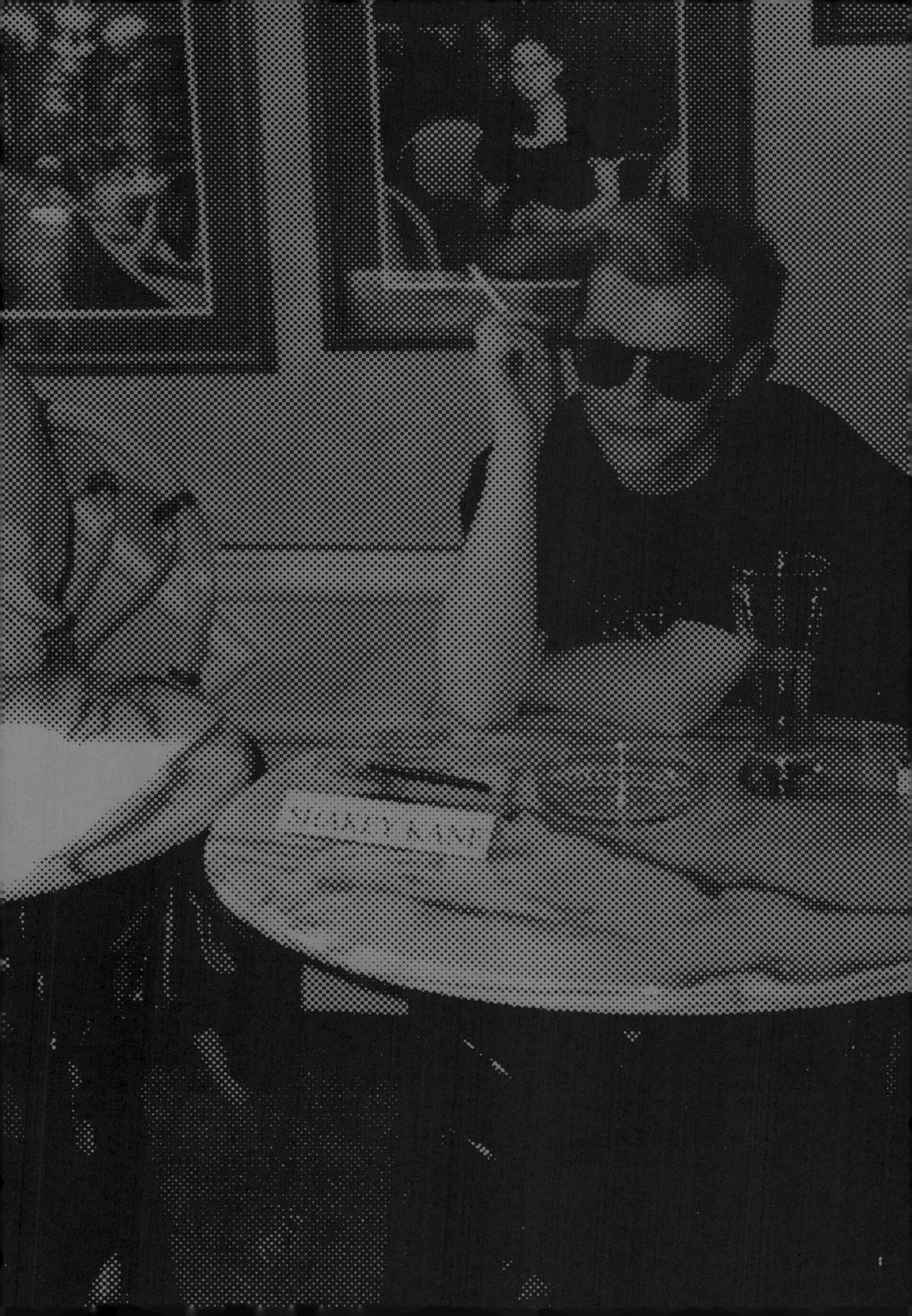

# Beyond Belief

**Page 30.** Through simply being in the right place, at the right time, namely riding the same bus as a friend of the art editors, I became a regular contributor to the New Musical Express. I'd draw one-off cartoons and spot illustrations for music-culture related articles. I can't imagine now how I thought them up, but I did this for a number of years, and I found it a fairly easy thing to do.

It was during this time that I put together a Xeroxed A4 fanzine entitled Beyond Belief! It was sort of a take on Ripley's Believe it or Not! It's a fairly common format to satirise, I suppose mine was bit more off the wall than most takes on the subject. I had about 20 copies run off on an office photocopier. I didn't really know what to do with them, so I left four or five on the counter of my local comic book shop in Seven Sisters, North London. I went in one day and was told that Brett Ewins had shown an interest, and had bought a copy. At the time Brett Ewins and Brendan McCarthy were about the only mainstream British comic book artists, whose work I actually had an interest in. I still vividly remembered Sometimes Stories and had sought out Cypher magazine because it featured Brendan's work. Somehow or other I got hold of Brett's phone number and we agreed to meet up, with the idea of collaborating on a strip something along the lines of The Electric Hoax which ran for a while in the weekly music paper Sounds. The strip idea we came up with, never worked out.

At one stage Peter Milligan was brought in as a script writer. Sky magazine showed an interest, but Pete had booked a holiday in Thailand, and had to defer on it, things sort of petered out and enthusiasm waned. But the good thing was I'd made contact. Brett told me, that along with Steve Dillon, he was putting together a monthly anthology tentatively entitled Deadline, and if I wanted to contribute something, I could pretty much draw whatever I wanted.

I was still working fulltime as an in-house designer at the Planning Department based in The Guildhall in the City of London. I spent most of my time there thinking about what I would draw when I got home from work. But what could I draw for Deadline? Working as a suit and tie John, I was still contributing to the NME, but to be honest, I was never much of an NME person. The only bands I actually liked at the time were Sigue Sigue Sputnik and Zodiac Mindwarp and the Love Reaction. I liked the way bands looked more than actually listening to them! My bad, I know.

I was walking to Moorgate Station, one evening, thinking what would be a good idea for a strip – I'd hardly ever drawn a sequential strip before – but I had a misguided belief in my own ability to pull it off somehow. I saw an Evening Standard headline in one of those stands the newspaper vendors use, which read "God's Cop". I had no idea who God's Cop was. Of course I soon found out about James Anderson, the Manchester Police Chief, and his homophobic belief that Aids was God's punishment on sexual deviants for "swirling in a cesspit of their own making". God's Cop – it sounded like a Video nasty. It was the simplest idea. What if the written word of the Bible was the word of the law? I had a terrible time trying to draw this stuff up. I couldn't hit on a drawing style. I was used to drawing one-off illustrations, drawing a whole strip was something completely different. Brett was really encouraging. At one stage he lent me a whole stack of pencils on tracing paper to work from. Brett worked in a mysterious way. As I understand the process, he would draw his characters, and then trace them off, positioning them on the page like a manual form of cut and paste.

I had all these Johnny Nemo pictures to work from. I worked over them to give them my own style, which at the time was fairly unsophisticated and raw. And the lettering? What a nightmare, trying to write neatly and fit it around the characters. I can only be grateful that as time went on it became a little easier.

**43.** Nuke Head was a character I'd come up with years earlier. I'd drawn a piece where Ronald Reagan was peeling off a rubber mask to reveal an alien head proclaiming, "It's time TEEN NUKE HEAD got to see what you've really fallen in love with!"

**48–49.** I always, and still do to a certain extent, run with the first idea I come up with. I was looking back to the drawings I liked as a kid. Looking to put a 'Kirby' spin into the drawings. Something recognizably American. Completely at odds with the Deadline house style. I was from a different generation from both Jamie Hewlett and Philip Bond. All of my artistic influences came from late sixties, early seventies comic book art, the Silver Age of comics. I'd try to put that into the mix. I was still literally making it up as I went along. I'd approach each strip as a blank canvas and draw, as it came to me, in one sitting.

**59.** "A swell guy from one of the top American publishing companies." I was at UKCAC (United Kingdom Comic Art Convention), and there was an editor there from DC comics, I think it was, who was doing portfolio reviews. It was much more casual in those days, you could just go up to him and show your wares. I showed him my artwork, just to see what he made of it – He wasn't exactly complimentary. He started telling me what comics "could be". I don't know what I was expecting. I figured then, that I was pretty much an Underground Cartoonist. Deadline was always Jamie Hewlett's magazine. I was beginning to wonder what I was doing in there. I suppose they had to fill the pages with something! A bit like the small ads in American comics. I was drawing the stink bomb adverts in Tank Girl magazine.

**61.** ALL HAIL THE PINHEAD! Again this is one of those things that happens when you have no idea of where the comic strip is heading. I spotted this article hidden away in The Guardian newspaper. "Eye Witness Reports of Pin-Head Aliens in Russia!" From this small germ of an idea I managed to get a regular strip in British comic magazine, Revolver, and featured the Pin-Head Alien in Grant Morrison's Doom Patrol from DC comics.

**62.** MONDO DALEK! I always liked the improbable helmets that Kirby would dress his characters in. If I flipped a Dalek, I found that the curve of the domed headpiece made the peak of a Police Officer's cap. Then following the inverted Dalek body it formed a headpiece which funnelled upward. Where does it end? I'd imagine that it just goes on and on out of panel.

**66–67.** Deadline Christmas card. I'd planned the art so that if it was folded, you read "I've been told to give you this" on the front of the card, with the caption "And this!" on the reverse. Doesn't really read viewed flattened out like this.

**68–69.** When I put my own A-MEN collection together, about ten years ago, I couldn't find this "Jesus Dead in Space" double page spread. I redrew it from memory (see opposite).

**70.** I started to add references to Becky the Monkey (Deadline's Tank Girl in residence) to my strips. I made a point of including people I liked into the art. Later I would actually draw them into the art. Maybe this was taking obsession too far…

**72–73.** At this stage I wanted to kill off The A-Men. I made the strip go full circle ending as it began, with the Night Canvassers "calling on people in the neighbourhood to discuss passages from the Good Book".

**74.** I drew The Shadowmen on a whim. It was taken from a memory of childhood night terrors, mixed with the feel of early Ditko/Kirby Strange Tales, condensed into a characteristically clumpy and fleeting read.

I'd started working slightly differently. Now I'd write down the prose and fit the image to flesh them out.

**77.** It was great to be given the opportunity to draw a Deadline cover. This image was painted pretty big in acrylic paint. I was determined to get a flat mass produced look to the colour. The pose was taken from a drawing of Skreemer, Brett and Steve's, Peter Milligan scripted gangland opus.

**81.** THE ATOMIC ERASER. Cultural shoplifting, I called it. The image of the Eraser was lifted directly from the cover of a vintage Batman book. I twisted the idea to ask the question – What would remain if we could erase the past?

**82–83.** Mr Destiny the man who forced the hand of chance!

**84–85.** Based on a painting showing an out-of-body experience. The astral body still attached to the corporeal form. I've always been a sucker for this kind of thing.

**92.** FRY IN HELL! Now this is where things started to go really weird! I'd always liked Goth, in a superficial way, in as much as I ever liked anything. To do a complete spin on The A-Men, I had the idea of Pagan Cops. Maybe a crazed detective, wearing a Wicker Man (as in the film of the same name) as a towering head piece! I'd call him The Wicca Man – "Fry in Hell, scum!" I thought it was a great idea… I thought it would lend itself to some great concepts.

At this time, Si Spencer had become editor at Deadline. I really wanted to draw something that was tightly scripted for a change. Something you could actually follow as a narrative script. Try to move away from the hit or miss random nature of my previous work. Si volunteered to script it for me. Now Si is a great guy, and it took the pressure off of me so I could concentrate on the visuals. when the script arrived I couldn't understand it! I thought it was me, that I was missing something. To this day, I've no idea what that strip was about…

**112–114.** TV FLY. Originally drawn for Alan Martin's Fanzine and Tape giveaway mail-in offer. I've no idea what happened here, only that it didn't materialize. So TV Fly ended up being printed in Deadline.

I'd given up my full time job and was working as a cartoonist from home. I'd fallen into the habit of drawing with the TV on. Australian soaps were a real fixture of daytime TV viewing, and against my better judgement I started to look forward to Home and Away coming on. Dannii Minogue played a character named Emma Jackson, before leaving to follow in her sister Kylie's footsteps as a regular pop star. Deadline said I should send a copy to her management, which I dutifully did with a note saying how much I liked watching the show and had followed her pop career. A couple

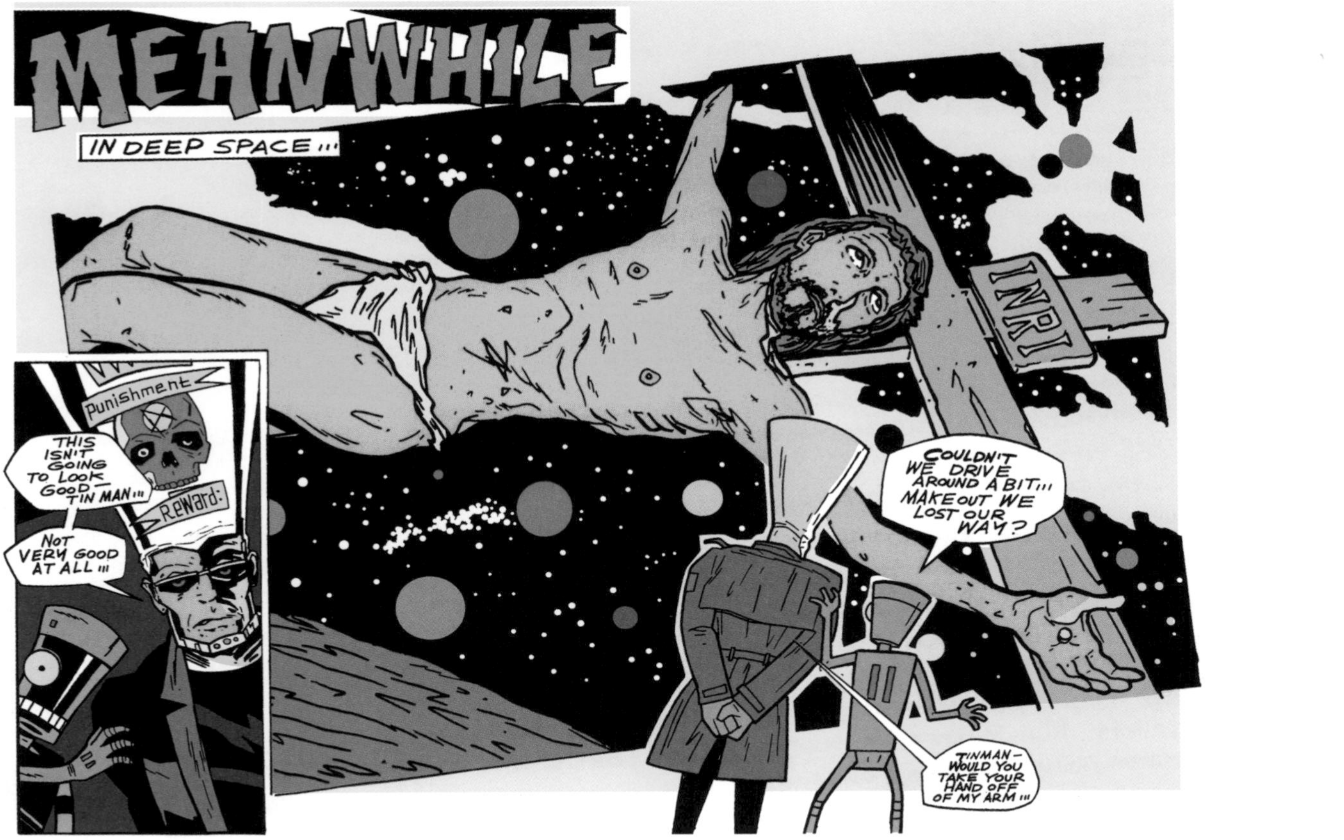
MEANWHILE
IN DEEP SPACE...
Punishment
THIS ISN'T GOING TO LOOK GOOD — TIN MAN...
REWARD:
NOT VERY GOOD AT ALL...
INRI
COULDN'T WE DRIVE AROUND A BIT... MAKE OUT WE LOST OUR WAY?
TINMAN — WOULD YOU TAKE YOUR HAND OFF OF MY ARM...

**68–69.** Jesus Dead in Space, 2002.

of weeks later I got a letter through the mail followed by signed photo. I think she was on tour in Hong Kong at the time! It was such a nice letter as well. A real sweetie.

**123–125.** Splitting from my wife and daughter, I spent the best part of two years, living at various addresses around the country. I moved from Tottenham to my brother's house in Hanwell. I moved back to Exeter for a period, and at one time rented Jamie Hewlett's old room, in a shared house in Worthing. Daytime TV and a fractured personal life. The theme tune from Home and Away, once trite, now mirrored my aspirations, becoming my own personal mantra.

**126–127.** Another Bambos/Kane joint effort. I'm not sure if it's apparent from the drawing, but this is Jayne Mansfield. Urban myth has it that she was decapitated in a horrific auto smash. To this day her head has never been found! I first met Bambos Georgiou at Brett's Birthday party. He was a professional comic artist and inker and we both shared a love for 50's retro.

We teamed up on a fair few occasions, he pencilled both the Icon Collision Earth (Jayne Mansfield) spread along with the Elvis versus Godzilla art.

Some of the panels in the G-Men strip were actually drawn by Bambos.

He inked the Deadline USA cover I drew with the HEX ON! Elvis picture. Still one of my favourite pieces, his inks lent the art a slickness that my work, at the time lacked

**130.** HOT TRIGGERS! Philip Bond sent me a fully realized, hand drawn breakdown for this strip. I drew it up using his guidelines. Somehow, the acetate layer slipped when the artwork was scanned, leaving the word balloons askew on the double page spread.

**133.** When this one was published I was approached by a guy from the magazine CU Amiga, who wanted to print t-shirts with the slogan "PEDESTRIANS MUST DIE!" He seemed to think that he could sell them to bicycle couriers! He bought the original art off of me. I can't imagine what happened with the venture. He seemed really keen, and for a while I ended up contributing to CU Amiga magazine, despite the fact that I'd never played a computer game in my life.

**134.** Graffiti, written on a condom vending machine in a public toilet, beneath the illustration for Nipple Head Delay–"THE MOST WANTED CREATURE IN THE UNIVERSE"!

**135.** I was always disappointed with the way this cover came out. I couldn't get the paint to work. It was based on a drawing which I enlarged on an art-o-scope for a Deadline display at UKCAC that year. I only wish computers were the thing back then, I could have really pumped the colour. I did a whole run of Elvis pictures.

**136–137.** SPACE BOSS! This was the first full colour spread I produced at Deadline. On the original as well as the caption "No more A-MEN!" the text read "No more Tank Girl!". I remember Brett picking the word balloon off!

**138–139.** THE FULL ELVIS! This celestial vision heralds the last days of The A-Men. I've since reworked this image a couple of times.

**140–141.** A collaboration with Bambos. He supplied the pencil and I supplied the inch-thick acrylics.

**142.** The robot illustration came from the box art of a wind-up robot I bought from a seaside gift shop. I like to mix things up a bit.

**143.** SATANIC ELVIS! This one got printed the wrong way up. If the Elvis head is viewed at first upside down, Elvis looks recognizably normal–it's only if you invert the image that his eyes are crazed!

**145–146.** I was asked to illustrate an article which in its own way was groundbreaking. As I remember it, it the article was a very well thought out piece which, in a nutshell, told how the author, credited as Samuel Adder Johnson, being a black British male, felt let down over the years with the way American comic books targeted a certain white audience. How, whenever black characters were featured they were always portrayed as 'exotic' and were only allowed a limited role in the main character's adventures. He actually phoned to thank me for contributing the art. What I liked mostly about this spread was the way the colour was added mechanically. It gave the drawings a mass produced look. A look which I couldn't have achieved myself with paints.

**147.** Si Spencer phoned out of the blue to conduct an interview. I asked him to leave me with the questions and phone back in an hour, and I'd have some answers. I came up with some sort of answers... The photograph is from a Deadline shoot by Lawrence Watson, who was a regular contributor to the NME.

**148.** I was attempting to use my regular Deadline pages to do something a bit more 'personal', something along the lines of genuine self-expression, rather than comic strips as such. I'd work from photographs I'd take on an Olympus Tripp camera. I'd work the photos into the art and get the whole page printed onto acetate. I'd paint onto the reverse of the art, in the way an animation cell is produced. I photographed Becky Ford (Deadline's design and advertising consultant, Becky the Monkey) and Matt Wakeham. I liked the way you could clearly see the clothes they were wearing, like the 'stand-ups' in ID magazine.

**151.** Becky contributed a regular strip which I added to my Deadline pages. I thought Becky's Mrs Macaroon strips were wonderful, contrasting with the darkening introverted themes of my own work.

**152.** Taken from a mis-remembering of the title of the Hare Krishna magazine "Back to Godhead". No internet back when I made that page!

**153.** I photographed my daughter Sophie holding a picture of The Sacred Heart of Jesus. I also took a picture of Becky, who always wore the coolest clothes. I wanted to be her.

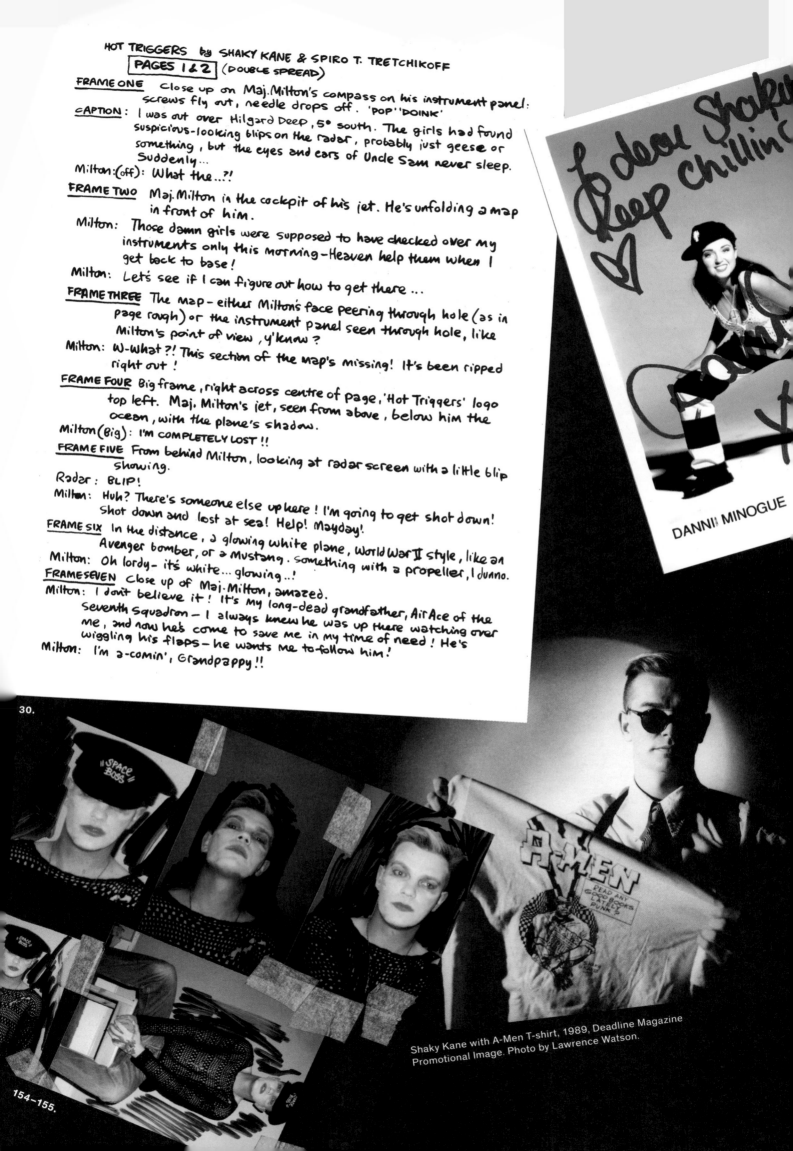

HOT TRIGGERS by SHAKY KANE & SPIRO T. TRETCHIKOFF

PAGES 1 & 2 (DOUBLE SPREAD)

FRAME ONE Close up on Maj. Milton's compass on his instrument panel: screws fly out, needle drops off. 'POP' 'DOINK'

CAPTION: I was out over Hilgard Deep, 5° south. The girls had found suspicious-looking blips on the radar, probably just geese or something, but the eyes and ears of Uncle Sam never sleep. Suddenly...

Milton:(off): What the...?!

FRAME TWO Maj. Milton in the cockpit of his jet. He's unfolding a map in front of him.

Milton: Those damn girls were supposed to have checked over my instruments only this morning – Heaven help them when I get back to base!

Milton: Let's see if I can figure out how to get there...

FRAME THREE The map – either Milton's face peering through hole (as in page rough) or the instrument panel seen through hole, like Milton's point of view, y'know?

Milton: W-What?! This section of the map's missing! It's been ripped right out!

FRAME FOUR Big frame, right across centre of page, 'Hot Triggers' logo top left. Maj. Milton's jet, seen from above, below him the ocean, with the plane's shadow.

Milton (Big): I'M COMPLETELY LOST!!

FRAME FIVE From behind Milton, looking at radar screen with a little blip showing.

Radar: BLIP!

Milton: Huh? There's someone else up here! I'm going to get shot down! Shot down and lost at sea! Help! Mayday!

FRAME SIX In the distance, a glowing white plane, World War II style, like an Avenger bomber, or a Mustang. Something with a propeller, I dunno.

Milton: Oh lordy – it's white... glowing...!

FRAME SEVEN Close up of Maj. Milton, amazed.

Milton: I don't believe it! It's my long-dead grandfather, Air Ace of the Seventh Squadron – I always knew he was up there watching over me, and now he's come to save me in my time of need! He's wiggling his flaps – he wants me to follow him!

Milton: I'm a-comin', Grandpappy!!

30.

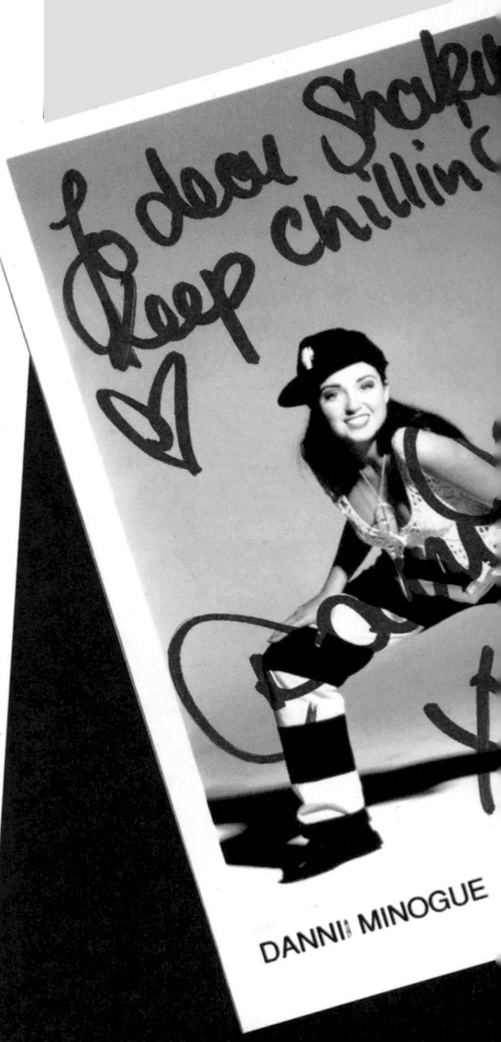

DANNII MINOGUE


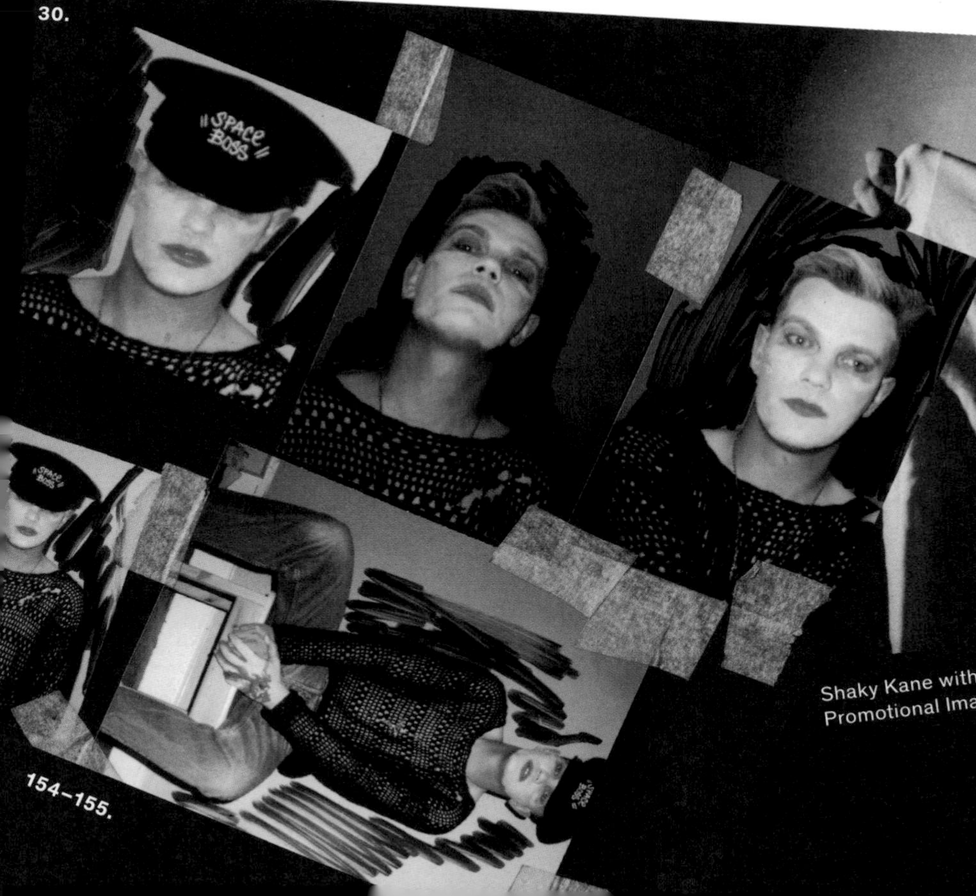

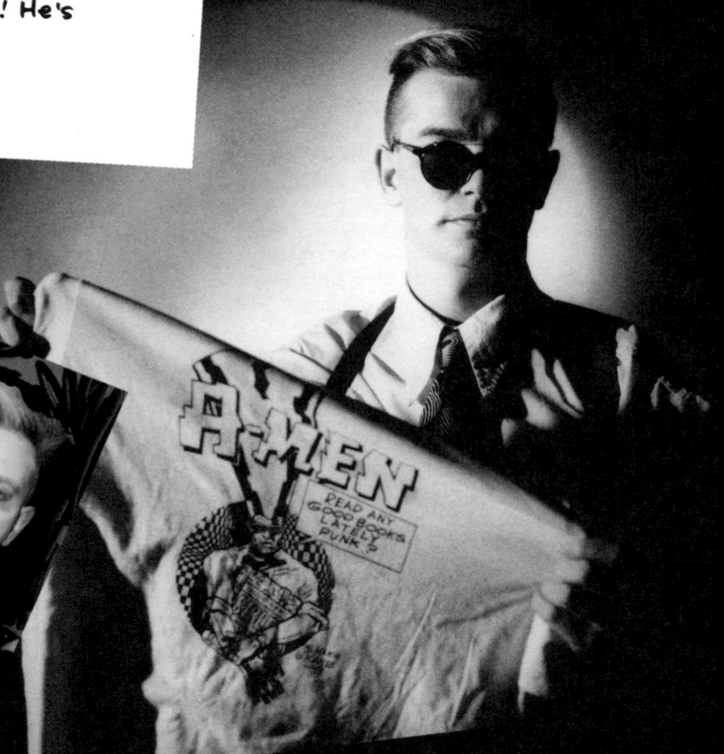

A-MEN


Shaky Kane with A-Men T-shirt, 1989, Deadline Magazine Promotional Image. Photo by Lawrence Watson.

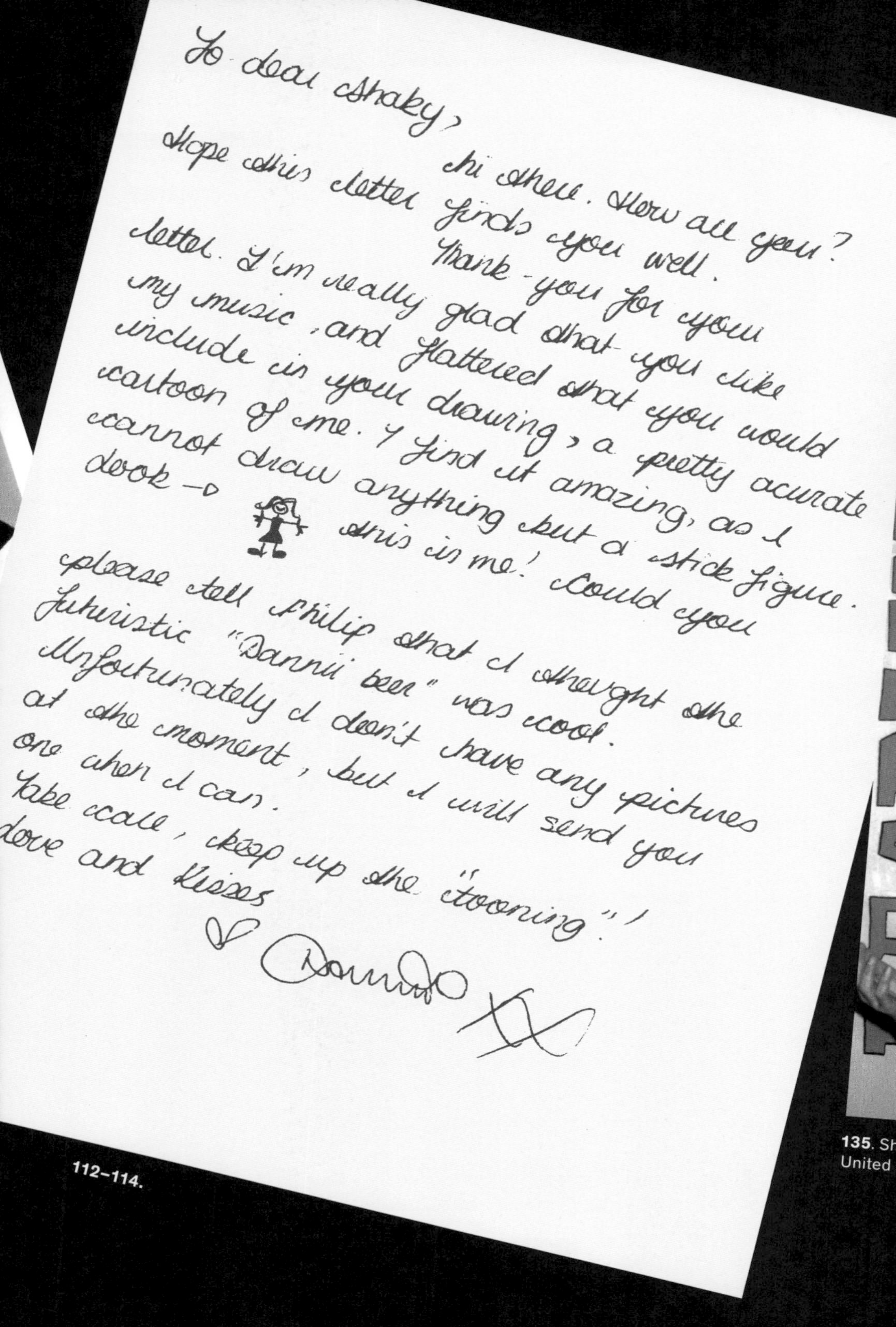

To dear Shaky,

Hi there. How are you?
Hope this letter finds you well.
Thank-you for your letter. I'm really glad that you like my music, and flattered that you would include in your drawing, a pretty accurate cartoon of me. I find it amazing, as I cannot draw anything but a stick figure. look ->

this is me! Could you please tell Philip that I thought the futuristic "Dannii beer" was cool. Unfortunately I don't have any pictures at the moment, but I will send you one when I can.
Take care, keep up the "tooning"!
Love and kisses
♡ Dannii xx

112–114.

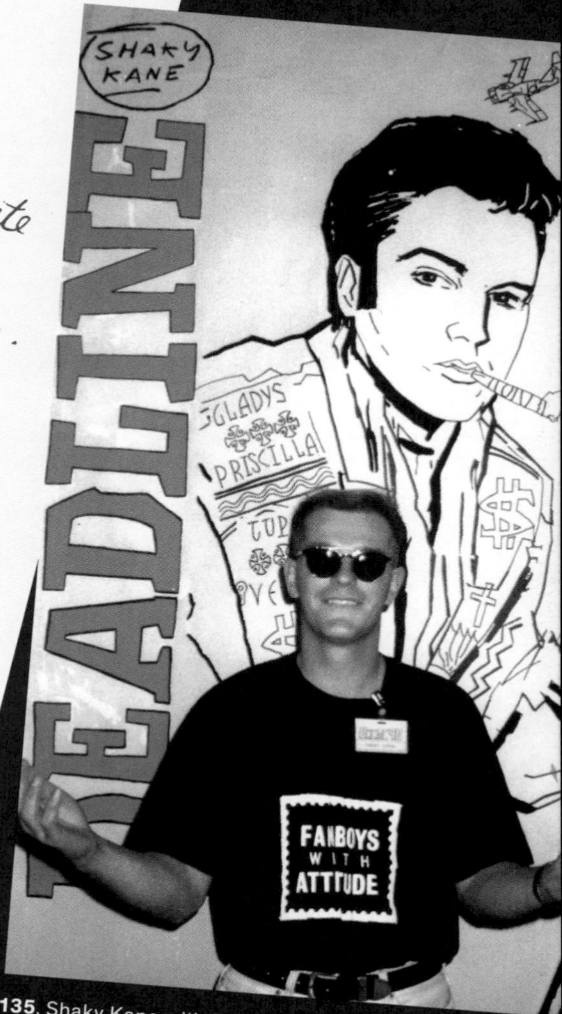
SHAKY KANE
DEADLINE
GLADYS
PRISCILLA
FANBOYS WITH ATTITUDE

**135**. Shaky Kane with Deadline display at United Kingdom Comic Art Convention, 1989.

**154–155.** I met Kate when she worked at Eternal Comics in Seven Sisters. Kate had this look which was way ahead of its time. Betty Page haircut, the whole look. To me she implied an alternative world. I really wanted her to be in my Deadline pages.

**156.** Philip Bond and Reverso Brendan McCarthy, two of my favourite comic book artists. I photographed them at a comic show at Alexandra Palace.

**158.** Through Kate I got interested in the Cinema of Transgression. She'd lent me Jörg Buttgereit's Nekromantik on VHS tape. I managed to get hold of Nekromantik 2, and Richard Kern's Films from the Deathtrip, through a small ad in the back of Darkside magazine.

**159.** I thought that if I were going to draw out-there comic strips I'd see how far I could push it. Best bit for me is the way you can see the newspaper I put on Kate's carpet to catch the blood-drips from the phoney stigmata hand-wound.

**160.** I like to imagine what it must be like to be dead. I do that a lot…

**163.** …while still featuring Becky's zany Mrs Macaroon strip.

**164.** I always liked the way makeup smells.

**165.** The Mothman appears here tortured by a Kate Fear doll. This was a continuation of a strip I submitted to Deadline entitled I am Mothman! Which was never used for one reason or another.

**166.** Kate posed mirroring the Space Boss pictures. I replaced The Sacred Heart picture with a photograph of the motor bike she pulled up on.

**168–169.** In my mind's eye, I returned to the Watch-tower from the A-MEN strips. I'd jot down a random chain of thoughts, presenting them against a backdrop of self-harm, self-abuse and self-immolation. Along with some Nazi nastiness and Bible fetish – I thought I was onto something here.

**172–173.** At this stage, I'd moved back to live in Devon. My nephew, Jordan used to come around to visit on a Saturday. We used to go to the local indoor market to buy horror videos. I had quite a collection. I asked him if he'd like to draw a strip that I could add to my pages, along the lines of the ones Becky drew. He came up with "You Die Now!" I thought it was the greatest. He was about 14 years old. I remember his mother was called into the school about his obsession with horror films and comics. She blamed me.

**176.** I had an idea to turn the nightmare back onto the perpetrator. I thought that it was fairly clear that the Prowler was trapped in a claustrophobic cycle of nightmarish events. Events familiar from low budget slasher movies. I thought at the time that it was a neat twist. I got a real dressing down from one reader. She tore the pages out of Deadline and posted them in along with a letter. I suppose she was right in a way, goes to show what thinking does for you.

**182–183.** The latex mask, once taken out of sexual context, serves its own purpose.

**184–193.** HOW FAR IS TOO FAR? Are we there yet? Page 186 is edited. I was told to black-in the suspended victim. I took it that drawings were just lines on paper and couldn't hurt anyone. I think I must have lost a sense of what was palatable to the reader. In the comic strip's defence, I think some of the dialogue is still funny…

**194.** I visited this weird British Elvis tribute store, in Shoreditch called Elvisly Yours. It was full of this appalling hand crafted Elvis kitsch. I read somewhere that Graceland Estates had tried to stop them trading, but the ruling was that Elvis was a historic figure, and Graceland didn't hold exclusive rights to Elvis memorabilia. Elvisly Yours sold a satin pillow with a screen printed image of The King, bearing the legend, "God knew Elvis was tired, so he took him to rest"! I thought this was such a great slogan, that I wanted to use it in my Deadline pages.

The Black Elvis, I drew, had no racial connotation. It was more a Negative Zone Elvis, an Earth Two Elvis. The Black being purely descriptive, echoing the Black Madonna from Medieval art.

**198.** Last night I dreamt of the twins. Hallucinations, guns, phantoms and the Ramsey Street twins, Gail and Gillian from the Australian soap opera Neighbours. What's not to like?

**202.** I was a hopeless romantic…

**209.** How big is a thought?

The Editor
Deadline
PO Box 435
London SE1 4SR

Jess Search
[redacted]
Sevenoaks
Kent
[redacted]

31st March 1993

Dear Editor,

<u>What is this shit?</u>

I've read Deadline for <u>years</u> and, although I've disliked the odd items from time to time, I've never had to wonder if I should stop buying it. It's this kind of rubbish that keeps comics in the dark ages read (and apparently drawn) by rape-obsessed 17 year old boys with emotional difficulties. Take it from me, many comic-reading women find this kind of thing inexcusably threatening and unpleasant.

Come on, I thought you guys were more progressive than that.

Yours sincerely

Jess Search

**176.**

## Spot Illustrations for Deadline Magazine Columns

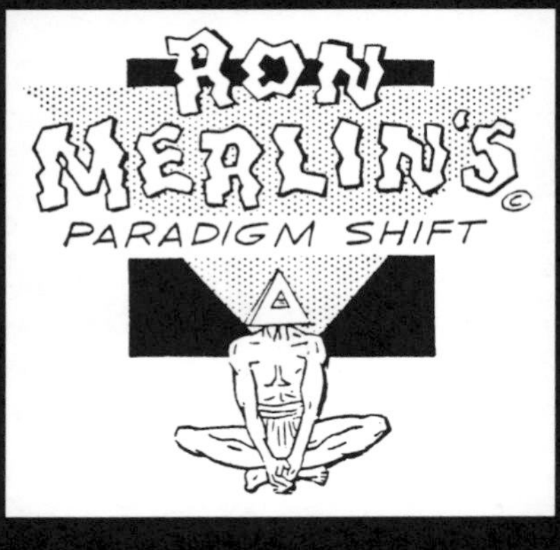
RON
MERLIN'S
©
PARADIGM SHIFT

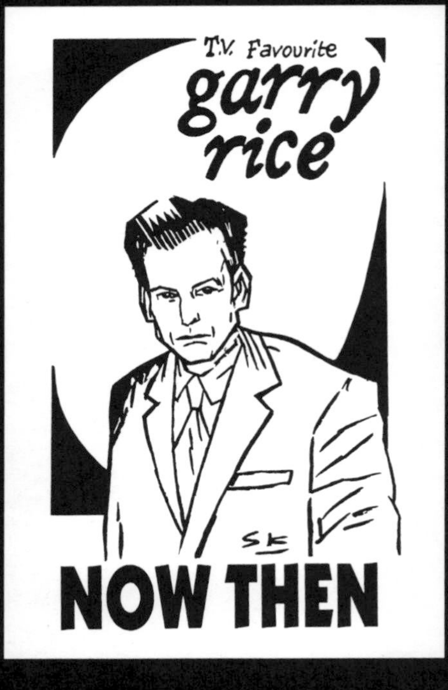
T.V. Favourite
garry
rice
SK
NOW THEN

# The Memory Man

Deadline kept an unsteady path, passing from one editor to another, until for one reason or another its glamour twinkled out.

Brett took the path less trodden  in search of The Ancient One and Steve? Steve left for Brigadoon.

I never made any effort to keep hold of the artwork I produced for Deadline, during the seven years spanning October 88 to the tail end of 1995.

I never much cared for the past, preferring the very here and now.

I shied from the idea of becoming a mythical Sisyphus, rolling the trappings of my past up the slope to my ultimate demise.

During the summer of 2002, the opportunity came up to produce a very small run comic book collection of my A-Men strips.

It was produced using Photostats of Deadline pages, from the copies I had in a box beneath the table, in the studio space I worked from, above The Cavern club, here in my hometown of Exeter.

It was incomplete, but in a way it gave me an opportunity to re-evaluate my contribution to a magazine which, regardless of its failings, still holds up as a cornerstone in the traffic cone crowned monument inscribed 'British Comics'.

A curious timepiece from a seminal time.

A time of Britpop and seaside revolution.

But mostly a time of unfettered optimism.

– Shaky Kane, 2017

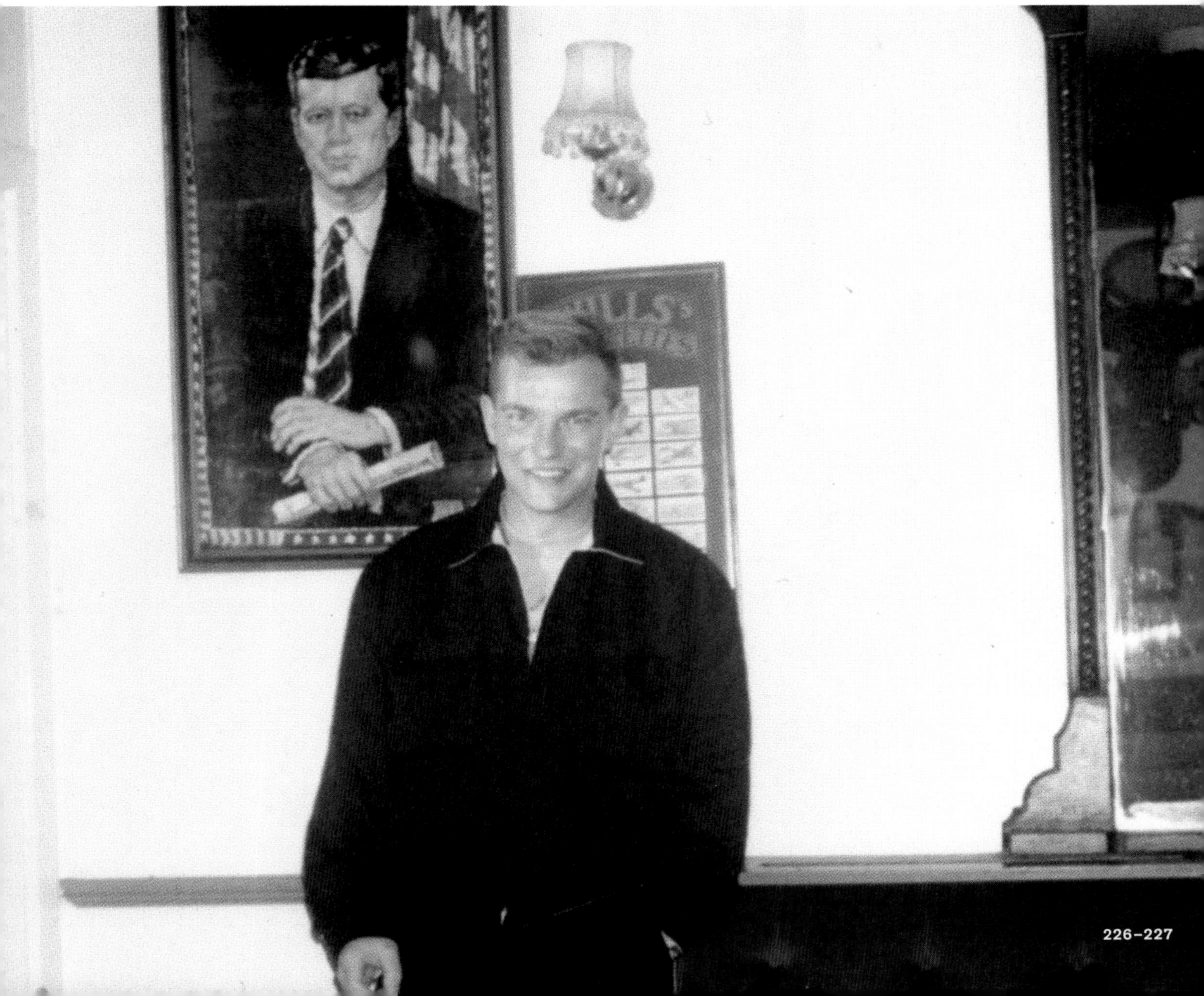

# Your Pal Shaky

Afterword by

## Frank Santoro

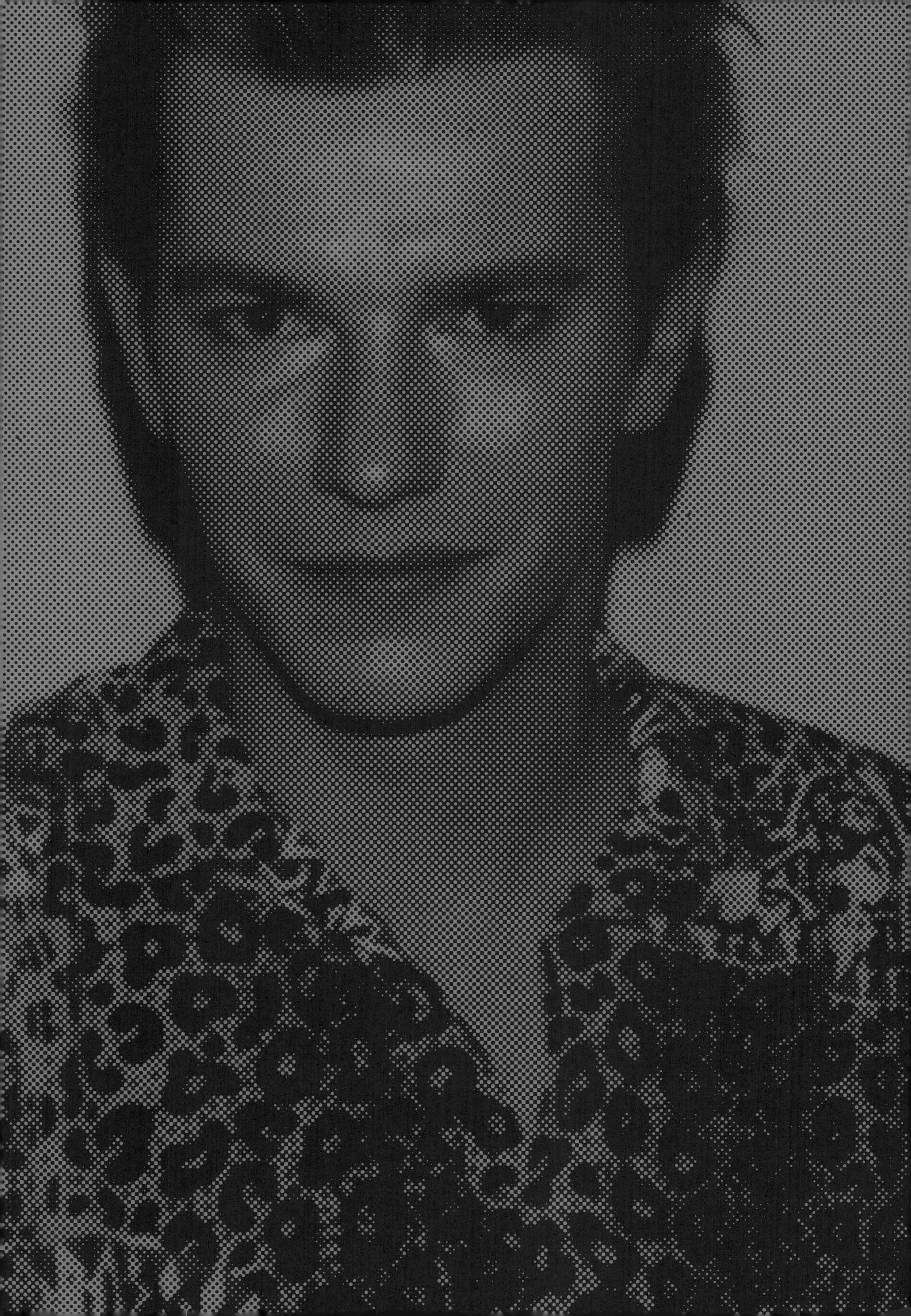

# SPECIAL BONUS PAGE!

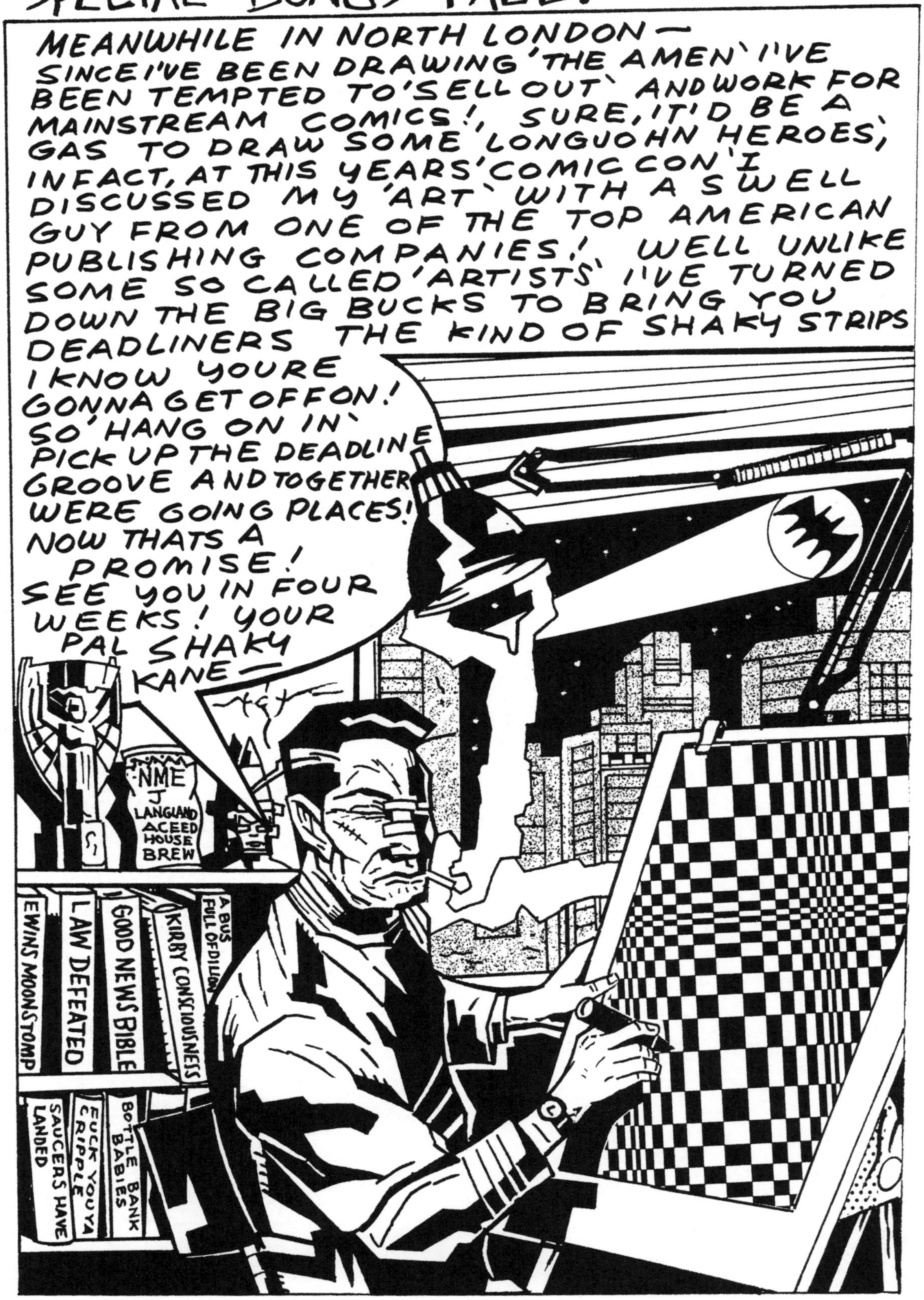

In this book there is a one panel cartoon of Shaky at his desk addressing the audience (p.59) . He says "Since I've been drawing 'The A Men' I've been tempted to 'sell out' and work for mainstream comics! Sure it'd be a blast to draw some 'longjohn heroes', in fact, at this year's 'comic con' I discussed my art with a swell guy from one of the top American companies! Well unlike some so called 'artists' I've turned down the big bucks to bring you Deadliners the kind of Shaky strips I know you're gonna get off on! So 'hang on in' pick up the Deadline groove and together we're going places! Now that's a promise! See you in four weeks! Your pal Shaky Kane – "

That was from 1989. Fast forward to 2015 and Shaky HAS worked for "one of the top American companies". But he didn't sell out. The mainstream just caught up to what he was laying down back in 1989.

Doing a monthly strip for Deadline back then was WAY cooler than doing work for some American company. I thought that then and I think that now. Shaky doing a mainstream comic for a major US publisher back then and adjusting who he was for them would have been a disaster. Of course, it's a joke; he's joking with us, the audience. He's saying that he is here for us – to preach the gospel of comics to us. That part is no joke. He was there for us. Or for me at least. Those of us who read Deadline off the newsstand back in the late '80s/early '90s remember how cool it was to see oversize colour comics printed in a slick magazine with "mainstream" trappings. Submitting to the dictates of a major US publisher back then would have distorted Shaky's message to such a degree that it would have really reached LESS people. Shaky made the right decision to stay where he was; more people heard the word, so to speak, and Shaky helped Comics to bust out of the ghetto; Armagetto, if you will.

Comics guru Bill Boichel was the only one Stateside who I knew boosting the Shaky signal back then. The strips were hard to find. Very few of us had a complete Deadline collection. Bill would make colour xerox enlargements of Shaky panels and hang them up in his comics shop. We would be excited when a new issue came out and Shaky was in it. Then, like many other forward thinking cartoonists of the period, Shaky seemed to simply vanish.

Fast forward to 2007. Rummaging around in an old box I find my cache of Deadline magazines. What struck me was how dated everything looked, except Shaky Kane's work. His colour and design and the humour of it all was quite striking. The work HELD UP after all these years. I excitedly began scanning images from the old mags and putting them on my blog. I begged anyone and everyone in comics to help me find Shaky Kane. We did an interview for the fanzine ComicsComics and Shaky bore witness to what he'd been through at Deadline and what he tried to accomplish there and where he'd been since. I'm going to effectively cannibalize it here to help provide some context for the work that is being reprinted in this volume from Breakdown Press.

When I look at Shaky's work now I think of Richard Hamilton, the British artist who is credited with making the first "Pop" artwork. They both had enough detachment from American culture, enough distance that they could "see" it in a way Rauschenberg, Rosenquist, Warhol, William Burroughs et al could not. Shaky Kane's contribution, for me, is an extension of this viewpoint into comics.

Shaky Kane's work used a Jack Kirby filter that carried with it a moral code – an invisible, massive language, cosmic in scale, that transcended any Pop Art or Comics reference. Shaky was deep. Profound. Ironic at times, but not to a fault. The cynicism was on the surface only. Beneath was a real sincerity to frame the redemptive spirit of the universe, as if some weary surfer of the stars writ poems to the earthman. And these fragments resonated within me. His choices, his intent, was felt by me. He drew cosmic gods and mortal men, fallible, human, a "Shadowman", a "Space Boss."

Ancient, modern and contemporary symbols collided in these fractured strips. The collage of styles unified by the Kirby line and colour, for me, was, and still is, what elevates the work. It's a brilliant, effortless choice for the medium of comics. As opposed to bringing art world concerns to comics through the introduction of painterly values like "The Studio" group and many others, Shaky Kane employed the very language of comics itself – most notably that of its founding father, Jack Kirby – to show us what was there all along, but what we, being too close to it, couldn't see: ourselves, in the mirror of comics we hadn't realised was there.

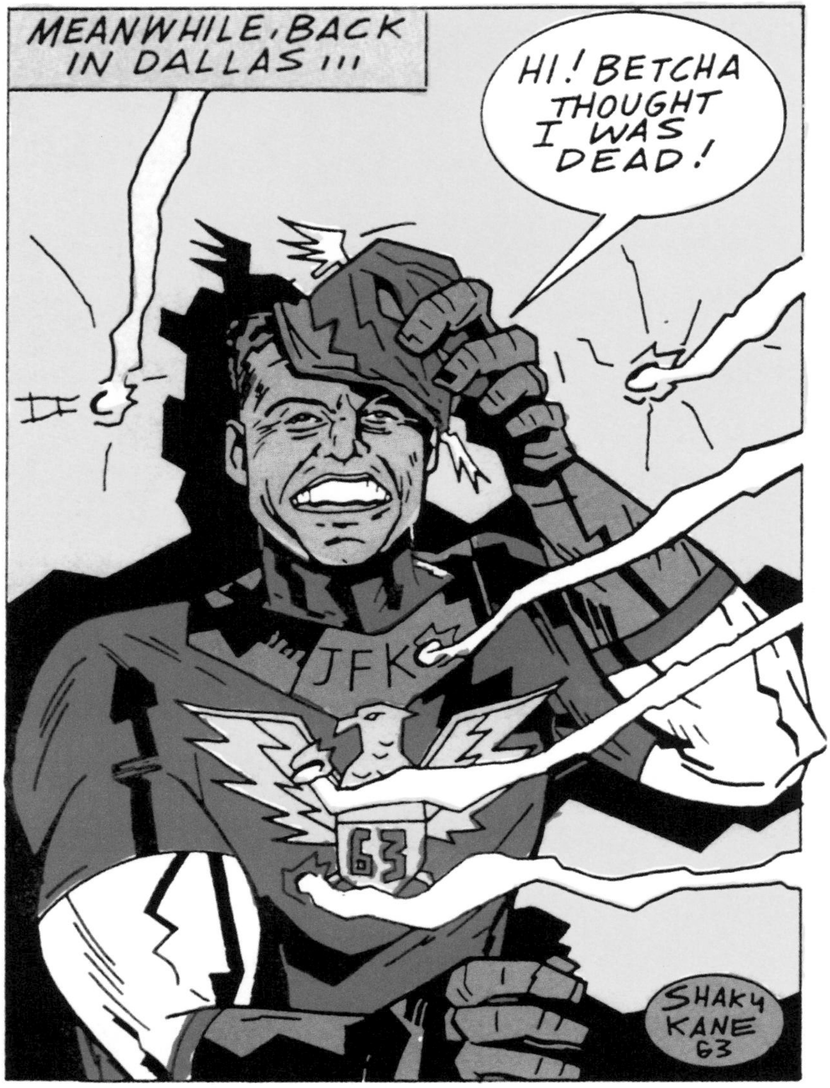
MEANWHILE, BACK IN DALLAS ...
HI! BETCHA THOUGHT I WAS DEAD!
JFK
63
SHAKY KANE 63

This language is codified, and for those initiated in Kirby's symbols, a doubly powerful layer emerges that is historical and imaginative; at once forward thinking and grounded in tradition. Something of a criteria, I believe, for great work. And remember: this was 1989, not '83 or even '87. Gary Panter and RAW magazine had been absorbed by the reading audience. The table was set for an image maker to reconstitute "America" in a way North American artists could not. For me, these hermetic symbols are very powerful and remain so today. JFK drawn in a Kirby manner, cryptically exclaiming "Hi! Betcha Thought I was Dead!" (p.145) is a remarkable image, something in the finer arts that would be used as an emblem of post modernism.

Shaky told me, "Jack Kirby was always on the surface of what I was doing. It was the stylistic device as you so rightly state it carried with it its own mythology/code. It was something that I felt an intuitive affinity with, rather than say Steve Ditko (who with his work spoke more for the "outsider" and would have had more appeal in the context of a magazine like Deadline!). William Burroughs was a definite influence on how I worked, more so (except maybe on a packaging stylistic level) than Punk, which most people associate me with! I think the important element I added to the mix was a sense of humour! It was when I was asked to produce work which simply stole from (or should I say "paid tribute to") Kirby that it fell to pieces and I felt it showed. Although, saying that, the work I did for 2000AD was the period when I actually made a living wage out of drawing! So it was difficult to have been choosy at the time!"

Shaky Kane has a very interesting place in comics history. Practically frozen in suspended animation for decades, his work didn't really age. The future simply caught up with him. It's the alchemy of the present colliding with the past – that's why the work holds up for me. The single page illustrations and various covers seem to presage the fragmentation of the digital world. The fragmented bits, the routines, the gags, they all manage to hold together in a way that straight forward non-serialized "graphic novels" do not and maybe cannot in this day and age. Each page of this collection feels self contained like you could pick it up and read it backwards or forwards from any random starting point and make it all make sense – to hang together.

The A Men reads like a contemporary webcomic glimpsed in bits and pieces online. His one panel gag comics read like internet memes.

Shaky was reflecting the change that was happening around him. Borrowing, sampling, and re-inserting the new collage back into the comics culture from whence it came. He may not have been the first comics artist to compose in this way, but he is definitely the preeminent example of the mid to late '80s sentiment stated above. His facility of line, colour and content were united in an effort to reposition the IMAGE in comics, to wrestle it back from a subordinate service to the narrative and reassert its status as an equal partner in the creation of meaning. Though few in number, the iconic works created by Shaky Kane, especially those for Deadline magazine, unlocked a significant and powerful mythic component that had accreted to certain key images, and so amply demonstrated the ability of comics imagery to contain and hold meaning as well as convey and communicate it. ∎

Frank Santoro is a cartoonist and educator based in Pittsburgh, PA. His works include *Storeyville* and *Pompeii*. He is the founder and head of The Comics Workbook Academy

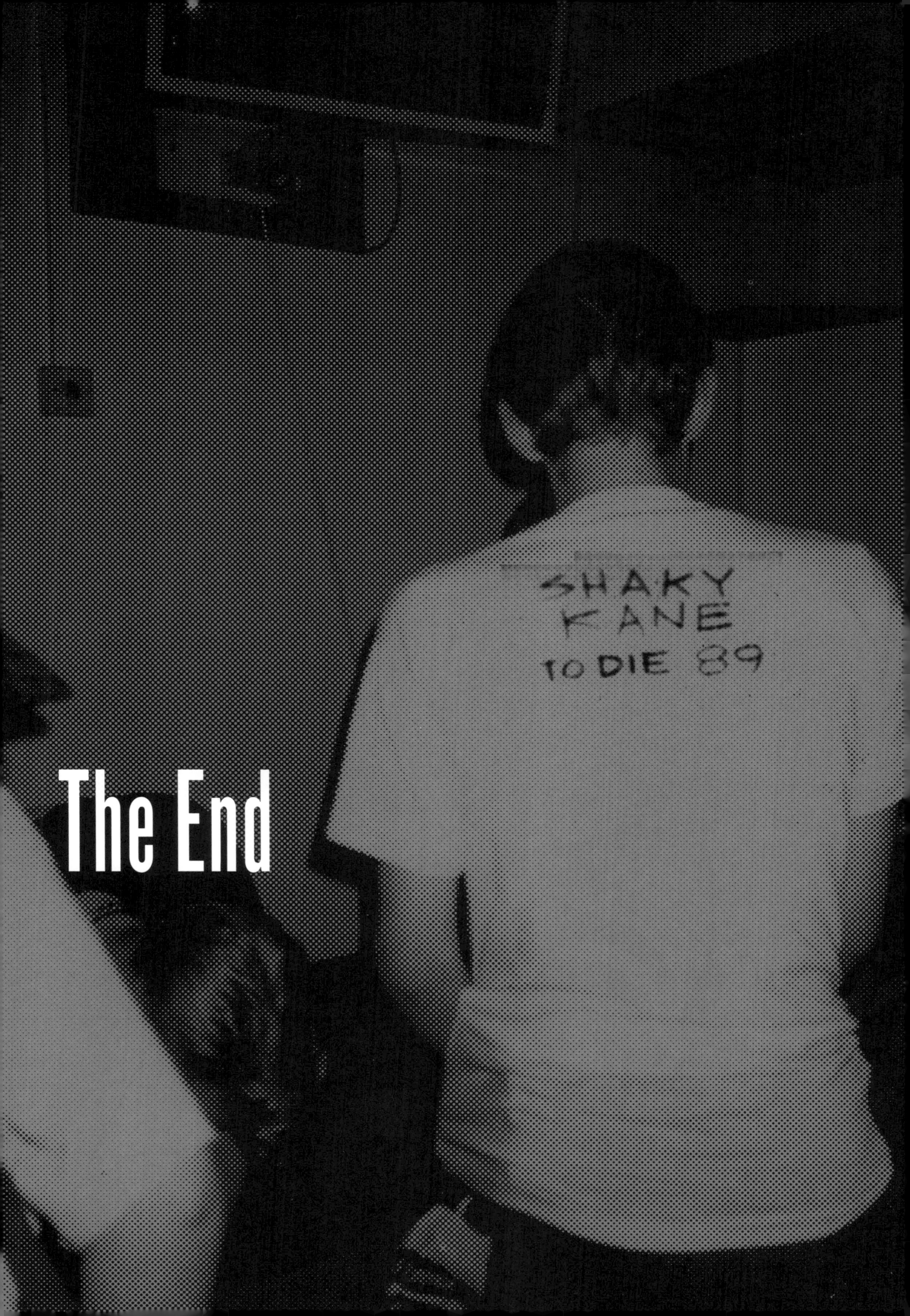
The End
SHAKY
KANE
TO DIE 89

# We Give Thanks

I'd work without rhyme or reason. Free from commercial consideration, in a shoe-box apartment in North London.

I had no concept of audience or readership, I simply drew what took my fancy. Approaching each strip as a blank canvas, drawing as my mind wandered. Undisciplined and unskilled in draughtsmanship, I could only draw large, filling in the pencil with a cheap fibre point pen.

But I kept at it for a number of years.

Looking back, I often wonder where my mind wandered.

Sometimes, just sometimes I felt I hit it right, and I'd see an echo of the comic books I'd read as a child in the drawings on the page. I'd see Kirby in the lines, only diluted down, like a homeopathic tincture. But usually it fell apart and I saw only soul destroying awkwardness and squandered opportunity.

But I kept at it for a number of years.

Thanks are due to Tom Astor, the unsung hero of Deadline who made Deadline possible. To Brett Ewins and Steve Dillon whose enthusiasm made it worthwhile. To Dave Elliot, Si Spencer and Frank Wynne who guided the Deadline enterprise through whatever course it took. Mentioning of course, Rebekah Ford, Kate Fear (I never knew her real name), Matt Wakeham, Bambos!, Ra Khan and the mighty Jordan Bruce, who while only fifteen years old shared my enthusiasm for market store videos.

– Shaky Kane

Breakdown Press would like to thank Nick Abadzis, Jason Atomic, John Bishop, Matthew Bookman, Steven Cook, Rufus Dayglo, Bambos Georgiou, Glyn Dillon, Joe Hales, Jim Hemmingfield, David Hine, Nicolas Papaconstantinou, David Quantick, Frank Santoro, Si Spencer, Lawrence Watson and Steve Welburn.

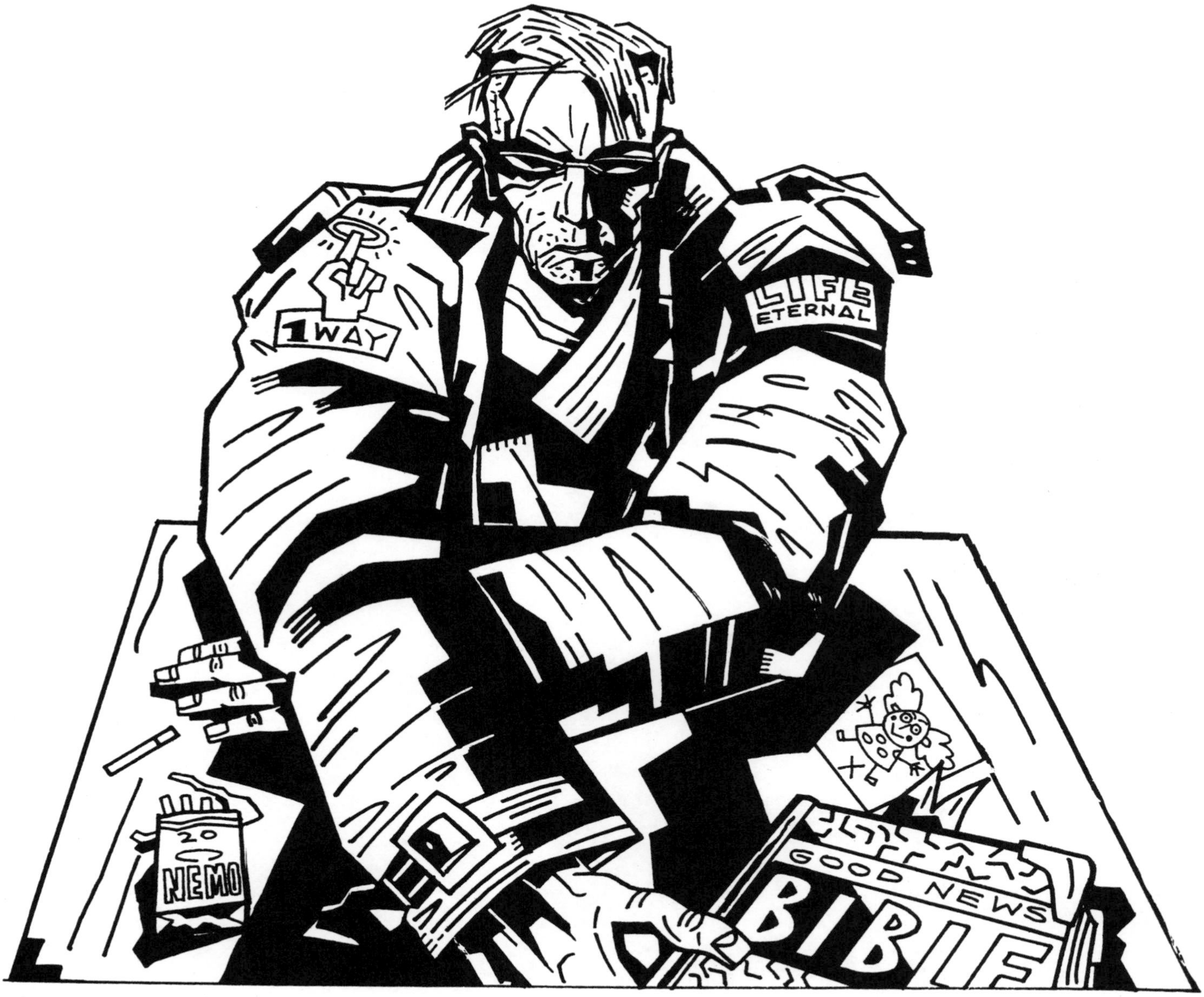
1WAY
LIFE ETERNAL
20
NEMO
GOOD NEWS

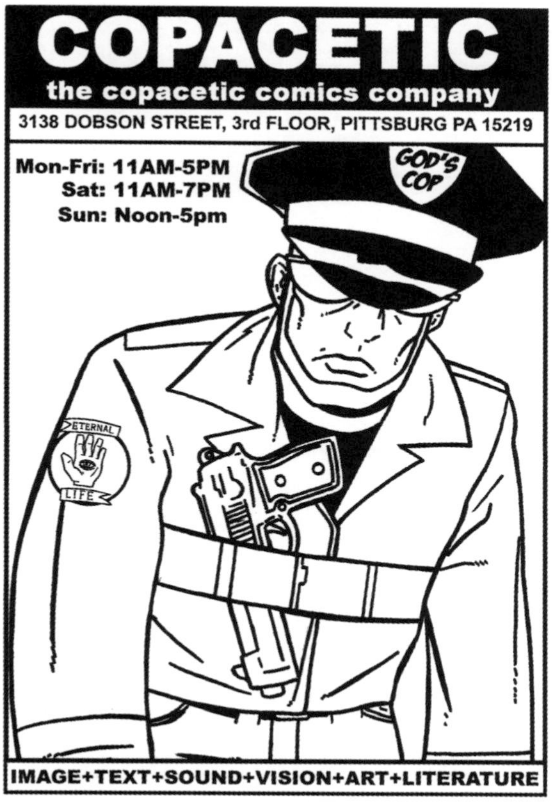

COPACETIC
the copacetic comics company
3138 DOBSON STREET, 3rd FLOOR, PITTSBURG PA 15219
Mon-Fri: 11AM-5PM
Sat: 11AM-7PM
Sun: Noon-5pm
GOD'S COP
ETERNAL LIFE
IMAGE+TEXT+SOUND+VISION+ART+LITERATURE


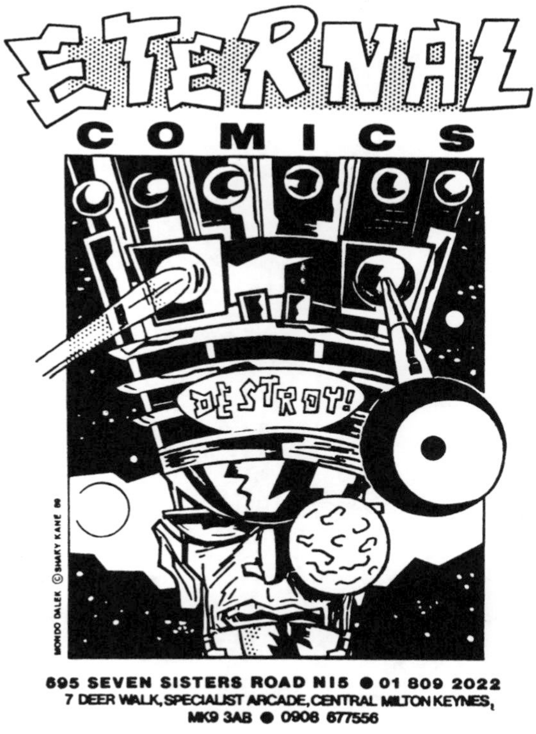

ETERNAL
COMICS
DESTROY!
695 SEVEN SISTERS ROAD N15 ● 01 809 2022
7 DEER WALK, SPECIALIST ARCADE, CENTRAL MILTON KEYNES,
MK9 3AB ● 0908 677556


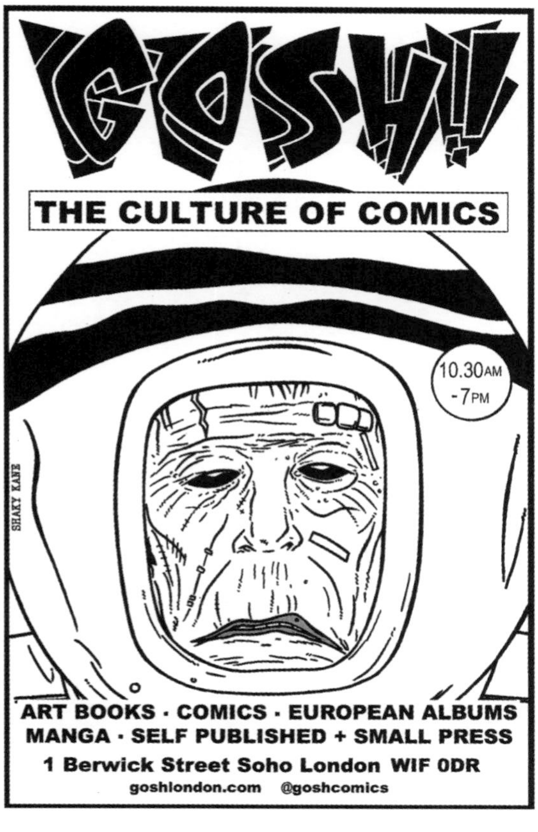

GOSH!
THE CULTURE OF COMICS
10.30AM -7PM
SHAKY KANE
ART BOOKS · COMICS · EUROPEAN ALBUMS
MANGA · SELF PUBLISHED + SMALL PRESS
1 Berwick Street Soho London WIF 0DR
goshlondon.com @goshcomics


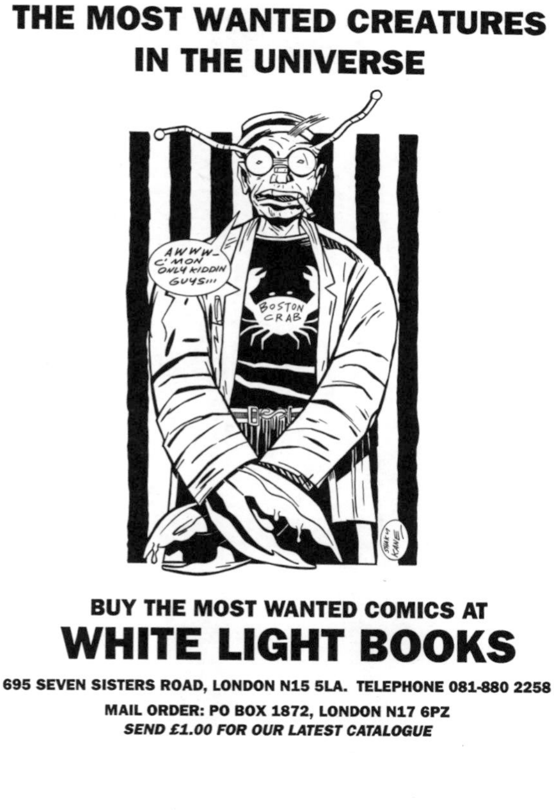

THE MOST WANTED CREATURES IN THE UNIVERSE
AWWW- C'MON ONLY KIDDIN GUYS!!!
BOSTON CRAB
BUY THE MOST WANTED COMICS AT
WHITE LIGHT BOOKS
695 SEVEN SISTERS ROAD, LONDON N15 5LA. TELEPHONE 081-880 2258
MAIL ORDER: PO BOX 1872, LONDON N17 6PZ
SEND £1.00 FOR OUR LATEST CATALOGUE

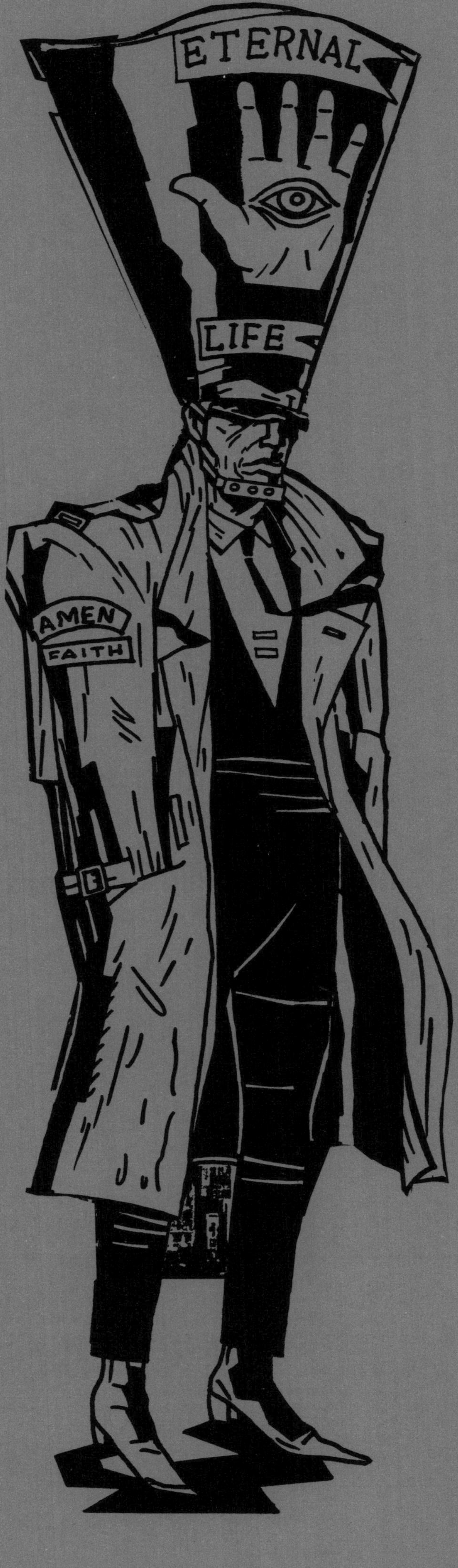
ETERNAL
LIFE
AMEN
FAITH

**Good News Bible:**
**The Complete Deadline Strips of Shaky Kane**
by Shaky Kane

Published by Breakdown Press
Designed by Joe Hales
Printed by Industria Grafica Siz, Verona

All photos unless otherwise credited by Shaky Kane.
Pictures of Shaky Kane taken on his camera by adoring fans.
Photo used on He Wore a Mask of Craters title page by
Lawrence Watson



ISBN: 9780957438149

Frst edition: August 2017

Breakdown Press
1 Berwick Street
London W1F 0RD

www.shakykane.com
www.breakdownpress.com

Learn more about the contributors to this book

Frank Santoro
www.comicsworkbook.com

Nick Abadzis
www.nickabadzis.com

Lawrence Watson
www.lawrencewatsonphotography.com

Steve Cook
www.steven-cook.com